TOMBS FOR THE LIVING:
ANDEAN MORTUARY PRACTICES

TOMBS FOR THE LIVING:
ANDEAN MORTUARY PRACTICES

A Symposium at Dumbarton Oaks
12TH AND 13TH OCTOBER 1991

Tom D. Dillehay, *Editor*

Dumbarton Oaks Research Library and Collection
Washington, D.C.

© 1995 Dumbarton Oaks Research Library
and Collection.
Trustees for Harvard University, Washington, D.C.
All rights reserved.

First paper edition, 2011.
Printed in the United States of America by
Thomson-Shore, Inc.

15 14 13 12 11   1 2 3 4 5

LIBRARY OF CONGRESS CATALOGING-IN-PUBLICATION DATA
Tombs for the living : Andean mortuary practices : a symposium at
    Dumbarton Oaks, 12th and 13th October 1991 / edited by Tom D.
    Dillehay.
        p. cm.
Includes bibliographical references and index.
    ISBN 978-0-88402-220-6 (hardcover : alk. paper)
    ISBN 978-0-88402-374-6 (paperback : alk. paper)
1. Indians of South America—Andes Region—Mortuary customs—
Congresses.
2. Indians of South America—Andes Region—Antiquities—Congresses.
3. Burial—Andes Region—Congresses.
4. Andes Region—Antiquities—Congresses.
I. Dillehay, Tom D.   II. Dumbarton Oaks.
F2230.1.M6T66   1994
393'.1'089983   dc20   93-29342

www.doaks.org/publications

Contents

PREFACE   vii

TOM D. DILLEHAY
Introduction   1

JOHN HOWLAND ROWE
Behavior and Belief in Ancient Peruvian Mortuary Practice   27

MARIO A. RIVERA
The Preceramic Chinchorro Mummy Complex of Northern Chile: Context, Style, and Purpose   43

ROBERT D. DRENNAN
Mortuary Practices in the Alto Magdalena: The Social Context of the "San Agustín Culture"   79

CHRISTOPHER B. DONNAN
Moche Funerary Practice   111

PATRICK H. CARMICHAEL
Nasca Burial Patterns: Social Structure and Mortuary Ideology   161

JOHN W. VERANO
Where Do They Rest? The Treatment of Human Offerings and Trophies in Ancient Peru   189

JANE E. BUIKSTRA
Tombs for the Living . . . or . . . For the Dead: The Osmore Ancestors   229

Contents

TOM D. DILLEHAY
Mounds of Social Death: Araucanian Funerary Rites
and Political Succession   281

FRANK SALOMON
"The Beautiful Grandparents": Andean Ancestor Shrines
and Mortuary Ritual as Seen Through Colonial Records   315

JOSEPH W. BASTIEN
The Mountain/Body Metaphor Expressed in a Kaatan Funeral   355

PATRICIA J. LYON
Death in the Andes   379

JAMES A. BROWN
Andean Mortuary Practices in Perspective   391

INDEX   407
Prepared by Lisa deLeonardis

Preface

THE IDEA FOR A SYMPOSIUM to focus on Andean mortuary practices began in conversations with Tom Dillehay in 1988. The Pre-Columbian program's Senior Fellows committee was looking to develop a symposium that drew upon recent research in the Andes and at the same time pushed researchers to expand their thinking about their own work. Dillehay and I had been discussing several ideas when he began to talk about a long-term interest of his: funerary practices. His work among the Mapuche, with their complex and costly burial practices, had made him realize how important and telling this aspect of a culture could be.

In spite of all the excavation—and all the looting—of cemeteries in the Andes, and in spite of the significance placed on burials by ancient Andean peoples, the theme of mortuary practices had never been thoroughly explored. The excavational material was potentially there, but analysis of that data in terms of the practices and beliefs lagged behind. The committee agreed fully with Dillehay's idea to organize a symposium for 1991 that would explore Andean mortuary practices and their social, economic, and religious implications, approached from a pan-Andean perspective.

As Dillehay has pointed out, in the Andes there is a long history of research on burial records and context for the purpose of reconstructing cultural affiliation, chronology, socioeconomic status, grave content, treatment of the human body, and specific burial context in various types of sites. Less attention has been paid to the larger question of how mortuary practices functioned in different cultures. The symposium, of which this volume is the result, focused on this broader issue by looking at linkages between the living and the dead (including ancestors) achieved through mortuary rites, the role of wealth and ancestors in cosmological schemes, the location and construction of tombs and cemeteries and their social and political implications, and the art and iconography of death. The speakers were chosen not for their geographic or culture coverage but because their work embraced different and complementary aspects of the topic. The speakers also brought their own perspectives and approaches, which makes for a richly textured volume.

Two features strike me about Andean mortuary evidence: the importance

Preface

of placement and the importance of preservation. Ancient Andeans must have considered them, too.

John Rowe, in his paper, perceptively highlights a fact we take for granted: objects and persons in burials were intentionally placed. Taking into account the natural settlement that occurs in burials and the potential for later disturbance, things in burials are found where they are, and the way they are, because someone thought to put them exactly there. Spatial placement and aspect are thus supremely important in funerary contexts and can reveal much about the motivations of those responsible for the burial. In this case, location carries meaning.

In the Andes, as practically nowhere else in the world, the preservation of organic materials is exceptional. The dry coastal desert and the frozen mountains at high altitude are ideal environments for preserving dead flora and fauna. Human remains, textiles, feathers, gourds, and animals buried in either location do not quickly deteriorate as they would in most other locations. The ancient inhabitants must have realized that things buried in these locations would not soon disappear. Rather the things (persons and materials) would still be with them on earth but would be physically separate from them. I do not know how this sense of enduring corporal existence affected individuals along the Andean coast. Esther Pasztory raised this question at the symposium, and it remains a consideration for thought. Certainly the Inka practice of curating the bodies of rulers tells us that very different ideas about death and decay were at work.

The title of the symposium, Tombs for the Living, reflects the understanding that elaborate burial rites, special accoutrements, and great funerary monuments all have social functions that go beyond their funerary purposes. Andrew Fleming of the University of Sheffield saw the megalithic chambered tombs of Western Europe as "tombs for the living" because their monumentality was clearly a conscious goal of the living members of the society and, therefore, must have served the interests of that society. Like Fleming, the participants in this volume are interested in understanding the social and economic roles of funerary practices. On the cultural level, tombs and burials actively serve the living just as they metaphorically serve the dead.

Elizabeth Hill Boone
Dumbarton Oaks

Introduction

TOM D. DILLEHAY
UNIVERSITY OF KENTUCKY

MORTUARY PRACTICE IS A TERM used with facility in everyday anthropological discourse, despite the considerable ambiguity surrounding it. All of us know that the term signifies interment of the dead and the context and ritual of burial. Although clear in what it signifies, the precise meaning of the practice eludes us; the broad meaning points to certain essential and terminal features of the life cycle of individuals in a society and to lasting linkages between the living and the dead. Only when death and mortuary practice and their broad meanings are elaborated as an interest of social and ideological research does the term become more clear, and we can begin to understand the empirical referents of the practice. This volume considers various aspects of the context and meaning of death and burial practice among different Pre-Columbian Andean peoples (Fig. 1) from the perspectives of archaeology, ethnohistory, and ethnography.

There are several different directions that this introduction could take. Ideally, its first aim would be to identify traditional cultural practices of death and treatment of the corpse among different past societies, and would be organized in terms of major mortuary practices for each culture developmental period in each area of the Andes. Another approach would be to provide a historical review of research on mortuary patterns, topics, and problems. Both of these approaches would require a great deal of discussion beyond the scope of this introduction. An alternative would be to apply broad theoretical and conceptual studies to Andean mortuary data, but that would be inappropriate for an introduction of this nature. Instead, I have combined aspects of all the above-mentioned approaches to reflect on the regional patterns and problems discussed in this volume: the material and symbolic aspects of death, organization of contexts of death and burial ritual, the transformative work that such contexts are thought to do, and the relationship of such contexts of transformation to social order. We know from the ethnohistoric and ethnographic records that the mortuary practices reported for many late pre-Hispanic, historic, and contemporary Andean

Fig. 1 Map of the archaeological, ethnohistorical, and ethnographic cultures or study areas covered in the text: (1) San Agustín culture; (2) north coast of Peru, including the Moche and Chimu cultures; (3) Nasca and Paracas cultures of the south-central coast of Peru; (4) the southern highlands of Peru; (5) the Moquegua Valley of the south coast of Peru; (6) the Aymara culture and altiplano area of Bolivia; (7) the Chinchorro culture of the north coast of Chile; (8) the Mapuche culture of south-central Chile.

Introduction

societies are instrumentally related to the structure of the kinship system, political alignments and territorial divisions, the organization of authority, and economic investment in burial rites and tomb construction. We also know that premonumental and monumental burial contexts and the quality of the mortuary data are important. This information is a necessary starting point for suggesting ways to attempt to reconstruct and explain major Andean mortuary practices.

PATCHY DATA AND CHRONOLOGIES

When we turn to the archaeological evidence for mortuary data, a serious discrepancy immediately becomes apparent. The ethnohistorical sources show a greater number of burial forms, ritual practices, and uses of mummified bodies in the rites of the living than is suggested by the archaeological data currently available. Many students of archaeology must experience a feeling of unreality as they turn the pages of the books of Bernabé Cobo and Pablo Joseph de Arriaga on Inka religious and mortuary practices, for instance. These observers of late Andean culture provide numerous references to death and burial practices of which little or nothing is known archaeologically. The opposite is true of archaeological records, such as for the Paracas culture of coastal Peru or the San Agustín culture of highland Colombia, for which we have burial data but little knowledge of the society. Extensive looting and destruction in many areas and the archaeological "invisibility" of graves, such as deep-shaft and other below-ground burials, compound these problems. There are other, similar problems that could be cited, but these few suffice to suggest the patchy state of archaeological and ethnohistorical knowledge on this subject, and the uneven distribution of research in the Andes, in both time and space.

Perhaps more than anyone else in this volume, John Rowe considers in detail the quality, patterning, and interpretative meaning of burial records in various areas of Peru, focusing specifically on the classic studies of archaeologists in the early decades of the discipline. His study provides good examples of the strengths and weaknesses of specific burial records, describes formal and informal burial types, associates mortuary variables with differing ritual and social contexts, and critically reconsiders some controversial data. Perhaps, above all, Rowe's contribution is in providing a backdrop to understanding the contexts and directions of scholarly research in the rich and complex field of mortuary practices, while cautioning that the discussion of the archaeological evidence for these practices is in danger of giving a distorted, or at least an incomplete, picture.

The chronological framework used by most contributors is that of Rowe's cultural developmental periodization (1962b). Though other schemes exist (e.g., Lumbreras 1974), Rowe's original framework is still the most regularly

Tom D. Dillehay

used by scholars working in the Central Andes. Rowe, Christopher Donnan, Jane Buikstra, Patrick Carmichael, and John Verano follow this scheme. Other contributors employ chronological frameworks developed for the countries or regions they discuss.

ANTHROPOLOGICAL CONCERNS AND ARCHAEOLOGICAL DIRECTIONS

Thinking in terms of interpretative approaches to Andean mortuary data, the traditional emphasis has been on context, variability, chronology, and description of tomb content and structure (e.g., Larco Hoyle 1945; Tello and Xesspe 1979; Kroeber 1925; Strong 1925; Rowe 1962a and this volume; Willey 1953; Bennett 1936, 1939; Donnan and Mackey 1978), and on the symbolic value of burial (e.g., Benson 1975; Donnan and Mackey 1978; Carrión Cachot 1948; Kauffman Doig 1979; Dwyer and Dwyer 1975; Greider 1978: 51–58; Greider et al. 1988; Paul 1990). Although the excavation and study of mortuary contexts were time-honored traditions in the early days of Andean archaeology, within the last four decades there has been less of an effort to understand the cultural and, especially, biological significance of human skeletal remains in light of their potential for the explanation of culture change and adaptation, and for the study of both pan-Andean and regional patterns. In the last decade, a greater effort has been made to focus more on the social aspect of death; the nature of the archaeological context of burial in terms of differential deposition, preservation, and recovery; the bioanthropological aspect of death and the evidence of group identity and associated material remains (see both Rivera and Buikstra, this volume); and the identification of interregional mortuary patterning. Little effort, however, has been made by archaeologists and other scholars, including several of the contributors to this volume, to bridge the gap between data and theory and between local and regional practices in order to reconstruct broader interpretative models of the meaning and context of death and burial in the Andes. Even less attention has been given to the types of burial forms characteristic of the different levels (types?) of chiefdom and state societies in the Andes.

As most of the papers in this book do not deal with model building but more with pattern recognition and interpretation, I will not provide a detailed discussion of general anthropological and archaeological thought on the meaning of mortuary practice. For such a discussion, the reader is referred to general publications on the subject (e.g., Bloch and Parry 1982; Bartel 1982; Brown 1981; Binford 1971; Chapman, Kinnes, and Randsborg 1981; O'Shea 1984; Tainter 1978). Several papers in the volume, however, deal with conceptual issues of general interest, including social differentiation, historical contingency, cosmology, social evolution, and hierarchies and inequalities (see Buikstra, Carmichael, Dillehay, Drennan, and Salo-

Introduction

mon). The commentaries of James Brown and Pat Lyon also touch on these issues. The remaining papers implicitly deal with these or other matters, but focus primarily on regional problems of an empirical and interpretative nature.

Discussed below are some general patterns of funerary practice and examples of sites that relate to them for the major culture developmental periods in the Andes. The reader should be aware that there are more specific patterns of tomb construction, body orientation, grave goods, and so forth than those presented here, if shorter time periods and smaller culture areas are used. (The case studies cited in each chapter should be consulted for details.)

Instead of reviewing the information on mortuary practices for the culture developmental periods in each area of the Andes, I will divide the discussion into premonumental and monumental patterns. This approach allows me to collapse the information into two broad stages of development without sacrificing historical accuracy.

PREMONUMENTAL CEMETERIES AND MONUMENTAL BURIALS

One theme shared by all areas of the Andes is the presence of premonumental and monumental burial contexts, a distinction that correlates roughly with presedentary societies of the Archaic period and with sedentary societies of the Formative and later periods, respectively. There is a pragmatic reason for highlighting this dichotomy and, particularly, burial monuments as conspicuous funerary contexts, for these settings provide most of the raw archaeological material for mortuary study. More emphasis on monumental tombs may seem to be a sampling problem at first, but the nature of our evidence probably reflects the actual priorities of many past Andean societies. That is, burial monuments were constructed to be more elaborate and more lasting than nonmonumental cemeteries, and they seemingly absorbed a far larger share of the energy budget.

Premonumental Forms of the Archaic Period

Although no human skeletal remains of reliable Pleistocene contexts have been found in the Andes, early to middle Archaic are relatively common (e.g., Allison 1985; Cardich 1964; Correal 1989; Engel 1960, 1963; Quilter 1989, 1991, n.d.; Stothert 1985; Rick 1980; Tattersall 1985; Bonavia 1982). My guess is that at least 800 burials have been found in reasonably well-defined archaeological contexts at various sites throughout the Andes. A few general patterns can be observed. There are both primary and secondary burials, with little variation in the orientation and treatment of the skeletons, including the presence of red ochre smeared on bones recovered at a few sites in northwest Argentina (González 1985), central Peru (Quilter

Tom D. Dillehay

1989), and northern Chile (Allison 1985). Most burials are individual, but some are multiple (Stothert 1985; Quilter 1989; Schiappacasse and Niemeyer 1984). Some skeletons are extended, others are tightly flexed, and the remainder are loosely contracted. Many burials have grave goods such as shell and bone ornaments, projectile points, stone adornments, or other items. Some site complexes, such as the Aguazuque burial complex in Colombia (Correal 1989) and the early Chinchorro complex in northern Chile are spectacular and associated with advanced treatment of the dead, including elaborate mummification in the latter case (see also Mario Rivera and Buikstra in this volume).

Chinchorro is among the most outstanding burial traditions of the Archaic period. Mario Rivera's chapter discusses the origin and meaning of this mortuary complex and how and why it changes through time. He includes archaeological, paleoecological, and biological evidence to study the demographic and social configuration of the Chinchorro mummies and formal cemetery areas, and overall ritual complex. In addition to mummification, some of the more important features are the use of hallucinogenic plants and paraphernalia and the placement of bodies in formal cemeteries. Evidence also suggests that the deceased were periodically removed from their tombs to participate in ritual among the living. Rivera postulates that aspects of this complex have their roots in early tropical forest cultures, as brought to the north coast of Chile by Preceramic migrants and/or by diffusion of cultural traits from the eastern side of the Andes. If this is the case, an early linkage is established between elaborate burial practice and continued use of the dead, perhaps in the context of intergroup contact and the need for local occupants to demonstrate their identity by displaying their dead. Buikstra adds in her paper that the Chinchorro practice probably symbolized corporate rights to resource use and/or control.

The Archaic period also showed conceptual changes in burial practice. For instance, people living at Las Vegas in southern Ecuador and at Chinchorro were purposely burying many of their dead, both adults and infants, in designated areas of residential sites. Although there is no uniform method of burial, some attention was often paid to the positioning of the body and to the objects left with it. Jewelry and other ornamental objects adorn some burials and have also been found in other deposits at these and other settlements. Representational art in several different media appeared for the first time in the middle Archaic period; for example, at Huaca Prieta (Bird 1963), figurines and other forms also indicate that some Andean people of the Archaic period used symbols to re-create the natural world. Such representations can be interpreted in a number of ways: most scholars might suggest that these symbolic forms possibly were elements in an early religion, perhaps based on food production fertility cults. Initial concepts of an

Introduction

afterlife, the control of death, and ancestor worship may be implied in these patterns as well.

Another important Archaic burial site is that of La Paloma, which has been dated between approximately 5000 and 2500 B.C. Although this site has been occupied by different cultural groups over time, its burial practices remained constant during its occupation (Quilter 1989, n.d.). Throughout the site the deceased were buried in the floor of huts. The bodies were occasionally salted to prevent decay; they were placed with their limbs flexed and mats tied around the body, and usually buried with very few grave goods. A pattern suggesting strong family ties is the sequential placement of burials along the inside of the hut walls, until all or most of the space beside the walls were occupied. An adult male was buried in the floor in the center of the hut, possibly symbolizing a family unit with the middle body representing the head of the household. After the placement of the central body, some huts were probably abandoned and burned. There also is some evidence of sexual equality in the Paloma community because of the minor amount of differentiation among grave goods associated with the early burials. The later burials suggest the appearance of differentiation between males and females.

In summary, the diversity of burial treatment during the Archaic period probably indicates that burial of the dead was a relatively formal custom and had not yet been culturally restricted to one form in most regions. The presence of both primary and secondary burial practices may be related to the nomadic to seminomadic nature of many Archaic period settlement patterns. At some sites, burials are characterized by standard burial positions. In other instances, rules stipulate burial in shallow pits or deep-storage pits within a few meters of the house, suggesting that the buried individuals were probably occupants of the nearest house. Other burials are associated with minor or major settlements, appearing to have been placed in a less patterned manner within sites. We also see during this period and during the early ceramic period in many areas (in Ecuador and Peru at least), the more regular appearance of formalized cemetery areas or, minimally, rules regarding where and how burials are placed.

Formal cemeteries continued to develop or remain in use after the residential sectors of late Archaic settlements had been abandoned, a pattern that also characterized the later ceramic periods (see Quilter 1991). At present it is not possible to determine whether this pattern reflects the distribution of settlements as a whole or whether cemeteries, in any context, took on very different and enduring meanings than residential areas. I suspect that these patterns probably relate to the development of urbanism in general and may have more meaning in areas like Peru, Ecuador, and Bolivia, where more complex chiefdom and state societies eventually emerged. Population growth, consolidation of authority, ancestor worship, and changing world views are other factors that should be considered as well.

Monumental Forms of the Formative and Later Periods

Monumental burial adds a different type of relationship between the living and the dead and between a place of burial and its use by the living after interment of the deceased. While premonumental cemeteries place the body below ground and usually closed the tomb permanently, monumental burial entails above-ground display and continued visibility, if not accessibility, of the tomb after burial. There are in the northern and central Andes a number of tombs placed in stone chambers (see Bruhns 1992; Drennan, this volume) which apparently were accessible for a much longer period of time, and may have been more expressive of labor investment and periodic rituals between the living and the dead. Nonmonumental cemeteries in villages and urban settlements also were apparently reused and possibly incorporated into ritual, as suggested at sites of the Nasca period in Peru (see both Rowe and Carmichael, this volume). These sites were utilized in other ways as well. After their abandonment, they apparently were considered either as sacred sites where later groups buried their dead or as opportunistic places for establishing ancestor linkages.

In fact, there seems to be something important about occupying the tomb of a competitor or predecessor and establishing one's own identity or historical placement in regional affairs. This could perhaps be described as a process of burial "sodalities" crosscutting previous particularistic ethnic-lineage divisions between the living and the dead or between religious and secular elite groups, which in turn is linked to the processes of ethnic expansion and consolidation. It also may relate to legitimation by foreign intruders. For instance, Buikstra observes in her chapter that foreign elites probably legitimized their primacy in the Moquegua region of south Peru through burial in local cemeteries (see Stanish n.d.). An attempt at legitimacy also may explain the placement of later elite burials in early cemetery sites or in the atrium of old burial monuments. Clearly, there is a greater need to reconsider the different forms of conspicuous and inconspicuous display of elites, in both life and death, and what they mean in terms of geopolitics and social transformation.

From a broader perspective, several studies in this volume (Salomon, Donnan, Carmichael, Buikstra, Rowe) suggest that the possible linkage between the living and the dead in different regions of early pre-state societies in Peru, such as the Moche, Nasca, and Recuay cultures (for discussions of regional patterns, see Proulx 1979; Silverman and Browne n.d.; Donnan and McClelland 1979; Strong and Evans 1952; Grieder 1978), took

Introduction

alternative courses, depending on whether the major emphasis fell on the manipulation of ancestry, control of ritual and ceremony, or the celebration of particular elite individuals. I suspect that each of these patterns probably corresponds to major changes in the forms of public monuments and in the character of burial rites. At the same time, certain traits were evidently shared between different regions, for instance, between the south coast and south-central highland cultures of Peru during the Middle Horizon and Late Intermediate Period, as Buikstra demonstrates in her paper. These links included different types of burial practices, as well as the artifacts with which they were associated.

Another issue requires brief discussion: it has long been assumed that there is an association between monumental burial and the rise of elites and their control over expanding agricultural (and maritime) populations (see Moseley 1975). If the construction of burial monuments can be treated as an indicator of social ranking and economic production, most of them should have been built by highly productive societies and generally located in rich and expansive agricultural and pastoral lands (see Joseph Bastien in this volume) and along well-endowed coastal areas for fishing and shellfish collecting. There should also be a direct correlation between the distribution of burial monuments and their size and scale and their location in high and low areas of productivity, which may not always be the case (see Dillehay 1990). It is also possible that some highly productive societies constructed elaborate tombs in areas of low productivity, such as distant desert lands and sacred mountain tops. Further, there is some evidence from Peru to question whether monumental elite burial existed in early Formative times (Initial Period and Early Horizon), and whether there is evidence of economic and social stratification (Moseley 1989; Quilter 1991; Burger, 1990, personal communication). There are no elaborate burials of rulers, for example, nor signs of the accumulation of luxury items for a select few at many early monuments. Instead of strict political rule, ideology might have been the organizing force behind their construction. It is not inconceivable that much infrastructure, including monuments, was achieved at an informally politicized, if not religionized, nonleader level, with more self-control exercised by an underlying population.

Perhaps some of the most impressive early tombs are on the Paracas peninsula (see both Verano and Carmichael, this volume), where two innovative methods of burial were established during the Early Intermediate Period: Paracas Cavernas and Paracas Necropolis. The Paracas Cavernas consists of deep domed-shaped chambers cut out of rock and containing numerous mummy bundles wrapped in many layers of cloth. The Paracas Necropolis is characterized by different sized, rectangular pits without roofs. The dead were wrapped in textiles (and occasionally placed in baskets) and placed in the pits, which were then filled with sand.

Tom D. Dillehay

Other impressive monumental burials are on the north coast of Peru where the later Moche and Chimu cultures constructed elaborate tombs and in Cuzco where the dead Inka lords were enshrined in opulent settings. Donnan's paper in this volume describes the burial tombs of the royal and mundane members of the Moche society. Rowe's paper briefly addresses the ruins of Chan Chan, the capital city of the Chimu. The city contains ten large compounds that are characterized by a series of internal storehouses and chambers, with the center of the structure belonging to the king as his royal living chamber and, later, as his burial place. The last of the great and lavish Andean funerary cultures were practiced by the Inka, who placed their mummified kings on golden thrones in the Temple del Sol (Korikancha).

Several issues and questions for future research may derive from these considerations, questions, and burial forms. What is "public" or "private" about premonumental burials and monumental burials in sites? What are the secular and sacred functions of these sites? How do these and other functions and relationships change through time? How do burial assemblages and nonburial assemblages reflect these relations through time and space? What do these sites tell us about the supernatural world? What do the scale of sites and the location of burials within them say about labor expenditure, duration of construction, and relation to the domestic settlement pattern? What is the relationship between single and multiple burials (and single and multiple monuments) and corporate labor? Can monuments constructed over several generations really be considered as corporate sites? How do we derive social and hierarchical meaning from death and ritual contexts? And what aspects of societies are hidden or disguised in mortuary practice?

RITUAL CONTEXTS AND SOCIAL DYNAMICS

Most archaeologists who have studied burial patterns agree that differences in mortuary practices must be understood in systems (e.g., Binford 1971; Saxe n.d.; Bartel 1982). Still one of the most widely cited approaches to burial data stems from the early work of Binford (1971), who suggested that the complexity of mortuary ritual reflects the social position achieved or ascribed by the deceased person. Variants of this approach include attempts to rank the dead according to the amount of energy expended in the funeral (Tainter 1978), or the variety and complexity of the surviving grave goods (O'Shea 1981). There are also several studies that place the emphasis on the relationship between monument building and the deceased as an important ancestor (Renfrew 1984), and others that attempt to assess different grave goods according to their frequency in the archaeological record (e.g., Kroeber 1927; Chapman, Kinnes, and Randsborg 1981; Bartel 1982).

Introduction

In the Andes, most research has dealt with the economic and demographic prehistory of specific cultural areas. Other than occasional and uncritical reference to the social evolutionary models of Elman Service, Ronald Cohen, and Morton Fried, little serious thinking has been given to the economic and ideological meaning of death and funerary rites. In most cases emphasis has been placed on the development of social ranking and stratification as a result of competition between individuals and groups of high status, as revealed by the ritual of burials (e.g., Donnan and McClelland 1979; Donnan, this volume), the construction of burial monuments (e.g., Duque and Cubillos 1979; Pozorski n.d.; Conrad n.d.; Donnan 1985; Arango 1984; Cubillos 1986; Dillehay 1990) and, sometimes, fortifications, and the consumption of prestige goods. There has also been little connection between the social dynamics inferred from burial and architectural data.

Although the more tractable vertical distinctions (e.g., rank and wealth) of Andean societies may be surmised archaeologically, other general indicators of social distinction have not been defined in terms of burial contexts—for example, corporate group membership, descent orientation, moiety affiliation, and society membership. Multistratified group cemeteries, like those found in many coastal and highland sites throughout the Andes (Bennett 1936; Kauffmann Doig 1973; Munizaga 1965; Stothert 1985; Ubelaker 1981; Engel 1966; Lubensky 1974; Donnan and Mackey 1978; Tello and Xesspe 1979), allow the possibility of studying these distinctions, as well as cultural identity and mortuary variability, from both synchronic and diachronic perspectives, as documented by several contributors to this volume.

The papers of Drennan and Buikstra, in particular, focus on these issues. Drennan examines the stone slab tombs and stone statues of the San Agustín culture (300 B.C. to A.D. 800) of Colombia. These tombs are covered by earthen barrows and are accompanied by stone statues of humans, animals, and anthropomorphic creatures. Most of the burial investment is associated with tomb construction; little grave furniture is included. To Drennan this pattern suggests little personal wealth for rulers and a political organization based on a highly personalized leadership in the context of relatively little economic differentiation. In such a system, the public commemoration of dead leaders in the form of elaborate above-ground tombs probably served to legitimize their successors. By extension, this process of legitimation of authority probably reflects incompletely or informally institutionalized positions of centralized political power. The disappearance of this practice around A.D. 800 probably signaled the demise of a centralized political organization. At the same time, there occurred an increase in settlement nucleation, suggesting more rather than less centralized patterns of social, economic, and political organization. Drennan believes that the changes taking place in settlement patterns and mortuary practices might reflect not the demise of political leadership, but rather its fuller institutionalization or its grounding in stronger economic differentiation, making legitimation by personal glorification of past leaders less relevant.

As part of a larger regional program developed by several scholars, Buikstra integrates biological and cultural perspectives concerning the Osmore Valley, focusing specifically on the Chiribaya culture, an Andean coastal polity of the Late Intermediate Period that emerged on the extreme south coast of Peru after the collapse of Tiwanaku. Her project is partially designed to distinguish between María Rostworowski de Diez Canseco's horizontal and John Murra's vertical strategies of social and economic organization. Rostworowski's model describes distinctive coastal polities dominated by local rulers. In her model, economic diversification and specialization create ethnically distinct farmers and fishers within local areas, as well as unequal distribution of resources within and between communities. Murra's approach entails cultural and biological diversity within ecological tiers, with observable interzonal linkages. Buikstra examined four grave sites for variation in tomb preparation, feature location, and content. She reports evidence for both vertical and horizontal differentiation. She also finds that above-ground burial display was important to resource control and to community identity, presumably in times of intergroup contact if not conflict.

Also focusing on vertical relationships is Donnan, who examines the aoche culture in terms of mortuary variability and the changing scale of the social system. Donnan brings together for the first time information on Moche burial practice to formulate a typology of burials that correlates to the wealth and social status of the deceased. Donnan discovers that most Moche burials are found in clusters, forming distinct cemetery areas comprising individuals of approximately the same social status. Although most cemeteries contain individuals of all ages and both sexes, a few contain only high-status adult males. The grave goods associated with this last group reflect individuals who were probably affiliated with a specific priesthood or ritual brotherhood. Donnan concludes that the relationship between the living and the organization of the burial points to scale and status in social life and to institutionalized redundancy of burial practice from elite to nonelite levels.

In a similar but less typological approach to the Nasca mortuary date, Carmichael examines burial patterns through time for continuity and change and how they reflect social structure and belief systems. He employs the relative amount of energy invested in the interment of an individual to categorize graves. He sees a direct correspondence between his burial categories and a loosely ranked social structure. While the burial data reflect a basic structural continuity in south coast society throughout the Early Intermediate Period, greater amounts of energy were invested in mortuary ritual during the middle part of the sequence. Carmichael believes that this empha-

Introduction

sizes intragroup pressures related to land ownership and inheritance of vital resources. The importance of ancestor worship as a means of validating ownership and status positions also is considered in light of mortuary-related iconography and archaeological evidence of tomb reentry, offering renewal, and secondary burial. Unlike the Moche case, the Nasca and Paracas burials seem to present an interesting case of disjuncture between political hierarchies and burial hierarchies in terms of the correspondence between conspicuous and elaborate burials and inconspicuous architecture.

An issue discussed by several contributors is the difference between the treatment of the dead and the burial of the dead, particularly in regard to social ranking and to our reading of the archaeological record. It is obvious that only part of a population received elaborate treatment in death and burial in monuments and cemeteries. For instance, the total number of burials in Moche and Nasca sites generally provides low population figures, and women and children are usually underrepresented. There is the further problem that different funerary practices within a single burial complex or among several complexes may have existed at the same time for the same group or for different groups. In the studies of Donnan, Carmichael, and Rowe, there is evidence to suggest that different societies may have interred different social groups in separate areas (see Brown 1981 for a similar pattern in other culture areas), several monuments, or parts of monuments, and that these monuments may have been utilized at different stages of ceremony or for different groups. It is also likely that burial clusters and compartmentalized tombs within the same site represent segmented societies (much like those in Africa), with each linked to a different ancestor lineage. We know from the ethnohistoric and ethnographic records that funerary rites may be spread over several ceremonies, which take place at different times and places (see Salomon and Dillehay, in this volume). It may even be possible to trace such a sequence in the archaeological record.

Burials also may have received preliminary treatment or bodily manipulation elsewhere, although it would be difficult to determine where and which practices were employed in other contexts. One argument for this kind of practice might come from the distribution of partial bodies, particularly in sites of the Formative period, such as those of the Initial Period (see Quilter 1991) and Early Horizon (see Lumbreras 1989) in Peru. The presence of particular bones in sites might mean that the near-complete body was buried elsewhere, that such remains were selected from ossuaries and did not result from burial or exposure at the tomb site itself.

It is during the Late Preceramic and Early Formative periods in many areas that an increase in bodily mutilation seems to have occurred (see Lumbreras 1989; Weiss 1962; Verano, Buikstra, and Carmichael in this volume). There also seem to be intermittent periods of mutilation, as suggested at several Middle Horizon sites on the coast of Peru and in many areas of the highlands. Although difficult to prove at present, intermittent mutilation and/or human sacrifice may demonstrate the power and wealth of new ruling groups and the lengths to which they would go to maintain power. It might also indicate changing ideologies and conflict between different ethnic groups. Furthermore, what may have started as a small-scale practice in earlier times or in local contexts—the ritualistic offering of wealth in exchange for recognized status—might have increased to include human sacrifice (and mutilation) and was elaborated until it assumed major and conspicuous importance. Clearly, as Verano suggests in his chapter on the treatment of human offerings and trophies, archaeologists must work harder to understand the context and meaning of bodily mutilation and unusually disarticulated and partial burials.

Verano shows that dedicatory burials, sacrifices, trophy heads, and other offerings of human remains constitute a unique category of archaeological features clearly distinct from standardized burial patterns. He also notes that human offerings normally assumed to be related to death under unusual circumstances are often categorized by archaeologists as "ritual death." Verano cautions that not all such features should be interpreted as reflecting sacrifices or ritual death, and that careful study of the physical remains is crucial to interpreting them. He also points out that the imprecise use of terms such as "trophy heads" has obscured the nature of these features.

Other aspects of monumental burial relate to architecture and art and their possible ritualistic functions. Examples are the cliff burials discovered in northeastern Peru by Federico Kaufmann Doig and his associates, and the iconographic depictions of human trophy heads and body parts either sculptured or etched in stone, such as those seen at Chavín de Huantar and Cerro Sechin in Peru. These features are examples of buildings or parts probably used for rituals, a development that apparently became more prevalent in subsequent cultures throughout the Peruvian highlands and coast.

At this point we can ask about the meaning of certain types of grave offerings and especially the style of goods found in tombs. A direct link between exotic goods and burials suggests that decorated artifact styles and their burial associations may possess a special character (*sensu* Menzel 1976). It is apparent that the styles of grave goods were as restricted in death as in life. We can also question whether ceramic styles, bodily positions, or other attributes, singularly or collectively, reflect ranking in the Andes, and to what extent grave goods even can be used to estimate rank and wealth. Central to this point is Drennan's study of the San Agustín burial monuments and offerings. As mentioned earlier, he does not believe that these features suggest great personal wealth of the deceased. Instead, he argues that they reflect a political organization based on a powerful but highly personalized leadership structure in a context of relatively little economic differentiation and an incompletely institutionalized political structure.

Introduction

In examining the social dimensions of Andean burial practices, we should bear in mind that the type and frequency of grave goods may be a poor method of determining the rank (see Tainter 1978) of the deceased, at least in comparison with studies on energy spent by the living to bury and commemorate the dead. More investigation into the nature and quantity of grave goods from both small-scale and large-scale sites should help in the study of ranking and social stratification. Such an approach also needs to be related to skeletal evidence concerning the age, sex, and diet of the deceased, but in the Andes such information is rare. A few skeletal studies (e.g., Ubelaker 1981; Munizaga 1965; Allison 1985; Allison and Gerszten 1982; Quilter 1989; Rothhammer et al. 1986; Weiss 1961, 1962) have provided some information on diet, disease, age profile, sex ratio, and sometimes social and cultural groups, but a much larger data base is required before reliable conclusions can be drawn. It also would be wise for Andeanists to consider the contextual and humanistic approaches of Ian Hodder (1986), which stress that material culture is not only a reflection of economic adaptation and political order, but also an active element in human relations, and that it can be used to disguise as well as reflect social relations and ideological schemes.

Last, from a broader social perspective it seems apparent that we need to view mortuary practices in terms of two general trends or trajectories that seemingly operated in Pre-Columbian times: (1) an alteration between periods of regionalization and centralization, in which social developments were essentially either small-scale or large-scale; and (2) periods in which parts of systems were integrated with ideological and economic networks reaching into distant areas, such as the eastern lowlands (see Rivera for the Chinchorro area) and other distant places (e.g., Buikstra for altiplano influence on the south coast of Peru). With possible exceptions, such as the Early Horizon in Peru, the major periods of economic growth in the Andes did not seem to occur when social systems were open to strong outside influence. Rather, some of the more important developments of a period, including elaborate mortuary practices, may have been stimulated by decreasing and selective contact with other areas. Although very little is known about these kinds of connections and how they operated at different temporal and spatial scales, it is interesting to contemplate how these trends might relate to selected mortuary practice, particularly if special exotic items were imported for grave contents and if an imported ideology determined the practice.

RITUAL FEASTING AND COSMOLOGICAL MEDIATION

Curiously, while many Western cultures have tried to liberate themselves from the tyranny of their own historical consequences, Andean cultures have seemingly thrived in it. If past Andean cultures were anything like their contemporary counterparts, the juxtaposition of the past and present in elaborate burial ceremony must have made people more conscious of their history by allowing them to step back from it temporarily. Burial feasts and ceremonies were not just public farewells to the deceased and political rallies for rulers; they also must have propelled people into the future and provided them with the form and the occasion for envisioning alternative life situations and reflecting on their history.

Several contributors (Bastien, Salomon, and Dillehay) suggest that Andean people conceived of time, death, and history in a present and nonpresent framework, which expressed social distance and social structure. These and other studies (e.g., Zuidema 1986; Murra 1977; Millones 1990; Netherly n.d.) point to the importance of Andean principles of social organization and conceptions of death in the afterworld and the role of burial ritual in linking the living and the dead. In particular, Bastien shows how Aymara burial rituals are replete with metaphors of fertility and social divisions. He sees ritual feasts among the dead as representing a metaphor for a cyclical process of life to death and death to life that is related to the Aymara's understanding of their role in the natural world. In the papers by Salomon and Dillehay, burial ritual, as the commemorative part of cosmology, seems to be an exercise of Andean society in search of temporal order. If this is the case, then monumental tomb construction can be considered an architectural cosmology that provided historical order among deceased leaders and, above all, established their historical place in society by visibly and permanently projecting people's concerns with death and the deceased upon the world. By extension, the construction phase can be seen as a process of transition through which the living and the dead are disentangled and defined contextually, with the former residing outside of the tomb and the latter remaining inside. These schema also might be reflected in the discussions of Donnan, Rowe, Verano, and Carmichael on the rites of different primary, secondary, and double burials among various Peruvian cultures. It may be that these rites frequently represent the dying and death as part of a cyclical process of life and death. And, as Rowe suggests, sequential burial contexts may indicate as much about the outside world of the living as they do about the order inside the world of the dead.

My own chapter reviews the archaeological, ethnohistoric, and ethnographic information on the Mapuche burial of paramount chiefs in earthen mounds and how mound burial reflects interlineage power relations and leadership succession. Chiefly, burial entails two funerary phases: rites associated with interment of the deceased in the mound, and postfunerary rites associated with the legitimation of the new ruler. In this case, postfunerary rites serve a lineage to time-extend the death of an important chief for the purpose of constituting and reconstituting enduring and productive social

Introduction

relations among allied kin groups, especially during times of war. These occasions also provide the opportunity for a new chief to establish his authority and attempt to extend it beyond his own group. Set in this context, mounds are products of regional interaction spheres, not local societies. Mounds are also considered to be historical signatures of power from which important lineages and new chiefs derive their authority. In this regard, mound building partially reflects a burial strategy employed for maintaining the institution of leadership following the death of incumbents.

WHEN DO THE DEAD DIE? TOMBS FOR THE LIVING

A major theme of several papers is the association of ancestor cults and mortuary practices, which links the living and the dead. We know from ethnographic research in the Andes that ancestor cults strengthen the cohesion of the community and its economy or political character (e.g., Salomon 1987 and this volume; Avila 1966); they also establish a community's claim to the resource zones which they control. This relationship is expressed in Bastien's paper. He shows how Aymara men establish patrilineal claims to land and how ancestral and permanent rights to property are founded on male descendants working the land and performing rituals, and ancestor burial in the community cemetery. His paper also demonstrates a close geographical relationship between a cemetery (as a monument) and local zones of resource productivity. Bastien also provides archaeologists with several good examples of Aymara-specific contextual and symbolic correlates for archaeological testing (see Cook 1993 for an archaeological study of Wari figurines and ancestor relations).

There is also the question of the role of ancestor worship in local mortuary practices and the continued use of ancestral monuments to make gains in the living world, themes discussed by Salomon and Dillehay. In his analysis of several regional societies, Salomon's paper shows that sacred shrines focused on ancestors and ancestor mummy cults were powerful forces of individual family and community action in late pre-Hispanic and colonial times. In the Andagua region of southern Peru, for instance, it seems that the economic flow of goods was directed through ancestors in the form of mummy cult endowments. The cults served to embody legitimacy in family and community titles to land and water. In effect, the ownership and cult control of important ancestor mummies gave principal families a historical precedence and claim to credit which enabled them to obtain major commitments of capital from the endowment fund and labor from the community. Salomon also notes that the opposite of ancestor cults—attacking and destroying the ancestors of outsiders—also played a major role in social change, as did the looting and destruction of the grave sites of non-locals. Salomon believes that such dynamics also played a key role in pre-Hispanic chiefdom societies, especially in regard to tribute-taking, ancestor worship, and public ceremony in the Inka state.

A subtle implication of these papers for archaeologists is how funerary ritual, as one aspect in which ancestor worship was carried out, can change once societies switched from primarily kin-based groups to non-kin tributary groups and, correspondingly, when more complex secular, urban settlements and production systems (e.g., Wari, Inka) came into being. The shift to more secular systems amd the demise of kin-based units in the overall power structure of society might suggest that differences of power and prestige were no longer expressed through ancestor celebration and conspicuous grave display. If so, we might expect several possible developments to occur. One is the gradual discontinuance of undifferentiated collective burial and the commemoration of specific individuals and perhaps lineage groups in monuments such as those seen in the San Agustín, Moche, and Mapuche cultures (see Drennan, this volume; Donnan, this volume; Dillehay 1990, 1992, and this volume). On the other hand, it might be that more recent funerary monuments, while taking the same architectural form as their predecessors (which might explain the horizontal and vertical accretion of burial monuments), no longer played the same role, but acted as a demonstration of an elite's power over corporate labor. And in some parts of the Andes the construction of large-scale burial monuments may be related to increased control over ritual and ceremony as a means of legitimizing and maintaining, if not building, a power base, a point suggested in my study of Mapuche mound building.

EPILOGUE

The Andean data on mortuary patterns suggest that our observations on death and the relationship between the living and the dead can be understood if the role of death and burial ritual is allowed to retain a central position in our analysis (see Lyon's commentary for a similar perspective). It is useful to know why the dead should assume prominence in different societies and what these differences tell us about the nature and organization of Andean society. More can be done to understand these differences, however. If we pay more attention to ritual action and its contextual sequencing, rather than to ideal-typical models of chiefdom and state forms derived from sociocultural developmental schema (*sensu* Fried, Service, Alfred Johnson, and Timothy Earle), certain patterning might stand out. More attention to context and ritual sequencing also might suggest more complex exchange of information and goods in the practice of known and unknown principles of the Andean world than any recognize previously.

There is an absence in this volume of papers focused on evolutionary schemes of chiefdom and state development. Perhaps most contributors are

Introduction

acutely aware of the limited utility of these schemes, or perhaps we sense that the Andean world, as represented by the burial practices studied in these papers, cannot always be understood in terms of general models. Within Andean tradition there must have been a competing set of models of the meaning of death, models which are firmly embedded in distinct social and cosmological (or philosophical) traditions. We must determine the structure and meaning of the various powers underlying them. Several papers, particularly those of Salomon, Carmichael, Dillehay, and Drennan, demonstrate the possibility that elite burial practices and cults played a significantly active part in achieving processes of social and cultural change. The question of understanding the role of death and burial ritual in maintaining the status quo or in bringing about change is a complex and significant one, to which archaeologists can contribute in various ways. But I suspect that given our current state of knowledge and interest in the Andes and the types of general models most Andeanists employ to interpret data—sociocultural developmental levels focused on chiefdom and state societies—we must rely on ethnohistorians and ethnographers to nudge us from our fixed positions to take bold steps to search for new directions.

Although archaeological burial records are ambiguous, they do, in principle, provide rich material for postulating baselines from which to evaluate likely conditions in time and space, which may be reinforced by the judicious use of ethnographic material (and ethnoarchaeological studies) as a means of thinking critically about possible alternative interpretations. While there are certain architectural and settlement forms associated with chiefdom and state societies, it is difficult to associate them with burial practices. Yet, as these introductory remarks seek to demonstrate, no truly universal group of categories such as chiefdom, state, and civilization is possible without considering the diversity of the forms of social, political, religious, and, I might add, death and mortuary dimensions, in terms of the entire history of a region. But the importance of death and burial may not lie in recognizing the similar and dissimilar processes in the San Agustín, Moche, Nasca, Mapuche, and other societies and in producing a common result—linking the living and the dead. Rather, burial practice should be seen as a process that is inextricably linked in fundamental conceptual terms with a larger enterprise, which places death and the whole of a group's history on a single agenda, one which was implemented through a variety of ritual, architectural, and symbolic linkages. Finally, from the many images of the past or future that must have influenced the actions of Andean societies, death was surely one of the most widespread and powerful ones. It must have been an ingredient of a social sense of historical time, whose horizons must have extended without limits into the future and the past, linking the dead and the living, as much as past and present cemeteries do today.

Although today Roman Catholicism has replaced many traditional belief

Tom D. Dillehay

systems in the Andes, when death occurs many communities still cling to old religious rites. These rites not only demonstrate how deeply rooted the cult of the dead is in Andean societies, but how death and, in the Mapuche case, the behavior of mourners may be politicized in the modern world. Beliefs about death surely provided a social basis for moral order in pre-Hispanic times and were vulnerable to manipulation by public leaders and priests. Future research should examine the politicization of death and public funerals and how it changed from the earlier theocratic chiefdom societies to the later secular urban societies. Research also is needed on the impact of increased urbanization, secularism, and regional religious differences and how they might have generated diverse attitudes toward death, causing funerals to evolve from local rituals into personalized symbolic events administered by the living rulers for dead rulers, for example, the burial of the Sipán lord being perhaps the most elaborate burial known. The development of monumental or public funerals and innovations in tomb administration probably suggest a new level of occupational specialization in politicized funeral arrangements. This display in turn probably demonstrates the importance of these events for defining social identity and political manipulation in pre-Hispanic times.

Acknowledgements I wish to thank Elizabeth Boone and the Senior Fellows of Dumbarton Oaks for inviting me to develop and chair an Andean symposium in the Pre-Columbian Studies Program. I am grateful to both Elizabeth Boone and the staff of Dumbarton Oaks for their congeniality, assistance, and hospitality. I also thank the anonymous reviewers for their helpful comments and suggestions on the individual chapters, including this introduction.

Introduction

BIBLIOGRAPHY

ALLISON, MARVIN J.
    1985   Chile's Ancient Mummies. *Natural History* 94: 74–81.

ALLISON, MARVIN J., AND ELIZABETH GERSZTEN
    1982   *Paleopathology in South American Mummies: Applications of Modern Techniques.* Medical College of Virginia, Richmond.

ARANGO, JORGE
    1984   *Reevaluación de las Antiques Cultures Aborigines de Colombia.* Bogotá.

AVILA, FRANCISCO DE
    1966   *Dioses y hombres de Huarochirí: Narración quechua recogida por Francisco de Avila (1598?).* (José María Arguedas, trans.). University of Texas Press, Austin.

BARTEL, BRAD
    1982   A Historical Review of Ethnological and Archaeological Analyses of Mortuary Practices. *Journal of Anthropological Archaeology* 1 (1): 32–58.

BENNETT, WENDELL C.
    1936   *Excavations in Bolivia.* Anthropological Papers of the American Museum of Natural History 35 (4). New York.
    1939   *Archaeology of the North Coast of Peru.* Anthropological Papers of the American Museum of Natural History 37 (1). New York.

BENSON, ELIZABETH (ED.)
    1975   *Death and the Afterlife in Pre-Columbian America.* Dumbarton Oaks, Washington, D.C.

BINFORD, LEWIS
    1971   Mortuary Practices: Their Study and Their Potential. In *Approaches to the Social Dimensions of Mortuary Practices* (James A. Brown, ed.). Memoirs of the Society for American Archaeology 25: 6–29. Washington, D.C.

BIRD, JUNIUS B.
    1963   Preceramic Art from Huaca Prieta, Chicama Valley. *Ñawpa Pacha* 1: 29–34.

BLOCH, MAURICE, AND JONATHAN PARRY (EDS.)
    1982   *Death and the Regeneration of Life.* Cambridge University Press, New York.

BONAVIA, DUCCIO
    1982   *Precerámico Peruano. Las Gavilanes: Mar, Desierto y Oasis en la Historia del Hombre.* Corporación Financiera de Desarrollo, Instituto Arqueológico Aleman, Lima.

BROWN, JAMES A.
    1981   The Search for Rank in Prehistoric Burials. In *The Archaeology of Death* (Richard Chapman, Ian Kinnes, and Klavs Randsborg, eds.): 25–37. Cambridge University Press, New York.

Bruhns, Karen
    1992   Monumental Sculpture as Evidence for Hierarchical Societies. In *Wealth and Hierarchy in the Intermediate Area* (Frederick Lange, ed.): 331–356. Dumbarton Oaks, Washington, D.C.

Cardich, Augusto
    1964   Lauricocha: Fundamentos para una prehistoria de los Andes Centrales. *Studia Praehistorica 3*.

Carrion Cachot, Rebeca
    1948   La Cultura Chavín: Dos Nuevas Colonias: Kuntur Wasi-Ancón. *Revista del Museo Nacional de Antropología Arqueología* 2 (1): 99–172.

Chapman, Richard, Ian Kinnes, and Klavs Randsborg (eds.)
    1981   *The Archaeology of Death*. Cambridge University Press, New York.

Conrad, Geoffrey
    n.d.   Burial Platforms and Related Structures on the North Coast of Peru: Some Social and Political Implications. Ph.D. dissertation, Harvard University, 1974.

Cook, Anita G.
    1993   The Stone Ancestors: Idioms of Imperial Attire and Rank among Huari Figurines. *Latin American Antiquity* 3: 341–371.

Correal U., Gonzalo
    1989   *Aquazuque: Evidencias de Cazadores-Recolectores y Plantadores el la Altiplanicie de la Cordillera Oriental*. Fundación de Investigaciones Arqueológicas Nacionales del Banco de la República, Bogotá.

Cubillos, J. César
    1986   *Arqueología de San Agustín*. Fundación de Investigaciones Arqueológicas Nacionales del Banco de la República, Bogotá.

Dillehay, Tom D.
    1990   Mapuche Ceremonial Landscape, Social Recruitment, and Resource Rights. *World Archaeology* 22 (2): 223–241.
    1992   Keeping Outsiders Out: Public Ceremony, Resource Rights, and Hierarchy in Historic and Contemporary Mapuche Society. In *Wealth and Hierarchy in the Intermediate Area* (Frederick Lange, ed.): 379–419. Dumbarton Oaks, Washington, D.C.

Dillehay, Tom D., and Patricia J. Netherly
    n.d.   Field Notes of the 1981 Survey Season in the Upper Zana Valley, Peru. Manuscript on file, University of Kentucky, Lexington, 1981.

Donnan, Christopher B. (ed.)
    1985   *Ceremonial Architecture in the Andes*. Dumbarton Oaks, Washington, D.C.

Donnan, Christopher B., and Carol Mackey
    1978   *Ancient Burial Patterns of the Moche Valley, Peru*. University of Texas Press, Austin.

Introduction

DONNAN, CHRISTOPHER B., AND DONNA MCCLELLAND
   1979   *The Burial Theme in Moche Iconography.* Studies in Pre-Columbian Art and Archaeology 21. Dumbarton Oaks, Washington, D.C.

DUQUE GOMEZ, LUIS, AND JULIO CÉSAR CUBILLOS
   1979   *Arqueología de San Agustín, Alto de Los Idolos, Montículos y Tumbas.* Fundación de Investigaciones Arqueológicas Nacionales del Banco de la República, Bogotá.

DWYER, EDWARD, AND JANE P. DWYER
   1975   The Paracas Cemeteries: Mortuary Patterns in a Peruvian South Coastal Tradition. In *Death and the Afterlife in Pre-Columbian America* (Elizabeth Benson, ed.): 145–161. Dumbarton Oaks, Washington, D.C.

ENGEL, FREDERIC A.
   1960   Un groupe humain de 5000 ans a Paracas, Perou. *Journal de la Société des Americanistes* 49: 7–35.
   1963   *A Preceramic Settlement on the Central Coast of Peru: Asia, Unit 1.* Transactions of the American Philosophical Society 53 (3). Philadelphia.
   1966   *Paracas, Cien Siglos de la Cultura Peruana.* Editorial Juan Mejía Baca, Lima.

GONZALÉZ, ALBERTO REX
   1985   Excavations in Bolivia. Anthropological Papers of the American Museum of Natural History 35: 329–507. New York.

GRIEDER, TERENCE
   1978   *The Art and Archaeology of Pashash.* University of Texas Press, Austin.

GRIEDER, TERENCE, ALBERTO B. MENDOZA, CHARLES E. SMITH, AND ROBERT M. MALINA
   1988   *La Galgada, Peru: A Preceramic Culture in Transition.* University of Texas Press, Austin.

HODDER, IAN
   1986   *Reading the Past.* Cambridge University Press, New York.

KAUFFMANN DOIG, FEDÉRICO
   1973   *Manual de Arqueología Peruana.* Ediciones PEISA, Lima.
   1979   Placas ceramicas de la Cueva de Chucu, Condesuyos. *Revista del Museo Nacional* 48: 187–194.

KROEBER, ALFRED L.
   1925   *The Uhle Pottery Collections from Moche.* University of California Publications in American Archaeology and Ethnology 21 (5). Berkeley.
   1927   Disposal of the Dead. *American Anthropologist* 28: 360–371.

LARCO HOYLE, RAFAEL
   1945   *La Cultura Viru.* Lima.

LUBENSKY, EDUARDO H.
   1974   Los Cementerios de Anllulla: Informe Preliminar sobre una Excavación Arqueológica. *Boletín de la Academia Nacional de Historia* 57 (123): 16–23. Bogotá.

LUMBRERAS, LUIS G.
- 1974 *The Peoples and Cultures of Ancient Peru* (Betty J. Meggers, trans.). Smithsonian Institution Press, Washington, D.C.
- 1989 *Chavín de Huántar en el Nacimiento de la Civilización Andina.* Instituto Andino de Estudios Arqueológicos, Ediciones INDEA, Lima.

MENZEL, DOROTHY
- 1976 *Pottery Style and Society in Ancient Peru.* University of California Press, Berkeley.

MILLONES, LUIS (ED.)
- 1990 *El Retorno de Las Huacas.* Instituto de Estudios Peruanos, Lima.

MOSELEY, MICHAEL E.
- 1975 *The Maritime Foundations of Andean Civilization.* Cummings Publishing Co., Menlo Park, Calif.
- 1989 Large Monuments and Precocious Formative Developments. *The Review of Archaeology* 10: 186–192.

MUNIZAGA, JUAN
- 1965 Skeletal Remains from Sites of Valdivia and Machalilla Phases. In *Early Formative Period of Coastal Ecuador: The Valdivia and Machalilla Phases* (Betty J. Meggers, Cliff Evans, and Emilio Estrada, eds.) 1: 129–234. Smithsonian Contributions to Anthropology, Washington, D.C.

MURRA, JOHN V.
- 1977 *La Organizacion Económica del estado Inca.* Siglo Vientiuno, Mexico City.

NETHERLY, PATRICIA
- n.d. Out of Many, Come One: The Organization of Rule in the North Coast Polities. Ph.D. dissertation, Cornell University, 1977.

O'SHEA, JOHN
- 1981 Social Configurations and the Archaeological Study of Mortuary Practices: A Case Study. In *The Archaeology of Death* (Richard Chapman, Ian Kinnes, and Klavs Randsborg, eds.): 39–52. Cambridge University Press, New York.
- 1984 *Mortuary Variability: An Archaeological Investigation.* Academic Press, New York.

PAUL, ANNE
- 1990 *Paracas Ritual Attire: Symbols of Authority in Ancient Peru.* University of Oklahoma Press, Norman.

POZORSKI, THOMAS
- n.d. Survey and Excavations of Burial Platforms at Chan Chan, Peru. B.A. thesis, Harvard University, 1971.

PROULX, DONALD A.
- 1979 *Nasca Gravelots in the Uhle Collection from the Ica Valley, Peru.* Department of Anthropology Research Reports 2. University of Massachusetts, Amherst.

QUILTER, JEFFREY
- 1989 *Life and Death at Palome: Society and Mortuary Practices in a Preceramic Peruvian Village.* University of Iowa Press, Iowa City.

1991 Late Preceramic Peru. *Journal of World Prehistory* 5: 387–438.
n.d. Paloma: Mortuary Practices and Social Organization of a Preceramic Peruvian Village. Ph.D. dissertation, University of California, Santa Barbara, 1984.

RENFREW, COLIN
1984 *Approaches to Social Archaeology.* Harvard University Press, Cambridge, Mass.

RICK, JOHN
1980 *Prehistoric Hunters of the High Andes.* Academic Press, New York.

ROTHHAMMER, FRANCISCO, CECELIA SILVA, JUAN COCILOVO, AND SYLVIA QUEVEDO
1986 Una hipotésis provesional sobre el poblamiento de Chile basada en el analísis multivariado de medidas craneométricas. *Chungará* 16–17: 183–198.

ROWE, JOHN H.
1962a Warsaae's Law and the Use of Grave Lots for Archaeological Dating. *American Antiquity* 28 (2): 129–137.
1962b Stages and Periods in Archaeological Interpretations. *Southwestern Journal of Anthropology* 18: 34–42.
1963 Urban Settlements in Ancient Peru. *Ñawpa Pacha* 1: 1–27.

SALOMON, FRANK
1987 Ancestor Cults and Resistance to the State in Arequipa, ca. 1748–1754. In *Resistance, Rebellion, and Consciousness in the Andean Peasant World: 18th to 20th Centuries* (Steve J. Stein, ed.): 148–165. University of Wisconsin Press, Madison.

SAXE, ARTHUR
n.d. Social Dimensions of Mortuary Practices. Ph.D. dissertation, University of Michigan, Ann Arbor, 1970.

SCHIAPPACASSE, VIRGILIO, AND HANS NIEMEYER
1984 *Descripción y Analísis Interpretativo de un sitio arcaico temprano en la Quebrada de Camarones.* Publicación Ocasional 41, Museo Nacional de Historia Natural, Santiago.

SILVERMAN, HELAINE, AND DAVID BROWNE
n.d. The Nascas. Manuscript on file at the University of Illinois, Urbana, 1991.

STANISH, CHARLES
n.d. Chulpa Tombs in Central Andean Prehistory. Manuscript, 1990.

STOTHERT, KAREN
1985 The Preceramic Las Vegas Culture of Coastal Ecuador. *American Antiquity* 50 (3): 613–637.

STRONG, WILLIAM D.
1925 *The Uhle Pottery Collections from Ancon.* University of California Publications in American Archaeology and Ethnology 21 (4): 135–190.

STRONG, WILLIAM D., AND CLIFFORD EVANS
1952 *Cultural Stratigraphy in the Viru Valley, Northern Peru: The Formative and*

Florescent Epochs. Columbia Studies in Archaeology and Ethnology 4. New York.

TAINTER, JOHN
1978 Mortuary Practices and the Study of Prehistoric Social Systems. In *Advances in Archaeological Method and Theory* 1 (Michael Schiffer, ed.): 105–141. Academic Press, New York.

TATTERSALL, IAN
1985 The Human Skeletons from Huaca Prieta, with a Note on Exostoses of the External Auditory Meatus. In Junius B. Bird, *The Preceramic Excavations at the Huaca Prieta, Chicama Valley, Peru* (John Hyslop, ed.). Anthropological Papers of the American Museum of Natural History 62 (1): 60–64. New York.

TELLO, JULIO C., AND T. MEJIA XESSPE
1979 *Paracas: Parte II, Cavernas y Necropolis*. Universidad Nacional Mayor de San Marcos, Lima.

UBELAKER, DOUGLAS H.
1981 *The Ayalan Cemetery: A Late Integration Period Burial Site on the South Coast of Ecuador*. Smithsonian Contributions to Anthropology 27. Washington, D.C.

WEISS, PEDRO
1961 *Osteología Cultural: Prácticas Cefálicas*. Universidad Nacional Mayor de San Marcos, Lima.
1962 *Las Trepanaciones de los Antiquos Peruanos: Estudios Osteo-Cultural*. Lima.

WILLEY, GORDON
1953 *Prehistoric Settlement Patterns in the Viru Valley, Peru*. Smithsonian Institution, Bureau of American Ethnology, Bulletin 155. Washington, D.C.

ZUIDEMA, TOM
1986 *The Inca Civilization of Cuzco*. University of Texas Press, Austin.

Behavior and Belief in Ancient Peruvian Mortuary Practice

JOHN HOWLAND ROWE

AS A CONTRIBUTION TO ARCHAEOLOGICAL THEORY, I want to discuss the inferences about behavior and belief that have been or can be made about ancient Peruvian mortuary practices from examining the archaeological evidence. I shall try to use disciplined logical and analogical arguments that avoid the realm of fantasy.

In excavating habitation refuse or house sites, whatever behavior we can see is the behavior of a group, a community, or a family. We do not see the behavior of individuals. If we find individual burials, however, we can distinguish one individual from another. If there is variation in the burials, we may be able to distinguish individual differences in burial practice. Differences in the selection of goods buried with different individuals may provide information on differences in behavior by sex or age and differences in occupation and status. These are excellent reasons for archaeologists to study ancient burials.

The position of objects in a refuse deposit provides no information about behavior or belief, because the placement of objects is not a consideration in refuse discard. Position is informative when we can argue that placement was deliberate. Such an argument can be made when we find a house or a settlement that was buried by a disaster, such as a landslide or a volcanic eruption. It can also be made for the contents of burials, including the bodies in them.

THE POSITION OF THE BODY

Let us consider, for example, the position of the body in ancient Peruvian interments. In Salinar, Gallinazo, and Moche burials, the body is consistently extended and supine, in essentially the same position used traditionally for Christian burials. This position is, for the living, one of rest associated with sleep. So is the position of a loosely flexed body lying on its side, a position observed by Augusto Cardich in burials in Cave L-2 at Lauricocha (Cardich 1964: 118).

A seated, flexed body carries a different message. The position is also one of rest for the living, but is assumed by people who are awake. Mummy bundles from the central coast of Peru in which the body is in a seated, flexed position sometimes have false faces or false heads attached to them on the outside, and the eyes in the faces are always open. Examples are illustrated by Dorothy Menzel (1977: figs. 45, 98).

In Lima burials on the central coast, the body is usually extended and prone, rarely on its back. In the prone burials, the head is turned to one side in some cases and is face down in others. The prone position with the head turned to one side is a position sometimes assumed by sleepers; I cannot explain the prone position with the face down on the evidence now available. A burial that was found at Ancon is suggestive for interpreting the prone position with the head turned to one side. In this burial (no. 415) there were three bodies. The principal one was of an adult woman, lying extended and prone, with her head turned to the left. At her head and facing her sat a young adult woman with her legs extended under the principal body. At the feet of the principal woman sat another young person, knees drawn up, also facing the principal woman. The arrangement of the bodies suggests that the two young people were attendants of the older woman and accompanied her in death: she slept and the young people watched over her (Ravines 1979–83, 43: 354–355).

In Initial Period burials at Waywaka, in the southern sierra, the bodies are very tightly flexed and placed in small pits in a variety of positions (Grossman 1985: 121–122). The pits in which the burials were placed were partially cut into bedrock. I infer from this that the important consideration for the survivors was to bury the dead with a minimum of digging.

In Middle Horizon 2, the traditional extended position used in earlier burials on the north and central coasts was replaced by the seated, flexed position. This position was traditional in the south and is that found in Huari burials (Lumbreras 1974: 181). The Huari empire had ruled the central and north coasts with a relatively light hand in Middle Horizon 1, but in Middle Horizon 2 it cracked down with enough authority to wake the dead.

TOMBS

In the basin of Lake Titicaca, and in some other places in southern Peru, it was customary in the Late Intermediate Period and Late Horizon to entomb the dead in structures of stone or clay built above ground (Tschopik 1946: 10–17). These structures characteristically had a vaulted roof and a single, small doorway at ground level on the east side. They are called "chullpas" in the archaeological literature; the people who built them called them 'amaya 'uta, "corpse house," in Aymara (Bertonio 1879, 1: 430; 2: 15). The dead were entombed in a seated position in these structures (Guaman Poma de Ayala 1936: 294 [296]). The surviving tombs of this kind have all been looted, so we are fortunate to have this historical testimony. Some of these tombs were barely big enough for one body; others were very large and could have held several.

Tombs above ground are monuments, helping to perpetuate the memory of the dead. In the climate of the Titicaca basin, a body protected by such a tomb dries out without decaying and keeps indefinitely. The tomb both preserves the body and makes it immediately accessible for the addition of offerings or participation in rituals. The dead man or woman is resting comfortably in his or her house.

The bodies of Nasca dead from the south coast, which were also in seated, flexed positions, were deposited in underground tomb chambers with roofs of stout poles that prevented sand from filling the chamber. Such chambers are also houses of the dead, but are hidden unless marked on the surface. Some Nasca tombs may have been marked with wooden posts (Neudecker 1979: 70–72).

Marking the location of a tomb makes it vulnerable to grave robbing, either for the looting of grave goods or the removal of skulls or other bones for unauthorized use. Menzel argued that certain rich Late Horizon tombs at Ica (Ti-5 and Tl-2) had been looted for bones before the arrival of the Spanish (Menzel 1976: 225–226).

People of wealth and power are always better able to leave monuments for themselves than ordinary folk, and as persons of prestige they are likely to be remembered and celebrated. A special case that we know of from Spanish records is that of the treatment required by deceased Inca rulers. The body of a dead Inca emperor was dried and preserved above ground, guarded by attendants, and treated as if the ruler were still alive. Inca rulers were worshiped as divine, and they could not wholly die. The palaces and other residences of a deceased ruler were not inherited by his successor, so the dead man could continue to occupy them; he was carried from one to another in a litter, as he had been carried in life. The bodies of all the dead rulers were taken to the temples for certain ceremonies and to the main plaza for others. The body itself preserved the memory of the dead ruler, and his descendants recited his deeds on public occasions. His residences were also his monuments. Indeed, we have the testimony of native witnesses that the Inca rulers built palaces in part so that they would be remembered. Since there were no Inca royal tombs, it is unlikely that this mortuary pattern could have been detected in the archaeological record without information from written sources.

At the Chimu site of Chan Chan, ancient Chimor, there are ten large compounds, nine of which are associated with platform mounds containing numerous chambers in which human remains were placed. Each mound has one principal chamber, larger than the others; all the principal chambers have been looted. One smaller chamber in the burial mound of Las Avispas was excavated and the human remains studied by Thomas Pozorski (1979). It contained the remains of 13 young women, stacked in three layers. Pozorski also studied the bones found in other excavations on the mound that he did not describe. He counted the minimum number of individuals in his sample as 93 and estimated that at least 300 persons had been buried in that mound, all young women. Bones of the person buried in the principal chamber were not found. Pozorski suggested that the person in the principal chamber could have been a king of Chimor, and that the young women could have been his wives or concubines, on the grounds that some of the bones had features suggesting that the women they belonged to had borne children.

Kent Day had proposed that the large compounds were royal palaces (Day 1982). Geoffrey Conrad accepted this idea, suggesting that there were so many compounds, because the kings of Chimor had a rule like the Inca one, and that a ruler could not inherit his predecessor's palace (Conrad 1982: 106–112). Unfortunately, Conrad did not fully understand the Inca case, perhaps because I had not fully explained it in the publications of mine that he cited. An Inca ruler could not inherit his predecessor's palace, because his predecessor was never buried and continued to occupy it. If the platform mounds associated with the large compounds were built for the burials of kings, as Pozorski suggested, there is no analogy with the Inca case. If each king built a new palace, it must have been for a different reason than the one that drove the Incas to do so; the kings of Chimor were buried.

There is also a problem with the idea advanced by Day and accepted by Conrad that the large compounds were royal palaces. If these compounds were palaces, where are the apartments that served as royal residences? Day describes the Rivero compound as comprising open areas, colonnades, U-shaped structures in small courtyards, and storerooms. The only area showing evidence of having been lived in is an enclosure at the south end of the compound. Day describes it as containing "walk-in wells, domestic debris, and remains of informal compactly arranged rooms." Such enclosures "apparently housed a resident population of low-status retainers . . . probably service and maintenance personnel" (Day 1982: 61).

As far as it goes, the evidence from Las Avispas supports Pozorski's conclusion that the mound could be a royal burial structure. The large compounds are closely associated with burial mounds; in seven cases, the mound is inside its compound and is the largest structure in it. We should consider the possibility that the entire compound is a funerary structure, that the ruler resided elsewhere, and that no one lived in the compound except the service personnel in the south enclosure.

Behavior and Belief in Ancient Peruvian Mortuary Practice

OBJECTS DEPOSITED WITH THE DEAD

Objects may be deposited with the dead so that the dead person may use them in an afterlife, or because personal property may not be inherited, or because objects that were used by someone who died are considered polluted or dangerous. In addition to, or instead of, objects used by or belonging to the specific person, we may find customary offerings, things that accompany most bodies. An example of a customary offering is the red powder found on the bones in Cupisnique burials (Larco Hoyle 1948: 154).

In Moche burials we find elaborately modeled vessels finished with great care, often depicting obviously mythical beings. We also find vessels of simple shapes, less carefully finished and painted with simple designs. A. L. Kroeber observed that the Moche pottery from the graves excavated by Max Uhle is "consistently of excellent quality as ware, but it is so regularly ornamented, in shape or color or both, that it obtrudes as essentially funerary apparatus. Very few vessels show signs of use; and nearly half are forms that could scarcely be put to daily, utilitarian employment" (Kroeber 1925: 202). Indeed, he considered only five vessels in the Uhle collection to be "domestic utensils" (202–203). These five are coarse, unpainted vessels with simple shapes; one, he said, is fire-blackened, and one "appears still to contain marks of food." Christopher Donnan, speaking of the vessels of the same collection, said, "For the most part, they are finely-made pieces which may have been produced specifically for burial purposes. Only one vessel in the entire collection shows any signs of use" (Donnan 1965: 115). Similar statements have been made by other archaeologists (Bennett 1939: 125; cf. Ford and Willey 1949: 21). Lawrence E. Dawson considered it worthwhile to examine the bottoms of the vessels from Uhle's burials to see which ones showed signs of wear. The project was carried out by Jeffrey B. Boynton, a student at Berkeley, as part of a study of technical aspects of Moche ceramics done in 1980. Boynton found signs of wear on a considerable number of the vessels he examined, including many of the most elaborately decorated and best finished ones. Subsequently I made my own observations on wear in this collection. Wear can be found on the bottoms of both elaborate and simple vessels, but it is more common on elaborate ones.

Some of the most elaborately modeled pieces show the greatest wear. Grave 12 was one of the richest burials that Uhle excavated at Moche site F, both in the number of pottery vessels it contained (59) and in the quality of the modeled pieces. F-12 is a Moche III lot. The modeling in this lot so impressed Kroeber that he illustrated ten vessels from F-12 in his report on the Uhle pottery collection from Moche (Kroeber 1925). Nine of the pieces illustrated by Kroeber show wear on the bottom, and six of them are heavily worn (figs. 53c, 54e, 56g and k, 57h, and 67b). Three are less heavily worn (figs. 53g, l, and k). One shows no wear (fig. 55b). There are two simple vessels in this lot, not illustrated by Kroeber, that show no wear (Hearst Museum 4-1983d and e). Wear occurs on vessels of all phases represented in the Uhle collection (Moche II, III, and IV).

Moche pottery was made in press molds, so the same shape could be repeated indefinitely. In some of the Uhle burials, there are sets of two to eight vessels that share the same shape and size and are decorated in the same way. Mostly, such sets consist of vessels with simple shapes and simple painted designs, not finished with great care. The sets I examined show no wear. Boynton made the reasonable inference that it was such pieces that were made especially for use as burial offerings. Kroeber and the others cited made a baseless assumption about use and did not think to look for wear.

It is possible to look at the assortments of pottery vessels deposited in burials and recognize sets of different shapes. Menzel recognized such sets in the pottery accompanying late burials from Chincha. She noted that a basic set for these burials consisted of one or two high ovoid jars, one or two squat ovoid jars without shoulder handles, one flask, one cup, and one complex rim bowl. The set also includes one figurine. She commented that in some burials miniatures were used as substitutes for vessels of one shape category. There are some incomplete sets and some burials with more than two of one or another of the shapes listed (Menzel 1967: 99).

It was Menzel's recognition of the set pattern that enabled her to see the function of the miniatures. The observation is important: it enables us to see a little more of human thought and behavior in ancient Chincha. Miniatures are always a problem requiring explanation.

In the Chancay Valley, Uhle excavated late burials at three sites: La Mina (Site A), La Calera de Lauren (Site B), and La Calera de Jegoan (Site C). At all three sites some burials contained vessels that had been overfired, some to the point that they had collapsed or were perforated. At La Mina, Grave 2 contained seven overfired vessels out of a total of 23; in Grave 3, one out of three vessels was overfired; and in Grave 4, two out of four were similarly defective. Graves 1 and 5 had only sound vessels. La Mina was evidently a place where pottery was being made; Max Uhle found a mold for plates in Grave 2, and Charlotte Uhle made a large collection of molds from the surface of the site. The Uhles did not report finding molds at the other two sites, and overfired pieces were more rare in the burials, although they did occur. What the overfired vessels have in common is that they are not broken in pieces, although the collapsed ones are useless as containers. It may be that there was some virtue in pieces that had come through the firing not broken but bent.

RANK AND POLITICS

Archaeologists commonly interpret differences in the quantity and quality of grave goods as reflecting differences in wealth and social position. In her monographic study, *Pottery Style and Society in Ancient Peru,* Menzel went much further. She interpreted the contents of late burials from Ica in terms of political loyalties and political movements as well as of rank. She was able to do so because she had made the most detailed and carefully documented style analysis of the pottery yet undertaken in the New World. Her study dealt with burials dating to just before the Inca conquest of Ica, ones dating to the period of Inca rule, identified by relating a phase of the local pottery style to imitations of Inca pottery and the presence of Inca style objects in the graves, and finally burials of the early Colonial Period, before conversion to Christianity led to the abandonment of the ancient cemeteries, identified by the association of another phase of the local pottery style with European glass trade beads.

Before the Inca conquest, Ica was under strong influence from Chincha. Menzel infers that Ica was not conquered by Chincha, because no actual Chincha pottery had been found at Ica, although Ica pottery was influenced by the Chincha style. After the Inca conquest the Chincha influence was eliminated (Menzel 1976: 234).

Menzel sorted the pottery of the period of Inca rule into a number of groupings based on the ways features of the native tradition and features relating to the Incas were combined. She found patterns of association of these groupings that enabled her to distinguish nobles of two ranks, their servants, a class of people identified with the Inca administration, probably civil servants, and the common people of Ica. The common people used only Ica style pottery; the upper classes enjoyed the prestige of using Inca and Inca-influenced pottery. All but one of the non-noble burials in the sample contained one or more antiques or imitation antiques. Menzel comments that this is "an extraordinary record of popularity for such an exotic practice." She infers that "it appears to have been an expression of a desire to return to earlier and better days, when the Ica Valley was free from pressure or domination by foreign powers" (1976: 241).

In the early Colonial Period, "A nativistic revival took place, in which the people of Ica reasserted their traditional artistic independence. The special trappings of the nobility and the civil servants were eliminated, as were the segregated communities. Eliminated were the Inca-associated vessel categories found regularly in pairs or multiples of pairs in Late Horizon graves of persons of distinction" (1976: 243). The potters of Ica swept away all Inca influence and tried to revive their native pottery tradition, going back to shapes and designs of pre-Inca phases. They did not simply copy old models, however; they made a new phase of the Ica style with old elements. Nothing like this nativistic revival happened at Chincha.

This is as close to political history as we are likely to get without a written record. No archaeologist whose pottery analysis consists of taxonomic types and statistical treatment of them would have been able to see the human behavior and thought revealed by Menzel's qualitative handling of style.

RITUAL

A ritual is a sequence of actions. In order to reconstruct a mortuary ritual, we must invoke a logic of sequence. The logic applicable in this case is that disarticulation of bones follows articulation. We are only going to be able to reconstruct a mortuary ritual if it involved a stage in which the bones were still articulated and a stage in which they had become disarticulated. Kathleen Kenyon reconstructed a mortuary ritual in Middle Bronze Age chamber tombs in Palestine. There was an average of 20 bodies in these tombs. What Kenyon found on opening one of these tombs was that there was the articulated skeleton of one person lying in the middle of the chamber. The bones of the rest were disarticulated and piled in a jumbled mass against the back and side walls of the chamber, mixed with grave goods. She argued that each body was laid in the middle of the chamber with its offerings. When the next body was brought in, the bones and offerings of the previous one were roughly pushed away to clear the space (Kenyon 1960: 189–190). Evidently, the body deserved respect only as long as it had flesh on its bones. Menzel used the same articulation logic to reconstruct a more complex ritual in the late Ica tombs.

Uhle excavated a number of large tombs at Soniche dating to the Late Horizon. In the undisturbed ones, Menzel noted two patterns of body treatment and grave goods, one represented by Grave Td-8 and the other by Grave Ta. In Td-8 there were three principal dead persons, the bodies seated and wrapped in mummy bundles. In front of them were three empty funerary urns, placed in one another. Beside the urns were the remains of several juveniles, not in mummy bundles. There were pottery vessels present but no metal dishes. In tombs of the other pattern, the funerary urns contained human bones painted red, along with gold or silver dishes; there were no mummy bundles, and the bones were disarticulated. In Grave Ta, the urns contained bones together with silver dishes and jewelry and a silver mask. Menzel thought that the silver mask indicated that the bones accompanying it were those of a principal dead person. She inferred that the two patterns represented two successive steps in a ritual sequence; that Ica nobles were originally buried in mummy bundles and without metal dishes; and that after the flesh had decayed the tombs were reentered, the bones cleaned, painted red, and deposited in the urns with the addition of metal dishes. She suggested that Grave Td-8 was closed prematurely to hide it from the Spanish, thus preserving the first stage (Menzel 1976: 223–225).

Behavior and Belief in Ancient Peruvian Mortuary Practice

OSSUARIES

Luis Llanos excavated two ossuaries near Calca (Cuzco) that contained disarticulated human bones, mostly crania (Llanos 1941). There were not enough mandibles to complete the skulls, suggesting that the bones were thrown into the ossuaries after the flesh had decayed. There were few objects with the bones. This combination of circumstances does not fit any pattern of disposal of the dead known from pre-Spanish Peru, and it puzzled me for a long time.

Finally, Patricia J. Lyon, who was going through a volume of legislation promulgated by Viceroy Francisco de Toledo, called my attention to an ordinance that he issued on 30 May 1580: "That the tombs be demolished and ossuaries be made in which to cast the bones of those who died infidels." The text of this ordinance reads in part: "Inasmuch as these Indians had a religious practice, much respected among them, of worshipping the dead from whom they were directly descended, . . . I order and command that each *corregidor* in his district have all the tower tombs demolished, and have a great hole made, in which all the bones of the deceased who died in their paganism shall be placed, mixed together" (Toledo 1989: 413–414). The ossuaries Llanos found, then, were not the product of some unknown native practice but of the efforts of the Spanish to "extirpate idolatry." Evidently, the *corregidor* of the Valley of Yucay, in whose jurisdiction Calca lay, had carried out the viceroy's order, more or less. His agents were more careful to collect crania than other bones, for whatever reason.

Archaeologists should be on the lookout for other examples of European meddling with native mortuary practices.

THE NECROPOLIS OF PARACAS

In 1927 Toribio Mejía Xesspe discovered two great concentrations of mummy bundles of Paracas. Counting outlying bundles, concentration A consisted of 325 bundles and concentration B of 126 bundles. This find became known as the Necropolis. The embroidered textiles from the Necropolis bundles are extraordinary, both on a technical and an aesthetic level. Some 47 of the bundles that have been opened have been dated by Jane Powell Dwyer and Anne Paul; the dates range from Epoch 10 of the Early Horizon to Epoch 2 of the Early Intermediate Period (Dwyer n.d.: 233a; Paul 1990: 60). A report on the excavations at Paracas was published by Julio C. Tello and Toribio Mejía Xesspe in 1979.

What do these concentrations of mummy bundles mean in terms of mortuary behavior? Were the concentrations formed gradually over some centuries, as people added a bundle at a time to the collection, or do they represent one or two events in which large numbers of bundles were collected and deposited together? The excavators assumed the former.

Unfortunately, the excavation report leaves much to be desired. The plans of the two concentrations of mummy bundles (Tello and Mejía Xesspe 1979: figs. 86, 87) are schematic; the bundles are indicated by circles of two standard sizes, many of which overlap others. If the overlaps gave an accurate picture of the way the bundles were piled up, we could draw some conclusions regarding the order of deposition. However, the depth at which the top of each mummy bundle was found is indicated in its circle, and the depths frequently contradict the overlaps. For example, how is it that mummy 265 in concentration B, found at a depth of 1.5 m, is overlapped by 295 (2 m), 298 (2.5 m), 292 (2.7 m), and 296 (3 m)? There are many other problems of this kind. Then there is a profile that purports to show a cross-section of concentration B (Tello and Mejía Xesspe 1979: fig. 89, p. 335). It is not consistent either with the plan or with the depth measurements given for individual mummies.

The mummy bundles were classified in three size categories at the time they were taken from the ground. The text of the report says that there were 19 mummies of the first category (large) removed from concentration A and seven from concentration B (Tello and Mejía Xesspe 1979: 322, 326). The plans, however, show 24 first category mummies in A and nine in B.

The two concentrations of mummy bundles at the Necropolis were deposited in and around rectangular buildings with field stone walls. The buildings were evidently in ruins when the mummy bundles were deposited there, for some bundles were placed on the lines of walls. An example specifically noted by Tello and Mejía Xesspe is mummy 27 (Early Intermediate Period 1B) in concentration A (1979: 436). Mummy 49 (Early Intermediate Period 1A) is said to have been found in a pit about half a meter deep in the floor of the same house (same page). The same authors say that the buildings were dwellings, and I also judged them to be dwellings when I surveyed the site. Tello and Mejía said further that the mummy bundles were buried in refuse (1979: 315, 335). A photograph taken during the excavation shows the mummy bundles in one of the concentrations packed tightly together and, as Tello said, "heaped up on one another" (Tello 1929: fig. 85 and p. 131).

I identified all the dated bundles on the published plans to see if there was a horizontal order in the deposition, older ones at one end and younger ones at the other. In concentration A, four of the five mummies that have been dated to Early Horizon 10A, the earliest time unit represented, are at the top edge of the concentration in the plan, fig. 86; the fifth is isolated close to the right edge in a small building. The 10B mummies are scattered through the concentration, intermingled with mummies of Early Intermediate Period 1A and 1B. The only Early Intermediate Period 2 mummy in this concentration is on the lower edge. In concentration B (Tello 1929: fig. 87), there are no 10A mummies, and the only 10B one is at the lower left corner. The

Behavior and Belief in Ancient Peruvian Mortuary Practice

Early Intermediate Period 1A and 1B mummies are scattered throughout the concentration, while the Early Intermediate Period 2 mummies are all along the lower edge. There is thus a possibility that some 10A mummies were deposited at A before the concentration was formed, and that the Early Intermediate Period 2 mummies were added after the formation of both concentrations. The marginal location of the four 10A mummies at the top of A may, however, be only an accident of the sample.

On the evidence now available, then, it appears likely that the concentrations of mummy bundles at the Necropolis represent one, two, or at most three events in which the bundles were removed from resting places elsewhere, brought to the abandoned houses, piled up in and around them, and buried in refuse. It is possible that the Early Intermediate Period 2 bundles were added one by one, but more likely that they were moved from somewhere else like the earlier ones. Isolated bundles, such as 349 (a 10A bundle) and 253 (an Early Intermediate Period 2 bundle), each buried alone in a house, may be unrelated to the concentrations they adjoin.

These Necropolis mummies are the remains of people of some distinction. Even the poorest ones that have been opened contain some offerings (Tello and Mejía Xesspe 1979: 446–454). In the early sixties, personnel of the Museo Regional de Ica excavated about a hundred burials in a cemetery at Chongos, in the valley of Pisco, most of which dated to Early Horizon 10. Some of the burials at Chongos were comparable to the small ones at the Necropolis. Others were much poorer; some had been covered with a layer of clay instead of cloth and had no offerings at all with them. At the other extreme are the large mummies of the Necropolis. For example, mummy 290, an Early Intermediate Period 1B mummy, had 97 specimens in it, including gold jewelry and 16 embroidered mantles (Tello and Mejía Xesspe 1979: 384–423). There is no reason to assume that these distinguished people lived in the desert on the Paracas Peninsula; they may very well have lived somewhere in the Pisco Valley, and they could have originally been buried there.

Jane and Edward Dwyer said of the Necropolis mummies that "several of the richest bundles . . . contain textiles among the outer wrappings that are stylistically later than those in the inner mass of decorated ones" (1975: 151). They suggested that the presence of later textiles on the outside of the bundles indicated that there had been a renewal of offerings (Dwyer and Dwyer 1975: 152). The bundles said to display this feature are not identified in the published article. If we are interested in mortuary behavior, the point is important.

Ann Rowe has made an index of the textiles from the Necropolis that have been published with their bundle associations. She was kind enough to check the Dwyers' statement against her sample. She found that there are some bundles with more advanced textiles in the outer layers and some with more conservative ones. She thinks it unlikely that additions were made to the bundles. Instead, she thinks that the stylistic differences result from a tendency to put impressive pieces (finely made, large, elaborately decorated ones) in the outer layers (personal communication).

HUMAN SACRIFICE

It was Max Uhle who first recognized human sacrifices in Peruvian archaeology. He found an Inca cemetery on the Temple of the Sun at Pachacamac that contained only sacrificed women. These women were dressed in Inca clothing, and each of them had been strangled with a knotted cloth. The cloths were still there, so Uhle was able to reconstruct the strangling process in detail (Uhle 1903: 85–86). He made a convincing case for Inca human sacrifice based on the archaeological evidence and then discussed how his findings related to the literary evidence, which was contradictory. The Inca Garcilaso had flatly denied that the Incas practiced human sacrifice, saying that Spanish reports of the practice were mistaken. Garcilaso's mother was an Inca princess, and he claimed special authority in consequence. The contradiction in the sources remained a problem for scholars until Uhle's find resolved it.

More recently, a number of human sacrifices have been found in Inca shrines on high mountains up and down the Andes. The best documented case is that of the sacrificed boy found frozen and well preserved on El Plomo in Chile, carefully studied by Grete Mostny and a team of Chilean experts (Mostny 1957). The boy was buried alive, presumably under the influence of alcohol, at an altitude of 5400 m. He froze to death and remained frozen until he was discovered.

In conclusion, ancient burials tell us directly about ancient behavior toward the dead, and sometimes about thought and belief about death. Because they enable us to see individuals, however, they allow us to draw a variety of inferences about the behavior of the living as well. The most impressive example of such inferences is certainly Menzel's use of burial data to show the Inca nobles imitating their Inca lords, while the common people were thinking nostalgically of an earlier time when they were not under the rule of foreigners.

BIBLIOGRAPHY

BENNETT, WENDELL C.
    1939   *Archaeology of the North Coast of Peru*. Anthropological Papers of the American Museum of Natural History 37 (1). New York.

BERTONIO, LUDOVICO
    1879   *Vocabulario de la lengua aymara*. B. G. Teubner, Leipzig.

CARDICH, AUGUSTO
    1964   *Lauricocha: Fundamentos para una prehistoria de los Andes centrales*. Centro Argentino de Estudios Prehistóricos, Studia Praehistorica 3. Buenos Aires.

CONRAD, GEOFFREY W.
    1982   The Burial Platforms of Chan Chan: Some Social and Political Implications. In *Chan Chan: Andean Desert City* (Michael E. Moseley and Kent C. Day, eds.): 87–117. University of New Mexico Press, Albuquerque.

DAY, KENT C.
    1982   Ciudadelas: Their Form and Function. In *Chan Chan: Andean Desert City* (Michael E. Moseley and Kent C. Day, eds.): 55–66. University of New Mexico Press, Albuquerque.

DONNAN, CHRISTOPHER BRUCE
    1965   Moche Ceramic Technology. *Ñawpa Pacha* 3: 115–134.

DWYER, JANE P.
    n.d.   Chronology and Iconography of Late Paracas and Early Nasca Textile Designs. Ph.D. dissertation, University of California, Berkeley, 1971.

DWYER, JANE P., AND EDWARD DWYER
    1975   The Paracas Cemeteries: Mortuary Patterns in a Peruvian South Coastal Tradition. In *Death and the Afterlife in Pre-Columbian America* (Elizabeth P. Benson, ed.): 145–161. Dumbarton Oaks, Washington, D.C.

FORD, JAMES ALFRED, AND GORDON R. WILLEY
    1949   *Surface Survey of the Viru Valley, Peru*. Anthropological Papers of the American Museum of Natural History 43 (1). New York.

GROSSMAN, JOEL WARREN
    1985   Demographic Change and Economic Transformation in the South-Central Highlands of Pre-Huari Peru. *Ñawpa Pacha* 21: 45–126.

GUAMAN POMA DE AYALA, FELIPE
    1936   *Nueva corónica y buen gobierno (Codex péruvien illustré)*. Travaux et Mémoires de l'Institut d'Ethnologie 23. Paris.

KENYON, KATHLEEN
    1960   *Archaeology in the Holy Land*. Frederick A. Praeger, New York.

KROEBER, ALFRED L.
    1925   *The Uhle Pottery Collections from Moche*. University of California Publications in American Archaeology and Ethnology 21 (5). Berkeley.

LARCO HOYLE, RAFAEL
1946 A Culture Sequence for the North Coast of Peru. In *Handbook of South American Indians* (Julian H. Steward, ed.). Smithsonian Institution. Bureau of American Ethnology, Bulletin 143 (2): 149–175. Washington, D.C.

LLANOS, LUIS A.
1941 Exploraciones arqueológicas en Quimsarumiyoc y Huaccanhuayco—Calca. *Revista del Museo Nacional* 10 (2): 240–262. Lima.

LUMBRERAS, LUIS G.
1974 *Las fundaciones de Huamanga: Hacia una prehistoria de Ayacucho.* Club Huamanga, Lima.

MENZEL, DOROTHY
1964 Style and Time in the Middle Horizon. *Ñawpa Pacha* 2: 1–106.
1967 The Pottery of Chincha. *Ñawpa Pacha* 4: 77–144.
1976 *Pottery Style and Society in Ancient Peru.* University of California Press, Berkeley.
1977 *The Archaeology of Ancient Peru and the Work of Max Uhle.* R. H. Lowie Museum of Anthropology, University of California, Berkeley.

MOSTNY, GRETE
1957 La momia del Cerro el Plomo (Grete Mostny, ed.). *Boletín del Museo Nacional de Historia Natural* 27 (1): i–iv, 1–120. Santiago de Chile.

NEUDECKER, ANGELIKA
1979 *Archäologische Forschungen im Nazca-Gebiet, Peru: Das Tal des Rio Santa Cruz in praespanischer Zeit aus der Sicht der Forschungen Professor Dr. Ubbelohde-Doerings im Jahre 1932.* Münchner Beitrage zur Amerikanistik 3. Klaus Renner Verlag, Hohenschäftlann.

PAUL, ANNE
1990 *Paracas Ritual Attire: Symbols of Authority in Ancient Peru.* University of Oklahoma Press, Norman.

POZORSKI, THOMAS
1979 The Las Avispas Burial Platform at Chan Chan, Peru. *Annals of the Carnegie Museum* 48 (8): 119–137. Pittsburgh.

RAVINES, ROGGER
1979–83 Prácticas funerarias en Ancón. *Revista del Museo Nacional* 43: 327–397; 45: 89–166. Lima.

TELLO, JULIO C.
1929 *Antiguo Perú: Primera época.* Comisión Organizadora del Segundo Congreso Sudamericano de Turismo, Lima.

TELLO, JULIO C., AND TORIBIO MEJÍA XESSPE
1979 *Paracas, segunda parte: Cavernas y Necrópolis.* Universidad Nacional Mayor de San Marcos, Dirección Universitaria de Biblioteca y Publicaciones, Lima.

TOLEDO, FRANCISCO DE
1989 *Disposiciones gubernativas para el virreinato del Perú, 1575–1580.* Publicaciones de la Escuela de Estudios Hispano-Americanos de Sevilla 347.

TSCHOPIK, MARION H.
    1946   *Some Notes on the Archaeology of the Department of Puno, Peru.* Papers of the Peabody Museum of American Archaeology and Ethnology, Harvard University 27 (3). Cambridge, Mass.

UHLE, MAX
    1903   *Pachacamac. Report of the William Pepper, M.D. LL.D. Peruvian Expedition of 1896.* Department of Archaeology, University of Pennsylvania, Philadelphia. Reprinted 1991 as University Museum Monograph 62.

The Preceramic Chinchorro Mummy Complex of Northern Chile: Context, Style, and Purpose

MARIO A. RIVERA

INTRODUCTION

THE PIONEERING WORK OF MAX UHLE (1919, 1922) and Junius Bird (1943) defined the Preceramic period for the extreme northern Chilean area. This research laid the foundation for my interpretation of this period, now known as the Chinchorro tradition (Rivera 1984, 1991). In recent years, studies of later ceramic societies have shown in situ processes of economic differentiation and increasing social complexity that have their roots in this earlier tradition. At present, detailed information on the socioeconomic organization and ritual practice of the Chinchorro culture is lacking. This paper presents a preliminary attempt to infer the social and religious meaning of Chinchorro mortuary customs and to describe their changes over time. An effort also is made to compare the Chinchorro mortuary customs to those of selected Preceramic societies in Ecuador and Peru.

As David H. Thomas has noted, ". . . persons who are treated differentially in life will be treated differentially in death" (Thomas 1991: 204). It is this social linkage between the living and the dead that reflects certain ceremonial and ritual aspects of society, and directs our attention to the mortuary custom and social structure of the Chinchorro people. Changes in this structure can be ascertained by comparing mortuary data from several Chinchorro cultural periods (*sensu* Binford 1971: 12–13; Brown 1971: 92–93; Saxe n.d.: 7–8; Renfrew 1974; Tainter 1978: 106–108; Hodder 1980, 1987) and by examining the artificial content and spatial distribution of human burials. Through the analysis of human remains it also is possible to examine evidence for differential health and fitness of Chinchorro people in both their natural and social environments. In particular, dietary, nutritional, pathological, and genetic studies can reveal interesting factors that contribute to our understanding of the quality of life of these ancient people.

The Chinchorro tradition (ca. 6000 to 500 B.C.) constitutes a crucial time for the increased social complexity that underlies such major achievements as the adoption of domesticated plants (i.e., maize, cotton, quinoa, potatoes, other Andean tubers) and animals (i.e., llamas, alpacas, guinea pigs). Metallurgy in copper, silver, and gold; basketry; and later, ceramics—along with an emerging village structure—also are associated with this tradition. Perhaps most significant, however, is the mortuary technology and ritual behavior associated with the disposal of the dead in planned cemeteries. Enough evidence is now available to suggest that the Chinchorro people manipulated afterlife through the apparent revitalization of the dead in the form of mummification and the use of mummies in rituals. (The term "mummification" is used here to imply a process by which the body is intentionally preserved; for example, the transformation of a dead body into a mummy [Binford 1971: 12]).

Examined below are aspects of the Chinchorro culture as they are represented at the major archaeological sites of the tradition. These sites are Playa Miller-8 (PLM-8), Chinchorro type-site, Morro-1 (MO-1), Camarones-14 (CAM-14), Camarones-15 (CAM-15), Quiani-2 (QUI-2), Quiani-7 (QUI-7), Playa Miller-7 (PLM-7), Pisagua-Viejo-1 (PIS-VJO-1), Patillos, Bajo Molle, Canastos-3, Caleta Huelén-42 (CAH-42), Antofagasta Hipodromo, and Taltal (Rivera 1991). Unfortunately, most of these sites have not been investigated systematically. Limited archaeological salvage work has been carried out at Morro-1, Playa Miller-8, Playa Miller-7, and Quiani.

Background on Chinchorro Research

The Chinchorro tradition extended along the entire north coast of Chile from about 18 to 20 degrees south latitude (Fig. 1). Jane Buikstra (this volume) also reports Chinchorro findings in the Moquegua-Ilo region, thus extending the presence of this tradition into southern Peru. The Chinchorro culture also is associated with adjacent highland environments (puna and altiplano) and possibly the *ceja de selva* and tropical forest formations, to the east of the altiplano. Descending westward from the altiplano, where the pre-Hispanic economy was based on herding and cultivation, there are several different environmental zones that extend to the coast. In the precordilleran basin, situated at 3,000 m in elevation, there is a pronounced rainy season, which is conducive to intensive high-altitude agriculture. At lower altitudes, the headwaters of the main streams flow to the coast, interconnecting with multiple environmental zones. Since early Preceramic times, both coastal and highland people simultaneously exploited all of these zones, a pattern known as ecological complementarity (Masuda, Shimada, and Morris 1985).

As discussed below, previous studies (Rivera n.d., 1975, 1991) already have dealt with the chronology and cultural development of the Chinchorro tradition. The tradition begins with an early period (9000 to 6000 B.C.), which is defined by hunters and gatherers in their early stages of adaptation

The Preceramic Chinchorro Mummy Complex of Northern Chile

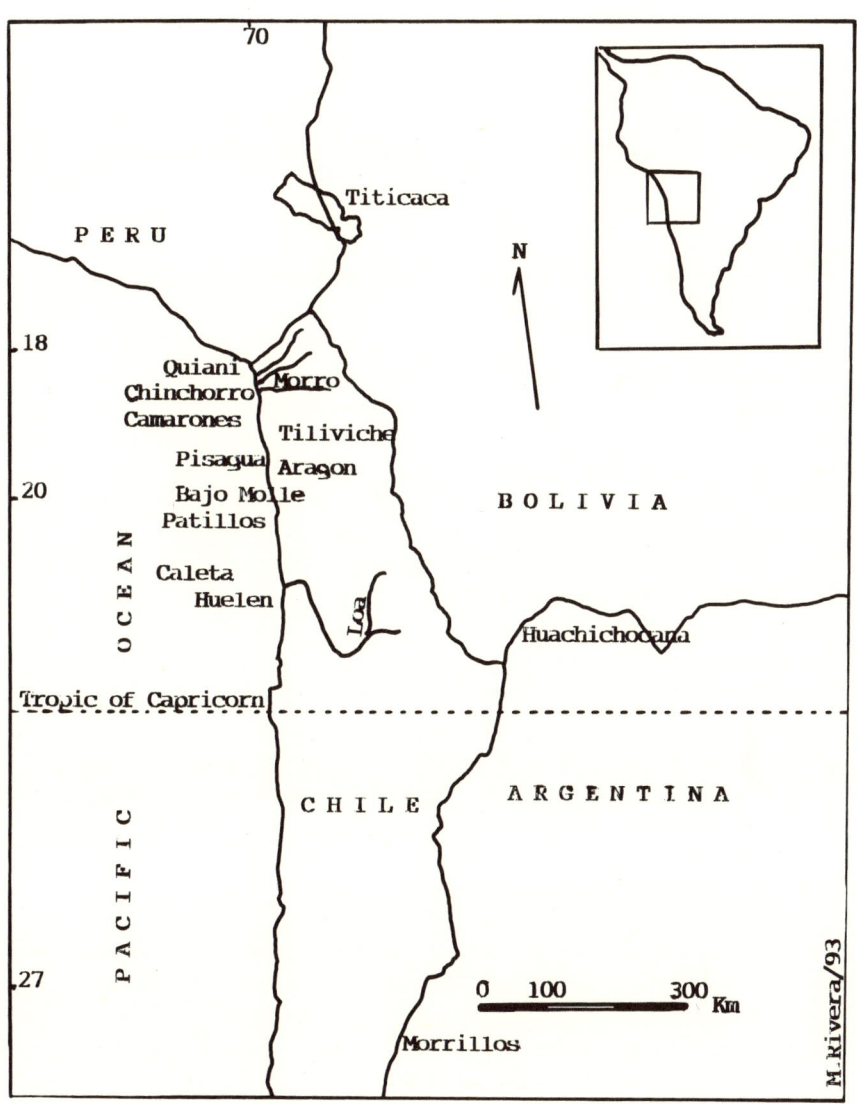

Fig. 1 Location of Chinchorro sites in northern Chile.

to the dry coastal environment of northern Chile. Between 6000 and 4000 B.C., a process of socioeconomic differentiation emerged in which some populations on the coast became fisher folk, while others in the interior valleys became gatherers (Fig. 2). This development began with the introduction of a sea-oriented technology consisting of shell fishhooks, grinding stones, harpoons, and mortars. One of the most important sites of this phase is Camarones-14. This site possibly developed from indirect contacts with eastern tropical forest groups, as well as local groups at the sites of Playa Miller-8, Morro-1, and Pisagua-Viejo-1. The archaeological assemblages from these sites include cephalic ornaments of tropical feathers, hallucinogenic snuff, snuff trays, tubes, spatulas, brushes, boxes, basketry, and spear throwers (Rivera 1975). The hallucinogenic equipment is particularly significant because it may have introduced practices related to public ritual and social differentiation.

Sometime between ca. 5000 and 500 B.C. the Chinchorro tradition developed to a full extent. In previous studies (Rivera 1984, 1991; Rivera and Rothhammer 1986), I suggested that the Chinchorro people were probably organized in small groups with a subsistence based on fishing and gathering. These groups were probably organized like the fishing communities along the north coast of Chile today (Fig. 3), where there is an emphasis on sea-oriented activities and economic specialization and mobility. Archaeologically speaking, this small-group organization is reflected in clustered circular houses with portable huts made of canes and matting, with stones as foundations. Evidence of such huts have been found at various sites along the coast, including Playa Miller-8, Acha, and Caleta Huelén-42 (Muñoz 1982; Dauelsberg 1974; Zlatar 1987). In Caleta Huelén-42, a coastal site of about 2,800 m square and radiocarbon dated to 2650 +/− 100 B.C. (GaK-3546) and 1830 +/− 90 B.C. (GaK-3545), houses are semisubterranean, with circular structures of stones showing a series of superimposed floors. The structures, measuring 2.5 × 2.0 m in diameter, are arranged around a central courtyard, which was probably the center of domestic activities. Dwellings contained plastered floors made of clay and seaweed. Extended burials were located under the floors, which, according to Zlatar (1983: 27), may indicate a more permanent residence pattern. It also is possible that semisedentary to sedentary groups were organized as small bands of four to five families, living near fresh-water sources at Camarones, El Morro, Chinchorro, and Pisagua. Beginning around 1000 B.C., a new tradition reached the coastal area. This is known as the Andean or altiplano tradition, which was derived from the area around Titicaca.

Chronology and Cultural Development

Based on the previous research carried out by Bittmann and Munizaga (1976), Núñez (1969), Alvarez (1969), Vera (1981), and Soto-Heim (1987), it

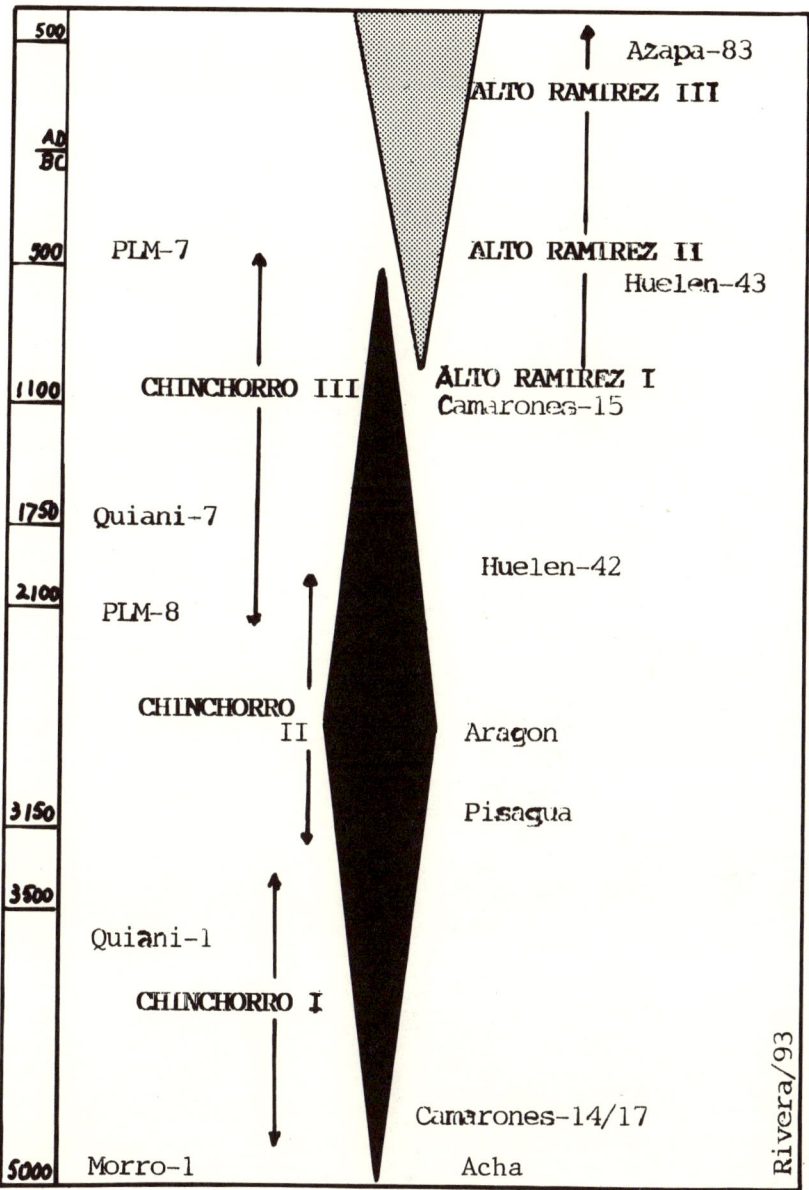

Fig. 2 Schematic development of the Chinchorro cultural phases.

Mario A. Rivera

Fig. 3 Modern Chinchorro fishermen on the Chinchorro beach, Arica.

is generally known that Chinchorro sites represent a long tradition of cultural development. Table 1 shows a series of 55 radiocarbon dates obtained from 20 different archaeological sites. (Samples were processed for carbon, wood, human tissue, and other types of organic materials, such as manioc tubers from the Playa Miller-8 site.) The samples from Camarones-15 and Morro-1 are derived from recent excavations, and thus represent more complete and reliable information. Other samples, however, are from early unsystematically studied collections (e.g., Patillos, Quiani, partially Playa Miller-8) with less reliable provenience, association, and context.

Three major problems occur with the dating and sequencing of the Chinchorro tradition and its three phases: (1) the above-mentioned difficulty of unreliable burial contexts and associations of grave offerings; (2) the long sequence of 55 radiocarbon dates covers a very long time span from approximately 7020 to 530 B.C.; and (3) at Morro-1, the ten radiocarbon dates range from 5850 to 1720 B.C., making it difficult to define each phase. It is highly probable that secondary deposition and reuse of the mummies account for the wide range of dates at sites. (Statistical analysis of the radiocarbon dates is being carried out to attempt to resolve the problems [Shea and Rivera n.d.].)

The Chinchorro Type-Site and Its Location

The type-site for the Chinchorro tradition was defined by Uhle (1919) when he discovered the first burials at the site of Chinchorro, on the northern outskirts of the city of Arica, northern Chile. This site, as well as most other Chinchorro localities excavated in the following years, were cemeteries. As a result of finding so many burial sites, archaeologists were initially uninformed about Chinchorro subsistence patterns, social organization, and cultural change in general. Later, when the Chinchorro shell middens were excavated, they were initially identified as a different culture and referred to by Bird as the early "Shell Fishing Culture" (Bird 1943). In recent years, however, we have been able to associate not only the shell midden and cemetery sites, but the residential sites as well within the Chinchorro tradition.

Chinchorro Mortuary Practices

Discussed below are the general features that characterize the Chinchorro sites in regard to their demographic structure, grave offerings, burial organization, and settlement patterns.

All burial sites are in locations that are difficult to access. Usually they are in steep dune slopes facing the ocean. This locality makes it very difficult to carry out stratigraphic and areal excavation and to correlate human bodies in situ. Almost all Chinchorro sites are single components. Exceptions are

TABLE 1. CHINCHORRO RADIOCARBON DATES, NORTHERN CHILE

Site	Sample	Absolute date	Reference
Playa Miller-7	GaK-5812	2480 +/− 100 B.P.	Rivera n.d.a
Morro 1-6-D, T-4	Beta-23401	2700 +/− 80	Focacci et al. n.d.
Morro 1-6-D, T-8	Beta-23403	2750 +/− 80	Focacci et al. n.d.
Morro 1-6-D, T-6	Beta-23402	2770 +/− 80	Focacci et al. n.d.
Camarones-15-D	GX-18257	2915 +/− 70	Rivera n.d.
Camarones-15-E	GaK-5813	3060 +/− 100	Rivera n.d.
Camarones-S	RL-2055	3060 +/− 380	Rivera 1991
Quiani-7	I-13655	3240 +/− 90	Focacci et al. n.d.
Quiani-7	I-13654	3280 +/− 90	Focacci et al. n.d.
Guasilla-1	B-3122	3490 +/− 290	Bittmann 1984
Morro 1-6, T-13	I-14958	3560 +/− 100	Focacci et al. n.d.
Quiani-7	GaK-5814	3590 +/− 100	Rivera n.d.
Camarones-15-D	RL-2054	3650 +/− 200	Rivera 1991
Morro-1	I-13651	3670 +/− 100	Allison et al. 1984
Morro 1-6	I-14957	3780 +/− 100	Focacci et al. n.d.
Caleta Huelén-42	GaK-3545	3780 +/− 90	Núñez 1976
Morro-1	I-13656	3790 +/− 140	Allison et al. 1984
Morro-1	I-13652	3830 +/− 100	Allison et al. 1984
Camarones-15-D	GX-18258	4010 +/− 75	Rivera n.d.
Morro-1	I-13543	4040 +/− 100	Allison et al. 1984
Playa Miller-8	GaK-5811	4090 +/− 105	Rivera n.d.
Morro-1	I-13541	4200 +/− 100	Allison et al. 1984
Camarones-15-D	GX-18256	4240 +/− 145	Rivera n.d.
Morro-1	I-13650	4350 +/− 280	Allison et al. 1984
Morro-1	I-14336	4360 +/− 110	Allison et al. 1984
Morro-1	I-13642	4570 +/− 100	Allison et al. 1984
Camarones-8	GX-15079	4635 +/− 90	Muñoz, Rocha, and Chacón 19
Guasilla-1	B-3121	4730 +/− 180	Bittmann 1984
Caleta Huelén-42	GaK-3546	4780 +/− 100	Núñez 1976
Pisagua Viejo	IVIC-170	4880 +/− 320	Núñez 1976
Cobija -1/S	B-3114	4880 +/− 90	Bittmann 1984
La Lisera	GaK-9903	5010 +/− 110	Vera 1981; Núñez 1967
Cobija-1/S	B-3117	5060 +/− 120	Bittmann 1984
Morro-1	I-13539	5160 +/− 110	Allison et al. 1984
Aragón-1	GaK-5965	5170 +/− 200	Núñez and Zlatar n.d.
Pisagua Viejo	IVIC-170	5220 +/− 245	Núñez 1976
La Lisera	GaK-9902	5240 +/− 230	Vera 1981; Núñez 1967
Cobija-1/S	B-3115	5440 +/− 150	Bittmann 1984
Cobija-1/S	B-3114	5460 +/− 140	Bittmann 1984
Cobija-1/S	B-3934	5510 +/− 60	Bittmann 1984
Chinchorro-1	GX-15083	5560 +/− 175	Múñoz et al. n.d.
Quiani-1	I-1349	5630 +/− 145	Bird 1967; Mostny 1964
Camarones-S	GaK-8645	5640 +/− 160	Rivera 1984
Cobija-1/S	B-3933	6030 +/− 70	Bittmann 1984
Chinchorro-1	GX-15084	6070 +/− 285	Muñoz et al. n.d.
Quiani-1	I-1348	6170 +/− 220	Bird 1967; Mostny 1964
Camarones-14	I-9816	6615 +/− 390	Schiappacasse 1984
Camarones-14	I-9817	6650 +/− 155	Schiappacasse 1984
Camarones-17	GX-15080	6780 +/− 110	Muñoz et al. n.d.
Camarones-17	GX-15081	6930 +/− 140	Muñoz et al. n.d.
Camarones-14	I-11431	7000 +/− 135	Schiappacasse 1984
Camarones-14	I-9999	7420 +/− 225	Schiappacasse 1984
Morro-1	I-13653	7810 +/− 180	Allison et al. 1984
Acha-2	I-15249	8900 +/− 150	Muñoz et al. n.d.
Acha-2	GX-15082	8970 +/− 255	Muñoz et al. n.d.

Camarones-15 and Pisagua-7, where Alto Ramirez phase burials (1000–500 B.C.) were placed adjacent to late Chinchorro burials (Phase III) (Aufderheide et al. n.d.b). Another exception is the Aragón site, where Núñez and Zlatar (n.d.) have postulated a Chinchorro Phase I component associated with early highland hunters.

The bodies in these sites are always in an extended position and organized in groups of several people of different age and sex. At present, we are attempting to determine genetically if these are, in fact, family members. Generally speaking, these groups consist of three to six children and two or more elders, representing both masculine and feminine sexes. It is difficult to establish age-sex relations among burial groups because there is no clear pattern of old and young, male and female, and small and large groups. There is, however, a high number of infants, and some fetuses, who were given special mortuary treatment.

In some cases piles of bodies were found with no preferred orientation (Morro-1), but in most sites the extended bodies face the sea. Bodies also are deposited on the sand, which makes it very difficult to record any superposition (Figs. 4 and 5). Generally, the bodies are placed on top of a reed matting, and when several bodies are buried together, an entire layer of matting can be seen. There are no indications of tomb shapes or burial chambers at Chinchorro sites.

At Morro-1 and other Chinchorro I sites, people disposed of the dead in special places that can be considered true cemeteries. Evidence of human tissue burning was obtained from several burials, and fireplaces, as well as a fair amount of carbon and ash, were noticed throughout many sites.

Contexts and Offerings

In following John Rowe (1962), two contextual issues require consideration. First is the direct association of artifacts with individual bodies. There is no reason to doubt that most of the artifacts on or immediately next to bodies belonged to the particular individual in life. In the case of secondary depositions, a time-space factor must be considered; new artifacts could have been added to the inventory as the body was reburied in a different place. This association may not be critical, however, if there was a short time period between primary and secondary deposition. And second, the associated artifacts must be seen as an assemblage that represents a coherent aspect of the Chinchorro tradition.

Although mummification techniques seem to occur throughout all three Chinchorro phases, burial offerings may suggest ranking within some Chinchorro populations (*sensu* Saxe n.d.: 226–227; Binford 1971: 12–13; Tainter 1978: 126). Commonly, offerings deposited with Chinchorro burials consisted of pieces of basketry rendered in the coiled technique, with both geometric and human designs, especially during Phase III. Bird skin with

Fig. 4 Excavation at Camarones 15-D site showing details of extended mummies of the Chinchorro Phase III.

The Preceramic Chinchorro Mummy Complex of Northern Chile

Fig. 5 Camarones 15-D showing details of Chinchorro Phase III mummies.

feathers attached and treated with red ochre was used as an inner wrapping. Matting was also used for wrapping bodies. In many cases, ribs and vertebrae of sea mammals were part of the offering. Bags (chinchorros) made of reed and finished in a netting technique, fishing lines made of cotton fibers, fishhooks (both thorn and shell), harpoons, spear throwers, darts, and grinding stones also were recovered. By Phase III, matting with geometric designs rendered with human hair, as well as pieces of cotton textiles, were present. In some cases, and apparently for very special people, necklaces of lapis lazuli and shell beads were recovered.

In one case at the site of Camarones-15, the bodies of two infants were deposited in wooden cradles (Rivera 1974: 84). These bodies show remains of complicated mummification with faces covered with clay and painted in red. Their heads were adorned with feathered crowns made in a very complicated technique with sewn yellow and blue feathers of tropical birds. Offerings included pieces of brown dotted pelt (probably from a feline). Water bags made of sea lion bladder, with snails used in the knob lacing of seams, were recovered, as well as figurines made of stone, wood, and bone (Núñez 1967-68: 87).

Perhaps the most distinctive Chinchorro feature is the preparation of the body and the inferred accompanying mortuary ritual. This feature led Uhle (1919) to define three types of body preparation: Type 1, bodies of simple preparation in which they are extended, tied, and covered with mats and clay (sites Quiani-7, Camarones-15); Type 2, bodies of complicated preparation with desiccation and evisceration and refill of empty cavities with straw, human hair, sticks, and shaping of a secondary restitution, including clay masks, wigs, and teeth (sites Playa Miller-8, Chinchorro type-site, Pisagua-Viejo-1, and Patillos); Type 3, extended bodies covered with clay and sand, wrapped in mats. In general terms, Uhle's proposed typology has been partially confirmed by our work at the site of Morro-1 (Allison et al. 1984).

Morro-1 is located at the base of Morro, Arica, a prominent rocky promontory that lies south of the city. The site was discovered by Uhle in 1914 when potable water tanks for the public service system were under construction. In 1983, when additional works for the same purpose were carried out by the Servicio Agua Potable de Arica, new archaeological evidence appeared. Beginning in November 1983, members of the Institute of Anthropology, the Universidad de Tarapacá (i.e., Vivian Standen, Guillermo Focacci, Marvin Allison, Raúl Rocha, Bernardo Arriaza) and Mario Rivera carried out limited but systematic excavation at the site. Ninety-six bodies were recovered from unstratified, mostly loose sand on the slope of the hill. The bodies were located well underground, at an average depth of 1.20 m. Of the total body count, 42 were children and 54 were adults. Among the adults, there were 27 women, 20 men, and seven bodies of indeterminate sex (Allison et al. 1984). Among the children, seven were female, 12 were male, and 23 were of indeterminate sex.

Two main areas were excavated at the Morro-1 site. One area contained groups of bodies, mainly children, in an extended position. The other area was characterized by piles of randomly oriented and extended mummies, most of which were wrapped in reed matting. Nine radiocarbon dates were obtained, ranging from 5860 to 1720 B.C. These dates suggest that the Chinchorro people were using the same site for more than 4,000 years.

Based upon the information available from the Morro-1 site, a revised typology of techniques of body treatment are presented below. Not discussed are the results of ongoing bioanthropological analyses of the body remains (Allison et al. 1984).

Type 1. Natural mummification, with no evidence of internal alteration of the body. The faces of some individuals are painted with red ochre. All Type I burials are extended, and sometimes slightly flexed. Several subtypes are divided by material used to wrap the body (Allison et al. 1984: 157). Our Type 1 is the same as Uhle's Type 1, with the difference being that he associated this type with the first Chinchorro settlements (Uhle 1922: 48–50).

Type 2. Artificial mummification with great variability in body treatment, particularly in the cavities (thorax, abdominal, pelvis, and cranium) and extremities. Both male and female sexual organs are modeled in clay. Other features include wigs; faces modeled with white or black clay (manganese), which sometimes outline eye features with incisions; noses slightly prominent and with nasal holes; and mouths opened or closed and outlined with incisions (Figs. 6–9).

The bodies were skinned and eviscerated, with the flesh peeled free of the bone. The bodies were then dried by using fire or hot ashes. Cavities were then dried and refilled with vegetal fibers and ashes, using straight sticks to keep the whole bundle well packed, when modeled with several layers of clay. Prepared bandages of human skin (presumably of the deceased) were applied to the body. There are several variations within this type, but in general it conforms to Uhle's Type 2, which he considered a logical evolution from the simpler Type 1.

Type 3. This type includes extended mummies, some characterized by fire-dried treatment of the body which produced an oil and ash concretion on the skin that added weight to the body. This type corresponds to Uhle's Type 3, which he viewed as a "degeneration" of Type 2 (Uhle 1922: 48–49).

Type 4. This group consists of bodies that were exposed to fire without further preparation. They appear as an unfinished Type 3 mummy. This group may belong to Uhle's Type 3 as well (Uhle 1922: 48–49, 66).

Data from the Morro-1 site yielded the following frequencies for each type of mummification: Type 1 with 37.5%, Type 2 with 36.4%, Type 3 with 19.17%, and Type 4 with 6.2% (Allison et al. 1984: 161).

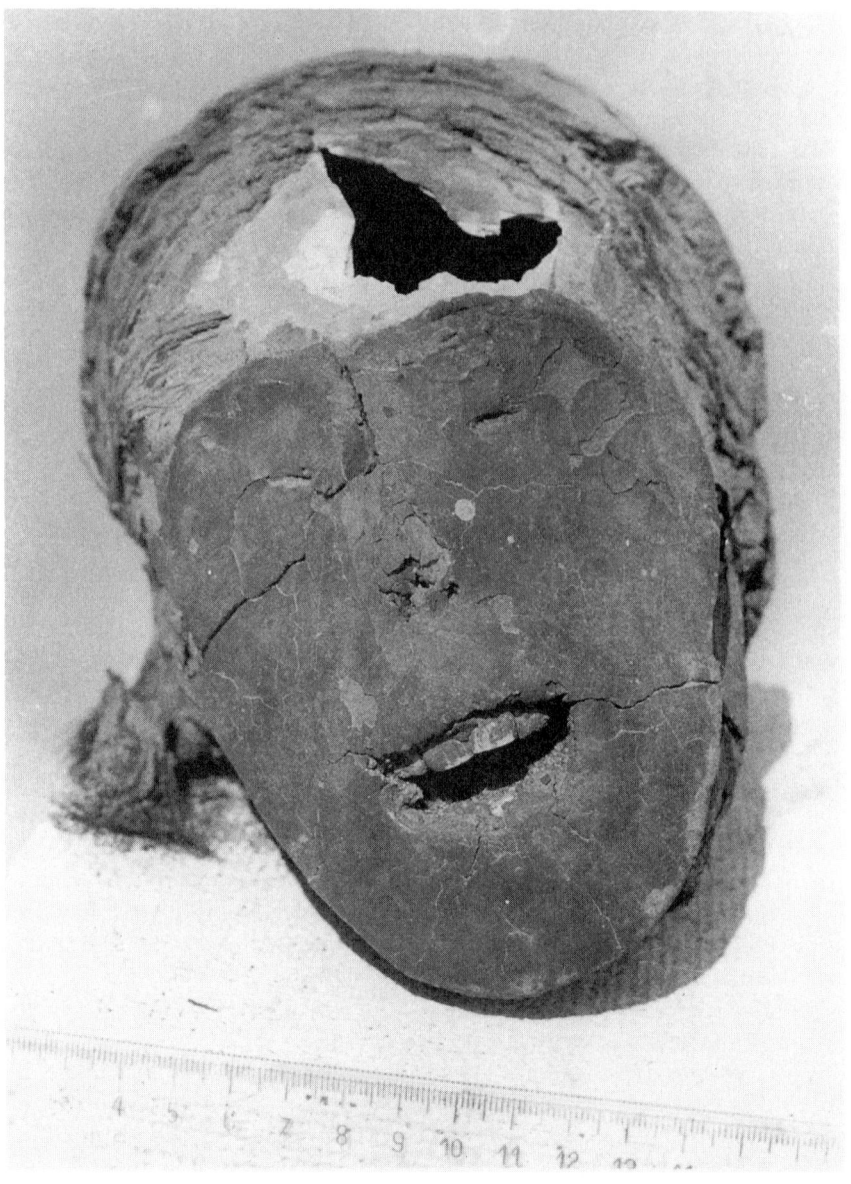

Fig. 6 Playa Miller-8 site showing Chinchorro Type 2 mummy. Note the clay mask covering the head of the body.

The Preceramic Chinchorro Mummy Complex of Northern Chile

Fig. 7 Morro-I site showing Chinchorro Type 2, Burial 23-10 with clay mask and wig. Note the skin bandages wrapped around the body (Collection of the Universidad de Tarapacá).

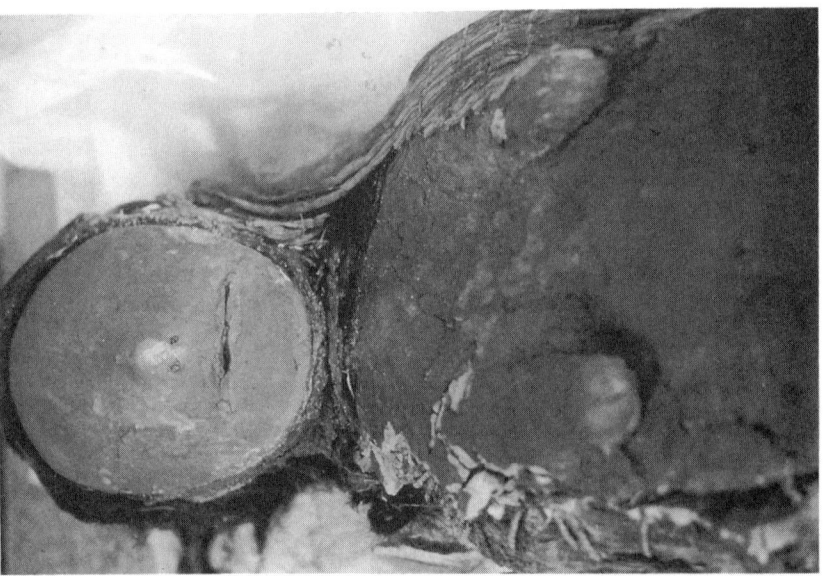

Fig. 8 Morro-I site showing Type 2 mummy, Burial 1-4 (Collection of the Universidad de Tarapacá).

The Preceramic Chinchorro Mummy Complex of Northern Chile

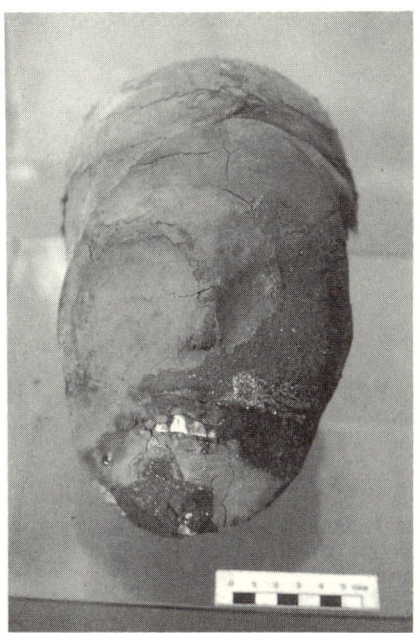

Fig. 9 Patillos site showing Chinchorro Type 2 mummy with clay mask covered with ochre (Collection of Anker Nielsen, Iquique).

In summary, Morro-1 represents the only extensive cemetery site ever excavated systematically. Because most other Chinchorro sites have not been studied cautiously and systematically, they cannot compare reliably with the Morro-1 findings. Thus, the present typology is derived only from the variety of techniques observed at a single site. Keeping this sampling bias in mind, I will now compare briefly the Chinchorro data with those from selected ethnographic cases and from other Preceramic cultures.

Despite the chronological and contextual problems with the Chinchorro sites, it is possible to use these sites to hypothesize three major mortuary patterns in body treatment and burial context (Fig. 2). These three trends correspond roughly with the three Chinchorro phases discussed earlier.

Pattern I (Chinchorro I). This pattern is characterized by extended bodies, with a few cases in which the orbital cavities were filled with clay, as well as a plaster-clay coating on the face. The burials are found in sites associated primarily with gathering activities (Rivera 1991) and a fishing technology consisting of shell fishhooks, lines, weights, and harpoons. There also are basketry and some cotton textiles. Most sites of this pattern are small cemeteries, such as Camarones-14, Morro-1, and Quiani-1. The average radiocarbon date from these sites is approximately 4600 B.C., although it may be earlier and correspond with Phase I.

Pattern II (Chinchorro II). During this phase, there was an apparent increase in the population with more sites located along the coast. The most characteristic feature is the complicated preparation of bodies, a trait that was defined by Uhle as "complicated mummification" (Uhle 1919). Bodies buried during this phase were found at the Chinchorro type-site, Playa Miller-8, Morro-1, Quiani-1, Pisagua-Viejo-1, Patillos, Bajo Molle, Aragón, and Caleta Huelén-42. Dwelling sites and cemeteries were more extensively and intensively occupied. Fishing equipment was technically more complete and efficient. Besides basketry and matting, spear throwers were known. Pattern II is radiocarbon dated between approximately 4000 and 2000 B.C.

Pattern III (Chinchorro III). This pattern is defined by extended as well as flexed bodies partially covered with clay and sand in what is believed to be a simplification of the earlier mummification patterns. Baskets were made with very fine techniques and textiles improved by the introduction of the belt loom. Besides cotton, wool was also used, as well as new techniques such as the "repp" geometric design in the direction of the weft. Hallucinogenic equipment, turbans, and cephalic ornaments are common. During this phase cultigens (e.g., manioc and quinoa) were introduced, and the Chinchorro people became more independent of marine resources. Later in this pattern, experimental pottery, characterized by a mixture of sand and algae temper, completed the technological advancement. The most representative sites are Playa Miller-7, Camarones-15, Quiani-7, Los Canastos, and Pisaqua. The pattern is radiocarbon dated between approximately 2000 and 500 B.C. (Rivera 1991: 15).

Comparisons of the Mortuary Data with Other Areas

Following Metraux (1947: 20–21), the term artificial "mummification" refers to deliberate measures to preserve the body from decay after death. Included here is the attempt to restore to the body some resemblance of the appearance it had during life. The specific methods employed to preserve the body are desiccation, evisceration, use of resinous substances, and stuffing with ashes, sand, or straw (Allison et al. 1984 : 157–160).

Mummification is different from the natural preservation that may result fortuitously from environmental conditions of climate, atmosphere, air, and soil that may cause desiccation, freezing, saponification, and tanning of the body.

Ethnographic cases provide useful information on the cultural techniques of mummification. For instance, the Chibcha and Sinu Indians of Colombia used evisceration and resinous substances, while the Quijo of Ecuador filled their dead with jewels (Metraux 1947: 20). Stuffing of the skin, body, and separate limbs also has been reported for various indigenous groups of Venezuela, Colombia, Ecuador, and the Inkas of Peru (Metraux 1947: 21; Bittmann and Munizaga 1976: 83). In some cases, mummification was reserved for captured enemies, and in others for the deceased of the tribe, commonly the chiefs. Also interesting are the ethnographic examples of the Vanuatu in the Pacific Islands. The Albert B. Lewis collection, gathered around 1910 with material from the Melanesian Islands (Field Museum of Natural History, Chicago), contains several examples of prepared bodies using methods that closely resemble those employed by the ancient Chinchorro people. Vanuatu mummies are extended so they could also remain in a standing posture. This gave them an appearance similar to the stone statues of Easter Island.

Perhaps the best known examples of mummification in South America are the shrunken heads of the Jivaro and neighboring people (Metraux 1947: 20). Mummified heads were also prepared by the Mundurucu in Brazil, who removed the brain and other soft parts, placed the head in oil, dried it in the sun, exposed it to smoke, and painted it. The brain cavity was filled with cotton, and artificial eyes were made by filling the sockets with wax upon which a tooth of an animal was placed to represent the pupil (Metraux 1947: 21).

As for the archaeological cases, in the Santa Elena Peninsula in southern Ecuador Karen Stothert (1985) has excavated the Las Vegas site, which dates between 6300 and 4650 B.C. There, Stothert defined a population with a broad-based subsistence pattern that included hunting and collecting. Most notable is the use of the bottle gourd, apparently domesticated, and phytolith evidence of maize agriculture. With respect to the burials, Stothert found that a high percentage were secondary, with many stripped of their flesh and showing signs of disarticulation and arrangement in groups and piles. Also, as in the Chinchorro case, many of the Las Vegas burials used red pigment and shell bead ornaments (Stothert 1985: 621).

Quilter, in comparing the Paloma (5000–2500 B.C.), Chinchorro, and Las Vegas burial patterns, found common traits such as group burials and special attention given to subadults (Quilter 1989: 70). Paloma revealed burial practices consistent for a long span of time, and showed a rather conservative mortuary tradition very much like that of Chinchorro. Among these practices were wrapping of bodies and burning in situ. Also important was the special treatment of infants and the use of red pigment, both features similar to Chinchorro. Contrary to the Paloma site, which was abandoned during the late Preceramic period, the Chinchorro sites show coexistence of Phase III burials with contemporary highlanders of the Alto Ramirez phase and with an incipient horticultural practice. Unlike the Paloma case, the Chinchorro people experienced the hypothetical change from a nomadic society to one which was horticultural and sedentary-based (Quilter 1989: 64–65).

Other possibly related sites are those located in Chilca (Engel 1984: 36) near Paloma. Here the most interesting feature is the circular-shaped, semisubterranean house (Donnan 1964: 127–144) with a conical structure made of junco, cane, and whalebones, in the same general pattern as those already described for Chinchorro (Rivera 1991: 18; Llagostera 1989: 71). At Chilca and at Las Haldas (Pozorski and Pozorski 1987: 20), infant burials, wrapped burials, and burning are also prevalent. In the upper Chilca Valley, at the Cave of Tres Ventanas, a site located 3,925 m above sea level, Engel (1987: 23) has reported bodies wrapped in camelid skins with radiocarbon dates of 6080 B.C. (Vallejos 1982: 21). Other high-altitude sites possibly representing a close connection to those of the Chinchorro tradition are situated in Jujuy, northwest Argentina, at the site of Huachichocana Cave 7 (Fernández 1974: 110, 124), and in San Juan, Argentina (Gambier and Sacchero 1969: figs. 1–4) at the Los Morrillos site. These two sites contain mummy bundles that are similar to those from Chinchorro. The goods that accompany the mummies, namely, basketry, featherwork, beads, nets, and others, also are similar and the radiocarbon dates are comparable (2460 +/− 150 B.C. for Morrillos, and 7670 +/− 130 B.C., 6720 +/− 550 B.C., for Huachichocana).

Other sites of the Peruvian coast also resemble Chinchorro mummies. For instance, at Paracas (Engel 1981: 31, 36), Asia (Engel 1976), Huaca Prieta (Bird 1985: 68, 74), and Bandurrias (Fung 1988: 77), extended bodies appear with mat wrappings that are very similar to those in Chinchorro.

The Preceramic Chinchorro Mummy Complex of Northern Chile

Interestingly, at Asia, aside from mummy wrappings, lithic blades (similar to Chinchorro knives), textiles, a baked clay tablet along with snuffing tubes, spears, and use of shark teeth occur as in late Chinchorro phases. Furthermore, in Asia as in some Chinchorro sites, signs of violence have been noticed, as well as headless bodies and trophy heads (Engel 1963: 47, 94–95, 100).

In concurring with Quilter (1989: 83–85), I see some common denominators for these collective burial patterns. First, there is an emphasis on fertility and possibly life after death, which could be interpreted from the high frequency of red pigment used, by painting faces and, in some cases, the rest of the body in the Chinchorro mummies. Pigment could symbolically represent blood, that is, vitality, regeneration, and movement. Second, infant burials may represent the symbol of potential life, that is, the recycling of generations (Quilter 1989: 83), an idea possibly supported by "feeding" the sea mammal bones to mummies and by making the mummies resemble their living bodies. It also is possible that the dead continued to play a role among the living, particularly if they were immortal. In this context, mummification may represent a "continuing existence" of the deceased. To speculate further, the high frequency of elaborated mummies of children is possibly related to "ancestor veneration."

Possible Origins of the Chinchorro Culture

Since the beginning of our research on the Chinchorro tradition, we have been puzzled by the sophisticated archaeological assemblages that characterized the Chinchorro sites. Traits such as hallucinogenic paraphernalia, along with spear throwers, well-developed basketry, featherwork, and even mummification itself, constitute remarkably complex features, as does the introduction of domesticated yucca (with estimated radiocarbon dates of about 2000 B.C.) and maize (with dates of approximately 3000 B.C. [see Rivera 1991: 15; Núñez 1989: 90; Bonavía and Grobman 1989: 468–469]). If all these traits are considered as part of a subtropical horticultural complex, then the whole question of the origins of the Chinchorro can be addressed in a rather different way.

Based on these traits and patterns, I previously have interpreted some socioeconomic aspects of the Chinchorro tradition as part of an eastern tropical lowland migration to or trade network with the Pacific coast in early Preceramic times (Rivera 1975: 28–29). In relation to certain archaeological traits of the tradition, hallucinogenic paraphernalia and its use must be considered as part of a complicated ritual that began as far back as Phase I of the Chinchorro tradition. This custom is possibly identified with eastern tropical forest groups.

Although spear throwers occur in many areas throughout Andean prehistory, they are most common in the archaeological record of northern Chile

Fig. 10 Patillos site showing Chinchorro mummy (p. 2569, 11-12-13-14/54). Buried with the body was a spear thrower (Collection of Anker Nielsen, Iquique).

and southern Peru during Chinchorro and early Alto Ramirez times. During Chinchorro times these weapons probably had both utilitarian and ceremonial uses. In the site of Patillos, Nielsen located a mummy (Fig. 10) with a complete spear thrower inserted inside the body next to the spinal column. Spear throwers also are well known among modern groups of the upper Xingu and Araguaya Rivers, as reported by Galvao (1950: 353–355) and Montandon (1934: 402) for the Kamaiura people of the Culuene River. The spear thrower also occurs in the neighboring area that extends from Panama, along the Magdalena River, to the upper Amazon at the foot of the Andes. Montandon (1934: 403) also recorded them among the Karaya people (Tupi-speaking) in the Xingu River, and among the Pouroupouroyu (Arawaks) of the Upper Amazon. Curiously enough, spear throwers used by these particular groups are similar in shape to the most typical ones from Chinchorro sites, namely Types A-1 and B, according to Rivera and Zlatar (1982: 27). Also, Uhle reported similar spear throwers from the south coast of Peru (Uhle 1907: 119–121) and northwest Argentina (Fernández 1977: 139).

Featherwork is also relevant in this context. There are several examples of associated material found with Chinchorro mummies at various sites in northern Chile. The best example is from the Camarones-15 site (Fig. 11). Two mummies of eight- to ten-year-old boys who wore feathered head ornaments of complicated manufacture were recovered (Rivera 1974: 80). The ornaments were made in the typical technique that several tropical forest groups exhibit today.

Whether these items reflect direct or indirect trade with tropical groups or actual migration of tropical groups to the coast is a matter of controversy (Brochado n.d.; Rouse 1986; Lathrap 1973: 176–182; Rivera and Rothhammer 1991: 254; Rothhamer and Silva 1992: 441–446). It is interesting to note, however, that recent evidence from studies on craniometrical distances using osteoarchaeological collections from several Preceramic sites (i.e., Camarones-14, Morro-1, Playa Miller-7 [northern Chile], Sambaquies Cabezuda [Brazil], Tiwanaku [Bolivia], Paucarcancha [Peru] [Rivera and Rothhammer 1986: 297]) suggests strong biological links between northern Chile and the eastern tropical lowlands.

Fig. 11 Sketch showing the distribution of the mummies at Camarones 15-D site (Based on field notes of Mario Rivera and Raúl Rocha).

Mario A. Rivera

In an attempt to understand these patterns and more of the biological makeup of the Chinchorro people, several exploratory studies are currently under way. These include research related to human populations living in coastal environments, to pneumonia frequencies and dust and smoke exposure contamination (Aufderheide et al. n.d.a), and to recovering DNA in hair from Chinchorro mummies. Another interesting development is that of coca use by prehistoric populations, which hypothetically could be tested through radioimmunoassay in human hair, under the assumption that the Chinchorro people were unaware of coca (Aufderheide et al. n.d.b; Cartmell et al. 1991). The result of these findings will be reported in future publications.

Discussion

In summary, the burial practices recorded at Morro-1, the most systematically studied site, reveal little variation in Chinchorro mortuary practices. The most common pattern of burial practices are Types 1 and 2, found among children and adults of both sexes. The most persistent practice is the extended body, wrapped in mattings and associated with limited offerings. Burial data from other Chinchorro sites reveal similar patterns, although these sites have not yet been studied systematically.

Despite the preliminary nature of the data, we may ask tentatively why the Chinchorro people maintained the same mortuary customs and rituals, and why they stored burials for living rituals. One possibility is that as groups moved to different site locations along the coast, they carried the more elaborate burials with them and copied their mummification technique. We have proposed previously (Allison et al. 1984) that the details in preparing the bodies suggest a deliberate attempt to make them as rigid as possible, perhaps for the purpose of transporting them from site to site and displaying them in an upright position. Additional evidence of secondary restitution, refinishing of facial clay masks, repainting of the body surface, and damaged bodies also supports this view (Figs. 6–9). Furthermore, it is becoming clearer that there is a temporal sequence of shaping mummies. In many cases, several layers of different types of clay were applied to the bodies. Since bodies were found in groups and composed of three to four adult males and females and two to five children, we surmise that the bodies of family units were finally disposed together, probably after some of them had traveled from settlement to settlement.

These customs take on more meaning when viewed from the concepts of Binford (1971), Tainter (1978), and Saxe (n.d.). Binford's concept of *social personae* is particularly significant in regard to the varying organizational complexity of populations and to their subsistence practices (Binford 1971: 18–19, 23). Recent results of our work in Pisagua (Aufderheide et al. n.d.b) reveal that the Chinchorro people hunted and gathered maritime products, as opposed to later Andean groups (e.g., Alto Ramirez) who based their subsistence primarily on agricultural products. For the Chinchorro people, a stable maritime economy probably did not require a complex social organization with repetitive structural changes. The elaborate treatment of infant bodies, however, might suggest a ranking system based on birth (Saxe n.d.: 8). And the exotic tropical feathered head ornaments worn by children buried at Camarones may suggest the symbolic meaning of social status. This procedure also may suggest a direct relation to corporate organization and the amount of energy expended on burial practices which, according to Tainter (1978: 125), indicates levels of social differentiation within a group, as well as levels of social involvement. Set in this context, differential burial treatment of the young could indicate a more direct relation to the ancestors. Useful here is Renfrew's proposition (Renfrew 1974: 74) of social differentiation, if we consider the Chinchorro people being composed of a mixture of group-oriented and individual-oriented bands, with communal work represented by mummification and socially differentiated cemeteries.

In returning to the previously mentioned elaborate burial of the two young boys in the Camarones-15 site, the offerings, which included high-quality feathered cephalic ornaments, feline furs as wrappings, outstanding pieces of basketry, and cotton-and-wool textiles, provide enough evidence to suggest that the youngsters belonged to a high-status group. The case of burial 1-4 from Morro-1, which belongs to a woman, suggests the same pattern (Fig. 8).

Two other examples, also from the Morro-1 site, are possibly indicative of social differentiation. Burial 10 shows a special treatment with a very elaborate offering consisting of sea lion skin wrappings on the body. Several pieces of a large sea mammal, probably a whale (Fig. 12), were placed on top of the body. Burial 28, from the same site, radiocarbon dated to 3680 +/− 100 B.C. (I-13652) (Arriaza 1988: 21), contained a male body that displayed a black tattooed moustache design. The offering also contained bird skin wrappings dyed with red ochre, sewn furs, probably from camelids, fish bone remains, shells containing red pigment, a bird bone tube used as receptacle for unknown substances, cotton-and-wool fiber textiles dyed yellow and red, fine pieces of basketry, and a black sea snail.

To summarize these points, the elaborate treatment of children, as well as women, may suggest the identification of a kin-related group based on power and prestige. To carry this interpretation a step further, the decrease in ritual burial during Chinchorro Phase III, or the terminal phase, could suggest increased social complexity associated with increased contact with agricultural groups (Alto Ramirez) and, as a result, a gradual shift to sedentism and a non-kin-based society.

Here our previously developed concept of primary division of labor (Rivera and Rothhammer 1986) centered on basic patterns of subsistence

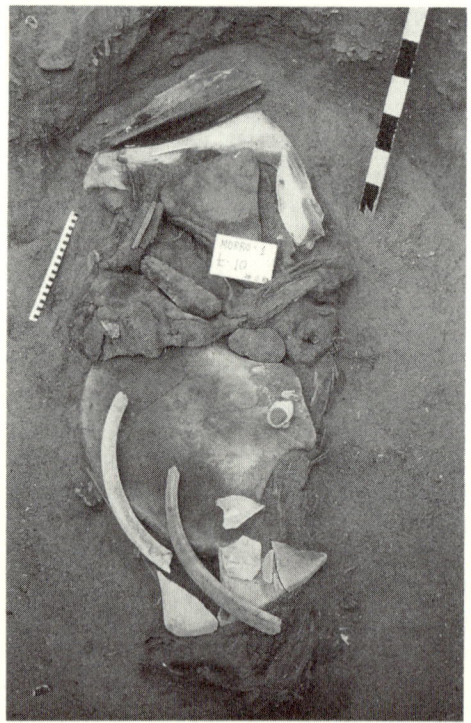

Fig. 12 Morro I site showing Chinchorro Burial 10 in association with sea mammal bones as offerings (Collection of the Universidad de Tarapacá).

and ritual is useful. This concept states that specialization in either economic or religious activities contributes to the identity of the group, certain territorialism, and spiritual cohesion. This may reflect a social group or community that shared a common spatial territory; that is, a territory that people traveled within and had resource rights to, for several continuous generations. Movement within this territory could be seasonal or cyclical, using a central base camp to develop a more efficient maritime and agricultural economy. Such a group structure would also have permitted the recognition of part-time leaders who perhaps based their authority on spiritual beliefs and corporate burial practices, with special tasks and special rights to subsistence sources.

Unfortunately, the lack of control over the contemporaneity of sites does not permit us to speculate on a more precise model of social differences and to suggest whether the observed differences are due to chronological sequences and/or functional distinctions. In several Chinchorro sites, however, we have recovered evidence of differential treatment of the bodies, either through mummification or associated offerings, which may be indicative of an incipient social ranking.

CONCLUSION

The Preceramic Chinchorro burial customs and rituals probably represent part of a complex process in which concepts of the afterlife played a central role. Practices related to mortuary rituals are part of a symbolic process. In this sense, it seems highly likely that the activities associated with the Chinchorro mortuary complex were part of what anthropologists call "religion." However, this system of beliefs and practices probably was not formalized as an institution, given the probable kin-based nature of Chinchorro society.

In addressing the structure of the Chinchorro society, Arriaza (1988: 25, 28–29) discussed the problem of social identity on the group and individual levels and their relation to the supernatural world. It is through the individuals themselves, and by preserving their bodies for the afterlife, that the group might have emphasized its cosmovision. A binary conception of life and death in which the soul finds its way to eternity could be taken from the observation that Chinchorro people were specialists in manipulating the human body and shaping a rigid mummy, solid and durable, with all the necessary requirements to beautify and carefully pack and bury it. This hypothesis is supported by the presence of figurines as offerings that display exactly the same attributes as the mummies. The figurines probably represent a close identification with children's burials and probably constitute symbols that recreate both the natural and social worlds. They also might represent a fertility cult, especially when the faces of both mummies and figurines are painted with red ochre and green colors.

Mario A. Rivera

As Rowe (this volume) has argued, it would have been important to know the sequence by which the Chinchorro mortuary rituals developed, and what roles the figurines and other objects played. Unfortunately, we lack clear evidence as to whether the bodies have been redeposited, or if there have been two or more stages of interment, or if the bodies had been utilized over several generations, and ultimately, if there have been several stages of the mummification process. Whatever the sequences, the whole process, including the use of figurines, is probably related to the re-creation of the continuing relationship between the living and the dead, including ancestors. We can surmise that beliefs in ancestors must have played an important role in the social structure of the Chinchorro society and in the use of formal cemeteries.

A link between formal cemeteries and territoriality in the Chinchorro tradition has been emphasized by Karen Wise (n.d.) and Jane Buikstra (this volume). Their main point, following Arthur Saxe (n.d.), is that by keeping a formal and permanent area for the disposal of the dead, public ritualization takes place. Buikstra (this volume) also suggests that both the elaborate Chinchorro mortuary ritual and the development of cemeteries probably constitute symbols of corporate rights over resource use and control.

To close, it is presently difficult to determine whether the variability of burial techniques in Chinchorro sites is due to regional, social, cultural, or temporal differences or any combination of these. More systematic studies of the ethnological and archaeological records are needed to understand the relationships between the religious and technological developments of mortuary practices and documented cultural changes in the Chinchorro society. Without any doubt, however, the mummification techniques and their implications for understanding Chinchorro society provide evidence of complex cultural development in early Andean times.

Acknowledgements Several persons have been involved with my Chinchorro research project and with the development of this paper. I would like to thank Vivian Standen and Raúl Rocha, my co-workers at the site of Morro-1, as well as Guillermo Focacci, my friend and colleague with whom I have shared many field seasons and discussions. I also thank Marvin Allison, Arthur Aufderheide, and Francisco Rothhammer for their contributions to the biological study of the bodies. Colleagues and friends from Instituto de Antropología Universidad de Tarapacá, Chile, are thanked for their collaboration both in the field and laboratory. The Research Committee of the Universidad de Tarapacá is acknowledged for funding part of the research. Marc Kelley, Jeffrey Shipman, Sean Murphy, Alvaro Carevic, and Iván Muñoz collaborated in the excavations at Camarones-15 and Pisagua. Jeffrey Quilter provided instructive comments and editorial observations, as did Tom Dillehay, Pat Lyon, and James Brown. Last, Elizabeth Boone and the staff of the Pre-Columbian Studies department at Dumbarton Oaks are thanked for inviting me to participate in this symposium. The ideas and interpretations expressed throughout this paper are my own responsibility.

BIBLIOGRAPHY

ALLISON, MARVIN J., GUILLERMO FOCACCI, BERNARDO ARRIAZA, VIVIAN STANDEN, MARIO RIVERA, AND JEROLD LOWENSTEIN
    1984   Chinchorro, momias de preparación complicada: Métodos de momificación. *Chungará* 13: 155–173.

ALVAREZ, LUIS
    1969   Un Cementerio Pre-Cerámico con Momias de Preparación Complicada. *Rehue* 2: 181–190.

ARRIAZA, BERNARDO
    1988   Modelo bioarqueológico para la búsqueda y acercamiento al individuo social. *Chungará* 21: 9–32.

AUFDERHEIDE, ARTHUR, MARVIN ALLISON, MARC KELLEY, MARIO RIVERA, JEFF SHIPMAN, AND LARRY TIESZEN
    n.d.a   The Prehistory of Pneumonia in the Atacama Desert. Manuscript on file, Paleopathology Lab, University of Minnesota, Duluth, 1990.

AUFDERHEIDE, ARTHUR, MARC KELLEY, MARIO RIVERA, H. ROY KROUSE, LARRY TIESZEN, LUZ GRAY, ELISHA IVERSEN, AND ALVARO CAREVIC
    n.d.b   The Bioanthropological Findings of Twelve Human Mummies from Pisagua, North Chile. Manuscript on file, Paleopathology Lab, University of Minnesota, Duluth, 1991.

BEARDSLEY, R., P. HOLDER, A. KRIESER, BETTY MEGGERS, J. RINALDO, AND PAUL KUTSCHE
    1955   Functional and Evolutionary Implications of Community Patterning. *Seminars in Archaeology* 22: 129–157. Society for American Archaeology, Washington, D.C.

BINFORD, LEWIS R.
    1971   Mortuary Practices: Their Study and Their Potential. In *Approaches to the Social Dimensions of Mortuary Practices* (James A. Brown, ed.). Memoirs of the Society for American Archaeology 25: 6–29. Washington, D.C.

BIRD, JUNIUS B.
    1943   Excavations in Northern Chile. Anthropological Papers of the American Museum of Natural History 38. New York.
    1967   Muestras de radiocarbono de un basural precerámico de Quiani, Arica. *Boletín Sociedad Arqueológica de Santiago* 4: 13–14.
    1985   *The Preceramic Excavations at the Huaca Prieta, Chicama Valley, Peru* (John Hyslop, ed.). Anthropological Papers of the American Museum of Natural History 62 (1). New York.

BIRD, JUNIUS B., AND MARIO A. RIVERA
    1988   *Excavaciones en el Norte de Chile*. Ediciones Universidad de Tarapacá, Arica.

BITTMANN, BENTE
    1984 El Proyecto Cobija: Investigaciones Antropológicas en la Costa del Desierto de Atacama (Chile). Ediciones Universidad del Norte, Antofagasta.
BITTMANN, BENTE, AND JUAN MUNIZAGA
    1976 The Earliest Artificial Mummification in the World? A Study of the Chinchorro Complex in Northern Chile. Folk 18: 61–92.
BONAVÍA, DUCCIO, AND ALEX GROBMAN
    1989 Andean Maize: Its Origins and Domestication. In Foraging and Farming: The Evolution of Plant Exploitation (Richard Harris and Glen C. Hillman, eds.): 456–470. Unwin Hyman, London.
BROCHADO, J. PROENZA
    n.d. An Ecological Model of the Spread of Pottery and Agriculture into Eastern South America. Ph.D. dissertation, University of Illinois-Urbana, 1984.
BROWN, JAMES A.
    1971 The Dimensions of Status in the Burials at Spiro. In Approaches to the Social Dimensions of Mortuary Practices (James A. Brown, ed.). Memoirs of the Society for American Archaeology 25: 92–112. Washington, D.C.
CARTMELL, LARRY W., ARTHUR AUFDERHEIDE, ANGELA SPRINGFIELD, CHERYL WEEMS, AND BERNARDO ARRIAZA
    1991 The Frequency and Antiquity of Prehistoric Coca Leaf Chewing Practices in Northern Chile: Radioimmunoassay of Cocaine Metabolite in Human-Mummy Hair. Latin American Antiquity 2: 260–268.
DAUELSBERG, PERCY
    1974 Excavaciones Arqueológicas en Quiani. Chungará 4: 7–38.
DONNAN, CHRISTOPHER
    1964 An Early House from Chilca, Peru. American Antiquity 30 (2): 137–144.
ENGEL, FREDERIC A.
    1963 A Preceramic Settlement on the Central Coast of Peru: Asia, Unit I. Transactions of the American Philosophical Society 53 (3). Philadelphia.
    1976 An Ancient World Preserved. Crown Publishing, New York.
    1981 Prehistoric Andean Ecology, Man, Settlement, and Environment in the Andes. The Deep South. Humanities Press, New York.
    1984 Chilca. Prehistoric Andean Ecology Series 4. Humanities Press, New York.
    1987 De las begonias al maíz, vida y producción en el Perú antiguo. Universidad Nacional Agraria, Lima.
FERNÁNDEZ, ALICIA
    1974 Excavaciones arqueológicas en la Cueva de Huachichocana, Departamento de Tumbaya, Prov. de Jujuy, Argentina. Relaciones 8: 101–126.
    1977 Nuevos hallazgos de estólicas en el borde de la Puna Jujeña (Argentina). In Actas VII Congreso Arqueología Chilena, Volume I (Hans Niemeyer, ed.): 131–165, Talca.

Focacci, Guillermo, Sergio Chacón, and Mario A. Rivera
   n.d. Excavaciones en Morro 1–6, Arica, Norte de Chile. Manuscript on file, Universidad de Tarapacá, Arica, 1988.

Fung, Rosa
   1988 The Late Preceramic and Initial Period. In *Peruvian Prehistory* (Richard W. Keatinge, ed.): 67–96. Cambridge University Press, Cambridge.

Galvao, Eduardo
   1950 O Uso de Propulsor entre as Tribus do Alto Xingu. *Revista Museu Paulista* 4: 353–368.

Gambier, Mariano, and Pablo Sacchero
   1969 Secuencias culturales y cronológicas para el sud oeste de la provincia de San Juan. *Hunuc-Huar* 1. San Juan.

Hodder, Ian
   1980 Social Structure and Cemeteries: A Critical Appraisal. In *Anglo-Saxon Cemeteries* (Peter Rahtz, Timothy Dickinson, and Larry Watts, eds.): 161–169. BAR British Series 82. Oxford.
   1987 *The Archaeology of Contextual Meanings*. Cambridge University Press, Cambridge.

Lathrap, Donald
   1973 The Antiquity and Importance of Long Distance Trade Relationships in the Moist Tropics of Pre-Columbian South America. *World Archaeology* 5 (2): 170–185.

Llagostera, Agustín
   1989 Caza y Pesca Marítima (9000 a 1000 A.C.) In *Culturas de Chile, Prehistoria* (Jorge Hidalgo, Virgilio Schiappacasse, Hans Niemeyer, Carlos Aldunate, and Ivan Solimano, eds.): 57–79. Santiago.

Martínez Compañón, Obispo
   1985 *Obra sobre Trujillo, siglo XVIII*. Edición Facsimilar, Ediciones Cultura Hispánica, Madrid.

Masuda, Shozo, Izumi Shimada, and Craig Morris (eds.)
   1985 *Andean Ecology and Civilization*. University of Tokyo Press.

Metraux, Alfred
   1947 Mourning Rites and Burial Forms of the South American Indians. *América Indígena* 7 (1): 7–44.

Montandon, George
   1934 *Traite d'Ethnologie cyclo-culturelle et d'ergologie systematique*. Payot, Paris.

Mostny, Grete
   1964 Anzuelos de Concha 6170 ± 220 años. *Noticiero Mensual Museo Nacional de Historia Natural* 98. Santiago.

Muñoz, Iván
   1982 Las Sociedades Costeras en el Litoral de Arica Durante el Período Arcaico Tardío y sus Vinculaciones en la Costa Peruana. *Chungará* 9: 124–173.

Muñoz, Iván, Raúl Rocha, and Sergio Chacón
    1991   Camarones 15: Asentamiento de Pescadores Correspondiente al Período Arcaico y Formativo en el extremo Norte de Chile. In *Actas XI Congreso Arqueología de Chile* (Hans Niemeyer, ed.): 1–24. Santiago.

Muñoz, Iván, Bernardo Arriaza, Juan Chacama, and Arthur Aufderheide
    n.d.   Los Orígenes del Poblamiento Humano en Arica. Manuscript on file, Universidad de Tarapacá, 1992.

Núñez, Lautaro
    1967/68   Figurinas Tempranas del Norte de Chile (Provincia de Tarapacá). *Estudios Arqueológicos* 3–4: 85–105.
    1969   El Primer Fechado Radiocarbónico del Complejo Faldas El Morro en el Sitio Tarapacá-40 y Algunas Discusiones Básicas. *Actas V Congreso Arqueologia Chilena*: 47–57. La Serena.
    1976   Registro Nacional de Fechas Radiocarbónicas en el Desierto Chileno. *Estudios Atacameños* 4: 74–123.
    1989   Hacia la Producción de Alimentos y la Vida Sedentaria (5000 A.C. a 900 A.C.). In *Culturas de Chile, Prehistoria* (Jorge Hidalgo, Virgilio Schiappacasse, Hans Niemeyer, Carlos Aldunate, and Ivan Solimano, eds.): 81–105. Santiago.

Núñez, Lautaro, and Cora Moragas
    n.d.   Reevaluación de los Primeros Poblamientos en las Tierras Bajas: Nuevas Evidencias de Maíz temprano en el Norte de Chile. *IV Congreso Arqueología Argentina*, San Rafael, 1976.

Núñez, Patricio, and Vjera Zlatar
    n.d.   Tiliviche 1-b y Aragón 1 (Estrato V): Dos Comunidades Precerámicas Coexistentes en Pampa del Tamarugal, Pisagua, Norte de Chile. *III Congreso Peruano del Hombre y la Cultura Andina*, Lima, 1977.

Pozorski, Sheila, and Thomas Pozorski
    1987   *Early Settlement and Subsistence in the Casma Valley, Peru*. University of Iowa Press, Iowa City.

Quilter, Jeffrey
    1989   *Life and Death at Paloma*. University of Iowa Press, Iowa City.

Renfrew, Colin
    1974   Beyond a Subsistence Economy: The Evolution of Social Organization in Prehistoric Europe. In *Reconstructing Complex Societies* (Christopher Moore, ed.). Bulletin of the American School of Oriental Research 20: 69–85 (supplement).

Rivera, Mario A.
    1974   Aspectos Sobre el Desarrollo Tecnológico del proceso de Agriculturización en el Norte Prehispano, Especialmente Arica (Chile). *Chungará* 3: 79–107.
    1975   Una Hipótesis Sobre Movimientos Poblacionales Altiplánicos y Transaltiplánicos a las Costas del Norte de Chile. *Chungará* 5: 7–31.
    1980   *Temas Antropológicos del Norte de Chile*. Ediciones Universidad de Chile, Antofagasta.

1984 Altiplano and Tropical Lowland Contacts in Northern Chile Prehistory: Chinchorro and Alto Ramirez Revisited. In *Social and Economic Organization in the Prehispanic Andes* (David Browman, Richard Burger, Mario Rivera, eds.). BAR International Series 194: 143–160. Oxford.
1991 The Prehistory of Northern Chile: A Synthesis. *Journal of World Prehistory* 5 (1): 1–47.
n.d. Prehistoric Chronology of Northern Chile. Ph.D. dissertation, University of Wisconsin–Madison, 1977.

RIVERA, MARIO A., AND FRANCISCO ROTHHAMMER
1986 Evaluación Biológica y Cultural de Poblaciones Chinchorro: Nuevos Elementos para la Hipótesis de Contactos Transaltiplánicos, Cuenca Amazonas-Costa Pacífico. *Chungará* 16–17: 295–306.
1991 The Chinchorro People of Northern Chile: 5000 BC–500 BC, a Review of Their Culture and Relationships. *International Journal of Anthropology* 6: 243–255.

RIVERA, MARIO A., AND VJERA ZLATAR
1982 Las Estólicas en el Desarrollo Cultural Temprano Prehispánico del Norte de Chile. *Boletín Museo La Serena* 18: 14–34.

ROTHHAMMER, FRANCISCO, AND CLAUDIO SILVA
1992 Gene Geography of South America: Testing Models of Population Displacement Based on Archaeological Evidence. *American Journal of Physical Anthropology* 89: 441–446.

ROUSE, IRVING
1986 *Migrations in Prehistory.* Yale University Press, New Haven, Connecticut.

ROWE, JOHN H.
1962 Warsaae's Law and the Use of Grave Lots for Archaeological Dating. *American Antiquity* 28 (2): 129–137.

SAXE, ARTHUR
n.d. Social Dimensions of Mortuary Practices. Ph.D. dissertation, University of Michigan, 1970.

SCHIAPPACASSE, VIRGILIO, AND HANS NIEMEYER
1984 *Estudio del Yacimiento Arqueológico Camarones 14.* Publicación Ocasional Museo Nacional Historia Natural, Santiago.

SHEA, DANIEL E., AND MARIO A. RIVERA
n.d. The Dating of the Chinchorro Mummy Complex: An Alternative Use of Radiocarbon Estimates. Manuscript on file, Department of Anthropology, Beloit College, 1992.

STAAL, CAROLINA
1974 Excavaciones en el sitio preagrícola Tiliviche 1-b. *Serie Documentos de Trabajos Universidad de Chile* 5: 14–26.

STOTHERT, KAREN
1985 The Preceramic Las Vegas Culture of Coastal Ecuador. *American Antiquity* 50 (3): 613–637.

SOTO-HEIM, PATRICIA
    1987   Evolución de Deformaciones Intencionales, Peinados, Tocados y Prácticas Funerarias en la Prehistoria de Arica. *Chungará* 19: 129–213.

TAINTER, JOSEPH
    1978   Mortuary Practices and the Study of Prehistoric Social Systems. In *Advances in Archaeological Method and Theory* 1 (Michael Schiffer, ed.): 105–141. Academic Press, New York.

THOMAS, DAVID H.
    1991   *Archaeology, Down to Earth*. Harcourt, Brace, and Jovanovich, Orlando, Fla.

UHLE, MAX
    1907   La Estólica en el Perú. *Revista Histórica* 2: 118–128.
    1919   *La Arqueología de Arica y Tacna*. Boletín Sociedad Ecuatoriana de Estudios Históricos Americanos 7–8, 1: 48. Quito.
    1922   *Fundamentos Etnicos y Arqueología de Arica y Tacna*, Quito.

VALLEJOS, MIRIAM A.
    1982   El Hombre Preagrícola de la Cueva Tres Ventanas de Chilca, Perú: Textilería. *Zonas Aridas* 2: 21–32.

VERA, JAIME
    1981   Momias Chinchorro de Preparación Complicada del Museo de Historia Natural de Valparaíso: 3.290 y 3.060 a.C. *Anales Museo Historia Natural Valparaíso* 14. Valparaíso.

WISE, KAREN
    n.d.   Preceramic Cultural Variability and Ethnic Diversity in the South Central Andes. Paper presented at 56th Annual Meeting of the Society for American Archaeology, New Orleans, April 1991.

ZLATAR, VJERA
    1983   Replanteamiento Sobre el Problema Caleta Huelén. *Chungará* 10: 21–28.
    1987   Un Yacimiento Precerámico y su Problemática desde la Perspectiva de sus Recintos Habitacionales. *Hombre y Desierto* 1: 1–36.

Mortuary Practices in the Alto Magdalena: The Social Context of the "San Agustín Culture"

ROBERT D. DRENNAN

UNIVERSITY OF PITTSBURGH

THE TOMBS OF COLOMBIA'S ALTO MAGDALENA region have always been the easiest aspect of its archaeological record to discuss. They are its only conspicuous monumental architectural remains, and they have been known and reported as curiosities since long before the beginnings of archaeology as a scholarly discipline. These tombs and the sculpture associated with them came to be the defining feature of the "San Agustín Culture," named after the modern town near which the largest number of most spectacular examples occurred. This archaeological culture has been defined, redefined, explicated, and compared to other archaeological cultures of the New World with primary reference to its tombs and its sculptural style (e.g., Preuss 1931; Pérez de Barradas 1943; Duque Gómez 1964; Reichel-Dolmatoff 1972; Hernández de Alba 1979; Duque Gómez and Cubillos 1979, 1983, 1988; Cubillos 1980; Gamboa Hinestrosa 1982; Sotomayor and Uribe 1987).

My attention here will be directed to the burial customs that the tombs represent and the ways in which consideration of these customs can help us understand the nature and development of the societies that produced them. I will summarize these burial customs and the archaeological remains they have left for us, but the real nature of the contribution that I hope to make involves placing these remains in the broader context of other kinds of archaeological information. In this effort, I will rely on results of relatively recent studies of residential zones and regional settlement patterns (e.g., Duque Gómez and Cubillos 1981; Llanos and Durán 1983; Drennan 1985; Llanos 1988, 1990; Herrera, Drennan, and Uribe 1989; Drennan et al. 1989, 1991). I will suggest some ways in which changes in burial customs in the Alto Magdalena might fit with other kinds of evidence of social, political, and economic change through time. And finally, I will discuss how such thinking helps to advance our understanding of early complex societies and their development.

Robert D. Drennan

I would prefer to start this discussion with the earliest known periods in the Alto Magdalena, and proceed chronologically through the sequence. It is the middle segment of the sequence, however, for which information is most abundant and which provides the best starting point for relating burial practice to other kinds of archaeological evidence. I have thus chosen to begin the story in the middle and to follow up with the beginning and the end. Available radiocarbon dates indicate that the monumental tombs of the Alto Magdalena were constructed primarily between about A.D. 1 and 800. I will refer to this period as the Regional Classic, adopting terminology most recently codified for the Alto Magdalena by Duque Gómez and Cubillos (1988), although my usage is not identical to theirs. My usage here is intended to make it easier to relate archaeological remains from the vicinity of San Agustín to those from the nearby Valle de la Plata (all within the Alto Magdalena, see Fig. 1). Unresolved issues of contemporaneity leave certain inconsistencies, particularly in when we date the beginning of the Regional Classic, but this is not an appropriate place to address those issues. Their ultimate resolution will not, in any event, affect the conclusions I arrive at here, and so for present purposes these inconsistencies do not matter.

Along similar lines, the length of the periods in the basic chronology available for the Alto Magdalena has bothered some scholars, in particular one of the discussants at the symposium for which this paper was written. We would, indeed, find greater chronological precision most helpful in studying various aspects of the sequence in the Alto Magdalena. For precisely that reason I have devoted considerable attention in my own work in the Valle de la Plata to chronological refinement. These efforts have met with some success (Drennan 1993). This is not an appropriate place to report them, however, because, among other reasons, greater chronological precision is not necessary to the achievement of the goals of this paper. The commonly used scheme of three long periods divides the sequence precisely where it needs to be divided to make the points I wish to make here. The fact is that the period when monumental tombs were commonly made in the Alto Magdalena is some 800 years long, and it is that period I wish to contrast with the preceding and following periods. There is no need here to subdivide it.

At the same time, it will be readily recognized that the picture of changing social patterns in the Alto Magdalena that can be painted at present is done in rather broad strokes. Many of the other contributors to this volume are able to discuss the social and symbolic context of mortuary practices with a richness of detail that still eludes us in the Alto Magdalena. To argue that we should not address such issues until our knowledge is much more detailed, however, is a prescription for halting progress in archaeology. To begin to paint the picture of society, even if the first strokes are broad, is the only way to determine what kind of archaeological information is needed to fill

Mortuary Practices in the Alto Magdalena

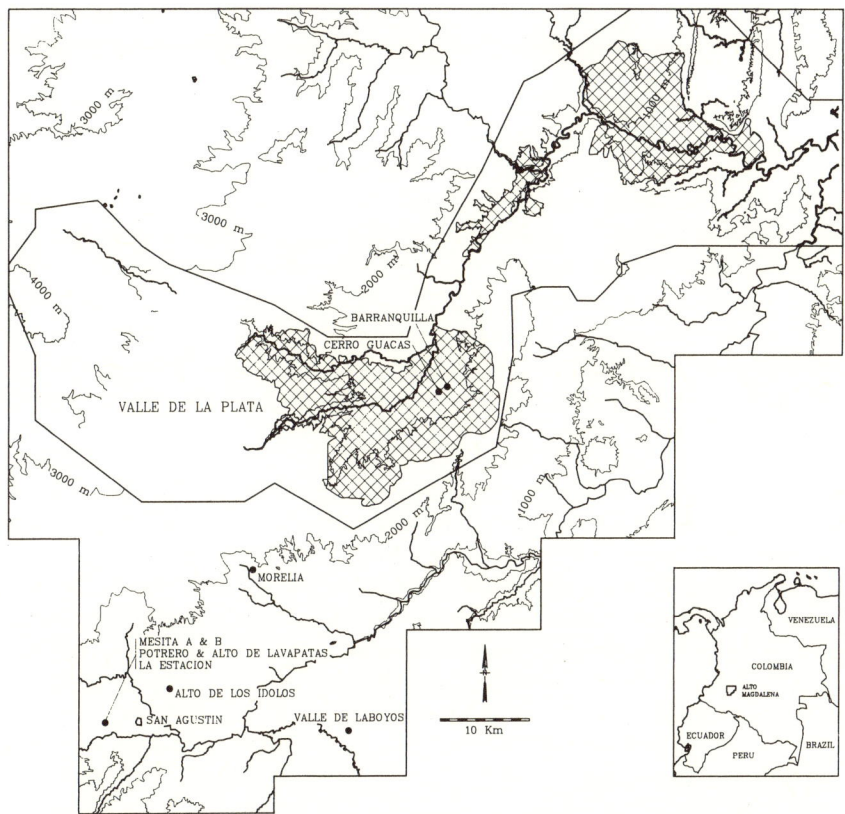

Fig. 1 Map of the Alto Magdalena showing archaeological sites mentioned in the text (solid circles), the Valle de la Plata study area, and zones of regional survey (crosshatched) within the Valle de la Plata.

in the details. And research conducted with no clear idea of what information is sought and why it is needed is more likely to confuse than enlighten. This paper, then, attempts to identify some broad changes in social organization in the Alto Magdalena sequence; it does not pretend to assign full meanings to all aspects of mortuary practices.

REGIONAL CLASSIC PERIOD MORTUARY PRACTICES

Any discussion of mortuary practices in the Alto Magdalena must recognize some deficiencies in this aspect of the region's archaeological record. In particular, preservation of bone is extremely poor as a consequence of very acid soils. This means that it is rare to actually recover skeletal remains, even from a carefully excavated tomb. What would, in many other regions, be well-preserved skeletons are, in the Alto Magdalena, faint powdery traces or less. It is only by the presence of grave goods and structures that burials are ordinarily recognized. Thus, it is usually necessary to work without even the most rudimentary information available from biological remains, such as age and sex or even position and number of individuals interred. Moreover, burials accompanied by no goods of a preservable character may be difficult to identify as burials at all. If such burials are simple inhumations in pits of modest size, even the pits can be mistaken for pits dug for other purposes (or, if one adopts a less conservative position on identifying graves, there is the risk that other kinds of pits will be counted as burials). It seems almost certain, then, that the burials of the majority of the population of the Alto Magdalena are systematically excluded from the evidence upon which the following discussion is based.

Another serious defect in the archaeological record for the Alto Magdalena is the extent to which its remains have been damaged by treasure hunters. The earliest known written account of the statues and tombs near San Agustín, that from the visit of Juan de Santa Gertrudis in 1758, speaks of the disappointment of the priest in San Agustín (then a hamlet of five houses) that the six experienced looters he had brought from Popayán had already opened 19 tombs, and found only one small ornament of gold (Santa Gertrudis 1970, 2: 97). The most extensive early campaign of archaeological fieldwork, led by Preuss in 1913 and 1914, expended considerable effort in documenting barrows already devastated by previous uncontrolled and undocumented excavations (Preuss 1931). Much of Preuss' documented work was subsequently undone by further vandalization of the tombs before adequate protection could be provided in such a remote region. (It took Preuss 16 days on muleback to reach San Agustín from the point where he had to abandon slightly more comfortable transportation.)

The extent of such looting, together with the poor preservation of skeletal remains, has led some scholars to apply the term "temple" to several monuments that were clearly tombs. It also means that, for all the most elaborate examples (which were looted), we have no information whatever about objects that may have been included with the principal burials. We do not even know for certain just what was the placement of the statues and stone slabs of which the architecture was composed, nor even what were the original dimensions of the earthen barrows that covered them.

Between 1970 and 1972, Duque Gómez and Cubillos (1979 and 1983) carefully collated the records of the various investigations suffered over 200 years by the elaborate tombs of the Mesita A, Mesita B, and Alto de los Idolos sites near San Agustín (Fig. 1). They conducted new excavations and attempted to replace the statues and stone slabs of which the tombs had been made in their original positions as nearly as could be determined. These

Mortuary Practices in the Alto Magdalena

now represent as good a guess as can be made about the characteristics of the largest and most elaborate tombs of the Alto Magdalena.

Figure 2 shows a plan and section of the West Mound at Mesita A as reconstructed by Duque Gómez and Cubillos. The tomb itself was a chamber some 1.5 × 3 m and not much over 1 m high. Its floor was of earth and its walls and roof were built of rough stone slabs (Fig. 3). Just beyond the northeastern end of this chamber were three large statues (Fig. 4). Two of

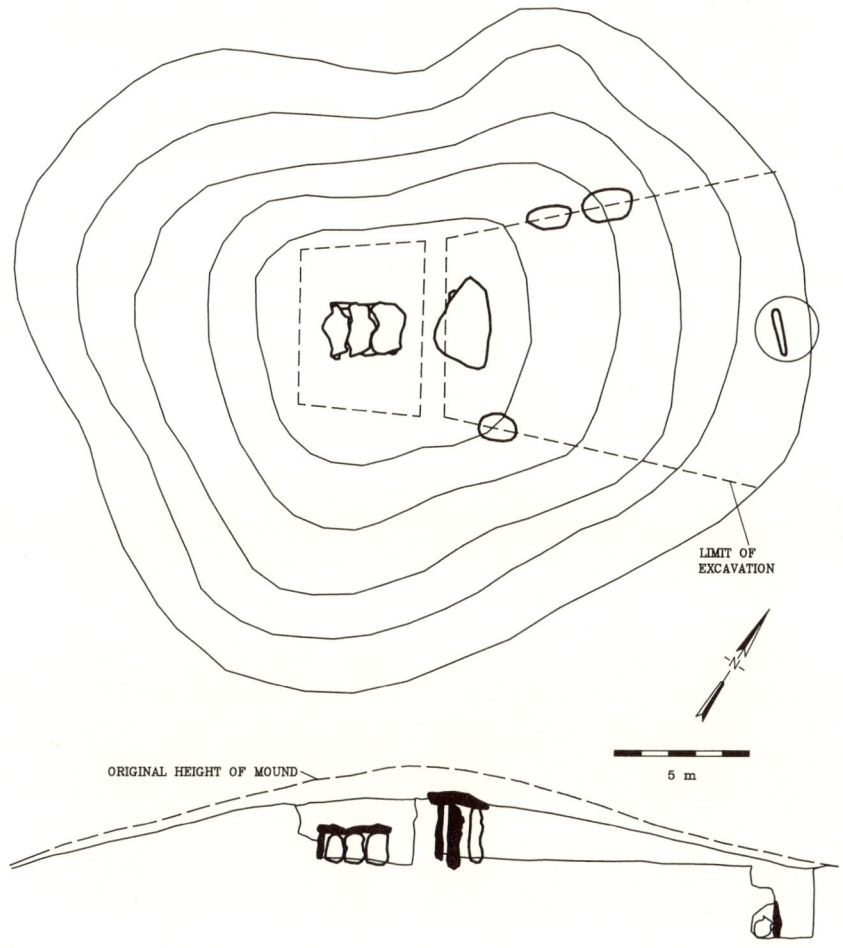

Fig. 2 Plan and section of West Mound at Mesita A (after Duque Gómez and Cubillos 1983: 79).

Fig. 3 Principal tomb chamber (*left*) and statues (*right*) in West Mound at Mesita A.

Fig. 4 Statues in West Mound at Mesita A.

Mortuary Practices in the Alto Magdalena

Fig. 5 General view of West Mound at Mesita A from the east.

them, together with two other vertically set stones, held up a single large slab which formed a roof over the central statue. This whole construction was at about the natural ground level. It was evidently originally covered over completely by an earthen barrow of irregular ovoid shape, perhaps 20 × 30 m (Fig. 5). Duque Gómez and Cubillos guess that it may have originally been about 3 m high at its peak. The barrow had been so thoroughly wrecked by previous excavation that no trace of any goods that might have been included with the burial was identifiable.

Figure 6 shows a plan and section of Mound 1 at Alto de los Idolos, also as reconstructed by Duque Gómez and Cubillos. Here the stone slab tomb chamber, similar in size to the one described above, contained a stone sarcophagus 2.5 × 0.6 m (Fig. 7). Preuss and the looters had been less thorough than usual in this case, and, in an undisturbed layer of artificially deposited soil around the sarcophagus, Duque Gómez and Cubillos found several small irregularly shaped thin pieces of gold with holes as if for sewing to clothing. There were also fragments of stone beads and sherds of pottery which may have been offerings destroyed by looters. A single statue stood beyond one end of the tomb chamber, also roofed by a large stone slab supported by four vertically set stones (Fig. 8). The distance of 4.5 m

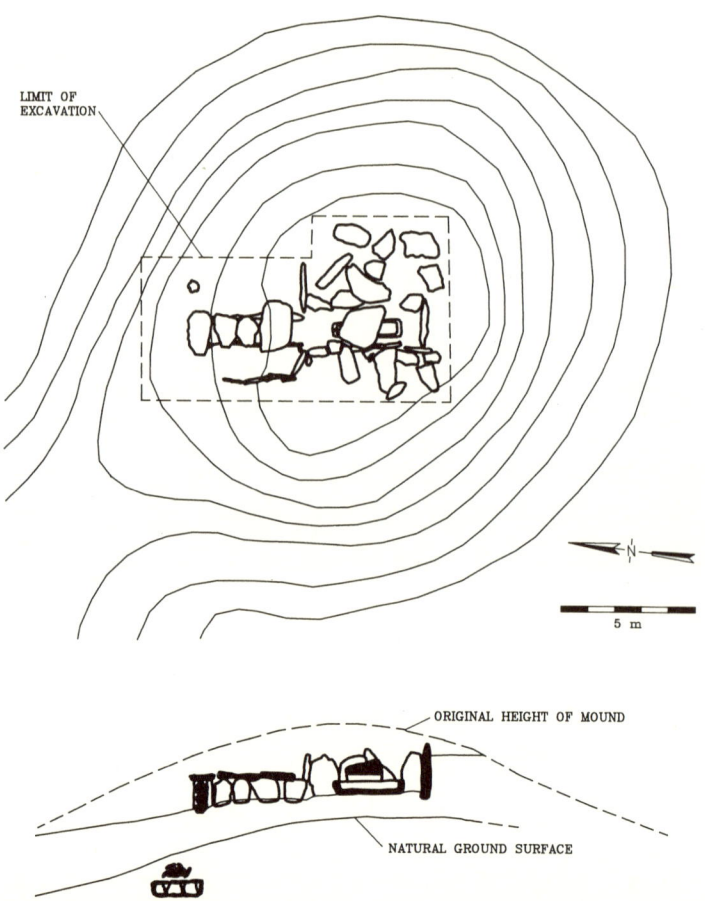

Fig. 6 Plan and section of Mound 1 at Alto de los Idolos (after Duque Gómez and Cubillos 1979: 19, 53, 64).

between the end of the tomb chamber and the statue was occupied by a narrow elongated chamber or passageway about 0.7 m high, walled and roofed with unmodified slabs. This chamber or passageway may not have been disturbed by looters before Duque Gómez and Cubillos uncovered it, but no trace of items that might have been placed in it remained. All this had been placed on a level surface created by artificial fill and was covered in turn by an earthen barrow perhaps 2.5 m high.

More than 2.5 m below these constructions of Mound 1, but following the same axis, was another tomb chamber. This small cist—1.8 m long ×

Mortuary Practices in the Alto Magdalena

Fig. 7 Remains of principal tomb chamber and stone sarcophagus in Mound 1 at Alto de los Idolos.

Fig. 8 View of excavated area in Mound 1 at Alto de los Idolos from the north.

Robert D. Drennan

0.5 m wide × 0.5 m high—had walls, floor, and roof of very small thin stone slabs. Above it, lying on its side, was a small statue. This tomb was undisturbed when Duque Gómez and Cubillos found it and contained two small beads in the form of fish covered with gold, one similar fish-shaped bead not covered with gold, one tubular stone bead, several tiny gold beads about 3 mm across, and a polishing stone.

Stone slab tombs and cists have been found at numerous sites throughout the Alto Magdalena. Figure 9 illustrates several such structures excavated by Duque Gómez (1964) at Mesita B. Those at Mesita B, of course, were in an area that contained barrows of the sort described above, but others occur at sites that have produced no statues or barrows. Their construction of stone slabs often approximates that of the main tomb chambers in the barrows;

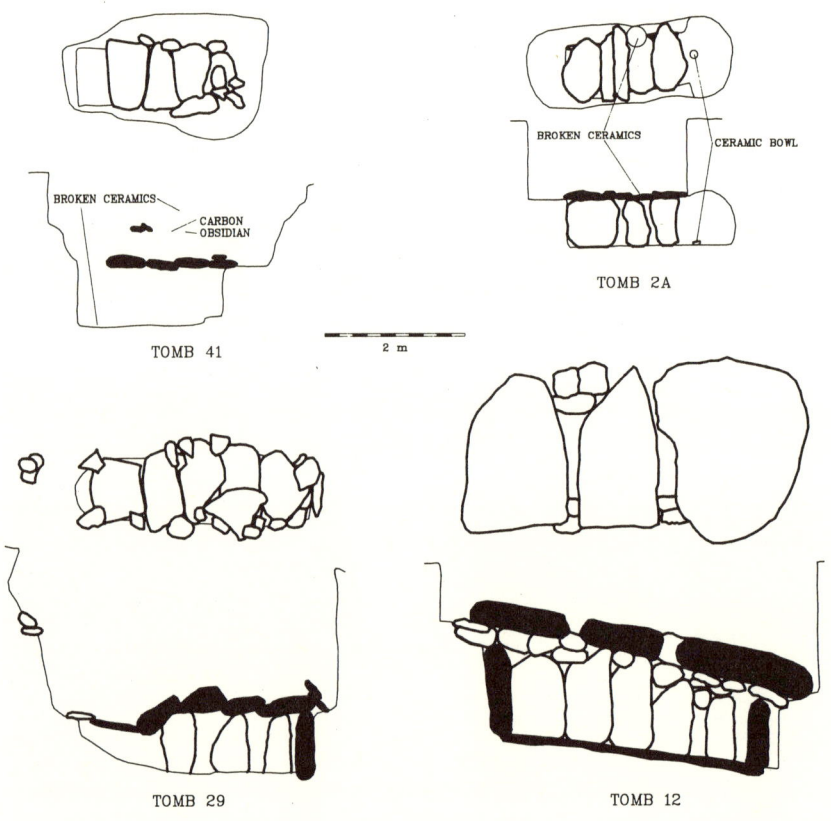

Fig. 9 Plans and sections of a few of the stone slab tombs at Mesita B (after Duque Gómez 1964: 45, 71, 85, 116).

sometimes the scale and elaborateness are similar, and sometimes they are considerably smaller and simpler (Figs. 10 and 11). Enough of them have been encountered in undisturbed condition to make it possible to discuss the goods included in them. These are remarkable chiefly for their modesty. A small number of ceramic vessels (rarely more than three or four in a single tomb), polished stone celts, beads, and sometimes small gold ornaments were included. A surprising number of apparently undisturbed tombs, including some chambers as large as those in the most elaborate barrows, contained no preserved goods at all. Burials in pits of rectangular or oval shape are also known from several sites of this period in the Alto Magdalena. Sometimes a partial roof over the pit was made of stone slabs, sometimes not. Modest offerings of the kinds mentioned earlier were included in some of them; others had none.

Regional Distribution of Tombs and Statues

The elaborate material remains of mortuary practices are scattered widely across the landscape in the Alto Magdalena. They cluster together in groups ranging from one or two barrows and a half-dozen or fewer statues to as many as ten barrows on a single hill with several dozen statues. The largest number of such groupings and those with the largest numbers of statues and barrows are in the vicinity of the modern town of San Agustín, but others occur throughout a zone some 120 km long lying on the eastern flank of the Central Andean cordillera at the headwaters of the Río Magdalena. Throughout the Alto Magdalena, which ranges in elevation from about 600 m to peaks more than 4,500 m above sea level, these funerary monuments concentrate heavily in the zone between 1,500 m and 2,000 m (cf. Sotomayor and Uribe 1987: 19).

The monuments defined small restricted ceremonial precincts associated with substantial evidence of human settlement. Excavations at Cerro Guacas in the Valle de la Plata produced little evidence of domestic activities immediately adjacent to such monuments. Here, at a modest monumental complex of only a pair of small barrows and probably originally no more than five or six statues, stratigraphic test pits in the immediate vicinity of the barrows revealed very shallow deposits and low artifact densities (Drennan 1993). Less than 100 m away, however, are abundant remains of residential activities, including posthole patterns of circular houses, recently excavated by Jeffrey Blick. At Morelia, Héctor Llanos (1988: 39–62) documented a similarly small-scale ceremonial complex attached to a residential zone of substantial size. Gerardo Reichel-Dolmatoff (1975) excavated stratigraphic trenches in deposits of residential refuse in the general vicinity of some of the largest and most elaborate tomb complexes near San Agustín.

Information at a larger geographic scale is available for one portion of the Alto Magdalena, the Valle de la Plata (Fig. 1), where systematic regional

Fig. 10 Stone slab tomb at Mesita A.

Mortuary Practices in the Alto Magdalena

Fig. 11 Stone slab tomb at VP0051 near the town of La Argentina in the Valle de la Plata.

survey has produced settlement pattern data for an area totaling more than 500 km² (Drennan, Herrera, and Piñeros 1989; Drennan et al. 1989, 1991). In the surveyed region, the broad pattern of population distribution during the Regional Classic was similar to the distribution of barrow tombs and statues in that both were heavily concentrated in the zone between about 1,500 and 2,000 m above sea level. Such a pattern of population distribution makes good environmental sense in the Valle de la Plata, since this elevation band contains the most promising agricultural resources for pre-Hispanic populations. In the lower part of the valley, higher temperatures, less available moisture, and smaller areas of fertile, easily worked soils place limitations on potential production. At the opposite extreme, above 2,000 m, low temperatures and waterlogged soils increasingly impede simple agriculture (Botero, León, and Moreno 1989). Between 1,500 and 2,000 m, though, temperature and moisture conditions are very good, and substantial areas of fertile, easily cultivated soils occur on relatively gentle slopes. This zone was very attractive to the pre-Hispanic inhabitants, and it was here that the societies of the Regional Classic period were focused.

Within this favored zone, further unevenness in settlement distribution provides clues to patterns of sociopolitical organization. Figure 12 illustrates the distribution of Regional Classic period settlement in a portion of the area surveyed in the Valle de la Plata. Elevations in this area range from about 1,400 to more than 2,400 m. Settlement, as just noted, was concentrated between 1,500 and 2,000 m, but even there its density varied considerably from place to place. Some of this variation corresponds to variability in topography and soils, but there remain clear concentrations of settlement unrelated to such environmental parameters. Between these settlement concentrations were areas where settlement was much less dense despite the fact that the agricultural resources they offered to their inhabitants were quite similar to those of the areas where the settlement concentrations occurred.

Regional Classic Social Organization

As can be seen in Figure 12, each of the Regional Classic ceremonial sites included in the surveyed area falls within one of these general settlement concentrations. From the opposite point of view, each of the settlement concentrations contains one site with barrow tombs and statues. What we seem to be seeing here is the representation in regional settlement patterns of several small separate chiefdoms. (I use the word "chiefdom" here simply as a convenient label for a highly diverse group of societies with many forms of complex hierarchical organization but without the bureaucratic political institutions of the state.) The concentrations of settlement within a few kilometers of each of the ceremonial sites represent the familiar centripetal tendency of complex societies to focus populations on central places.

Mortuary Practices in the Alto Magdalena

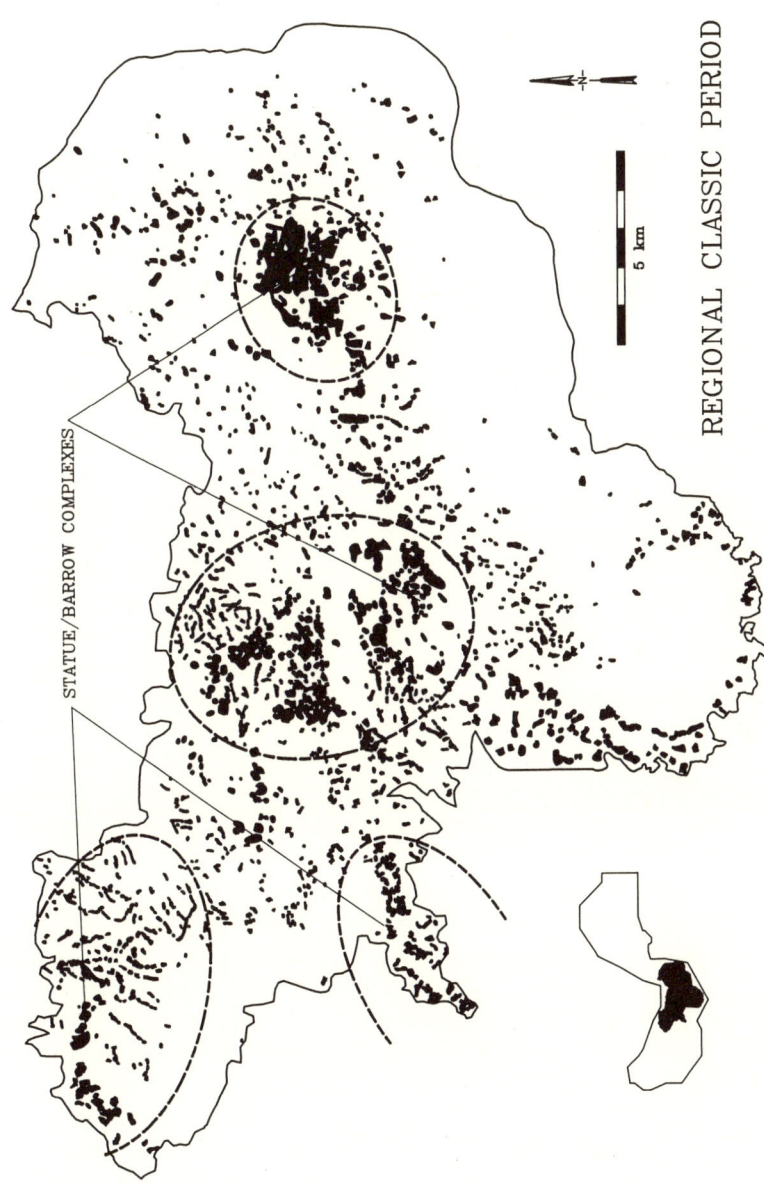

Fig. 12 Map of Regional Classic period settlement distribution in one of the regional survey zones in the Valle de la Plata.

Robert D. Drennan

Although I describe these as concentrations of settlement, residences within them were still dispersed with considerable open space between them. Hermann Trimborn (1949: 129–130) has compiled evidence from several early conquest period eyewitness accounts of such concentrations of dispersed settlement in southwestern Colombia. Houses in some places were not clustered tightly enough together that early chroniclers were comfortable calling the settlements "pueblos," but they did form clearly defined communities that the same authors identified without hesitation as "pueblos" in the other sense of the word, emphasizing social rather than spatial relations. Although the zones between the settlement concentrations of the Regional Classic in the Valle de la Plata were by no means deserted, occupation was noticeably less dense than within the concentrations, and this suggests the separateness (and quite possibly from time to time the competitiveness) of these chiefdoms. Each chiefdom would have consisted of a few thousand people in a settlement concentration with a radius of no more than about 10 km.

The individuals buried in the Valle de la Plata's elaborate tombs seem most likely to have been the leaders (or "chiefs") of these societies. Presumably they lived in the general vicinities of the ceremonial locations where monuments marked the burial places of their predecessors and where they themselves would eventually be interred. The monumental nature of these burials made an emphatic and permanent statement about the importance of the individuals so commemorated. If we adopt the perspective suggested to us by the title of this symposium, "Tombs for the Living," we are led to think why such a statement might have been so important to the survivors of a deceased leader. It was, after all, those who survived who surely shouldered the principal responsibility for this elaborate mortuary treatment. And whatever message may have been communicated by this behavior, it was communicated to those who lived on after the leader's death.

Providing permanent reminders of the importance of specific past leaders is likely to be of particular importance in societies where leadership is a highly personal affair—that is, in societies where the institution of leadership is not highly developed. If leadership positions are fully institutionalized, the demise of a leader automatically creates a vacancy to be filled. Chiefdoms, however, often lack such a high degree of institutionalized leadership, which would seem logically related to the established bureaucratic systems of states. Each chief may have to do more than claim the position; he may have to create or at least actively maintain the position so that it is there for him to occupy. In such a situation, not only who is chief, but also how powerful the chief is, or even whether there is a chief at all, depends to some extent on the personal abilities of the individual chief to persuade his people of his legitimacy and to exercise effectively whatever actual power he has—in general to use whatever means are at his disposal to induce cooperation or compliance from the people he purports to lead.

One such means is to forge strong links between himself and previous effective chiefs. The commemoration of individual predecessors through permanent public monuments provides a chief (or hopeful chief) with the opportunity simultaneously to glorify these predecessors who were effective leaders (and thus their actions) and to attach himself to their tradition. It is, of course, not a novel observation that such activities are important in maintaining and reinforcing leadership and the social order in general in many societies, and it has long been noticed that deaths of leaders were pivotal events in the societies of the northern Andes. Early conquest period accounts pay considerable attention to the elaborate treatment accorded deceased leaders in native Colombian societies (cf. Trimborn 1949: 226–332), and the Andes in general have been characterized as having a similar preoccupation.

A focus on connections to previous leaders and their power can thus be a powerful political tool in the hands of those leaders' descendants. Such legitimation is not necessarily incompatible with other means of exercising leadership, and may well combine with them. In the Alto Magdalena, however, the only works of a permanent, monumental character of which we have archaeological evidence are funerary monuments created to commemorate specific individuals. There are no permanent monumental remains in the Alto Magdalena of the temples, plazas, palaces, or other kinds of structures (often of unclear function) that appear in the archaeological record of some complex societies elsewhere in the Andes and in other parts of the world. It is reasonable to suggest, then, that the societies of the Alto Magdalena during the Regional Classic were ones in which the basis of leadership was highly personal (as opposed to institutional)—that these were what Colin Renfrew (1974) has labeled "individualizing" chiefdoms, ones heavily focused on status rivalries between individual chiefs or aspiring chiefs, as opposed to "group-oriented" chiefdoms, where leadership seems to have a more collective and less personalized basis.

Up to now I have concentrated primarily on the monumental character of the tombs in which important individuals were buried in the Alto Magdalena during the Regional Classic and of the statues associated with these burials. The nature of the offerings included with the burials also presents us with some interesting indications of the basis for leadership in these societies. Perhaps the most salient characteristic of these offerings is their sparseness. Compared with the architectural and sculptural elaboration of the tombs, the inventories of objects included as offerings with the corpses seem quite impoverished. This remains true, even after making allowances for the fact that the largest and most elaborate tombs were looted long ago.

Archaeologists are ordinarily accustomed to encounter much richer offerings in tombs far less distinguished in terms of their construction, their placement in ceremonial precincts, and their sculptural associations. Pedro de Cieza de León, along with other sixteenth-century chroniclers, makes much of the richness of the chiefs he observed in southern Colombia and the quantity of elaborate material goods included with their burials: "They have their mortuaries and tombs, in the custom of their land, with vaulted chambers, very deep, and with the opening to the east. When a lord or *principal* has died, they place him inside with many tears, leaving with him all the arms and clothing and gold that he has, and food as well" (Cieza de León 1553: 113 [chap. XV]). In the Alto Magdalena, however, during the Regional Classic, a good number of fairly elaborate tombs contained no non-perishable offerings at all, even though the usual range of non-perishable artifacts (including pottery, flaked stone, stone beads and pendants, and gold ornaments) were clearly regarded as appropriate burial offerings and were included in modest quantities in some tombs.

Such patterns of burial offerings are consistent with the notion that the basis of acquiring and exercising leadership in the Alto Magdalena during the Regional Classic, however personal or attached to individuals it may have been, was not primarily through the accumulation of personal wealth. While the individuals buried in the tombs clearly had great personal prestige, there is little to suggest that they possessed much wealth. The commemoration of individuals suggested is rather of their public stature and supernatural characteristics or connections of some kind. One general point on which all interpretations of the Alto Magdalena's sculpture agree is that the themes represented are in some way supernatural—it would seem hard to argue otherwise for representations of people with long fangs or with two-headed crocodiles clinging to their backs and peering fiercely over their heads. Sculpture with broadly similar characteristics has been argued to be particularly appropriate in sanctifying a social order and the role of leaders in it, for example, in the case of Olmec art (Coe 1972; Drennan 1976). These artistic expressions of the supernatural characteristics or connections of certain individuals spring from and reinforce the beliefs that provide the reasons why ordinary people are willing to follow these individuals' leadership.

Belief (often religious) in the legitimacy of leaders and their directives certainly makes people more likely to heed them, and attainment of such legitimacy is often posed as an alternative to use of coercive force or control over basic resources (which makes coercive force possible) as a means of social control. Processes of sanctification could, of course, operate either in tandem with considerable concentration of resource control in the hands of leaders (i.e., personal wealth) or in lieu of much resource control. The archaeological evidence just described leads one to think in the latter terms—of social integration more heavily dependent on ideological/religious bases than on economic ones.

The mortuary practices of the Alto Magdalena, then, form a basis for suggesting that societies of the Regional Classic period were characterized by minimally institutionalized leadership roles rather dependent for their force and even continued existence on justification in personal or individual terms. The principal foundation of this largely personal leadership would seem to lie in the realm of belief systems rather than in an ability to exercise force or control basic resources, and leaders, despite the individualized nature of their positions, would seem to have had relatively little personal wealth. These suggestions derive from a number of different characteristics of the mortuary evidence, including the architectural elaboration of tombs, their associated sculpture, their location in apparent ceremonial precincts at the heart of regional settlement concentrations that seem to represent social units, the paucity of offerings included with burials, and the absence of archaeological remains of any other kinds of permanent monuments.

Increasing Confidence in Our Social Reconstructions

There are, of course, other possible interpretations of such mortuary patterns. For instance, one can imagine a society with marked wealth differentiation—indeed, in which wealth differences were a major organizing principle—but with an ideology denying the legitimacy or even the very existence of those wealth differences. In such a society the rule of behavior for the wealthy would not be conspicuous consumption, but rather covert consumption. Measures might be taken to prevent any obvious display of wealth, and such measures would probably extend to the treatment wealthy individuals received after death as well. Some archaeologists are tireless in their efforts not only to imagine such counterexamples to the apparent indications of the archaeological record, but also to find ethnographic instances to prove that the imagined counterexamples are more than just pipe dreams.

Could the Regional Classic societies of the Alto Magdalena be such a counterexample? It certainly must be recognized as a possibility. Is there some other way of looking at mortuary practices that would enable us to come to a more certain reconstruction of social patterns? It is surely more productive to look instead at other, independent lines of evidence. No matter how careful we are at sorting out the mortuary evidence, and no matter how clever we are at thinking of ways in which the conclusions we base on it could be in error, we will probably never succeed in completely eliminating the possibility that the pre-Hispanic inhabitants of the region are telling lies by the way they buried their dead. After all, an important point of departure for this symposium is consideration of the role that public mortuary ritual plays in living societies, that is, the kinds of public statements that mortuary practices make about establishing and reaffirming the social order.

When the material remains we study as archaeologists are shaped by their role in making public statements about social facts, then we risk being taken in by statements that are self-serving or worse. This realization need not cause a sort of nihilistic paralysis in archaeology. After all, ethnographers have always risked being lied to in depending primarily on asking a small number of informants about what people think, say, and do in the societies those informants are taken to represent. The solution to the ethnographer's problem is not to connect informants to polygraphs (if for no other reason than that informants may really believe in the truth of the lies they may tell). Similarly, the solution to the archaeologist's problem is not a rigorous crosscultural search for "material correlates" of particular behaviors for which there is never a counterexample. The solution, for ethnographer and archaeologist alike, is to pay attention not only to the statements people make but also to observe their behavior in as many different ways as possible—in short, to seek different, independent lines of evidence bearing on the conclusions we wish to make.

To return to the reconstruction of some aspects of social organization I have drawn out of the mortuary evidence from the Alto Magdalena, we must recognize that it is based on several different, but only partially independent, lines of evidence, all concerned with burial practices. The route toward being more certain of the reconstruction I have suggested (or alternatively toward rejecting it in favor of something else) lies not in worrying the burial evidence to death. It lies in turning to other completely unrelated kinds of archaeological evidence. At least two principal directions immediately suggest themselves.

In the first place, because of their generally conspicuous character in the archaeological record, we are well aware of the tombs and statues of the Regional Classic. That no obvious, monumental, and permanent constructions for other kinds of public, ritual, or communal activities have been noted for the Regional Classic, however, does not necessarily mean that such activities were not conducted. Temples may have been constructed of perishable materials, as were residences; plazas for public assembly of one kind or another may have been integrated into residential zones; and so on. The fact that such features did not have the permanent monumental character of chiefly burials has implications for the personalized nature of leadership, as argued above, but knowledge of the size, location, and character of spaces created for other public, ritual, or communal activities would help us to arrive at a more complete picture of sociopolitical organization. The lack of evidence for such things may indicate a truly overwhelming focus of public life on burial-related commemoration of specific individuals. On the other hand, this lack may simply be a consequence of the absence of detailed community-level studies applying such standard archaeological approaches as intensive surface survey of single communities (with a much higher level of resolution than that possible in regional-scale survey) and excavation of substantial areas in residential zones.

A second major direction in which future gathering of evidence should proceed focuses on other ways of using archaeological remains to reconstruct aspects of wealth differentiation. Despite the obvious differences in prestige between inhabitants of the Regional Classic societies of the Alto Magdalena, the burial evidence has suggested little or no wealth differentiation. If this reconstruction is accurate, then there should be other evidence of evenness of wealth distribution. We would expect to see little variation in house size or construction, we would expect deposits of household refuse to yield similar ranges and frequencies of possible luxury goods for all households, we would expect remains of likely preferred foods to be fairly evenly distributed, and so on. At least some of these independent lines of evidence would not be at risk from the kind of lying discussed above, since people are unlikely, for example, to be consciously or unconsciously making any kind of statement by disposing of household garbage. Similarly, the independence of such lines of evidence makes it likely that they will escape other sources of confusion or error to which the interpretation of the burial evidence may be subject.

On both these scores, the relevant evidence is not currently available for the Alto Magdalena. It does not come from the excavation of tombs or from regional survey, although both of these have contributed mightily to our knowledge thus far. It can only come from intensive attention to use of space at the community level, painstaking exposure of residential architecture, rigorous reporting of artifact inventories organized not simply for purposes of stylistic description but in meaningful units for purposes of social reconstruction, careful recovery and quantitative analysis of several kinds of food remains, and so on. This will require patient excavation of substantial areas at several different sites of the Regional Classic period. Some such excavation is being carried out in the Valle de la Plata as this paper is being written; more is planned, and still more will surely be required to provide the necessary complement to the information already obtained. There is no need to wait for ethnoarchaeological study of households, the development of new archaeological methods, or the elaboration of more sophisticated conceptual tools. We simply need to practice certain aspects of what has fairly widely been preached in archaeology for at least two decades.

THE FORMATIVE PERIOD

Taking a broader diachronic view is difficult, because our ability to discuss either patterns of social organization generally or mortuary practices specifically for the Formative period (here taken to be before about A.D. 1) is quite limited. Surface collections, shovel tests, and small-scale stratigraphic excavations in the Valle de la Plata show a clear association of sites with statues and barrow tombs to the Regional Classic, although it would be premature to assert that the beginnings of these practices do not reach back into the Formative. Available radiocarbon dates associated with the tomb and statue complexes are strongly clustered in the first few centuries A.D. A few fall slightly earlier, back to 150 B.C. Duque Gómez and Cubillos (1988: 106) report a date of 800 B.C. +/− 30 for a slab tomb in a barrow at Alto de las Piedras, but they provide no information about the nature of the carbon sample or its context. A date of 555 B.C. +/− 50 (Duque Gómez 1964: 456) has a somewhat dubious history, coming from a wooden sarcophagus obtained in 1937 by Pérez de Barradas (1943: 109) at Alto de Lavapatas. Duque Gómez and Cubillos (1988: 107) attribute its actual excavation to looters.

In all it seems likely that the mortuary practices our attention has been focused on up to now began around the time of Christ or possibly slightly before. Since the only direct evidence for complex social organization in the Alto Magdalena has until recently been the tomb and statue complexes that flourished in the Regional Classic, it has been customary to treat the Formative implicitly as a period of egalitarian societies. In the Valle de la Plata survey area, population at the end of the Formative was probably less than one-fifth the size it reached in the Regional Classic, so the region's demographic scale was certainly much smaller then.

On the other hand, the distinct settlement concentrations that seem to correspond to small chiefdoms in the Regional Classic are clearly present in the settlement pattern maps of the middle and later Formative as well. This suggests that such centralized social organization had its beginnings well back in the Formative period. If chiefdoms did come into existence by the middle of the Formative, then they apparently managed successfully without the elaborate mortuary practices of the Regional Classic. Such issues as the extent of prestige accumulated by leaders and the existence of differentiation of wealth or resource control, however, remain entirely undocumented. To begin to deal with these subjects, we will need the kind of information called for above to complement the burial and regional survey data for the Regional Classic. I will pass on, then, from discussion of the Formative, simply noting that the beginnings of complex societies in the Alto Magdalena may well antedate by a substantial margin the appearance of the tombs and statues that, simply because of their conspicuous nature, have always seemed such a watershed in the region's archaeological record.

THE RECENT PERIOD

Following A.D. 800 or so, the construction of the permanent funerary monuments that have been the focus of this paper ceased. The suggestions that the people who created these monuments disappeared and that the Alto Magdalena was abandoned have been fueled by a documentable long period of near-total abandonment after the Spanish conquest and by unclear and incomplete accounts of the nature and distribution of population in the Alto

Mortuary Practices in the Alto Magdalena

Magdalena in the 1530s when the Conquistadores first arrived. As archaeological attention turned from a single-minded focus on tombs and statues to systematic efforts to build chronology, it became clear that there were, indeed, archaeological remains of habitation in the region after the end of the Regional Classic (Duque Gómez 1964; Reichel-Dolmatoff 1975), in a period that has come to be called simply "Recent."

In the Valle de la Plata survey area, not only were these remains present, but it is quite clear that population levels were at least as high as they had been during the Regional Classic and probably somewhat higher. Llanos (1990: 51) also notes an abundance of Recent settlements in the Valle de Laboyos. As Figure 13 shows, population distribution in the Valle de la Plata during the Recent period has the same tendency to form settlement concentrations as it did before. Indeed, this tendency is even stronger, in that the settlement concentrations are now smaller and denser, and the intervening areas more sparsely settled than before. This finding is not consistent with notions of "cultural decline" or "social collapse" spawned by the disappearance of the conspicuous evidence of complex organization provided by the monumental burials of the previous period. Instead, it suggests a form of organization even more centralized in some way than its predecessor.

Mortuary practices were quite different. A narrow shaft with a small side tomb chamber from the site of Barranquilla is illustrated in Figures 14 and 15. Offerings, consisting of a *metate,* two *manos,* and four ceramic vessels, had been placed in the fill of the shaft 60 to 90 cm below its top (Drennan 1985: 127–129). Other, larger, tombs of similar design have been opened by looters at the same site both prior to and following the 1984 excavations (Drennan 1985: 123). Figure 14 also shows Tomb 47, excavated at Alto de Lavapatas. It is a shallower, somewhat larger tomb chamber, also with an entrance shaft or step to one side. The only indication of offerings was a pile of carbonized wood and other plant matter, including maize cobs, some with kernels still attached (Duque Gómez and Cubillos 1988: 174, 187–188).

There is no indication that such tombs of the Recent period were marked by any kind of permanent monuments visible on the surface after the tombs had been filled in. These tombs, then, would not have functioned to reinforce the roles of leaders nearly as well as those of the Regional Classic. And yet the intensification of the pattern of concentrated settlement seen earlier suggests that centralized leadership continued to exist, possibly in even stronger form. The changes in mortuary practices raise the possibility of changes in the base upon which chiefs' ability to exercise their leadership rested. Personal claims to legitimacy, previously bolstered through mortuary practices commemorating past leaders, may have become less important. It is easy to think of at least two bases for leadership that may have become more important. The first is more complete institutionalization of positions of leadership, giving them an existence and power apart from their

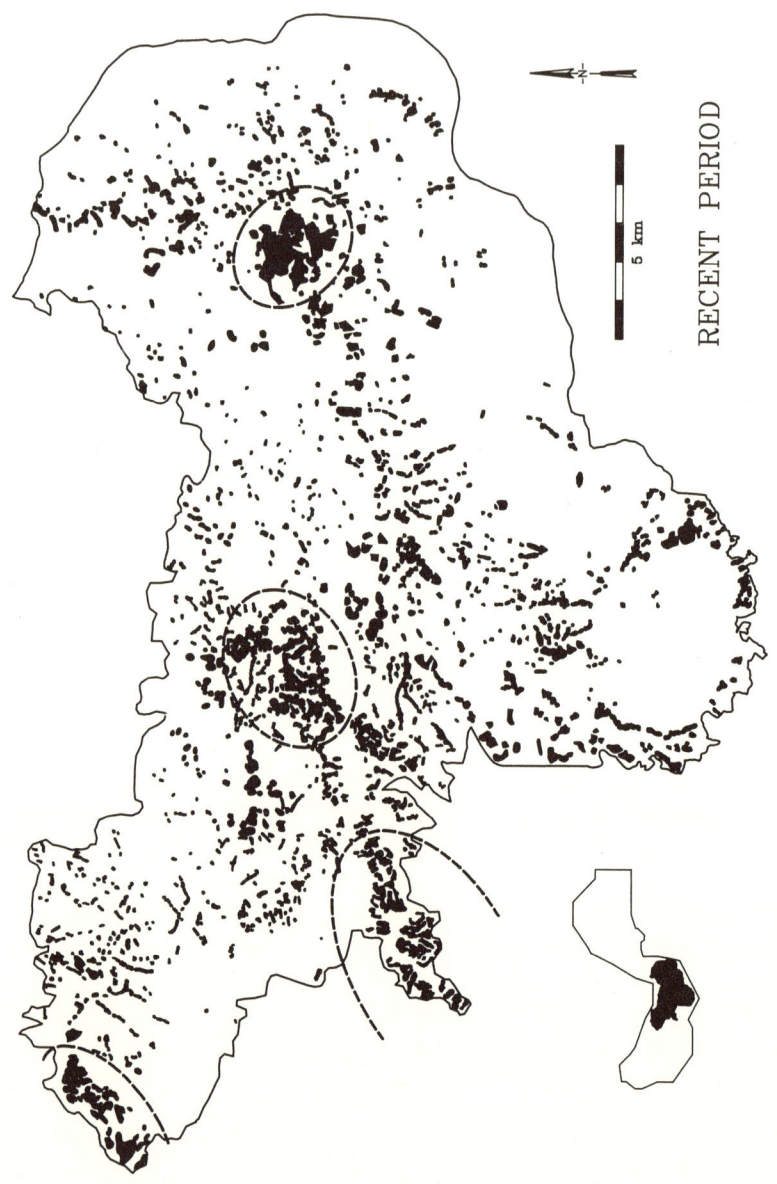

Fig. 13 Map of Recent period settlement distribution in one of the regional survey zones in the Valle de la Plata.

Mortuary Practices in the Alto Magdalena

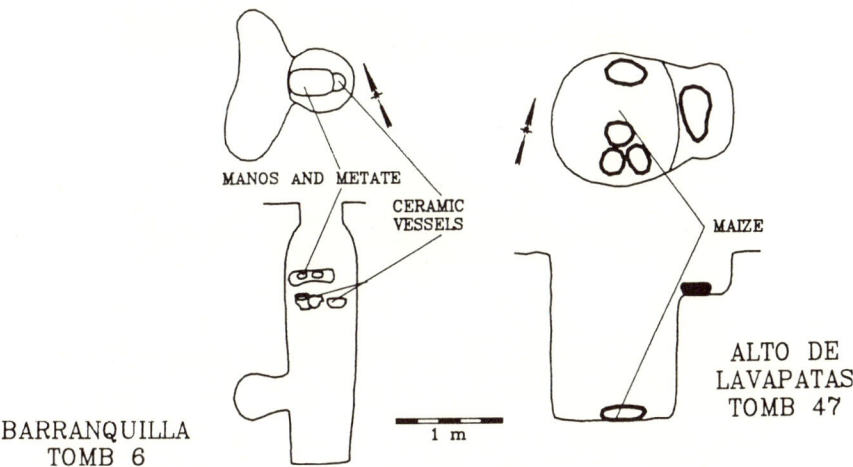

Fig. 14 Recent period tombs at Barranquilla (VP0002) in the Valle de la Plata and at Alto de Lavapatas near San Agustín (after Drennan 1985: 127, and Duque Gómez and Cubillos 1988: 174 and 187).

individual occupants. The second is expanded exercise of economic forms of control. Increased development of either of these would not necessarily imply that legitimation through connections to previous leaders disappeared entirely—only that it may have lost some of the centrality I have argued that it had previously.

We might expect greater institutionalization of leadership to be reflected in more standardized symbols of the office occupied—symbols likely to be more important and conspicuous during the lifetime of a chief than after his death. Things like the nature of the chief's house, special activities conducted there, and special artifacts that he used might set him apart more markedly. Precisely such things characterized some southern Colombian societies at the time of the conquest: "The lords or chiefs and their captains have very large houses, and at their doors are placed thick canes of the kind they have there, which resemble small beams; on the tops of these they have placed many heads of their enemies" (Cieza de León 1553: 112–113 [chap. XV]). Trimborn (1949: 217–220) lists fine cotton garments, elaborate feathers, gold implements and ornaments, and other special symbols of authority used by conquest period chiefs according to various early accounts. Very similar kinds of evidence could also relate to economic power as reflected in greater wealth accumulated by the chief and passed down to his descendants.

Robert D. Drennan

Fig. 15 View of Tomb 6 at Barranquilla.

Solidification of institutions of leadership might call for increased emphasis on activities of a communal or ritual nature focused on those institutions rather than on deceased individual chiefs. Plazas, temples, or other spaces might be created for the regular occurrence of such activities. Chroniclers such as Cieza de León often note the absence of temples, but chiefs' houses are described as having cages for captives taken in war: "They feed them very well and when they are fat they take them out to the plazas, which are next to the houses, and on feast days they kill them with great cruelty and eat them" (Cieza de León 1553: 128 [chap. XX]).

Unfortunately, the conquest period societies of the Alto Magdalena are not among those for which highly useful eyewitness accounts are available, so we must rely on multiple lines of archaeological evidence to reconstruct them. At least a little archaeological evidence aside from mortuary patterns and settlement distribution already referred to is available. Ordinary residences of the Recent period have been excavated at Potrero de Lavapatas (Duque Gómez 1964: 232–241), La Estación (Duque Gómez and Cubillos 1981: 19–110), and Quinchana (Llanos and Durán 1983: 35–60). These houses, evidenced by posthole patterns, were circular, ranging in diameter from about 2.5 to 5.5 m. Tombs of the general sort already described for the Recent period were intermingled with residences at all these sites. Although the small stratigraphic tests at Barranquilla were not large enough to reveal the posthole patterns of houses, tombs were spread through an area of dense residential debris (Drennan 1985: 117–129).

At La Estación, a single, larger circular structure, some 9 m in diameter, was also uncovered (Duque Gómez and Cubillos 1981: 25–36). Whether this was a ceremonial structure or chief's house (both of which notions have been suggested by its excavators) or something else altogether is not entirely clear, but it could be evidence for the kind of social changes postulated. (We do not, of course, know that such structures were not present during the Regional Classic, owing to the small amount of excavation data available for residential areas.) The general range of offerings in Recent period tombs, like those of the Regional Classic, is limited, however, and this lends little support to the notion of increased unevenness in the distribution of wealth, but complementary data from such sources as refuse associated with different houses are not available. The notions suggested, then, about social changes from the Regional Classic to the Recent periods require further investigation.

CONCLUSION

Consideration of mortuary practices in combination with other kinds of archaeological evidence has led me to suggest that the Regional Classic in the Alto Magdalena, and perhaps the Formative before it as well, were periods of vigorous development of small-scale chiefdoms. In some respects these chiefdoms resembled those documented in written sources for the early sixteenth century in the northern Andes. They may have differed, however, particularly in the extent to which accumulation of personal wealth was an important principle of social organization and possibly in the extent to which positions of leadership were institutionalized. Subsequent societies of the Recent period in the Alto Magdalena may have shown greater development of one or both of these features, although even the archaeological evidence available at present fails to fit perfectly with what we would expect of societies like those that populate the written accounts of the sixteenth century for the northern Andes. The notion of associating the most spectacular monumental remains with a period of relatively undeveloped institutions of leadership runs counter to the implicit assumptions most often made about the Alto Magdalena, but it strongly parallels Dillehay's analysis of Mapuche mound building in this volume. If the outline of social evolution I have sketched for the Alto Magdalena is confirmed (in some of the ways I have suggested above), it raises questions whose answers have implications for our understanding of the nature and processes of development of early complex societies.

The course of development from Formative through Regional Classic times can be seen as fairly consistent and continually in the direction of larger-scale and more complex forms of organization. There is, however, a marked change at around the beginning of the Regional Classic, when population levels soared and the construction of monumental burial complexes flourished. This development did not burst upon the scene with no prior warning; its roots are clearly in the Formative. And yet we cannot say to what extent it involved qualitatively new forms of social, political, or economic organization and to what extent it was simply the intensification of previously existing patterns. We do not understand the nature of the relationship between the surge in population and the conspicuous monumental manifestation of hierarchical organization. Was one the cause of the other? If so, which one? Were both the result of some other process among the several that have been suggested to bring chiefdoms into being? If the Regional Classic was characterized by only very limited accumulation of personal wealth, then resource control and economic advantage generally probably did not play a major role in the emergence of the earliest chiefdoms in this region. Such a view was once argued as a generalization about chiefdoms, but it has recently been vigorously challenged.

The end of the Regional Classic may mark an even more dramatic point of change in the sequence. This time, however, the change is not primarily one of demographic scale or degree of complexity, as the beginning of the Regional Classic seems to have been. To judge from the regional settlement pattern evidence, societies of the Recent period were only very slightly larger and more centralized than those of the Regional Classic. Instead, the change I have suggested is a qualitative one in the basis of the social hierarchy: increased institutionalization of positions of leadership and/or increased economic differentiation. Such changes are taken by some to be involved in the shift from chiefdom to state, but this was clearly not such a shift. This change took place within the class of chiefdom. (Or, to put it another way in case misunderstandings or disagreements about how to use the word "chiefdom" may cloud my meaning, societies of both the Regional Classic and

Recent periods in the Alto Magdalena fall toward the simple end of the complex society scale.)

The sequence of social change in the Alto Magdalena, then, seems not to be adequately characterized simply as movement along an axis running from small-scale simple organization to large-scale complex organization. While several kinds of cultural evolutionary approaches have made a valuable contribution in calling our attention to this axis, they have encouraged us to overlook variation along other axes not parallel to this one. This consideration of changing mortuary patterns in the Alto Magdalena, as related to some other categories of archaeological evidence presently available, raises issues of varying bases for authority or power in social hierarchies—varying bases not necessarily related to or best studied in the context of either the initial emergence of chiefdoms or their transformation into states. More subtle variations in organization, like those discussed here, and a recognition of axes of variation that do not simply correspond to level of complexity, offer us an opportunity to raise (and try to answer) somewhat different questions about the fundamental processes of social change.

BIBLIOGRAPHY

BOTERO, PEDRO JOSÉ, JONÁS C. LEÓN P., AND JULIO CÉSAR MORENO
    1989   Soils and Great Landscapes. In *Prehispanic Chiefdoms in the Valle de la Plata, Volume 1: The Environmental Context of Human Habitation* (Luisa Fernanda Herrera, Robert D. Drennan, and Carlos A. Uribe, eds.). University of Pittsburgh Memoirs in Latin American Archaeology 2: 1–14.

CIEZA DE LEÓN, PEDRO DE
    1553   *La Crónica del Perú*. Edición de Manuel Ballesteros. Historia 16 (In-
    [1984] formación y Revistas, S.A.), Madrid.

COE, MICHAEL D.
    1972   Olmec Jaguars and Olmec Kings. In *The Cult of the Feline* (Elizabeth Benson, ed.): 1–12. Dumbarton Oaks, Washington, D.C.

CUBILLOS, JULIO CÉSAR
    1980   *Arqueología de San Agustín*. Fundación de Investigaciones Arqueológicas Nacionales del Banco de la República, Bogotá.

DRENNAN, ROBERT D.
    1976   Religion and Social Evolution in Formative Mesoamerica. In *The Early Mesoamerican Village* (Kent V. Flannery, ed.): 345–368. Academic Press, New York.
    1985   Archeological Survey and Excavation. In *Regional Archeology in the Valle de la Plata, Colombia: A Preliminary Report on the 1984 Season of the Proyecto Arqueológico Valle de la Plata* (Robert D. Drennan, ed.): 117–180. Museum of Anthropology, University of Michigan, Technical Reports 16. Ann Arbor.
    1993   Ceramic Classification, Stratigraphy, and Chronology. In *Prehispanic Chiefdoms in the Valle de la Plata, Volume 2: Ceramics–Chronology and Craft Production* (Robert D. Drennan, Mary M. Taft, and Carlos A. Uribe, eds.). University of Pittsburgh Memoirs in Latin American Archaeology 5.

DRENNAN, ROBERT D., LUISA FERNANDA HERRERA, AND FERNANDO PIÑEROS S.
    1989   Environment and Human Occupation. In *Prehispanic Chiefdoms in the Valle de la Plata, Volume 1: The Environmental Context of Human Habitation* (Luisa Fernanda Herrera, Robert D. Drennan, and Carlos A. Uribe, eds.). University of Pittsburgh Memoirs in Latin American Archaeology 2: 228–234.

DRENNAN, ROBERT D., LUIS GONZALO JARAMILLO, ELIZABETH RAMOS, CARLOS AUGUSTO SÁNCHEZ, MARÍA ANGELA RAMÍREZ, AND CARLOS A. URIBE
    1989   Reconocimiento Arqueológico en las Alturas Medias del Valle de la Plata. In *V Congreso Nacional de Antropología: Memorias del Simposio de Arqueología y Antropología Física* (Santiago Mora C., Felipe Cárdenas

A., and Miguel Angel Roldán, eds.): 119–157. Instituto Colombiano de Antropología and Universidad de los Andes, Bogotá.
1991   Regional Dynamics of Chiefdoms in the Valle de la Plata, Colombia. *Journal of Field Archaeology* 18: 297–317.

DUQUE GÓMEZ, LUIS
1964   *Exploraciones Arqueológicas en San Agustín*. Revista Colombiana de Antropología, Suplemento No. 1. Imprenta Nacional, Bogotá.

DUQUE GÓMEZ, LUIS, AND JULIO CÉSAR CUBILLOS
1979   *Arqueología de San Agustín: Alto de los Idolos, Montículos y Tumbas*. Fundación de Investigaciones Arqueológicas Nacionales del Banco de la República, Bogotá.
1981   *Arqueología de San Agustín: La Estación*. Fundación de Investigaciones Arqueológicas Nacionales del Banco de la República, Bogotá.
1983   *Arqueología de San Agustín: Exploraciones y Trabajos de Reconstrucción en las Mesitas A y B*. Fundación de Investigaciones Arqueológicas Nacionales del Banco de la República, Bogotá.
1988   *Arqueólogia de San Agustín: Alto de Lavapatas*. Fundación de Investigaciones Arqueológicas Nacionales del Banco de La República, Bogotá.

GAMBOA HINESTROSA, PABLO
1982   *La Escultura en la Sociedad Agustiniana*. Ediciones Centro de Investigación y Educación Cooperativas, Universidad Nacional de Colombia, Bogotá.

HERNÁNDEZ DE ALBA, GREGORIO
1979   *La Cultura Arqueológica de San Agustín*. Carlos Valencia Editores, Bogotá.

HERRERA, LUISA FERNANDA, ROBERT D. DRENNAN, AND CARLOS A. URIBE (EDS.)
1989   *Prehispanic Chiefdoms in the Valle de la Plata, Volume 1: The Environmental Context of Human Habitation*. University of Pittsburgh Memoirs in Latin American Archaeology 2.

LLANOS VARGAS, HÉCTOR
1988   *Arqueología de San Agustín: Pautas de Asentamiento en el Cañon del Río Granates—Saladoblanco*. Fundación de Investigaciones Arqueológicas Nacionales del Banco de la República, Bogotá.
1990   *Proceso Histórico Prehispánico de San Agustín en el Valle de Laboyos (Pitalito—Huila)*. Fundación de Investigaciones Arqueológicas Nacionales del Banco de la República, Bogotá.

LLANOS VARGAS, HECTOR, AND ANABELLA DURÁN DE GÓMEZ
1983   *Asentamientos Prehispánicos de Quinchana, San Agustín*. Fundación de Investigaciones Arqueológicas Nacionales del Banco de la República, Bogotá.

PÉREZ DE BARRADAS, JOSÉ
1943   *Arqueología Agustiniana: Excavaciones Arqueológicas Realizadas de Marzo a Diciembre 1937*. Imprenta Nacional, Bogotá.

PREUSS, KONRAD THEODOR
1931   *Arte Monumental Prehistórico: Excavaciones Hechas en el Alto Magdalena y San Agustín (Colombia). Comparación Arqueológica con las Manifestaciones*

Artísticas de las Demás Civilizaciones Americanas. Escuelas Salesianas de Tipografía y Fotograbado, Bogotá.

REICHEL-DOLMATOFF, GERARDO
  1972 *San Agustín: A Culture of Colombia.* Praeger, New York.
  1975 *Contribuciones al Conocimiento de la Estratigrafía Cerámica de San Agustín, Colombia.* Biblioteca Banco Popular, Bogotá.

RENFREW, COLIN
  1974 Beyond a Subsistence Economy: The Evolution of Social Organization in Prehistoric Europe. In *Reconstructing Complex Societies: An Archaeological Colloquium* (Charlotte B. Moore, ed.): 69–85. Supplement to the *Bulletin of the American Schools of Oriental Research* 20.

SANTA GERTRUDIS, FRAY JUAN DE
  1970 *Maravillas de la Naturaleza,* 4 vols. Biblioteca Banco Popular, Bogotá.

SOTOMAYOR, MARÍA LUCÍA, AND MARÍA VICTORIA URIBE
  1987 *Estatuaria del Macizo Colombiano.* Instituto Colombiano de Antropología, Bogotá.

TRIMBORN, HERMANN
  1949 *Señorío y Barbarie en el Valle del Cauca: Estudio sobre la Antigua Civilización Quimbaya y Grupos Afines del Oeste de Colombia.* Translated from the German by José María Gimeno Capella. Consejo Superior de Investigaciones Científicas, Instituto Gonzalo Fernández de Oviedo, Madrid.

Moche Funerary Practice

CHRISTOPHER B. DONNAN
UNIVERSITY OF CALIFORNIA, LOS ANGELES

THOUSANDS OF MOCHE BURIALS have been looted since Europeans entered Peru in the early sixteenth century, but relatively few have been excavated archaeologically and recorded systematically. Nevertheless, a detailed analysis of all Moche graves for which at least some information is available makes it possible to identify the characteristics of Moche funerary practice, and to define a range of elaboration in treatment of the corpse, grave architecture, and associated grave contents. This, combined with what is currently known about Moche cemeteries, provides important information about Moche culture.

SAMPLE

Before beginning with a description of Moche funerary practice, it is important to review the data on which this description is based. There are 326 Moche burials that have been excavated and for which at least some documentation is available.[1] These have been compiled into Table 1, "Moche Burial Sample," where each burial is assigned a number. Throughout this report, reference to specific burials will be made by citing the number assigned to them in Table 1.

Great variation exists in the amount of information accessible for burials in the sample. For some, the only available record is a single photograph taken when the grave was exposed and its contents were in situ. For others, only the associated grave contents are known; there is virtually no information about the grave itself. The quality of the archaeological record increases from this rather minimal documentation to burials where the entire contents are illustrated, both in situ and individually, along with the exact location, form, and size of the burial chamber. In a few instances, the age, sex, and pathologies of the corpse are also provided.

Manuscript completed June 1991 and revised for publication May 1992.
[1] This is the total number of individuals excavated. In some instances, two or more skeletons were found in a single grave. The number does not include severed heads, hands, or feet that had been placed in graves.

Table 1. Moche Burial Sample

#	VALLEY	SITE	BURIAL #	PHASE	SOURCE	NOTES
1	La Leche	Huaca Lucia	Burial II	V	Shimada et al., 1981: 426-428	1
2	La Leche	Huaca Soledad	Burial 1	V	Shimada (n.d.)	1
3	La Leche	Huaca Soledad	Burial 2	V	Shimada (n.d.)	1
4	Reque	Sipán	Warrior Priest a	III	Alva 1988	1, 2
5	Reque	Sipán	Warrior Priest b	III	Alva 1988	1, 2
6	Reque	Sipán	Warrior Priest c	III	Alva 1988	1, 2
7	Reque	Sipán	Warrior Priest d	III	Alva 1988	1, 2
8	Reque	Sipán	Warrior Priest e	III	Alva 1988	1, 2
9	Reque	Sipán	Warrior Priest f	III	Alva 1988	1, 2
10	Reque	Sipán	Warrior Priest g	III	Alva 1988	1, 2
11	Reque	Sipán	Warrior Priest h	III	Alva 1988	1, 2
12	Reque	Sipán	Priest a	III	Alva (n.d.)	1, 2
13	Reque	Sipán	Priest b	III	Alva (n.d.)	1, 2
14	Reque	Sipán	Priest c	III	Alva (n.d.)	1, 2
15	Reque	Sipán	Priest d	III	Alva (n.d.)	1, 2
16	Reque	Sipán	Priest e	III	Alva (n.d.)	1, 2
17	Reque	Sipán	Priest f	III	Alva (n.d.)	1, 2
18	Reque	Sipán	Priest g	III	Alva (n.d.)	1, 2
19	Reque	Sipán	Old Lord a	III	Alva 1990	1, 2
20	Reque	Sipán	Old Lord b	III	Alva 1990	1, 2
21	Reque	Sipán	Burial 1	III	Alva (n.d.)	1
22	Reque	Sipán	Burial 2	III	Alva (n.d.)	1
23	Reque	Sipán	Burial 3	III	Alva (n.d.)	1
24	Reque	Sipán	Burial 4	III	Alva (n.d.)	1
25	Reque	Sipán	Burial 5	III	Alva (n.d.)	1
26	Reque	Sipán	Burial 6	III	Alva (n.d.)	1
27	Reque	Sipán	Burial 7	III	Alva (n.d.)	1
28	Jequetepeque	La Mina	Not given	I?	Narvaez 1989	1
29	Jequetepeque	San José de Moro	U11-E1	V	Donnan and Castillo (n.d.)	1
30	Jequetepeque	San José de Moro	U13-E1	V	Donnan and Castillo (n.d.)	1
31	Jequetepeque	San José de Moro	U15-E1	V	Donnan and Castillo (n.d.)	1, 2
32	Jequetepeque	San José de Moro	U15-E2	V	Donnan and Castillo (n.d.)	1, 2
33	Jequetepeque	San José de Moro	U15-E3	V	Donnan and Castillo (n.d.)	1, 2
34	Jequetepeque	San José de Moro	U26-E1	V	Donnan and Castillo (n.d.)	1, 2
35	Jequetepeque	San José de Moro	U26-E2	V	Donnan and Castillo (n.d.)	1, 2
36	Jequetepeque	San José de Moro	U26-E3	V	Donnan and Castillo (n.d.)	1, 2
37	Jequetepeque	San José de Moro	U26-E4	V	Donnan and Castillo (n.d.)	1, 2
38	Jequetepeque	San José de Moro	U26-E5	V	Donnan and Castillo (n.d.)	1, 2
39	Jequetepeque	San José de Moro	U26-E6	V	Donnan and Castillo (n.d.)	1, 2
40	Jequetepeque	San José de Moro	U26-E7	V	Donnan and Castillo (n.d.)	1, 2
41	Jequetepeque	San José de Moro	U27-E1	V	Donnan and Castillo (n.d.)	1
42	Jequetepeque	San José de Moro	U28-E1	V	Donnan and Castillo (n.d.)	1
43	Jequetepeque	San José de Moro	U29-E1	V	Donnan and Castillo (n.d.)	1
44	Jequetepeque	San José de Moro	U30-E1	V	Donnan and Castillo (n.d.)	1, 2
45	Jequetepeque	San José de Moro	U30-E2	V	Donnan and Castillo (n.d.)	1, 2
46	Jequetepeque	San José de Moro	U30-E3	V	Donnan and Castillo (n.d.)	1, 2
47	Jequetepeque	San José de Moro	U30-E4	V	Donnan and Castillo (n.d.)	1, 2
48	Jequetepeque	San José de Moro	U30-E5	V	Donnan and Castillo (n.d.)	1, 2
49	Jequetepeque	San José de Moro	U30-E6	V	Donnan and Castillo (n.d.)	1, 2
50	Jequetepeque	San José de Moro	U30-E7	V	Donnan and Castillo (n.d.)	1, 2
51	Jequetepeque	San José de Moro	U31-E1	V	Donnan and Castillo (n.d.)	1

Moche Funerary Practice

Table 1 cont.

#	VALLEY	SITE	BURIAL #	PHASE	SOURCE	NOTES
52	Jequetepeque	San José de Moro	U32-E1	V	Donnan and Castillo (n.d.)	1
53	Jequetepeque	San José de Moro	U38-E1	V	Donnan and Castillo (n.d.)	1
54	Jequetepeque	San José de Moro	U39-E2	V	Donnan and Castillo (n.d.)	1
55	Jequetepeque	San José de Moro	U41-E1	V	Donnan and Castillo (n.d.)	1, 2
56	Jequetepeque	San José de Moro	U41-E2	V	Donnan and Castillo (n.d.)	1, 2
57	Jequetepeque	San José de Moro	U41-E3	V	Donnan and Castillo (n.d.)	1, 2
58	Jequetepeque	San José de Moro	U41-E4	V	Donnan and Castillo (n.d.)	1, 2
59	Jequetepeque	San José de Moro	U41-E5	V	Donnan and Castillo (n.d.)	1, 2
60	Jequetepeque	San José de Moro	U50-E1	V	Donnan and Castillo (n.d.)	1
61	Jequetepeque	San José de Moro	U50-E2	V	Donnan and Castillo (n.d.)	1
62	Jequetepeque	Pacatnamu	A I	III	Ubbelohde-Doering 1983: 41	1
63	Jequetepeque	Pacatnamu	A II	V	Ubbelohde-Doering 1983: 41	1
64	Jequetepeque	Pacatnamu	A III	III	Ubbelohde-Doering 1983: 41	1
65	Jequetepeque	Pacatnamu	A IV	III	Ubbelohde-Doering 1983: 44	1
66	Jequetepeque	Pacatnamu	A V	III	Ubbelohde-Doering 1983: 44	1
67	Jequetepeque	Pacatnamu	A VI	III	Ubbelohde-Doering 1983: 44-48	1
68	Jequetepeque	Pacatnamu	A VII	III	Ubbelohde-Doering 1983: 48	1
69	Jequetepeque	Pacatnamu	A VIII	III	Ubbelohde-Doering 1983: 48	1
70	Jequetepeque	Pacatnamu	D IV	V	Ubbelohde-Doering 1983: 50	1
71	Jequetepeque	Pacatnamu	D V	V	Ubbelohde-Doering 1983: 50-52	1
72	Jequetepeque	Pacatnamu	D VI a	V	Ubbelohde-Doering 1983: 52	1, 2
73	Jequetepeque	Pacatnamu	D VI b	V	Ubbelohde-Doering 1983: 52	1, 2
74	Jequetepeque	Pacatnamu	E I a	III	Ubbelohde-Doering 1983: 52-85	1, 2
75	Jequetepeque	Pacatnamu	E I b	III	Ubbelohde-Doering 1983: 89	1, 2
76	Jequetepeque	Pacatnamu	E I c	III	Ubbelohde-Doering 1983: 89-90	1, 2
77	Jequetepeque	Pacatnamu	E I d a	III	Ubbelohde-Doering 1983: 90	1, 2
78	Jequetepeque	Pacatnamu	E I d b	III	Ubbelohde-Doering 1983: 90-91	1, 2
79	Jequetepeque	Pacatnamu	E I e	III	Ubbelohde-Doering 1983: 91	1, 2
80	Jequetepeque	Pacatnamu	E I f	III	Ubbelohde-Doering 1983: 91	1, 2
81	Jequetepeque	Pacatnamu	E I g	III	Ubbelohde-Doering 1983: 91-92	1, 2
82	Jequetepeque	Pacatnamu	E I h	III	Ubbelohde-Doering 1983: 92	1, 2
83	Jequetepeque	Pacatnamu	E I sacrifice a	III	Ubbelohde-Doering 1983: 53	1, 2
84	Jequetepeque	Pacatnamu	E I sacrifice b	III	Ubbelohde-Doering 1983: 53	1, 2
85	Jequetepeque	Pacatnamu	E I sacrifice c	III	Ubbelohde-Doering 1983: 53	1, 2
86	Jequetepeque	Pacatnamu	E II	III	Ubbelohde-Doering 1983: 92	1
87	Jequetepeque	Pacatnamu	F II	V	Ubbelohde-Doering 1983: 92	1
88	Jequetepeque	Pacatnamu	L II	V	Ubbelohde-Doering 1983: 97	1
89	Jequetepeque	Pacatnamu	L III	V	Ubbelohde-Doering 1983: 97	1
90	Jequetepeque	Pacatnamu	L V	V	Ubbelohde-Doering 1983: 97	1
91	Jequetepeque	Pacatnamu	M XI a	V	Ubbelohde-Doering 1983: 107-113	1, 2
92	Jequetepeque	Pacatnamu	M XI b	V	Ubbelohde-Doering 1983: 107-113	1, 2
93	Jequetepeque	Pacatnamu	M XI c	V	Ubbelohde-Doering 1983: 107-113	1, 2
94	Jequetepeque	Pacatnamu	M XI d	V	Ubbelohde-Doering 1983: 107-113	1, 2
95	Jequetepeque	Pacatnamu	M XI e	V	Ubbelohde-Doering 1983: 107-113	1, 2
96	Jequetepeque	Pacatnamu	M XII a	V	Ubbelohde-Doering 1983: 107-113	1, 2
97	Jequetepeque	Pacatnamu	M XII b	III	Ubbelohde-Doering 1983: 113-122	1
98	Jequetepeque	Pacatnamu	V I	III	Ubbelohde-Doering 1983: 126	1
99	Jequetepeque	Pacatnamu	V II	V	Ubbelohde-Doering 1983: 126	1
100	Jequetepeque	Pacatnamu	V IV	III	Ubbelohde-Doering 1983: 126	1
101	Jequetepeque	Pacatnamu	V V	III	Ubbelohde-Doering 1983: 126	1
102	Jequetepeque	Pacatnamu	V VI	III	Ubbelohde-Doering 1983: 126	1

Christopher B. Donnan

Table 1 cont.

#	VALLEY	SITE	BURIAL #	PHASE	SOURCE	NOTES
103	Jequetepeque	Pacatnamu	V VII	I?	Ubbelohde-Doering 1983: 126-129	1
104	Jequetepeque	Pacatnamu	V VIII	V	Ubbelohde-Doering 1983: 129	1
105	Jequetepeque	Pacatnamu	V IX	III	Ubbelohde-Doering 1983: 129	1
106	Jequetepeque	Pacatnamu	H1R5 B1a	V	Donnan and McClelland (n.d.)	1, 2
107	Jequetepeque	Pacatnamu	H1R5 B1b	V	Donnan and McClelland (n.d.)	1, 2
108	Jequetepeque	Pacatnamu	H1R5 B2	V	Donnan and McClelland (n.d.)	1
109	Jequetepeque	Pacatnamu	H2 B1	V	Donnan and McClelland (n.d.)	1
110	Jequetepeque	Pacatnamu	H2 B2	V	Donnan and McClelland (n.d.)	1
111	Jequetepeque	Pacatnamu	H2 B3	V	Donnan and McClelland (n.d.)	1
112	Jequetepeque	Pacatnamu	H20 B1	V	Donnan and McClelland (n.d.)	1
113	Jequetepeque	Pacatnamu	H26 B1	V	Donnan and McClelland (n.d.)	1
114	Jequetepeque	Pacatnamu	H26 B2	V	Donnan and McClelland (n.d.)	1
115	Jequetepeque	Pacatnamu	H26 B3	V	Donnan and McClelland (n.d.)	1
116	Jequetepeque	Pacatnamu	H28 B1	V	Donnan and McClelland (n.d.)	1
117	Jequetepeque	Pacatnamu	H28 B2	V	Donnan and McClelland (n.d.)	1
118	Jequetepeque	Pacatnamu	H31 B11	V	Donnan and McClelland (n.d.)	1
119	Jequetepeque	Pacatnamu	H45CM1 B1	III	Donnan and McClelland (n.d.)	1
120	Jequetepeque	Pacatnamu	H45CM1 B2	III	Donnan and McClelland (n.d.)	1
121	Jequetepeque	Pacatnamu	H45CM1 B3	III	Donnan and McClelland (n.d.)	1
122	Jequetepeque	Pacatnamu	H45CM1 B4	III	Donnan and McClelland (n.d.)	1
123	Jequetepeque	Pacatnamu	H45CM1 B5	III	Donnan and McClelland (n.d.)	1
124	Jequetepeque	Pacatnamu	H45CM1 B6	III	Donnan and McClelland (n.d.)	1
125	Jequetepeque	Pacatnamu	H45CM1 B7	III	Donnan and McClelland (n.d.)	1
126	Jequetepeque	Pacatnamu	H45CM1 B8	III	Donnan and McClelland (n.d.)	1
127	Jequetepeque	Pacatnamu	H45CM1 B9	III	Donnan and McClelland (n.d.)	1
128	Jequetepeque	Pacatnamu	H45CM1 B10	III	Donnan and McClelland (n.d.)	1
129	Jequetepeque	Pacatnamu	H45CM1 B11	I?	Donnan and McClelland (n.d.)	1
130	Jequetepeque	Pacatnamu	H45CM1 B12	III	Donnan and McClelland (n.d.)	1
131	Jequetepeque	Pacatnamu	H45CM1 B13	III	Donnan and McClelland (n.d.)	1
132	Jequetepeque	Pacatnamu	H45CM1 B14	III	Donnan and McClelland (n.d.)	1
133	Jequetepeque	Pacatnamu	H45CM1 B15	III	Donnan and McClelland (n.d.)	1
134	Jequetepeque	Pacatnamu	H45CM1 B16	III	Donnan and McClelland (n.d.)	1
135	Jequetepeque	Pacatnamu	H45CM1 B17	III	Donnan and McClelland (n.d.)	1
136	Jequetepeque	Pacatnamu	H45CM1 B18	III	Donnan and McClelland (n.d.)	1
137	Jequetepeque	Pacatnamu	H45CM1 B19	III	Donnan and McClelland (n.d.)	1
138	Jequetepeque	Pacatnamu	H45CM1 B20	III	Donnan and McClelland (n.d.)	1
139	Jequetepeque	Pacatnamu	H45CM1 B21	III	Donnan and McClelland (n.d.)	1
140	Jequetepeque	Pacatnamu	H45CM1 B22	III	Donnan and McClelland (n.d.)	1
141	Jequetepeque	Pacatnamu	H45CM1 B23	III	Donnan and McClelland (n.d.)	1
142	Jequetepeque	Pacatnamu	H45CM1 B24	III	Donnan and McClelland (n.d.)	1
143	Jequetepeque	Pacatnamu	H45CM1 B25a	III	Donnan and McClelland (n.d.)	1, 2
144	Jequetepeque	Pacatnamu	H45CM1 B25b	III	Donnan and McClelland (n.d.)	1, 2
145	Jequetepeque	Pacatnamu	H45CM1 B26	III	Donnan and McClelland (n.d.)	1
146	Jequetepeque	Pacatnamu	H45CM1 B27	III	Donnan and McClelland (n.d.)	1
147	Jequetepeque	Pacatnamu	H45CM1 B28	III	Donnan and McClelland (n.d.)	1
148	Jequetepeque	Pacatnamu	H45CM1 B29	I?	Donnan and McClelland (n.d.)	1
149	Jequetepeque	Pacatnamu	H45CM1 B30	III	Donnan and McClelland (n.d.)	1
150	Jequetepeque	Pacatnamu	H45CM1 B31	III	Donnan and McClelland (n.d.)	1
151	Jequetepeque	Pacatnamu	H45CM1 B32	III	Donnan and McClelland (n.d.)	1
152	Jequetepeque	Pacatnamu	H45CM1 B33	III	Donnan and McClelland (n.d.)	1
153	Jequetepeque	Pacatnamu	H45CM1 B34	III	Donnan and McClelland (n.d.)	1

Moche Funerary Practice

Table 1 cont.

#	VALLEY	SITE	BURIAL #	PHASE	SOURCE	NOTES
154	Jequetepeque	Pacatnamu	H45CM1 B35	III	Donnan and McClelland (n.d.)	1
155	Jequetepeque	Pacatnamu	H45CM1 B36	III	Donnan and McClelland (n.d.)	1
156	Jequetepeque	Pacatnamu	H45CM1 B37	III	Donnan and McClelland (n.d.)	1
157	Jequetepeque	Pacatnamu	H45CM1 B38	III	Donnan and McClelland (n.d.)	1
158	Jequetepeque	Pacatnamu	H45CM1 B39	III	Donnan and McClelland (n.d.)	1
159	Jequetepeque	Pacatnamu	H45CM1 B40	III	Donnan and McClelland (n.d.)	1
160	Jequetepeque	Pacatnamu	H45CM1 B41	III	Donnan and McClelland (n.d.)	1
161	Jequetepeque	Pacatnamu	H45CM1 B42	III	Donnan and McClelland (n.d.)	1
162	Jequetepeque	Pacatnamu	H45CM1 B43	III	Donnan and McClelland (n.d.)	1
163	Jequetepeque	Pacatnamu	H45CM1 B44	III	Donnan and McClelland (n.d.)	1
164	Jequetepeque	Pacatnamu	H45CM1 B45	III	Donnan and McClelland (n.d.)	1
165	Jequetepeque	Pacatnamu	H45CM1 B46	III	Donnan and McClelland (n.d.)	1
166	Jequetepeque	Pacatnamu	H45CM1 B47	III	Donnan and McClelland (n.d.)	1
167	Jequetepeque	Pacatnamu	H45CM1 B48	III	Donnan and McClelland (n.d.)	1
168	Jequetepeque	Pacatnamu	H45CM1 B49	III	Donnan and McClelland (n.d.)	1
169	Jequetepeque	Pacatnamu	H45CM1 B50	III	Donnan and McClelland (n.d.)	1
170	Jequetepeque	Pacatnamu	H45CM1 B51	III	Donnan and McClelland (n.d.)	1
171	Jequetepeque	Pacatnamu	H45CM1 B52	III	Donnan and McClelland (n.d.)	1
172	Jequetepeque	Pacatnamu	H45CM1 B53	III	Donnan and McClelland (n.d.)	1
173	Jequetepeque	Pacatnamu	H45CM1 B54	III	Donnan and McClelland (n.d.)	1
174	Jequetepeque	Pacatnamu	H45CM1 B55	III	Donnan and McClelland (n.d.)	1
175	Jequetepeque	Pacatnamu	H45CM1 B56	III	Donnan and McClelland (n.d.)	1
176	Jequetepeque	Pacatnamu	H45CM1 B58	III	Donnan and McClelland (n.d.)	1
177	Jequetepeque	Pacatnamu	H45CM1 B59	III	Donnan and McClelland (n.d.)	1
178	Jequetepeque	Pacatnamu	H45CM1 B60	III	Donnan and McClelland (n.d.)	1
179	Jequetepeque	Pacatnamu	H45CM1 B61	III	Donnan and McClelland (n.d.)	1
180	Jequetepeque	Pacatnamu	H45CM1 B62	III	Donnan and McClelland (n.d.)	1
181	Jequetepeque	Pacatnamu	H45CM1 B63	III	Donnan and McClelland (n.d.)	1
182	Jequetepeque	Pacatnamu	H45CM1 B64	III	Donnan and McClelland (n.d.)	1
183	Jequetepeque	Pacatnamu	H45CM1 B65	III	Donnan and McClelland (n.d.)	1
184	Jequetepeque	Pacatnamu	H45CM1 B66	III	Donnan and McClelland (n.d.)	1
185	Jequetepeque	Pacatnamu	H45CM1 B67	III	Donnan and McClelland (n.d.)	1
186	Jequetepeque	Pacatnamu	RG79 B1	V	Donnan and McClelland (n.d.)	1
187	Jequetepeque	Pacatnamu	RG79 B2	V	Donnan and McClelland (n.d.)	1
188	Jequetepeque	Pacatnamu	RG79 B3	V	Donnan and McClelland (n.d.)	1
189	Jequetepeque	Pacatnamu	RG79 B4	V	Donnan and McClelland (n.d.)	1
190	Chicama	Magdalena de Cao	Not given	IV	Diaz 1939	
191	Chicama	Pampa de Chicama	Not given	IV	Bennett 1939: 89	
192	Chicama	Salamanca Playa	Not given	IV	Bennett 1939: 86	
193	Moche	Caballo Muerto	M III 4	III	Donnan and Mackey 1978: 82-85	
194	Moche	Cerro Blanco	M IV 18	IV	Donnan and Mackey 1978: 184-187	2
195	Moche	Cerro Blanco	M IV 19	IV	Donnan and Mackey 1978: 184-187	2
196	Moche	Galindo	Not given	V	Bawden n.d.: 364-367	
197	Moche	Galindo	Not given	V	Bawden n.d.: 367	
198	Moche	Galindo	Not given	V	Bawden n.d.: 368-369	
199	Moche	Galindo	Not given	V	Bawden n.d.: 368-369	
200	Moche	Huanchaco	M IV 20	IV	Donnan and Mackey 1978: 190-191	
201	Moche	Huanchaco	M IV 21	IV	Donnan and Mackey 1978: 192-193	
202	Moche	Huanchaco	M IV 22	IV	Donnan and Mackey 1978: 194-195	
203	Moche	Huanchaco	M IV 23	IV	Donnan and Mackey 1978: 196-197	
204	Moche	Huanchaco	M IV 24	IV	Donnan and Mackey 1978: 199	

Christopher B. Donnan

Table 1 cont.

#	VALLEY	SITE	BURIAL #	PHASE	SOURCE	NOTES
205	Moche	Huanchaco	M IV 25	IV	Donnan and Mackey 1978: 200-207	2
206	Moche	Huanchaco	M IV 26	IV	Donnan and Mackey 1978: 200-207	2
207	Moche	Huanchaco	M IV 27	IV	Donnan and Mackey 1978: 200-207	2
208	Moche	Huanchaco	M IV 28	IV	Donnan and Mackey 1978: 200-207	2
209	Moche	Huanchaco	Grave 1A	IV	Iriarte (n.d.)	
210	Moche	Huanchaco	Grave 2	IV	Iriarte (n.d.)	
211	Moche	Huanchaco	Grave 2A	IV	Iriarte (n.d.)	
212	Moche	Huanchaco	Grave 3	IV	Iriarte (n.d.)	
213	Moche	Huanchaco	Grave 4	IV	Iriarte (n.d.)	
214	Moche	Huanchaco	Grave 5	IV	Iriarte (n.d.)	
215	Moche	Huanchaco	Grave 6	IV	Iriarte (n.d.)	
216	Moche	Huanchaco	Grave 7	IV	Iriarte (n.d.)	
217	Moche	Huanchaco	Grave 8	IV	Iriarte (n.d.)	
218	Moche	Huanchaco	Grave 9	IV	Iriarte (n.d.)	
219	Moche	Huanchaco	Grave 10	IV	Iriarte (n.d.)	
220	Moche	Huanchaco	Grave 13	IV	Iriarte (n.d.)	
221	Moche	Pyramids of Moche	Grave 1		Topic n.d.: 397	
222	Moche	Pyramids of Moche	Grave 2	I	Topic n.d.: 398	
223	Moche	Pyramids of Moche	Grave A		Bennett 1939: 84	
224	Moche	Pyramids of Moche	Grave B		Bennett 1939: 84	
225	Moche	Pyramids of Moche	M I 1	I	Donnan and Mackey 1978: 60-61	
226	Moche	Pyramids of Moche	M III 1	III	Donnan and Mackey 1978: 66-69	
227	Moche	Pyramids of Moche	M III 2	III	Donnan and Mackey 1978: 72-75	
228	Moche	Pyramids of Moche	M III 3	III	Donnan and Mackey 1978: 78-79	
229	Moche	Pyramids of Moche	M IV 1	IV	Donnan and Mackey 1978: 92-99	2
230	Moche	Pyramids of Moche	M IV 2	IV	Donnan and Mackey 1978: 92-99	2
231	Moche	Pyramids of Moche	M IV 3	IV	Donnan and Mackey 1978: 102-115	
232	Moche	Pyramids of Moche	M IV 4	IV	Donnan and Mackey 1978: 116-119	
233	Moche	Pyramids of Moche	M IV 5	IV	Donnan and Mackey 1978: 120-127	
234	Moche	Pyramids of Moche	M IV 6	IV	Donnan and Mackey 1978: 128-131	
235	Moche	Pyramids of Moche	M IV 7	IV	Donnan and Mackey 1978: 132-139	
236	Moche	Pyramids of Moche	M IV 8	IV	Donnan and Mackey 1978: 140-143	
237	Moche	Pyramids of Moche	M IV 9	IV	Donnan and Mackey 1978: 144-149	
238	Moche	Pyramids of Moche	M IV 10	IV	Donnan and Mackey 1978: 150-153	
239	Moche	Pyramids of Moche	M IV 11	IV	Donnan and Mackey 1978: 154-159	
240	Moche	Pyramids of Moche	M IV 12	IV	Donnan and Mackey 1978: 160-161	
241	Moche	Pyramids of Moche	M IV 13	IV	Donnan and Mackey 1978: 164-167	
242	Moche	Pyramids of Moche	M IV 14	IV	Donnan and Mackey 1978: 168-174	2
243	Moche	Pyramids of Moche	M IV 15	IV	Donnan and Mackey 1978: 168-174	2
244	Moche	Pyramids of Moche	M IV 16	IV	Donnan and Mackey 1978: 176-179	
245	Moche	Pyramids of Moche	M IV 17	IV	Donnan and Mackey 1978: 180-182	
246	Moche	Pyramids of Moche	Site F Grave 1		Uhle (n.d.)	3
247	Moche	Pyramids of Moche	Site F Grave 2	III	Uhle (n.d.)	3
248	Moche	Pyramids of Moche	Site F Grave 3	III	Uhle (n.d.)	3
249	Moche	Pyramids of Moche	Site F Grave 4	III	Uhle (n.d.)	3
250	Moche	Pyramids of Moche	Site F Grave 5	III	Uhle (n.d.)	3
251	Moche	Pyramids of Moche	Site F Grave 6	IV	Uhle (n.d.)	3
252	Moche	Pyramids of Moche	Site F Grave 7	IV	Uhle (n.d.)	3
253	Moche	Pyramids of Moche	Site F Grave 8	IV	Uhle (n.d.)	3
254	Moche	Pyramids of Moche	Site F Grave 9	IV	Uhle (n.d.)	3
255	Moche	Pyramids of Moche	Site F Grave 10	III	Uhle (n.d.)	3

Moche Funerary Practice

Table 1 cont.

#	VALLEY	SITE	BURIAL #	PHASE	SOURCE	NOTES
256	Moche	Pyramids of Moche	Site F Grave 11	III	Uhle (n.d.)	3
257	Moche	Pyramids of Moche	Site F Grave 12	III	Uhle (n.d.)	3
258	Moche	Pyramids of Moche	Site F Grave 13	II	Uhle (n.d.)	3
259	Moche	Pyramids of Moche	Site F Grave 14	II	Uhle (n.d.)	3
260	Moche	Pyramids of Moche	Site F Grave 15	IV	Uhle (n.d.)	3
261	Moche	Pyramids of Moche	Site F Grave 16	III	Uhle (n.d.)	3
262	Moche	Pyramids of Moche	Site F Grave 17		Uhle (n.d.)	3
263	Moche	Pyramids of Moche	Site F Grave 18	IV	Uhle (n.d.)	3
264	Moche	Pyramids of Moche	Site F Grave 19	IV	Uhle (n.d.)	3
265	Moche	Pyramids of Moche	Site F Grave 20	II	Uhle (n.d.)	3
266	Moche	Pyramids of Moche	Site F Grave 21	III	Uhle (n.d.)	3
267	Moche	Pyramids of Moche	Site F Grave 22	III	Uhle (n.d.)	3
268	Moche	Pyramids of Moche	Site F Grave 23	IV	Uhle (n.d.)	3
269	Moche	Pyramids of Moche	Site F Grave 25	IV	Uhle (n.d.)	3
270	Moche	Pyramids of Moche	Site F Grave 26	III	Uhle (n.d.)	3
271	Moche	Pyramids of Moche	Site F Grave 27	III	Uhle (n.d.)	3
272	Moche	Pyramids of Moche	Site F Grave 28	III	Uhle (n.d.)	3
273	Moche	Pyramids of Moche	Site F Grave 29	III	Uhle (n.d.)	3
274	Moche	Pyramids of Moche	Site F Grave 30	II	Uhle (n.d.)	3
275	Moche	Pyramids of Moche	Site F Grave 32	III	Uhle (n.d.)	3
276	Moche	Pyramids of Moche	Site F Grave 33	III	Uhle (n.d.)	3
277	Moche	Pyramids of Moche	Site G Grave 1		Uhle (n.d.)	3
278	Moche	Pyramids of Moche	Site G Grave 2		Uhle (n.d.)	3
279	Moche	Pyramids of Moche	Site G Grave 3		Uhle (n.d.)	3
280	Moche	Pyramids of Moche	Not given	IV	Larco 1945: 34 above	
281	Viru	Castillo de Tomaval	Burial Site 2	IV	Strong and Evans 1952: 108-109	
282	Viru	Huaca de la Cruz	Burial 11 A 1	III	Bennett 1939: 30-31	
283	Viru	Huaca de la Cruz	Burial 11 A 2	III	Bennett 1939: 30-31	
284	Viru	Huaca de la Cruz	Burial 1	IV	Strong and Evans 1952: 139-140	
285	Viru	Huaca de la Cruz	Burial 3	IV	Strong and Evans 1952: 140-141	
286	Viru	Huaca de la Cruz	Burial 4	IV	Strong and Evans 1952: 141	
287	Viru	Huaca de la Cruz	Burial 5	IV	Strong and Evans 1952: 141-145	
288	Viru	Huaca de la Cruz	Burial 6	IV	Strong and Evans 1952: 145-146	
289	Viru	Huaca de la Cruz	Burial 7	IV	Strong and Evans 1952: 146	
290	Viru	Huaca de la Cruz	Burial 9	IV	Strong and Evans 1952: 146-147	
291	Viru	Huaca de la Cruz	Burial 10	IV	Strong and Evans 1952: 147-149	
292	Viru	Huaca de la Cruz	Burial 11	IV	Strong and Evans 1952: 149-150	
293	Viru	Huaca de la Cruz	Burial 12	IV	Strong and Evans 1952: 150-167	2
294	Viru	Huaca de la Cruz	Burial 13	IV	Strong and Evans 1952: 150-167	2
295	Viru	Huaca de la Cruz	Burial 14	IV	Strong and Evans 1952: 150-167	2
296	Viru	Huaca de la Cruz	Burial 15	IV	Strong and Evans 1952: 150-167	2
297	Viru	Huaca de la Cruz	Burial 16	IV	Strong and Evans 1952: 150-167	2
298	Santa	Pampa Blanca	PV28-64 Grave 1	IV	Donnan 1973: 132	
299	Santa	Pampa Blanca	PV28-64 Grave 2	IV	Donnan 1973: 132	
300	Santa	Pampa Blanca	PV28-64 Grave 3	IV	Donnan 1973: 132	
301	Santa	Pampa Blanca	PV28-100 Grave 1	IV	Donnan 1973: 132	
302	Santa	Pampa Blanca	PV28-122 Grave 1	IV	Donnan 1973: 132	
303	Santa	Pampa Blanca	PV28-122 Grave 2	IV	Donnan 1973: 132-133	
304	Santa	Pampa Blanca	PV28-122 Grave 3	IV	Donnan 1973: 133	
305	Santa	Pampa Blanca	PV28-122 Grave 4	IV	Donnan 1973: 133	
306	Santa	Pampa Blanca	PV28-122 Grave 5	IV	Donnan 1973: 133	

TABLE 1 cont.

#	VALLEY	SITE	BURIAL #	PHASE	SOURCE	NOTES
307	Santa	Pampa Blanca	PV28-122 Grave 6	IV	Donnan 1973: 133	
308	Santa	Pampa Blanca	PV28-122 Grave 7	IV	Donnan 1973: 133	
309	Santa	Pampa Blanca	PV28-122 Grave 8	IV	Donnan 1973: 133	
310	Santa	Pampa Blanca	PV28-122 Grave 9	IV	Donnan 1973: 133	
311	Santa	Pampa Blanca	PV28-123 Grave 1	IV	Donnan 1973: 133	
312	Santa	Pampa Blanca	PV28-123 Grave 2	IV	Donnan 1973: 133	
313	Santa	Pampa Blanca	PV28-123 Grave 3	IV	Donnan 1973: 133-134	
314	Santa	Pampa Blanca	PV28-123 Grave 4	IV	Donnan 1973: 134	
315	Santa	Pampa de los Incas	PV28-156 Grave 1	IV	Donnan 1973: 134	
316	Casma	San Diego	Not given	IV	Pozorski & Pozorski (n.d.)	
317	Unknown	Unknown	Not given		Larco 1945: 34 below	
318	Unknown	Unknown	Not given		Larco 1945: 36 above	
319	Unknown	Unknown	Not given		Larco 1945: 37 left	
320	Unknown	Unknown	Not given		Larco 1945: 37 right	
321	Unknown	Unknown	Not given		Larco 1945: 38 above	
322	Unknown	Unknown	Not given		Larco 1945: 38 below	
323	Unknown	Unknown	Not given		Larco 1945: 39	
324	Unknown	Unknown	Not given		Larco 1945: 40 above	
325	Unknown	Unknown	Not given		Larco 1945: 40 below	
326	Unknown	Unknown	Not given		Larco 1945: 41	

1. See footnote 2 in text.

2. Burials in brackets in the Burial # column are individuals that were buried together.

3. Uhle's field catalog, along with the collection from his Moche excavations, are at the Lowie Museum of Anthropology at the University of California, Berkeley. His field notes, which may contain more information about individual graves, are in the Ibero-American Institute in Berlin. At the present time, the field notes are not available for study.

The sample of Moche burials comes from only 18 archaeological sites, distributed in eight of the 13 river valleys that were once inhabited by the Moche (Fig. 1, Table 2). More than 75% of the burials are from only two of the valleys: Moche and Jequetepeque. Furthermore, more than 55% of the burials are from only two sites: the Pyramids at Moche in the Moche Valley, and Pacatnamu in the Jequetepeque Valley. Clearly, the sample is not evenly distributed geographically.

The burial sample is also unevenly distributed temporally. Accurate absolute dates for most of the burials are not available, but their distribution according to the five-phase chronology defined by Rafael Larco (1948) re-

Moche Funerary Practice

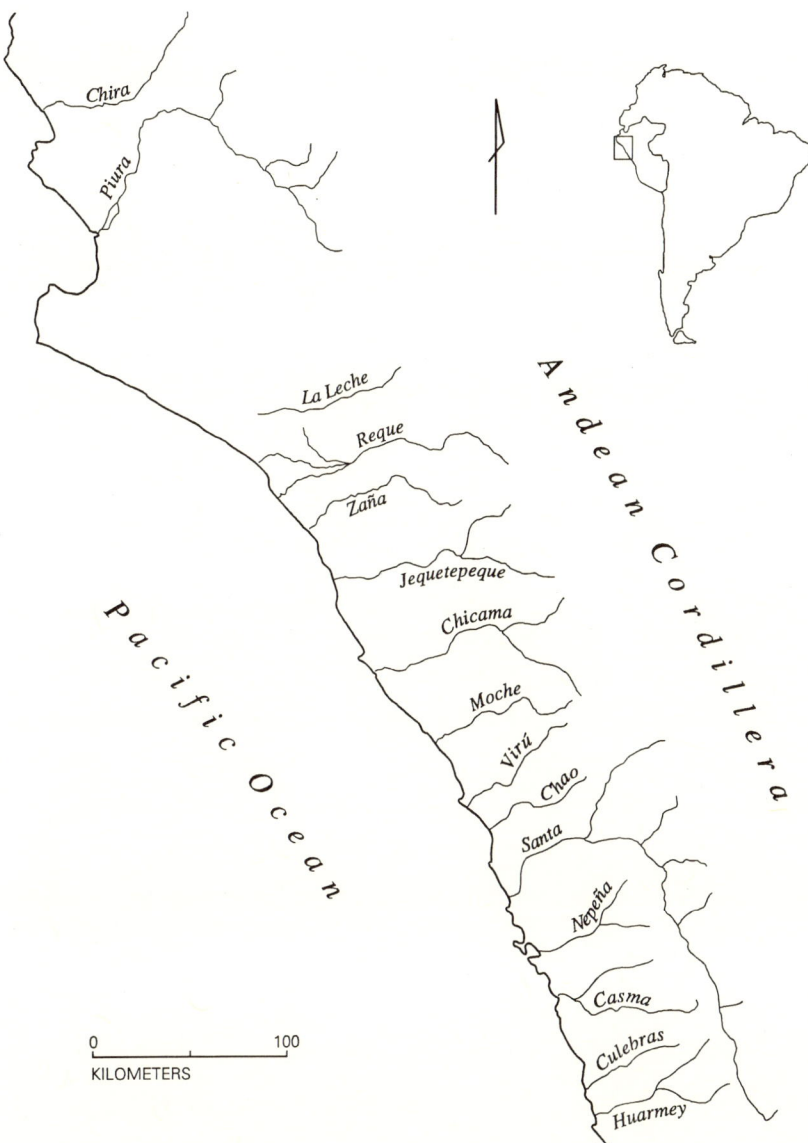

Fig. 1 Map of the north coast of Peru.

Christopher B. Donnan

TABLE 2. GEOGRAPHICAL DISTRIBUTION OF THE MOCHE BURIAL SAMPLE

VALLEY	GRAVES	%
Piura	0	0.0%
La Leche	3	0.9%
Reque	24	7.4%
Saña	0	0.0%
Jequetepeque	162	49.7%
Chicama	3	0.9%
Moche	88	27.0%
Viru	17	5.2%
Chao	0	0.0%
Santa	18	5.5%
Nepeña	0	0.0%
Casma	1	0.3%
Huarmey	0	0.0%
Unknown	10	3.1%
TOTAL	326	100.0%

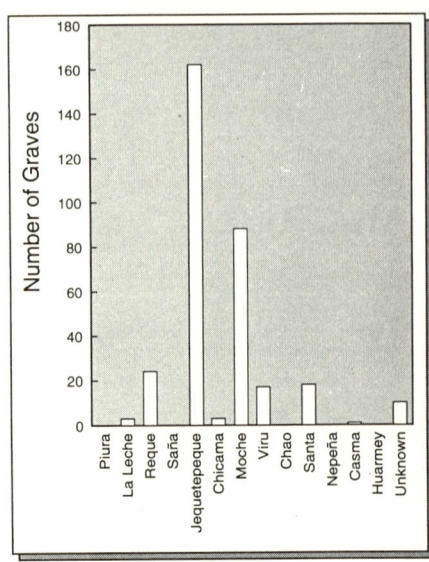

veals that less than 25% of them are Phase V, and fewer than 2% are Phase I (Table 3).[2]

Another variable that significantly affects the burial sample is the degree of preservation. Most Moche burials that have been excavated were found in poor condition—organic materials such as textiles, basketry, cordage, leather, feathers, and gourd containers were decomposed, and little or no evidence of them remained. This distorts not only the reconstruction of the original grave contents, but also removes information about how the corpse

[2] Larco's chronology appears to be valid only for the southern valleys, from Chicama to Huarmey (Donnan n.d.). The northern valleys, from Jequetepeque to Piura, have a ceramic tradition that does not conform to the Larco chronology. For the purposes of this paper, however, an attempt has been made to assign Larco's phase designations to burials found in the northern valleys. The burials excavated by Izumi Shimada at La Leche are late and would most likely correlate to Larco's Phase V. A radiocarbon date from one of the burials at Sipán (no. 4) is A.D. 260 +/- 50 years, and we have assigned the Sipán burials to Larco's Phase III. The burial from La Mina may be contemporary with Larco's Phase I. Since many of the burials from Pacatnamu and Moro are late, and must be approximately contemporary with Larco's Phase V, they have been assigned to this phase. The others are somewhat earlier, and have been assigned to Phase III. As more archaeological evidence for the chronology of the northern valleys is available, and a chronological sequence for this area is defined, it should be possible to correlate it with Larco's chronology for the southern valleys. Ultimately, this may revise the temporal placement of the northern burials in Table 1.

Moche Funerary Practice

TABLE 3. TEMPORAL DISTRIBUTION OF THE MOCHE BURIAL SAMPLE

PHASE	GRAVES	%
I	6	1.9%
II	4	1.2%
III	137	42.0%
IV	87	26.7%
V	74	22.7%
Unknown	18	5.5%
TOTAL	326	100.0%

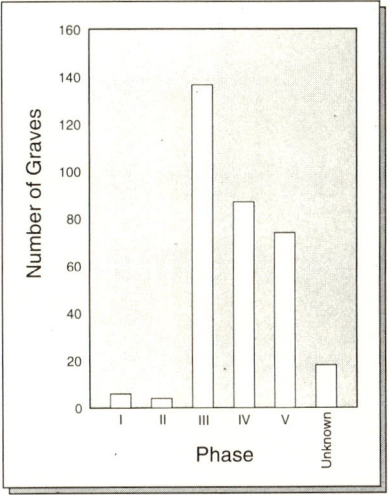

may have been dressed, wrapped in shrouds, and/or placed in a cane or wood coffin.

In a few instances, however, the organic material is preserved remarkably well, and it is possible to make a detailed reconstruction of the grave contents and treatment of the corpse. The well-preserved burials indicate that those without good preservation were considerably more complex, contained a much greater range of grave contents, and involved a much more elaborate preparation of the corpse than is reflected in the existing archaeological record.

FUNERARY PRACTICE

To understand the variations in Moche funerary practice, it is worthwhile to consider five distinct aspects of burial (Fig. 2): (1) preparation of the corpse; (2) encasing the corpse; (3) funerary chambers; (4) quantity and quality of grave goods; and (5) location.

Preparation of the Corpse

On the north coast of Peru, at the time of European contact, it is said that the death of an individual was followed by a five-day mourning period when the corpse was washed and prepared for burial (Calancha 1977–81: 1247). It is not known if the Moche practiced a similar mourning period or if they washed the corpse, but on the basis of the few well-preserved graves

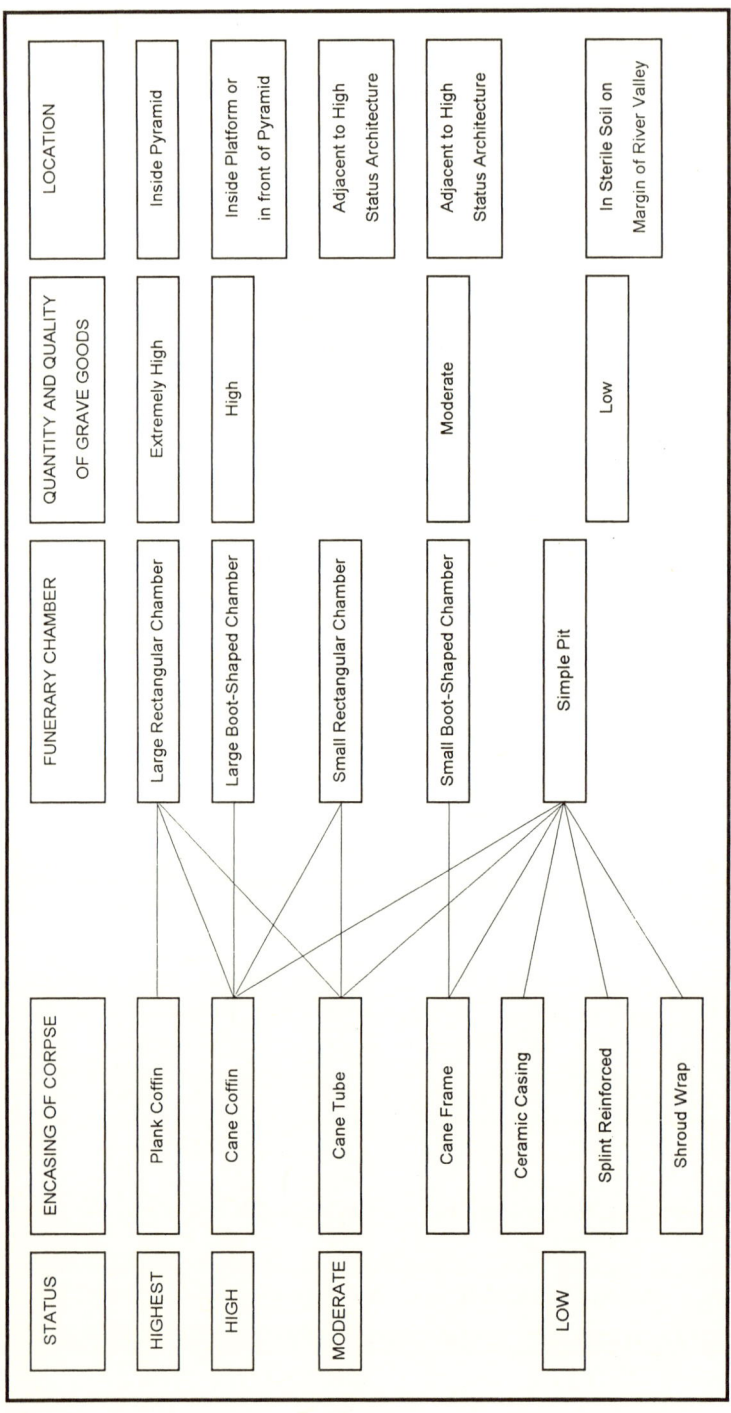

Fig. 2 Moche funerary practice.

that have been recorded it is possible to note some procedures that were taken to prepare the corpse for burial.

Three burials have been found where the hair treatment could be observed. All three were women. Two had the hair divided into two long bunches, one along each side of the head (nos. 285, 286). The other (no. 174) had the hair braided.

Red pigment adhering to the forehead and facial bones of the skull on several burials indicates that the face of the deceased was sometimes painted this color at the time of burial. This practice has been noted on one nine-month-old infant (no. 31), one child from three to five years old (no. 257), one child approximately 11 years old (no. 50), one 18-year-old female (no. 75), and two adult males (nos. 4, 290).

Often wool yarn was wrapped around the head, hands, wrists, ankles, or feet. The head was wrapped with multiple windings around the forehead (nos. 149, 158, 173), or with multiple strands of yarn (at least 20) that formed a headband knotted at the center of the forehead (no. 165). Each hand was wrapped individually around the palm and the back of the hand, leaving the thumb free. When the wrist was wrapped, the wrapping sometimes extended over the palm of the hand. Each foot was wrapped separately, below the arch and over the top of the foot.[3]

It is not clear how frequently the deceased were buried wearing articles of clothing. Most of the well-preserved burials that have been found were not dressed. In a few instances, however, there was clear evidence that the corpse was wearing a shirt (nos. 133, 165), a loincloth (no. 118), or both (no. 111).

The Moche normally buried their dead in a fully extended position, lying on their back, with the hands at the sides or over the pelvic area. The ankles sometimes were crossed, but more commonly were side by side. Two burials are reported to have had the legs and ankles tied together with sashes of cloth (nos. 293, 294).

There are very few Moche burials where the body was not in a fully extended position. Most of those were secondary individuals, buried in elaborate graves of individuals of high status. In only two instances were the individuals buried alone. One was an adult male found seated in a flexed position, knees folded close to the body, arms at the sides, with the hands resting on the floor of the grave pit (no. 281). The other was a young adult male, lying on his side in a flexed position, with the torso twisted and the head facing down (no. 311).

Many of the well-preserved Moche burials had unspun cotton placed over

---

[3] Heads, hands, and feet are also taken as trophies in Moche ritual, suggesting that these three parts of the body were considered to be the location of the essence, or power, of the individual (see Donnan 1978: figs. 273, 274).

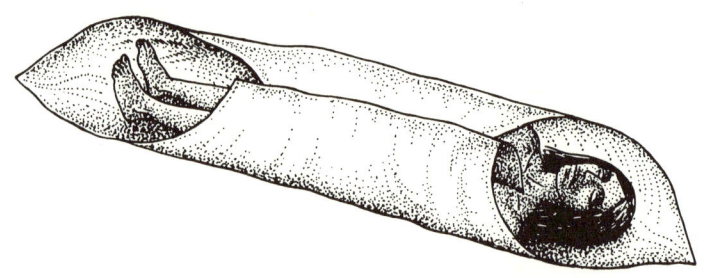

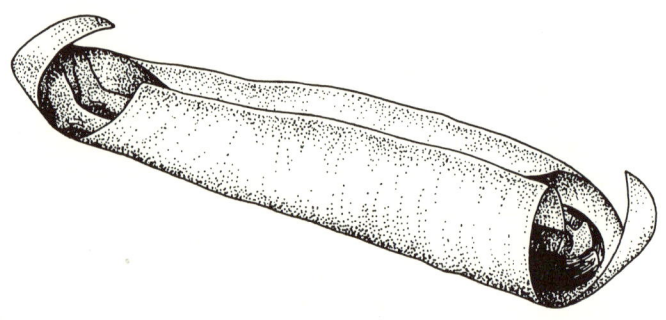

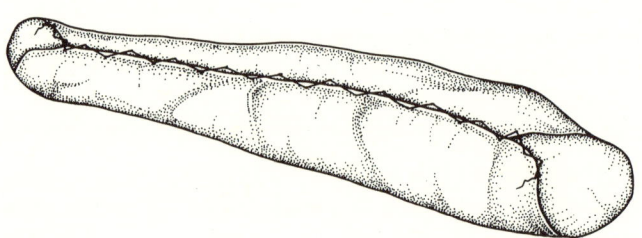

Fig. 3 Shroud wrap.

Moche Funerary Practice

the eyes or face before the body was wrapped in textiles. Several burials had unspun cotton under the head as though serving as a pillow, or had a thin layer of unspun cotton placed under the entire body. In other burials the head was resting on a stack of textiles, and occasionally one or more textiles were folded and placed beneath the entire body. Textiles also were frequently placed over the face or wrapped around the head.

Encasing the Corpse

There appear to have been seven distinct procedures used to encase the corpse for burial (Fig. 2). These seven procedures reflect an increasing complexity of funerary practice with an increase in the amount of both raw materials and labor invested.

Shroud Wrap. The simplest procedure was to wrap the body in a plain cotton shroud and subsequently sew the shroud closed along the top of the bundle (Fig. 3). Sometimes the wrapping consisted of two textiles, an inner shroud and an outer shroud. In these cases the inner shroud was usually a finer weave than the outer shroud, and was sometimes decorated with a woven design. It was not sewn closed.

Splint reinforced. The body was encased in a shroud wrap. Wood or cane splints were then tied to the outside of the bundle, keeping the body rigid (Fig. 4).

Cane frame. The body was encased in a shroud wrap, and the completed bundle was then placed on a rigid cane frame. The bundle and frame were subsequently wrapped in another large textile that was sewn shut (Fig. 5).

Cane tube. The body was encased in a shroud wrap. The completed bundle was then wrapped in canes that previously had been twined together. The twined canes formed a tube around the bundle. The ends of the tube sometimes were closed with shallow gourd plates (Fig. 6).

A variation on the cane tube procedure was to wrap a mat around the shroud wrap, which was then tied with rope. Finally, the bundle was wrapped in the roll of canes, forming a tube (Fig. 7; nos. 285, 293).

One cane tube burial (no. 290) ultimately was wrapped along its length with sedge rope, creating an elaborate exterior pattern. Two others (nos. 289, 290) are said to have had a coarse cotton textile over the cane tube, but it is not clear whether these textiles actually were wrapped around the cane tubes as a final casing or if they simply were placed on top of the cane tubes.

Ceramic casing. The corpse was enclosed in two large, open mouth ceramic jars, positioned on their sides so the mouths of the jars were joined (no. 319). This formed a large egg-shaped enclosure (Fig. 8).[4]

---

[4] The reconstruction of this type of burial chamber is based on two sources: Larco's text and photograph of this type of tomb published in 1945 (no. 286), and the scale model of this tomb type that currently is on display in the Museo Rafael Larco Herrera in Lima. The placement of ceramic fragments around the mouths of the two jars is a detail specifically shown in the scale model.

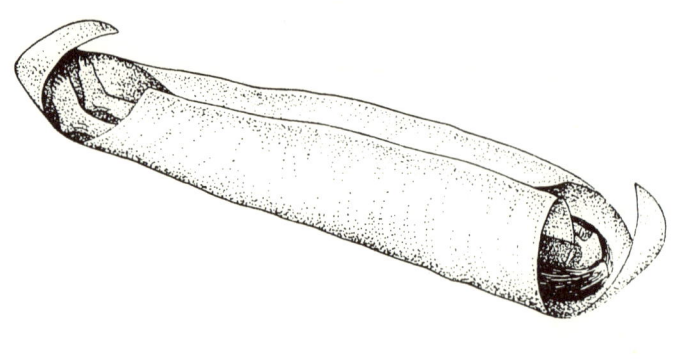

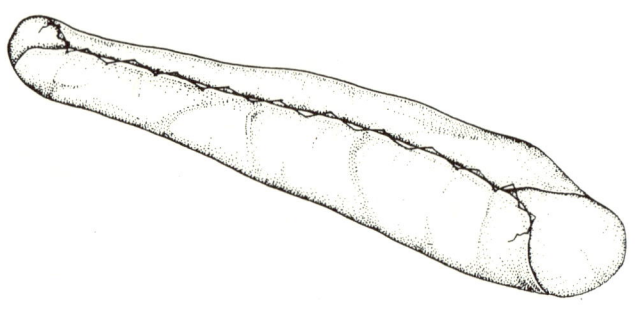

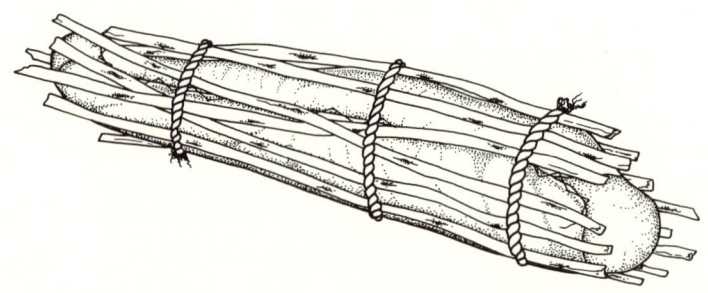

Fig. 4 Splint reinforced.

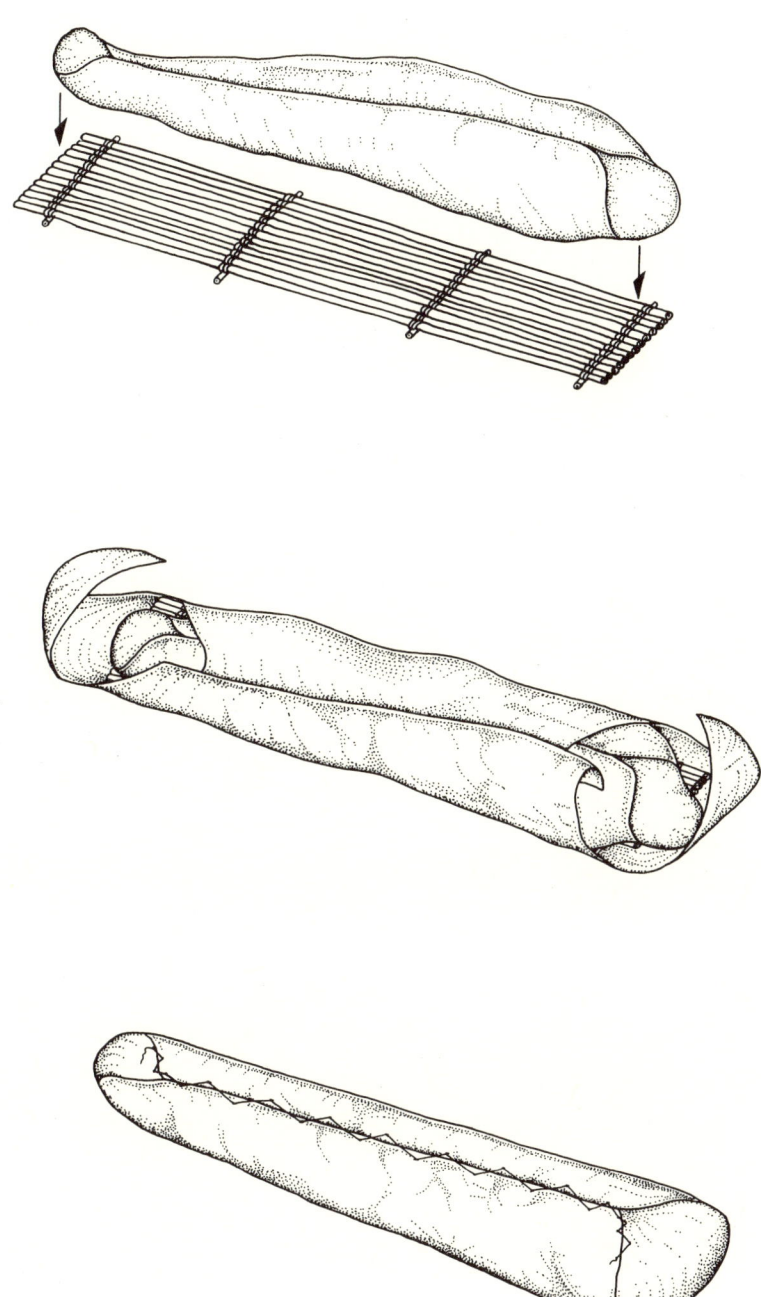

Fig. 5 Cane frame.

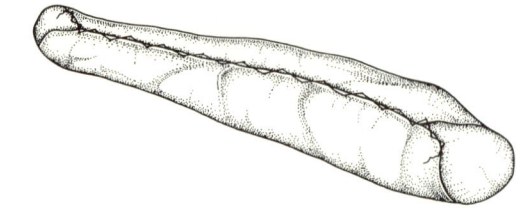

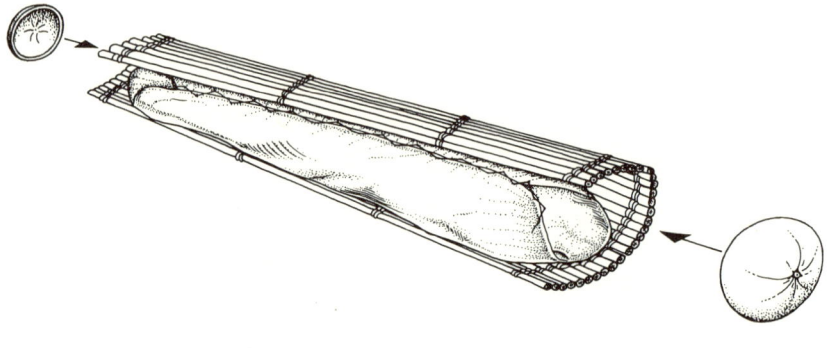

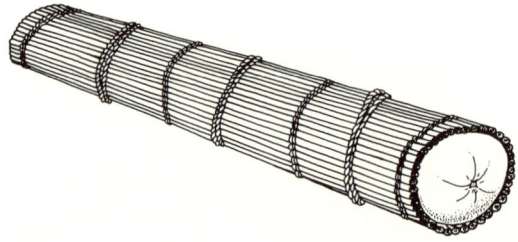

Fig. 6 Cane tube.

Moche Funerary Practice

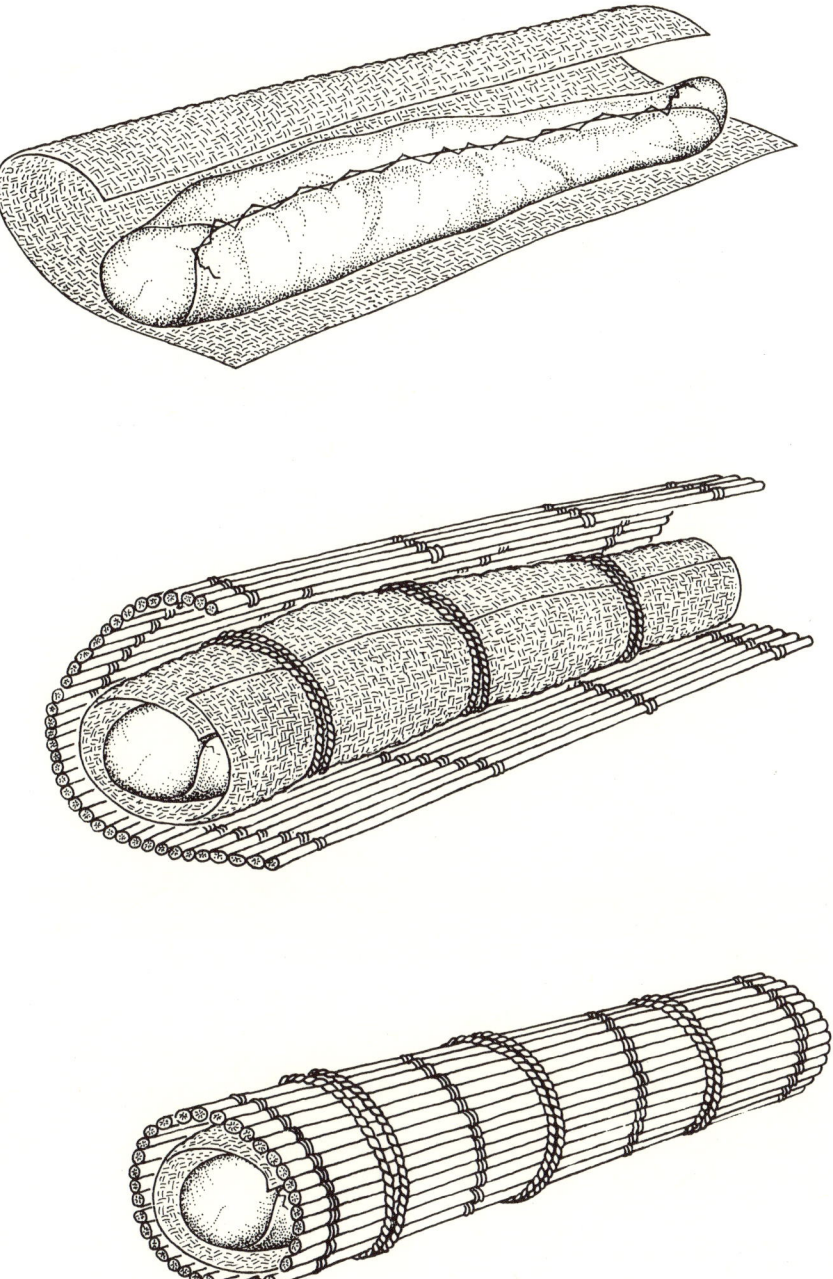

Fig. 7 Cane tube alternative.

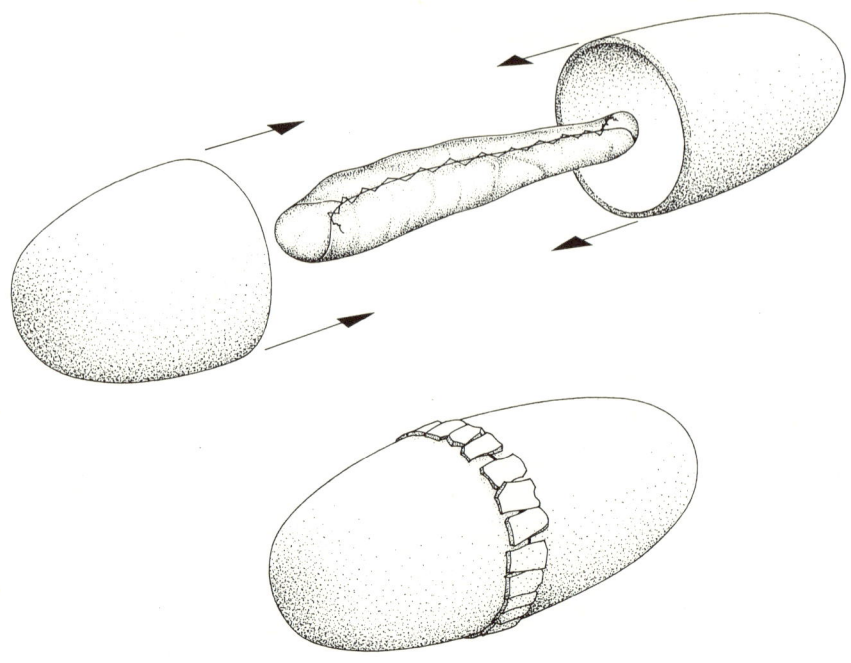

Fig. 8 Ceramic casing.

A variation on this procedure was to place the body inside a series of smaller stacked jars or cooking ollas with the bases broken out (no. 320). The horizontal stack of ceramic vessels formed a segmented casing around the body.

Another variation of ceramic casing was to place the corpse in a large, upright jar. Only one example of this procedure has been documented. It was the burial of an infant (no. 291).[5]

It is likely that the corpses in all ceramic casing burials were wrapped in shrouds, but in no instance have they been reported in sufficient detail for this to be documented.

Cane coffin. The body was encased in a shroud wrap. Then it was wrapped with a large cane frame that had been crimped to fold into four sections forming the sides, top, and bottom of a cane coffin (Fig. 9). The two ends of the coffin consisted of separate cane frames which were tied into

---

[5] William Strong and Clifford Evans (1952: 196) claim to have excavated a Moche urn burial at Castillo de Tomoval, Site 1. This burial was of an adult female sitting in a semiflexed position inside a large olla (Strong and Evans 1952: 107–108). There is no direct evidence, however, that this is a Moche burial.

Moche Funerary Practice

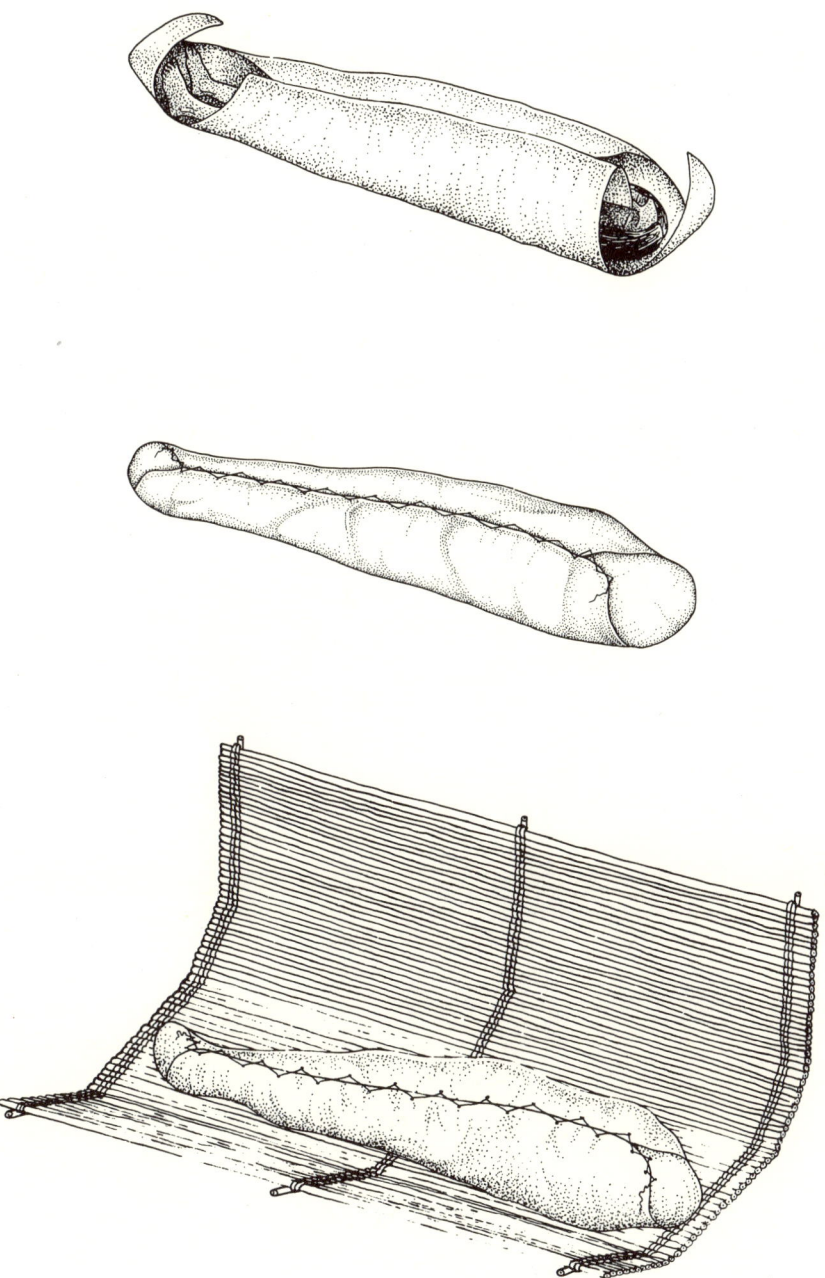

Fig. 9 Cane coffin.

Christopher B. Donnan

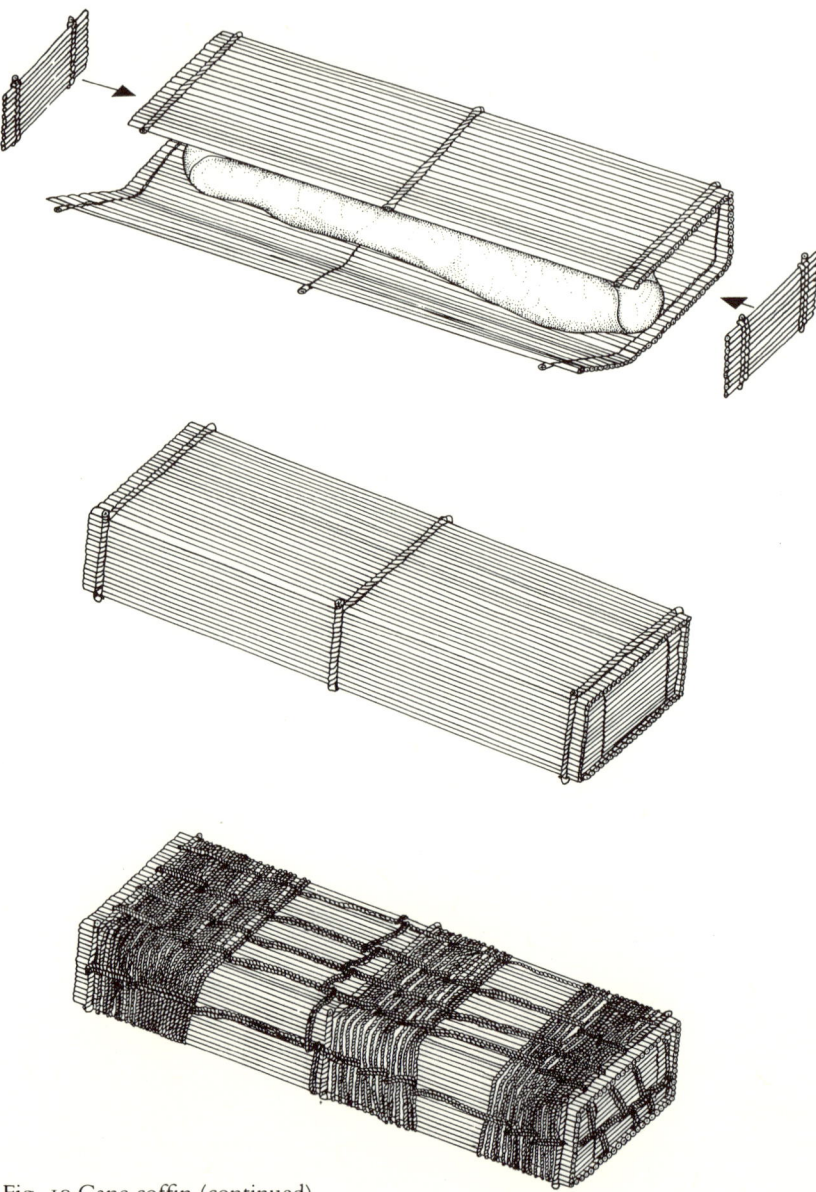

Fig. 10 Cane coffin (continued).

place as the larger frame was wrapped around the corpse (Fig. 10). In some cases, the cane coffin then was wrapped with rope, creating an elaborate pattern on the exterior surface.

A variation on the cane coffin procedure was to wrap the body first in a plain cotton textile and then wrap it in a mat. The mat wrapping was tied with rope and subsequently placed in the cane coffin (no. 294).

One burial has been reported in which an adult and a child were wrapped individually in cotton textiles and then put in a single cane coffin (nos. 294, 297). The adult was placed on the bottom, with the child above. They were separated by a cane mat that was placed on top of the adult bundle. In this instance, once the lid was closed and tied shut, the coffin was covered with another textile wrapping.

Plank coffin. Only two examples of this type have been excavated (nos. 4, 12), and neither was sufficiently well preserved so that the precise wrapping of the corpse could be reconstructed. Both examples, however, had evidence of a rigid wood frame placed under the corpse (Fig. 11), similar to the cane frame burial treatment illustrated in Figure 5. It is assumed that the body was wrapped first in a large textile and placed on the frame, and that both the frame and bundle were then wrapped a second time. This created a larger bundle which subsequently was placed inside the plank coffin.

Plank coffins were made of large wood planks tied together with copper straps (Fig. 11). The straps tied the planks at the corners of the coffin, and midway along each of its sides. Although the precise sequence for assembling the coffins could not be reconstructed, they appear to have been tied together in situ with the corpse inside rather than fabricated elsewhere and transported to the burial site already assembled (Walter Alva, personal communication, 1990).

It is possible that some corpses were buried without a wrapping, ceramic casing, or coffin—essentially placed nude in a burial chamber. However, there is no good archaeological evidence for this. Nor is there any evidence for a corpse being buried wearing clothing, but not wrapped or placed in a coffin. It was not unusual to include garments and headdresses inside the wrapping or coffin, but in only a few instances was the corpse wearing them. In most cases, the body was not dressed, but simply wrapped in textiles. The wrapping of the body is so universal in the sample of well-preserved Moche burials that it seems probable that it was a standard aspect of Moche funerary practice.

The seven procedures for encasing the corpse probably correlate to economic and social status as well as age. Infants and young children normally were buried with shroud wrap, splint reinforced, and ceramic casing burial procedures, and tended to have few, if any, objects accompanying them. When adults were buried with the shroud wrap procedure, they also had

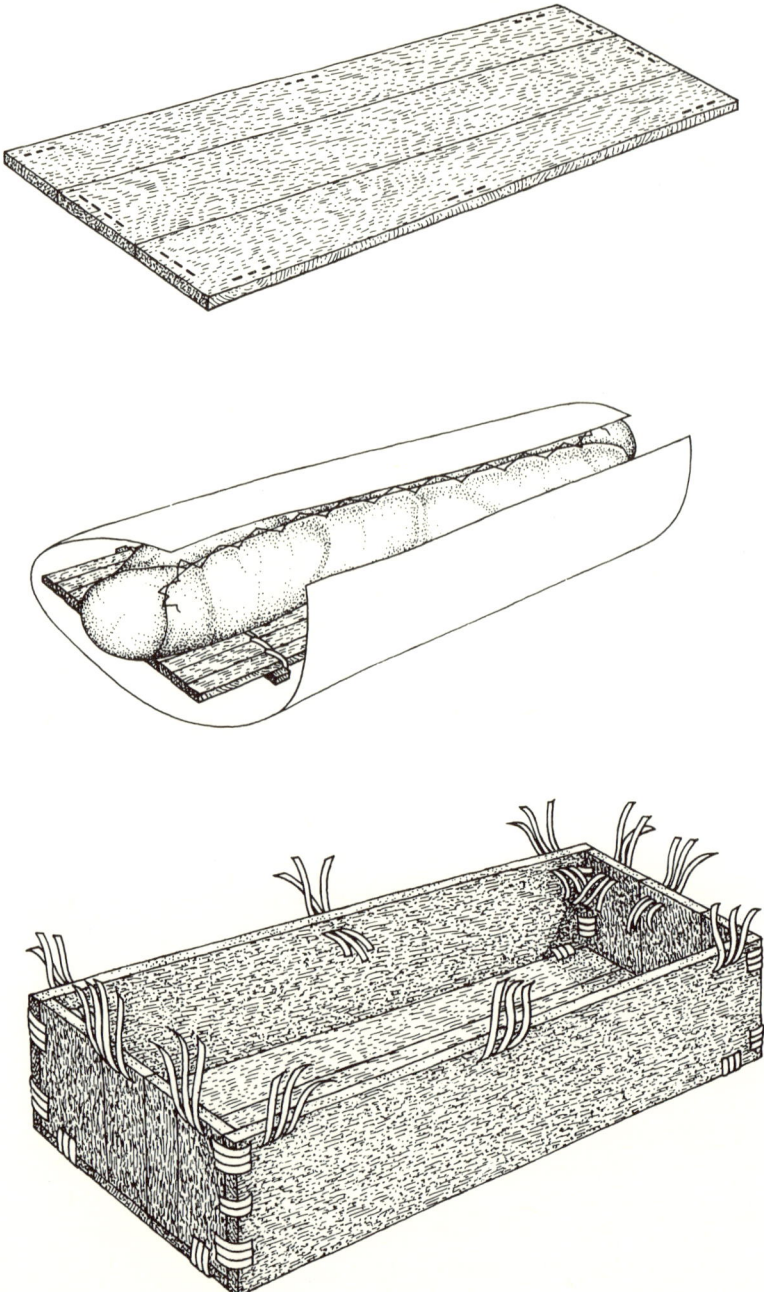

Fig. 11 Plank coffin.

few, if any, objects accompanying them, and the objects were generally of poor quality.

Cane frame, crane wrap, and cane tube burial procedures normally were used for burial of individuals older than 15 years of age and generally had more grave goods than shroud wrap, splint reinforced, and ceramic casing burials. This is particularly true of cane tube burials, some of which were accompanied by a remarkable quantity and quality of grave goods (e.g., no. 285).

Cane coffin burials were exclusively those of adults and invariably were accompanied by numerous grave goods, many of which were more elaborate and/or better crafted than those found in the simpler burials.

The two plank coffin burials that have been excavated are clearly of adult males of the highest social rank. They contained great quantities of grave goods, including gold, silver, and copper jewelry. They also contained retainer burials in cane coffins.

Funerary Chambers

There are four types of funerary chambers. These range from a simple shallow pit to a large room-like funerary vault. As with the procedures for encasing the corpse, the sequential types of funerary chambers reflect an increase in the amount of both raw materials and labor invested.

Simple pit. The most rudimentary form of burial chamber is a simple pit. It is generally rectangular or oval-shaped; the floor is flat or slightly concave. The pits are generally not much larger than the bundles, ceramic casings, or coffins that were placed in them, and are generally rather shallow—from 40 to 100 cm deep.

Simple pits were always used for bodies prepared with shroud wrap, splint reinforced, ceramic casing, and cane frame burial procedures. Bodies with cane tube and cane coffin burial procedures also were found occasionally in simple pits.

Boot-shaped chambers. Some Moche graves have been found in shaft tombs consisting of a vertical shaft with an enlarged chamber at the bottom, making them boot-shaped in profile (Fig. 12). To date, this form has been well documented only for Moche graves excavated at Pacatnamu and San José de Moro in the lower part of the Jequetepeque Valley.[6] Some boot-shaped chambers which were intended for burial of a single body are small and rather shallow. The vertical shaft is from 90 to 170 cm deep, and the chamber at the bottom of the shaft is from 80 to 210 cm long, 40 to 150 cm

---

[6] A possible occurrence of Moche boot-shaped chamber tombs has been reported from the Vicus area in the Piura Valley (Horkheimer 1965; Matos 1965–66). However, there is no direct evidence that the Moche ceramics from this area were actually found in tombs of this type.

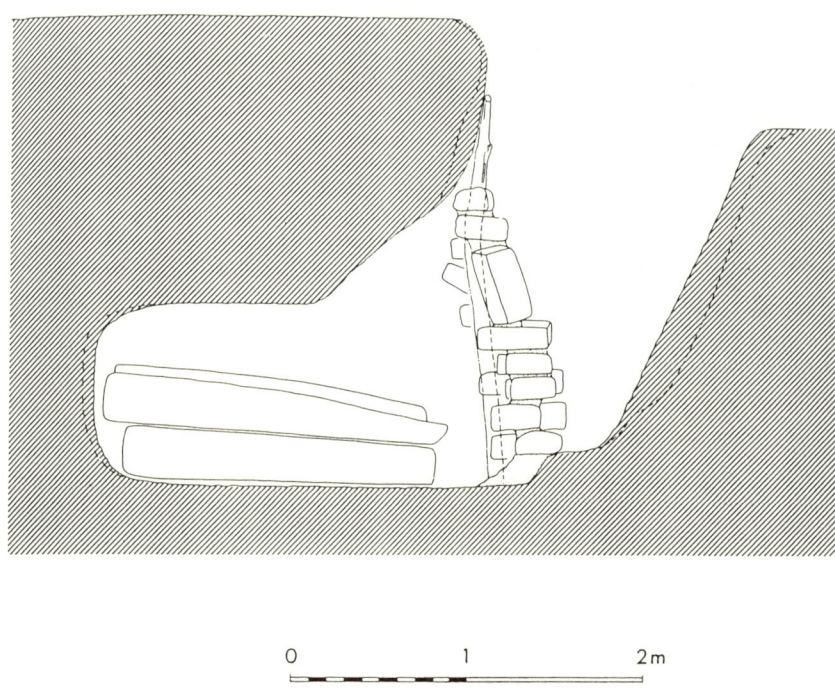

Fig. 12 Boot-shaped chamber (nos. 74–85; after Ubbelohde-Doering 1983: 55).

wide, and 60 to 110 cm high. The chamber normally is sealed from the base of the shaft by an irregular wall of mud bricks.

Larger and deeper boot-shaped chambers have been reported. They appear to have been used for multiple burials. The best reports on these are from Pacatnamu (Ubbelohde-Doering 1959, 1967, 1983) and San José de Moro (Donnan and Castillo n.d.). The largest (nos. 74–85) had a shaft approximately 2.5 m deep, providing access to the burial chamber which was approximately 2 m long and 3 m wide. An irregular wall made of wood beams and mud bricks sealed the chamber at the bottom of the shaft (Fig. 12). Inside the chamber was a stack of nine cane coffins and a large assortment of grave contents (Fig. 13). Three other shaft tombs also contained multiple burials. One (nos. 91–96) had a wall of plastered reed and mud bricks separating the shaft from the chamber. The walls of the others (nos. 31–33, 75–85) were only mud bricks.

Rectangular chamber. This type of tomb was constructed by two distinct methods. The simpler method was to remove mud bricks from a mud-brick pyramid or large mud-brick platform to create the rectangular chamber

Moche Funerary Practice

Fig. 13 Inside boot-shaped chamber (nos. 74–85; after Ubbelohde-Doering 1967: 62).

(Donnan and Mackey 1978: 101–157). The more complex method involved excavating a rectangular-shaped pit and lining the walls with rocks (Fig. 14) or mud bricks (Fig. 15) set in mud mortar. All rectangular chambers appear to have been roofed with cane or wood beams.

There is considerable variation in the size of rectangular chambers. Most of them contain only a single burial and vary from 180 to 230 cm in length, from 70 to 110 cm in width, and from 50 to 95 cm in height. The largest rectangular chambers contain between five and seven individuals, and are the most elaborate Moche tombs that have ever been excavated. Two of them (nos. 4, 12) contained a principal burial in a plank coffin, surrounded by retainer burials in cane coffins. One of these two was approximately 4 × 4 m in area, and approximately 3.5 m deep (no. 4; Fig. 16).

Niches are found in many of the rectangular chambers (Fig. 17). In the smaller examples, made for one body, there are from one to three niches on the sides and sometimes one niche at the head of the chamber (nos. 28, 191, 192). The larger tombs containing multiple burials had from two to six

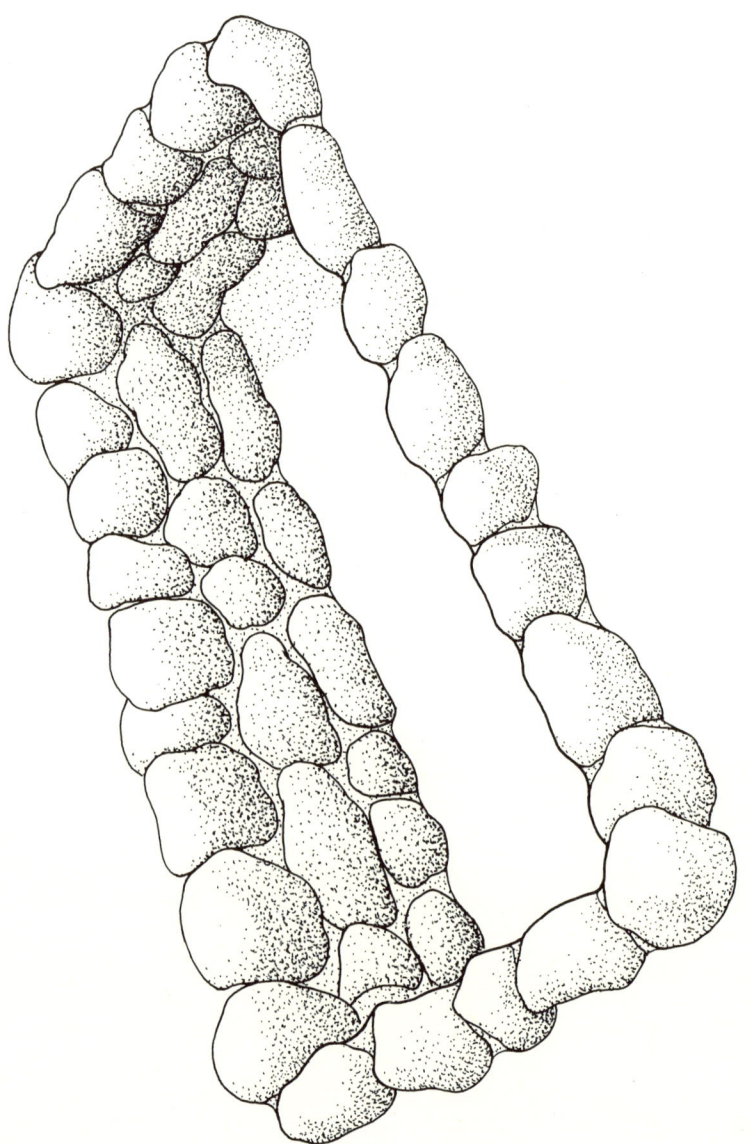

Fig. 14 Rectangular chamber lined with rocks.

Moche Funerary Practice

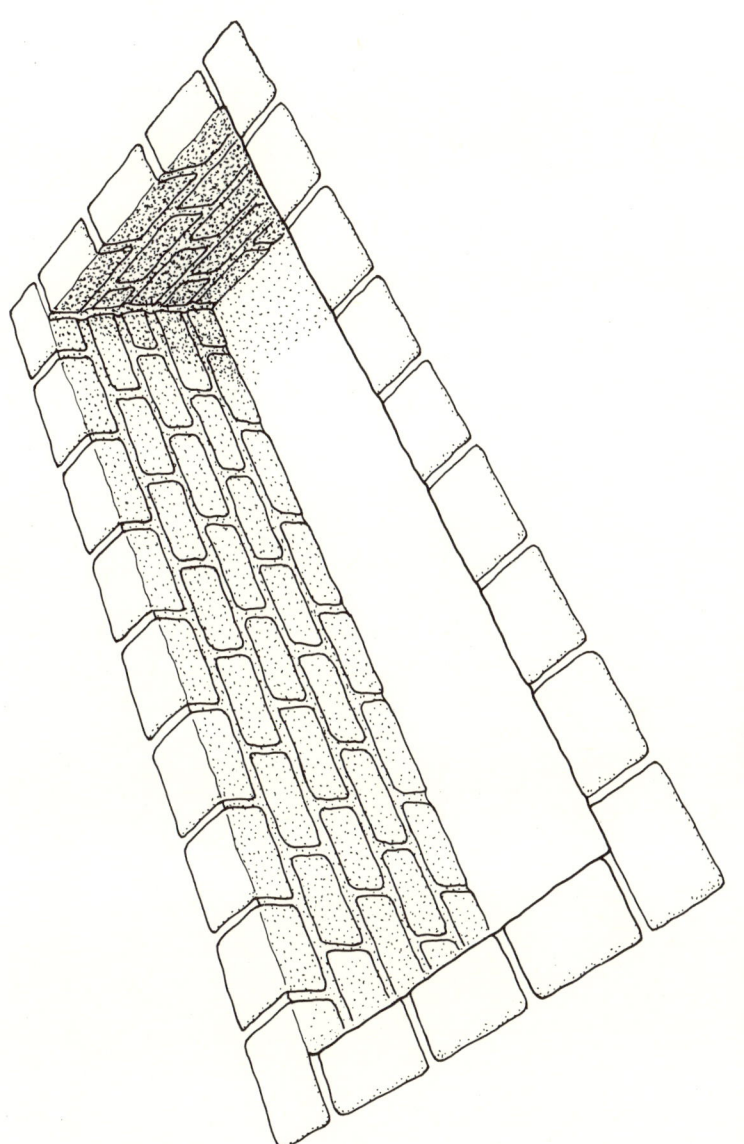

Fig. 15 Rectangular chamber lined with mud bricks.

Christopher B. Donnan

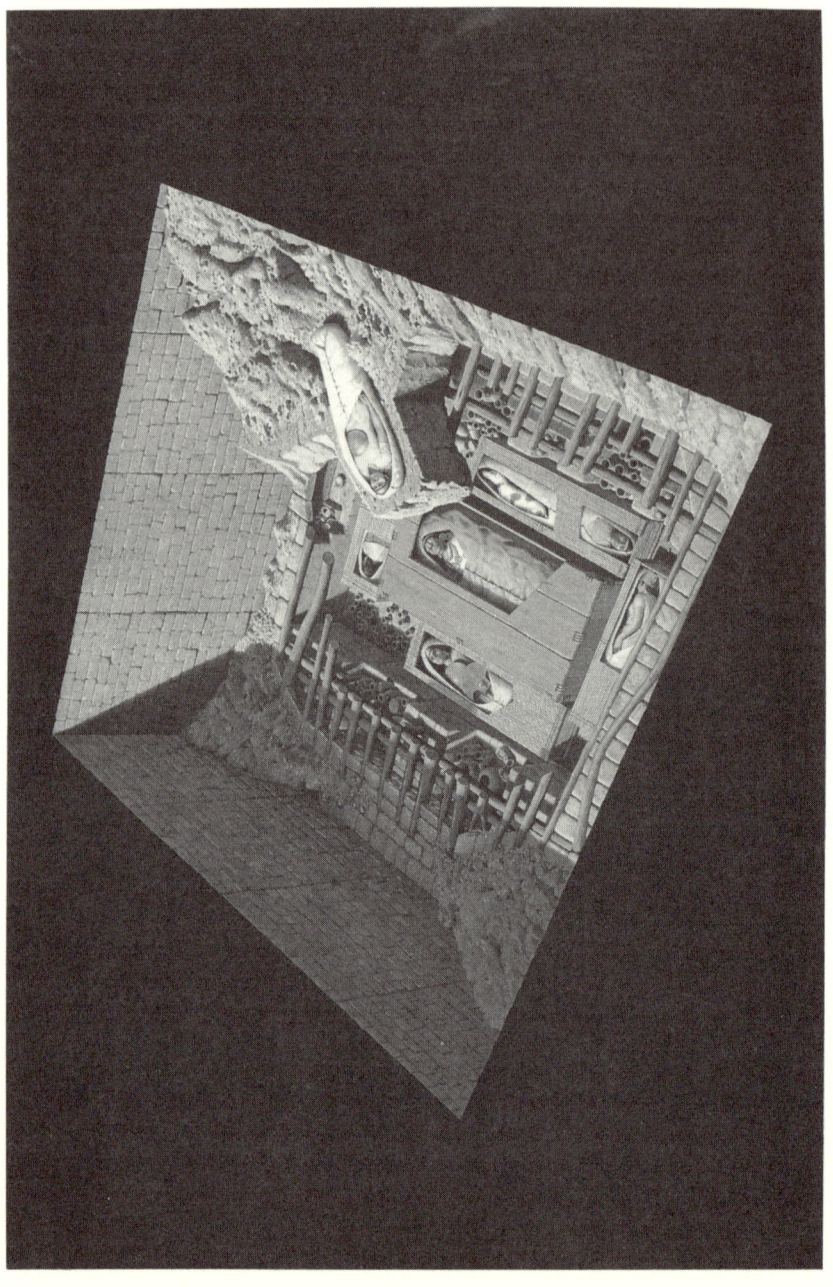

Moche Funerary Practice

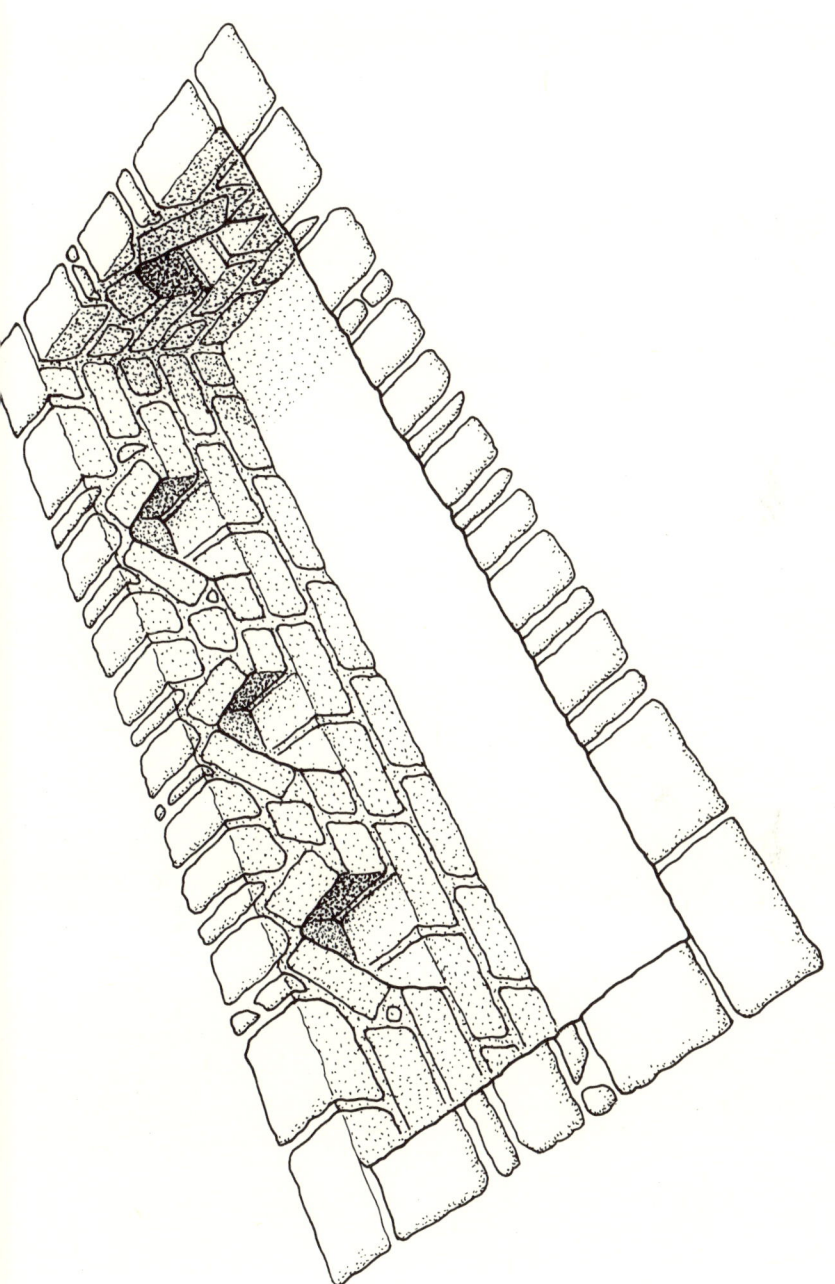

Fig. 17 Rectangular chamber with niches.

niches on each side, and from one to four niches at the head of the chamber. The greatest number ever recorded from a single tomb (nos. 55–59) was 16—six on each side and four at the head of the chamber. No tomb has been recorded with a niche at the foot of the chamber. The niches sometimes contained ceramics, llama bones, copper, and/or clay architectural models. Sometimes a niche was left empty.

One other example of a Moche tomb with a very large rectangular chamber was looted by grave robbers in the lower Jequetepeque Valley at the site of La Mina (no. 28; Narvaez 1989). It was constructed by digging a large pit at the base of a conical hill overlooking the valley floor. Inside the pit, a room was built with mud bricks. It was approximately 3 × 2 m in area, and approximately 4 m deep. There were no niches in the sides of the room, but all four sides had been plastered and painted with colorful geometric murals. The room was roofed with large wood beams approximately 2 m above its plastered floor. Above the beams was a dome-shaped pile of rock and gravel that effectively served to seal the tomb from above.

One final aspect of Moche funerary chambers that should be considered is the presence or absence of grave markers. Larco (1945: 51) states that Moche graves were marked with canes that connected to the mouth of the deceased in order to continue offering the person food and drink. However, he provides no examples of this practice. A cane grave marker was noted by Strong and Evans in their excavations of a grave (no. 287) at Huaca de la Cruz in the Viru Valley. It was reported to have been a "heavy bamboo-like cane, 9 centimeters in diameter . . . above and to the right of the head and not over the face" (Strong and Evans 1952: 141). Five other burials at the same site (nos. 282–284, 288, 293) had vertical wood posts above them. In most instances, the vertical posts were at or near the head end of the burial. The wood posts in three of the graves (nos. 283, 288, 293) were *algarroba*. It is not known whether the cane and wood posts were actually grave markers, or if they served some symbolic meaning, such as permitting contact with the deceased.

Quantity and Quality of Grave Goods

There is a considerable range in both the quantity and quality of objects placed in Moche graves. To some extent this is due to differences in preservation—only a few graves are sufficiently well preserved that the full range of their goods can be identified. Often, it is only the objects of ceramic, stone, and bone that survive. Nevertheless, on the basis of evidence currently available, various observations can be made about the objects that the Moche considered appropriate for placement in burials.

Ceramic vessels are the most commonly found artifacts in Moche graves. The number of ceramic vessels in a single grave varies considerably. Twenty-eight graves have been reported that did not contain any ceramic vessels. There were 83 ceramic vessels in a burial (no. 268) at the Pyramids at Moche. Most burials, however, have fewer than five ceramic vessels. In general, the graves of adult males contain more ceramics than those of females, and the graves of children contain the fewest.

The inventory of ceramic objects tends to vary from grave to grave in terms of the relative percentage of vessel forms such as stirrup spout bottles, flaring bowls, and jars. There appears to be no clear distinction in the frequency of vessel forms found in the graves of males as opposed to females or adults as opposed to children.[7] This suggests that there were no standards regarding an appropriate inventory of ceramic forms.

For the most part, the variety of ceramic objects is directly proportional to the number of ceramic objects; apparently, a variety of vessel forms in the grave was preferable to multiple examples of a limited number of forms. There are, however, exceptions to this, such as a burial of a male and female together (nos. 229, 230) which contained 35 plain jars, one modeled jar, and one stirrup spout bottle.

In many Moche graves, one can observe a propensity for pairing ceramic vessels: pairs of jars, pairs of flaring bowls, pairs of stirrup spout bottles, etc. While this is not adhered to slavishly such that the entire inventory of vessels can be divided into pairs, it does appear to account for many of the vessels included in a given burial.[8]

In most graves, there is no obvious correlation between the iconography of ceramic vessels in a burial and the role or status of the deceased. In the burial of one infant (no. 306), for example, there was a spout and handle bottle depicting an adult male riding a llama, and in a burial of a woman and child together (nos. 242, 243), there was a jar in the form of a prisoner.

In a few instances, however, the iconography does appear to relate directly to the role and status of the individual. Perhaps the best example of this is a burial of an adult male (no. 239) who was buried with a disk headdress identical to those worn in the Bean Runner ceremony (Fig. 18; Larco 1942: 93–103; 1943: 1–36). He was also buried with a bottle painted with a scene of Bean Runners.

Gourd containers are found in nearly all Moche burials with good preservation of organic materials. Most of these were cups, bowls, and plates (Fig. 19a–c), generally ranging in size from 10 to 20 cm in diameter and 2 to 7 cm in depth. Bottle-shaped gourd containers were also found (Fig. 19d), rang-

---

[7] Strong and Evans (1952: 201) suggest that there may be some correlation between stirrup spout bottles with chambers in the form of jars, and burials of women. In their sample from Huaca de la Cruz in the Viru Valley, all four ceramic vessels of this form were associated with women (nos. 287, 288, 296, 297). However, in the sample from the Moche Valley, this form occurs in three burials of men (nos. 230, 235, 239).

[8] In one instance (no. 219), a pair of vessels consists of two from the same mold. One of the pair is well made, painted, polished, and fired, while the other is significantly inferior in quality.

Christopher B. Donnan

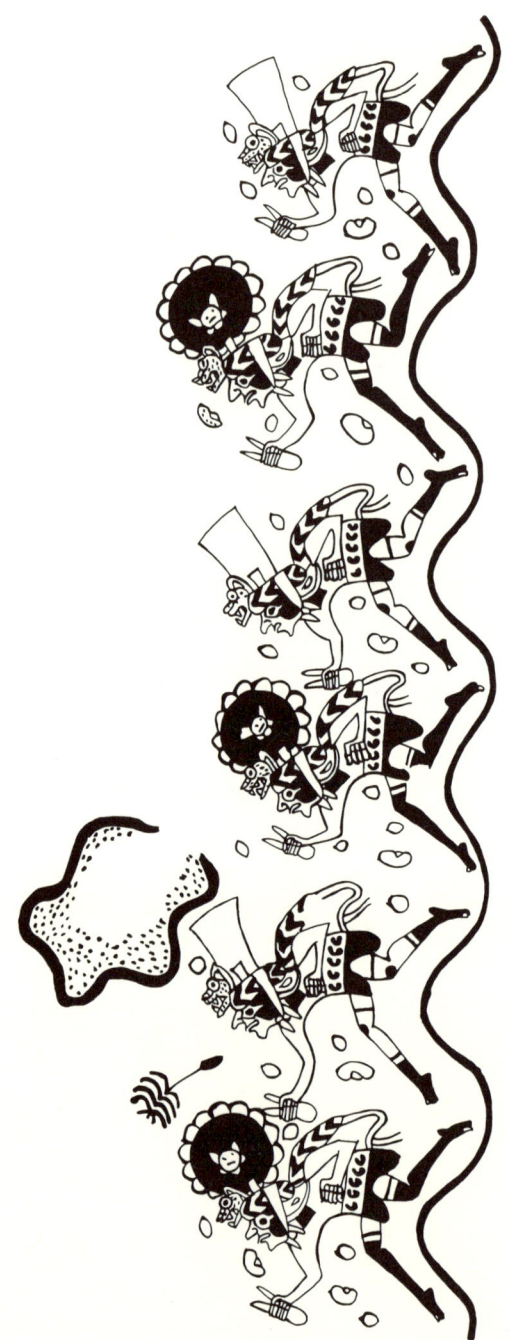

Fig. 18 The Bean Runner Ceremony.

Moche Funerary Practice

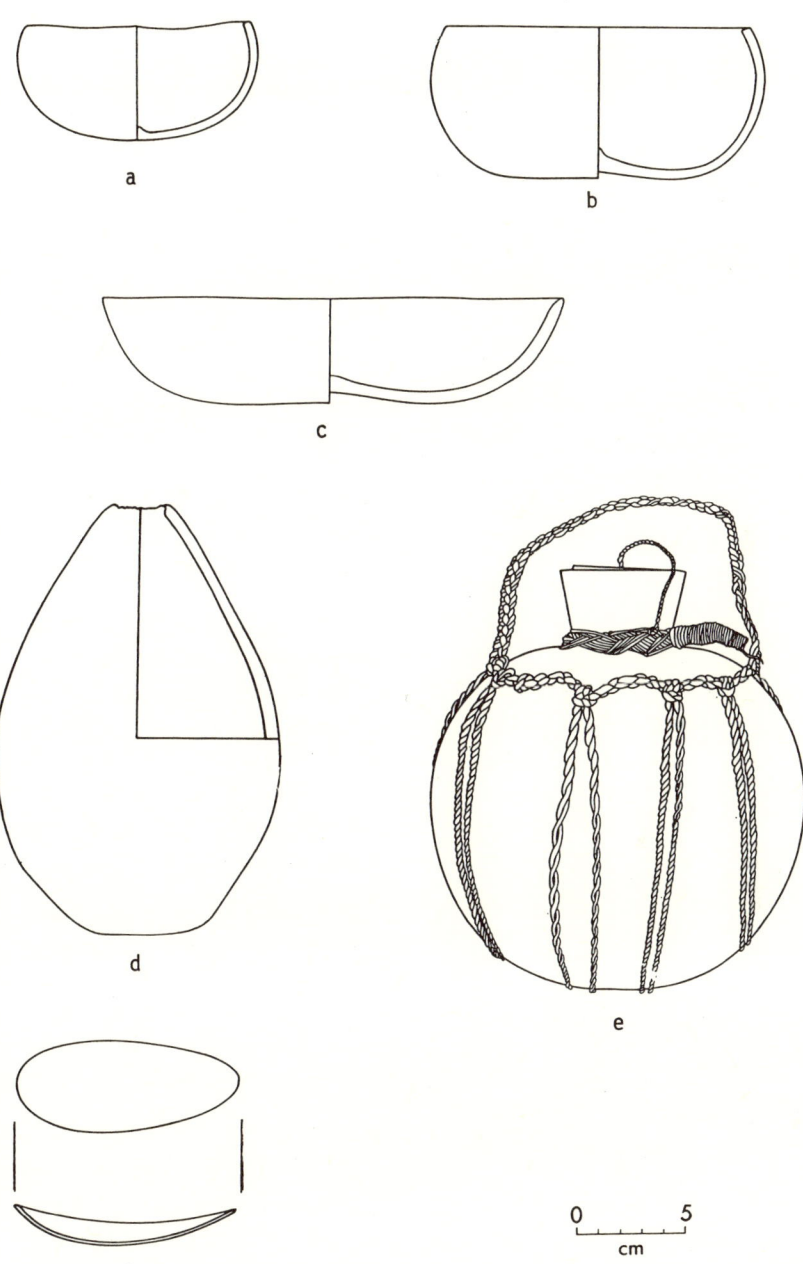

Fig. 19 Gourds from Moche burials.

ing from 9 to 15 cm in height, and 4 to 8 cm in diameter. One gourd container was a jar with a stopper (Fig. 19e), which had a carrying harness of sedge rope. Two graves (nos. 121, 291) contained shallow gourd spoons (Fig. 19f).

The bowls and plates were often empty, but sometimes contained corn, beans, cotton seeds, edible seaweed, whole fish, or llama bones. Sometimes the gourds were turned upside down on top of bottles or jars to serve as lids. Bowls and plates were also very often turned upside down over the face of the deceased or used to cover other parts of the body. This occurred with burials of both sexes and all ages. Sometimes gourds were inside the burial shrouds; in other cases they were put on top of the textile wrappings. Many burials were found with the head resting in a shallow gourd plate.

Plants other than gourds are seldom recovered and are only found in graves that have good preservation. They are normally placed in gourd or ceramic containers, although in a few cases corn cobs have been found wrapped in textiles (no. 160), yarn (no. 160), or cotton (no. 174). The most common plant remains are maize (almost always on the cob), beans, peanuts, and edible seaweed. Less commonly found are the seeds of squash, lucuma, and gourd as well as the remains of chili peppers, and avocados (Gumerman n.d.). There was no consistent combination of plants selected, and in no instance were large quantities of plant foods recovered. Generally there was scarcely enough plant food in a grave to provide a small meal.

Animals, both complete and partial, were found in many of the Moche graves that have been excavated, including those of men, women, and children. The most frequently identified animals are llamas—perhaps because their bones are large and tend to be preserved when smaller skeletal materials may have decomposed or been overlooked during the excavation. In simple graves with few grave goods, only parts of the llamas were found, most frequently the skull, scapulae, lower legs, feet, and teeth.[9] When one considers how little meat is on these parts of the llama, it would appear that they were not placed in the graves because of their food value. The animal parts are generally found outside the textile wrappings, but can be either inside or outside of the cane tubes or coffins. A common offering of llama parts consists of the four lower legs (with toes) and the head. These are stacked alongside the human corpse.

In the most elaborate Moche burials, whole llamas (nos. 4–11, 12–18, 34–40, 44–50, 287), or llamas with only the head missing (nos. 293–297) are sometimes found. Normally these are associated with burials in large rectangular chambers (nos. 4–11, 12–18, 34–40, 44–50), or burials that have cane coffins with large quantities of grave goods (nos. 293–297). Occasionally the llamas are wrapped in textiles (no. 125). Elaborate Moche burials also

---

[9] In one instance (no. 118), ribs were found.

Moche Funerary Practice

have parts of butchered llamas. In contrast to simple Moche graves, however, they normally have parts with substantial quantities of meat: upper legs, ribs, and neck.

Other than llama bones, animal skeletal material is rarely reported from Moche burials. Only two burials (nos. 118, 231) were found to contain guinea pig bones, and unidentified small animal bones were found in another (nos. 205–208). Fish were found in several burials at Pacatnamu (nos. 74–85, 109, 112) and fish skin was found on one of the cane coffin burials (no. 76). Two burials (nos. 6, 55–59) contained a dog, and another (no. 149) contained a dog skull. One (no. 74) contained the skull of a sea lion, another (no. 57) a sea lion scapula, and one contained a snake (no. 16).

Metal objects are frequently found in Moche graves, but only the graves of people of high status contain metal in quantity. Lower-status burials generally contain only copper objects; those of higher status may include objects of gilded copper, silver, and gold. Only the highest status graves (nos. 4, 12, 19, 28, 55) have an abundance of gold and silver objects. Copper objects were generally bent or broken prior to placement in the graves, while objects of gold and silver were generally not damaged.

When only a few objects of metal were put in the grave, they were generally placed in the mouth and hands of the deceased. Sometimes they were also placed near the feet. These were normally folded metal sheets, broken or bent implements or ornaments, or amorphous lumps of metal (often whole or partial ingots). They often had textile fragments, yarn, or unspun cotton fiber around them, and sometimes were held in place with multiple wrappings of yarn.

Metal sandals were worn by the deceased in two of the highest status adult male graves at Sipán (nos. 4, 12). Other pairs are reported from high-status graves at Pacatnamu (no. 97) and Moro (no. 55). In more modest burials (nos. 287, 292) small sheets of copper were placed against the bottom of the feet. Perhaps these were meant to be the equivalent of the sandals in the more elaborate burials.

Several Moche graves, including those of men, women, and children, were reported to have a metal mask over the face. Sometimes it was simply a sheet of copper (nos. 287, 292). In other instances (nos. 237, 238, 239, 245, 297) it was a large circular copper disk of the type frequently depicted being worn as a headdress by Bean Runners (Fig. 20). In one grave (no. 4), the lower part of the face and neck was covered with a mask of gold.

In tombs where there were often multiple sets of elaborate gold, silver, and gilded copper jewelry, the objects generally were placed in the vicinity of the body where they would have been worn. Thus headdresses, nose ornaments, and ear ornaments were placed over and around the head. Necklaces and pectorals were placed near the neck and upper torso, rattles and spatulas near the hands, bells and warrior backflaps near the waist, and

Christopher B. Donnan

Fig. 20 The Sacrifice Ceremony.

Moche Funerary Practice

metal sandals near the feet. Armaments, such as war clubs, *atl-atls,* and darts were generally placed parallel to the body, either above it or at the sides.

Jewelry in Moche culture consisted basically of ear ornaments, nose ornaments, necklaces, and bracelets. Ear ornaments are not found in the graves of infants or children, but are common in the graves of both male and female adults. They are found in a great variety of sizes, forms, and raw materials. The sample of ear ornaments that has been recorded from graves does not indicate that specific types were associated exclusively with males or females. However, the ear ornaments in simple graves tended to be made of wood or bone, and contain inlay of shell, iron pyrite, and malachite, while the more elaborate graves tended to have earspools of gold, silver, and copper, with inlay that often included turquoise, lapis lazuli, *Spondylus,* and gold.

Nose ornaments are much less common than ear ornaments and appear to be found only in the burials of adult males of high status. All nose ornaments are made of gold, silver, and copper. The most elaborate nose ornaments often combine gold and silver, and are inlaid with shell and semiprecious stone.

Necklaces and bracelets are quite varied. The most elaborate bracelets are of sheet gold with superbly crafted repoussé designs, or thousands of tiny turquoise beads on multiple strings that are kept evenly spaced by gold spacer bars. The most elaborate necklaces consist of large gold or silver beads which have been exquisitely fashioned in the form of feline, human, or deity heads. Some necklaces consist of thousands of small beads of shell, stone, or metal that have been strung on multiple strings to form large pectorals to cover the chest and shoulders of the wearer.

Bracelets and necklaces are found in the graves of both males and females, but tend to be associated only with individuals of high status. Many of the infants and children in the sample were found with a "bead string" tied around their wrists and neck. In contrast to the adult jewelry, these consist of three to 30 beads, generally of varying size, color, and material, that are strung in a random sequence. They may have been used to amuse or entertain the child. With the exception of the burial shroud, a bead string around the wrist or neck is the artifact most commonly associated with infant and child burials.

Headdresses and headcloths are reported from several burials of adults, but not from burials of children. One of the high-status tombs at Sipán (no. 4) contained three headdresses, while another (no. 12) contained only one. Two of the retainer burials at Sipán (nos. 6, 7) also contained headdresses. A major tomb at Huaca de la Cruz in the Viru Valley (no. 294) contained at least five headdresses, and four burials (nos. 237, 238, 239, 245) at the Pyramids at Moche each contained one headdress.

Headcloths were identified on three adult males from Pacatnamu (nos. 78, 163, 97). These consisted of a large openweave fabric with an elaborate tapestry weave border. Two adult burials from Pacatnamu had caps. One of these (no. 66) was made of fibers and the other (no. 81) of reeds.

Spinning and weaving implements were often placed in graves of females, but were found in only one male grave (no. 231). One infant burial (no. 41) and one juvenile burial (no. 62) contained spindle whorls, but in all other instances they were found in burials of adults. In most instances their position suggests that they were on wood spindles when they were placed in the graves. When there was good preservation of organic materials, complete spindles and yarn were recovered. Fifteen wooden spindles and several balls of yarn were found in a large gourd bowl in one grave (no. 288). In another (no. 287), two weaving baskets were found, one of which contained several spindles and a few strands of cotton.

A very elaborate burial of a woman with a remarkable array of grave goods (no. 291) contained a weaving basket with three spindles, two needles, and a gourd spoon. A mass of unspun cotton had been placed in a large gourd bowl, and an elaborately carved weaving staff was resting on the woman's pelvis and chest. These weaving implements, found in what appears to be the grave of a high-status woman, suggest that spinning and weaving were not activities restricted to the middle and lower classes, but were also practiced by the elite.

Fishing implements frequently were found in the burials at Pacatnamu, but are not reported from burials at any other site. The most common implement was a *mallero,* a flat rectangular object of bone, stone, or wood that is used in tying fishing nets to maintain a consistent mesh size. These appear to have been as exclusive to male graves as weaving implements were to women's graves.

Net sinkers were found in two graves (nos. 62, 72), which were presumably of women since they also contained spindle whorls. A copper fishhook also was found in the burial of an adult female (no. 127).

Sacrificed humans were found in several of the burials in the sample. A well-documented instance of this is the elaborate tomb of a man and child at Huaca de la Cruz (nos. 293–297). This tomb included the bodies of two adult females (nos. 295, 296) who appear to have been sacrificed.[10] Their bodies were shoved into the spaces just beyond the head and foot of the coffin containing the principal figure.

At Huanchaco, an adult male (no. 205) was buried with three extra human hands. Two of the hands apparently had been removed from an adult female (no. 206) whose dismembered body was buried in a flexed position above his burial chamber. The third hand came from a second victim whose body was not present.

---

[10] One of the women (no. 295) had a cotton sash wrapped around her neck, possibly indicating strangulation (Strong and Evans 1952: 152).

Moche Funerary Practice

In a large tomb at Pacatnamu, Heinrich Ubbelohde-Doering found the skeletons of three persons (nos. 83, 84, 85) that he believed had been sacrificed. In the same tomb he found a human skull wrapped in a textile, and inside one of the cane coffins (no. 77 or 78) was the skull of a child. In another tomb at Pacatnamu were four individuals that presumably were sacrificed (nos. 92, 93, 95, 96). One of these (no. 93) was a small child (Hecker and Hecker 1992).

The placement of sacrificed females in elaborate Moche tombs does not appear to have antecedents in the cultures of northern Peru, and thus may have been innovated by the Moche. It appears to be the precedent for elaborate Chimu tombs that contained a high-status male buried with numerous females (Conrad n.d.; Pozorski n.d.). It is not known who the sacrificed females were, nor their relationship to the principal male. In Inka culture, however, it is said that some of a noble's wives and servants sometimes were killed and buried with him (Cobo 1964: 274–275).

Multiple Burials. In addition to the Moche graves containing what appear to be sacrificed humans, there are a number of instances where two or more individuals appear simply to have been buried together. These multiple burials take many forms, and probably resulted from a variety of circumstances. The most elaborate Moche burials, those in deep boot-shaped chambers and large rectangular chambers, are always multiple. The best documented tombs of this type are the large rectangular chambers at Sipán (nos. 4–11, 12–18) and San José de Moro (nos. 34–40, 44–50, 55–59). Each of these tombs contained the body of a principal figure—an adult male or female, and in one case a child—with between five and seven secondary individuals.

In some instances, it is clear that the secondary individuals had been dead for a considerable time before being placed in the grave. Their bones, particularly in the torso, were disarticulated and jumbled, indicating that the bodies had been moved *after* decomposition (Verano n.d.: 12–15). This strongly implies that the bodies of these individuals had been kept for a considerable time before being placed in the high-status tomb. Their relationship to the primary individual is not clear. Perhaps they died or were sacrificed at different times during his lifetime. It is also possible that they were not of his generation, but had died before he was born. Nevertheless, the practice of keeping a corpse for some time and later burying it along with another clearly was practiced by the Moche, and may have been fairly common.[11]

---

[11] Some of the individuals in multiple burials whose bones were not jumbled also may have been dead long before the others they were buried with, but well-preserved soft tissue and/or careful handling of the body as it was transported to the grave maintained the bones in their natural position. It is also likely that disarticulation and jumbling of the bones has often gone unnoticed by the archaeologists excavating Moche burials.

Multiple burials do not occur exclusively in the most elaborate Moche tombs. They have also been noted in more modest burials, including simple interments of what were apparently common people. There are three instances of an adult male and an adult female buried together (nos. 32, 33; 230, 231; 181, 182). Two of these burials (nos. 32, 33, and 181, 182) contained an infant as well. In most other cases, the multiple burial is of one adult with either a child, an infant, or one or more fetuses. There are three instances of adult males buried with children (nos. 299, 300; 194, 195; 294, 297), one of a male buried with two fetuses (nos. 205, 206, 207), one of a female and a fetus (nos. 106, 108), two of a female buried with a child (nos. 143, 144; 242, 243), and one of a child buried with an infant (nos. 203, 204). In addition, there may have been one instance of an infant buried with another infant (nos. 282, 283).

Here again, we must consider the possibility that some of the individuals in these multiple burials had been dead for a considerable time before being placed in the grave. Early accounts of the native people in the Andean area report that the bodies of certain stillborn infants were kept in households as sacred objects (Arriaga 1968: 31). It may be that some of the infants in the multiple Moche burials had been kept as sacred objects prior to burial. In this regard, it is interesting to note that most of the Moche infants that have been excavated were buried in multiple burials rather than buried alone.

Orientation. There was considerable variation in the orientation of Moche burials relative to the cardinal points, but burials at a given site tended to conform to a single orientation. At Sipán in the Reque Valley and at Pacatnamu and San José de Moro in the Jequetepeque Valley, the burials were oriented north-south with the head to the south. In the Moche Valley, burials from the Pyramids at Moche were approximately north-south with the head to the southwest, and those from Huanchaco were approximately north-south with the head to the southeast. At Huaca de la Cruz in the Viru Valley, and at Pampa Blanca in the Santa Valley, the burials tended to be east-west with the head to the west. Thus, the shared orientation of Moche burials at a given site appears to have been widespread, if not universal.

Location

There is considerable variation in the location of Moche burials, and their location tends to correlate with their degree of elaboration. Relatively simple Moche burials are found often in cemeteries located on the periphery of the river valleys, outside the area of cultivation. The cemeteries often are situated on river terraces or in dry ravines and are generally near, but not actually within, small Moche settlements. The burials almost always are prepared with shroud wrap, splint wrap, cane frame, or cane tube procedures, although occasionally a cane coffin burial also is reported. They are placed in simple pit graves and accompanied by relatively few associated grave goods.

Many Moche burials are located in Moche settlements, often in refuse or under the floors of houses. These burials tend to be similar to those found in Moche cemeteries located on the margin of the river valleys. However, a few are somewhat more elaborate, with rectangular burial chambers lined with rocks or mud bricks set in mud mortar. In general, if the settlement is large and includes pyramids, platforms, and other elaborate architecture, there is a greater probability that the graves located there are elaborate.

The most elaborate Moche graves generally are found at or near settlements with large pyramids and platforms. Within these sites, however, there is again a range of elaboration based on proximity of the burials to the pyramids and platforms. If the burials are not located near a pyramid or platform, they tend to be relatively simple, and placed in shallow pits or small boot-shaped chambers. More elaborate graves generally are found at the base of the pyramids or inside pyramids or platforms.

One other aspect of burial location that tends to correlate with elaboration, and hence status, is the depth of the burial beneath the ground surface. To some extent this results from the nature of the grave itself. For example, simple pit graves can be much more shallow than room-sized burial chambers. But if one measures the depth from ground surface to the *top* of the funeral chamber, the depth becomes an independent variable that tends to correlate with burial elaboration: the greater the depth, the greater the elaboration.

Specialized Cemeteries

Nearly all Moche cemeteries have both male and female burials as well as burials of adults, children, and infants. Generally, they also represent a range of status. Some burials are very simple and without many grave goods; others are more elaborate, with multiple grave goods. There are three Moche cemeteries, however, that appear to have been used exclusively for the burial of a distinct set of individuals.

The first observed occurrence of such a cemetery was at the Pyramids at Moche. There, in 1972, excavation of a mud-brick platform located on the plain between the Pyramid of the Sun and the Pyramid of the Moon yielded only adult male burials (nos. 231–239). These were all individuals of high status, and three of them (nos. 237–239) were buried with large copper disk headdresses like those worn by the Bean Runners shown in Moche art (Fig. 18; Larco 1942, 1943). The concentration of these burials in the mud brick platform suggests that this was a cemetery reserved exclusively for males affiliated with the Bean Runner ceremony.

Christopher B. Donnan

Another instance of a specialized cemetery is the site of Sipán, where three extremely high-status adult male burials have been excavated (nos. 4, 12, 19), along with a number of retainer burials that accompanied them. The high-status burials were of individuals who evidently participated in a ceremony where prisoners of war were sacrificed (Donnan 1988). The Sacrifice Ceremony, which is depicted clearly in Moche art (Fig. 20; Donnan 1978), apparently was conducted at Sipán, and this site was a designated burial place for the high-status individuals who participated.

Finally, a discrete cemetery of three infant burials found at Pacatnamu (nos. 113, 114, 115) suggests that there may have been more cemeteries that were restricted to this age grade.

A Shared Funerary Tradition

While there is considerable variation in Moche burials, the full range of data available at this time demonstrates a remarkable consistency in funerary practices. This suggests that Moche burial practices were shared over a large area of the north coast, rather than each local region developing its own distinctive pattern.

The options selected for the burial of a given individual almost certainly were indicative of his or her role or social position. Men tended to be buried with somewhat more elaborate procedures and to have more grave goods than women, although some very elaborate, high-status female burials have been reported. Children tended to be buried with simple procedures and few grave goods. Only one rich child burial has been reported (no. 50).

The variations in burial procedure clearly reflect a continuum from the most simple to the most elaborate, with subtle gradations resulting from increasing amounts of time and materials invested. As demonstrated above, this continuum is based on variations in four of the five aspects of funerary ritual: how the body was encased, the nature of the burial chamber, the quantity and quality of associated grave goods, and the location of the grave. Once understood, it is possible to observe a specific grave and appreciate how it might have been different if the deceased had been slightly higher or lower on the social scale.

Perhaps the best way of demonstrating the cohesiveness of Moche funerary practice is to discuss briefly two of the burials in the sample: one of an adult male who probably lived at the top of the Moche economic and social world (no. 4), and the other of an elderly woman who probably lived at or near the very bottom (no. 128).

The adult male grave is the richest Moche tomb ever recorded. In 1987 when it was first uncovered at Sipán, it appeared to be aberrant in many respects—the known sample of Moche burials included no examples of large room-sized burial chambers, plank coffins, retainer burials in cane coffins, or many of the grave goods associated with the primary individual.

Moche Funerary Practice

On closer consideration, however, it became clear that this tomb was different simply in degree, not in kind. It was much more elaborate than any previously known Moche burial and had resulted from a vastly greater investment of labor and raw materials. Yet virtually every aspect of the burial was simply a wealthier manifestation of Moche funerary practices that had been observed repeatedly in more modest Moche graves.

The large, room-sized burial chamber is an enlargement of the smaller rectangular burial chambers that had been noted previously, some of which, like the Sipán tomb, had been created by removing mud bricks from solid mud-brick structures. The niches on the two sides and at the head of the burial chamber are an elaboration of the niches found in smaller mud-brick chambers (Fig. 17). Whereas the latter occasionally contain a ceramic vessel, in the Sipán tomb they contained *many* ceramic vessels.

The plank coffin, tied together with a copper strapping, is similar to a cane coffin tied together with sedge rope. It simply required a much greater investment of labor and raw materials. Inside it, the deceased was lying on his back in the typical Moche burial position, wrapped in multiple shrouds. These shrouds happened to be covered with platelets of gilded copper; nevertheless, they wrapped the body in the prescribed fashion. It is interesting that the body was on a wood frame, an upscale version of the cane frame that characterized the much simpler encasing procedure illustrated in Figure 5.

Beneath the head of the deceased was a gold dish-shaped object which seemed unique. However, it is simply an elaborate version of the gourd plate that frequently was placed under the head of the corpse. The metal sandals tied to the feet of the principal figure are unusual, but three elaborate graves, one from Pacatnamu (no. 97), one from San José de Moro (no. 55), and one other from Sipán (no. 12), had similar metal sandals, while more modest burials at Huaca de la Cruz had small sheets of copper at the bottom of the feet (nos. 287, 292).

The principal figure had a large gold ingot on his right hand and a large silver ingot on his left hand. These are simply an elaboration on the practice, frequently noted in more modest Moche graves, of placing copper (often whole or partial ingots) in or near the hands of the deceased. Similarly, the gold mask covering the lower face and neck in this royal tomb is an elaboration of the custom of placing a sheet of copper over the face of the deceased.

Many other examples could be cited, but it is evident that the tomb is in no way aberrant. On the contrary, all the elements in this tomb are simply richer or more elaborate versions of corresponding elements in more simple Moche tombs.

The burial of an elderly female (no. 128), who probably was near the bottom of the social and economic scale, demonstrates how the appropriate Moche funerary practices were maintained even in the poorest graves. The woman was buried with minimal procedures, in a simple pit dug into windblown sand that had accumulated along the bottom of a dry ravine. The textile that was used for her single shroud was tattered and frayed, and had been mended and patched on numerous occasions.

Only a broken and mended gourd plate had been placed in the grave pit outside her shroud. There were, however, two objects inside her shroud. Next to her torso was a section of a corn cob with a broken stick through its center—clearly a hastily made, non-functional version of the spindle with spindle whorl that is appropriately placed in graves of women. The second object was in her hand, where one normally finds a piece of copper wrapped in either unspun cotton or a fragment of textile. In this instance, the hand was clutching unspun cotton, wrapped around a small, plain pottery sherd.

Clearly, the people that buried this woman were adhering to standard Moche funerary practices. Yet they were able to downscale the spindle and spindle whorl, as well as the copper in the hand, by substituting quickly fabricated replicas made of worthless materials. The fact that they included these replicas in her grave rather than burying her with nothing suggests that the patterns of appropriate funerary practice were well established and well understood by the Moche people, and that it was important to comply with those practices.

Although these two individuals represent opposite ends of the economic and status scales, their burials demonstrate the remarkable continuity and consistency of Moche funerary practice for more than half a millennium throughout the north coast of Peru.

Acknowledgments I would like to express my appreciation to Luis Jaime Castillo, Guillermo Cock, Alana Cordy-Collins, Lawrence Dawson, Betsy Escandor, Geraldine Ford, Donna and Don McClelland, and Lorna Profant for their generous assistance and suggestions in the preparation of this report; Luis Jaime Castillo for helping to create Tables 1–3 and Figure 2; Patrick Finnerty for helping to create Figures 3–15, 17, and 21; and Donna McClelland for Figures 19, 20, and 22. I am also grateful to Walter Alva, Shelia and Thomas Pozorski, and Izumi Shimada for allowing me to include unpublished information on Moche burials they have excavated.

BIBLIOGRAPHY

ALVA, WALTER
- 1988 Discovering the New World's Richest Unlooted Tomb. *National Geographic* 174 (4): 509–550.
- 1990 New Tomb of Royal Splendor. *National Geographic* 177 (6): 2–15.
- n.d. Notas de Campo de las Excavaciones en Sipán. Manuscript, 1987–89.

ARRIAGA, PABLO JOSEPH DE
- 1968 *The Extirpation of Idolatry in Peru* (L. Clark Keating, ed. and trans.). University of Kentucky Press, Lexington.

BAWDEN, GARTH
- n.d. Galindo and the Nature of the Middle Horizon in Northern Coastal Peru. Ph.D. dissertation, Harvard University, 1977.

BENNETT, WENDELL C.
- 1939 *Archaeology of the North Coast of Peru.* Anthropological Papers of the American Museum of Natural History 37 (1). New York.

CALANCHA, FRAY ANTONIO DE LA (OSA)
- 1977–81 [1638] Crónica Moralizada. In *Crónicas del Perú* 4–9 (Ignacio Prado Pastor, ed.). Universidad Nacional Mayor de San Marcos, Lima.

COBO, BERNABÉ
- 1964 [1653] *Historia del nuevo mundo.* Biblioteca de Autores Españoles. Ediciones Atlas, Madrid.

CONRAD, GEOFFREY W.
- n.d. Burial Platforms and Related Structures on the North Coast of Peru: Some Social and Political Implications. Ph.D. dissertation, Harvard University, 1974.

DIAZ, MAX R.
- 1939 Una Tumba perteneciente a la Cultura Mochica. *Actas del XXVII Congreso Internacional de Americanistas* 1: 551–558. Lima.

DONNAN, CHRISTOPHER B.
- 1973 *Moche Occupation of the Santa Valley, Peru.* University of California Press, Berkeley.
- 1978 *Moche Art of Peru.* Museum of Cultural History, University of California, Los Angeles.
- 1988 Unraveling the Mystery of the Warrior-Priest. *National Geographic* 174 (4): 550–555.
- 1990 Masterworks of Art Reveal a Remarkable Pre-Inca Culture. *National Geographic* 177 (6): 16–33.
- n.d. A Reassessment of Moche, Phase I. Manuscript, 1991.

DONNAN, CHRISTOPHER B., AND LUIS JAIME CASTILLO
- n.d. Field Notes on the Excavations of Moche Burials at San José de Moro. Manuscript, 1991.

DONNAN, CHRISTOPHER B., AND CAROL MACKEY
  1978 *Ancient Burial Patterns in the Moche Valley, Perú*. University of Texas Press, Austin.
DONNAN, CHRISTOPHER B., AND DONNA MCCLELLAND
  1979 *The Burial Theme in Moche Iconography*. Studies in Pre-Columbian Art and Archaeology 21, Dumbarton Oaks, Washington, D.C.
  n.d. Field Notes on the Excavations of Moche Burials at Pacatnamu. Manuscript, 1983–88.
GUMERMAN IV, GEORGE
  n.d. Corn for the Dead: The Significance of *Zea mays* in Moche Burial Offerings. Paper presented at Corn and Culture in the Prehistoric New World Conference, Minneapolis, May 11–13, 1990.
HECKER, GIESELA, AND WOLFGANG HECKER
  1992 *Huesos humanos como ofrendas mortuorias y uso repetido de vasijas*. Baessler-Archiv. Neue Folge 40: 171–195. Berlin.
HORKHEIMER, HANS
  1965 *Vicus*. Serie Orígenes del Arte Peruano Ediciones del Instituto de Arte Contemperáneo de Lima.
IRIARTE B., FRANCISCO
  n.d. Notas de Campo de las Excavaciones en Huanchaco. Museo de Sitio en Chanchan. Trujillo. Manuscript, 1965.
KROEBER, ALFRED L.
  1925 *The Uhle Pottery Collections from Moche*. University of California Publications in American Archaeology and Ethnology 21 (5): 235–264. Berkeley.
LARCO, RAFAEL
  1942 La Escritura Mochica Sobre Pallares. *Revista Geográfica Americana*, Año 9, 18: 93–103. Buenos Aires.
  1943 La Escritura Peruana Sobre Pallares. *Revista Geográfica Americana*, Año 11, 20: 1–36. Buenos Aires.
  1945 *Los Mochicas (Pre-Chimú, de Uhle y Early Chimú, de Kroeber)*. Sociedad Geográfica Americana, Buenos Aires.
  1948 *Cronología Arqueológica del Norte del Perú*. Biblioteca del Museo de Arqueología Rafael Larco Herrera, Hacienda Chiclín, Trujillo. Sociedad Geográfica Americana, Buenos Aires.
MATOS MENDIETA, RAMIRO
  1965–66 Algunas consideraciones sobre el estilo Vicus. *Revista del Museo Nacional* 34: 89–130. Lima.
MCCLELLAND, DONNA
  1990 A Maritime Passage from Moche to Chimu. In *The Northern Dynasties: Kingship and Statecraft in Chimor* (Michael E. Moseley and Alana Cordy-Collins, eds.): 75–106. Dumbarton Oaks, Washington, D.C.
NARVAEZ, ALFREDO
  1989 Pintura Mural en La Mina. *Lundero* 12 (141): 8–9. La Industria. Chiclayo y Trujillo.

POZORSKI, THOMAS
  n.d. Survey and Excavations of Burial Platforms at Chan Chan, Peru. B.A. thesis, Harvard University, 1971.

POZORSKI, THOMAS, AND SHELIA POZORSKI
  n.d. Recent Discoveries of Moche Ceramics in the Casma Valley, Peru. Manuscript, 1989.

ROWE, JOHN H.
  1946 Inca Culture at the Time of the Spanish Conquest. In *Handbook of South American Indians* 2 (Julian H. Steward, ed.): 183–330. Smithsonian Institution, Bureau of American Ethnology, Bulletin 143, Washington, D.C.

SHIMADA, IZUMI
  n.d. Field Notes on the Excavations at Huaca Soledad. Manuscript, 1984.

SHIMADA, IZUMI, ET AL.
  1981 The Batán Grande-La Leche Archaeological Project: The First Two Seasons. *Journal of Field Archaeology* 8: 405–446.

STRONG, WILLIAM D., AND CLIFFORD EVANS, JR.
  1952 *Cultural Stratigraphy in the Virú Valley, Northern Perú*. Columbia University Studies in Archaeology and Ethnology 4. New York.

TOPIC, TERESA L.
  n.d. Excavations at Moche. Ph.D. dissertation, Harvard University, 1977.

UBBELOHDE-DOERING, HEINRICH
  1959 Bericht über archäologische Feldarbeiten in Perú (II). *Ethnos:* 24 (1–2): 1–32. Stockholm.
  1967 *On the Royal Highways of the Inca*. Frederick A. Praeger, New York.
  1983 *Vorspanische Gräber von Pacatnamú, Nordperu*. Materialien zur Allgemeinen und Vergleichenden Archäologie 26. Verlag C. H. Beck, München.

UHLE, FRIEDRICH MAX
  1913 Die Ruinen von Moche. *Journal de la Société des Américanistes de París* 10: 95–117.
  n.d. Field Catalog of the Excavations at Moche. Lowie Museum of Anthropology, University of California, Berkeley. Manuscript, 1899–1900.

VERANO, JOHN W.
  n.d. Human Skeletal Remains from Tomb 1, Sipán. Manuscript, 1989.

Nasca Burial Patterns: Social Structure and Mortuary Ideology

PATRICK H. CARMICHAEL
UNIVERSITY OF CALGARY

For much of this century the ancient Nasca of the Peruvian south coast were a classic "cemetery culture," known only from vast burial grounds (Early Intermediate Period; hereafter EIP, ca. A.D. 1–700). Settlement pattern studies and stratigraphic excavations were not initiated until the 1950s; thereafter followed a twenty-year research hiatus, but the 1980s witnessed renewed interest in the south coast and a series of recent studies have contributed much new data on settlement distributions and economy. In this chapter I return to the mortuary evidence, most of which remains unpublished and therefore less accessible to modern scholars. Drawing upon a large, excavated sample, I review Nasca burial practices and evidence of associated belief systems. It will become evident that for the Nasca the dead played a vital role among the living. The question of ranking versus stratification in Nasca social structure, and its attendant implications for sociopolitical reconstructions, provides a major focus throughout this chapter. At issue is the scale of Nasca society. Specifically, I will address the question of whether, at any time, Nasca approximated a state-level society (Lanning 1967; Proulx 1968, 1983, 1989; Massey n.d.; Silverman 1987, 1988b).[1] While the terms "state" and "regional state" have been used casually in the literature and seldom qualified, at base they imply a hierarchically

---

[1] Donald Proulx (n.d.: 6) now states that ". . . politically [Nasca] was at best a Chiefdom, not a state level society."

Helaine Silverman points out that her position has wavered back and forth on the issue (1990b, 1992). In her earlier work she envisioned Nasca society as a chiefdom or confederacy of chiefdoms, later as a state or regional state, and more recently as a complex society with all of the trappings of "civilization" (1990b: 452). In her most recent review (Silverman 1992), she sees strong support for the Nasca state concept with the proviso that if Nasca was a state, it was different from Wari, Chimu, or Inka.

The Nasca state label has become embedded in the literature and continues to circulate (see Patterson 1991: 32; Moseley 1992a: 186).

stratified social structure. This model will be weighed against the mortuary evidence.

SOCIAL STRUCTURE

A clear distinction should be drawn between ranking and stratification at the outset. In Morton Fried's (1967) original definitions, the difference was based on differential access to basic resources. Following Elman Service (1971: 149), a further basic distinction is added here: a ranked society is a graded society, while a stratified society is divided. The distinction is that of degree and kind. Ranked societies follow a continuous status gradient, while stratified societies contain discontinuous status groupings. Among the Chimu, class divisions were even sanctioned by a myth which claimed totally separate creations for nobles and commoners (Rowe 1948: 47).

The Inka are the best documented example of a stratified Andean society. Inka social structure had two classes of nobility—Inkas by birth and Inkas by privilege, each with a series of ranks corresponding to levels in the administrative bureaucracy—and a commoner class with additional ranking depending on occupation and local custom. Special groups such as the Yanacona and state-supported artisans formed additional components in society. The divisions within and between classes were symbolized by differing rules of dress, ornamentation, marriage, and taxation. The circulation of certain materials, such as gold and silver, was also restricted within the class structure (Rowe 1946).

Mortuary Correlates

> "To put it simply, a person treated differentially in death was probably also so treated in life; this differential treatment reflects the social structure of the society" (Goldstein 1981: 54).

In a mortuary population, status hierarchies may be identified by segregated burial locations, restricted distributions of artifact types, variation in body treatment and tomb form, and differential expenditures of energy on the interment (also see Goldstein 1981: 59). A hierarchy is indicated where such factors cluster at different levels of intensity to partition the mortuary domain. These groupings reflect vertical social structure. Their number and the degree to which they are formally differentiated indicates relative structural complexity. Horizontal structure may be expressed by symbols which are of approximately equal intensity (units of equivalency) which crosscut age, sex, and status categories (O'Shea 1981: 41). Examples of such units are age grades, sodalities, task groups, moieties, and lineages. The current study is primarily concerned with vertical structure.

Lewis Binford (1971) proposed that the size and composition of the group

Nasca Burial Patterns: Social Structure and Mortuary Ideology

owing status duties to the deceased, and the extent to which burial ritual interfered with normal activities, would vary with the relative status of the individual. Joseph Tainter (1973) operationalized Binford's hypothesis by suggesting that the amount of corporate involvement and the degree of activity disruption would correspond to the amount of energy expended on the mortuary ritual and thereby imply status. A pertinent example of Tainter's principle is provided by Pedro de Cieza de León's observation (1864: 229) that along the Peruvian coast the length of the mourning period varied with status, retainers and quantities of grave goods accompanied a lord, some goods were burned, and the tombs were later reopened for offering renewals. The principle of energy expenditure is well suited to archaeological detection, for it recognizes several measures of status, including complexity of body treatment and construction and placement of interment facility, in addition to material contributions to the burial (Tainter n.d.: 55; 1978: 126–127). Because of the vicissitudes of archaeological recovery, the precise measure of energy expenditure is extremely difficult to quantify. In the current work it is treated as a relative measure.

The considerations listed above have been examined and critiqued in detail elsewhere (Brown 1971a, 1971b, 1981; Tainter 1978; Chapman and Randsborg 1981; Bartel 1982; O'Shea 1984; Morris 1989). It is evident that a variety of factors such as status masking (Morris 1989: 38–39, 186) and cycles of mortuary elaboration and restraint (Cannon 1989) may obscure the relation between burial patterning and social structure in some cases. Fortunately, this study is not concerned with Archaic Greece or Victorian England. While cautionary tales are always kept in mind, the immediate concern is with mortuary behaviors in an Andean context. The general concepts developed by James Brown, Binford, Tainter, and others are applicable in the Andes. To demonstrate this point and provide a comparative base for later discussion of Nasca practices, a brief summary of Dorothy Menzel's (1976) classic study of Late Intermediate Period and Late Horizon burials from Ica now follows (also see Rowe, this volume).

Menzel's Late Horizon burials are particularly illustrative of social differentiation expressed in mortuary symbolism. As an Inka province, Ica was subject to the organizing principles and policies of the state. Degrees of affinity with the Inka system were expressed in pottery associations and metal artifact distributions. In addition to state-sanctioned markers, Menzel was able to clearly identify the local hierarchy on the basis of indigenous symbols of status and authority. The nobility were buried in large, structured tombs at depths of 4.5 to 6.5 m, which penetrated the clay subsoil. Human remains underwent a multistage program of modification involving tomb reentry and were accompanied by retainer and animal sacrifices. Grave posts were buried above the chamber, and grave goods included artifacts of gold and silver, large wooden carvings with metal sheathing, and distinct pottery types (i.e., Ica-Inka A and Imitation Chimu). A second form of burial probably corresponds to civil servants with ties to the local nobility and Inka hierarchy. These were primary burials in urns at depths of 2.5 to 4.0 m (above the clay subsoil). Grave goods included copper artifacts and tall wooden carvings without metal sheathing, wooden keros, khipus, and distinct pottery styles (i.e., Chimu-Inka and Cuzco Inka). Commoners received primary burial in shallow pits. Pottery associations were mainly in the Ica 9 style, but included antique and imitation antique vessels (summarized from Menzel 1976: chaps. 1 and 5).

Menzel's Ica study illustrates the manner in which social divisions may be symbolized in mortuary treatments. While this brief summary does not do justice to the intricacies of her analysis, it serves to establish a comparative reference. In present terminology, the social structure of Late Horizon Ica is reflected in restricted artifact distributions, differences in body treatments and tomb forms, and variations in energy expenditures in the burial complex. Under Inka rule Ica society was stratified, as would be anticipated from ethnohistoric accounts. This is shown by absolute differences in burial customs which sharply delineate the social hierarchy. As Menzel has pointed out, there are also indications in her sample of additional internal ranking among the nobility and commoners (1976: 224, 232).

THE NASCA EVIDENCE: SAMPLE AND OBJECTIVES

The principles of mortuary analysis outlined above were applied to a large sample of Nasca burials. The primary objectives were to examine the nature of Nasca social structure as revealed in mortuary patterning, elucidate the ideological component encoded in burial ritual, and document changes and/or stability in the mortuary complex through time. The burials represent Nasca stylistic Phases 1–8. The first seven phases correspond to the epochs of the EIP. Phase 8 is now assigned to the Middle Horizon.[2]

Results pertaining to social structure are derived from a core sample of 168 burials representing Phases 2–8. An additional 35 graves representing multiple and secondary burials, empty graves, and unique body positions, and eight Phase 1 interments are considered separately in the latter sections of this chapter.

The burials derive from 14 sites in the Rio Grande de Nazca Drainage Basin (hereafter Nazca Basin) and five sites in the Ocucaje oasis near Ica (Fig. 1). Recoveries were made over a 60-year period by several researchers,

---

[2] Phase 8 was included in the EIP during the original analysis (1985–87), but absolute dating and stylistic evidence now indicates it is better considered within the Middle Horizon (Silverman 1988a). Seventeen Phase 8 interments were used in this study. They do not differ in any substantial way from the Phase 2–7 burials, although tombs containing two or more individuals (multiple interments) are more common (six of ten Nazca Basin examples).

Nasca Burial Patterns: Social Structure and Mortuary Ideology

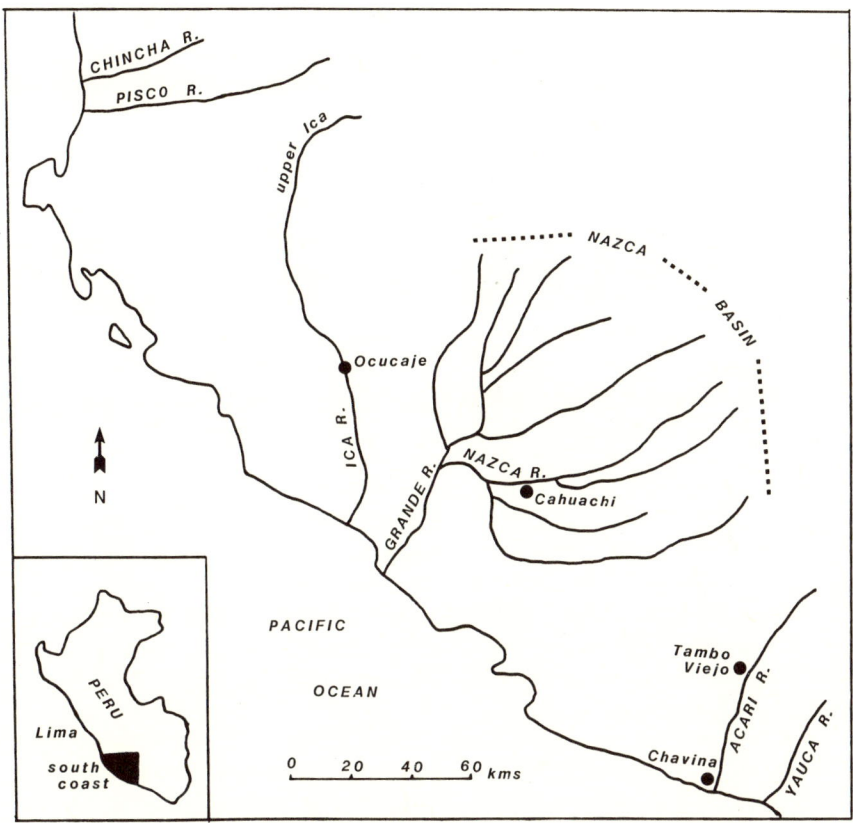

Fig. 1 Map of the south coast.

but remain unpublished. The principal investigators and dates of these studies are William Farabee, 1922; Alfred Kroeber, 1926; Heinrich Ubbelohde-Doering, 1932; Duncan Strong, 1952; Aldo Rubini, 1956; and Guiseppe Orefici, 1982–85 (for site locations and history of investigations see Carmichael n.d.: 117–166). Variations in recording styles and looting at nearly all of the sites render this sample far from ideal, however, it represents the bulk of documented Nasca burials available at this time. When possible, the contents of each tomb were reexamined and noted in detail.

As in the preceding example of Late Horizon Ica society, the Nasca sample was examined to determine whether status hierarchies could be identified by restricted artifact distributions, differences in body treatments and tomb forms, and differential energy expenditures in the mortuary complex. Burial locations, biological age, and sex and chronological variations were also taken into account (hereafter collectively referred to as the factors of analysis). Burials were assigned to discrete stylistic phases on the basis of associated pottery. When pottery was not present but the associated graves clustered around contiguous phases, relative assignments were made: Early, Phases 2–4; Middle, Phases 5–6; and Late, Phases 7–8.[3]

Some burial traits were found to have numerically minor representation while others showed a range of expressions which become lost when reduced to aggregate numbers. In view of this, no statistical methods beyond descriptive statistics were employed. The presence or absence of trait correlations was established by visually inspecting cross-tabulations of the data. This approach is less likely to be deceptive given the nature of the data under consideration.

Burial Patterns

The standard burial posture for all members of society throughout Phases 2–8 was a seated and flexed position, with knees drawn up to the chest.[4] Generally, the arms were flexed with hands resting on or around the knees, but in some instances the hands were placed against the chest, between the thighs, or crossed beneath the legs. The body was then wrapped in one or several shrouds consisting of plain cloth and/or textile garments.

The presence or absence of cranial deformation[5] did not correlate with any of the factors of analysis, nor did facing (the compass direction which the skull faced).[6] The majority faced south (47%), west (19%), and southwest (15%), but examples of individuals facing all other directions were present.

Interments were placed in graves ranging from less than 1 to 4.5 m in depth. Some of the graves had roofs consisting of branches or small poles, while others were constructed of heavy logs overlaid with a cap of mud and stones. The shafts were vertical with no appreciable variation in width below the roof. On average they ranged from 0.50 to 1.20 m in diameter and varied in shape from round to square. On occasion the lower portion, which held the body, was adobe or stone-lined, and a clean layer of sand or leaves was sometimes placed on the floor. Burial chambers may be open

---

[3] These phase groupings were arranged to meet the requirements of this particular sample. I now advocate relative assignments as follows: Proto-Nasca, Phase 1; Early, Phases 2–4; Middle, Phase 5 (including late 4 and early 6); Late, Phases 6–7; Middle Horizon, Phases 8–9.

[4] The number of observations on different traits varies according to preservation and the recording styles of the original excavators. Conclusions on body posture are based on 72 observations.

[5] One hundred fifteen observations.

[6] Ninety-four observations.

Nasca Burial Patterns: Social Structure and Mortuary Ideology

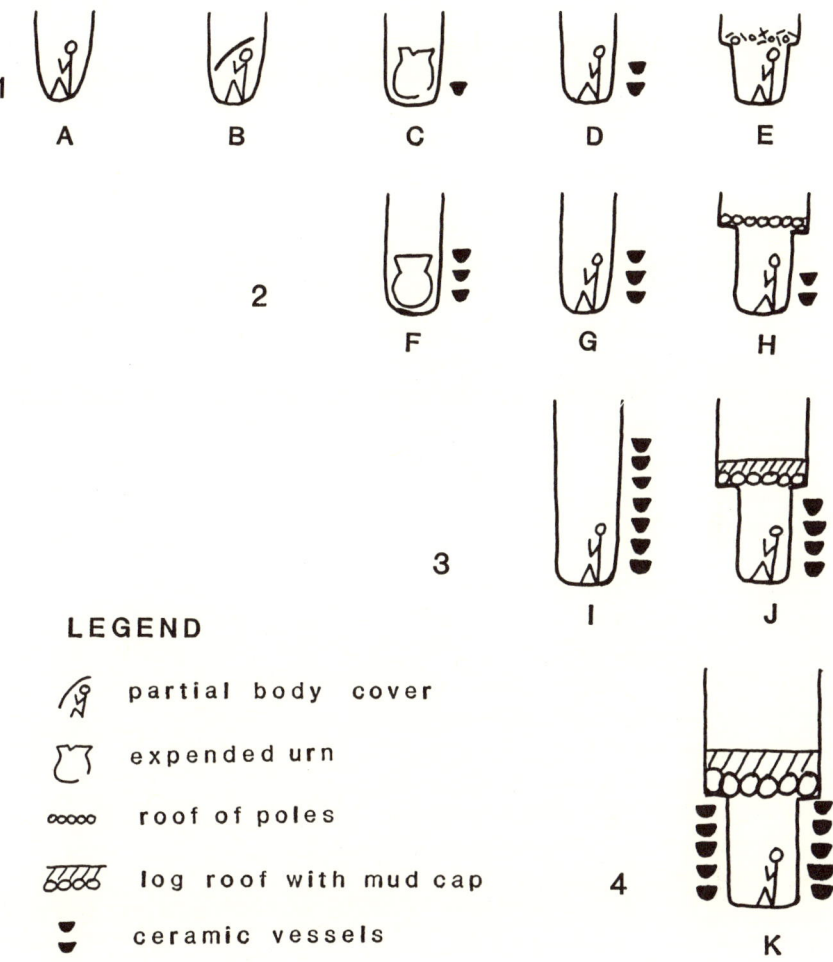

Fig. 2 Grave forms and burial categories.

spaces below roofs, but even when roofs are present solid-fill chambers are more common. Some individuals were buried in urns within pit or shaft graves. The tendency was to use expended cooking ollas for children and serviceable storage jars for adults. Persons in shallow graves lacking roofs were sometimes partially covered by objects such as a section of an urn, loose adobes, cane, leaves, etc., occurring individually or in combinations. All of the above tomb forms were used for both sexes and all age groups throughout Phases 2–8 (Fig. 2).

Patrick H. Carmichael

Markers were sometimes placed in the shaft above the chamber, presumably to indicate the presence of a tomb below. There is great variety in the positioning and types of objects used as shaft markers. Examples are a single cane projecting vertically from the top of the roof; one or several vertical sticks, poles, or logs in the upper shaft; a single horizontal log or adobe in the upper shaft; and piles of loose adobes not far below the ground surface. Only 29 graves contained such devices, and there were no correlations with the other factors of analysis.

A considerable variety of grave goods were recorded. Many of these were organic materials such as textiles, gourd containers, baskets, feathers, raw cotton, bundles of human hair, and plant remains. Although the arid south coast is renowned for preservation of organic artifacts, the degree of preservation varies a great deal according to the circumstances of location and tomb depth. In some areas deeper burials are closer to the water table and no organic material survives, however, when burials were placed on dry hills, virtually all of the tomb contents are preserved intact. Unfortunately, due to the vagaries of preservation, organic artifacts could not be used as a common basis for comparison.

Pottery was given special attention in this study because it is a common and less perishable form of grave inclusion and provides a number of variables (wares, shapes, and motifs) that may have been used as social markers. In the total sample, 561 vessels were classified (29 plainware and 532 fineware) into four major shape categories (bowls, jars, vases, and bottles) with 22 vessel forms (i.e., cup bowl, flaring bowl; necked jar, collared jar). Iconography was successively classified by theme categories[7] (supernatural, referential, abstract), major themes (i.e., birds, plants), and specific motifs (i.e., hummingbird, condor; beans, lucuma). None of these variables with significant representation correlated with age, sex, tomb form, or location.

Burial locations were classified as domestic habitation areas; non-domestic architecture (artificial mounds); adjacent to non-domestic architecture (within a 100 m radius of the feature); and isolated locations (more than 100 m from the nearest habitation or non-domestic architectural unit). No correlations with any of the factors of analysis could be identified within or between these locales, and all were used throughout Phases 2–8.

ANALYSIS AND INTERPRETATIONS

Control of the time factor is crucial in mortuary analysis. In order to identify chronological variations in mortuary patterning the observations on each burial were studied and compared with all other burials within and between phases. The burials were then reorganized into Early, Middle, and

---

[7] I now regard these theme categories as misleading and have abandoned their use (Carmichael 1992b, 1993).

Nasca Burial Patterns: Social Structure and Mortuary Ideology

Late groupings for further comparison. At both levels the results were uniform. In this sample all forms of burial, including body posture, tomb construction, pottery inclusions, and location were present throughout Phases 2–8. No forms of burial were added or deleted, and there is no indication that identifiable status markers changed. In the absence of appreciable change through time, the sample was collapsed and treated as a unit in order to classify the burials on the basis of the amount of energy expended on each interment. The archaeological measure of energy expenditure must rely on physical evidence which is not susceptible to decay and can be distinguished by identifiable variations in energy intensity. Further, in order to be useful for establishing similarities and differences the selected traits should be common to a number of graves, but have discontinuous distributions within the sample. Many of the factors noted in this study did not meet these criteria. For example, variations in body posture were absent, while the vagaries of preservation hindered the usefulness of organic artifacts as a common basis for distinguishing status differences. The variables which provided the most useful measure of energy expenditure were those related to grave depth, tomb construction, and ceramic volume. Observations on the presence and extent of these variables could be made for all graves, and, therefore, provided a common basis for comparison.

Taking the above factors into account, the sample was partitioned into burial categories on the basis of differential energy expenditures identified through visually inspecting cross-tabulations of the data (Tables 1–3; Fig. 2). The purpose of this exercise was to determine whether discrete groupings could be identified and to provide a further basis for trait comparisons. While the burials in each category are considered to reflect approximately equal amounts of energy expenditure, it was found that the point of division between each group had to be established arbitrarily. As shown in Table 1, a burial with five pots was placed in category 2, while a grave with six pots was assigned to category 3. In terms of numbers the difference is negligible; this example highlights the arbitrary nature of the divisions. However, in general terms, as the graves become deeper they tend to contain more pottery and have successively more substantial roofs (Fig. 2; Tables 1, 2). The two extremes are shown by illustrations A and K in Figure 2. Typical of burial form A would be an adult interred at a depth of 0.75 m without body cover, urn, roof, or pots, while K represents an adult in a tomb 4.0 m deep with a roof of large logs covered with a thick layer of mud and stones, and accompanied by 10 vessels. In terms of energy expenditure these two burials are clearly differentiated. However, the other burials in this sample form a graded continuum between these extremes. The dividing points between burial categories is therefore artificial, but the categories nonetheless serve as useful points of reference for trait comparisons. Finer divisions could be made, but the numbers involved would become increasingly meaningless. As presented, the

Table 1. Burial Categories and Relative Status

Burial Category	Relative Status
1 — N=74 — A) simple burial B) body cover only C) urn with 1 pot D) 1–2 pots only E) light roof only	Low
2 — N=37 — F) urn with 2–5 pots G) 3–5 pots only H) roof with 1–2 pots	Mid
3 — N=33 — I) 6–8 pots only J) roof with 3–5 pots	High
4 — N=24 — K) roof with 6+ pots	

Table 2. Summary of Tomb Depths by Burial Categories
(Depth shown in Meters)

Burial Category	Range	Mean	Mode
1	0.50–2.50	1.35	0.70–1.50
2	1.30–2.70	1.81	1.40–2.10
3	1.40–3.60	2.28	2.00–3.00
4	1.80–4.50	2.97	2.50–4.50

Table 3. Age and Sex Distributions by Burial Categories

Burial Category	Indeterminate Sex and Age	Male	Female	Adults Unsexed	Subadults	Total
1	5	5	9	19	36	7_
2	4	9	8	10	6	3_
3	8	6	5	10	4	3_
4	10	5	2	7	0	2_
TOTALS	27	25	24	46	46	16_

Nasca Burial Patterns: Social Structure and Mortuary Ideology

categories could be amalgamated into tripartite or bipartite divisions (i.e., 1, 2–3, 4, or 1–2, 3–4), and an equally good case could be made for each of these scenarios. But no matter which series of divisions is chosen, the highly graded nature of the sample will always present a number of borderline cases, which, in the final analysis, will require arbitrary designations.

The right-hand column in Table 1 shows approximations of relative status. The terms "low," "mid," and "high" do not imply fixed parameters corresponding to homogeneous social groups (ranks), rather, they are simply applied as relative terms of comparison to facilitate discussion.

All burial categories were represented at all sites with substantial samples. It is therefore concluded that status differences were not symbolized by formal separation involving interment at different localities. Data from three of the better documented cemeteries yielding clusters of undisturbed graves were examined to determine whether individuals of different status were spatially separated within the cemetery. The three sites included an isolated cemetery (Kroeber, Aja B, Phases 2–3), a cemetery adjacent to non-domestic architecture (Strong, Cahuachi Burial Area 1, Phases 5–6), and a cemetery in non-domestic architecture (Kroeber, Cahuachi A, Phase 3). It was found that members of each burial category occurred in association with members of all other categories. Evidence for intrasite spatial patterning on the basis of status is therefore absent. Nasca cemetery compositions were likely based on something akin to the historic Andean ayllu with membership, as opposed to status within the group, being the only criterion for inclusion within the group's common cemetery.

Skull deformation, facing, shaft markers, open or filled burial chambers, and prepared chamber surfaces did not correlate with the burial categories, nor with any other factors of analysis.

Ceramic Analysis

The distribution of elements considered in the ceramic analysis were also compared with the burial categories. It was found that vessel shapes and iconographic units with significant representation in this sample did not correlate with any of the burial categories. The ceramic complex appears to have been an open, shared system to which all members of society had access. Two exceptions should be noted: miniatures and vessel pairs.

Virtually all vessel shapes were skillfully reproduced in miniature. Conventional wisdom has long held that these were simply children's toys. In this sample miniature vessels occurred with two subadults (both in burial category 3) and three adults (all in category 4). The significance of these tiny vessels appears to lie more with status than age.

Matched pairs of vessels (almost identical in shape, size, and decoration) tended to correlate with mid- to high-status graves. Paired vessels were present in 34 graves, of which only four were in category 2, and these were among the most elaborate in this category. The remainder occurred in category 3 and 4 burials. The presence of matched pairs is not strictly a numbers-dependent variable. There are examples of graves in which a pair were the only vessels present and others which contained many vessels but no pairs. Limited occurrence and restricted distribution indicate that vessel pairs held some meaning beyond utilitarian function. The question is best considered together with evidence on partial vessels and tombs linked by articulating sherds.

Alfred Kroeber was the first to recognize that adjacent graves are sometimes linked by articulating sherds (Kroeber n.d.). The sherds may reconstitute a nearly complete vessel, but frequently several pieces or entire sections are absent (presumably deposited in other burials). Some of these sherds exhibit sharp, clean, edge breaks, while articulating sherds from adjacent graves have heavily worn edges suggesting that they were curated for some time before being deposited. In light of these observations, the presence of individual sherds and partial vessels in graves takes on new significance. It may be conjectured that a custom prevailed whereby pottery vessels were broken during the interment ceremony and pieces were kept by one or more participants for eventual placement in other graves. Thus, pottery was used to signal some form of relationship between individuals, and a link was maintained between the living and the dead.

The clearest examples of tombs linked by articulating sherds were two Phase 5 graves, both in burial category 4, and three Phase 3 graves, one in burial category 4 and two in category 2. This small sample does not allow generalizations; however, the Phase 3 graves indicate that the custom was not restricted and allowed persons of lesser status to signify a relationship with persons of higher status.

Partial vessels (sections constituting 33% or more of the original vessel) were present in graves from all burial categories; however, as a percentage of the total number of graves in each category, they were most common in mid- to high-status burials (category 1—8% of burials; category 2—14%; category 3—21%; category 4—33%). The presence of three or more partial vessels in a grave always correlated with mid to high status, and among high-status burials as many as seven partial vessels were found in a single grave. To some extent the distribution of partial vessels among the burial categories may be a numbers-dependent variable; however, as discussed above, broken pottery was used to symbolize relationships. In this context, partial vessels may represent individuals who wished to affirm a special familial bond or status-duty relationship with the deceased. The number and importance of such affirmations is likely to increase with the status of the deceased, for the act could be seen as a means of legitimizing the current status and future aspirations of the contributor.

In light of the foregoing, it is possible that vessel pairs were also used to symbolize relationships. The vessels which constitute a pair are virtually identical; however, close examination reveals minor differences in size and slight variations in decorative details. When such vessels are found together they are classified as a pair, but when virtually identical vessels are recovered from separate graves they are referred to as products of the same workshop. Vessels of this nature may well have constituted a pair at one time. There are several examples in the current study of strikingly similar vessels recovered from separate graves within the same cemetery. If familial or social relationships were symbolized by dividing individual vessels, it is plausible that pairs may have been used in a similar manner. As a corollary, it may be postulated that at times the separation of pairs occurred during the lifetime of both individuals, and that the two original vessels were sometimes united again upon the death of one of the participants. Such speculations are consistent with Nasca practice and, as with partial vessels, the number of relationships requiring symbolic recognition is likely to increase with the status of the deceased. A scenario of this kind would account for the covariance of paired vessels with mid- to high-status burials.

Hair Analysis

Human-hair wigs, tresses, braided twine, and small bundles of hair occur in some well-preserved Nasca graves. Samples from three adult graves were submitted for forensic analysis to determine whether the various hair artifacts from individual tombs were derived from the scalp hair of one person (the deceased?) or represented several individuals (Carmichael, Kennedy, and Lacapra n.d.). At present the results of such analyses are not considered definitive in a legal sense, but can indicate whether two samples are consistent or inconsistent with a common source. Results of the current study suggest that hair samples from each of the graves came from different individuals (i.e., they were not consistent with having derived from a common source).

In the Andean tradition hair was the object of much pride and ritual ceremony and, as it was believed to contain the essence of a person's life force, it was also the object of both malevolent and benign sorcery (Cobo 1893: 158, 177; Arriaga 1968: 54, 58, 86; Zárate 1968: 96; Millones and Pratt 1989: 57–60). Bernabé Cobo states that women cut their hair as a sign of mourning when their husbands died (1893: 237). The Nasca apparently had similar customs, although we can only speculate on the precise nature of their beliefs.

In addition to pottery, the results of the hair analysis provide further evidence that in some cases a number of individuals contributed to the grave contents. Human hair, perhaps the most sacred and personal gift an individual could offer, served as another symbolic link between the living and the dead.

Two of the graves used in the hair analysis were adjacent in a line of four Phase 3 graves excavated by Kroeber at Cahuachi. All four of these interments were interconnected by pottery (articulating sherds and virtually identical vessels). While analysis indicates that the hair artifacts within each of the sampled graves (Burial 12—5 samples; Burial 13—5 samples) represent several persons, two samples from Burial 12 matched two samples from Burial 13 (i.e., they were consistent with having derived from the same sources). One of these matches indicates that the same person contributed a hair bundle to Burial 12 and another to Burial 13. The other match involves scalp hairs from one of the deceased in Burial 13 (there were three adult males in this tomb) and a hair bundle in Burial 12 (which contained one adult male). One scenario suggests that a man who contributed a hair bundle to Burial 12 was later interred in an adjacent grave. The occupants of these four Cahuachi tombs were clearly related. Close affinities were symbolized by grave location (contiguous alignment within a structurally bounded area), and intergrave connections of pottery and hair artifacts. These persons may have belonged to an immediate family, or been members of the same lineage/ayllu.

Status and Burial Customs

In the current sample no absolute differences could be detected in burial locations, tomb forms, grave goods, or body treatments that would clearly distinguish one status group from another. When the sample is reordered on the basis of relative energy expenditures, differences become apparent; however, these differences are expressed in degrees of intensity that form a smoothly graded continuum. Although four burial categories were identified to facilitate discussion, it has been stressed that these artificial groupings blend into one another and lack finite boundaries. Evidence of stratification is entirely absent. The implications of this finding and possible biases in the data base will be discussed in the concluding section.

Social ranks are composed of both sexes and all age groups (Brown 1981: 30). Formalized ranks could not be identified in this sample. The age and sex distributions shown in Table 3 illustrate that, as a group, subadults did not participate equally with adults in the status hierarchy. This is shown by the small numbers of subadults in burial categories 2 and 3, and their absence in category 4. The fact that ten subadults in categories 2 and 3 received greater mortuary attention than 33 adults in category 1 may indicate that a system of ascribed status at birth was operative. Males and females are present at all levels of the hierarchy, but overall figures tend to favor males in high-status positions (however, the most elaborate burial in this sample was female).

It may be concluded that ranking was present in Nasca society, but there was a low degree of formalized social differentiation in the status hierarchy. On the basis of current evidence it is not possible to speak of discrete social ranks; rather, status positions form a gradient which is better described as a status continuum.

Temporal Variation

Structural uniformity in the mortuary program through time indicates continuity in the basic social structure. However, while absolute differences in kind were not present in this sample, temporal variations in degree of intensity were observed. The samples from Phases 3 and 5 best illustrate these trends. In comparison with the averages for Phase 3, Phase 5 burials are deeper, have heavier roofs, and contain more pottery. These trends are present in all burial categories, but are most pronounced among high-status interments. Status markers remained the same, and no new forms of burial were added. The burial complex, therefore, remained structurally unchanged, but greater amounts of energy were being expended within the existing structure during Phase 5, especially among the elites. Increased emphases of this nature are often related to group pressures involving land ownership and the inheritance of vital resources (Morris 1989: 34, 42).

Shifts in settlement patterns (Schreiber and Lancho 1988) and radical trends in ceramic styles (Roark 1965; Blagg n.d.) were also taking place during Phase 5. Environmental data indicate prolonged periods of severe drought in the Peruvian Andes during the sixth century A.D. (Shimada 1991: 47–48), the approximate time frame of Phase 5. This would have significantly reduced water availability along the south coast and further impoverished an already tenuous environment. While the systemic processes are not yet clarified, climatic anomalies appear to be a root factor behind changes in the settlement, iconographic, and mortuary complexes during Phase 5. Although the burial samples are more limited for the following phases, there are indications that average grave depths and pottery inclusions returned to Phase 3 levels during Phases 6 and 7, with a slight resurgence in Phase 8.

Mortuary Variation

The burials used in the preceding analysis represent the common forms of interments during Phases 2–8 in the Nazca Basin; however, additional forms are known from within and outside of this area. Variations in the Nazca region include multiple interments, secondary burial, empty graves, and individuals in unique burial postures (these were not included in the sample previously discussed). The limited number of examples and range of variation in each group indicate they were uncommon treatments accorded under special circumstances. They are worthy of note as elements within the mortuary complex, but, short of individual description and speculation, are only briefly mentioned here (details are given in Carmichael n.d.: 345–366).

Because these are small, internally diverse samples they are not comparable with the burial categories discussed above.

Multiple interments in the same burial chamber (2–5 individuals) occurred throughout Phases 2–8, although six of the ten Nazca Basin examples date to Phase 8. The available documentation did not make it possible to determine whether the individuals in a grave were buried together or added sequentially (single event or family sepulcher?), or whether one or more of the deceased were retainer sacrifices. There are examples of adults with adults and children with adults. It was seldom possible to determine which grave goods were associated with individuals. If multiple burials were assigned to the burial categories, examples would be placed in categories 2 to 4.

Secondary burials contained disarticulated and incomplete skeletal remains (usually only long bones, sometimes bundled together), and the bones were noticeably drier than those in surrounding graves. The four clear examples of secondary burial were all adults from the early part of the EIP. Two additional burials appear to have been shifted from their original positions to make room for later burials. The presence of ochre on bone surfaces in three other graves may imply secondary burial, treatment in situ, or, as a mineral pigment, the ochre may have been applied at the time of burial and simply adhered to the bone after the flesh decayed.

There were five examples of empty graves. In each case the excavator encountered what appeared to be a pristine tomb complete with grave goods, but there was no body. In one instance a few adult metacarpals were also present. These tombs may represent the initial resting place of what later became secondary burials, or perhaps they were symbolic, representing individuals who died some distance away or could not be recovered.

Unique postures were recorded for 11 adults and three subadults. The range of individual variation defies generalization; however, examples of fully extended positions (both face up and face down) and side-flexed positions (both left and right) were noted. Some had limbs askew, ". . . right arm doubled in with hand near chest, left thrown above head," and one elderly man was ". . . thrown into pit head first." Such burials seldom have associated artifacts and are generally less than 1 m in depth. One receives the impression that these individuals were casually "dumped," perhaps with haste and disdain, and with little regard for their earthly remains. They may represent criminals, sacrificial victims, or, as Silverman (1990a: 237) suggests, "bad deaths" (also see Verano, this volume).

Protracted Ceremony

Some grave shafts contain evidence of sequential fill, which may indicate that the entombment ceremony took place over a period of time. Sequential fill can take the form of artifacts situated at the level of the waist, chest, or head of the deceased, or ash lenses and discrete soil layers above the chamber.

Nasca Burial Patterns: Social Structure and Mortuary Ideology

It is not possible to determine whether these events took place in one day or over a longer period of time. Only 43 burials contained evidence of sequential fill, and no correlations with the other factors of analysis or status could be identified. It is possible that protracted entombment ceremonies were granted to all persons, but these did not all follow a standard program, and only those more obvious forms are detectable in the archaeological record.

Tomb Reentry

There is some evidence that a few of the high-status tombs in this sample were reentered after initial closure. Ubbelohde-Doering (1958) excavated a large tomb at Cahuachi in which the deceased was reportedly seated on a basketry "throne," but the head and upper body were missing and the grave goods were in disarray. Ubbelohde-Doering is quite specific in stating that the large log roof was intact and showed no signs of disturbance. A number of vessels and quantities of textiles and other artifacts were found in this tomb. In spite of this, he concluded that the grave must have been plundered in historic times to obtain hypothetical gold jewelry from the body. It appears more likely that reentry took place in antiquity, perhaps as part of a multistage ritual involving secondary burial and ancestor worship. Even if this tomb had been opened before pottery was valued, looters are not known to cart off sections of bodies or carefully restore large log roofs. Furthermore, some of the pottery recovered from this grave can be dated on stylistic grounds to Phase 7, while other vessels belong to Phase 8. This suggests that additional offerings were added at a later date, perhaps when portions of the body were removed. Similar circumstances were noted for three other high-status burials in this sample, and Samuel Lothrop and Joy Mahler (1957) report parallel conditions in some of the Acarí cist tombs. The custom of opening tombs to renew offerings was still being practiced in the early sixteenth century (Cieza de León 1864: 229).

Tomb reentries raise the issue of grave good deletions or additions, and the effect on relative status assessments. In the current sample only four of 168 graves showed evidence of reentry, and even after the pottery from a later phase is excluded, these would still be classified as category 4 burials. In a few other instances objects were found on top of grave roofs (e.g., two gourds wrapped in cloth, a spear thrower and darts, pacay seeds, a pottery vessel). In each case the presence of such objects did not alter the burial category classification.

Regional Differences

The basic EIP tomb forms that have been described for the Nazca Basin are also found over a wider area of the south coast, but some important regional variations should be noted. Sarah Massey (n.d.: 323) describes EIP

3 and 4 graves in the upper Ica Valley as stone-lined pits covered by stone slabs and outlined on the surface by spaced stones. Farther to the south in the Acarí Valley, contiguous adobe cist tombs with interments in a side-flexed posture have been reported at Chaviña (Lothrop and Mahler 1957; Valdez n.d.). Associated pottery crossdates to Nasca Phases 7 and 8. A number of side-flexed interments in shallow pits dating to the late EIP/early Middle Horizon have also been recovered at the Acarí site of Tambo Viejo (Shumate n.d.; Kent and Kowta 1993). None of the above-mentioned burial forms has been documented for the EIP in the Nazca Basin. Although south coast EIP societies shared a number of generic traits, regional differences of this nature suggest strong local autonomy.

Early Intermediate Period One

Only eight burials dating to the beginning of the EIP were documented in this study. They were all recovered by Aldo Rubini at three sites in Ocucaje (Fig. 1). This small, spatially discrete sample shows greater affinities with the local Paracas tradition than with the ensuing phases of the EIP in the Nazca Basin. The following grave forms have been recorded: (1) shallow interment with the body covered by rushes, (2) shaft grave 1.5 m deep with a roof of cane and mud, (3) urn burial with the mouth of the urn covered by an animal skin and cane, and (4) single and double chamber cist tombs (all forms are illustrated in Carmichael n.d.). The cist tombs are subterranean chambers approximately 2 m deep with walls of adobe or laced cane and mud plaster, and roofs of logs. In the double-chambered form the chambers are set one atop the other with human remains above and a single vessel in the vault below.

According to Rubini's notes, Ocucaje burials from the late Early Horizon and EIP 1 occur at the same cemeteries and in close proximity to each other. With the exception of single-chambered cist tombs, all of the burial forms reported for EIP 1 were present in the Early Horizon. Other similarities include relatively few ceramic inclusions (0–4 vessels per burial), and a relative abundance of gold artifacts (present in three of the eight EIP 1 graves; in the sample of 168 burials from Phases 2–8, only one contained a gold object). Several additional EIP 1 burials in Rubini's notes also contained gold, while gold is common in his Early Horizon grave lots where it even occurs in simple, shallow interments. Edward Dwyer and Jane Dwyer (1975) discuss several other forms of burial practiced during EIP 1. Jonathan Kent and Makoto Kowta (1993) describe an extended interment at Tambo Viejo dated to A.D. 20, which I would place in EIP 1.

CONCLUSIONS

The conclusions reached in this study regarding the nature of Nasca social structure are based on the following assertions: (1) social structure is symbolized in mortuary patterning, (2) status markers in this sample were correctly identified, and (3) the sample is representative. In an earlier section, Menzel's study (1976) of Late Horizon burials from Ica was cited as an example of how the social structure of a stratified Andean society may be expressed in burial patterns, and the Chimu provide an additional example (compare Donnan and Mackay 1978 with Pozorski 1979 and Conrad 1982). Status in these societies was clearly symbolized by mortuary customs that varied not only in degree but in kind. Absolute differences which divide the mortuary domain and vary significantly in energy expenditure demarcate the boundaries of these vertically stratified societies. Until contrary cases are documented, it is reasonable to assert that in the Central Andean tradition social structure was symbolized in mortuary patterning.

A series of factors may obscure the identification of status markers, not the least of which are postdepositional agencies of cultural or natural origin (O'Shea 1984: 24–26). Preservation is an important variable as status may be symbolized in perishable materials such as textiles or featherwork. However, in the Ica and Chimu examples social strata were clearly differentiated in a manner readily detectable in the archaeological record. Failure to identify ranks in the current sample may be the result of poor preservation, and in some instances poor recording on the part of the original excavators, but the sample of 168 burials is deemed sufficient to identify general patterns. The status indicators identified in this study (grave depth, tomb structure, and ceramic volume) were operative social markers in other Andean cultures (Menzel 1976; Donnan, this volume) and, after careful consideration of all available evidence, were found to be the only distinguishable variables in this sample.

The greatest potential flaw in this study is whether the sample is truly representative of all forms of burial. It is possible that more elaborate graves remain to be discovered. In this case the question will be whether such tombs vary in degree or in kind from the patterns identified here. Given the tremendous amount of looting that has taken place it is also possible that extremely rich burials have been eliminated from the archaeological record. This speculation will always remain viable. I can only claim to have examined the bulk of documented graves available at this time. In any event, it can be stated that the current mortuary evidence provides no support for the theory that Nasca society was stratified.

The contention that the Nasca formed a state-level society assumes the presence of stratification. As defined here, social stratification is present in all early state formations and may be considered among the fundamental characteristics, although it is not limited to states, for it also occurs in complex chiefdoms. While the current study found no evidence of stratification, it may always be argued that this is due to sample limitations. No single line of evidence should be relied upon exclusively in archaeological reconstructions. However, the current findings are congruent with all other forms of evidence.

Recent surveys in the Nazca Basin have not located the patterns associated with state-level societies. There is no evidence of full-time craft specialization. A few mounds at Cahuachi have been described as "monumental," but these pale in comparison with EIP constructions on the central and north coasts, and are unique to Cahuachi: there is no pattern of monumental mound construction in the Nazca Basin. It has been demonstrated that the famous Nazca geoglyphs, which are truly impressive in size, did not require extensive labor investments (Silverman 1990b: 441; Aveni 1990: 24). The aqueduct systems described by Katherine Schreiber and Josué Lancho (1988) represent a certain labor expenditure and coordination, but again, need hardly imply state-level organization. "Monumental" is a highly subjective term. When used to infer large, centralized political systems such as the state, it is not the simple presence or absence of a few large features, nor the magnitude of individual works; rather, it is an extensive and repetitive pattern of such undertakings over a region which mark the hand of centralized authority and vast labor pools.

Settlement patterns can also provide clues to the nature of social formations. In the Nazca Basin, EIP settlement is characterized by villages and a few large villages or towns, cemeteries, and ceremonial areas (geoglyphs and/or low mounds). On the basis of surface observations, Silverman (1990b, 1992) has tentatively described a Nasca site in the Ingenio Valley as urban, but cautions that excavations will be required to determine whether it meets her criteria for an urban center (Silverman 1988b: 404). In any event, the issue is not the presence or absence of a single trait (i.e., an "urban" settlement), but the extent to which formalized configurations are expressed in repetitive, regional patterns. The EIP settlement patterns in the Nazca Basin do not parallel those of state-level polities elsewhere in the Andes.

The geographical extent of Nasca hegemony needs to be reconsidered. In the traditional view, a Nasca polity centered in the Nazca Basin exerted direct control southward into the Acarí Valley.[8] Numerous field studies in recent years have failed to substantiate this hypothesis. Acarí researchers now state there is no evidence of Nasca political or socioeconomic intervention in the valley (Kent and Kowta 1993, and see Carmichael 1992a). Some writers have implied that Pisco was also within the Nasca sphere. This inference is based on similarities between contemporary ceramic styles and the distribution of trade vessels. There is no direct evidence of Nasca control in the Pisco Valley. Much confusion in the literature has resulted from using "Nasca" as a generic term for all EIP remains along the south coast (Carmi-

---

[8] Rowe (1963) first suggested this as a possibility. Others have repeated it as established fact.

chael 1992a). As local sequences are refined the territorial limits of the Nasca tradition are being reduced.

I have considered applying the label "complex society" to Nasca, but choose not to adopt this term because it is generally understood to include the complex chiefdom–early state continuum, and I see no evidence that Nasca was anywhere near this level of complexity. However, there is no universal definition of complex society and others may define it as they wish. I offer the following definition based on Tainter (1990) to clarify my position; others may disagree, but there should be no confusion about my use of the term.

Complex societies are those in which hierarchically ordered social components exhibit marked functional differentiation and specialization. The components are therefore functionally interdependent in that no individual or group can fulfill all of the required roles and duties. One measure of complexity is shown by the number of specialized, full-time occupations (i.e., farmer, fisherman, potter, metalsmith, weaver, builder, administrator, priest). In the ancient world heterogeneous societies of this nature are inevitably stratified and cover the spectrum from complex chiefdoms to mature states. The identification of complex societies is not contingent on the presence or absence of a single trait; it is the extent of formalization within and between a series of related factors that distinguishes this form of society.

The weight of current evidence indicates that the Nasca lived in societies with ranking, and ascribed status may have been operative. Other labels, if the reader prefers, would be middle-range societies or chiefdoms. However, the chiefdom label is also vague for it covers a tremendous range of social formations. As Timothy Earle (1987: 288) points out, chiefdoms include societies of around a thousand persons in several villages (simple chiefdoms) to polities integrating tens of thousands (complex chiefdoms). Robert Carneiro (1981: 47) provides a more graded typology of minimal, typical, and maximal chiefdoms. Complex or maximal chiefdoms, those approaching statehood, may be described as complex societies, but the minimal and typical forms fall below this threshold as defined above. On the basis of current evidence I would place Nasca on the mid to low end of the chiefdom continuum. Throughout the seven centuries of the EIP there may have been several small chiefdoms in the Ica Valley and Nazca Basin that periodically coalesced into larger confederations, but the extent to which these groups were united or independent during the EIP remains to be demonstrated. It is in the nature of such societies to periodically coalesce and then fragment back into their constituent parts.

While we will never escape crosscultural comparisons and their attendant typologies, there has been a growing consensus among Andean archaeologists that Andean social structures must be considered in the Andean context (Moseley 1992b; Silverman 1992), and the utility of this approach has been demonstrated for the south coast in works by Silverman (1990a) and Gary Urton (1990). Ethnohistoric studies by María Rostworowski (1977, 1978, 1983) and others provide excellent models, even allowing for Inka and Spanish alterations. The Andean señorío or curacazgo equates roughly with chiefdom, but contains dual and quadripartite divisions of leadership, in addition to numerous local and temporary positions. I am in complete agreement that we need to develop Andean models for Andean data, but caution that, as with chiefdoms, there was considerable range in the scale of señoríos (Rostworowski 1983) that must be taken into account and specified when applied to archaeological reconstructions. Urton (1990) provides a plausible model of structural organization in the Nazca Basin during the early historic period. The extent to which this model may be applied to the EIP is a matter of speculation, but the basic principles of Andean organization surely obtained. It may be conjectured that in the Nazca Basin EIP society structurally resembled one or several small señoríos, but the size and density of populations at any point in time remains to be determined.

The central importance of ancestor worship among Andean peoples is well documented in the ethnohistoric and ethnographic literature. The ancestors collectively watch over the flocks, fields, and harvests, insuring growth and fertility (Harris 1982: 48, 56, 61; Allen 1988: 59–60; Rasnake 1988: 179; Salomon, this volume). Among the Laymi, burial is also semantically and conceptually linked with the acts of cultivation and planting (Harris 1982: 52). Two of the major festivals held each year throughout the Central Andes are the Festival with the Dead (All Saints' Day and All Souls' Day), held at the beginning of the rainy season when planting is underway (Harris 1982: 54; Allen 1988: 164; Rasnake 1988: 178; Bastien, this volume), and the Festival of First Fruits (Carnival), which takes place at the end of the rainy season to celebrate the harvest (Harris 1982: 57–58; Allen 1988: 165, 182; Rasnake 1988: 242). The main focus of both festivals is ancestor homage and invocation. The well-being of each community rests with its dead. Although the Nasca are too far removed in time to assume direct historical continuity, the archaeological record suggests strong conceptual parallels between ancient and contemporary traditions (Donnan 1978; Carmichael 1992b, 1993).

The considerable time depth of the Central Andean tradition is shown by many elements in the Nasca mortuary complex. Above all is the deep concern with death and ancestor worship. Ties between the living and the dead were demonstrated and maintained through symbolic use of pottery and hair offerings. It may be conjectured that such ritual also served to validate the status and land tenure claims of living relatives, while in death the ancestors provided supernatural aid in the struggles of life.

BIBLIOGRAPHY

ALLEN, CATHERINE J.
    1988   *The Hold Life Has*. Smithsonian Institution Press, Washington, D.C.

ARRIAGA, PABLO JOSEPH DE
    1968   *The Extirpation of Idolatry in Peru* (L. Clark Keating, ed. and trans.). University of Kentucky Press, Lexington.

AVENI, ANTHONY
    1990   An Assessment of Previous Studies of the Nazca Geoglyphs. In *The Lines of Nazca* (Anthony Aveni, ed.): 1–40. The American Philosophical Society, Philadelphia.

BARTEL, BRAD
    1982   A Historical Review of Ethnological and Archaeological Analyses of Mortuary Practice. *Journal of Anthropological Archaeology* 1 (1): 32–58.

BINFORD, LEWIS R.
    1971   Mortuary Practices: Their Study and Their Potential. In *Approaches to the Social Dimensions of Mortuary Practices* (James A. Brown, ed.). Memoirs of the Society for American Archaeology 25: 6–29. Washington, D.C.

BLAGG, MARY M.
    n.d.   The Bizarre Innovation in Nasca Pottery. M.A. thesis, University of Texas at Austin, 1975.

BROWN, JAMES A.
    1971a   Introduction. In *Approaches to the Social Dimensions of Mortuary Practices* (James A. Brown, ed.). Memoirs of the Society for American Archaeology 25: 1–5. Washington, D.C.
    1971b   The Dimensions of Status at Spiro. In *Approaches to the Social Dimensions of Mortuary Practices* (James A. Brown, ed.). Memoirs of the Society for American Archaeology 25: 92–112. Washington, D.C.
    1981   The Search for Rank in Prehistoric Burials. In *The Archaeology of Death* (Robert Chapman, Ian Kinnes, and Klavs Randsborg, eds.): 25–38. Cambridge University Press, New York.

CANNON, AUBREY
    1989   The Historical Dimension in Mortuary Expressions of Status and Sentiment. *Current Anthropology* 30 (4): 437–447.

CARMICHAEL, PATRICK H.
    1992a   Local Traditions on the South Coast of Peru During the Early Intermediate Period. *Willay* 37–38: 4–6.
    1992b   Interpreting Nasca Iconography. In *Ancient Images, Ancient Thought: The Archaeology of Ideology* (A. Shawn Goldsmith, Sandra Garvie, David Selin, and Jeanette Smith, eds.): 187–197. Chacmool, Department of Archaeology, University of Calgary.

Patrick H. Carmichael

> 1993 The Life from Death Continuum in Nasca Imagery. *Andean Past* 4, in press.
> n.d. Nasca Mortuary Customs: Death and Ancient Society on the South Coast of Peru. Ph.D. dissertation, University of Calgary, 1988.

CARMICHAEL, PATRICK H., BRENDA V. KENNEDY, AND JANICE D. LACAPRA
> n.d. Unbraiding the Past: A Forensic Examination of Nasca Hair Artifacts. Manuscript on file, Department of Archaeology, University of Calgary, 1992.

CARNEIRO, ROBERT L.
> 1981 The Chiefdom: Precursor of the State. In *The Transition to Statehood in the New World* (Grant Jones and Robert Kautz, eds.): 37–79. Cambridge University Press, New York.

CHAPMAN, ROBERT, AND KLAVS RANDSBORG
> 1981 Approaches to the Archaeology of Death. In *The Archaeology of Death* (Robert Chapman, Ian Kinnes, and Klavs Randsborg, eds.): 1–24. Cambridge University Press, New York.

CIEZA DE LEÓN, PEDRO DE
> 1864 *The Travels of Pedro de Cieza de León, A.D. 1532–50: Contained in the First Part of His Chronicle of Peru* (Clements R. Markham, ed. and trans.). The Hakluyt Society, London.

COBO, BERNABÉ
> 1893 [1653] *Historia del nuevo mundo* 4 (Don Marcos Jimenez de la Espada, ed.). Sociedad de Bibliofilos Ambulances, Seville.

CONRAD, GEOFFREY W.
> 1982 The Burial Platforms of Chan Chan: Some Social and Political Implications. In *Chan Chan: Andean Desert City* (Michael E. Moseley and Kent C. Day, eds.): 87–117. University of New Mexico Press, Albuquerque.

DONNAN, CHRISTOPHER B.
> 1978 *Moche Art of Peru*. Museum of Cultural History, University of California, Los Angeles.

DONNAN, CHRISTOPHER B., AND CAROL J. MACKAY
> 1978 *Ancient Burial Patterns in the Moche Valley, Peru*. University of Texas Press, Austin.

DWYER, EDWARD, AND JANE P. DWYER
> 1975 The Paracas Cemeteries: Mortuary Patterns in a Peruvian South Coastal Tradition. In *Death and the Afterlife in Pre-Columbian America* (Elizabeth Benson, ed.): 145–161. Dumbarton Oaks, Washington, D.C.

EARLE, TIMOTHY K.
> 1987 Chiefdoms in Archaeological and Ethnohistoric Perspective. *Annual Review of Anthropology* 16: 279–308.

FRIED, MORTON
> 1967 *The Evolution of Political Society*. Random House, New York.

GOLDSTEIN, LYNNE
> 1981 One-Dimensional Archaeology and Multi-Dimensional People: Spatial Organization and Mortuary Analysis. In *The Archaeology of Death* (Rob-

ert Chapman, Ian Kinnes, and Klavs Randsborg, eds.): 53–69. Cambridge University Press, New York.

HARRIS, OLIVIA
- 1982 The Dead and the Devils among the Bolivian Laymi. In *Death and the Regeneration of Life* (Maurice Bloch and Jonathan Parry, eds.): 45–73. Cambridge University Press, New York.

KENT, JONATHAN, AND MAKOTO KOWTA
- 1993 Gods, Graves and Cists at Tambo Viejo, Acarí Valley, Peru. *Andean Past* 4, in press.

KROEBER, ALFRED L.
- n.d. Archaeological Explorations in Nazca Peru: The 1926 Marshall Field Expedition, with Donald Collier (Patrick H. Carmichael, ed.). *Fieldiana*, Anthropology Series, Field Museum of Natural History, Chicago. (forthcoming)

LANNING, EDWARD P.
- 1967 *Peru Before The Incas*. Prentice-Hall, Inc., Englewood Cliffs, N. J.

LOTHROP, SAMUEL K., AND JOY MAHLER
- 1957 *Late Nazca Burials in Chaviña, Peru*. Papers of the Peabody Museum of Archaeology and Ethnology 50 (1). Harvard University, Cambridge, Mass.

MASSEY, SARAH A.
- n.d. Sociopolitical Change in the Upper Ica Valley, B.C. 400 to 400 A.D.: Regional States on the South Coast of Peru. Ph.D. dissertation, University of California, Los Angeles, 1986.

MENZEL, DOROTHY
- 1976 *Pottery Style and Society in Ancient Peru*. University of California Press, Berkeley.

MILLONES, LUIS, AND MARY PRATT
- 1989 *Amor Brujo: Imagen y Cultura del Amor en los Andes*. Instituto de Estudios Peruanos, Lima.

MORRIS, IAN
- 1989 *Burial and Ancient Society* (2nd ed.). Cambridge University Press, New York.

MOSELEY, MICHAEL E.
- 1992a *The Incas and Their Ancestors*. Thames and Hudson, New York.
- 1992b Maritime Foundations and Multilinear Evolution: Retrospect and Prospect. *Andean Past* 3: 5–42.

O'SHEA, JOHN M.
- 1981 Social Configurations and the Archaeological Study of Mortuary Practices: A Case Study. In *The Archaeology of Death* (Robert Chapman, Ian Kinnes, and Klavs Randsborg, eds.): 39–52. Cambridge University Press, New York.
- 1984 *Mortuary Variability*. Academic Press, Toronto and New York.

PATTERSON, THOMAS C.
- 1991 *The Inca Empire*. Berg, St. Martin's Press, New York.

POZORSKI, THOMAS
    1979 The Las Avispas Burial Platform at Chan Chan, Peru. *Annals of the Carnegie Museum* 48 (8): 119–137. Pittsburgh.

PROULX, DONALD
    1968 *Local Differences and Time Differences in Nasca Pottery.* University of California Publications in Anthropology 5. Berkeley.
    1983 The Nasca Style. In *Art of the Andes: Pre-Columbian Sculptured and Painted Ceramics from the Arthur M. Sackler Collections* (Lois Katz, ed.): 87–105. Arthur M. Sackler Foundation, Washington, D.C.
    1989 Nasca Trophy Heads: Victims of Warfare or Ritual Sacrifice? In *Cultures in Conflict* (Diana Tkaczuk and Brian Vivian, eds.): 73–85. University of Calgary Archaeological Association.
    n.d. Representations of Humans in Nasca Ceramic Art. Paper presented at the 11th Annual Meeting of the Northeast Conference on Andean and Amazonian Archaeology and Ethnohistory, Colgate University, 1992.

RASNAKE, ROGER N.
    1988 *Domination and Cultural Resistance.* Duke University Press, Durham and London.

ROARK, RICHARD P.
    1965 From Monumental to Proliferous in Nasca Pottery. *Ñawpa Pacha* 3: 1–92.

ROSTWOROWSKI, MARÍA DE DIEZ CANSECO
    1977 *Etnía y Sociedad, Costa Peruana Prehispánica.* Instituto de Estudios Peruanos, Lima.
    1978 *Señoríos Indigenas de Lima y Canta.* Instituto de Estudios Peruanos, Lima.
    1983 *Estructuras Andinas del Poder.* Instituto de Estudios Peruanos, Lima.

ROWE, JOHN H.
    1946 Inca Culture at the Time of the Spanish Conquest. In *Handbook of South American Indians* (Julian H. Stewart, ed.). Smithsonian Institution, Bureau of American Ethnology, Bulletin 143: 183–330, Washington, D.C.
    1948 The Kingdom of Chimor. *Acta Americana* 6 (1–2): 26–59.
    1963 Urban Settlements in Ancient Peru. *Ñawpa Pacha* 1: 1–28.

SCHREIBER, KATHERINE J., AND JOSUÉ LANCHO ROJAS
    1988 Los Puquios de Nasca: Un Sistema de Galerías Filtrantes. *Boletín de Lima* 59: 51–62.

SERVICE, ELMAN R.
    1971 *Primitive Social Organization* (2nd ed.). Random House, New York.

SHIMADA, IZUMI
    1991 Pachacamac Archaeology: Retrospect and Prospect. In *Pachacamac and Pachacamac Archaeology* (reprint of the 1903 edition by Max Uhle with an introduction by Izumi Shimada): 14–66. University Museum Monograph 62. The University Museum of Archaeology and Anthropology, University of Pennsylvania, Philadelphia.

SHUMATE, SCOTT M.
    n.d.   The Continued Salvage Excavation of the Late Nasca Cemetery at Tambo Viejo. In *Archaeological Investigations in the Acari Valley, Peru: A Field Report, 1989* (Francis Riddell, ed.): 5–13. In-house document produced by the California Institute for Peruvian Studies, Sacramento, 1989.

SILVERMAN, HELAINE
    1987   A Nasca 8 Occupation at an Early Nasca Site: The Room of the Posts at Cahuachi. *Andean Past* 1: 5–55.
    1988a   Nasca 8: A Reassessment of Its Chronological Placement and Cultural Significance. In *Michigan Discussions in Anthropology: Multidisciplinary Studies in Andean Anthropology* 8 (Virginia Vitzthum, ed.): 23–32.
    1988b   Cahuachi: Non-Urban Cultural Complexity on the South Coast of Peru. *Journal of Field Archaeology* 15 (4): 403–430.
    1990a   The Early Nasca Pilgrimage Center of Cahuachi and the Nazca Lines: Anthropological and Archaeological Perspectives. In *The Lines of Nazca* (Anthony Aveni, ed.): 209–244. The American Philosophical Society, Philadelphia.
    1990b   Beyond the Pampa: The Geoglyphs in the Valleys of Nazca. *National Geographic Research* 6 (4): 435–456.
    1992   Estudio de los Patrones de Asentamiento y Reconstruccion de la Antigua Sociedad Nasca. *Boletín de Lima* 82: 33–44.

TAINTER, JOSEPH
    1973   The Social Correlates of Mortuary Patterning at Kaloko, North Kona, Hawaii. *Archaeology and Physical Anthropology in Oceania* 8 (1): 1–11.
    1978   Mortuary Practices and the Study of Prehistoric Social Systems. *Advances in Archaeological Method and Theory* 1: 105–141.
    1990   *The Collapse of Complex Societies* (3rd ed.). Cambridge University Press, New York.
    n.d.   The Archaeological Study of Social Change: Woodland Systems in West-Central Illinois. Ph.D. dissertation, Northwestern University, 1975.

UBBELOHDE-DOERING, HEINRICH
    1958   Bericht über archäologische Feldarbeiten in Perú. *Ethnos* 23: 67–99.

URTON, GARY
    1990   Andean Social Organization and the Maintenance of the Nazca Lines. In *The Lines of Nazca* (Anthony Aveni, ed.): 175–206. The American Philosophical Society, Philadelphia.

VALDEZ, LIDIO M.
    n.d.   Informe de los Trabajos de Campo de la Temporada de 1990 del "Proyecto Arqueológica Acarí, Yauca, Atiquipa y Chala." In-house document, the California Institute for Peruvian Studies, Sacramento, 1990.

ZÁRATE, AGUSTÍN DE
    1968   *The Discovery and Conquest of Peru* (J. M. Cohen, trans.). Penguin Books, Baltimore.

Where Do They Rest?
The Treatment of Human Offerings and Trophies in Ancient Peru

JOHN W. VERANO

SMITHSONIAN INSTITUTION

INTRODUCTION

As ITS TITLE IMPLIES, A PRINCIPAL FOCUS of this volume is how mortuary practices reflect the dynamic relationship between the living, the dead, and the supernatural in the Andean world. The ritual offering of human remains, or of human lives, also appears to have functioned as an important mediator between these entities. This paper will focus on the treatment of the human body in contexts outside the boundaries of standard Andean mortuary behavior. Examples include human sacrifice, dedicatory burials, secondary offerings of human remains, and the collection and curation of human body parts. In some cases, these bodies, or body parts, were treated in a similar fashion to normal burials. In other cases, however, non-standard treatment suggests that human remains were being thought of in a very different manner.

There are three principal sources of information on these practices—ethnohistoric accounts from the early colonial period, iconographic depictions of sacrifice and related themes, and archaeological evidence of the activities themselves. Ethnohistoric accounts speak primarily about the Inka, although some chroniclers described pre-Inka practices as well. The iconographic record is relatively uninformative for the Inka, because Inka art was largely non-representational, but it is particularly valuable for earlier cultures such as the Moche and Nasca. Data from archaeological excavations are limited by several factors, including preservation, the destruction of sites by urban expansion and looting, the lack of context in materials excavated unscientifically, and by variability in the observational and recording skills of archaeologists. Although all three data sources have inherent limitations, each provides information on the different ways in which human remains were treated in ancient Peru.

John W. Verano

THE ETHNOHISTORIC RECORD

Human Sacrifice

Chroniclers who described human sacrifice in the Inka empire indicated that it was not a frequent practice, but was reserved for times of great crisis, such as famines, epidemics, or major defeats on the battlefield (Rowe 1946; Fig. 1). It was reported that following important military victories, the Inka brought war prisoners and individuals selected from the defeated population to Cuzco for sacrifice (Cobo [1653] 1990: 111). In general, however, individuals chosen for sacrifice were children or young women selected from various parts of the empire during regular taxation. Hundreds of children were reportedly sacrificed following the death of an Inka ruler and during ceremonies associated with the coronation of his successor (Rowe 1946: 305–306). According to Bernabé Cobo, the bodies of sacrificed individuals "were buried with gold and silver and other things and with special superstitions" (Cobo [1653] 1990: 112). The remains of relatively few Inka sacrificial victims have been found archaeologically, although those that have are generally consistent with Cobo's description. One of the earliest discoveries was made by Max Uhle, who found the bodies of numerous sacrificed women buried at the temple of Pachacamac (Uhle 1903: 84–88). Excellent preservational conditions and careful observation by Uhle allowed him to determine that the women had been strangled with knotted ligatures. As John Rowe points out in this volume, Uhle's discovery was important in refuting Garcilaso de la Vega's claim that the Inka did not practice human sacrifice.

Inka child sacrifices have been found at several high-altitude Inka shrines in Chile and Argentina. The best documented is the child of Cerro El Plomo, discovered in 1954 in the highlands of central Chile (Mostny 1957; Rowe, this volume). The Cerro El Plomo child, an eight- to nine-year-old boy, was buried in a llama wool tunic, accompanied by gold, silver, and *Spondylus* shell figurines, and leather bags that contained coca leaves, hair, fingernail clippings, and deciduous teeth of the child. Other child sacrifices from high-altitude sites in Chile and Argentina contain similar offerings (Schobinger 1991; Reinhard 1992). The context and contents of these child burials are consistent with ethnohistoric descriptions of the Inka sacrificial cycle of *capac hucha*, in which children selected from distinct parts of the Inka empire were brought to Cuzco and then sent back to their native regions to be buried alive as sacrifices (Duviols 1976; Besom n.d.; Solomon, this volume).

While sacrifices such as the Cerro El Plomo child received elaborate mortuary treatment, this was probably not the case with war captives chosen for sacrifice. It is more likely in these cases that the body was not given a ceremonious burial. Intentional exposure of the corpse to vultures and other

Fig. 1 Offering of a child sacrifice to Pachacamac (after Guaman Poma de Ayala 1980, 1: 268 [266]).

scavengers was a frequently described punishment for individuals who had committed serious crimes against the Inka state (Basadre 1937: 207–210; Cieza de León 1941: chap. 70; Guaman Poma de Ayala 1980: 187ff). *Portions* of enemies, however, were occasionally retained for ritual or display purposes (Fig. 2). War trophies collected by the Inka included necklaces of human teeth, human skin (used to cover drums or stuffed with straw to create a mannequin), and flutes made of human bones (Rowe 1946: 279). A building in Cuzco is reported to have housed the skulls of conquered enemies (Lastres 1951: 65). A more elaborate treatment of an enemy's head was reserved for particularly important individuals:

> One of Atahualpa's favourite possessions was the head of Atoc, one of Huascar's generals. . . . Cristóbal de Mena saw this "head with its skin, dried flesh and hair. Its teeth were closed and held a silver spout. On top of the head a golden bowl was attached. Atahualpa used to drink from it when he was reminded of the wars waged against him by his brother." (Hemming 1970: 54)

Only a few examples of Inka war trophies are known. Uhle found necklaces of human teeth in his excavations at the Inka fortress of Saqsawaman (Tello 1918). A flute made of a human arm bone is in the collections of the Amano Museum in Lima, and the Museum of Archaeology at the University of San Antonio Abad, Cuzco, has a skull which may have been modified as a drinking vessel (McIntyre 1975: 59).

Human Sacrifice in Pre-Inka Times

Ethnohistoric data on human sacrifice before Inka times are limited to a few accounts, such as Fray Antonio de la Calancha's description of a temple in the Jequetepeque Valley on the north coast of Peru, where child sacrifices were reportedly made (Rowe 1948: 50). However, depictions of severed human heads, mutilated bodies, and scenes showing the capture and sacrifice of war prisoners can be found in the iconography of many ancient Andean societies. In Moche art, for example, the capture, arraignment, and sacrifice of war prisoners are common themes (Fig. 3), as are scenes showing victims being exposed to vultures (Donnan 1978: fig. 147; Donnan 1990). Supernatural figures holding human heads, and depictions of severed heads and limbs are also known from Moche art (Kutscher 1954: pl. 25b; Moser 1974; Donnan 1978: figs. 151, 152), and earlier Formative cultures on the north coast of Peru (Cordy-Collins 1992). Scenes involving the sacrifice and mutilation of bound captives are also known from Chimu iconography (Verano 1986; Lapiner 1976: 279–282), suggesting some continuity of themes seen in Moche art.

A recent discovery of a mass burial of mutilated individuals at the site of Pacatnamu in the Jequetepeque River Valley suggests that scenes of prisoner

Fig. 2 Head of an enemy being presented to the Inka Capac Yupanqui by his son, Topa Inka Yupanqui (after Guaman Poma de Ayala 1980, 1: 130 [153]).

John W. Verano

Fig. 3 Rollout of a Moche IV fineline drawing showing prisoners being brought before an elaborately dressed figure seated atop ceremonial architecture. Surrounding scenes depict splayed bodies, a disembodied head (*lower right*), and activities related to sacrifice. Associated with these activities are anthropomorphized black birds, possibly vultures. American Museum of Natural History, New York (illustration by Donna McClelland).

sacrifice, mutilation, and exposure of the body to scavengers are not merely symbolic statements or depictions of mythical events. In 1984, the remains of 14 adolescent and young adult males were found at Pacatnamu in the bottom of a trench outside the entrance to the principal ceremonial complex (Verano 1986). The deposit, which dates to the Late Intermediate Period (ca. A.D. 1150–1250), consists of three superimposed groups of skeletons (Fig. 4). Evidence indicates that on at least three distinct occasions, individuals were sacrificed, mutilated, and deposited in the trench. Insect remains found with the skeletons and surface weathering of bones indicate that the bodies of the victims were left exposed to scavengers rather than being promptly buried (Faulkner 1986). The skeletons show evidence of multiple injuries, including stab and cut wounds, fractures, and forced dismemberment. Two individuals had their throats slit, two were decapitated, and five appear to have had their chests cut open (Verano 1986). The radius, one of the bones of the forearm, had been forcibly removed from four of the individuals. The missing radii were not found elsewhere in the deposit, suggesting that they were intentionally collected from the victims. The articulated skeletons of two black vultures were also found associated with the human remains in the Pacatnamu mass burial. Initially assumed to be the remains of opportunistic scavengers, a detailed examination of the vulture skeletons revealed multiple fresh fractures and penetrating wounds, suggesting that the vultures had been sacrificed as well (Rea 1986).

The identity and origin of the mass burial is not known, although their ages and sex (adolescent and young adult males), and contextual evidence, such as ropes found around their ankles, suggest that they may have been war prisoners. Biometric comparisons between the mass burial victims and contemporary skeletal samples from Pacatnamu and adjacent coastal and highland sites were not conclusive in determining their population origin. However, an analysis of the isotopic composition of their bone collagen revealed that six of the 14 victims showed a nitrogen isotopic composition more than two standard deviations away from mean isotopic ratios for a contemporary sample of Pacatnamu burials (Verano and DeNiro 1993). The results suggest that these individuals had a different dietary history (and by implication, geographic origin) from the local population at Pacatnamu, and lend support to the hypothesis that these were war captives rather than members of the local population. The Pacatnamu mass burial shows a close correspondence to events depicted in scenes of prisoner sacrifice in Moche and Chimu iconography, as well as to north coast ethnohistoric descriptions of punishments involving mutilation and exposure of the body to scavengers (Rowe 1948: 49). It is important in that it provides archaeological documentation of activities previously known only indirectly from iconographic and ethnohistoric sources.

John W. Verano

Fig. 4 The Pacatnamu mass burial during excavation.

Retainer Burial

Spanish chroniclers noted that upon the death of a prominent Inka lord, certain of his wives, relatives, and servants were expected to accompany him to the grave (Cobo [1653] 1990: 251). Of course, this was not strictly true in the case of the Inka rulers, who in fact were not buried but continued to occupy their palaces in mummified form. Their sacrificed wives and retainers were buried elsewhere (see Rowe and Solomon, this volume). At the funeral of the Inka Atahualpa, following his garroting by the Spanish, Lucas Martínez Vegaso observed:

> When we were in the church singing the funeral service for Atahualpa with his body present, certain ladies—his sisters, wives and other intimates—arrived with great clamour. . . . They said that the tomb must be made much larger: for it was the custom when the chief lord died for all who loved him to be buried alive with him. (Hemming 1970: 79)

Retainer burial was not a practice unique to the Inkas, but was a deeply rooted tradition in the Andes. Cieza de León, describing traditional burial practices on the south coast of Peru, noted: "In these valleys the custom is very general of burying precious things with the dead, as well as many women and the most confidential servants possessed by the chief when alive" (Dwyer and Dwyer 1975: 145). Tombs of high-status individuals with accompanying retainer burials have been reported from a number of Andean archaeological sites (Rowe, Donnan, this volume). The presence of multiple primary interments in a single tomb does not, of course, necessarily imply sacrifice of retainers. Contextual clues such as unusual body position or the absence of grave goods may identify retainer burials. An example is the tomb of the Warrior Priest excavated at Huaca de la Cruz in the Viru Valley, where a high-status male was buried with four other individuals—an eight- to ten-year-old child, two adult females, and one adult male (Strong and Evans 1952; Donnan, this volume). The child and adult male were placed carefully in the tomb extended on their backs in standard Moche burial position, while the two females appear to have been forced into the corners, suggesting that they were retainers to the principal burial. Elsewhere in this volume, John Rowe describes a Lima period burial from the central coast of an old adult female with two retainers, identified as such by their unusual burial position.

Three high-status Moche tombs recently excavated at Sipán in the Reque Valley include retainer burials (Alva 1988, 1990; Verano n.d.a; Donnan, this volume). The two large chamber tombs (Tombs 1 and 2) each had a "guard" above the roof of the chamber and multiple burials surrounding the principal interment. Tomb 3, that of the "Old Lord" of Sipán, had a single retainer, a young female. In most cases, the bodies accompanying the principal burial appear to have been given careful mortuary treatment. Female retainers in the Sipán tombs showed substantial variability, however. The skeletons of the three females in Tomb 1 showed patterns of disarticulation suggesting that they were secondary burials, placed in the tomb after substantial soft tissue decomposition had already taken place (Verano n.d.a; Donnan, this volume). The young adult female in the second chamber tomb lay sprawled face down (Fig. 5) in a position suggesting casual treatment of the body rather than careful placement. The female retainer buried with the "Old Lord" was tightly flexed and forced face down into a small space at one end of the tomb. It is unclear why female retainers in the Sipán tombs were given such diverse treatment, although Donnan (this volume) suggests several possible explanations for the presence of secondary burials in the tomb of the Warrior Priest.

In highland Ecuador, deep shaft tombs containing elite burials and sacrificed retainers have been reported from the site of La Florida (Doyon 1988). Six high-status tombs, which date to the Regional Development period (500 B.C.–A.D. 500), contained numerous articulated skeletons that appear to be sacrifices placed with the principal burials. Articulated crania and mandi-

John W. Verano

Fig. 5 Female retainer burial in Tomb 2, Sipán (photo by the author, courtesy of Walter Alva).

bles, as well as disassociated skeletal elements, were also found in the upper shaft of some of the tombs, suggesting that some individuals were decapitated and dismembered. Most of the articulated skeletons believed to be sacrifices were young females, whereas the articulated skulls and mandibles were of males (Ubelaker n.d.).

Chan Chan

The most impressive example of retainer burial in the Andean archaeological record is found in the royal burial platforms at Chan Chan. The platforms, which are generally considered to have been the burial places of the kings of Chimor, are associated with nine of the ten large compounds at the site (Conrad 1982; Rowe, this volume). Intensively looted during the early colonial period, most have received little systematic study by archaeologists. The Las Avispas burial platform, associated with the Laberinto Compound, has been most extensively excavated. Excavations conducted by Thomas Pozorski revealed that the structure consisted of a series of 24 rectangular cells surrounding a central T-shaped chamber. The central chamber is believed to have once held the remains of one of the kings of Chimor

Where Do They Rest?

(Pozorski n.d.; Conrad 1982). In the disturbed fill of the surrounding cells, Pozorski recovered skeletal material from at least 93 individuals. All of the bones examined were judged to be females, and approximately two-thirds were estimated to have been between 17 and 24 years of age (Pozorski n.d.). Only about 25% of the fill from the Avispas platform was excavated, and the structure originally may have contained 200–300 burials (Conrad 1982: 100).

The young females in the burial platforms at Chan Chan are believed to be sacrificial victims placed in the platforms upon the death of the king.[1] Presumably they were interred in the secondary cells surrounding the principal burial chamber, although looting of the platforms has destroyed or thoroughly jumbled their internal contents. Pozorski was fortunate to find 13 articulated skeletons in one of the cells of the Las Avispas platform. The bodies had been placed in the cell extended on their backs, rather than seated and flexed, as is the normal Chimu burial position. Geoffrey Conrad describes them as being stacked one on top of another "like cordwood" (Conrad 1982: 99). The unusual burial position and stacking of the bodies in the cells is certainly suggestive of sacrifice.

Some of the burial platforms at Chan Chan had more than 40 secondary cells. If one assumes that all of these contained sacrificed victims, the scale of retainer burial at Chan Chan is truly impressive. Impressive also is the restricted age and sex distribution of the retainers. Pozorski's age and sex determinations of the skeletal remains from Las Avispas indicate that only a select category of individuals was considered appropriate for such sacrifice.[2]

Dedicatory Burials

In addition to the individuals placed in the burial platforms, young females have also been found as offerings placed under architectural features at Chan Chan. These burials contained fine textiles, ceramics, and other offerings, which might initially suggest that they were high-status individuals. However, the location and context in which they are found indicates that they were sacrifices. The burials are found in subfloor pits under U-shaped structures, or *audiencias,* as well as under ramps leading from courtyard floors to benches in the large compounds or *ciudadelas,* and appear to have been placed as offerings at the time of construction (Andrews 1974; Day 1982). Andrews concluded that all of the dedicatory burials were adolescent females, based on his examination of the skeletal remains (Andrews 1974: 250).

---

[1] Eight of the nine burial platforms had additional cells added on to the original structure, suggesting that more sacrifices may have been made on later occasions.

[2] Pozorski was an undergraduate student with limited training in osteology when he studied the skeletal material from Las Avispas. Reexamination of the Avispas material by a specialist in human osteology would be helpful in confirming the accuracy of his age and sex determinations.

John W. Verano

Burials of adolescent or young adult females with elaborate grave goods have also been found under *audiencias* at the sites of Farfán (Keatinge and Conrad 1983) and Pacatnamu (Bruce 1986) in the Jequetepeque Valley, indicating that the practice was not limited to the Chimu capital. Chimu dedicatory burials share some common features with the individuals interred in the royal burial platforms, in age and sex, as well as in the types of grave goods with which they were interred. Clearly, the dedication of certain buildings was an occasion of great ritual significance, involving both human sacrifice and the offering of textiles, ceramics, and other elite goods.

ISOLATED BONES AND BODY PARTS

Isolated human remains occur outside normal burial contexts at many Andean archaeological sites. In attempting to classify these features, it is important to distinguish between incidental inclusions of isolated human bones or bone fragments in architectural fill or occupational refuse, and human remains, whether partial or complete, that were intentionally buried or incorporated into architectural features.

Isolated human bones are commonly found at archaeological sites with multiple or extended periods of occupation. In most cases, such findings have been interpreted as the result of the accidental disturbance of earlier burials by later occupants of a site (Strong and Evans 1952: 41; Feldman n.d.: 121–122; Wing 1980: 234; Bonavia 1982: 397; Shimada 1982, 1985). Other possible explanations, such as cannibalism, have occasionally been suggested—particularly in the case of human bones found in domestic refuse deposits (Uhle 1925; Strong and Evans 1952). Although there has been a recent revival of the cannibalism hypothesis (Lumbreras 1989: 206–211), most cases of isolated human bones in fill or refuse are probably best explained as disturbance of earlier burials. What is of interest here is evidence of the intentional manipulation, modification, or redeposition of human remains.

Burned Human Bone

As Rowe notes in his chapter, cremation was not a customary mortuary practice in ancient Peru. Deposits of burned human bone have been found within the context of ritual offerings, however. One such offering has been described from the Galería de las Ofrendas at Chavín de Huantar (Lumbreras 1989). A 15 to 20 cm thick deposit containing ceramics, human and animal bone, shell, and small stone objects was found covering the floor of the gallery. The human bone consisted of small fragments that showed various degrees of burning. Fracture patterns on the bones indicate that they were dry and not fleshed when burned, indicating that human skeletal material, rather than bodies or body parts, were burned and later deposited in the gallery.

Where Do They Rest?

Secondary cremations of human skeletal remains have also been found at two sites in the lower Jequetepeque Valley on the north coast of Peru. In 1987, the cremated remains of a partial adult skeleton were found in a deposit of ash and burned earth on the summit of an Initial Period mound located approximately 1 km east of the site of Pacatnamu (Verano and Cordy-Collins n.d.). Like the human remains at the Galería de las Ofrendas, the bones showed no warping or transverse fracture lines, indicating that they were not covered with flesh at the time of burning (Baby 1954; Binford 1963). Carbonized fragments of textile were found with the bones, suggesting that they had been wrapped in a bundle and burned. The remains were then placed on the summit of the mound and capped with a pavement of field stones. Secondary cremations of human remains have also been found in a Middle Horizon context at Pacatnamu. In this case, several bundles containing partial skeletons of adults were placed in a room along with ceramic vessels, camelid limb segments, and other offerings. The room and its contents then appears to have been intentionally burned and abandoned (Cordy-Collins n.d.).

Secondary Deposits of Bone

Linda Manzanilla and Eric Woodard have recently reported the discovery of the partial skeletal remains of 17 individuals buried around the temple of Akapana at Tiwanaku (Manzanilla and Woodard 1990). The remains, about half of which were children and the other half adults of both sexes, were represented by partial skeletons and disarticulated skeletal elements. While the deposit was initially thought to represent sacrifice and dismemberment, no evidence of cut marks or fresh fractures was found on the bones. Manzanilla and Woodard suggest that the remains represent offerings of secondary burials made to the temple. Rowe (this volume) describes several Late Horizon ossuaries excavated by Luis Llanos near Calca, which also appear to represent the collection and secondary burial of human skeletal remains.

Isolated Skulls and Headless Burials

Burials of isolated skulls have been reported from various Andean archaeological sites. Some of these appear to represent the secondary burial of skulls as dedicatory offerings. Richard Burger found four isolated skulls in the fill of a platform at Chavín de Huantar (Burger 1984: 31), and burials of single skulls and skull caches have been reported from the Middle Horizon sites of Wari and Pikillacta (Brewster-Ray 1983; McEwan 1987: 39). At Wari, isolated skulls were found in pits under the floors of rooms and courtyards of an architectural compound. Although most had been disturbed, one skull was found intact, wrapped in cloth pinned with four copper *tupus*. At Pikillacta, a single cache of ten skulls was found in a pit in the corner of a large room. A metal spike was the only object found associated with them, although the cache was disturbed and objects may have been removed. The skulls lacked mandibles, and no cut marks or other evidence of trauma was present. While the source of the skulls is unknown, the practice of removing skulls from tombs in pre-Hispanic times has been reported from various Andean sites. Jane Buikstra, for example, reports evidence of skulls being removed in ancient times from tombs in Initial Period cemeteries in southern coastal Peru and northern Chile. She suggests that this may have been done to preserve portions of the ancestors as reminders of intergenerational relationships (Buikstra, this volume). Dorothy Menzel reported similar examples of the removal of skulls and other bones from Late Horizon tombs in the Ica Valley (Rowe, this volume), and Patrick Carmichael (this volume) describes both the removal of skulls and discoveries of empty tombs (grave goods but no occupant) in some Nasca cemeteries. Occasionally, additional skeletal material (or articulated body parts) were added to tombs, such as in the case of a Moche tomb from Huanchaco, described by Christopher Donnan (this volume), which contained three additional hands.

The burial of isolated skulls in ceremonial architecture may reflect mortuary behavior related to the honoring of ancestors, but clearly not in all cases. Five skulls found at the Formative period site of Wichquana in the Ayacucho Basin appear to reflect the burial of freshly disembodied heads rather than the secondary reburial of skulls (Lumbreras 1981). The Wichquana skulls were found in individual pits that had been cut into the floor of a U-shaped ceremonial structure. Each skull had one or more cervical vertebrae still articulated, indicating that soft tissue was still present at the time of burial. Lumbreras believes that the disembodied heads were sacrifices placed as offerings during a period of modification of the structure, sometime between 1150 and 750 B.C.

In many cases it is not clear whether isolated skulls and headless skeletons represent sacrificed individuals, secondary burials, or disturbed interments. In his excavations of a Preceramic cemetery at the site of Asia on the central coast, Frederic Engel found two headless skeletons and a total of eight isolated skulls (Engel 1963). In each case, the remains were wrapped in fiber mats and buried in a similar fashion as other individuals in the cemetery. The two headless skeletons were both of adults. One had associated grave goods, including textiles and a tooth pendant; the other was simply wrapped in a fiber mat. The eight skulls were judged by Engel to pertain to three adults, two children, and three infants. Two of the skulls were individually wrapped and buried in separate pits, one bundle contained two skulls (one child and one adult), and another contained four (one adult and three infants).

Where Do They Rest?

The bundle with four skulls was noteworthy in several respects. In it were found the remains of several textiles, including two twined cloaks, as well as "an engraved tray holding a mirror, a necklace of bone disks, shell pendants, a bone pin, feathers, and red pigment" (Engel 1963: 95). The quantity and quality of objects buried with these four skulls indicate elaborate treatment of the remains. Some features of the adult skull, however, suggest a more complex scenario. In examining the specimen, which had desiccated skin and hair still adhering to the bone, Engel noted a deep cut across the forehead. Below the cut mark the skin of the face was missing. Engel hypothesized that the face had been intentionally flayed (Engel 1963: fig. 185). Such mutilation of the head seems inconsistent with the otherwise careful treatment of the remains and associated offerings. Perhaps the skull belonged to a member of the Asia community who was killed and mutilated elsewhere, and whose head was later recovered and buried.

It is difficult to interpret the headless skeletons and isolated skulls at Asia due to a lack of detail in the published descriptions. A general report on the skeletal material from the site has been published (Hartweg 1958), but no detailed study of the isolated skulls and headless skeletons is available. It is not clear whether any cervical vertebrae were found with the isolated skulls, or whether an examination was made for cut marks or damage to the base of the skulls. Cut marks on the cervical vertebrae of the two headless skeletons would distinguish intentional decapitation from postmortem disturbance and reinterment. Further examination of this material is needed.

TROPHY HEADS

Spanish chroniclers reported that the practice of taking and preserving the heads of enemies was common among some Ecuadorian populations in the sixteenth century. Head-hunting continued to be practiced by some Amazonian groups until the early twentieth century. In the case of the Shuar of Ecuador, heads of enemies taken in raids were prepared by removing the skin from the skull and shrinking it (Stirling 1938; Harner 1972). In the case of the Mundurucú of Brazil, the brain was removed, but the skin and skull were otherwise left intact, resulting in a full-size preserved head (Ihering 1907).

Although common in Andean iconography, actual examples of severed human heads are rare in the Andean archaeological record, with the exception of the Paracas and Nasca cultures of the south coast of Peru. Since the first Nasca trophy heads were described by Uhle and Julio C. Tello early in this century (Uhle 1914; Tello 1918), many more examples have been discovered and described (Proulx 1971, 1989; Coelho 1972; Neira and Coelho 1972; Silverman n.d.a; Baraybar 1987, n.d.). Most of these are associated with the Nasca culture (ca. A.D. 1–800), but some have been found in Paracas contexts (ca. 600–200 B.C.) as well.

Over the past several years I have examined collections of trophy heads in the Museo Nacional de Antropología y Arqueología and the Museo Arqueológico de la Universidad Mayor de San Marcos in Lima, the Museo Regional de Ica, and the Field Museum of Natural History in Chicago. In addition, I have completed a preliminary analysis of a cache of 48 trophy heads found in 1989 at Cerro Carapo, in the modern town of Palpa (Silverman n.d.b; Verano n.d.b). The following description of Nasca trophy heads is based on my examination of 84 specimens, as well as on a review of published and unpublished reports on other examples.[3]

Diagnostic Features

Trophy heads from the south coast of Peru can be recognized by the presence of two diagnostic features: (1) damage to the base of the skull, which can vary from slight enlargement of the foramen magnum to the complete removal of the base and posterior portion of the skull; and (2) a hole broken through the frontal bone (Fig. 6). These two features are important, since they are recognizable even in incomplete or poorly preserved specimens.

Well-preserved trophy heads have desiccated skin and hair, as well as other features which are useful in understanding the way in which the heads were prepared. The general procedure for trophy heads preparation can be reconstructed as follows. The head was first severed at the neck, and remaining cervical vertebrae and soft tissue structures at the base of the skull (muscles, throat structures, the tongue) were removed. The base of the skull was then broken open and the brain and supporting membranes evacuated through the opening. A hole was punched through the frontal bone in the approximate center of the forehead for the attachment of a suspensory cord. The lips, and occasionally the eyelids, were pinned shut with huarango spines. The end result of this procedure was a head complete with skin and hair, with a cord permitting easy carrying or display (Fig. 7).

One of the objectives of those who prepared Nasca trophy heads appears to have been to preserve the natural appearance of the head. The lower jaw was frequently tied to the zygomatic arches to retain it in proper articulation, with the mouth closed. Wads of textile or other materials were often stuffed in the cheeks and eye sockets to maintain a full and lifelike appearance of the face (Fig. 8). The pinning shut of the mouth and eyelids presumably functioned to prevent their retraction during desiccation of the head.

---

[3] I am grateful to José Pablo Baraybar and Helaine Silverman for sharing their unpublished material on trophy heads.

Where Do They Rest?

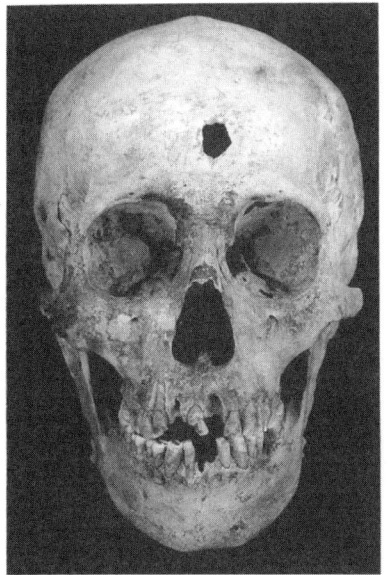 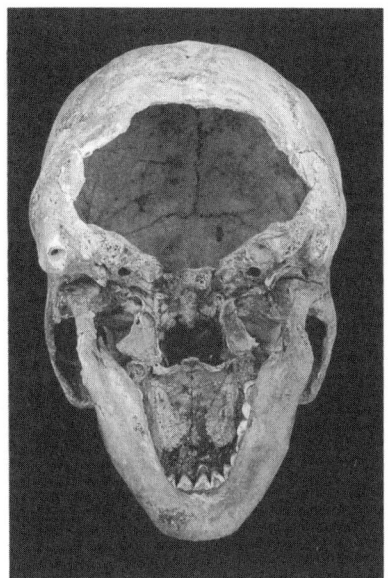

Fig. 6 Front and basal view of a Nasca trophy head (skull without preserved soft tissue) showing the diagnostic features of a hole through the frontal bone and damage to base of the skull. P538-3, Palpa.

The result was a neutral, stoic facial expression that is characteristic of Nasca trophy heads.[4]

Nasca trophy heads show some variations in preparation details. The suspensory cord, for example, can be made of twined vegetable fiber, cotton textile, or hair cut from the victim's head. The cord may be very simple, or it may have tassels or other objects attached to it. In two cases I have examined, a desiccated tongue, presumably that of the victim, was tied to the suspensory cord (Fig. 9).

Trophy Heads and Trophy Skulls

Several investigators have noted the presence of cut marks on the external surfaces of the skull and mandible of some trophy heads (Coelho 1972; Baraybar 1987, n.d.). Baraybar found that cut marks were most numerous around attachment sites of the major neck and chewing muscles, and concluded that the marks were the result of the dissection of these muscles from the skull and mandible. He noted, however, that cut marks are sometimes

---

[4] The Shuar are known to pin, and later sew, shut the lips of shrunken heads to prevent the soul of the victim from escaping and causing harm (Stirling 1938). Donald Proulx (1989) has suggested that a similar concept may have existed among the Nasca.

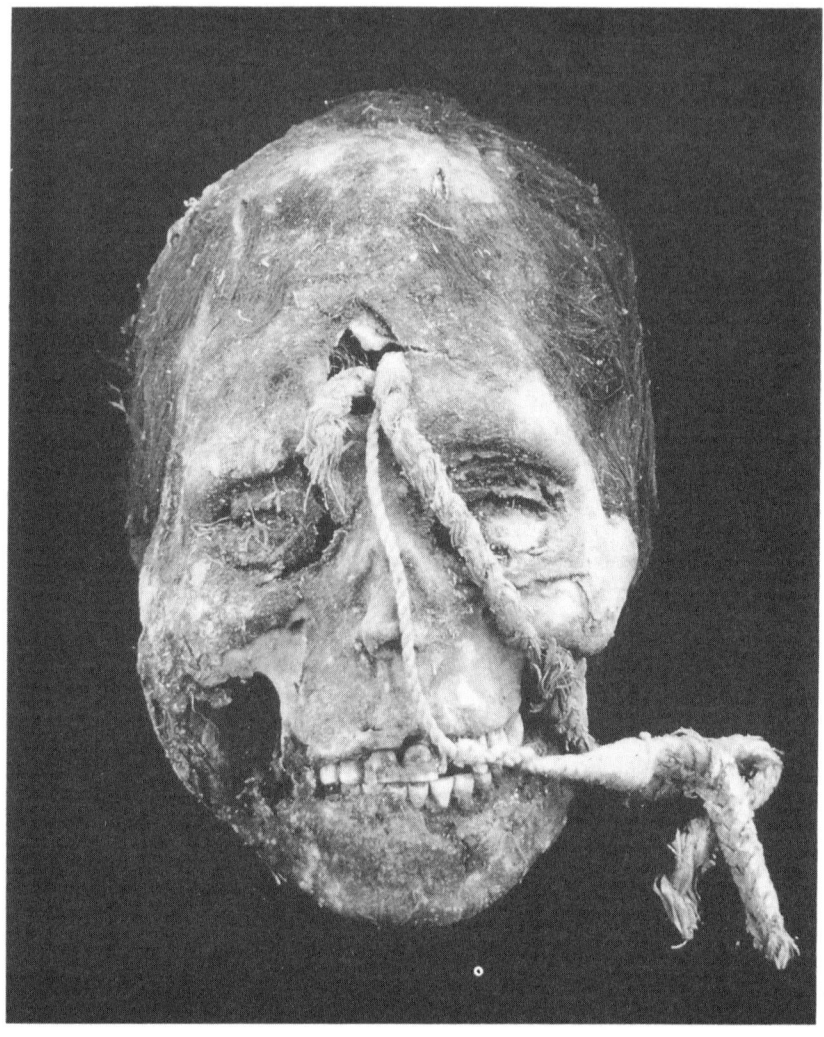

Fig. 7 Well-preserved Nasca trophy head with desiccated skin and hair and carrying cord. Museo Nacional de Antropología y Arqueología, AF: 7047.

Where Do They Rest?

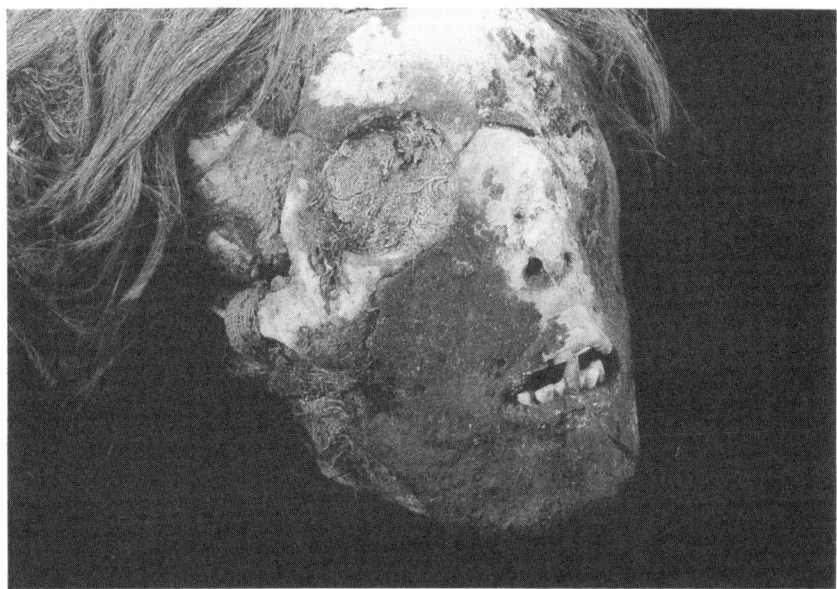

Fig. 8 Nasca trophy head. The cheeks and eye orbits are stuffed with textile and the mandible is tied to the zygomatic arches. Museo Nacional de Antropología y Arqueología, AF: 7053.

found on areas of the skull vault, face, and mandible that are not sites of muscle attachment, and suggested that some trophy heads may have been intentionally defleshed. Such defleshing would result in a trophy "skull" rather than a mummified head. Were some heads mummified and others defleshed? Unfortunately, cut marks can only be examined on trophy heads without overlying soft tissue. While archaeological preservation is generally excellent on the south coast of Peru, organic remains, including the skin and hair of trophy heads, are not always preserved. In the case of an isolated skull with cut marks, but no soft tissue preserved, it is difficult to know whether the head was actually defleshed, or whether the skin and hair decomposed following burial. It is possible that the skin was retracted to allow muscles and other subcutaneous tissues to be cut and scraped away, and then the skin was replaced over the skull.

A trophy head I examined in the Field Museum of Natural History suggests a solution to the defleshing question. It is a relatively well-preserved specimen, with hair, scalp, and some facial skin preserved. Close inspection of the head reveals that a plainweave textile lies *between* the exterior surface of the skull and the scalp (Fig. 10). Its presence between the scalp and bone

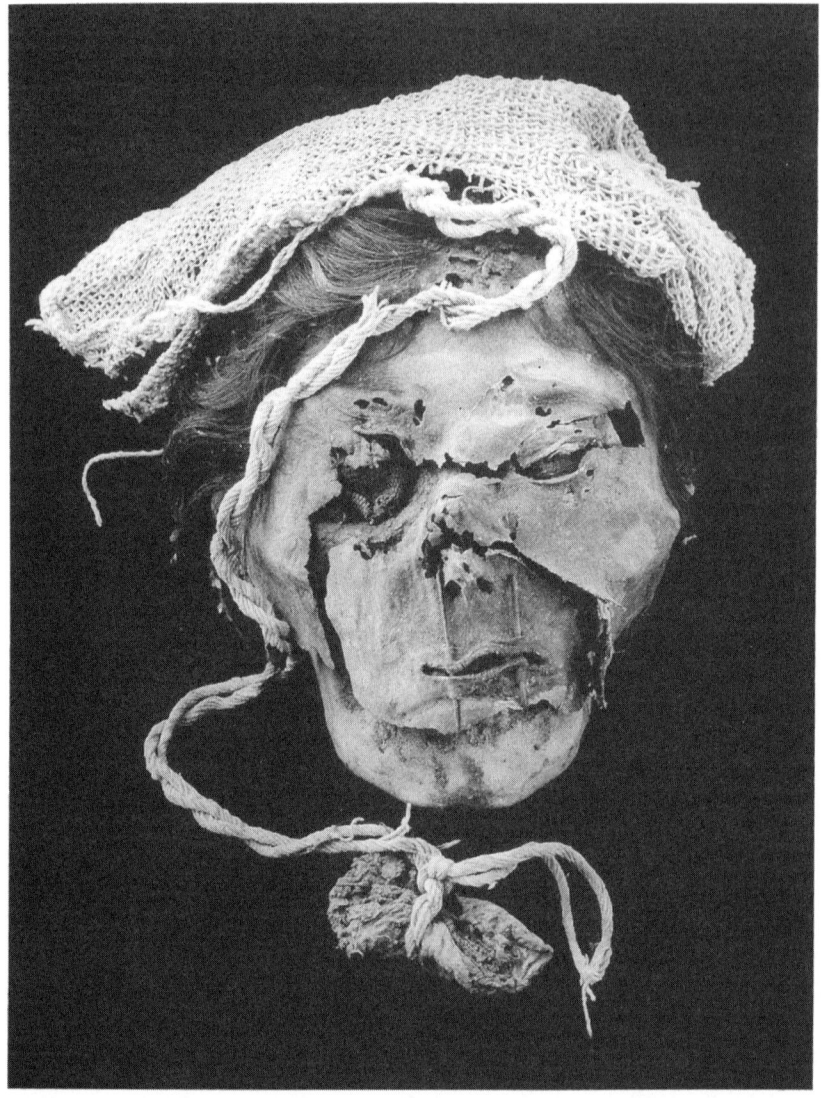

Fig. 9 Nasca trophy head with a desiccated tongue tied to the suspensory cord. Museo Nacional de Antropología y Arqueología, AF: 7508.

Where Do They Rest?

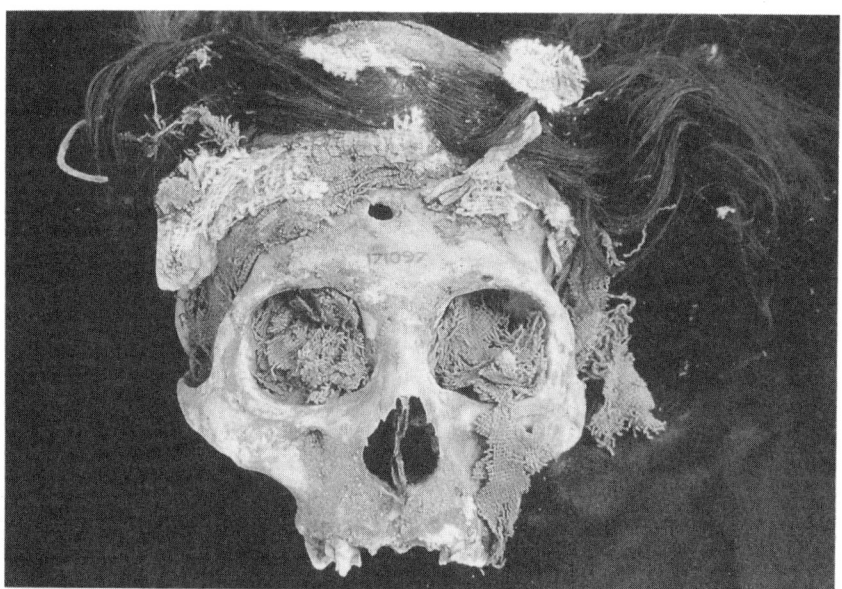

Fig. 10 Nasca trophy head from Cahuachi that shows a layer of textile (a) lying between the external surface of the skull vault (b) and the scalp (c). Field Museum of Natural History, Chicago, 171097.

suggests that in this case, at least, preparation of the head involved removing the skin, cleaning the skull and covering it with textile, and then replacing the skin over the skull.

Although the Field Museum specimen is a single case, it is consistent with certain observations I have made on "defleshed" specimens. If some trophy heads were in fact defleshed, and the skulls curated and handled over an extended period of time, one might expect to see some evidence of surface polishing on the bone. Such polish is a diagnostic feature of trophy skulls from other areas of the world, for example, Melanesia (White and Toth 1991). I have not seen any evidence of surface wear or of environmental exposure (sun bleaching or surface cracking) on any Nasca specimens I have examined,[5] and I am not aware of any depictions of trophy "skulls" in Nasca iconography. Trophy heads, when shown, are fleshed and with hair—they are never, to my knowledge, shown as skulls.

TROPHY HEADS IN THE ARCHAEOLOGICAL RECORD

Although commonly depicted in Paracas iconography, relatively few trophy heads have been recovered from Paracas contexts. Alejandro Pezzia has described two trophy head caches discovered on the Hacienda Ocucaje in the Ica Valley (Pezzia 1968). In 1956, he found two trophy heads lying on a thick layer of pacae leaves in a shallow pit in a looted Paracas cemetery on Cerro Max Uhle. In 1966, he recovered a cache of 13 covered with a plainweave cotton textile in a looted Paracas cemetery on Cerro de la Cruz. The 13 specimens consisted of the frontal and facial portions of the skull only, with well-preserved skin and hair. All were lying face up under the textile. It is interesting that while both caches found by Pezzia were in cemeteries, they were not associated with burials but appear to have been isolated offerings. Five trophy heads that date to either late Paracas or Early Nasca were found during excavations at Tambo Viejo in the Acarí Valley (Riddel and Belan n.d.). The heads were buried in ceramic ollas, in clay or rock-lined pits under the floor of four rooms Riddel excavated. Some of the heads were wrapped in plain cotton textile, but no other objects were associated with them. Other examples of Paracas trophy heads probably exist in museum and private collections, but the lack of provenience and associations for most specimens make it difficult to distinguish them from Nasca examples.

A large number of trophy heads have been recovered from Nasca sites. José Pablo Baraybar, who has made a concerted effort to track down and study trophy head collections, has documented more than 70 specimens (Baraybar 1987, n.d.). Combined with a recently discovered cache from

---

[5] This is not to be confused with the sun bleaching and weathering commonly seen on looted specimens due to recent surface exposure.

Where Do They Rest?

Palpa (described below), a conservative estimate places the number of Nasca trophy heads in museums and private collections at more than 120 specimens. Unfortunately, much of this sample comes from looted sites, and few specimens have good archaeological documentation. Some have been excavated scientifically, however, and these provide some information on burial context.

Until recently, the largest sample of provenienced trophy heads came from the site of Cahuachi in the Nazca Valley. Twenty-one specimens have been recovered in site surveys and excavations conducted by archaeologists Alfred Kroeber, Duncan Strong, Helaine Silverman, and Giuseppe Orefici (Baraybar 1987, n.d.; Silverman n.d.; Carmichael 1988; Proulx 1989). Some were found on the surface and lack specific context. Others, like those found by Kroeber, have not been published in detail. Most examples for which excavation data are available were isolated specimens found in the architectural fill of platforms, or in small pits dug into hardened dirt floors. An exception was a cache of nine heads found in a high-status tomb (Carmichael 1988: 482–483). Two trophy heads found by Silverman were wrapped in cotton textile, while those found by Orefici do not appear to have been wrapped.

Eleven trophy heads were found by Máximo Neira and Vera Coelho during excavations on the periphery of a Nasca cemetery at Chaviña in the Acarí Valley (Neira and Coelho 1972; Coelho 1972). The heads were arranged in a linear fashion along the western face of a mud brick wall. Nine had been placed in small circular pits dug through a hard caliche floor, while the remaining two were placed on the hardened surface and covered with sand and domestic refuse. One head was buried inside a broken ceramic olla. Most of the heads were wrapped in plain cotton textile. One was wrapped in a dark blue textile with polychrome borders, and fragments of polychrome textile were found with another. Additional objects were found in the small pits in which the heads were placed, and within the textile wrappings themselves. Two of the pits contained guinea pig skeletons, and chili peppers were found in the textile wrappings of three of the heads. Pairs of huarango spines were also found in the mouth area of three heads. The cranial cavity of one head was filled with a variety of plant material, including corn leaves, peanut shells, pacae husks, cactus spines, and other plant remains. The authors describe these inclusions as intentional "offerings," although they may simply represent materials used to dry and conserve the head.

The limited nature of Neira and Coelho's excavations did not establish the specific nature of the architecture with which the trophy heads were associated. The mud brick wall was located on the perimeter of a looted cemetery, and was covered by a deposit of occupational refuse containing diagnostic Nasca ceramic sherds. The authors hypothesize that the wall was part of some ceremonial structure, and that the trophy heads were offerings associated with it. A radiocarbon determination on one of the textile wrappings gave a date of A.D. 450 +/− 70 (Neira and Coelho 1972).

Cerro Carapo, Palpa

A recently discovered group of trophy heads from Cerro Carapo, outside the town of Palpa in the Ingenio Valley, constitutes the largest single cache of Nasca trophy heads known (Silverman n.d.a; Verano n.d.b). The cache was discovered by clandestine excavators, digging on Cerro Carapo above the modern community cemetery of Palpa in 1989. Archaeologists Helaine Silverman, David Browne, and Rubén García were informed of the discovery and conducted a salvage excavation of the site. Excavation revealed a large oval pit that had been dug into a natural deposit of sand, gravel, and boulders on the side of the hill. Twenty-six trophy heads and two mandibles were found in situ; 22 others were scattered in the looters' backdirt. Although the original pit had been disturbed, the position of the undisturbed heads suggested that they were originally arranged in two concentric rings. In total, the cache contained 48 trophy heads. The only cultural material associated with the cache were remains of suspensory cords attached to some of the heads, and a Nasca 5 sherd found in a level above the pit fill (Silverman n.d.a). The Nasca 5 sherd provides a terminus post quem for the deposit; radiocarbon dating of small wooden crossmembers tied to the suspensory cords may provide a more specific date for the deposit.

The Cerro Carapo trophy head cache is an isolated find without clear links to architectural features, tombs, or other evidence of cultural activity. Strata below the cache pit were sterile, and due to the salvage nature of the operation, excavations were not extended beyond the pit area. Further excavation might establish some context for the deposit. For the present, however, the importance of the Cerro Carapo trophy head cache lies in the fact that it represents an unusually large sample from a single archaeological context.

I had the opportunity to examine the trophy heads in Palpa shortly after they had been excavated, and later to clean and study them in Lima. Organic preservation was not good at the Palpa site, and textiles, if they had been present, were not preserved. Some fragments of suspensory cords, consisting of simple braided rope, were still present, as were small wooden crossmembers used to anchor the rope inside the skull. No soft tissue was preserved on the skulls, but traces of hair, and hair impressions were present in the adherent soil matrix, indicating that hair and scalp had been present on the heads at the time they were buried. Examination of the skulls revealed cut marks distributed widely over the external surfaces of the skull vault, face, and mandible, suggesting that the heads had been prepared in a complex manner, involving flaying of the skin, scraping away of underlying soft tissue, and replacement of the skin over the skull. All 48 of the Palpa skulls showed similar patterns of cut marks, in addition to the diagnostic features of a broken skull base and a perforation through the frontal bone.

Examination of the Palpa skulls indicated that all were males between the ages of approximately 20 and 45 years,[6] with the exception of one individual 12 to 15 years old, of indeterminate sex. Most skulls showed artificial cranial deformation of characteristic Nasca form (Weiss 1958; Allison et al. 1981; Baraybar 1987, n.d.). Other than cut marks and breakage related to their preparation as trophy heads, few skulls showed evidence of violent injuries. Two skulls had healed depressed fractures, and a third had a fresh depressed fracture on the occipital bone, which may have occurred at or around the time of death.

Trophy Heads, Warfare, and Nasca Society

Since the earliest descriptions by Tello, there has been continuing debate over how trophy heads were collected and how they functioned in Nasca society. Tello argued that mummified Nasca heads were not simply war trophies, but were important religious and power symbols: "La cabeza ha sido ante todo un símbolo religioso; un símbolo de poder; fué el más preciado atributo de los dioses" (Tello 1918: 58). Such an assertion is certainly supported by the prominent association between trophy heads and supernatural beings in Paracas and Nasca art (Dwyer and Dwyer 1975; Proulx 1971; Silverman n.d.). Tello noted that in the sample of eight trophy heads he examined, one was a child and three appeared to be female. He noted also that all eight heads were deformed in the Nasca style, and concluded that they were likely not the heads of enemies of the Nasca people.

With the discovery of more trophy heads in recent decades, the debate over whether Nasca trophy heads were really "war trophies" has continued. Vera Penteado Coelho (Coelho 1972; Neira and Coelho 1972) has argued, largely on the basis of the 11 heads found at Chaviña, that mummified Nasca heads were ritual offerings rather than war trophies. Coelho argues that the Chaviña heads are better interpreted as ritual offerings than as war trophies because they were buried with offerings, no weapons were found with them, and several females and a child, as well as males, were present. Coelho's argument has been questioned on various grounds (Proulx 1989; Baraybar n.d.), but I would like to focus on the issue of age and sex.

Table 1 presents the age and sex distribution of 84 trophy heads I have examined. This is an adequate sample size to approach the question; the

---

[6] Age estimates were based on dental eruption and tooth wear, and degree of closure of the spheno-occipital and vault sutures. Sex determinations were based on morphological characteristics of the skull, including general size and robusticity of muscle attachment areas.

John W. Verano

TABLE 1. AGE AND SEX OF TROPHY HEADS EXAMINED BY THE AUTHOR

AGE

Collection	Under 12 Years	12-20 Years	Adults
Museo Nacional de Antropología y Arqueología	1	3	21
Field Museum of Natural History	-	-	8
Museo Regional de Ica	1	-	2
Cerro Carapo, Palpa	-	-	48
Total	2	3	79
Percentage	2.4	3.6	94.0

SEX

Collection	Male	Female	Male?	Female?	?
Museo Nacional de Antropología y Arqueología	16	4	1	2	2
Field Museum of Natural History	7	1	-	-	-
Museo Regional de Ica	1	-	-	-	2
Cerro Carapo, Palpa	48	-	-	-	-
Total	72	5	1	2	4
Percentage	85.7	6.0	1.2	2.4	4.8

small samples examined by Tello (N = 8) and Coelho (Chaviña N = 11) are not. As Table 1 indicates, trophy heads of children and adolescents, while occasionally found, are quite rare. Children under 12 years of age make up less than 3% of the sample I examined; adolescents less than 4%. At the other end of the age spectrum, old adults (over 50 years) are notably absent. In terms of sex distribution, males substantially outnumber females (85% vs. 6%). From these data it is clear that Nasca trophy heads are not a random sampling of a living population, nor do they fit the profile of revered elders; with few exceptions they are young adult males.

Such an age and sex distribution is consistent with the hypothesis that Nasca trophy heads were collected from enemy combatants rather than from revered ancestors. There is some debate, however, over whether the

Where Do They Rest?

Fig. 11 Nasca 7 ceramic vessel with decapitation scene. Amano Museum, Lima, Catalog No. 037 (photo by author, courtesy of the Amano Museum).

victims were killed and decapitated on the battlefield, or whether they were captured and later ritually sacrificed. Nasca iconography is not particularly useful in providing an answer to this question. While depictions of supernatural beings or human figures holding trophy heads are common in Nasca art, scenes showing the act of decapitation are very rare. One of the best known examples is found on a ceramic vessel in the Amano Museum in Lima (Fig. 11). Illustrated on the vessel chamber are several elaborately dressed figures holding enemies by the hair and preparing to decapitate them with serrated knives. The scene can be interpreted as either a battle scene, as Proulx (1989) does, or as the sacrifice of prisoners. The latter interpretation is suggested by the fact that one of the elaborately dressed figures appears to be standing on elevated architecture. Several other Nasca depictions of decapitation or headless bodies have been illustrated by Proulx, who interprets them as battle scenes.

Based on his examination of actual trophy heads, José Pablo Baraybar is convinced that they are the product of ritual sacrifice rather than items brought back from the battlefield (Baraybar 1987, n.d.). He argues that cut marks he has observed on the scalp of some specimens were made while the

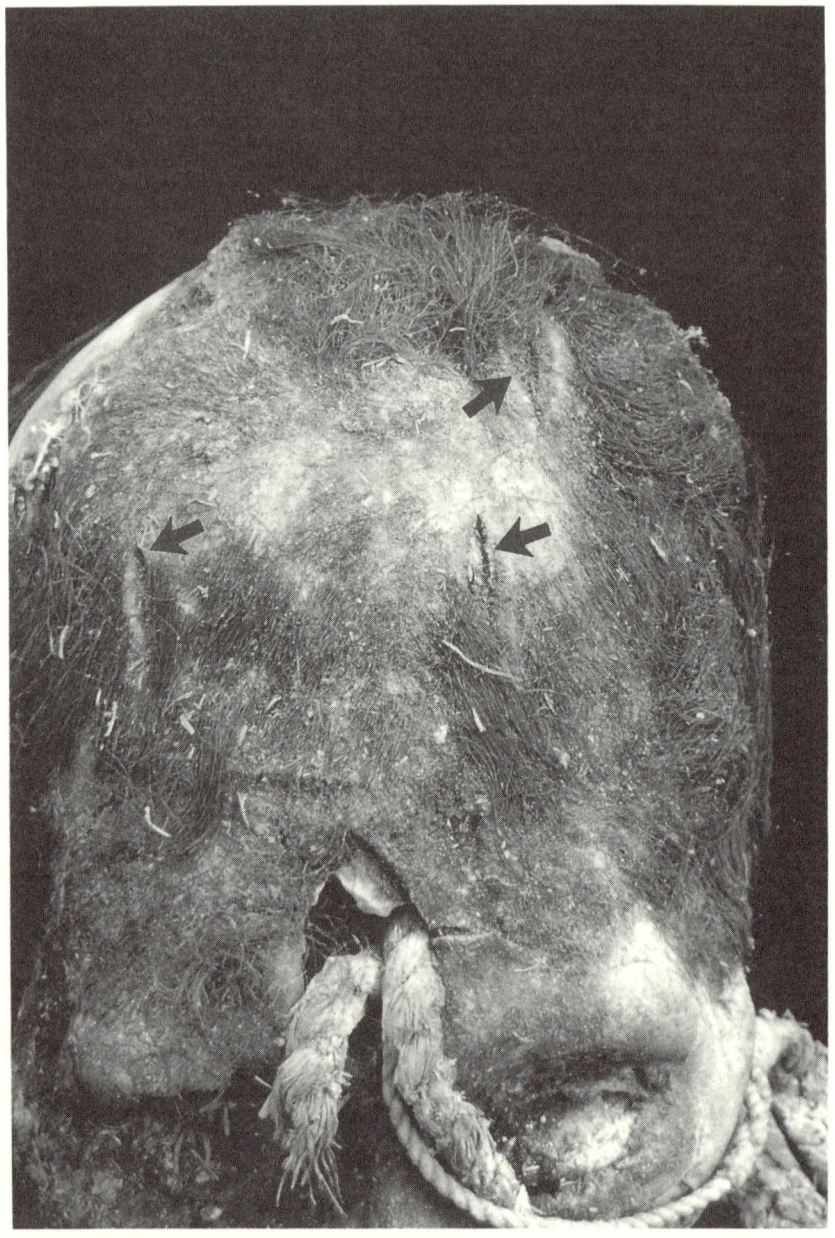

Fig. 12 Nasca trophy head showing cuts through the scalp (arrows). Museo Nacional de Antropología y Arqueología, AF: 7047.

Where Do They Rest?

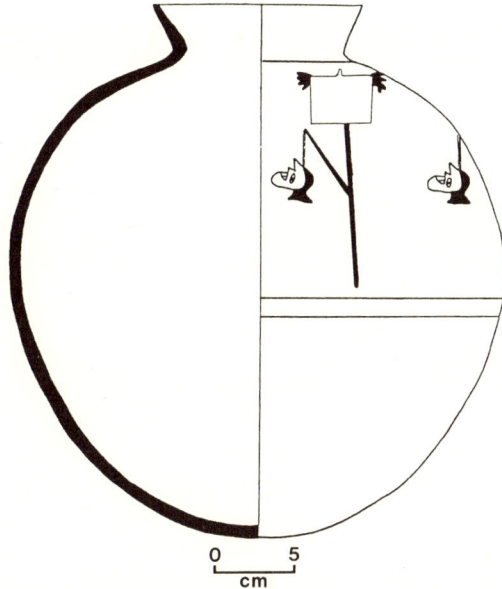

Fig. 13 Nasca ceramic vessel showing suspended trophy heads. Museo de América, Madrid (drawing after Blasco and Ramos 1974: fig. III).

victims were still alive (Fig. 12), and suggests that these individuals were intentionally "bled" before being decapitated, as part of a ritual that involved the public display of bloodied victims, followed by their sacrifice.[7]

Baraybar's hypothesis is interesting, although it is a difficult one to test. Proulx is skeptical, arguing that he finds no convincing evidence of human sacrifice among the Nasca (Proulx 1989). From the perspective of physical anthropology, the critical issue is whether or not one can confidently distinguish between antemortem and postmortem flesh wounds on a mummified head. Baraybar argues that the cuts are antemortem, because the margins of the wounds are retracted, and that stains around some of them show a positive reaction to a chemical test for blood. I believe that neither observation is sufficient to establish a confident antemortem diagnosis. Retraction of the edges of cuts are likely to have occurred during desiccation of the soft tissues, regardless of whether the cuts were made before or after death, and blood residues are certainly to be expected on a head that was detached from

---

[7] A similar observation was made previously by Pedro Weiss: "La retracción de los bordes en estas heridas de las cabezas trofeos indica que fueron hechas en vida de la víctima" (Weiss 1961: 134).

a living or recently deceased body. Given our lack of detailed knowledge of how Nasca trophy heads were prepared, manipulated, and curated, it is perhaps overly optimistic to attempt to distinguish antemortem and postmortem flesh wounds. The cut marks do exist, however, and Baraybar's hypothesis remains a possible explanation for their presence.

Curation and Burial of Trophy Heads

Nasca trophy heads show evidence of having been carefully prepared and curated. The complex treatment of the head, which included removal of the brain, major muscles, and other soft tissue structures at the base of the skull, as well as the stuffing of the cheeks and eye orbits, implies that trophy heads were prepared with long-term curation in mind. How, where, and for how long trophy heads were kept and displayed is a matter of conjecture. In Nasca iconography, trophy heads are most frequently shown being held in the hands of supernatural beings or, less commonly, humans. A ceramic olla in the Museum of the Americas in Madrid (Fig. 13) shows trophy heads suspended from poles which also support some form of banner. The latter suggests that heads were prominently displayed on certain occasions. Archaeological evidence indicates that after some period of time, the heads were ritually buried, rather than being discarded or intentionally destroyed. The most commonly observed pattern is the burial of individual heads or caches of heads under floors and within the fill of ceremonial architecture. Although three caches of trophy heads have been found in cemeteries, only rarely do such heads occur as grave offerings in Nasca tombs. In a study by Patrick Carmichael of the contents of 213 Nasca tombs, only four included trophy heads, and in one of the four cases the head appeared to belong to the tomb's occupant, reunited with its decapitated body (Carmichael 1988: 481–483). Perhaps trophy heads were not considered to be appropriate grave offerings except in unusual circumstances. Alternatively, trophy heads may have been perceived as community property rather than as the possessions of a particular individual.

The iconography of Paracas and Nasca trophy heads, particularly their association with supernatural beings, indicates that they were important objects of ritual power, and not simply war trophies. However, their age and sex characteristics are consistent with Proulx's assertion that they were collected from enemy combatants. The population affiliation of trophy head victims remains a problem. Cranial deformation, when present, is of Nasca style, indicating that the victims were of south coast origin. A number of headless Nasca burials are known (Carmichael 1988), suggesting a source for at least some trophy heads. However, there are few well-documented skeletal collections from the south coast of Peru with which to make comparisons.

CONCLUSION

This paper has focused on the treatment of human remains outside the boundaries of standard Andean mortuary practices. The topic is a broad one, encompassing behaviors related to human sacrifice, warfare, the collection of body parts, and the ritual reinterment of human remains. Ethnohistoric sources on the Inka provide a basic framework for understanding these practices, although the iconographic and archaeological record of pre-Inka societies provides much of the physical evidence, as well as important time depth, for such behaviors.

Human sacrifice was known to have been practiced by the Inka in times of crisis, and to commemorate significant events such as the coronation or death of an Inka emperor. Archaeological evidence of human sacrifice in pre-Inka times is limited for the most part to retainer burials in high-status tombs. Retainer burial reached its most extreme form in the royal burial platforms at Chan Chan, where hundreds of individuals were sacrificed upon the death of a king. The sacrifice and burial of young females as dedicatory offerings under architecture was also common at Chan Chan and other Chimu sites on the north coast of Peru.

The Inka are also known to have sacrificed war prisoners following important military victories. Certain war prisoners, as well as individuals convicted of serious crimes, were further punished by the deliberate mutilation and exposure of the body to scavengers, preventing proper burial. Artistic representations of prisoner sacrifice may date as far back as the Initial Period at the site of Cerro Sechin (Tello 1956), and they become important themes in the art of some later cultures such as the Moche. Desecration of the body by exposure to vultures is often associated with scenes of prisoner sacrifice, and the denial of proper mortuary treatment appears to have been an essential part of the ritual. A mass burial of sacrificed prisoners at Pacatnamu suggests that sacrificial scenes depicted in Moche and Chimu art were not mythical events or metaphorical statements, but are depictions of events that actually occurred.

Ritual decapitation is seen in the iconography of many ancient Andean cultures. Indeed, decapitation at the hands of supernaturals appears to be the most pervasive Andean metaphor for ritual death. The importance of the head is underscored by the Inka practice of preserving and modifying the heads of important enemies as war trophies. Similar practices have been documented in pre-Inka societies. The earliest archaeological evidence of decapitated individuals and disembodied heads may be present at the Preceramic site of Asia, on the central coast of Peru. It is among the Paracas and Nasca cultures of the south coast of Peru, however, that the iconography of decapitation and the display of disembodied heads is most closely paralleled by the physical evidence.

John W. Verano

Offerings of isolated skulls, caches of skulls, secondary burials and burned human bone have been found associated with ceremonial architecture at a number of Andean sites. These offerings can be distinguished from sacrifices by the lack of evidence of cut marks or other trauma, the disarticulated and incomplete nature of the remains (indicating secondary burial), and by the nature of burning (dry bones vs. fleshed remains). Such offerings appear to represent rituals of a different nature from those involving the sacrifice of living victims, and perhaps are better interpreted within the framework of ancestor worship.

In discussing Andean mortuary practices, it must be kept in mind that certain individuals never reached the cemetery. Others arrived incomplete, and others still were disinterred and reburied elsewhere. Human remains were treated in very diverse ways depending on the nature and meaning of a particular human death. These non-standard treatments must be kept in mind when considering the broader subject of Andean mortuary behavior.

BIBLIOGRAPHY

ALLISON, MARVIN J., ENRIQUE GERSZTEN, JUAN MUNIZAGA, CALOGERO SANTORO, AND GUILLERMO FOCACCI
   1981   La Práctica de la Deformación Craneana entre los Pueblos Andinos Precolombinos. *Chungará* 7: 238–260.

ALVA, WALTER
   1988   Discovering the New World's Richest Unlooted Tomb. *National Geographic* 174 (4): 510–549.
   1990   New Tomb of Royal Splendor. *National Geographic* 177 (6): 2–15.

ANDREWS, ANTHONY P.
   1974   The U-Shaped Structures at Chan Chan, Peru. *Journal of Field Archaeology* 1: 241–264.

BABY, RAYMOND S.
   1954   *Hopewell Cremation Practices.* The Ohio Historical Society, Papers in Archaeology 1.

BARAYBAR, JOSÉ PABLO
   1987   Cabezas Trofeo Nasca: Nuevas Evidencias. *Gaceta Arqueológica Andina* 15: 6–10.
   n.d.   Late Paracas and Early Nasca Trophy-Heads: The Evidence for Human Sacrifice. In *Symbolism of Trophy Heads and Decapitation in the Americas* (Elizabeth Baquedano, ed.). Oxbow Books, Oxford (in preparation).

BASADRE, JORGE
   1937   *Historia del Derecho Peruano.* Biblioteca Peruana de Ciencias Juridicas y Sociales. Editorial Antena, Lima.

BESOM, THOMAS
   n.d.   The Capac Hucha of Collasuyu. Paper presented at the Northeastern Conference on Andean and Amazonian Archaeology and Ethnohistory, SUNY-Binghamton, 1990.

BINFORD, LEWIS R.
   1963   An Analysis of Cremations From Three Michigan Sites. *Wisconsin Archeologist* 44: 98–110.

BLASCO, CONCEPCIÓN, AND LUIS J. RAMOS
   1974   Cabezas Cortadas en la Cerámica Nazca Según la Colección del Museo de América de Madrid. *Cuadernos Prehispánicos* (Valladolid) 2: 29–79.
   1980   *Cerámica Nazca.* Seminario Americanista de la Universidad de Valladolid, Spain.

BONAVIA, DUCCIO
   1982   *Los Gavilanes.* Corporación Financiera de Desarrollo S.A. Cofide and Instituto Arqueológico Aleman, Lima.

BREWSTER-WRAY, CHRISTINE C.
    1983   Spatial Patterning and the Function of a Huari Architectural Compound. In *Investigations of the Andean Past* (Daniel Sandweiss, ed.). Cornell University Press, Ithaca.

BRUCE, SUSAN L.
    1986   The Audiencia Room of the Huaca 1 Complex. In *The Pacatnamu Papers* 1 (Christopher B. Donnan and Guillermo A. Cock, eds.): 95–108. Museum of Cultural History, Los Angeles.

BURGER, RICHARD L.
    1984   *The Prehistoric Occupation of Chavín de Huántar, Peru*. University of California Press, Berkeley.

CARMICHAEL, PATRICK H.
    n.d.   Nasca Mortuary Customs: Death and Ancient Society on the South Coast of Peru. Ph.D. dissertation, University of Calgary, 1988.

CIEZA DE LEÓN, PEDRO DE
    1941   *La Crónica del Perú* (3rd ed.). Espasa-Calpe, Madrid.

COBO, BERNABÉ
    1990   *Inca Religion and Customs* (Roland Hamilton, ed. and trans.). University of Texas Press, Austin.

COELHO, VERA PENTEADO
    n.d.   Enterramentos de Cabeças da Cultura Nasca. Tese de Doutoramento Apresentada ao Departamento de Comunicaçoes e Artes da Universidad de Sao Paulo, 1972.

CONRAD, GEOFFREY W.
    1982   The Burial Platforms of Chan Chan: Some Social and Political Implications. In *Chan Chan: Andean Desert City* (Michael E. Moseley and Kent C. Day, eds.): 87–117. University of New Mexico Press, Albuquerque.

CORDY-COLLINS, ALANA K.
    n.d.   The Offering Room at Pacatnamu, Peru. Dumbarton Oaks Tertulia, Washington, D.C., November, 1987.
    1992   Archaism or Tradition? The Decapitation Theme in Cupisnique and Moche Iconography. *Latin American Antiquity* 3 (3): 206–220.

DAY, KENT C.
    1982   Ciudadelas: Their Form and Function. In *Chan Chan: Andean Desert City* (Michael E. Moseley and Kent C. Day, eds.): 55–66. University of New Mexico Press, Albuquerque.

DONNAN, CHRISTOPHER B.
    1978   *Moche Art of Peru*. Museum of Cultural History, Los Angeles.
    1986   Introduction. In *The Pacatnamu Papers* 1 (Christopher B. Donnan and Guillermo A. Cock, eds.): 19–26. Museum of Cultural History, Los Angeles.
    1990   Masterworks Reveal a Pre-Inca World. *National Geographic* 177 (6): 17–33.

DONNAN, CHRISTOPHER B., AND DONNA MCCLELLAND
    1979   *The Burial Theme in Moche Iconography*. Studies in Pre-Columbian Art and Archaeology 21. Dumbarton Oaks, Washington, D.C.

DOYON, LEÓN G.
    1988   Tumbas de la Nobleza en La Florida. In *Quito Antes de Benalcázar*. Centro Cultural Artes Serie Monográfica 1—Año 1: 51–66. Quito.

DUVIOLS, PIERRE
    1976   La Capacocha. *Revista Allpanchis* (Cuzco) 9: 11–57.

DWYER, EDWARD, AND JANE P. DWYER
    1975   The Paracas Cemeteries: Mortuary Patterns in a Peruvian South Coastal Tradition. In *Death and the Afterlife in Pre-Columbian America* (Elizabeth Benson, ed.): 145–161. Dumbarton Oaks, Washington, D.C.

ENGEL, FREDERIC
    1963   *A Preceramic Settlement on the Central Coast of Peru: Asia, Unit 1*. Transactions of the American Philosophical Society 53 (3): 3–139. Philadelphia.

FAULKNER, DAVID K.
    1986   The Mass Burial: An Entomological Perspective. In *The Pacatnamu Papers* 1 (Christopher B. Donnan and Guillermo A. Cock, eds.): 45–150. Museum of Cultural History, Los Angeles.

FELDMAN, ROBERT A.
    n.d.   Aspero, Perú: Architecture, Subsistence Economy, and Other Artifacts of a Pre-Ceramic Maritime Chiefdom. Ph.D. dissertation, Harvard University, 1980.

GUAMAN POMA DE AYALA, FELIPE
    1980   *El Primer Nueva Corónica y Buen Gobierno*. 3 Vols. (John V. Murra and Rolena Adorno, eds.). Siglo XXI, Mexico.

HARNER, MICHAEL J.
    1972   *The Jivaro: People of the Sacred Waterfalls*. Doubleday/Natural History Press, Garden City, New York.

HARTWEG, RAOUL
    1958   Les Squelettes des Sites Sans Céramique de la Côte du Pérou. *Journal de la Société des Américanistes* 47: 179–202.

HEMMING, JOHN
    1970   *The Conquest of the Incas*. Harcourt Brace Jovanovich, New York.

IHERING, RODOLPHO VON
    1907   As Cabeças Mumificadas Pelos Indios Mundurucús. *Revista do Museu Paulista* 7: 179–201.

IZUMI, SEIICHI, PEDRO J. CUCULIZA, AND CHIAKI KANO
    1972   *Excavations at Shillacoto, Huanuco, Peru*. University of Tokyo Press.

KEATINGE, RICHARD W.
    1986   The Huaca 4 Complex. In *The Pacatnamu Papers* (Christopher B. Donnan and Guillermo A. Cock, eds.): 151–160. Museum of Cultural History, Los Angeles.

KEATINGE, RICHARD W., AND GEOFFREY W. CONRAD
  1983   Imperialist Expansion in Peruvian Prehistory: Chimu Administration of a Conquered Territory. *Journal of Field Archaeology* 10 (3): 255–283.

KUTSCHER, GERDT
  1954   *Nordperuanische Keramik.* Casa Editora, Gebr. Mann., Berlin.

LAPINER, ALAN C.
  1976   *Pre-Columbian Art of South America.* H. N. Abrams, New York.

LASTRES, JUAN B.
  1951   *Historia de la Medicina Peruana, Volumen I: La Medicina Incaica.* Imprenta Santa Maria, Lima.

LAVACHERY, HENRI A.
  1929   *Las artes antiguas de América en el Museo Arqueológico de Madrid.* Ediciones De Sikkel, Amberes.

LUMBRERAS, LUIS G.
  1981   The Stratigraphy of the Open Sites. In *Prehistory of the Ayacucho Basin, Peru, Volume II: Excavations and Chronology* (Richard S. MacNeish, ed.): 167–198. University of Michigan Press, Ann Arbor.
  1989   *Chavin de Huantar en el Nacimiento de la Civilización Andina.* Instituto Andino de Estudios Arqueológicos, Lima.

MANZANILLA, LINDA, AND ERIC WOODARD
  1990   Restos humanos asociados a la Pirámide de Akapana (Tiwanaku, Bolivia). *Latin American Antiquity* 1 (2): 133–149.

MCEWAN, GORDON
  1987   *The Middle Horizon in the Valley of Cuzco, Peru: The Impact of the Wari Occupation of Pikillacta in the Lucre Basin.* BAR International Series 372, Oxford.

MCINTYRE, LOREN
  1975   *The Incredible Incas and Their Timeless Land.* National Geographic Society, Washington, D.C.

MORIMOTO, IWATARO, AND SHUNJI YOSHIDA
  1985   The Human Skeletal Remains From the 1982 Excavations at Huacaloma and Kolguitin, Peru. In *The Formative Period in the Cajamarca Basin, Peru: Excavations at Huacaloma and Layzon, 1982* (Kazuo Terada and Yoshio Onuki, eds.): 283–287. University of Tokyo Press.

MOSER, CHRISTOPHER L.
  1974   Ritual Decapitation in Moche Art. *Archaeology* 27 (1): 30–37.

MOSTNY, GRETE
  1957   La Momia del Cerro el Plomo (ed.). *Boletín del Museo Nacional de Historia Natural* 27 (1): 1–120.

NEIRA, MÁXIMO, AND VERA P. COELHO
  1972   Enterramientos de Cabezas de la Cultura Nasca. *Revista do Museu Paulista*, n.s. 20: 109–142.

PEZZIA ASSERETO, ALEJANDRO
    1968   *Ica y el Perú Precolombino,* Tomo I, Arqueología de la Provincia de Ica. Editora Ojeda, S.A., Ica.

POZORSKI, THOMAS
    n.d.   Survey and Excavations of Burial Platforms at Chan Chan, Peru. B.A. thesis, Harvard University, 1971.

PROULX, DONALD A.
    1971   Headhunting in Ancient Peru. *Archaeology* 24 (1): 16–21.
    1989   Nasca Trophy Heads: Victims of Warfare or Ritual Sacrifice? In *Cultures in Conflict: Current Archaeological Perspectives* (Diana C. Tkaczuk and Brian C. Vivian, eds.): 73–85. University of Calgary Archaeological Association.

REA, AMADEO M.
    1986   Black Vultures and Human Victims: Archaeological Evidence From Pacatnamu. In *The Pacatnamu Papers* 1 (Christopher B. Donnan and Guillermo A. Cock, eds.): 139–144. Museum of Cultural History, Los Angeles.

REINHARD, JOHAN
    1992   Sacred Peaks of the Andes. *National Geographic* 181 (3): 84–111.

RIDDEL, FRANCIS, AND A. BELAN
    n.d.   Informe del Proyecto de Rescate Arqueológico INC-CIPS en el Sitio de Tambo Viejo (PV-74-1) Valle de Acarí, Departamento de Arequipa. Report to the Instituto Nacional de Cultura, Lima, 1987.

ROWE, JOHN H.
    1946   Inca Culture at the Time of the Spanish Conquest. In *Handbook of South American Indians* 2 (Julian H. Steward, ed.): 183–330. Smithsonian Institution, Bureau of American Ethnology, Bulletin 143, Washington, D.C.
    1948   The Kingdom of Chimor. *Acta Americana* 6 (12): 26–59.

SANTILLAN, FERNANDO DE
    1927   Relacion. In *Historia de los Incas y Relación de su Gobierno* (Juan Santa Cruz Pachacuti and Fernando de Santillan, eds.). Imprenta y Libreria Sanmarti, Lima.

SCHOBINGER, JUAN
    1991   Sacrifices of the High Andes. *Natural History,* April: 63–69.

SHIMADA, MELODY
    1982   Zooarchaeology of Huacaloma: Behavioral and Cultural Implications. In *Excavations at Huacaloma in the Cajamarca Valley, Peru, 1979* (Kazuo Terada and Yoshio Onuki, eds.): 303–336. University of Tokyo Press.
    1985   Continuities and Changes in Patterns of Faunal Resource Utilization: Formative Through Cajamarca Periods. In *The Formative Period in the Cajamarca Basin, Peru: Excavations at Huacaloma and Layzon, 1982* (Kazuo Terada and Yoshio Onuki, eds.): 289–310. University of Tokyo Press.

SILVERMAN, HELAINE
    n.d.a   Cahuachi: An Andean Ceremonial Center. Ph.D. dissertation, University of Texas at Austin, 1986.
    n.d.b   Getting Ahead in Ancient Peru: Nasca Trophy Head Taking. In *Symbolism of Trophy Heads and Decapitation in the Americas* (Elizabeth Baquedano, ed.). Oxbow Books, Oxford (in press).

STIRLING, M.W.
    1938   *Historical and Ethnographical Material on the Jivaro Indians.* Smithsonian Institution, Bureau of American Ethnology, Bulletin 117. Washington, D.C.

STRONG, WILLIAM D., AND CLIFFORD EVANS, JR.
    1952   *Cultural Stratigraphy in the Virú Valley, Northern Peru.* Columbia University Press, New York.

TELLO, JULIO C.
    1918   *El uso de las Cabezas Humanas Artificialmente Momificadas y su Representación en el Antiguo Arte Peruano.* Ernesto R. Villaran, Lima.
    1956   *Arqueología de Valle de Casma.* Editorial San Marcos, Lima.

UBELAKER, DOUGLAS H.
    n.d.   Human Remains From La Florida, Quito, Ecuador. Manuscript on file, Department of Anthropology, National Museum of Natural History, Smithsonian Institution. Washington, D.C., 1991.

UHLE, MAX
    1903   *Pachacamac. Report of the William Pepper, M.D. LL.D. Peruvian Expedition of 1896.* Department of Archaeology, University of Pennsylvania, Philadelphia.
    1914   The Nazca Pottery of Ancient Peru. *Proceedings of the Davenport Academy of Sciences* 13: 1–46.
    1925   Report on Explorations at Supe. *University of California Publications in American Archaeology and Ethnology* 21 (6): 257–263.

VALCARCEL, LUIS E.
    1971   *Historia del Peru Antiguo.* Editorial Juan Mejia Baca, Lima.

VERANO, JOHN W.
    1986   A Mass Burial of Mutilated Individuals at Pacatnamu. In *The Pacatnamu Papers* 1 (Christopher B. Donnan and Guillermo A. Cock, eds.): 117–138. Museum of Cultural History, Los Angeles.
    n.d.a   Human Skeletal Remains from Tomb 1, Sipán. Manuscript submitted to University of Mainz for volume (in prep.) on Tomb 1, Sipán.
    n.d.b   A Cache of 48 Trophy Heads from Cerro Carapo, Peru. Paper presented at the 18th Annual Midwest Conference on Andean and Amazonian Archaeology and Ethnohistory, Chicago, 1989.

VERANO, JOHN W., AND MICHAEL J. DENIRO
    1993   Locals or Foreigners? Morphological, Biometric, and Isotopic Approaches to the Question of Group Affinity in Human Skeletal Remains Recovered from Unusual Archaeological Contexts. In *Investiga-*

tions of Ancient Human Tissue: Chemical Analysis in Anthropology (Mary K. Sandford, ed.): 361–386. Gordon and Breach, New York.

VERANO, JOHN W., AND ALANA CORDY-COLLINS
n.d. Preliminary Report on Chavin Sites in the Lower Jequetepeque Valley. Manuscript on file at the Museum of Cultural History, Los Angeles.

WEISS, PEDRO
1958 *Osteología Cultural: Prácticas Cefálicas.* Universidad Nacional Mayor de San Marcos, Lima.
1961 *Osteología Cultural: Prácticas Cefálicas.* 2nda. Parte. Universidad Nacional Mayor de San Marcos, Lima.

WHITE, TIM D., AND NICHOLAS TOTH
1991 The Question of Cannibalism at Grotta Guattari. *Current Anthropology* 32 (2): 118–138.

WING, ELIZABETH S.
1980 Faunal Remains. In *Guitarrero Cave: Early Man in the Andes* (Thomas F. Lynch, ed.): 149–172. Academic Press, New York.

Tombs for the Living ... or ... for the Dead: The Osmore Ancestors

JANE E. BUIKSTRA
UNIVERSITY OF CHICAGO

... near *Arica,* above the Church of *Hilo,* and all along the Shore ... being an infinite Number of Tombs, where they bury'd themſelves alive with their Families and Goods; which is the Reaſon that when they happened to dig at this very Time, they find Bodies almoſt entire with their Cloaths, and very often Gold and Silver Veſſels. Thoſe I have ſeen are dug in the Sand the depth of a Man, and incloſed with a Wall of dry Stone: They are cover'd with Wattles of Canes, on which there is a Bed or Layer of Earth, and Sand laid over, to the end the Place where they were, might not be obſerv'd ...

We are here to obſerve, that there is much Difference between these Voluntary Tombs, and thoſe they erected for Men of Note; the latter are above the Ground, built with unburnt Bricks and round, like little Pigeon Houſes ....

Frézier 1717: 177–178

ALTHOUGH PLENTIFUL, CEMETERIES from the south-central Andes are seldom characterized by monumentality. Amédée François Frézier—an engineer to the French king—visited the region in 1713 and observed that the majority of graves seemed, in fact, specially designed to guard against discovery by the living. Thus, the few occasions of monumental mortuary architecture—Frézier's "Pigeon Houſes"—assumed special significance. The visibility of these structures, which we recognize as chullpas, led Frézier to emphasize differences of status and presumably wealth even in the face of precious metals recovered from the hidden graves.

With today's wisdom, we recognize that Frézier had been misled by the remarkable preservation of Andean coastal sites and had, therefore, reduced millennia of rich and complex prehistory to an instant of very recent time. Influenced by European burial customs, while assuming contemporaneity between obscure cist tombs and highly visible mortuary structures, he inferred that monumental architecture was uniquely associated with "men of note."

As in Frézier's time, funerary monumentality and elaborate grave goods influence contemporary interpretations of ancient south-central Andean peoples. Recent critical review of assumptions commonly made in cemetery studies has, however, led to theories of mortuary behavior that place disposal areas (graves) and death rituals within broader interpretive contexts. Such approaches, which emphasize the role of the mourners as well as the history of the deceased, hold promise for enriching our interpretation of south-central Andean mortuary monuments, including both the elaborate above-ground chullpas *and* the simple subterranean tombs.

Using the Osmore drainage as an example, we find that monumental architecture is extremely rare, only twice directly associated with disposal of the dead: once at the Middle Horizon site of Omo and again as a generalized phenomenon—chullpas—during very late prehistory. At Omo, a Tiwanaku V (Chen Chen phase) plaza and complex structure surrounded by both cemeteries and domestic precincts may signal an intrusive rather than a local development (P. Goldstein n.d.). The Late Period chullpas and "proto-chullpas" are also thought to represent architectural styles adapted from highland contexts (Stanish n.d.b).

To understand such rare, but highly visible, monumental features, we must become immersed in the broader context of regional mortuary traditions. The dynamic relationship between social order and such archaeologically discoverable phenomena as architectural forms and material culture can only be understood in diachronic perspective. From such contextual treatments emerges a clear sense of importance for even the less-than-monumental tombs, where the relationships of the living to the dead were symbolically represented—just as at the monumental facilities.

This paper considers and interprets the diachronic sequence of cemeteries excavated within the lower and middle Osmore drainage (Fig. 1) in southern Peru as a case study of a south-central Andean region. Since systematic excavation and population-based interpretation of mortuary sites is only lately developed in this area—attributable perhaps to the absence of monumentality described above—we are relying primarily upon data from very recent and ongoing excavations. Our conclusions should therefore be considered preliminary observations that will be refined in the course of subsequent study.

THEORETICAL CONCERNS

The theories embodied in *Approaches to the Social Dimensions of Mortuary Practices* (Brown 1971) and related works (Saxe n.d.) have influenced a generation of archaeological scholarship. Based upon observations of cross-

Tombs for the Living ... or ... for the Dead: The Osmore Ancestors

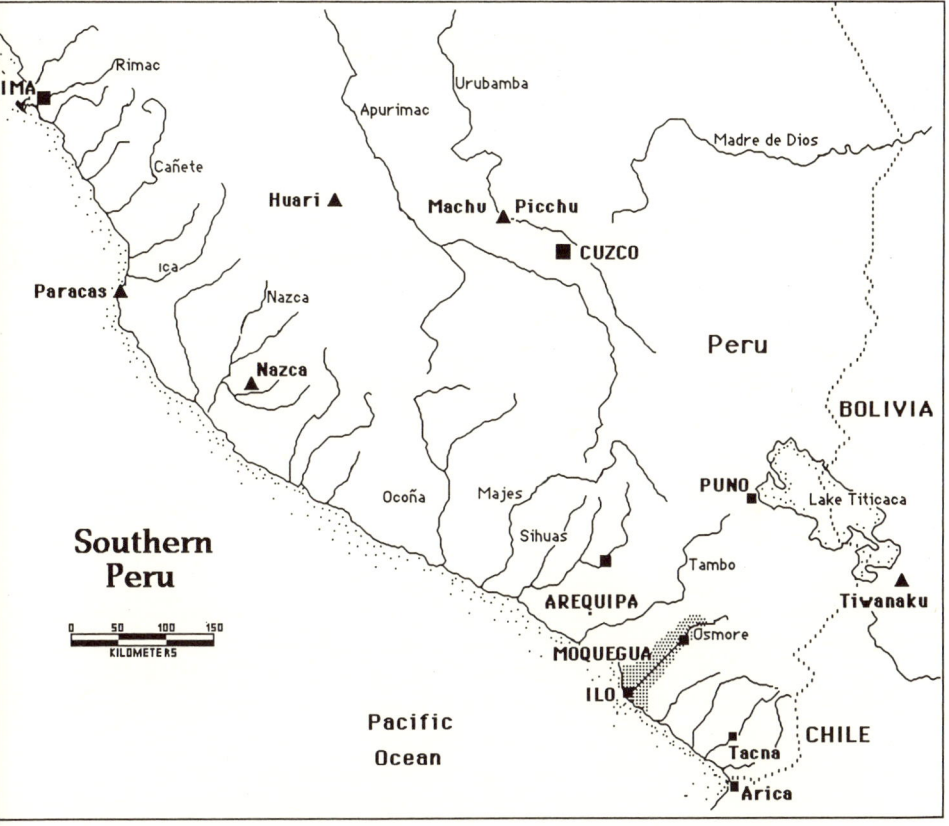

Fig. 1 Location of the study area.

cultural regularities in disposal practices, the Saxe–Binford "school" has encouraged inferences about social complexity based upon mortuary site structure and content. While this development is largely North American, the influence of V. Gordon Childe (1945) and Colin Renfrew (1973, 1976, 1984) has led British scholars to similar interpretive models. These "new" or "social archaeological" developments have enhanced the visibility of mortuary archaeology, thus encouraging extensive cemetery excavations through emphasis upon intrasite variability and structure. The integration of biological data (age/sex/health status) with cultural attributes describing tomb form, corpse treatment, and grave wealth led physical anthropologists out of the appendices of site reports and into nearly equal partnership with archaeologist-excavators (Blakely 1977; Powell, Mires, and Bridges 1991).

Jane E. Buikstra

The productive offspring of the Saxe-Binford school have made major contributions to our appreciation of ancient lifeways (e.g., Bradley 1984; Chapman, Kinnes, and Randsborg 1981; Charles and Buikstra 1983; L. Goldstein n.d., 1980; O'Shea 1984; Tainter 1977a, 1977b), yet they are not without their critics (Braun 1981; Hodder 1980, 1981, 1982a, 1982b). The most severe criticism has been leveled by members of the postprocessual/contextual school(s) who have called attention to the imperfect relationship between social forms and mortuary treatment (Hodder 1980, 1981, 1982a, 1982b, 1986, 1987a, 1987b; Miller and Tilley 1984; Shanks and Tilley 1987). While the most extreme postprocessualists, as Trigger (1990: 119) emphasizes, "appear to be so determined to affirm cultural particularities that they overlook or deny cross-cultural uniformities," some of their cautions are just. Particularly useful in achieving the fullest possible interpretive richness from the archaeological record is the postprocessualist emphasis on context and the appreciation of traditions in interpreting temporal sequences. Equally important is their concern for the dynamic relationship between social order and mortuary customs.

Binford (1971) and Saxe (n.d.) emphasized the *social persona* of the deceased, with the mourners assuming secondary importance. The postprocessualists have shifted the balance back to the mourners, sometimes to a fault, with the deceased becoming a shadow behind the political machinations of the living. Yet it *is* the living who create tombs, prepare corpses, and engage in either brief or extended mortuary rituals. They may "use" any aspect of the ritual to enhance or otherwise symbolize their political fortunes, as in Dillehay's (1990, this volume) Mapuche example. Or they may simply choose to represent directly the lifetime achievements of the deceased and so leave archaeologists a rather direct map for inferring activities and social order. Influenced both by tradition and by current social, political, and economic circumstances, the living mourners thus create the record that may be read many generations in the future, necessarily distorted by the numerous factors that influence archaeological preservation (O'Shea 1984). The challenge for the archaeologist of death is to establish the nature of the coded message left us by the living. Where on the continuum of possible behaviors—from direct representation of the deceased individual's composite roles to deliberate distortion—does our ancient burial program fall?

Even in the absence of monumental mortuary architecture, the extensive archaeological record from the Osmore drainage provides ample opportunity to use cemetery data for investigating long-term changes in the Andean social landscape. In this paper, we focus upon the meaning inherent in certain mortuary forms: evidence of extended mortuary ritual, monumental architecture, and chullpas. In addition, following Binford (1971) and Saxe (n.d.), we assume that increased social complexity is associated with restricted access of specific age/sex groups to specialized forms of burial treatment. Thus, when sufficiently large and well-documented cemetery samples are available, we will focus first upon defining modal interment behaviors within cemeteries, as structured by age and sex of the deceased. The meaning assigned to aberrations from modal behaviors requires sensitivity to context and local traditions.

THE OSMORE DRAINAGE

The mortuary sites considered in this paper are located within the 139 km drainage of the Rio Osmore and its tributaries (Fig. 2).[1] This drainage complex extends from the cordillera at ca. 5,100 m above mean sea level (AMSL) to the coast, entering the Pacific Ocean near the present-day city of Ilo. The midvalley zone, at 1,000 to 2,000 m AMSL, comprises the Moquegua Valley, where agricultural productivity—enhanced in both ancient and modern times by extensive irrigation systems—is greatest. The upper limit of the midvalley zone is defined by the confluence of three tributaries above the present-day city of Moquegua: the Huaracane, the Torata, and the Tumilaca rivers. Although evidence of ancient human habitation extends throughout the Osmore drainage (Watanabe, Moseley, and Cabieses 1990), few of the sites considered here occur in the upper valley, above 2,000 m AMSL. The exception is the cluster of sites excavated by Stanish (n.d.a; 1989) in the Otora Valley, which is a small, upper sierra tributary, located between 2,300 and 3,000 m AMSL.

Forty-five km from the coast, a formidable sand-and-rock escarpment serves as an effective barrier, separating the middle and lower Osmore valleys. Here the river disappears into an aquifer, reappearing 17 km from its mouth. Although less productive than the broad floodplain dominating the middle valley, the lower valley supported agriculture, intensified during Late Intermediate times. Marine resources show a longer history of harvest from coastal locations beginning in the late Preceramic period. The chronology and phase names for the three sections of the Osmore drainage are illustrated in Table 1 (after Stanish and Rice 1989: 14), which also presents the sequence for adjacent northern Chile.

The Osmore drainage has recently been the subject of intensive archaeological investigation by scholars operating under the "umbrella" of Programa Contisuyu (Stanish and Rice 1989: 3). The Programa is a loose coalition of Peruvian and North American institutions that facilitates research through logistical support. Projects are funded independently, but are coordinated through the Programa. Under Programa sponsorship, initial archaeological surveys were conducted in 1982, followed by excavations in later years.

[1] After P. Goldstein n.d.; Rice 1989; Williams n.d.

Jane E. Buikstra

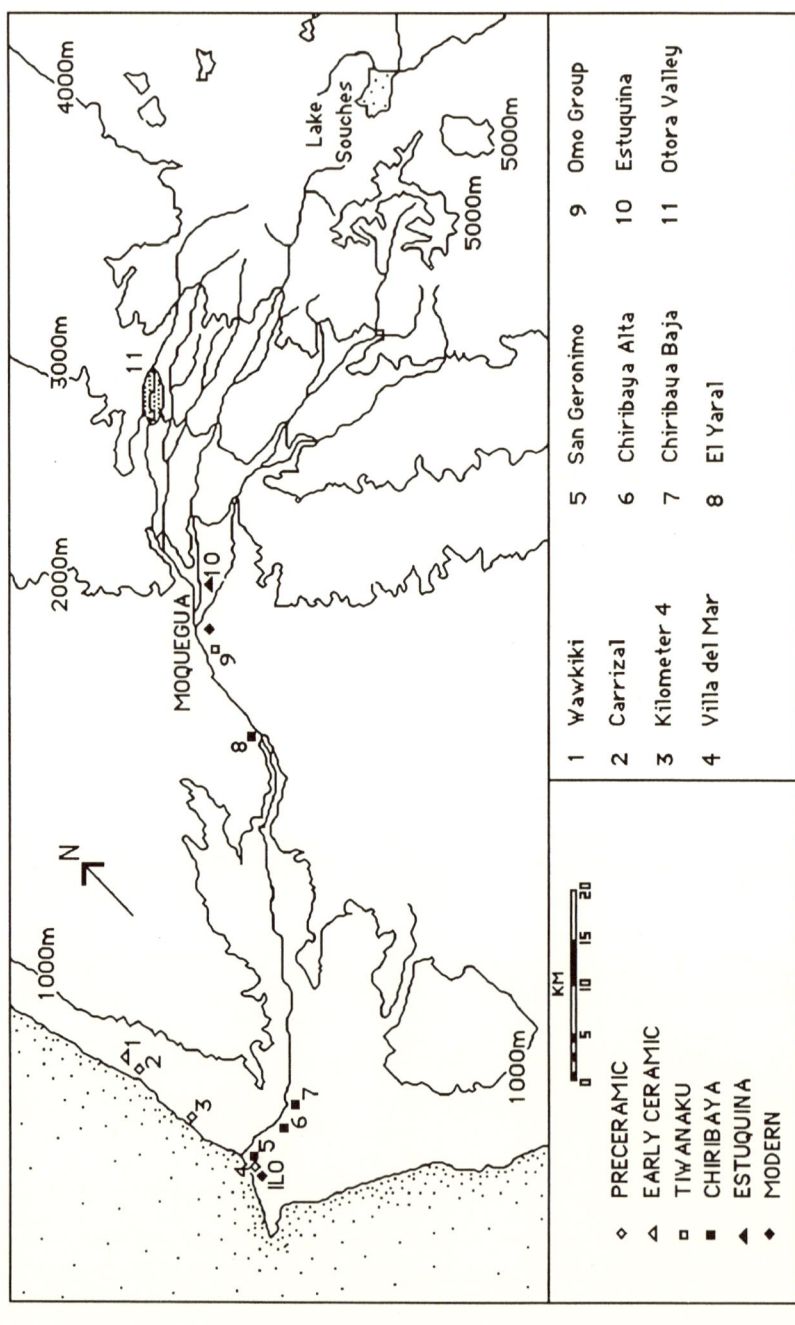

Fig. 2 Osmore drainage and associated mortuary sites.

TABLE 1. CHRONOLOGY OF CULTURAL DEVELOPMENT WITHIN THE OSMORE
DRAINAGE AND ADJACENT NORTHERN CHILE

PERIODS	PHASE NAMES BY REGION			
	LOWER VALLEY	MID-VALLEY	UPPER VALLEY	N CHILE
Late Horizon —1500—	*Inca*	*Inca*	*Inca*	*Inca*
L. Intermediate —1000—	*Chiribaya*	*Estuquiña* *Tumilaca*	*Estuquiña* *Otoro*	*Gentilar* *San Miguel*
Middle Horizon	*Loreto Viejo*	*Chen Chen* *Omo*	*Tumilaca*	*Maytas* *Cabuza*
—500— E. Intermediate —AD/BC—		*Huaracane*		*Faldas del Morro* *Alto Ramirez*
—500— Early Horizon		*Trapiche*		
—1000— Initial Period —1500—				
—2000— ⋮ —9500—	*Chinchorro* ↕			*Chinchorro* ↕

Jane E. Buikstra

THE FIRST FORMAL MORTUARY RITUAL

Within the Osmore drainage, the earliest evidence of mortuary ritual develops from late Preceramic coastal graves, during a period characterized by increasing sedentism and intensification of fishing (Bawden 1989a, 1989b; Sandweiss et al. 1989; Torres Pino et al. 1990a, 1990b; Wise 1989, n.d.a, n.d.b; Wise and Clark n.d.). An interment from the site of Carrizal has been recovered from a midden dating between 4350 and 4810 B.P. (Bawden 1989b; Stanish and Rice 1989). The elderly (50+ years) female had been buried in a pit lined with vegetal fiber, her head covered by a fiber hat. At the site of Kilometer 4 (K4), a single grave has been excavated from a domestic terrace, in association with midden dated to 4620+/− 90 B.P. (Wise n.d.b). The K4 grave contained a male (45–50 years) dressed in a cotton loincloth, covered with a large, plain cloak and interred with numerous artifacts: a projectile point, ten bone artifacts including hollow bone tubes, two stone beads, a concentration of mussel-shell valves, a possible animal-hide bag, six distinctive textiles, and a cluster of unidentified plant materials—all recovered from a layered concentration at the northern aspect of the pit. Both the K4 and the Carrizal remains were excavated from midden contexts, not discrete disposal areas (Wise and Clark n.d.; Wise n.d.b). These graves resemble the slightly more recent interments from the site of Quiani 7 in northern Chile (Llagostera 1989; Muñoz 1982; Nuñez 1976).

Burial features clustered within a third residential site, Villa del Mar, may represent a formally bounded cemetery area (Wise n.d.b). A single burial excavated in 1986 contained the remains of a 17 to 20-year-old female and an adolescent (12–14 years) of indeterminate sex, both buried in extended positions, heads to the northeast. The adolescent was associated with numerous artifacts: two pieces of cotton fabric, one decorated with wool; 33 shell beads; a basalt bead; and a harpoon shaft (Torres Pino 1990a, 1990b; Wise n.d.b). Other extended remains without artificial mummification have been recovered from north Chilean Preceramic sites such as Acha (9000 B.P., A. Aufderheide, personal communication) and Morro (7810-4040 B.P., Allison et al. 1984).

Two features excavated at Villa del Mar during 1989–90 were found to contain a six-month-old infant (Tomb 1), and a triple burial of a 5-year-old child, a 45-year-old female, and an infant (Tomb 2) (Wise n.d.b). All interments in Tomb 2 were in an extended position. The infant in Tomb 1 was buried in the style commonly termed Chinchorro, including clay molded over the skull and the use of red pigment (Allison et al. 1984; Bittman 1982; Bittman and Munizaga 1976, 1979; Llagostera 1989; Rivera 1984, this volume; Rivera and Rothhammer 1986; Uhle 1919, 1922; Wise n.d.b).

Wise (n.d.b) links the emergence of formally bounded cemeteries and the Chinchorro tradition with territoriality, following a Saxe–Binford theoretical approach. In a refinement of Saxe's Hypothesis 8, Lynne Goldstein has

Tombs for the Living . . . or . . . for the Dead: The Osmore Ancestors

generated a tripartite reformulation concerning the relationship between cemeteries, mortuary ritual, and crucial resources (after Charles and Buikstra 1983: 119).

> 1. To the degree that rights of corporate groups to use and/or control crucial but restricted resource(s) are attained and/or legitimized by lineal descent from the dead (i.e., lineal ties to ancestors), such groups will, by popular religion and its ritualization, regularly reaffirm the lineal corporate groups and its rights. *One* means of ritualization that is often but not always employed is the maintenance of a permanent, specialized, bounded area for the exclusive disposal of their dead.
> 2. If a permanent, specialized, bounded area for the exclusive disposal of the group's dead exists, then it is likely that the corporate group has rights over the use and/or control of crucial but restricted resource(s). This corporate control is most likely attained and/or legitimized by lineal descent from the dead, either through an actual lineage or through a strong, established tradition that the critical resource passes from parent to offspring.
> 3. The more structured and formal the disposal area, the fewer the alternative explanations of social organization, and conversely. (L. Goldstein 1980: 8; cited in Charles and Buikstra 1983: 119)

Applications of this model in North America have focused primarily upon explanations of Preceramic Middle Archaic cemeteries that commonly take the form of burial mounds (Charles and Buikstra 1983; Buikstra 1988). Mound building is thus characterized as a monumental mortuary tradition that signals the reaffirmation of group rights to control scarce or crucial resources. In the Andean cases cited here, *both* the elaborate Chinchorro mortuary ritual and the development of formally bounded disposal areas appear to be symbols of corporate rights over resource use and/or control. While less archaeologically visible than the North American tumuli, the Chinchorro interments are clearly the products of extended ritual processes that similarly served to link corporate rights and the ancestors. Such interpretations develop from our theoretical focus upon actions of the living, rather than simply the residue recovered through archaeological excavations.

Bente Bittmann (Bittmann 1982; Bittmann and Munizaga 1976, 1979) proposes that the most intense expression of the Chinchorro mummification tradition, including elaborate cleansing of flesh from bones and re-creation of the individual using materials of permanence, occurs at the earliest phase of the sequence. Complex treatments, for example, are reported for the north Chilean sites of Camarones 14 (7000 B.P.) and Morro 1 (7810-4040 B.P.) (Llagostera 1989; Schiappacasse and Niemeyer 1984). Even though Rivera (Rivera 1984, this volume; Rivera and Rothhammer 1986), following

Jane E. Buikstra

Uhle (1919, 1922), argues that the most elaborate Chinchorro corpse disposal ritual occurs slightly later, it is clear that complex treatments emerge relatively early, frequently associated with the development of distinctive cemetery areas. Such initial, elaborate mortuary practices are predicted by Childe (1945), and noted in this volume by Dillehay for Araucanian earthen mounds. Evidence for an extended period of above-ground display prior to interment, as indicated by surface cracking and repainting of facial masks (Allison et al. 1984; Bird 1943; Mostny 1944), also underscores the significance of this elaborate burial treatment in the lives of early coastal peoples.

Chinchorro cemeteries appear at a time when coastal population density is increasing (Rivera 1984, this volume; Rivera and Rothhammer 1986), presumably in association with local competition for resources, such as access to fresh water and fishing territories (Wise n.d.b). An association with sedentism and territorial exclusivity is therefore predictable, following a model proposed by Charles and Buikstra (1983) for Middle Archaic populations from midcontinental North America. Andean ethnographic and ethnohistoric sources cited in this volume also underscore links between funerary rites and access to land and water (Bastien, Salomon), while emphasizing that political stresses may encourage mortuary elaboration (Dillehay, Salomon). In an archaeological example, Carmichael (this volume) relates burial complexity to "group pressures involving land ownership and the inheritance of vital resources" among Nasca V peoples.

Preceramic artifactual remains provide evidence of tools used for hunting, fishing, and utilization of shellfish among both Chinchorro juveniles and adults. A limited number of tool kits designed to facilitate the use of hallucinogenic drugs also occur among Chinchorro adult remains, suggesting the presence of a class of ritual specialists whose power emanates from their special relationship to altered states of awareness (Guillén n.d.). Thus, in these subsistence and ritual examples, grave goods relate primarily to the necessary maintenance activities of the dead individual, while lengthy corpse preparation rituals and cemetery formations are charged with meaning for the living descendants. In this matter, both the deceased's persona and the politics of the living are symbolized in the Preceramic archaeological record for the south-central Andes.

EARLY PRECERAMIC COASTAL SITES

Thirty km north of Ilo and 1 km inland is the earliest known coastal burial aggregation that is clearly defined as a formally bounded cemetery located outside a domestic context. With a date of 1610+/− 70 B.P. (Stanish and Rice 1989), the Wawakiki burial complex has been partially excavated, thus far yielding the remains of 17 individuals recovered from 16 graves (Bawden 1989a, 1989b; O'Donnabháin and Lozada Cerna n.d.; O'Donnabháin, Lozada Cerna, and Buikstra n.d.). An unexplored portion of the site may contain 40 to 60 additional interments (O'Donnabháin and Lozada Cerna n.d.). Within this Early Ceramic burial complex are individuals of both genders and all age groups, suggesting that Wawakiki was an inclusive community cemetery.

The predominant grave goods for the Wawakiki site were undecorated ollas (Bawden 1989a, 1989b; O'Donnabháin, Lozada Cerna, and Buikstra n.d.). The only other ceramic is a painted bowl that Bawden uses to strengthen his argument for autonomous coastal traditions (Bawden 1989a, 1989b). Cotton textiles, animal skins, and feathers had been used to wrap the bodies; reeds or grasses commonly lined burial pits. A copper ornament was recovered during excavations conducted in 1988 (O'Donnabháin and Lozada Cerna n.d.). Annular cranial deformation discernible in two Wawakiki skulls contrasts with the Preceramic "tabular erect" form characteristic of remains from Villa del Mar (O'Donnabháin and Lozada Cerna n.d.; Torres et al. 1990a, 1990b).

The Wawakiki cemetery provides evidence for skull removal following a period of corpse deterioration, as indicated by the presence of intact tombs containing articulated skeletons without crania and with mandibles still in place. Similar occurrences have been noted in both Chinchorro and Early Ceramic Chilean contexts (Guillén n.d.; Meighan 1980; O'Donnabháin, Lozada Cerna, and Buikstra n.d.), as well as in a Nasca example excavated from the site of Cahauchi (Carmichael, this volume). Such treatment suggests that portions of the ancestors were removed for display purposes, thus serving as visible reminders to the living of intergenerational relationships. Further details concerning the final disposal of bones subject to such removals are considered by John Verano (this volume).

Other examples of mortuary ritual elaboration include the presence of artifact caches—a basket containing fish hooks; a cluster of seashells surrounding a rolled pebble—excavated from within the cemetery precinct outside tomb boundaries. These doubtless signify the importance of marine resources to the group who buried at Wawakiki.

HUARACANE PHASE CEMETERIES

The first cemeteries reported for the midvalley region of the Osmore drainage are associated with "Huaracane" residential terraces and olla plainwares (Feldman 1989, 1990a, 1990b). The Huaracane type-site cluster (M22–28) includes heavily disturbed tombs with multiple burials in round semisubterranean structures (M29), as well as a series of unmarked tombs with individual burials on the side of a low ridge (M30) (Feldman 1989: 212). Looted in antiquity,[2] the M30 burial features produced no pottery;

---

[2] The volcano Huana Putina erupted during February of 1600, scattering a fine, gray volcanic ash across the Osmore midvalley. Although the Spanish entered this area prior to 1600, it

wrist or ankle bracelets of tubular bone beads were recovered from two graves (Feldman 1989: 212). Additional, intensely disturbed masonry features of the Pampa Huaracane group, which Feldman describes as "either destroyed large platform structures or collapsed complexes of closely packed small round structures," include fiber-tempered sherds, beads, and bone fragments—suggesting that these too may have been tombs (Feldman 1989: 211).

Predating the extensive Tiwanaku V occupation of Omo site M10 are a series of six Huaracane "boot tombs"—deep shafts with small side chambers (P. Goldstein n.d.). Other examples of boot tombs are cited by Christopher Donnan (this volume) as one of four types of funerary chambers recorded for contemporary Moche peoples from the north coast of Peru. Looted in antiquity, the Omo M10 Huaracane tombs contained multiple interments of male and female adults, as well as juveniles. The least disturbed structures, Tombs 4, 5, and 6, served as burial facilities for a minimum of five, eight, and five individuals, respectively. Four skulls (three adult males and one infant) from Tomb 6 present similar patterns of artificial cranial deformation: two pads placed bilaterally high on the frontal with a complementary triangular pad mitigating pressure centered on the squamous portion of the occiput.

In addition to incomplete human remains (primarily foot bones), fragments of ceramic vessels, beads, decorated baskets, and elaborate textiles have been recovered from the Huaracane component of M10. Ceramic analyses link Huaracane styles with both altiplano (Chiripa and Wankarani) and coastal sites. Similar fiber-tempered vessels are termed "Faldas del Morro" in northern Chile (Feldman 1989, 1990a, 1990b; P. Goldstein 1989, n.d.).

Both altiplano and coastal associations are suggested by the M10 Huaracane Phase non-ceramic artifacts. Similar tubular bone beads and drilled stone disks have been recovered from Chiripa sites, while elaborately embroidered sections of a loosely woven cotton fabric are of a Paracas-derived style (P. Goldstein n.d.: 59). A finely woven, hemispherical basket recovered intact near the base of Tomb 5 contained a small wooden cup, which may have served as a llipta or cal receptacle. A stopper with a carved reptile face recovered from the tomb floor is probably associated with the cup, providing indirect evidence for coca use. A copper ring was also recovered from Tomb 5. Lucuma pits, squash seeds, and fragments of maize and gourds were associated with tomb fill. Based on a fragment of wooden roofing material, Tomb 6 has been dated to A.D. 50 +/− 70 (dendrochronologically corrected) (P. Goldstein n.d; Stanish and Rice 1989).

---

can safely be assumed that most disturbed contexts covered by ash lenses were "looted in antiquity," that is, prior to the European presence.

Tombs for the Living . . . or . . . for the Dead: The Osmore Ancestors

Huaracane phase residential and cemetery sites are located on escarpments adjacent to the fertile valley floor. The heavily looted stone complexes of the Huaracane M29 site, along with the "rings or polygons with wattle and daub roofing" that Paul Goldstein describes for Omo M10, comprise visible mortuary structures in locations adjacent to cultivated fields. Although looted in antiquity, these tombs apparently served as sequential mortuaries for a single descent group. Following the same theoretical argument developed for the coast Chinchorro materials, it is probable that these facilities served not only to receive corpses but also to ritually legitimize linkages to scarce or crucial resources, in this case the arable land of the Moquegua Valley.

The below-ground tombs for individual interments at Huaracane M30 do not conform to the pattern common to M29 and M10. While the elaborate stone structures of M29 likely represent the ongoing intergenerational linkages between the living and the dead, the isolated graves of M30 apparently contained individuals adorned only with personal items. Whether vertical status distinctions among contemporaneous descent groups or temporal trends in mortuary customs are represented here requires additional excavations and analysis. The M30 interments may, for example, predate the competitive displays represented by the M29 and Omo M10 sites.

Both coastal and altiplano elements are represented in these Huaracane phase tombs, especially those from Omo M10. Paul Goldstein (n.d.) argues for social differences between the groups who buried at the Omo and Huaracane sites, with the Omo metals, complex tombs, elaborate jewelry, and imported textiles reflecting an elite whose wealth extended beyond local resources. Arguments such as these are representational, with emphasis upon the persona of the deceased. A competing interpretation invokes broader consideration of the Huaracane mourners and their relationship to the presence of another ceramic tradition and perhaps another people within the region during late Early Horizon/Early Intermediate times.

Robert Feldman (1989) reports that a distinctive ceramic tradition, termed Trapiche and thought to represent a locally produced variant of the altiplano Pukara style, occurs at several midvalley Osmore sites. Wool textiles recovered from the same Trapiche sites are linked with the Pukara tradition, being most similar to Pukara fabrics recovered from Chilean Alto Ramiréz phase sites. As emphasized by Feldman, dating of the Trapiche phase "is not secure, although a rough consensus is that it dates to after or about 300 B.C." (Feldman 1989: 215).

It thus appears that the midvalley Osmore region was populated, at least during part of late Early Horizon/Early Intermediate times, by two distinctive ethnic groups. The elaborate Huaracane phase tombs may have developed in this competitive atmosphere as symbolic representations of territorial control, legitimized by the presence of ancestors. While Huaracane residential sites are not fortified, the standing walls still visible at the Trapiche type-site of Cerro Trapiche suggest a competitive stance. If the M30 Huaracane phase cemeteries are more recent than those at M29 and M10, it may indicate a relaxation of regional tensions. Alternatively, the M30 interments may predate the Trapiche incursion.

MIDDLE HORIZON: THE OMO CEMETERIES

Investigations of cemetery organization, grave contents, and human biology hold excellent promise for resolving persistent controversies in Middle Horizon archaeology. One such issue involves the relationship between complex altiplano urban centers, such as Tiwanaku, and distant contemporary communities that show evidence of similar cultural forms, such as those from the midvalley Osmore drainage. In this context, Murra's "vertical archipelago" model has gained great popularity in recent years (Murra 1964, 1968, 1972), taking focus upon Tiwanaku in the work of Elías Mujica, Mario Rivera, and Thomas Lynch (1983).

Paul Goldstein (1989, 1990a, 1990b, n.d.) has sought evidence for altiplano-inspired local productive centers as one of three competing models for the relationship between Osmore drainage midvalley Tiwanaku sites and the altiplano state. Another, less intrusive possibility is that trade between communities facilitated by llama caravans explained the distribution of goods beyond zones of local production (Browman 1980, 1984, 1985). More extreme would be the development of state-run provinces, whose leadership received direction from Tiwanaku (P. Goldstein n.d.).

The oasis of San Pedro de Atacama in northern Chile serves as a convincing Middle Horizon example of trade between local centers and the altiplano encouraging increased integration of local leaders into "frontier client" relationships (P. Goldstein n.d.). Interpretations of mortuary site data are essential to this argument, which is buttressed by the presence of portable sumptuary goods in elite burial contexts (Browman 1985; Mujica 1985; P. Goldstein n.d.). Elías Mujica (1985: 116, as cited in P. Goldstein n.d.: 42–43) notes:

> In San Pedro, Tiwanaku materials that do not appear in coastal valleys predominate, such as finely made pottery, *rapé* snuff tubes and palettes, gold *keros,* and other wood objects finely worked and decorated with feline faces, human heads, and personages such as the sacrifice(r) or the staff personage of the Tiwanaku sun gate. Moreover, even if these objects come from burials, no purely Tiwanaku cemetery is yet known, nor is there even a Tiwanaku settlement.

The limited presence of such items in a small number of graves from a few Middle Horizon San Pedro cemeteries appears to identify elites from competing descent groups who were empowered by their special relationships with the distant altiplano polity, or as Paul Goldstein (n.d.: 44) suggests, "Tiwanaku played preferential politics with the various San Pedro ayllus to guarantee the efficient access to the oasis and points beyond." Thus, the discontinuous distribution of specific "elite" items recovered from graves is used to argue for a system of indirect influence. In this case, the placement of rare and iconographically rich items in tombs no doubt communicated to the living information about key intergenerational linkages among those whose power was enhanced by special relationships to altiplano centers via trading partnerships.

While the San Pedro de Atacama case appears to fulfill our expectations for indirect highland influence, no similar examples occur in the archaeological record for the Osmore Valley (P. Goldstein n.d.). The two remaining models—vertical archipelagos or provincial centers—require further consideration. In the zonal complementarity example, we might expect that *mitmaquna*-like colonists would fiercely guard their ethnic identity through specific burial rituals and cemetery structure. A further, traditional means of specifying group identity—cranial deformation—would likely distinguish colonists from different locations.

A provincial center, on the other hand, could be expected to replicate—in simplified detail—the structure of the capital (P. Goldstein n.d.). Interment forms should resemble those common to the altiplano center, with visible distinctions between elites and those less powerful. While mortuary data from the site of Tiwanaku itself is incomplete, there *is* evidence of extended mortuary rituals and the dedication of human remains to specific structures, including the Akapana itself (Manzanilla and Woodard 1990). It will be extremely important for the interpretation of Osmore Middle Horizon sites to have further detailed knowledge concerning altiplano burial rituals and thus to establish the degree to which provincial burial programs symbolically represent distinctions important at the Tiwanaku core.

Although the archaeological record for mortuary sites within the Osmore drainage is relatively silent during Early Intermediate times, Middle Horizon ceramics have, however, been identified throughout the drainage. The most extensive documentation of Osmore Middle Horizon cemetery areas features the midvalley Omo site group (Fig. 2). The relatively extensive Omo data base (Fig. 3, after P. Goldstein 1989, n.d.) will, therefore, serve to anchor the present discussion.

As indicated in Table 1, the first Osmore midvalley Tiwanaku-like ceramic tradition is termed "Omo phase" and corresponds to Phase IV of the Bolivian Tiwanaku sequence, ca. A.D. 375–725 (P. Goldstein n.d.). Best known from locations M12, M13, and M16 of the Omo site group, Omo

Jane E. Buikstra

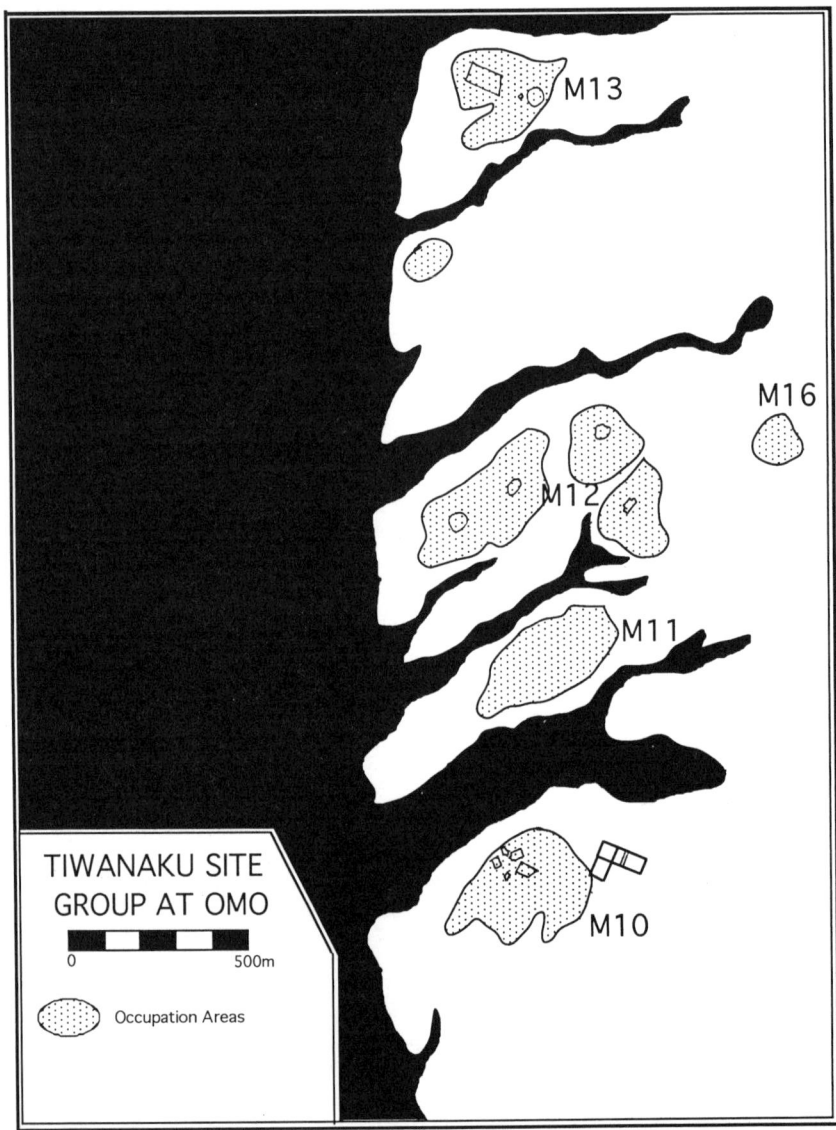

Fig. 3 Omo site group (after P. Goldstein n.d.).

phase peoples apparently farmed valley bottom land with little evidence of terraced irrigation systems. Paul Goldstein identifies the presence of dispersed homesteads and hamlets, as well as a much larger settlement at the Omo site; the absence of fortifications provides evidence of a stable political environment (n.d.: 61).

Even though Omo phase Tiwanaku IV residential areas are readily identified, no contemporary cemeteries have been isolated. Enthusiasm on the part of local collectors and archaeologists alike for grave goods suggests that Omo phase interments are invisible either because corpses were interred with diagnostic artifacts or that remains were removed to other contexts for final disposal. Certainly, there are no highly visible Omo phase cemeteries in the Osmore midvalley, all the more striking in the presence of the earlier Huaracane phase boot tombs and the extensive subsequent Tiwanaku V cemeteries, for example, Chen Chen and Omo M10. Such a pattern is not unexpected, however, given evidence for peaceful coexistence in a resource-rich environment. In the absence of active competition for resources, the Omo phase Tiwanaku IV ancestors were simply not used to validate either access to resources or the status of their descendants.

The situation changes, however, during Tiwanaku V times, locally termed the Chen Chen phase. With an "explosive Tiwanaku V expansion" in the midvalley region (P. Goldstein n.d.), separate cemetery areas are visibly associated with a number of large domestic sites, including Omo and Chen Chen (Disselhoff 1968; P. Goldstein 1989, n.d.; Ishida 1960). One of these site complexes—Omo M10—also includes a large ceremonial structure, which is said to indicate that Omo served as a regional administrative center (P. Goldstein n.d.: 70). A structural post from M10 has yielded a dendrochronologically corrected date of A.D. 900 +/− 60 (P. Goldstein n.d.: 69). Omo M10, including the distribution of both domestic and mortuary features, is illustrated in Figure 4.

The "monumental core" of the M10 site—termed Complex A—includes an adobe-walled compound 120 m in length. Composed of three walled courts, each at a different level, the structure ascends the eastern hill of the M10 bluff. The upper level includes a central semisubterranean court which may have been the site of a carved stone structure that had been destroyed during late Tiwanaku V times. The remains of a llama fetus and a starfish recovered just above the lower plaster floor of this complex is interpreted as an offering that symbolically links the altiplano with the coast (P. Goldstein n.d.: 153). Paul Goldstein argues, however, that the architectural model for Complex A is clearly in the altiplano, perhaps the three-tiered terrace conformation of the Akapana itself (P. Goldstein n.d.: 154–157).

M10 is the most thoroughly reported of the Tiwanaku V sites within the Osmore drainage. Along with 7.75 hectares of domestic occupation, M10 also includes 19 separate cemeteries—one Huaracane phase cluster (dis-

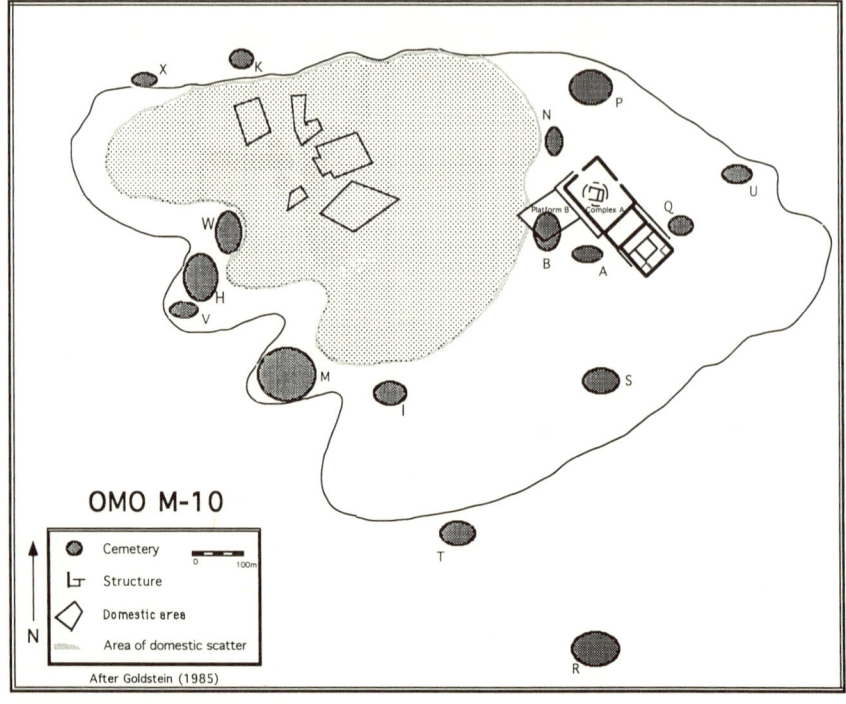

Fig. 4 Omo M10 (after P. Goldstein n.d.).

cussed above) and 18 from Middle Horizon times. Seven hundred and seventy-five tomb depressions have been recorded. One hundred four disturbed Tiwanaku tombs from nine of the M10 cemeteries (A,B,M,N,P,Q,R,S,T) were examined in 1984 by archaeologists working with the Programa Contisuyu. Sixty-seven graves were judged to be sufficiently complete for (re)excavation (P. Goldstein n.d.).

Details for the excavated tombs and their contents are reported by Paul Goldstein (n.d.: 282–305). This work is exemplary in its detailed representation of each interment and is constrained only by an excavation strategy limited to previously looted areas. More recently, block excavation techniques implemented at the Estuquiña site cemeteries (Williams, Clark, and Buikstra 1990; Williams et al. 1989) and subsequently applied at the mortuary components of Chiribaya Alta (Williams and Buikstra n.d.) and El Yaral (Lozada Cerna and Torres Pino n.d.) have identified undisturbed tombs, even in heavily looted cemeteries. Systematic sampling of intact tombs is obviously an advantageous strategy for most fully representing the richness of the archaeological record.

The M10 Tiwakanu V tombs are all cylindrical cists, usually with single burials. Stones commonly line the tombs and/or encircle their mouths. Common tomb types include (1) unlined pits with surface rings (n = 22); (2) stone-lined tombs, with or without surface courses (n = 25); and (3) slab cists, which include both surface rings and internal stonework, dominated by vertically placed large stone slabs (n = 7). Additional tomb ornamentation, common in Tumilaca cemetery M11 and M10-N, incorporates additional stone rings or collars. Broken wooden sticks found in M10-M are interpreted as marker poles. Although none of the tombs reported here was found with capstone in place, the presence of large slablike boulders in fill and near tombs suggests that these massive rocks were originally used as roofing material (P. Goldstein n.d.).

A variety of tomb forms is apparent in each disposal area. The most completely excavated cemetery, M10-M, comprises four slab cists, six stone-lined cists, two with plaster floors, and two with surface rings. Other cemeteries show a similar range of tomb types. The notable exception is M10-Q, where three of the five reported tombs are unlined pits. One M10-Q tomb is lined with stones and another presents a collar. In four of the five reported instances, human remains were interred face down, an anomalous burial posture for Middle Horizon times. Individuals buried in this unusual position included an adult female with a fetus, who presumably died in childbirth. Paul Goldstein (n.d.: 164), using ethnographic analogy—"In 1984, eight Peruvian journalists mistaken for Sendero Luminoso terrorists were murdered by villagers in the Ayacucho hamlet of Uchurracay and buried face down"—suggests that "the Q cemetery was reserved for outcast or taboo individuals." Given that spatial segregation is a dimension of mortuary activity commonly used to symbolize circumstances of death (Binford 1971; Saxe n.d.), it would seem that the nature of the mortal event may be the most likely explanation for the spatial circumscription of Cemetery Q and its contents. Similar "bad deaths" are also considered in this volume by Patrick Carmichael. The fact that the only skull observable for cranial deformation (Q4) presents a form similar to that for individuals from Cemeteries P, R, and T supports the notion that remains interred in the Omo M10-Q cemetery were drawn from the local community.

Given the disturbed nature of the M10 tombs, grave good assemblages are undoubtedly impoverished. Looters in antiquity apparently focused on metal objects, as witnessed by the absence of such items except when in hidden contexts (M10-M7). Spindle whorls are found only with females (R8, 35–45 female; T2, 50+ female); complete keros are recovered only from the graves of males and juveniles (B7, 7–9 years; M1, 50+ male; M4, 18–22 male; M10, empty; N3, old adult male; N5, adult male; S1, 7–9 years). Both coastal and altiplano resources receive symbolic representation: a monkey-headed vessel (R2, 47+ male); flamingo motifs on tazons (N9, young adult female; R1, adult); feline motifs (M1, 50+ male; N5, adult male); and spoons with carved llama images (M10, no human remains; M16 adult <30 years; M17 no human remains; N9, young adult female; P2, 7–9 year old). A 50+ female designated T2 was interred with a rich artifact assemblage that included fine textiles; a basket; a gourd dipper; a pigment box; a spindle whorl; and a bag with "leaf" fragments, presumably coca. The single metal item—a silver earspool—was excavated from the grave of an adult male (M7), 35 to 40 years of age, where textiles, a quartz projectile point, and a llama bone were also found. A set of cane pan pipes were recovered from the grave (B7) of a 7- to 9-year-old child. As in the B7 example, artifact assemblages of children generally appear as replete as those of adults. While llama and guinea pig bones as well as maize cobs occur within tomb fill, vegetal items are reported to have been much less common than in Late Intermediate Chiribaya or Estuquiña tombs (P. Goldstein n.d.), although this may to some degree reflect the disturbed nature of the Omo site graves.

Given the disturbance evident in the Omo site tombs, it is difficult to draw distinctions based upon grave construction and associated items. If any of these Chen Chen phase cemeteries suggest the presence of an elite, this would be the M10-M cemetery, where marker poles and a metal item have been recovered (P. Goldstein n.d.).

The question of lineage or ethnic distinctions between the Omo site cemeteries can also be addressed through the study of cranial deformation (Hoshower et al. n.d.). Virtually all skulls from the Andean region present evidence for the use of deforming devices during infancy, thus producing a culturally determined cranial (head) shape. Following researchers such as Marvin Allison et al. (1981), Ales Hrdlicka (1912), José Imbelloni (1925, 1932, 1933, 1934, 1937), Juan Munizaga (1964), Rudolph Virchow (1892), and Pedro Weiss (1961), this discussion will focus upon the structure of deforming devices rather than nuances of ultimate shape and form. Technology-based differences in adult skull appearance are, of course, created during infancy and early childhood with the ensuing culturally determined form persisting as a lifelong symbol of group identity. Garcilaso de la Vega reported that people of the province of Palta presented uniquely shaped heads because "From birth they pressed their children's skulls between two planks tied together at the ends, which they tightened a little every day. . . . After three years, a child's skull was deformed for life . . . ([1607]1961: 301). The importance of head shape as a symbol of group identity is also emphasized by de las Casas, who indicates that "individuals from each province had to form their heads in the same way so that they could be recognized by their neighbors" (1892[1561]: 174–175).

Tombs for the Living . . . or . . . for the Dead: The Osmore Ancestors

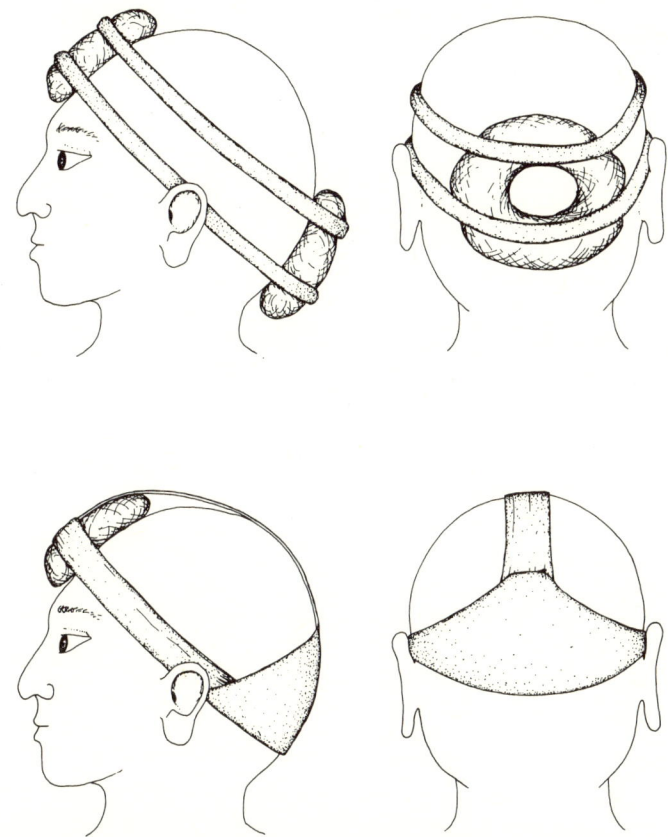

Fig. 5 Contrastive cranial deformation forms from Omo M10.

Within the Omo series, distinctive technological differences are apparent in the placement of deforming pads on the frontal and occipital regions of the skull (Hoshower et al. n.d.). One or two pads were used at the front of the deforming device, either placed high adjacent to the coronal suture or lower, in the region of the frontal bosses. Postcoronal constriction was a constant feature, present in all crania. A linear depression following the sagittal suture, frequent within this sample, is though to reflect pressures from the deforming device. At the posterior aspect of the skull, pads were either triangular or ring-shaped, as illustrated in Figure 5. Triangular pads were positioned either at the posterior occipital protuberance, locally de-

TABLE 2. DEFORMATION FORMS FROM OMO CEMETERY M10[1]

Cemetery B: (n = 3: B3, B5, B7) All individuals show two pads bilaterally placed high on the forehead, with circular deformation of the occiput.

Cemetery M: (n = 8: M1, M2, M4, M5, M6, M7, M20, M24) Four (M1, M4, M6, M20) show evidence of two pads placed in the central portion of the frontal; the remainder reflect a single pad placed in a similar location. At the posterior aspect of the skull, five display the effect of triangular pads, two (M1, M2) at lambda and three (M5, M20, and M24) centrally on the squamous portion. The remaining three (M4, M6, and M7) exhibit relatively faint ring-shaped pad impressions.

Cemetery N: (n = 3: N2, N3, N9) Two pads placed at middle point of forehead and pressure at lambda are indicated in all individuals.

Cemetery P: (n = 1: P3) Two pads were placed high on the forehead, with a triangular pad used on the squamous portion of the occiput.

Cemetery Q: (n = 1: Q4) Two pads were placed high on the frontal; a triangular pad at the occiput produced a flattened region extending from lambda to the inferior nuchal crest.

Cemetery R: (n = 4: R2, R3, R7, R8) All present evidence of two pads placed high on the forehead. Occipitals were flattened from lambda to the inferior nuchal crest, mediated by a triangular pad centered in the squamous portion of the occiput. These individuals present a classic tabular erect pattern.

Cemetery S: (n = 4: S1, S2, S6, S8) S2 presents no evidence of cranial deformation. The remainder present evidence for two pads placed high on the forehead and circular, bun-type deformation of the occiput.

Cemetery T: (n = 4: T1, T2, T3, T4) All present evidence of two pads on the frontal with a triangular pad centering either on the squamous portion (T1, T2, T4) or at lambda (T3). The frontal pads of T3 were placed lower than those of the remaining individuals.

[1] After Hoshower et al. n.d.

pressing the planum occipital; or higher, near lambda, and thus more extensively affecting the full squamous portion of the occipital bone. Based on shape and location of the deforming apparatus, three basic forms of occipital deformation can be identified: (1) pressure at lambda only, (2) ring-shaped or circular deformation that produced distinct bunning, and (3) a triangular pad with primary pressure at opisthocranion. As illustrated in Table 2, intracemetery homogeneity and intercemetery heterogeneity is the rule.

Of the six cemeteries that contain more than one observable individual, five show remarkable within-group homogeneity of deformation type, which crosscut age and gender. Cemetery R, for example, includes an elderly male (R2), a middle-aged female (R8), a child of six to eight years (R3), and an adolescent (R7). All present virtually identical "tabular erect" cranial deformation. Similarly diverse age-sex distributions characterize Cemetery T, where occipital flattening is also mediated by triangular pads, and Cemetery S, where the three deformed individuals have circular bunning of the occipital. Individual S2 is the only remains from the sample that presents no indication of deformation. Patterns such as this suggest that each Omo M10 cemetery contains the remains of a distinctive corporate group, where all individuals—male and female, young and old—shared a similar cranial shape created by deformation technology.

A more enigmatic situation exists uniquely in Cemetery M, where a considerably more heterogeneous distribution of deformation procedures is evident. The three styles of occipital pads which are otherwise confined to specific cemeteries are all evident, while both single and double pads were used to mitigate the impact of the deforming device on the frontal bone. No other cemetery presents evidence for the use of a single frontal pad. There is an additional subtle distinction: the pads on the frontal bone are placed relatively low, in the central part of the forehead, rather than nearer the coronal suture, as is characteristic of most other Omo M10 cemeteries. This clearly suggests that the M10-M cemetery interments had origins distinct—either by ethnicity, lineage, or time—from those of other cemeteries. If this is an elite group, as Paul Goldstein suggests, then it does not appear to have been drawn from the same communities that buried their dead in the other portions of the M10 site.

Cranial deformation technology thus defines three distinctive physical groupings: (1) Cemeteries B and S, with bun-shaped occiputs; (2) Cemeteries N, R, and T, with flattened occiputs; and (3) Cemetery M, with its diversity of deformation forms. The isolated individuals from Cemeteries P and Q resemble the second group. Proper interpretation of these differences requires further consideration of the chronological sequence for the domestic areas and cemeteries in relationship to the central platform.

Paul Goldstein has argued that Cemetery N is relatively recent, perhaps even Tumilaca phase, based upon tomb typology; textile preservation suggests a similar temporal association for Cemetery Q (n.d. 283). Cemetery B, located within Platform B and thus postdating both the construction of Complex A and the original use of Platform B, is therefore also relatively late. Thus—depending upon the chronological placement of cemeteries S and M—we have increased diversity of deformation forms through time, as the central monumental structure undergoes adaptive reuse. Such increased diversity might indicate the addition of distinctive ethnicities and/or descent groups drawn from a larger region. The use of the triangular pad among the earlier groups (Cemeteries R and T) produces a deformation type similar to that of the Early Ceramic Huaracane boot tombs, possibly identifying a stable, local style. Interestingly, the Omo M10 cemeteries suggested to be relatively late—B, N, and Q—are also located near Platform A. Perhaps the original administrative function of this structure had become redirected to ritual functions, a shift in emphasis from secular to sacred.

Having considered the broad outlines of mortuary data from the Omo site, we may now return to the three relational/administrative models presented at the beginning of this section. Clearly there is no support here for the type of patron-client relationship reported in the San Pedro de Atacama archaeological record. The large cemetery complexes at Omo, without evidence of special Tiwanaku sumptuary goods, argue for a more structured, complex association. Paul Goldstein, based on the presence of monumental architecture on so vast a site, characterizes Omo as an administrative center for colonists from the altiplano rather than representing a less structured collection of archipelago colonies. The plaza complex is said to symbolize the central authority and hierarchical control typical of such contexts. Data derived from the Omo cemeteries is important in further exploring the implications of the alternative administrative and archipelago models.

Both altiplano and coastal motifs find representation within the Chen Chen phase cemeteries, just as the conjoined offering of a llama fetus and a starfish within the highest plaza of the central structure symbolize Omo as an important intermediary between coast and altiplano. Thus far, no clear between-cemetery patterned distinctions have emerged either for tomb form (except for anomalous Cemetery Q) or grave wealth across the M10 site. The possible exception is M10-M, where poles and one metal item provided slim evidence for a special elite context (P. Goldstein n.d.).

Across-site homogeneity of tombs and grave goods contrasts with the patterning evident in cranial deformation forms, which appears strongly linked with cemetery membership. Identical head forms within but not between cemeteries argues for a culturally mediated physical distinction that has strong cultural meaning. Thus, if contemporary, the people buried in the various cemeteries may represent different communities, lineages, or perhaps craft specializations. Following an archipelago model, we might suggest the presence of culturally distinct groups from the coast and the sierra. More subtle would be distinctions based on occupational specializations, such as weaving and herding. The artifact record, seeming homogeneous across the site, provides no convincing support for either interpretation. Tomb forms and artifact styles do not covary with cranial deformation, and although Marc Bermann et al. (1989: 272) identify craft specialization at M10, the only evidence within the grave good assemblages appears to be gender-related. It is, therefore, more likely that these distinctive traditions of cranial deformation signify different descent groups that together formed a structured Tiwanaku V community. (Carmichael, in this volume, also concludes that burial within the three "better documented" Nasca cemeteries is based upon ayllu-like group membership. In Carmichael's examples, however, deformation forms do not vary across other burial categories.)

Three possible scenarios might explain the presence of these distinctive M10 kin groups. The similarity of deformation forms in skulls from the Huaracane Tomb 6 and Omo M10 Chen Chen phase cemeteries P, R, and T could indicate the presence of an indigenous population, complemented during Middle Horizon times by foreign settlers from the altiplano. The rela-

Tombs for the Living . . . or . . . for the Dead: The Osmore Ancestors

tively homogeneous artifact assemblage across all the M10 cemeteries does not, however, identify the deeply rooted ethnic distinctions one might expect in this example. Alternatively, the distinctive head forms may have been present in a heterogeneous founding altiplano population with ayllu-like systems for representing social distinctions. Finally, there may be a sequence of distinctive deformation styles represented, reflecting the shifting fortunes of different lineages or ethnicities. Refined chronological control and assessments of genetic relationships are necessary before these alternative explanations can be fully evaluated.

Even though our data are incomplete, it is tempting to develop an analogy between the Omo M10 community and the local ceremonial centers described by Salomon (this volume). Omo M10, located within the fertile Moquegua Valley, appears to be a core location that served as a permanent or seasonal residential complex for small groups of related individuals who were not distinguished by material culture. The only obvious point of differentiation between these groups involved culturally determined head shapes, one of which strongly resembled forms long common within the region. This traditional physiognomy contrasts with another which may have been considered a cultural inheritance from immigrant conquerors whose origin lay in the heights of Titicaca or other montane lands (Salomon, this volume). The Omo M10 data are compatible with this view.

As noted above, there is no strong indication of differential treatment for truly elite individuals in the Omo M10 cemeteries. Perhaps affirmation of status did not include burial rituals, or perhaps the most honored dead were interred in a location presently unknown. Further knowledge of burial programs within altiplano centers is essential to future interpretations of the intriguing yet enigmatic absence of obvious status-based distinctions in mortuary ritual for the Omo site.

The monumentality of Complex A at Omo M10 is indeed a strong declarative statement concerning a relationship between the Moquegua Valley and the altiplano early in the Tiwanaku V sequence. Artifact styles also affirm important linkages with distant highland peoples, as well as with others in coastal environments. Descent groups drawn to the Omo site apparently shared a number of beliefs about gender-based roles and mortuary rituals, while maintaining physical distinctions symbolic of kin and/or ethnic relations. While elite statuses may have been represented in daily life, as yet no parallel distinctive mortuary rituals have been identified. Obvious, too, is the fact that the structure and function of Omo M10's central monument—Complex A—changed during the Tiwanaku V sequence. Once a vigorous symbol of highland authority, the structure later served as a source of building materials for tombs, while an adjacent platform became pocked with burial cists. Thus, with time, a monument constructed to signify the power and authority of a foreign state was modified to serve the needs of the local ancestors and their descendants.

Jane E. Buikstra

THE LATE INTERMEDIATE PERIOD

Many of the social and political issues raised for Tiwanaku continue to dominate discussions of the Late Intermediate archaeological record. Even without the monolithic presence of the Tiwanaku state, an economic imperative for distant resources has clearly affected social and political relationships between more recent Osmore communities. The form taken by such interactions has been modeled in various ways, including Murra's vertical archipelago construct, which has ethnohistoric validation for the Moquegua region (Stanish 1989). Colonization based upon economic complementarity has been posited to explain patterns seen in both the middle and lower valley during Late Intermediate times (Conrad and Rice 1989; Stanish 1989). A competing model for the lower valley, favored by María Rostworowski (1977, 1981, 1988) and Garth Bawden (1989a, 1989b), emphasizes independent coastal traditions with considerable time depth and efficiency—a "horizontal model"—that contrasts with the vertical relationships implied by zonal complementarity. Each holds implications for the structure and contents of mortuary sites.

Ethnically distinct colonists exploiting local resources would be expected to display their contrastive traditions in mortuary ritual. In fact, if there is significant competition for local resources, this display would be expected to be effusive, with emphasis upon signals of distinctive group identities. Rostworowski's contrastive horizontality model (1977, 1981, 1988) describes distinctive coastal polities dominated by endogamous elites. Economic diversification and specialization so extreme as to create ethnically distinct farmers and fishers within local areas is implied, as is unequal distribution of resources within and between communities. Such specialization should be played out in grave contents, where tool kits and occupational symbols will be conspicuous. More rare will be the symbols of elite status, nevertheless visibly displayed. Local cemeteries should present evidence of stable, long-term mortuary traditions. The major source of intercemetery variation should be discovered between local productive zones, rather than within them—as one might expect in the verticality model.

Chiribaya

Chiribaya sites dominate the archaeological record for the lower Osmore Valley during the Late Intermediate Period. Initially defined by Humberto Ghersi Barrera (1956) on the basis of ceramic vessels recovered from grave lots, Chiribaya sites are now known to include extensive residential terraces, deep middens, and even fortification walls. Thus, Chiribaya is considered a distinctive Late Intermediate cultural entity whose influence extended from the Tambo to the Azapa valleys (Dauelsberg 1960, 1973a, 1973b; Focacci 1980; Jessup 1990; Lumbreras 1989; Muñoz 1983; Tartaglia 1980).

Tombs for the Living . . . or . . . for the Dead: The Osmore Ancestors

Their distribution centered in the lower Osmore Valley; Chiribaya ceramics have been recovered from many midvalley sites, with at least one Chiribaya occupation reported for the Otora Valley above Moquegua at 2,300 m AMSL (Stanish 1989, n.d.a, n.d.b).

Although Chiribaya cemeteries initially received disproportionate archaeological attention (Belan 1981; Ghersi 1956; Santos Ramirez 1983), more recent surveys and excavations conducted by scholars working with Programa Contisuyu document extensive domestic areas and complex architecture (Bawden 1989a, 1989b; Jessup n.d.; Lozada Cerna and Torres Pino n.d.; Williams and Buikstra n.d.). The origins of Chiribaya peoples is unclear, with both Tiwanaku (Stanish n.d.a) and coastal (Bawden 1989a, 1989b) precursors posited. Archaeological investigations have recently been designed to examine the proposition that Chiribaya peoples comprise basal nodes for Late Intermediate "vertical" economic strategies (Rice, Conrad, and Watanabe 1990). Others, such as Bawden (1989a, 1989b), emphasize evidence for distinctive coastal traditions and invoke Rostworowski's horizontality model. Chiribaya mortuary site data are germane to these issues.

Extensive cemetery excavations have occurred at three Chiribaya sites: San Gerónimo, Chiribaya Alta, and El Yaral (see Fig. 2). Since fieldwork has only recently been completed, the results discussed here will necessarily be preliminary. In addition, systematic excavations of domestic areas of Chiribaya Baja, the original type-site excavated by Ghersi (1956), have been conducted by Jessup (1990, n.d.), who reports the presence of two interments. At least one human burial was discovered in a domestic context during 1986 excavations at the midvalley site of El Yaral (Garcia n.d.; Rice, Conrad, and Watanabe 1990). Two cemeteries associated with Chiribaya Baja were excavated during 1991.

A 21 × 21 m block rescue excavation was executed in 1988 within the site of San Gerónimo, located ca. 200 m from the ocean at the mouth of the Rio Osmore (Jessup 1990; Jessup and Torres n.d.). A total of 92 graves (56 intact; 33 disturbed; three burial urns) were recovered from within midden deposits. During 1989 and 1990, excavations were conducted at Chiribaya Alta (Fig. 6), which is both the largest and the most complex Chiribaya site discovered to date (Williams and Buikstra n.d.). As indicated in Figure 6, Chiribaya Alta includes nine distinctive cemeteries, numerous complex domestic structures, and a defensive wall, all of which extend over an area approximately 600 × 600 m. Table 3 reports the distribution of the 307 tombs that were excavated from the nine Chiribaya Alta cemeteries. The two disposal areas of El Yaral (Fig. 7), located at the lowest point of the midvalley Osmore Valley, were also sampled in 1990 (Lozada Cerna and Torres n.d.). Remains of 99 individuals were recovered; 47 from Cemetery 1 and 52 from Cemetery 2. Cemetery 1 included a few remains from Late Tiwanaku (Tumilaca) times.

Jane E. Buikstra

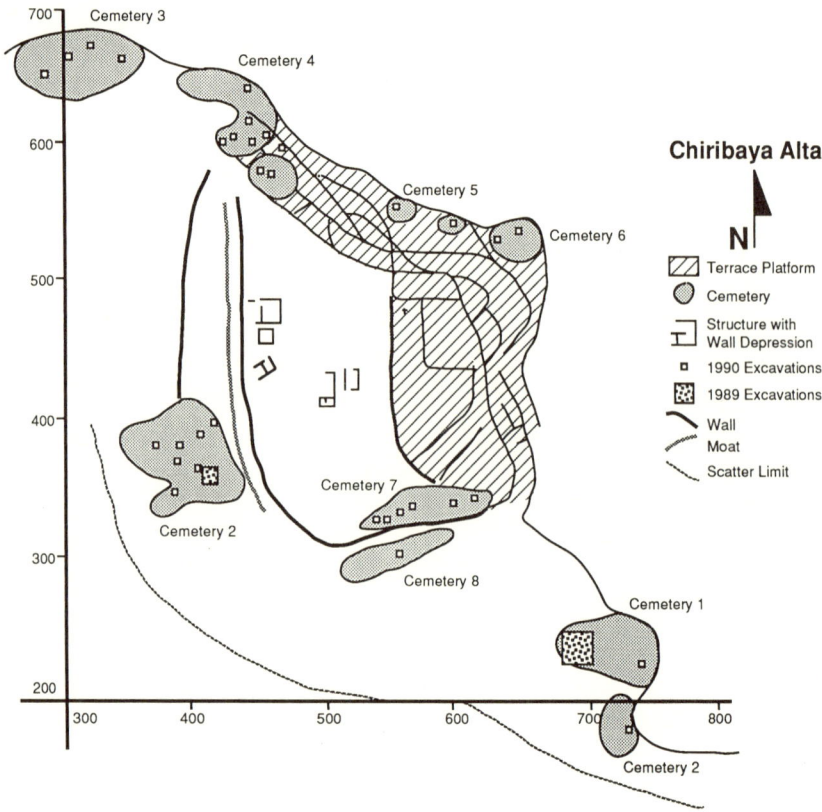

Fig. 6 Chiribaya Alta site.

TABLE 3. TOMBS FROM CHIRIBAYA ALTA

Cemetery #	Intact Tombs	Disturbed Tombs	?
1	14	34	50
2	4	68	72
3	8	23	31
4	8	34	42
5	5	15	20
6	2	11	13
7	15	48	63
8	3	6	9
9	1	6	7
	60	245	307

Tombs for the Living . . . or . . . for the Dead: The Osmore Ancestors

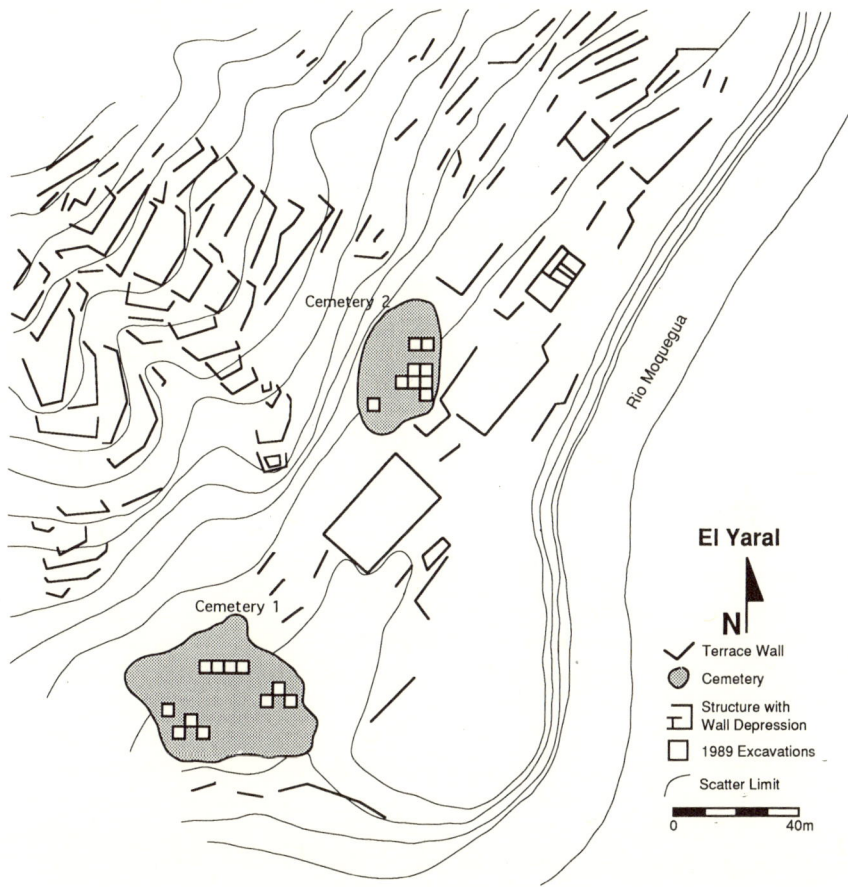

Fig. 7 El Yaral site.

Although a full discussion of Chiribaya mortuary data must await the completion of fieldwork and data analysis, we can offer a few observations relevant to ongoing discussions of contrastive social and economic models. The following questions will be addressed:

1. How similar were the formal attributes of the three Chiribaya cemeteries under discussion here?
2. What evidence is there for site-specific occupational specializations?

Jane E. Buikstra

3. Is there evidence for status distinctions that crosscut gender-specific roles?
4. How conspicuous are non-local resources within grave lots?

While Chiribaya ceramics may reflect a unified tradition, there exists significant variation in mortuary practices between Chiribaya sites. First of all, while El Yaral, Chiribaya Alta, and Chiribaya Baja contain formally bounded cemeteries adjacent to residential terraces, the situation is different at San Gerónimo. The numerous burials from San Gerónimo were recovered from midden contexts, which also included many non-mortuary features. Evidence from 1986 public works trenches also suggests that interments were scattered through the site. Thus, at the site of San Gerónimo the ancestors were not being used to make the same declarative statement concerning resource access that is apparent in other Chiribaya contexts.

Grave form and orientation vary between El Yaral and the lower valley sites. At El Yaral, circular to oval cists with diameters of 0.5 to 0.6 m dominate the distribution. Seventeen examples of collared tombs, five in Cemetery 1 and 12 in Cemetery 2, are similar to Otora phase examples from the upper Osmore drainage. With few exceptions, all El Yaral interments were of single remains, seated in a flexed position and facing east. Individualized treatments also characterize most Chiribaya Alta and San Gerónimo burials, most commonly flexed remains facing either south or east. Important, however, is the fact that lower valley Chiribaya tombs are typically rectangular. Only eight rectangular tombs were encountered within the two El Yaral cemeteries. Thus, the interment facilities at El Yaral resemble most closely earlier midvalley tomb forms, contrasting with the lower valley and coastal sites.

The El Yaral cemeteries contain "collar tombs," which are defined by above-ground rings of either angular stones or cobbles surrounding below-ground burial cists. Although multiple interments have been recovered from collar tombs at Estuquiña phase sites, the El Yaral examples contained single interments as do the earliest collar tombs Stanish reports for the Otora Valley (Stanish n.d.a, n.d.b, 1989).

Stanish (n.d.a, n.d.b) links collar tombs or "protochulpas" with altiplano traditions, such as those reported by John Hyslop (1977). He argues that "the symbolic importance of the proto-chulpa and the presumed ideological change associated with it was not bound to a particular ethnic or cultural affiliation. The construction of above-ground tombs was part of an interethnic process in the sierra, altiplano and coast" (Stanish n.d.a: 48). A proposed direct altiplano linkage is, however, difficult to reconcile with the relatively early appearance of the El Yaral tombs, which are either contemporary with or even earlier than altiplano chullpas. Even more problematic is the obvious similarity between the collar tombs and earlier Osmore midvalley interment facilities. Tumilaca tombs are regularly associated with circumferential flat stone surfaces, for example, and Huaracane phase mortuary structures included rings of large stones beyond the tomb mouth. Similarly, invoking an "inter-ethnic process" does not really explain why groups should accept new interment forms. Such requires consideration of contextual variables linking political, social, and economic domains.

More convincing is Stanish's argument that collar tombs imply a significant restructuring of mortuary ritual. A sacred precinct has been created near the corpse, where offerings could be placed and replenished at appropriate intervals. Linkages to the ancestors were thus visibly maintained, frequently at locations either near community boundaries or within cemetery areas, as they were at El Yaral. Accessible burial structures thus facilitated the use of extended mortuary rituals to reaffirm rights, likely to both land and water, as well as relationships among the living. Abundant ethnohistoric and ethnographic documentation exists for protracted interment rituals among Andean peoples, including examples cited in this volume by Bastien, Dillehay, and Salomon.

The grave good assemblages at El Yaral are relatively impoverished, compared to those for San Gerónimo and Chiribaya Alta. Typically, each cist at El Yaral contained a ceramic vessel, a gourd, and a wooden spoon. Additional items appear gender-specific and likely vocational: spindle whorls with five juveniles and five females; camelid bones with three adult males. Somewhat more enigmatic are the associations between camelid hoofs (seven juveniles and one young adult female) and vegetal fiber "boats" (three juveniles and two elderly females). Keros were found with juveniles (seven), adult males (four), and adult females (two).

Quantities of grave goods at the lower valley sites varied widely, with some graves containing few items, as was the case at El Yaral. Others, however, were filled with vessels and other grave goods. The average number of grave goods for San Gerónimo, for instance, was more than 30 (Jessup 1990; Jessup and Torres n.d.).

As was the case at El Yaral, the artifact assemblage at San Gerónimo largely reflects gender-based occupational specializations. A maritime focus is indicated by the inclusion of harpoons, fishhooks, weights, and string with males. Miniature wood boats were recovered from the tombs of both males and females. Gender differences are reinforced by manner of dress, including systematic variation in shirt form, head coverings, and belts. Females, for example, were always buried with their faces covered, their shirts tied with a wide belt, and often were accompanied by looms and a number of large ceramic vessels. Males were typically interred with faces exposed and heads covered with hats. Certain males were accompanied by non-utilitarian axes in addition to fishing kits. Imported items were rare and limited strictly to contemporaneous coastal stylistic traditions. A few crosscutting status distinctions are suggested through patterned distributions of metal items and other ornaments, number and quantity of items overall, and camelid remains. Most notable in this regard was the inclusion of nine camelid crania with an elderly male who was also interred with a metal plate headdress (Jessup 1990; Jessup and Torres n.d.). Litters were included in many tombs, suggesting that the corpse had been part of a funerary procession and was thus displayed prior to interment, reminiscent of the earlier Chinchorro pattern.

Analysis of grave goods from Chiribaya Alta is not yet complete, although a few generalizations can be made. While some tombs were simply adorned with a few ceramic vessels, many included quantities of ceramics, tools, ornaments, and food items. Several graves were marked by numerous camelid skulls, more rarely immature camelids were recovered intact. One of the richest tombs was excavated from Cemetery 4 (no. 419) and included the remains of three adults (one male and two females). Closed by large rocks and mortar layered over three cane stretchers, this rectangular tomb was oriented northeast to southwest with the interments facing northeast. Each body had been individually wrapped with textiles, and quantities of grave goods were placed on the tomb floor near the feet. The male's head covering was a four-pointed hat, while the females wore metal bands across their foreheads. Wide, heavily decorated belts were also associated with the females. A total of 32 ceramic vessels, 20 baskets, 25 textiles, and six metal items along with other artifacts were recovered from within the feature. External offerings included four camelid crania, camelid feet, and a large ceramic sherd—all located near the capstone (Williams and Buikstra n.d.).

If Jessup's (n.d.) ceramic seriation is correct, the cemeteries of Chiribaya Alta can be divided into an earlier and a later group, with Cemeteries 1, 2, 3, and 9 predating 4, 5, and 6. The rich assemblage of grave wealth within Tomb no. 419 thus argues for the presence of elite mourners late within the Chiribaya sequence.

The recovery of camelid bones with certain interments at San Gerónimo and Chiribaya Alta suggests that a period of feasting was associated with the mortuary festival. The large number of *manos* and *metates* recovered from the surface of Chiribaya Alta argues for specialized production of chicha, with consumption anticipated in ritual contexts. The special importance of camelids is also apparent at El Yaral, though not within cemetery precincts. Garcia (n.d.) reports the remains of at least nine complete camelids recovered from a single domestic structure. An anomalous human male burial (30–35 years), extended and wrapped in a camelid skin, had also been interred under a house floor within the domestic area (D. Rice, personal communication). The symbolic importance of camelids was thus celebrated at El Yaral, but the ritual took a form different from that of Chiribaya peoples at lower altitudes. Whether camelids were or were not living year round on the Osmore coast during Late Intermediate times, the ubiquitous presence of remains within both cemeteries and residential areas argues for both economic and ritual significance. Salomon (this volume) reports ethnohistoric sources indicating that the head of the llama was served to the dead as a propitiation, and other meat portions and coca were given to already-mummified ancestors. What was burned in the fire was said to be food for the dead. In an archaeological example, Donnan (this volume) reports that among the Moche the less meaty parts were found within less elaborate tombs, while whole llamas, llamas only missing the head, or butchered meaty parts were recovered from rich interment contexts.

Very few Chiribaya graves present evidence of non-local items other than camelid remains, if camelids should indeed be considered exotic during the Late Intermediate Period. Even the ubiquitous bags of coca contain leaves of a coastal plant variety. *Spondylus* shells from coastal Ecuador and remains of birds from the eastern slopes of the Andes represent very minor portions of the archaeological record. A monkey interred in the manner of a human fardo within the domestic terraces of Chiribaya Baja presents an isolated instance of a rare item assuming special importance (Jessup n.d.).

In summary, mortuary contexts provide evidence for Chiribaya as a distinctive political entity composed of economically specialized communities. In this sense, Rostworowski's model is supported, although the degree of craft specialization is less elaborated than in her example. Camelids, important both for food and wool, may also have served to facilitate transportation and trade with distant groups. In the absence of abundant exotic materials or craft items, we must, however, conclude that vertical trade was relatively attenuated, occurring primarily within the lower valley and the sierra (Jessup n.d.). Relatively late within the Chiribaya sequence fortification walls were built at the Chiribaya Alta site, in parallel with the presence of elaborate tombs at the edge of the Pampa de Descanso escarpment, overlooking the Osmore Valley. The development of a visible elite, symbolically guarding the interests of both living and dead, apparently emerged under pressure from other Late Intermediate peoples. This consolidation of power did not, however, succeed in ensuring the long-term viability of Chiribayan culture, which had largely disappeared by A.D. 1350—a demise perhaps influenced by cataclysmic environmental events (M. Moseley, personal communication).

The Midvalley Sequence

Tiwanaku influence in the midvalley Osmore drainage is commonly cited as ending ca. A.D. 1000, perhaps two centuries earlier than in the altiplano centers (Bermann et al. 1989: 271–272). This inference is apparently based on the fact that the first Chiribaya dates for the site of El Yaral include the early eleventh century: A.D. 999–1166; A.D. 1012–1153; A.D. 1216–1270 (Stanish and Rice 1989). The site of El Yaral, however, is located at the extreme southern periphery of the midvalley, where initial Chiribaya influence is likely to have occurred. Two Omo M10 Tiwanaku V dates reach into the second half of the tenth century, with calibrated ranges of A.D. 880–986 and A.D. 776–961, and there are two Chen Chen site dates with calibrated ranges from A.D. 956–1020 and A.D. 1020–1175 (Stanish and Rice 1989). Uncorrected dates of 1040 +/− 65 and 930 +/− 65 are also reported for the Tiwanaku component of the Trapiche site (M7) (Bermann, Watanabe, and Goldstein 1990). It would therefore seem likely that Tumilaca phase sites were occupied well into the eleventh and perhaps even the twelfth century. For this reason, the Tumilaca burial program will be discussed in relationship to other midvalley Late Intermediate interment patterns.

Characteristically fortified and/or in strategic locations, Tumilaca sites continued much of the Tiwanaku V mortuary tradition, including the presence of formally bounded cemeteries adjacent to residential areas (Bawden 1989a; Bermann et al. 1989; P. Goldstein n.d., 1989, 1990a, 1990b). Thus, the symbolic relationship between the living and the dead that characterized Tiwanaku V peoples was maintained into Tumilaca times. This continuity is apparent at the Omo M11 cemetery, which includes the variety of tomb forms reported for the nearby Tiwanaku V M10 site. The M11 cemetery was constructed outside the fortification wall, a pattern that is repeated in more recent Estuquiña phase sites. Separate surface collars become much more prevalent at M11, where only two of 72 graves have been excavated. As emphasized by Paul Goldstein (n.d.: 208), the "protochulpa" form linked by Charles Stanish (1989, n.d.b) with the altiplano is quite similar to the Chen Chen phase stone collars which became increasingly popular during Tumilaca times.

Within the Otora Valley, above the confluence of the Tumilaca, Torata, and Huaracane rivers (see Fig. 2 for site location), a series of 17 Middle Horizon, Late Intermediate, and Late Period sites have been investigated by Stanish (n.d.a, 1989). Stanish argues that the valley was originally settled during Tumilaca times by individuals who left no recognizable burials nor any evidence of defensive architecture. Even though some Tumilaca sites are fortified (e.g., M11 from the Omo group), the remote location of Otora Valley site P5 was apparently sufficient to buffer intercommunity tensions. The absence of formally organized cemeteries is scarcely surprising in this context, given no tangible need to legitimize access to land through mortuary ritual. This parallels the situation for Tiwanaku IV peoples within the region, who also present no evidence of formal cemetery construction (P. Goldstein n.d.).

Following Tumilaca times, Stanish (1989, n.d.a, n.d.b) argues that the Otora Valley was colonized by individuals from the coast (site P4) and the altiplano (P8). Diagnostic ceramics are said to identify P4 with the Chiribaya tradition, while both ceramic styles, funerary architecture, and room construction link P8 with the Colla, a polity found on the northern side of the Lake Titicaca Basin. A third contemporaneous site, P7, is thought to reflect a local development based in the Tumilaca tradition. Interestingly, the only interment within P7 was a neonate recovered from within a domestic structure.

Stanish identifies Otora Valley collar tombs or "protochulpas" as markers of altiplano traditions. Typically, Otora Valley collar tombs include a central, subfloor cist containing a single interment. Prepared floors surround the cist, which is in turn bounded by a low stone wall approximately 2 m in diameter. The single intact collar tomb (P8-4) from the Otora Valley included a cist 65 cm in diameter and 70 cm deep. The round exterior wall was 2.2 m in diameter. Llama phalanges were recovered from the cist, with a ceramic vessel recovered from the prepared floor within the exterior wall. The tomb contained the remains of an adult male.

Both collar and cist tombs occur at P4, while only collar tombs were located at P8. Even though P4 is said to be a colonial Chiribaya site, nine collar tombs are reported. Collar tombs are clearly not typical lower valley Chiribaya grave forms, although they are found at the site of El Yaral, presumably very early within the Late Intermediate sequence.

Stanish theorizes that the presence of true chullpas and perhaps even collar tombs in the Osmore drainage is associated with the presence of elites who legitimize their primacy through the use of altiplano symbols (Stanish n.d.b). This argument is intriguing and appears least problematic in the more complex situation of the Estuquiña site (see below). Stanish's theory does not, however, fully explain the Otora collar tombs as exclusive interment forms, as they apparently are at P8. The identification of an elite presence within a community comprising a few households is also problematic.

An alternative speculative model for the Otora, based upon territorial models of mortuary behavior, would support Stanish's notions concerning the Tumilaca peoples as the first settlers. Without competition, corpse disposal was casual and formally bounded cemetery areas are absent. The daughter settlement of P7, also facing no competition, continued the practice of casual disposal. With increased colonization at P4 and then P8, formally bounded cemeteries expressed the declarative statement predicted by mortuary theory. The earliest intrusive community (P4) established a cemetery of cist tombs to legitimize their presence. Following the entrada of P8 peoples, the P4 community also established more visible mortuaries and their attendant rituals as a more florid representation of their rights to local resources.

Stanish (n.d.a) argues that the subsequent Estuquiña phase communities emerge as an indigenous sierra culture developed from the various colonial ethnicities that characterize the early Late Intermediate Period. In a contrasting argument, direct altiplano influences are cited by Bawden (1989a: 301), who believes that "shortly following the end of the Tumilaca Phase migrants entered the upper Moquegua drainage from the highlands, settling in the small fortified villages of the Estuquiña period bringing with them a very different cultural tradition from that of earlier occupants of the region. In all probability this pattern of communally self-reliant intrusion represents the operation of the 'vertical archipelago' model of ecological and economic interaction with colonists linked with their highland core societies by ethnic and kinship ties as opposed to the political ties of the Tiahuanaco period."

Often contained within fortification walls or in defensible locations, Estuquiña phase sites are thought to be much less hierarchical than Tumilaca. Influenced by the sequential components of the Tumilaca site, Bawden (1989a, 1990a, 1990b) sees Tumilaca domestic space formally structured according to a pattern reminiscent of earlier Tiwanaku V sites. The subsequent Estuquiña phase portion of the Tumilaca site, with partially partitioned domestic units loosely organized within walled enclosures separated by open space, suggests to Bawden a much less complex social organization, probably kin and perhaps ayllu-based. Estuquiña phase collar tombs are scattered over the site, rather than being structured within formal cemeteries (Bawden 1989a: 292).

Interpretations of the recently excavated Estuquiña site, located in the Moquegua Valley (Fig. 2), are important in this context (Rice, Conrad, and Buikstra 1990; Clark n.d.; Williams et al. 1989; Williams, Clark, and Buikstra 1990; Williams n.d.). The Estuquiña site includes a domestic area with 38 rooms of various sizes. As illustrated in Figure 8, there are three spatially distinct cemetery areas, Nos. 1 and 2 to the west and No. 3 to the east. In addition, burials were recovered from domestic areas, including within-room contexts. Ten distinctive tomb types have been identified, with many falling into a limited number of categories. Most prevalent were the below-ground cist tombs extending approximately 0.5 m below the ground surface, capped by one or two large stone slabs, and frequently associated with both internal and external offerings. Above-ground collared tombs were located in Cemeteries 1 and 2, including a cluster of 14 that defined the eastern boundary of Cemetery 1. Three collar tombs are located near the boundary between Cemeteries 1 and 2. Cemetery 2 is positioned between two defensive walls; Cemetery 1 is beyond the fortified areas. Cemeteries 1 and 2 thus stand with fortification walls in symbolic defense of the Estuquiña community. Estuquiña was not only defended by its walls and living inhabitants, but by the ancestors as well (Moseley 1990).

Grave goods recovered from the Estuquiña site included a variety of utilitarian items, such as spindle whorls and other artifacts associated with textile production—most commonly recovered from the tombs of adult females. Plant and animal offerings represent both altiplano and coastal resources, with llama feet as a ubiquitous feature. Food containers including ceramic vessels—whole or in sections—and gourds frequently presented

Tombs for the Living ... or ... for the Dead: The Osmore Ancestors

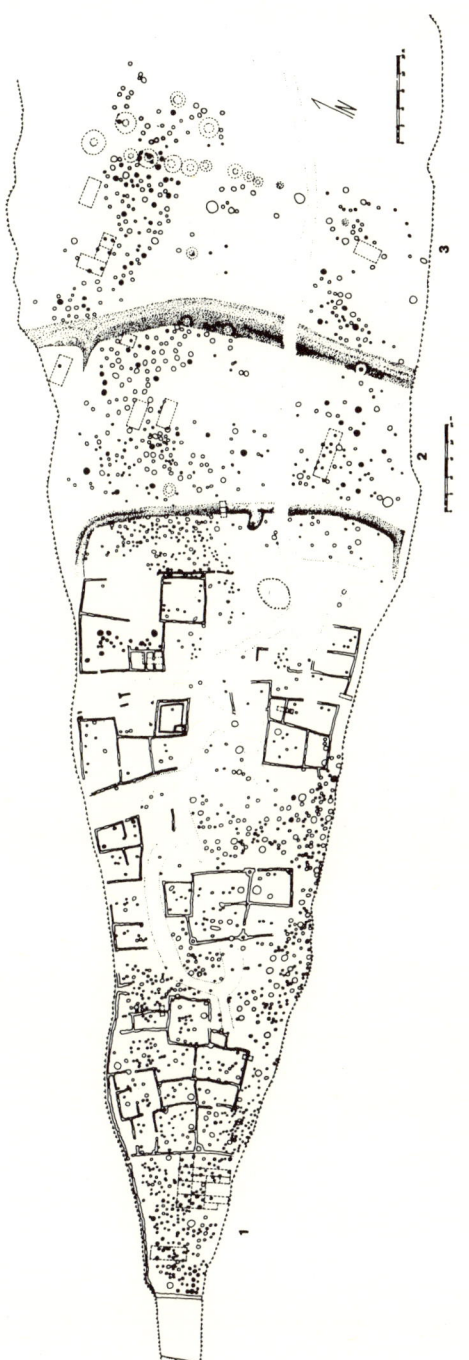

Fig. 8 Estuquiña site.

Jane E. Buikstra

evidence of foodstuffs (Williams et al. 1989). Textiles, though occasionally new, frequently were used garments woven from wool (Williams et al. 1989; Clark 1990).

Although we have at present no means of reconstructing within-site chronological sequences, we might suspect that the earliest habitation and mortuary activity occurred at the western aspect of the site. A portion of Cemetery 3 appears to comprise a disposal area for infants and young children, a mortuary custom likely predicated by the shallow persona of the deceased. Placing burials within houses, also characteristic of the Estuquiña phase component of the Tumilaca site (Bawden 1989a), is a remarkable break with earlier interment traditions. In fact, this shift is so extreme that it may reflect deliberate political manipulation of mortuary ritual as a means of either establishing or legitimizing power. The relatively common appearance of metal within domestic area burials (Bürgi et al. 1989; Williams et al 1989) also suggests that there is a special agenda behind the domestic area burials. If Bawden is correct in his characterization of domestic space use and the strong influence of descent groups in organizing that space, perhaps the ancestors were also being used to validate the authority of the kin group. Competition between kin groups could encourage ritual displays of this type.

The apparent simplification of mortuary ritual represented by Estuquiña phase residential interments should not be accepted uncritically as de facto evidence for less differentiated social structures. Elite groups will, under certain conditions, deliberately simplify mortuary ritual displays in order to distance themselves from non-elites (Cannon 1989). In the face of rapid social change, mortuary customs may also become restructured relatively quickly without necessarily implicating population replacement, as in the Temuan ethnographic example cited by Arthur Saxe and Patricia Gall (1977). Less than a generation was required for the Temuan to move from a relatively unstructured burial program to the development of formally bounded cemeteries.

Returning to our speculative history of the Estuquiña site, we believe that through time, perhaps with the emergence of a stronger overarching authority structure, formal cemeteries again assumed prominence. Increased competition with neighboring communities may have served to stimulate cemetery development, although Bawden's notion of Chiribaya raiders (Bawden 1989a: 298) appears anachronistic in the face of the current radiocarbon dates. Initially Cemetery 2 was established beyond the first defensive wall. When Cemetery 2 was saturated, the mortuary area was extended beyond the second wall into Cemetery 1.

Among the most recent mortuary events was the construction of collar tombs, which in the Estuquiña site example included multiple remains— typically of six to seven individuals who represent both sexes and all ages.

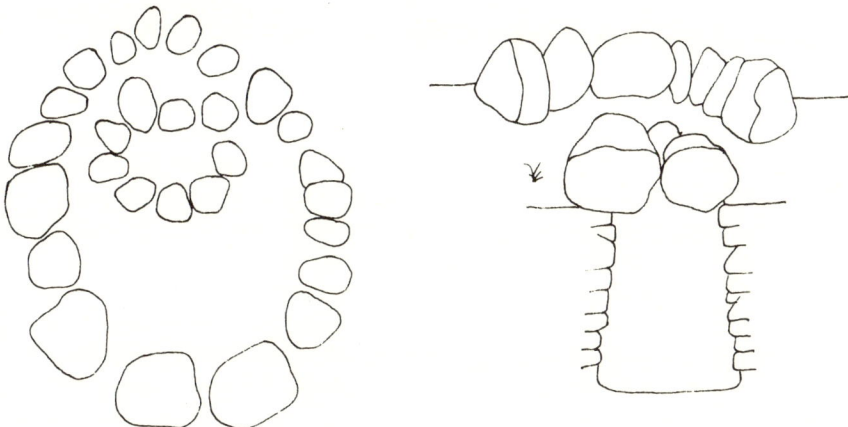

Fig. 9 Collar tomb from the Estuquiña site (after Clark n.d.).

An example of this impressive tomb form is illustrated in Figure 9. The remains recovered from the collar tombs probably represent members of a single descent group whose corporate nature is emphasized by monumental architecture. With maximum external diameters of one to two m, the Estuquiña collar tombs were highly visible monuments. Opening to the east, in parallel to the eastern orientation of individual interments within the cist and other subfloor tombs, these elaborate graves both established boundaries and reaffirmed intergenerational linkages.

Even more monumental are the "chulpas" reported by Stanish for Estuquiña phase sites from the Otora Valley. These above-ground stone cists resemble the Estuquiña site collar tombs by having doors facing east and containing the remains of several individuals. Heavily looted, the Otora Valley chullpas had a base diameter of approximately 2 to 2.5 m and were constructed of pirca fieldstone masonry. A chullpa from the Porobaya site (P1-CH2) appears to have been more than 2 m in height. Only the top section of this chullpa had been looted; the sealed bottom chamber contained a minimum of five individuals, including three adults, one child, and one infant. Also recovered were bones representing 27 llama feet, guinea pig remains, maize cobs, gourd fragments, textiles, wood, freshwater shrimp, a wooden spoon, marine shell fragments, 15 cactus spine needles, guinea pig feces, a cryptocrystalline quartz knife, and a ceramic jar. The Otora Valley Estuquiña phase burial program apparently included both cist tombs and chullpas, most commonly in cemetery clusters at site peripheries. The single

Jane E. Buikstra

dendrocalibrated radiocarbon date for the P1 site of A.D. 1398–1454 suggests that this site is contemporaneous with the later occupations of the Estuquiña site.

At P2 (Colana site), chullpas were either strategically located on principal access routes or on agricultural terraces (Stanish n.d.a: 49). Both situations suggest that these Estuquiña phase chullpas were legitimizing access to resources by symbolically representing links to the ancestors, with the burial structure serving as the collective cemetery for a corporate group.

Stanish (n.d.b) argues eloquently for chullpas as elite constructions that belonged to select corporate groups and symbolized alliance formation between elites from different regions. "The distribution of this burial practice is a result of a highly structured diffusion process in which emergent elite groups adopted a non-local ideology, a component of the more general cultural process of the development of sociopolitical hierarchies in complex non-market societies" (Stanish n.d.b: 19). This argument parallels that of Mary Helms (1979, n.d. cited in Stanish n.d.b), who emphasizes the special value placed on foreign goods by elites and the fact that they frequently legitimize authority through "genetic" links to exotic areas. In this context, chullpa burial practices are said to represent a "foreign" elite ideology, derived from the altiplano (Stanish n.d.b).

However intriguing this model may seem, it must be interpreted in the history of tomb development within the Osmore drainage. Stanish's emphasis upon the collar tomb and the chullpa as "new forms" would seem somewhat overdrawn, given the resemblance between Otora phase collar tombs and Tumilaca graves, such as those at M11 (P. Goldstein n.d.) and the Chiribaya collar tombs from El Yaral. The rings of stones surrounding the Huaracane Phase graves at Omo M10 and within the Huaracane site cemetery M29 (Feldman 1989) are also significant above-ground interment structures. There is a clear tradition of visible, above-ground mortuary monuments within the Osmore midvalley, which gradually changes form. Even the corporate nature and extended use of the tombs develops slowly, with the first collar tombs including only cist tombs for single Otora phase interments. Fully developed chullpa forms with multiple interments emerge very late, relative to other Estuquiña phase mortuary structures. Does one need to invoke a "pan-ethnic ideology" (Stanish n.d.a) to explain their existence?

A "pan-ethnic" ideology, as a monolithic construct, threatens to impose a veneer of unified meaning that is not yet supported by other classes of archaeologically recoverable data. The presence of collar tombs and chullpas does, no doubt, identify the emergence of a preeminent descent group whose monumental tombs served to facilitate local (within and between-community) communication about corporate status and control. And Stanish may be correct in inferring that alliance formation with distant elites could have functioned to reinforce status distinctions among certain Late Intermediate families. Rather than proposing a "pan-ethnic ideology," however, we would emphasize the process by which monumental tombs developed and be careful not to impute a common rationalization for their use sustained across many generations and distinctive ethnicities. The extended burial rituals associated with the above-ground mortuary monuments of the Osmore Valley during the Late Intermediate Period, even if symbolically linked to altiplano sources, were undoubtedly reinterpreted according to local belief systems and social relations. As in Salomon's ethnohistoric examples (this volume), powerful ancestors were evoked by prosperous descendants, who thus legitimized their good fortune. In this manner, the cemeteries and the ancestors served well the needs of the living, the chullpas remaining as monuments symbolic of this dynamic relationship.

CONCLUDING STATEMENT

In this survey of Osmore Valley cemeteries, we have reported and interpreted both below-ground cists—which are indeed plentiful—and above-ground mortuaries that resemble the "little Pigeon Houfes" reported by Frezier in 1717. Drawing on multiple classes of archaeologically recoverable data—both biological and cultural—our inferences are informed by both processual and postprocessual theories. We believe that in most instances the Osmore mourners chose to represent directly the deceased persona, as evidenced by tools and items of personal adornment. That interments were commonly grouped in formally bounded cemetery areas is a stong declarative statement about ancient communities and their relationship to scarce and/or important resources.

The earliest Osmore mortuary rituals—those of Preceramic peoples—appear to have been protracted, with final corpse disposal less important than intermediate stages of body preparation and display. The ancestors of Chinchorro peoples were thus visible reminders of their descendants' access to scarce resources, including fresh water and fishing territories. More recent Early Ceramic coastal cemeteries similarly provide evidence that ancestral remains were maintained among the living.

Midvalley Early Ceramic period cemeteries were strategically located in positions symbolizing corporate control of arable land. Such strong declarative statements were followed by centuries of archaeological silence concerning funerary rites, times when the ancestors were apparently not invoked to legitimize the claims of the living. During the Middle Horizon tantalizing—though incomplete—mortuary data record ethnic differentiation within Tiwanaku V sites of the Omo group, where intercemetery distinctions in cranial form are significant. Such highly visible markers of group identity are not paralleled, however, by differences in material culture.

Jane E. Buikstra

Ritual displays including quantities of grave goods become prominent among coastal Late Intermediate Chiribaya peoples, contrasting with Chiribaya mortuary procedures within the Moquegua Valley. During the latter part of the Estuquiña phase descent groups of paramount importance apparently emerged—their status perhaps enhanced by relationships with distant elites. Osmore Valley elites chose to elevate their ancestors above ground, locating remains in highly visible tombs that served as symbols of village access and community limits. Lengthy Estuquiña phase funerary rituals also included periodic visits by mourners who replenished offerings at the periphery of interment facilities. At such times, the Osmore ancestors were ceremonially invited to participate in the lives of their descendents, thus following a pervasive—and persistent—Andean tradition.

Acknowledgements The research reported here has been generously supported by the Southern Peru Copper Company; the National Science Foundation; the Bioanthropology Foundation of Sausalito, California; the Lichtstern Committee of the Department of Anthropology at the University of Chicago; and the Committee on Latin American Studies at the University of Chicago. The intellectual and administrative leadership of Fernando Cabieses, Michael Moseley, Don Rice, and Geoffrey Conrad within Programa Contisuyu Proyecto Osmore have been essential for the archaeological investigations described in this report. This manuscript has benefited from the comments of Shelley Burgess, Douglas Charles, Niki Clark, Sonia Guillen, Lisa Hoshower, and Maria Cecilia Lozada Cerna, who are responsible for none of its shortcomings.

A special debt of gratitude is owed to Sr. Manuel Pacheco, whose enthusiasm for the lives of the Osmore ancestors is a source of constant inspiration to Programa Contisuyu scholars.

BIBLIOGRAPHY

Allison, Marvin J., Enrique Gerszten, Juan Munizaga, Calogero Santoro, and Guillermo Focacci
    1981   La práctica de la deformación craneana entre los pueblos Andinos Precolumbinos. *Chungará* 7: 238–260.

Allison, Marvin J., Guillermo Focacci, Bernardo Arriaza, Vivian Standen, Mario Rivera, and Jerold Lowenstein
    1984   Chinchorro, Momias de Preparación Complicada: Métodos de Momificación. *Chungará* 13: 155–174.

Bawden, Garth
    1989a   The Tumilaca Site and Post-Tiahuanaco Occupational Stratigraphy in the Moquegua Drainage. In *Ecology, Settlement and History in the Osmore Drainage, Peru* (Don S. Rice, Charles Stanish, and Phillip R. Scarr, eds.): 287–302. BAR International Series 545 (2). Oxford.
    1989b   Settlement Survey and Ecological Dynamics on the Peruvian South Coast. *Andean Past* 2: 39–67.
    1990a   El Sitio Tumilaca. In *Trabajos Arqueológicos en Moquegua* 2 (Luis Watanabe, Michael Moseley, and Fernando Cabieses, eds.): 69–74. Lima.
    1990b   Tumilaca: Un Sitio de las Fases Tiwanaku y Estuquiña en el Valle de Moquegua. *Gaceta Arqueológica Andina* 18-19: 105–113.

Belan Franco, L. Augusto
    1981   *Chiribaya: Apuntes para el Conocimiento de la Arqueología Surperuana.* Editorial "Arqueos," Arequipa.

Bermann, Marc, Paul Goldstein, Charles Stanish, and Luis Watanabe
    1989   The Collapse of the Tiwanaku State: A View from the Osmore Drainage. In *Ecology, Settlement and History in the Osmore Drainage, Peru* (Don S. Rice, Charles Stanish, and Phillip R. Scarr, eds.): 269–285. BAR International Series 545 (2). Oxford.

Bermann, Marc, Luis Watanabe, and Paul Goldstein
    1990   Algunos Entierros Tiwanaku y del Período Intermedio Tardío en Moquegua. In *Trabajos Arqueológicos en Moquegua* 2 (Luis Watanabe, Michael Moseley, and Fernando Cabieses, eds.): 97–113. Lima.

Binford, Lewis R.
    1971   Mortuary Practices: Their Study and Their Potential. In *Approaches to the Social Dimensions of Mortuary Practices* (James A. Brown, ed.). Memoirs of the Society for American Archaeology 25: 6–29. Washington, D.C.

Bird, Junius B.
    1943   Excavations in Northern Chile. *Excavations at Quiani.* Anthropological Papers of the American Museum of Natural History, Bulletin 38 (4): 232–250. New York.

BITTMAN, BENTE
    1982   Revisión del Problema Chinchorro. *Chungará* 9: 46–79.
BITTMAN, BENTE, AND JUAN MUNIZAGA
    1976   The Earliest Artificial Mummification in the World? A Study of the Chinchorro Complex in Northern Chile. *Folk* 18: 61–92.
    1979   El Arco en América, Evidencia Temprana y Directa de la Cultura Chinchorro. *Indiana* 5: 229–251.
BLAKELY, ROBERT L.
    1977   *Biocultural Adaptation in Prehistoric America.* Southern Anthropological Society, Proceedings 11.
BRADLEY, RICHARD
    1984   *The Social Foundations of Prehistoric Britain.* Longmans, London.
BRAUN, DAVID P.
    1981   A Critique of Some Recent North American Mortuary Studies. *American Antiquity* 46: 398–416.
BROWMAN, DAVID L.
    1980   Tiwanaku Expansion and Altiplano Economic Patterns. *Estudios Arqueológicos* 5: 107–120.
    1984   Tiwanaku: Development of Interzonal Trade and Economic Expansion in the Altiplano. In *Social and Economic Organization in the Prehispanic Andes* (David L. Browman, Ronald Burger, and Mario Rivera, eds.): 117–142. BAR International Series 194. Oxford.
    1985   Cultural Primacy of Tiwanaku in the Development of Later Peruvian States. In *La Problemática Tiwanaku-Huari en el Contexto Panandino del Desarollo Cultural.* Dialogo Andino No. 4, Arica.
BROWN, JAMES A. (ED.)
    1971   *Approaches to the Social Dimensions of Mortuary Practices.* Memoirs of the Society for American Archaeology 25. Washington, D.C.
BUIKSTRA, JANE E.
    1988   *The Mound-Builders of Eastern North America: A Regional Perspective.* Institute for the Study of Pre- and Protohistory. University of Amsterdam, The Netherlands.
BÜRGI, PETER T., SLOAN A. WILLIAMS, JANE E. BUIKSTRA, NIKI R. CLARK, MARIA C. LOZADA CERNA, AND ELVA TORRES PINO
    1989   Aspects of Mortuary Differentiation at the Site of Estuquiña, Southern Peru. In *Ecology, Settlement and History in the Osmore Drainage, Peru* (Don S. Rice, Charles Stanish, and Phillip R. Scarr, eds.): 347–369. BAR International Series 545 (2). Oxford.
CANNON, AUBREY
    1989   The Historical Dimension in Mortuary Expressions of Status and Sentiment. *Current Anthropology* 30: 437–458.
CHAPMAN, ROBERT, IAN KINNES, AND KLAVS RANDSBORG (EDS.)
    1981   *The Archaeology of Death.* Cambridge University Press, New York.

CHARLES, DOUGLAS K., AND JANE E. BUIKSTRA
　1983　Archaic Mortuary Sites in the Central Mississippi Drainage: Distribution, Structure, and Behavioral Implications. In *Archaic Hunters and Gatherers in the American Midwest* (James L. Phillips and James A. Brown, eds.): 117–145. Academic Press, New York.

CHILDE, VERE GORDON
　1945　Directional Changes in Funerary Practices during 50,000 Years. *Man* 45: 13–19.

CLARK, NIKI R.
　1990　Textiles Arqueológicos en su Contexto Socio-cultural. In *Trabajos Arqueológicos en Moquegua* 3 (Luis Watanabe, Michael Moseley, and Fernando Cabieses, eds.): 123–137. Lima.
　n.d.　The Estuquiña Textile Tradition: Cultural Patterning in Late Prehistoric Fabrics Moquegua, Far South Peru. Ph.D. dissertation, Washington University, St. Louis, 1993.

CONRAD, GEOFFREY W., AND DON S. RICE
　1989　Proyecto Osmore: Introduction to the Study of Late Prehistoric Vertical Connections. In *Ecology, Settlement and History in the Osmore Drainage, Peru* (Don S. Rice, Charles Stanish, and Phillip R. Scarr, eds.): 321–327. BAR International Series 545 (2). Oxford.

DAUELSBERG, PERCY
　1960　Algunos Problemas sobre la Cerámica de Arica. *Boletín del Museo Regional de Arica* 5: 7–17.
　1973a　La Cerámica de Arica y su Situación Cronológica. *Chungará* 1-2: 17–24.
　1973b　Carta Respuesta a Luis Lumbreras "Sobre Problemática Arqueológica de Arica." *Chungará* 1-2: 32–37.

DE LAS CASAS, FR. BARTOLOME
　1892　*De las Antiguas Gentes del Perú.* Manuel G. Hernandes, Madrid.
　[1561]

DILLEHAY, TOM D.
　1990　Mapuche Ceremonial Landscapes, Social Recruitment and Resource Rights. *World Archaeology* 22: 223–241.

DISSELHOFF, HANS D.
　1968　Huari und Tiahuanaco: Grabungen und Funde in Sud-Peru. *Zeitschrift für Ethnologie* 93: 207–216.

FELDMAN, ROBERT A.
　1989　The Early Ceramic Periods of Moquegua. In *Ecology, Settlement and History in the Osmore Drainage, Peru* (Don S. Rice, Charles Stanish, and Phillip R. Scarr, eds.): 207–217. BAR International Series 545 (2). Oxford.
　1990a　La Cerámica del Período Temprano de Moquegua. In *Trabajos Arqueológicos en Moquegua* 1 (Luis Watanabe, Michael Moseley, and Fernando Cabieses, eds.): 227–235. Lima.
　1990b　Ocupaciones del Período Cerámico Temprano en Moquegua. *Gaceta Arqueológica Andina* 18-19: 65–73.

FOCACCI ASTE, GUILLERMO
   1980   Síntesis de la Arqueología de Extremo Norte de Chile. *Chungará* 6: 3–23.
FRÉZIER, AMÉDÉE FRANÇOIS
   1717   *A Voyage to the South-Sea, and along the Coasts of Chili and Peru, in the years 1712, 1713, and 1714.* Jonah Bowyer, London.
GARCIA, MANUEL
   n.d.   La Excavación de Dos Estructuras de la Yaral. Tesis Bachiller, Universidad Católica Santa Maria, Arequipa 1988.
GARCILASO DE LA VEGA, E.
   1961   [1609] *The Incas: The Royal Commentaries of the Inca* (M. Jolas, trans.; A Gheerbrandt, ed.). The Orion Press, New York.
GHERSI BARRERA, HUMBERTO
   1956   Informe sobre las Excavaciones en Chiribaya. *Revista del Museo Nacional* 25: 89–119.
GOLDSTEIN, LYNNE G.
   n.d.   Spatial Structure and Social Organization: Regional Manifestations of Mississippian Society. Ph.D. dissertation, Northwestern University, 1976.
   1980   *Mississippian Mortuary Practices: A Case Study of Two Cemeteries in the Lower Illinois Valley.* Northwestern University Archeological Program, Evanston, Ill.
GOLDSTEIN, PAUL
   1989   The Tiwanaku Occupation of Moquegua. In *Ecology, Settlement and History in the Osmore Drainage, Peru* (Don S. Rice, Charles Stanish, and Phillip R. Scarr, eds.): 219–255. BAR International Series 545 (2). Oxford.
   1990a La Occupación Tiwanaku en Moquegua. *Gaceta Arqueológica Andina* 18-19: 75–104.
   1990b La Cultura Tiwanaku y la Relación de Sus Fases Cerámicas en Moquegua. In *Trabajos Arqueológicos en Moquegua* 2 (Luis Watanabe, Michael Moseley, and Fernando Cabieses, eds.): 31–58. Lima.
   n.d.   Omo, A Tiwanaku Provincial Center in Moquegua, Peru. Ph.D. dissertation, University of Chicago, 1989.
GUILLÉN, SONIA
   n.d.   The Chinchorro Adaptation to the Environment of the South Central Andes. Ph.D. dissertation, University of Michigan, 1992.
HELMS, MARY W.
   1979   *Ancient Panama: Chiefs in Search of Power.* University of Texas Press, Austin.
HODDER, IAN
   1980   Social Structure and Cemeteries: A Critical Appraisal. In *Anglo-Saxon Cemeteries* (Philip Rahtz, Tania Dickinson, and Lorna Watts, eds.): 161–169. BAR British Series, 82. Oxford.
   1981   Towards a Mature Archaeology. In *Patterns of the Past* (Ian Hodder,

Glynn Isaac, and Norman Hammond, eds.): 1–13. Cambridge University Press, Cambridge.
- 1982a *Symbols in Action.* Cambridge University Press, Cambridge.
- 1982b Theoretical Archaeology: A Reactionary View. In *Symbolic and Structural Archaeology* (Ian Hodder, ed.): 1–16. Cambridge University Press, Cambridge.
- 1986 *Reading the Past.* Cambridge University Press, Cambridge.
- 1987a *Archaeology as Long-term History* (ed.). Cambridge University Press, Cambridge.
- 1987b *The Archaeology of Contextual Meanings* (ed.). Cambridge University Press, Cambridge.

HOSHOWER, LISA, JANE E. BUIKSTRA, PAUL GOLDSTEIN, AND ANN D. WEBSTER
- n.d. Artificial Cranial Deformation at the Omo M10 Site: A Tiwanaku Complex from the Moquegua Valley, Peru. Manuscript.

HRDLICKA, ALES
- 1912 Artificial Deformations of the Human Skull with Special Reference to America. *Conferencia Internacional de Americanistas:* 147–149. Buenos Aires.

HYSLOP, JOHN
- 1977 Chulpas of the Lupaca Zone of the Peruvian High Plateau. *Journal of Field Archaeology* 4: 218–225.

IMBELLONI, JOSÉ
- 1925 Deformaciones Intencionales del Cráneo en Sud-America: Polígonos Craneanos Aberrantes. *Revista del Museo de la Plata* 28: 329–407.
- 1932 Las Deformaciones Corporales en la Estética de los Pueblos Bárbaros y Civilizados. *Ciclo de Conferencias Dictadas en el Museo Argentino de Ciencias Naturales.* Buenos Aires.
- 1933 Los Pueblos Deformadores de los Andes. *Antropología, Etnología, y Arqueología* 75: 209–257.
- 1934 Ueber Formen, Wesen und Methodik der Absichtlichen Deformationen. *Zeitschrift für Morphologie und Anthropologie* 33: 164–189.
- 1937 Deformaciones Intencionales del Cráneo en Sud America. *Helmintología* 6: 330–406.

ISHIDA, EIICHIRO
- 1960 *Andes, the Report of the University of Tokyo Scientific Expedition to the Andes, 1958.* University of Tokyo.

JESSUP, DAVID
- 1990 Rescate Arqueológico en el Museo de Sitio de San Gerónimo, Ilo. In Trabajos Arqueológicos en Moquegua 3 (Luis Watanabe, Michael Moseley, and Fernando Cabieses, eds.): 151–165. Lima.
- n.d. Desarollos Generales en el Intermedio Tardío, Ilo. Informe Interno del Programa Contisuyu, 1990.

JESSUP, DAVID, AND ELVA TORRES PINO
- n.d. Sumario de las Excavaciones en el Museo de Sitio, San Gerónimo, Ilo, 1990.

LLAGOSTERA, AGUSTÍN
    1989   Caza y Pesca Marítima. In *Culturas de Chile, Prehistoria* (Jorge Hidalgo, Virglio Schiappacasse, Hans Niemeyer, Carlos Aldunate, and Iván Solomano, eds.): 57–79. Editorial Andrés Bello, Santiago.

LOZADA CERNA, MARIA C., AND ELVA TORRES PINO
    n.d.   Mortuary Excavations at La Yaral, Southern Peru. Manuscript, 1991.

LUMBRERAS, LUIS
    1989   *The Peoples and Cultures of Ancient Peru* (eighth printing, Betty Meggars, trans.). Smithsonian Institution Press, Washington, D.C.

MANZANILLA, LINDA, AND ERIC WOODARD
    1990   Restos Humanos Asociados a la Pirámide de Akapana (Tiwanaku, Bolivia). *Latin American Antiquity* 1 (2): 133–149.

MEIGHAN, CLEMENT W.
    1980   Archaeology of Guatacondo, Chile. In *Prehistoric Trails of Atacama: Archaeology of Northern Chile* (Clement W. Meighan and Delbert L. True, eds.): 99–126. Institute of Archaeology, The University of California, Los Angeles.

MILLER, DANIEL, AND CHRISTOPHER TILLEY (EDS.)
    1984   *Ideology, Power and Prehistory*. Cambridge University Press, Cambridge.

MOSELEY, MICHAEL
    1990   Fortificaciones Prehispánicas y la Evolución de Tácticas Militares en al Valle de Moquegua. In *Trabajos Arqueológicos en Moquegua* 1 (Luis Watanabe, Michael Moseley, and Fernando Cabieses, eds.): 237–252. Lima.

MOSTNY, GRETE
    1944   Excavaciones en Arica. *Boletín del Museo Nacional Historia Natural* 22: 135–145. Santiago.

MUJICA, ELÍAS
    1985   Altiplano-Coast Relationships in the South-Central Andes: From Indirect to Direct Complementarity. In *Andean Ecology and Civilization* (Shozo Masuda, Izumi Shimada, and Craig Morris, eds.): 103–140. University of Tokyo Press.

MUJICA, ELÍAS, MARIO A. RIVERA, AND THOMAS F. LYNCH
    1983   Proyecto de Estudio sobre la Complementaridad Económica Tiwanaku en los Valles Occidentales del Centro-Sur Andino. *Chungará* 11: 85–109.

MUNIZAGA, JUAN R.
    1964   Deformación Cefálica Intencional. *Antropología* 2: 5–17.

MUÑOZ, IVÁN
    1982   Las Sociedades Costeras en el Litoral de Arica durante el Período Arcaico Tardío y sus Vinculaciones con la Costa Peruana. *Chungará* 9: 124–151.
    1983   El Poblamiento Aldeano en el Valle de Azapa y sus Vinculaciones con Tiwanaku (Arica-Chile). *Asentamientos Aldeanos en los Valles Costeros de*

Arica. Documentos de Trabajo 3: 43–93. Universidad de Tarapacá, Instituto de Anthropología y Arqueología.

MURRA, JOHN
- 1964 Una Apreciación Etnológica de la Visita. In *Visita Hecha a la Provincia de Chucuito por Garcí Díez de San Miguel en al Año 1567* (John Murra, ed.): 419–442. Casa del la Cultural del Perú, Lima.
- 1968 An Aymara Kingdom in 1567. *Ethnohistory* 15: 115–151.
- 1972 El 'Control Vertical' de un Máximo de Pisos Ecológicos en la Economía de las Sociedades Andinas. In *Visita de la Provincia de León de Huánuco en 1562* (John Murra, ed.): 427–476. Documentos para la Historia y Etnología de Huánuco y la Selva Central 2, Universidad Nacional Hermilio Valdizán, Huanuco.

NUÑEZ A., LAUTARO
- 1976 Registro Nacional de Fechas Radiocarbónicas del Norte de Chile. *Estudios Atacameños* 4. San Pedro de Atacama.

O'DONNABHÁIN, BARRA, AND MARIA C. LOZADA CERNA
- n.d. Excavations at an Early Ceramic Cemetery at Wawakiki, Ilo, Peru. Manuscript on file, Department of Anthropology, University of Chicago, 1989.

O'DONNABHÁIN, BARRA, MARIA C. LOZADA CERNA, AND JANE E. BUIKSTRA
- n.d. Recent Excavations of an Early Ceramic Cemetery at Wawakiki, Ilo, Peru. Paper Presented at the 56th Annual Meeting of the Society for American Archaeology, New Orleans, April 1991.

O'SHEA, JOHN M.
- 1984 *Mortuary Variability: An Archaeological Investigation*. Academic Press, New York.

POWELL, MARY L., ANN M. MIRES, AND PATRICIA BRIDGES (EDS).
- 1991 *What Mean These Bones?* University of Alabama Press, Tuscaloosa.

RENFREW, COLIN
- 1973 Monuments, Mobilization and Social Organization in Neolithic Wessex. In *The Explanation of Culture Change* (Colin Renfrew, ed.): 539–558. Duckworth, London.
- 1976 Megaliths, Territories and Populations. In *Acculturation and Continuity in Atlantic Europe* (Sigfried J. De Laet, ed.): De Tempel, Brugge.
- 1984 *Social Archaeology*. Edinburgh University Press.

RICE, DON S.
- 1989 Osmore Drainage, Peru: The Ecological Setting. In *Ecology, Settlement and History in the Osmore Drainage, Peru* (Don S. Rice, Charles Stanish, and Philip R. Scarr, eds.): 17–33. BAR International Series 545 (2). Oxford.

RICE, DON S., GEOFFREY W. CONRAD, AND JANE E. BUIKSTRA
- 1990 Investigaciones en Estuquiña, Descripciones Preliminares 1985-1986. In *Trabajos Arqueológicos en Moquegua 3* (Luis Watanabe, Michael Moseley, and Fernando Cabieses, eds.): 39–93. Lima.

RICE, DON S., GEOFFREY W. CONRAD, AND LUIS WATANABE
    1990   Proyecto Osmore: Un Estudio del Programa Contisuyu sobre la Complementariedad Económica en la Prehistoria Tardía de la Cuenca del Osmore, Moquegua, Perú. In *Trabajos Arqueológicos en Moquegua* 3 (Luis Watanabe, Michael Moseley, and Fernando Cabieses, eds.): 7–37. Lima.

RIVERA, MARIO A.
    1984   Altiplano and Tropical Lowland Contacts in Northern Chile Prehistory: Chinchorro and Alto Ramirez Revisited. In *Social and Economic Organization in the Prehispanic Andes* (David L. Browman, Richard L. Burger, and Mario A. Rivera, eds.): 143–160. BAR International Series 194. Oxford.

RIVERA, MARIO A., AND FRANCISCO ROTHHAMMER
    1986   Evaluación Biológica y Cultural de Poblaciones Chinchorro: Nuevos Elementos para la Hipótesis de Contactos Transaltiplánicos, Cuenca Amazonas-Costa Pacífico. *Chungará* 16-17: 295–306.

ROSTWOROWSKI, MARÍA
    1977   *Étnia y Sociedad: Costa Peruana Prehispánica.* Instituto de Estudios Peruanos, Lima.
    1981   *Recursos Naturales Renovables y Pesca, Siglos XVI y XVII.* Instituto de Estudios Peruanos, Lima.
    1988   *Historia de Tahuantinsuyu.* Instituto de Estudios Peruanos, Lima.

SANDWEISS, DANIEL H., JAMES B. RICHARDSON III, ELIZABETH J. REITZ, JEFFREY T. HSU, AND ROBERT A. FELDMAN
    1989   Early Maritime Adaptations in the Andes: Preliminary Studies at the Ring Site, Peru. In *Ecology, Settlement and History in the Osmore Drainage, Peru* (Don S. Rice, Charles Stanish, and Phillip R. Scarr, eds.): 35–84. BAR International Series 545 (2). Oxford.

SANTOS RAMIREZ, R.
    1983   Rescate e Investigación arqueológica en Ilo, Moquegua. *Praxis* 2, Arequipa.

SAXE, ARTHUR A.
    n.d.   Social Dimensions of Mortuary Practices. Ph.D. dissertation, University of Michigan, 1970.

SAXE, ARTHUR A., AND PATRICIA L. GALL
    1977   Ecological Determinants of Mortuary Practices: The Temuan of Malaysia. In *Cultural-ecological Perspectives on Southeast Asia* (William H. Wood, ed.). Papers in International Southeast Asia Studies 41: 74–82. Ohio University, Athens, Ohio.

SCHIAPPACASSE, VIRGILIO, AND HANS NIEMEYER
    1984   *Descripción y Análisis Interpretativo de un Sitio Arcaico Temprano en la Quebrada de Camarones.* Publicación Ocasional 41. Museo Nacional de Historia Natural, Santiago.

SHANKS, MICHAEL, AND CHRISTOPHER TILLEY
    1987   *Re-Constructing Archaeology.* Cambridge University Press, Cambridge.

STANISH, CHARLES
    1989   An Archaeological Evaluation of an Ethnohistorical Model. In *Ecology, Settlement and History in the Osmore Drainage, Peru* (Don S. Rice, Charles Stanish, and Phillip R. Scarr, eds.): 303–320. BAR International Series 545 (2). Oxford.
    n.d.a   Post-Tiwanaku Regional Economies in the Otora Valley, Southern Peru. Ph.D. dissertation, University of Chicago, 1985.
    n.d.b   Chulpa Tombs in the Central Andes. Paper given at the annual meeting of the Society for American Archaeology, New Orleans, 1991.

STANISH, CHARLES, AND DON S. RICE
    1989   The Osmore Drainage, Peru: An Introduction to the Work of Programa Contisuyu. In *Ecology, Settlement and History in the Osmore Drainage, Peru* (Don S. Rice, Charles Stanish, and Phillip R. Scarr, eds.): 1–14. BAR International Series 545 (2). Oxford.

TAINTER, JOSEPH A.
    1977a   Modeling Change in Prehistoric Social Systems. In *For Theory Building in Archaeology* (Lewis R. Binford, ed.): 327–351. Academic Press, New York.
    1977b   Woodland Social Change in West-central Illinois. *Mid-Continental Journal of Archaeology* 2: 67–98.

TARTAGLIA, LOUIS J.
    1980   A Revised C14 Chronology for Northern Chile. In *Prehistoric Trails of Atacama: Archaeology of Northern Chile* (Clement W. Meighan and Delbert L. True, eds.): 5–22. Institute of Archaeology, University of California, Los Angeles.

TRIGGER, BRUCE G.
    1990   Monumental Architecture: A Thermodynamic Explanation of Symbolic Behavior. *World Archaeology* 22: 119–132.

TORRES PINO, ELVA, CHRIS O. CLEMENT, NIKI R. CLARK, AND JUAN C. TELLO
    1990a   Entierro Precerámico Doble en Ilo, Perú: Reporte Preliminar. In *Trabajos Arqueológicos en Moquegua* 1 (Luis Watanabe, Michael Moseley, and Fernando Cabieses, eds.): 177–183. Lima.
    1990b   Un Entierro Precerámico Doble en Villa del Mar, Ilo: Informe Preliminar. *Gaceta Arqueológica Andina* 18-19: 59–64.

UHLE, MAX
    1919   La Arqueología de Arica y Tacna. *Boletín Sociedad Ecuatoriana de Estudios Históricos Americanistas* 3 (7–8): 1–48.
    1922   *Fundamentos Etnicos y Arqueología de Arica y Tacna*. Universidad Central, Quito.

VIRCHOW, RUDOLPH
    1892   *Crania Ethnica Americana*. A. Asher and Co., Berlin.

WATANABE, LUIS, MICHAEL MOSELEY, AND FERNANDO CABIESES (EDS.)
    1990   *Trabajos Arqueológicos en Moquegua*, 3 vols. Lima.

WEISS, PEDRO
    1961   Osteología Cultural, Prácticas Cefálicas. *Anales de la Facultad de Medicina*, 133–136. Lima.

Jane E. Buikstra

WILLIAMS, SLOAN R.
    n.d.   The Skeletal Biology of Estuquiña: A Late Intermediate Period Site in Southern Peru. Ph.D. dissertation, Northwestern University, 1990.

WILLIAMS, SLOAN R., AND JANE E. BUIKSTRA (EDS.)
    n.d.   Mortuary Investigations at Chiribaya Alta: A Late Intermediate Period Site near Ilo, Perú. (in preparation)

WILLIAMS, SLOAN R., NIKI R. CLARK, AND JANE E. BUIKSTRA
    1990   Excavaciones en los Cementerios de Estuquiña, Moquegua, sur del Perú. In *Trabajos Arqueológicos en Moquegua* 3 (Luis Watanabe, Michael Moseley, and Fernando Cabieses, eds.): 95–122. Lima.

WILLIAMS, SLOAN R., JANE E. BUIKSTRA, NIKI R. CLARK, MARIA C. LOZADA CERNA, AND ELVA TORRES PINO
    1989   Mortuary Site Excavations and Skeletal Biology in the Osmore Project. In *Ecology, Settlement and History in the Osmore Drainage, Peru* (Don S. Rice, Charles Stanish, and Phillip R. Scarr, eds.): 329–346. BAR International Series 545 (2). Oxford.

WISE, KAREN
    1989   Archaic Period Research in the Lower Osmore Region. In *Ecology, Settlement and History in the Osmore Drainage, Peru* (Don S. Rice, Charles Stanish, and Phillip R. Scarr, eds.): 85–99. BAR International Series 545 (2). Oxford.
    n.d.a   Late Archaic Period Maritime Subsistence Strategies in the South-Central Andes. Ph.D. dissertation, Northwestern University, 1990.
    n.d.b   Preceramic Cultural Variability and Ethnic Diversity in the South-Central Andes. Paper presented at the 56th Annual Meeting of the Society for American Archaeology, New Orleans, April 1991.

WISE, KAREN, AND NIKI CLARK
    n.d.   The Cotton Preceramic Period in the South-Central Andes. Paper Presented at the 55th Annual Meeting of the Society for American Archaeology, Las Vegas, April 1990.

Mounds of Social Death: Araucanian Funerary Rites and Political Succession

TOM D. DILLEHAY

UNIVERSITY OF KENTUCKY

INTRODUCTION

ONE OF THE MOST PERSISTENT, though least acknowledged, research themes in Andean archaeology is mortuary treatment. An important trend in the first half of this century was the excavation of burials for the purpose of reconstructing context, regional chronological sequences, and different archaeological cultures (e.g., Uhle 1903; Strong and Evans 1952; Bennett 1939; Estrada 1957; Rowe 1962; Tello and Xesspe 1979; Willey 1953). While much Andean research over the past few decades has focused on settlement and subsistence issues, there has been a resurgence of mortuary studies in other areas of the world (e.g., Bartel 1982; Brown 1981; Chapman 1981; O'Shea 1984; Tainter 1978) and from other anthropological perspectives (e.g., Blakely 1977; Cannon 1989; Powell, Mires, and Bridges 1991). Burial data are now seen as important analytical tools that allow increasing accuracy in the elucidation of other aspects of human behavior—social status and nutrition, the social narration of death, the investment of tomb construction, the role of the deceased in the past, division of labor, warfare, social class structure, centralization of power, and cosmology, to name only a few examples. With the exception of a few studies (Conrad n.d.; Donnan and Mackey 1978; Donnan and McClelland 1979; Quilter 1989; Buikstra 1990 and this volume), it has only been recently that Andeanists have given more comprehensive coverage to these topics.

The initial stage of archaeological research in south-central Chile, or the Araucanian culture area (Fig. 1), is similar to that of other Andean areas. The investigation of cemetery sites initially yielded only the recognition of different archaeological cultures. Recently interest has turned to social distinctions in the burial record (Gordon n.d., 1975, 1978, 1984), and to broader problems reflected in the rich ethnohistoric and ethnographic source material on Araucanian mortuary practice. Analysis of these sources

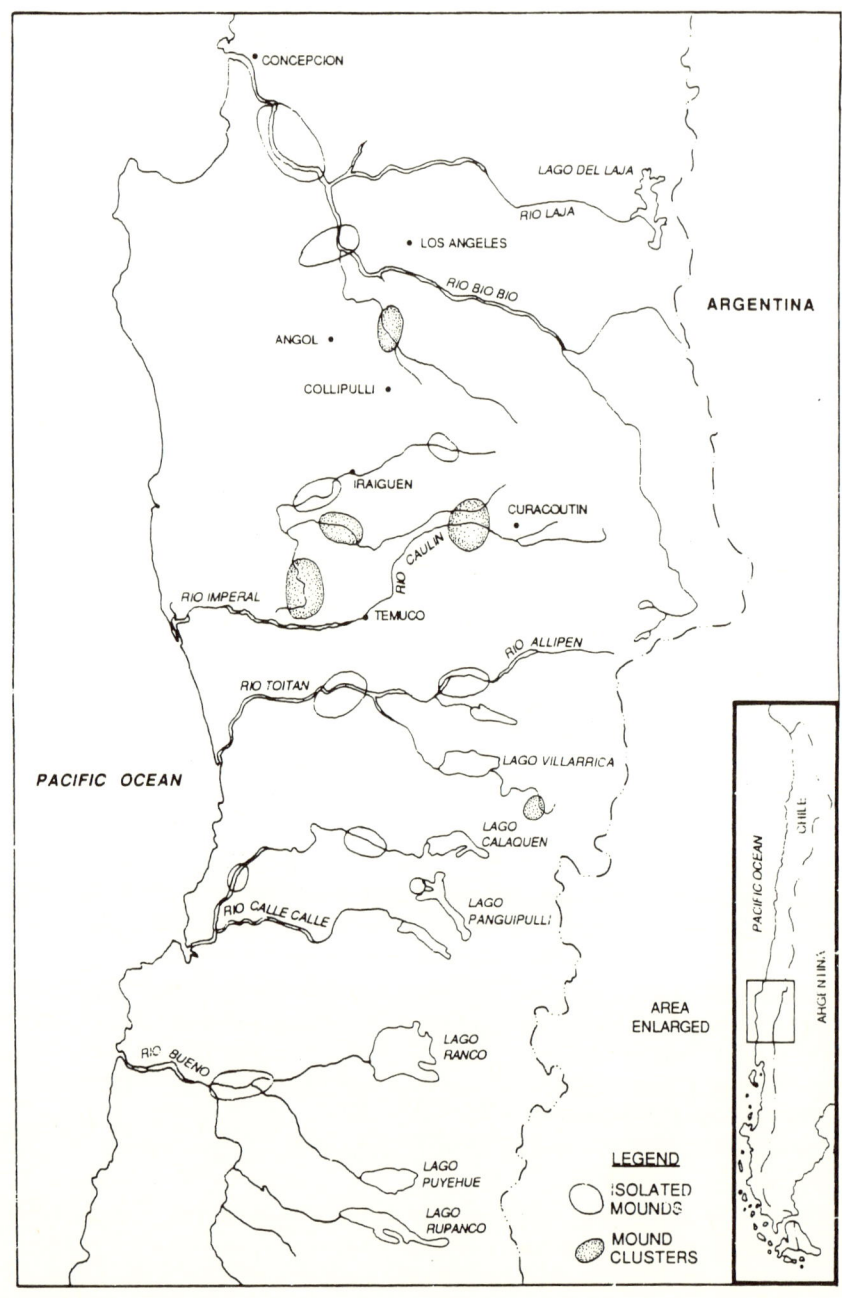

Fig. 1 Location map of study area showing the major river valleys and areas of mound concentration.

Mounds of Social Death: Araucanian Funerary Rites and Political Succession

reveals that death was part of a long, transformative process involving a number of stages which marked different points of articulation between the living and the dead and their religious ideas and political organization. These records also show that the Araucanians practiced elaborate funerary rites and built impressive earthen burial mounds for paramount chiefs (Dillehay 1985, 1990). Mounds were constructed primarily during the late prehistoric and historic periods of demographic and political turmoil, although the tradition continued into the present century and still exists as "remembered culture" in a few areas (Latcham 1928; Dillehay 1985, 1990).

It is the intent of this paper to examine the Araucanian data for the context and meaning of time-extended funerary rites of ancesteral worship, mound construction, and corollary acts (e.g., animal sacrifice, feasting) associated with the burial of important war chiefs. Imperative to this study is the distinction between funerary and postfunerary rites. The former are related to the interment of lower-ranking chiefs and other lineage members. Once interred, no postfunerary rites are performed at their tombs. In this case, burial is a statement of the final biological and social conditions of the deceased. The latter involves the time-extended construction of a mound over the tomb of a high-ranking chief. This activity transforms the defunct leader into an authentic ancestor, and prolongs his "social death" for the explicit purposes of (1) installing a new leader, (2) legitimizing and extending the authority of the installed leader beyond his local kin group, and (3) maintaining (or building) alliances between his and other lineages. Set in this context, postfunerary rites and burial mounds (called *cuel* in Mapudungun, the Araucanian language) were sources of authority and inspiration produced by regional alliances, not local groups. Alliances depended for their survival upon public ceremonial congregation and upon strong warrior leadership and the maintenance of politicoreligious relations among lineages, especially during times of conflict and internal stress.

In regard to the last point, it is important to remember that the Araucanians were the only large-scale ethnic population in South America that repulsed the Inka and later the Spanish. They regained control of their own territory in the early 1600s, reinstated their ethnic identity, and expanded geographically (into Argentina) with a mixed set of political and cultural institutions introduced by the Inka and Spanish (see Cooper 1946). It was not until the late nineteenth century that the Araucanians were finally defeated by the Chilean army (e.g., Villalobos 1982, 1989).

RELEVANT THEMES OF MORTUARY ANALYSIS

A brief summation of mortuary studies specifically relevant to this paper is sufficient as background to the discussion of general archaeological and ethnological literature. This discussion focuses on four aspects: meaning and

Tom D. Dillehay

expression of death in regard to individual and group relations: monumental burial forms; the role of ancestors in burial rites; and chiefly burial and installation rites.

In recent years, much of our anthropological thinking about the meaning of death in traditional societies has altered. We have learned that the death of an individual was a long and gradual social process and that a consistent relationship existed between the world of the living and that of the dead (e.g., Hertz 1960; Huntington and Metcalfe 1979; Turner 1969; Chapman, Kinnes, and Randsborg 1981; Tainter 1978; O'Shea 1984). It also is recognized that the death of important persons may change the relations between individuals and between different sectors in a society, thus representing a traumatic period when potential conflict may arise between groups. Participation in burial ritual also may increase or decrease during this period because of sorcery, destruction, warfare, and environmental disasters (Bloch and Parry 1982).

More specifically related to the archaeology of death is the analysis of mortuary ritual and symbolism and the hierarchical dimension of burial records. Perhaps the most widely studied approach to these dimensions in burial practice has developed from the work of Binford (1971), who suggested that the complexity of mortuary ritual (i.e., grave style and content) reflects the social position held by the deceased individual. It also has been recognized that the rank of the dead may covary with the amount of energy expended in the funeral (see Tainter 1978), and that the variety and complexity of grave goods (O'Shea 1984) are generally reliable indicators of rank. Others, including structuralists (e.g., Godelier [1977] in social anthropology and Hodder [1984] in archaeology), believe that the content and context of graves is not merely a reflection of sociopolitical organization but an active element in human relations, and that they can be used to reflect, disguise, or manipulate social ideals rather than social reality.

Of additional interest are analyses that have focused on formal burial structures as reflections of important linkages, events, and critical resources. Such cultural elaborations as earthen mounds and other monuments are frequently explained by increasing subsistence development (agriculture) and greater social differentiation and by ancestral worship and territorial claims. One of the most insightful archaeological studies of the relationship between ancestral cults and resource claims is Renfrew's work on the development of monumental tombs in a European context. He suggests that elaborate tombs are territorial markers in "small-scale segmentary societies, by which the territorial division of the terrain is given symbolic expression" (Renfrew 1976: 206). This line of thinking generally follows Sahlins (1961) in linking ancestral cults and monumental tombs. He suggested that in areas in which competition for resources occurs, dispersed communities are likely to stress links with an ancestral lineage as a way of claiming a territory. In this expression, ancestral cults are seen as developing primarily in agricultural societies that have continuous investment in the land and a developed genealogical system to relate group membership to relations of production and cooperation and to hierarchical structures (see also Meillassoux 1972, 1968).

Burial monuments have also been seen as communal status markers and historic monuments. Presumably, comparison of their number and configuration within an overall area reveals data about the historical context and event of monumental burial (Kossak 1974; Fleming 1972; Bradley 1990). Kossak, in particular, has suggested that monuments as "display graves" are built during times of excessive cultural contact, or a period of military, social, or political change. This point is particularly relevant to the historic Araucanian case.

In my previous studies of burial mounds in Mapuche society (Dillehay 1986 and 1990), I focused on the main variables accounting for mound-building rites (*cueltun*) and for the limited distribution of these structures (Fig. 1). I postulated that mound building is related to the changing social relations between different lineages and to a set of historically contingent factors, that is, long-term kinship sedimentation, residential contiguity of related lineages, protection of land-use rights, and profitable alliance making and trade-exchange affairs. It was also suggested that increased social and political complexity was achieved by a few lineages when they regulated the annual itinerary of multiple ceremonial events at sacred sites. My previous work did not address the specific relationships between warfare, ancestry, postburial rites, and political succession except in terms of the development of dynastic chiefdoms and mound clusters in areas where conflict had not interrupted the residential permanency of lineages. I also did not consider the potential political gains made by new leaders who administered the periodic construction of earthen mounds over their predecessors. As discussed below, sufficient archaeological, ethnohistoric, and ethnographic evidence is becoming available to suggest that mound building also was a corporate ritual regulated by succeeding leaders who sought to legitimize their authority and to expand it beyond the lineage level. The scant number and uneven distribution of historic mound sites in the study area suggest that very few segments of the Araucanian population ever experienced this type of leadership behavior.

In synthesis, these and other studies have been valuable in broadening the conceptual framework of archaeological mortuary practices and relating them to changes in population size, critical resources (e.g., land scarcity), sociopolitical organization, formal disposal of the dead, descent groups, control and transfer of land, and ideological practices. As far as I am aware, there have been no archaeological attempts, however, to study the relationship between mortuary and installation rites of chiefs, and the political benefits reaped by leaders who oversee postfunerary rites at the tomb of their predecessor. For information on this practice, we must turn to ethnographic work.

Ethnographic studies of African, Asian, and South Asian chiefdoms (Goody 1966; Buxton 1963; Arhem 1988) have shown that the death and funerary rituals for a deceased leader and the installation of his successor are often politically unstable times and are connected as a single sequence. Installation of a successor is a public event administered during the mortuary rite and attended by rival chiefs and other dignitaries. Such occasion allows a new ruler to demonstrate his ancestral affinity to the deceased chief and to define (and expand) his own power base. For instance, in her analysis of the Mandari chiefdom of east Africa, Buxton (1963: 83–87) noted that upon the death of a leader, he must be replaced immediately in the interests of orderly social and political relations among chiefdoms. If not, chiefdoms are weakened and their people are derived of leadership, especially when an important chief dies and his successor is, as yet, of unknown quality. It is the duty of the new chief, although endowed by birth with potential leadership qualities, "to prove to members of neighbouring chiefdoms, as well as to those of his own," that he is worthy of rule and that he can sustain the alliances established between his predecessor and them. Buxton and others show that in order to legitimize their new authority and to maintain alliances, chief-elects must draw on a continuous source of power, which is ritually linked to their predecessors and to the grave sites of those predecessors. This linkage, established in funerary and postfunerary ceremonies, reflects the ambivalent relations between chiefly groups during the time of death of an important leader. Without these ceremonies, there would be few lasting alliances between lineages.

TRADITIONAL ARAUCANIAN SOCIETY: ANCESTORS, FUNERALS, AND LEADERS

In terms of traditional social organization, the proto-Araucanians and contemporary Mapuche are made up of patrilineal kin groups that can be considered a patchwork of autonomous, small- to medium-scale horticultural units roughly organized on a moderately advanced chiefdom level of society. As Cooper noted about the historic period:

> Some major features of the system . . . are quite clear. There was no peacetime over-all chief, no centralization of authority . . . in any one individual or administrative body. Furthermore, such authority as was vested in kinship heads and local "chiefs" was very limited—exclusively or almost exclusively consultative and persuasive, with little or no coercive power.
>
> Supreme military commanders in important campaigns or in general uprisings against the Spaniards were usually elected in

open assembly by choice of the leaders, but kinship heads and other "chiefs" were as a general rule hereditary. On the death of such a kinship head or "chief," his eldest or most capable son ordinarily succeeded him. . . . In some cases, where the heir was unfit or incompetent, some other man would assume the office (rather than of authority proper) embracing higher and lower heads and "chiefs". . . . (Cooper 1946: 724–725)

Although the Araucanians have always lacked the structured control hierarchy typical of states, they were characterized by relations of social and economic dominance and subordination, and by a level of organization consisting of lineages of different social and economic scales. The relations between lineages are similar in some ways to what Colin Renfrew and S. Shennan (1982: 1–18) have described for European societies as roughly comparable "peer-polities," or in this case, peer-chieflets (Dillehay 1992).

In summarizing the territorial organization of Araucanian society, Cooper states that:

The largest geographical division among the *Mapuche-Huilliche* was the *vutanmapu* (? + country). Three such divisions were recognized in earlier times, constituting longitudinal strips along the Coast, the central valley, and the sub-Andean region . . . to which were later added a fourth embracing the *Huilliche* country . . . and a fifth, the Andean Cordillera region. These great divisions functioned chiefly, it would seem, in times of war. (Cooper 1946: 724–725; also see Molina 1795: 114)

It can be determined from the written documentation that formal marriage and exchange relations between lineages were organized primarily along river valleys, which extended from the Andes to the east down to the Pacific Ocean to the west. For reasons not yet well understood, the religious and military alliances of lineages were oriented in the opposite direction, in correspondence with the north to south *butalmapu* divisions. In other words, socioeconomic cohesion was strongest at the local level and weakest at the regional level. Religious and military cohesion, on the other hand, was strongest at the interregional level and weakest at the local level.

In more specific terms, the historic sociopolitical organization of the Araucanians was divided into four apparently ranked groups, each with internal ranking: chiefs (*lonko, toqui*), eminent men (*weupin, ulmen*), shamans (*machi*), and commoners. During the early historic period, rank was achieved, sometimes through personal exploits but most commonly through ascribed membership in patrilineal groups (Faron 1961). Technically, such a system is non-hereditary, but the access to important positions by descendants of powerful lineages suggests that the system also had some hereditary tendencies (see Bengoa 1985: 62–67, for a summary of this process), whereby chiefly rule was passed along male lines (i.e., eldest sons). War parties during this period were organized and led by powerful *toqui* war chiefs, who may or may not have been peacetime lineage heads or *lonko*. As Diego de Rosales has described:

> There are only *lonko* chiefs and *Toqui* chiefs. They are dignified, respected and well-known persons. . . . Chiefs are head of the families and lineages. No paramount chief resides over the lineage chief; lineage heads are in charge during times of peace. . . .
>
> Among the chiefs is a principal *Toqui* who also is a *lonko*. He is head of his own lineage and presides over other chiefs in times of war. *Toqui* possess a stone axe [*toquicura*] . . . this *toqui* represents the emblem of his lineage . . . .
>
> *Toqui*, or war chiefs, inherit their position; hence, upon the death of a chief, his first son or the most capable son takes over as chief. . . . (Diego de Rosales 1989 [1877–78]: 136–137)

Toqui were often drawn from senior lineages, and regional politics were usually played out among their lineages. *Lonko* apparently had little real power beyond their own kin. In effect, *toqui* chiefs were expected to make alliances with other chiefs and lineages. These alliances formed the basis of a network of chiefs who would respond to calls for economic assistance and military support in the expectation of future returns.

More locally, the role of both *toqui* and *lonko* chiefs, as guardians of their lineages, extended to the dead and to deities, as well as the living. Much of this role was and still is ceremonial; that is, the power of chiefs is based heavily on their regulation of ceremonial and ancestral history, and on the manipulation of chiefly symbols (e.g., *chemamüll* statues of ancestor heroes, sacred ponchos, and sacred stones, the *toquicura*). This role also is closely linked to the manipulation of these symbols to regulate land claims and land distribution among lineage members. That is, leaders guarantee through public ritual participation that a cultivated religious landscape of ancestral iconography exists, in the form of *ñguillatun* (a fertility rite hosted by a *trokinche* unit[1]) ceremonial fields, earthen burial mounds (*cuel*), and wooden

---

[1] Although there is disagreement among ethnographers and historians about the validity and meaning of the term *trokinche,* I have employed it here and elsewhere (Dillehay 1990, 1991) to refer to the corporate group of three different lineages that annually host a *ñguillatun* ceremony. The present-day Mapuche do not have a term for this corporate ritual grouping, though elders claim a name once existed. Today, in literal translation, *trokinche* means division of people. For the purpose of convenience and consistency, I will continue to use the term *trokinche* to refer specifically to the tripartite grouping of host lineages. Faron (1964: 111) has observed that more than three lineages may make up a *ñguillatun*. I have seen as many as nine lineages hosting the event, but this occurred in areas where leaders were weak and required the services of peers, or the economic conditions were so bad that several lineages had to share the cost of the feast.

statues of ancestors (*chemamüll*) (Figs. 2–5). Participation in these ceremonies was (and still is) important because every lineage derived its identity and its claim to land from a recognized ancestor, local or pan-Araucanian.

The remnants of this traditional organization on the minimal level can be observed today in more isolated areas, in *reducciones* that have maintained at least some of the social and religious landscape. The more mobile and extensive social and political units, from the scale of chiefly alliances to that of war groups, obviously no longer exist. At this more extensive level, the scale of operation itself meant a change from the level of personal relations among specific chiefs to that of interlineage political structure and broader interregional ceremonial contexts. It is this latter scale, in the context of chiefly mortuary ritual and succession of leaders in times of warfare, that I will attempt to reconstruct and analyze from the archaeological, ethnohistoric, and ethnographic data.

ARCHAEOLOGY AND ETHNOHISTORY

Archaeology

The study of archaeological mortuary behavior is limited by a small sample of excavated cemetery sites, by the poor preservation of skeletal remains in the wet forested areas of south-central Chile, and by the inaccessible location of many cemetery and mound sites on Mapuche lands. Despite these problems, the archaeological data have confirmed much of the ethnohistorical assertions concerning the manner in which social differentiation is expressed in the mortuary treatment.

Specifically, several pre-Hispanic and historic burial treatments have been recognized in the archaeological record, including urn, stone cistern, dugout canoe, wooden coffin, earthen mound, and simple pit burials. It is possible in historic sites and possibly some prehistoric sites to distinguish female and male burials if earrings and/or female-specific *quetru metawe* vessels (Dillehay and Gordon 1977) are present. It has also been surmised that some elements of social ranking are identifiable by the content and quantity or grave offerings, as well as some elements symbolic of social units and horizontal differentiation (Gordon 1978, 1984). Social ranking in terms of leadership has also been hypothesized for earthen mounds (Dillehay 1985, 1990).

Looking briefly at the chronology and distribution of burial mounds from an archaeological perspective, three significant patterns emerge. First, the earliest indications of farming in the south appear in the first half of the second millennium A.D., possibly about the same time that the first burial mounds were built. Second, the majority of the mounds appear to belong to a late pre-Hispanic ceramic phase, probably dating around A.D. 1300 to 1500 and lasting until the late historic period. And third, most mounds are con-

Tom D. Dillehay

Fig. 2 U-shaped *ñguillatun* ceremonial field located in the highlands above Curacautin.

Fig. 3 Early historic earthen burial mound located in the vicinity of Lumaco.

Fig. 4 Dual *chemamüll* ancestral figures located on a boundary line between two wife-giving and wife-receiving lineages.

Fig. 5 Nineteenth-century Mapuche cemetery showing *chemamüll* grave markers. Photograph courtesy of the Museo Chileno de Arte PreColombino.

fined to river valleys, although it is difficult to relate them entirely to agricultural subsistence. In fact, some of the largest mound clusters are found in external zones of the historic Araucanian territory, at the fringes of the main river valleys. There are indications that the political edges of this territory, or "la Frontera" as it came to be known during the traumatic historic era (Villalobos 1989), were possibly the most politically regulated and integrated from the mid-1600s to the late 1800s, while the center or heartland was less organized. As discussed later, this period might be related to intensified mound building and clustering.

Ethnohistory

The ethnohistoric data reveal that the Mapuche divided mortuary practice into treatment which all individuals received and treatment given only to elites (e.g., *lonko, toqui*) of the population. Information on the treatment of commoners is fairly abundant and repetitious, suggesting that single, primary burial in group cemeteries was the common mode of body disposal. Burial structures and burial coverings are mentioned often, the latter usually consisting of stone cisterns, urns, wooden canoes, and simple graves. Little information is available on burial orientation and specific grave offerings, however.

Elaborated mortuary treatment was restricted primarily to important chiefs, including the sons of these chiefs. As described below, war chiefs (*toqui*) and occasionally *lonko* of high rank were accorded particularly elaborate burial rites, involving the whole of the community. These rites often included a time-elapsed burial process related to the construction and maintenance of earthen mounds, to enduring kin and non-kin relations, and to animal sacrifice and chicha consumption over the grave. It is also clear from these accounts that not all chiefs had mounds built over their tombs and that these practices continued throughout the historic period and into the present century.

The earliest and most detailed passage regarding these matters is from the sixteenth-century chronicler Diego de Rosales. He states:

> They bury dead chiefs in their best cloths and with their best ornaments, arms, and food. Kinsmen place chicha vessels and containers with meat, corn, flour, and other food in the grave. Each person attending the funeral places items in the grave. . . .
> The burial of chiefs lasts 3–4 days, during which time the mourners drink heavily and sing about the deeds of the defunct chief. . . .
> After a period of one year, kinsmen and friends come together again to drink, to feast and to mourn in the name of the dead chief. They also placed sheep, meat and chicha in the tomb. The defunct chief is renourished by pouring the blood of sacrificed sheep on

Mounds of Social Death: Araucanian Funerary Rites and Political Succession

[and into] the tomb. Afterwards, the mourners dance around the tomb, carrying chicha vessels, worshipping their ancestors, and informing the interred chief of events that have happened since his death. Lastly, they pour chicha on the grave, telling the dead chief that he will not be hungry or thirsty because they have given him food and drink. . . . To assure that dead chiefs will always be remembered by other chiefs and by noble persons, they bury the *toqui* in places on high hills where kinsmen come together to play *chueca* [a ritual game for warriors], perform the *Regues* [major public ceremony, probably the *ñguillatun*], and hold their administrative meetings. Each relative of the interred chief breaks a chicha jar over the tomb, toasting to the defunct chief. . . .

For the dead chief, kinsmen and friends prepare tables and benches outside their homes . . . for visiting dignitaries and others to eat, drink, dance and sleep. . . . The [new] chief, who oversees the ritual, pays the poets and orators for their commemorative services during the interment of a principal [*toqui*] chief. (Diego de Rosales 1989: 137–157)

Jeronimo Quiroga (1979: 293) and Francisco Nuñez De Pineda y Bascúñan have observed similar patterns during the same period. In describing the funeral of a chief's son, Pineda y Bascúñan (1973) noted that the Araucanians carried "the body to a high place where the marked graves of their ancestors are located and can be seen from the homes of the living." He also provided information on mound construction and on the deliberate breakage of chicha jars over the grave, the latter confirmed by archaeological research at several late pre-Hispanic and early historic cemetery sites (Gordon 1985). After closing the coffin,

. . . the first person to throw soil on the tomb was the father. This act initiated the war crys. All participants then covered the tomb with earth, forming a large elevated mound that served as a mediating line between houses which could be seen from several directions. . . . After this, they sat at the base of the circular mound, placing all of the chicha jars in proper order [along kin lines?]. Because the funeral ritual was attended by more than 200 persons, they quickly broke their chicha vessels over the tomb. . . . (Pineda y Bascúñan 1973: 187–1930)

Writing in the eighteenth century, Juan Ignacio Molina (1795) commented that "after interring the body they again covered it with earth and stones to form a 'piramidel' (mound), upon which they broke many chicha vessels." In the following century, Pascual Cona (1973: 395–415) described in great detail the burial of a *toqui* war chief, also emphasizing the construction of an earthen mound over the tomb, the enduring links between the living and the dead, and the role of living chiefs in the burial ceremony.

R. Latcham, perhaps the most astute observer of early twentieth-century Mapuche culture, commented on the continuity of these burial practices. He stated: "Until recently [early part of the present century], they followed this custom [mound building] . . ." (Latcham 1928: 761). He also says that the burial of important persons such as chiefs and landholders (*ulmen*) "could last several weeks or months" (Latcham 1928: 748). It was custom

> . . . in some areas to participate in the festivals and celebrations of the dead. . . . they placed plates of food and chicha jars on the tomb. One year after the burial, they again opened the tomb to place new offerings in the grave . . . and when it was the grave of an important person, they repeated this ritual for several years. . . . (Latcham 1928: 767)

Latcham (1928: 763) also provided information on wooden ancestral statues, or *chemamüll,* placed on graves: "they placed wooden figures and crosses on the mound."

R. Emile Housse, also writing in the early part of this century, commented on similar practices at the tomb of defunct chiefs:

> In the past, the Araucanians followed the custom of the Inca in constructing a mound of loose stones on the grave and breaking chicha vessels on it. For a long time now, they [Araucanians] have replaced the mound with a long wooden pole carved in the form of a human [*chemamüll*]. (Housse 1940: 332)

Viewed from both the archaeological and ethnohistorical records, we know that mound building was associated primarily with the interment of paramount *toqui* chiefs. Latcham (1928) has recovered polished stone axes, or *toquicura,* from several mound sites near Temuco and Tirua. (As noted earlier, these stones have been identified ethnohistorically and ethnographically as the symbol of power of *toqui* war chiefs.) We also know from the written records and oral tradition that not all chiefs had mounds constructed over their tombs and that only a small number of *toqui* ever became dominant enough to form regional war and political alliances (Dillehay 1990).

These few passages suffice to give a general idea of the time-extended nature of chiefly burial during the past few centuries and the funerary context of ancestral worship, mound building, animal sacrifice, and chicha consumption.

Unfortunately, no known written record (including contemporary ethnographers) tells us why chiefly burials were prolonged. Several chroniclers document the role of succeeding chiefs (including the eldest sons or brothers of defunct chiefs) in performing funerary and postfunerary celebrations at

Mounds of Social Death: Araucanian Funerary Rites and Political Succession

grave sites, but they do not provide information on the broader significance of this responsibility. It is clear, however, from these data that these events were attended by a large number of people (Fig. 6), which, we can assume, required a considerable amount of communication and planning on an interlineage and probably regional level, and that living chiefs had an important role in the mortuary and postmortuary ceremonies of dead chiefs.

Quite possibly the chroniclers played down the role of new chiefs (and shamans) in these ceremonies lest they undermine the Spanish Crown's attempt to extirpate indigenous cults of the dead. It is more understandable why Latcham and other ethnographers (e.g., Titiev 1951; Faron 1964) never emphasized the administrative role of chief-elects in rites. Most ethnographers have been more interested in other themes (i.e., kinship, acculturation), and they worked with the Mapuche when the role and power of leaders had been diminished considerably by the *reducción* system. A few ethnographers, notably Faron and Latcham, have observed that shaman (*machi*) give prayer at the funeral of an important leader, but almost always under the auspices of a local chief, usually the eldest sons, or the chief-elect, of the dead.

Fig. 6 Nineteenth-century burial ceremony of a Mapuche chief. Photograph courtesy of the Museo Nacional de Historia.

Tom D. Dillehay

To gain additional insight into these issues, we must look to the ethnoarchaeological and ethnographic records, which provide information obtained from interviews with Mapuche elders who either participated in mound-building rites when they were young or, through oral tradition, remember stories about them.

ETHNOGRAPHY AND ETHNOARCHAEOLOGY

The brief reconstruction I present below of the burial mound construction is based on examination of some of the detailed published works on the Mapuche. My principal sources are Latcham (1915), Tomás Guevara Silva (1913), and Cona (1973) (see Dillehay 1985, 1990, 1992).

As I have described elsewhere (Dillehay 1986, 1990), there are a few areas where earthen mounds are still utilized by local Mapuche groups. Informants in one area, Lumaco, report that these structures were built over the past few centuries and that the remains of *toqui* chiefs are interred under them. Today, periodic earth-capping rites, called *cueltun,* are performed at two mounds and are attended by local and non-local lineage members. These rites are reported to have a dual function. They symbolically lift the spirit of the corpse into the upper world (*wenumapu*) of the ancestors, transforming the chief into an authentic ancestor, and they sustain links between the living and the dead. (It also should be pointed out that in his dictionary of the Mapuche language, Esteban Erize (1987) translates *cuel* as a "tumulo" or mound that forms a "borde" or "limite" between lineages.)

We also have learned that the funerary and postfunerary rites associated with these structures are ritually and architecturally separated. That is, the tomb, or *eltun,* containing the body is different from the earth layers (i.e., the "mound") superimposed on it. The tomb relates specifically to the *awn* funerary rite of interment of the deceased; the mound, or *cuel,* is the aboveground structure formed by the postfunerary *cueltun* earth-capping rite carried out by kinsmen and non-kinsmen of the deceased. Although these episodes are often administered ritually by *machi,* they are organized secularly by *lonko,* and presumably, in times past, by *toqui.*

In this context, it must be emphasized that earthen mounds are not true "burial mounds" but structures formed by periodic activities associated with postfuneary functions and meanings. Based on oral tradition, we can surmise that these functions served a lineage to time- and occasion-extend the death of an important chief for the purpose of constituting and reconstituting enduring and productive social relations among kin and non-kin affiliates, to recruit new affiliates, and to legitimize and extend the authority of the chief-elect, usually the eldest son of the deceased. Such episodes brought together large numbers of powerful people who were obligated to focus prayer and alliance building in the name of the defunct chief and of his lineage. Only the death of important war chiefs, who were backed by large

Mounds of Social Death: Araucanian Funerary Rites and Political Succession

kin and non-kin groups, provided such opportunities to the less important lineages. The funerals of less important chiefs and common lineage members were attended by fewer people and were of much less political and religious significance.

There are other important dimensions to the relations between death ritual and ancestor worship that reveal more about the mortuary rites of dead chiefs, the rites of installation of chief-elects, and the linkage and responsibility of chiefs to the ceremonial landscape and to those who live in it. These dimensions are animal sacrifice, chicha consumption, and, in the immediate past, the placement of wooden *chemamüll* statues of ancestor heroes on the tombs of chiefs.

Machi informants in Lumaco state that every four years two sheep are sacrificed over actively used mounds of interred chiefs, and both animal blood (*ñache*) and chicha (*mudai*) are poured into vertically placed holes in the mounds in the name of the lineage ancestral spirits of the deceased. When animals are sacrificed on mounds, everyone dances in a close circle around the mound and gives prayer to the spirits of the dead, all of which forms a series of ancestral and community-extended linkages (see Housse 1939: 155–159 and Cona 1973: 405 for descriptions of these practices in the last century). Although *machi* legitimize the ceremony through prayer and through communication with ancestral spirits, it is the *lonko* (as *ñguillatufe*) who kills and defleshes the animal and distributes parts to lineage members and visiting dignitaries.

Associated with animal sacrifice are several hours of drinking and dancing and, occasionally, the deliberate breakage of chicha vessels over the tomb. *Machi* claim that in the past large quantities of chicha vessels were smashed over both the grave and the new layer of soil periodically placed over the tomb. The first vessel is reported to have been broken by the chief-elect. Today, informants speculate that the breakage of vessels over tombs probably signified the departure of the spirit of the deceased to the ancestral world and the final act of communion between the living and the dead. Vessel breakage on tombs is described by numerous chroniclers and ethnographers (e.g., Diego de Rosales, Pineda y Bascúñan, Latcham), and also is documented at several archaeological cemeteries (Gordon et al. 1972–73: 64; Gordon 1978, 1984, n.d.).

Linkages between the living and the dead extend well beyond the grave site, and beyond the chicha consumption and bloodletting rites associated with it, to include a much wider setting. This setting is a cultivated landscape of ancestral imagery in the form of ceremonial fields, mounds, volcanoes, and *chemamüll*. Ceremonial fields and mounds have already been discussed.

The most prevalent form is the carved wooden *chemamüll* statue (Erize 1987: 106–107), often placed in fields and, until recently, on the graves of chiefs. *Chemamüll* usually occur in pairs and are said to represent important ancestors, usually *lonko*. Informants report that these statues oversee and protect lineage lands, and that they represent land markers located between *lonkos* standing in a fixed dual relationship to each other. Today, as in the past, dances and prayer, and, occasionally, animal sacrifice, are performed around these figures, all in the name of local ancestors.

There is also a strong relationship between ancestor deity worship and reverence of volcanoes (see María Ester Grebe, personal communication, 1990). Spatially, the ancestral spirits of important people are associated with higher elevations, because these places are closest to the ancestor spirits in the sky. For this reason, it is reported that burial mounds are placed on high terraces and hilltops within sight of volcanoes and other mounds, if the latter are present.

Collectively, all of these features and forms are historical symbols that embody linkages between time and place and encode past, present, and future Mapuche generations. As such, they establish the coordinates of a sacred politicohistorical landscape that forms an overarching regional system of pan-Mapuche architectural icons and ancestral land markers, which are manipulated by chiefs to legitimize their authority and extend their power to others. All of this provides an interpretative framework or a core of continuity utilized by different lineages to make sense of their relationships to each other and their relationships with the political environment.

Although the tradition of sculpturing the landscape and of building mounds has nearly disappeared, the burial of important chiefs is still a major event associated with interlineage relations and the display of succeeding leaders. In recent years, I have had two opportunities to participate in the burial ceremony of chiefs in the Chol-Chol and Queule areas. Both funerals were attended by more than 1,000 persons, some traveling more than 200 km to participate (Fig. 7). Large quantities of food and drink were consumed at the funerals, and animals were sacrificed.

All prayer at the funerals was conducted by *machi*. Planning and administration of the funerals, however, were handled by the eldest sons, or "chief-elects," of the deceased. The sons arranged the funeral, selected the grave site, obtained and organized the food and drink, and received all participants, especially *lonko* and dignitaries from distant areas. Despite the moderate to heavy acculturation in both areas, it was clear at both funerals that the eldest sons were very aware of the chiefly administrative position they were about to assume. Throughout the entire funerary process, they assured trade partners, friends, and others that they would honor the linkages their fathers had established with them.

I was told by the eldest son at the Queule funeral that dance, festival, and animal sacrifice will be repeated in future years at the grave of his father. I asked him if a mound would eventually be built over the tomb of his father. Although he never mentioned a *cuel,* he did say that the tomb must be

Mounds of Social Death: Araucanian Funerary Rites and Political Succession

Fig. 7 Present-day Mapuche interment ceremony in mounded cemetery. Photograph courtesy of Rene San Martín.

distinguished from others, visible from a distance, and curated for several years to come. I took it to mean that the grave site would be modified in some form or fashion. Once the grave has been curated socially, the dead chief can finally die. No additional rites were planned for the Chol-Chol burial, where Christian influence is much heavier.

The present-day funerals revealed that burial of important persons is still a pretext to focus attention on a new leader and, above all, to test his generosity and his potential leadership quality. It was evident at both funerals that the traditional forging of links between new leaders and the members of other lineages still demands in Mapuche terms feasting and the mutual consumption of food and drink. As R. Latcham, M. Titiev, L. Faron, R. San Martin, and other ethnographers have commented before, feasting and the offering of food and drink to the living and the dead was and still is a sign of chiefly wealth and power. During times of war in the historic past (and to a much lesser extent today), the new chief who met these obligations established credit among his peers, kinsmen, friends, and allies. If not, he ran the risk of resentment and anger within a social system in which political cohesion depended upon the support of other chiefs and their followers.

HISTORIC CONTEXT OF FUNERARY RITUALS AND LEADERSHIP

At this point, I will attempt to infer the meaning of these mortuary features and social patterns in terms of the history and the culture logic of the Araucanians. To speculate on the broader meaning of the postulated relationship between time-extended funerary rites and the expansion of chiefly authority during times of political stress, we must return to events and circumstances of the historic period of warfare (A.D. 1600-1850). As noted by several historians (e.g., Villalobos 1989; Pinto 1988; León 1991; Bengoa 1985; Canals Frau 1946), this period involved a radical transformation of Araucanian society in which many of the social and economic principles typical of a local society were gradually submerged by those of a regional level, primarily for the purposes of territorial defense and later of a raiding economy in foreign lands (see León 1991). In this society, characterized by political pressure and warfare, weak leadership at the supralineage level would have taken on greater meaning: the power and alliance of a lineage could be threatened within the regional population.

These circumstances made it necessary for Araucanian leaders to forge new mechanisms that functioned to maintain societal cohesion in the face of these pressures. The situation called for a means of greater social interaction and political unification and, above all, for a new form of leadership to emerge, one which could strengthen social control and politicomilitary authority on a regional basis (a form probably similar to the *butalmapu* territorial divisions mentioned by Diego de Rosales and Molina in the mid-1700s). To develop a leadership capable of military defense, chiefs not only had to solidify their power among their own kin but extend their authority beyond the boundaries of their own lineage. This feat depended upon the reputation of new leaders as warriors and household heads, and, above all, the closeness of their kinship ties to high-ranking chiefs and ancestor heroes. The opportune institutional contexts for new leaders to legitimize their claim to power and the attempt to extend it to others were the *awn* burial and *cueltun* mound-building services at the grave sites of their defunct predecessors. These rites were the only such contexts because they were the only public events bringing together numerous lineages and chiefs, and they were the places that provided linkages between the old and new leadership and between the living and the dead. As such, these services focused the communal will and effort on a single act of political integration that hopefully would endure and carry over into other relations. They also gave both lineages and chiefs the opportunity to redefine their interests and relations. Such interaction and reflection were required if new chiefs were to become successful rulers.

If indeed public ceremonies were the occasions for extending chiefly authority to non-kinsmen, then the scant presence of mounds in the study area suggests that there must have been limited times and places when these services were performed, and that, as the historical documents indicate, few leaders ever achieved a supralineage position, or what the Spanish called a "*Toqui* principal." We can surmise from the documents that the social status and political power of leaders were not passed on to their heirs. Sons, as chief-elects, were undoubtedly respected, but they had to prove their own capabilities as leaders. That is, while chiefly position was ascribed, status was achieved. Status building began with the funerary services of predecessors, which created a period of grace for new chiefs, a sort of dress rehearsal or pretext of leadership, at a time of potential decay in the social fabric of lineage alliances. Those chief-elects who fully utilized this period and worked hard to sustain alliances gained status and were more likely to be successful. Powerful lineages with a dynastic string of competitive chiefs and continued success in marriage alliances, economic activities, and warfare were able to monopolize local and regional events and, above all, to survive as productive social units.

During the late historic period, as a result of success in warfare, some *toqui* leaders evidently developed limited coercive power, but had no extended centralized authority. Nonetheless, the participation of leaders in interlocking sets of public ceremonies (e.g., Dillehay 1990, 1992) seems to have developed a chiefly brotherhood and solidarity at a higher level in the society. The administration of these ceremonies emphasized the separation of the chiefly elite from the rest of the population, a separation probably necessitated by regional political tension and formal leadership directed beyond the local group and expressed through the foundation of long-distance alliances on an elite *toqui* level, not a local level. This separation, in the form of regional elite alliances, appears to be reflected in the *butalmapu* divisions. Such divisions apparently were not territorial groups defined by centralized administrative units but lineages interlocked in ritual ceremony, and, in historic times, bonded by direct cooperation among *toqui* war chiefs (Faron 1961). Together, these relations are encoded historically by the mounds and *chemamüll,* which reflect an architectural and symbolic landscape conditioned by warfare and regional political integration, and hence a hierarchical Araucanian territory in general.

To summarize, in the historic Araucanian society, there was a recognized loose hierarchy consisting of major and minor authorities who apparently controlled major and minor subdivisions of the population (Aguirre 1907; Best 1960; Bengoa 1985; León 1991). Such an arrangement was, in effect, a chain of command, linking leaders at different regional and local levels. It seems clear from the written records for the early historic period that the rapid intensification of warfare in the seventeenth century was a critical factor in the development of this hierarchy and its corresponding architectural structures and ancestral symbols. We can associate these developments with a weakly institutionalized political organization, which was forced to organize and defend itself militarily and to search for ways economically to support its campaigns against the Spanish and later Chilean armies. This support came primarily from raiding Spanish homesteads along the Chilean frontier and in the Argentina pampas (Cabrera 1934; Villalobos 1989; León 1991).

Although the raiding economy was a possible intensifier of chiefly political power in times of war, it seemingly had little initial influence on the territorial defense of Araucanian society. Instead, I am convinced that the initial linkage of large-scale public religious foundations, political defense, and the extension of leadership authority beyond local communities had more to do with the problem of geopolitics among competing lineages than with a changing or developing political economy and social ranking. This is not to deny the role of these factors; but the present evidence suggests that this linkage was achieved first through an ideopolitical process, not a socioeconomic one.

DISCUSSION AND CONCLUSION

In this paper, I have reviewed some recent work in south-central Chile, suggesting how the archaeological, ethnohistorical, and ethnographic records of the late historic and early modern periods relate to postfunerary rites of paramount chiefs and chiefly political installation and political succession and extension. I also have suggested that the patterns described above are largely the product of the differences between two contemporary and contrasting societies. The patterns discussed changed drastically when the

Mounds of Social Death: Araucanian Funerary Rites and Political Succession

Araucanians were pacified in the late 1800s. *Toqui* leaders disappeared and the power of *lonko* and other chiefs was reduced. Similarly, it is obvious that the type of cultivated ancestral landscape which developed in the study area during the past few centuries, with its *cuel* mounds, *chemamüll* figures, and *ñguillatun* fields, could not have remained intact very long except in isolated and traditional areas where some customs are maintained. Despite heavy acculturation throughout the present century, there is still enough traditional material and spatial evidence available to suggest that any study of the historic relationships among ancestors, leadership, elaborate graves, and geopolitical boundaries must be cast over a wide social field. In casting a study, these findings suggest that the location of sets of contemporaneous mounds and associated habitational sites may reveal much about the political order and events of a particular epoch. Survey and excavation of these sites in the archaeological past must be carried out, however, before I can demonstrate the origins and time depth of this model and test many of its specific implications.

Although not discussed above, I am concerned about the broad 300-year time span of the model presented here and the unknown aspects of mortuary practices. Due to the lack of archaeological research on mound sites in the study area, I cannot link specific historic events and periods with specific mound sites, or say that there is a horizon of mound building. The scant evidence available suggests that the sequence of developments varied over different parts of the study area. It may be that the uneven distribution of mounds reflects preference for certain lineages and their leaders or for demographic stability. It may also suggest differences in mortuary practice and political behavior along internal and external frontiers. We can surmise that there must have been selective forces favoring the rise of certain chiefs and lineages in certain places at certain times (see Dillehay 1990), because not all leaders were vying for extended power and mounds do not occur in all valleys.

I am also concerned about other possible ritual or symbolic practices that may express similar mortuary forms and political processes. Despite the continuity in content and form of burial practices observed in the archaeological, ethnohistoric, and ethnographic records, there must have been many important changes in mortuary practice, ancestral worship, and political organization which are not being detected and which may explain the findings in different ways. For instance, extended mortuary rites undoubtedly involved the preparation of dead chiefs and their spirits for the afterworld. Was this involvement more important than the pretext of leadership afforded to his successor? Is there cause to believe that burial contexts provided new chiefs with the opportunity to attract and retain the nonmilitary labor of followers through which privileged access to material wealth, prestige, and ultimately political power became possible? Although we do not have answers to these questions at present, neither the archaeological nor the ethnohistorical records reflect an accumulation of chiefly wealth which is commensurate with political power.

These questions lead us to another issue. It is insufficient to explain the Mapuche rites of chiefly burial and the installation of new rulers exclusively in terms of ancestral worship services dedicated to defunct chiefs, or for that matter, any single variable. The general approach adopted in this paper has been to argue that these rites, in the context of mound building, reflect a need formally to install, legitimize, and expand the authority of local chiefs during periods of political stress (i.e., primarily territorial defense in the Araucanian case). As suggested in the ethnohistorical and archaeological records, a new regional politicomilitary organization was created for this defense, one which was associated with different forms of external and internal (lineage) boundaries marked by mounds, wooden statues, and public ceremonial fields. Extended funerary rites of chiefs at mound sites became the symbolic lattices through which different parts of the political system were linked. These rites, however, were much more than mere political rallies. They were also rites of social transformation and models for the fate of local political alliances, in that alliances were manipulated through the death of a paramount chief. In effect, these were the contexts within which leaders reworked social relationships by creating shifting coalitions, none of which probably lasted very long. These rites also had a cosmological meaning: they reaffirmed the perpetuity of the lineage by transforming new chiefly ancestors into old ones, thereby creating a sense of time-depth and prolonged history against which the future was projected. In this sense, extended mortuary practices brought about change in political organization and demographic structure, and made use of the past (through ancestral rites and recounting events) to determine the future. They, like the display burial mounds where they were performed, reflected time and history, and, as such, conveyed a concern with permanence and suggested a temporal reality.

All of this is intuitively evident. We have said that the political system derived its authority from lineage history (*admapu*) and from the plans of participating lineages, as seen by their members. In the sense of Kossak's and Renfrew's notions of conspicuous ancestor monuments, the display of monumental graves was intended to secure for the members of the lineages the benefits of the rituals in perpetuity, even when the rituals were not being performed at the mound. It is in this regard that mound building was a way of time, or history, reckoning, and that monumental graves became time markers, just as they were space markers (Dillehay 1990). Mounds, particularly a suite of mounds, represented a continuum of political eschatologies, marking the end of some chiefly regimes, and political cosmogenies, marking the beginning of others. This continuum is reflected in the spatial layout and indigenous nomenclature of mounds. For instance, as I have noted previously for a family suite of mounds in Lumaco (Dillehay 1990: 232), the older, informantly named structures of the early historic period have the prefix *kuifil*,[2] meaning ancient or long ago, before their names. The younger mounds including those still in use today, have active names more indicative of their specific ritual function. Within this suite of structures, some mounds are sacred architectural memorabilia that commemorate past leaders and past times; others simply mark present social history. All of this suggests a very different organizational level of time or history and a Mapuche sense of the human locus in the supramatrix of space-time. It is not the same type of time associated with rhythms of the seasons, with plants and animals, and with harvest cycles. It is a ritualized socialization of time segregated by sequential burial of chiefs at monumental grave sites. Temporal segregation through political eschatologies and cosmogenies, as continually manifested in monumental burials, was a powerful means of creating and maintaining lineage distinction, recounting achievement of ancestors, and recording social history. As such, the distribution of mounds in space is the same as the distribution of the historical behavior of lineages in time. Hence, a spatial pattern of mound burials is interchangeable with a temporal or historical pattern of lineage history.

We can say then that those lineages manipulating chiefly burials at public places to inaugurate a new chief and actively change (or even maintain) the structure and direction of social events were *mound literate,* so to speak. As I have discussed before (Dillehay 1990, 1992), mounds and mound-related rituals had (and still have) a life beyond the theme of death and burial; they were memorabilia and ceremonial places actively used and, through the death of a leader and the reconstruction of alliances by new leaders, actively restructured who participated in ceremony. Mound politics culturally transformed social structure as death did political structure. Thus, mound literacy—knowing how to use mounds socially to maintain the status quo or bring change for one's lineage—became as much of a prerequisite for the political conduct of a group as did technological literacy (weapons, irrigation systems) and economic literacy (monetary exchange, resource values). Each of these devices demanded a special way of human interaction in Mapuche society, and, for the archaeologist, a special way of perceiving the archaeological record.

[2] Informants in the Lumaco area referred to two usages of the term *kuifil,* expressed here as *kuifil cuel,* and the other as *cuelku.* Informants used both terms to refer to the oldest mounds. Although I recognize that the terms may have different meanings and that one may be more grammatically correct than the other, I use *kuifil cuel* because it was identified by shamans and by more elders.

Finally, although it is not the place in this paper to discuss the broader archaeological patterns and meaning of mound building, these issues reflect on some of the primary concerns of recent mortuary studies. There has been a construction and partial testing of relationships linking social structure, economic investment, resource stress, and mortuary treatment within broader anthropological contexts (O'Shea 1984; Tainter 1978; Chapman, Kinnes, and Randsborg 1981; Bartel 1982). The findings of the Mapuche study tend to support some ideas of Renfrew, Hodder, and Kossak that monumental burial forms represent territorial markers and that the "display" (and I would add continued use) of monuments was important to historical events and circumstances in the society. It also seems that the organizational processes occurring on the macro level of chiefly political organization were partially isolated from the micro level of domestic affairs. This is not to imply a complete separation, for it is obvious that the two levels must have functioned in unison in order to meet their goals. Rather, I believe that Araucanian leadership in the form of chiefly associations, perhaps like the interregional *butalmapu* system, consolidated first on a regional level of interlineage relations, then perhaps began to scale down into local parts. It is possible that the size of mounds relates to this scaling-down effect. Preliminary archaeological findings suggest that the large, more elaborate mounds were produced in the earlier periods (Latcham 1928; Dillehay 1990), probably when integration among groups was more regionally based and was achieved through extended death rituals of paramount chiefs, not through the political structure itself. As chiefly military and economic networks developed further and the chiefly office became more formalized and secure, for reasons not completely understood at present, there was probably less need for large mounds. It was likely that once chiefly authority was manifested in other ways, either through an elaborate political symbolic system or through more formal secular architectural forms (e.g., formal village layout), mound building probably disappeared altogether in some areas, shrunk in size in others, or was transformed into other sacred or secular systems. From this perspective, we can envision continued use of the same mound, its growth through burial accretion, and the construction of an architectural design to allow ceremony to occur around and on top of it. We can also envision a point when a mound is abandoned or its use increased by part-time residency commensurate with architectural growth and modification and with greater public participation suited to this purpose. Obviously, these suppositions require more rigorous archaeological and ethnohistorical testing before we can consider their fuller implications.

To conclude, it is somewhat difficult to extend these findings to other Andean areas. Without comparative written records in areas where other early complex societies emerged, it is difficult to designate warfare and the

Mounds of Social Death: Araucanian Funerary Rites and Political Succession

stress of a frontier situation as the primary conditions accounting for the events and patterns studied here. Although I do not claim to have tested any specific hypotheses related to Andean studies, we can see in this study certain Andean traditions (e.g., animal sacrifice, intentional vessel breakage, chicha consumption) that are important to political power and public ceremony. In attempting to offer broad correlations between specific types of mortuary contexts and particular procedures of social cohesion, I suggest that we pay more strict attention to the architectural separation between the tomb and its contents and the elaborate monument built over it. Although they are linked in many obvious ways, each relates to the achievements and images of different generations of leaders and to historical events that extend well beyond the death of the interred. Hopefully the potential of these findings will stimulate constructive comment and productive research on similar themes in other areas.

In recent years, Araucanian specialists have begun to realize that the proto-Mapuche society was much more economically and politically complex than previously believed. This realization has come about largely through concerted efforts to revise the extant archaeological (e.g., Dillehay 1981, 1990) and ethnohistorical records (e.g., León 1991; Dillehay 1990), and perhaps above all, to understand the local context within which the Mapuche culture and society emerged. No doubt, as more information becomes available on the archaeology and history of the Araucanians, specialists also will realize that the pre-Hispanic societies of the south-central Andes were southern expressions of deeply rooted demographic and social processes which have their roots in an often inconspicuous and hybrid pattern of interaction between Andean and eastern tropical forest societies. This is not to deny the contribution made by local societies, but rather to identify the catalyst that gave them this expression.

Acknowledgements I wish to thank Tom Hakansson for reading an earlier draft of this manuscript. Also thanked are Rene San Martin, Kenneth Hirth, William Y. Adams, Berle Clay, David Pollack, José Peréz Gollan, and Nancy O'Malley for sharing their knowledge of archaeological mound cultures with me.

BIBLIOGRAPHY

AGUIRRE, MIGUEL DE
    1907   Población de Valdivia, 1646. Colección de Historiadores y de Documentos Relativos a la Historia Nacional 45. Santiago.

ARHEM, KAJ
    1988   Into the Realm of the Sacred: An Interpretation of Khasi Funerary Ritual. In *On the Meaning of Death* (Sven Cederroth, Claes Corlin, and Jan Lindstrom, eds.): 257–300. Uppsala Studies in Cultural Anthropology 8. Stockholm.

BARTEL, BRAD
    1982   A Historical Review of Ethnological and Archaeological Analyses of Mortuary Practices. *Journal of Anthropological Archaeology* 1: 32–58.

BASCÚÑAN, FRANCISCO NÚÑEZ DE PINEDA Y
    1973   [1865] *Cautiverio Feliz.* Editorial de la Universidad de Chile, Santiago.

BENGOA, JOSE
    1985   *Historia del Pueblo Mapuche: Siglo XIX y XX.* Ediciones Sur, Santiago.

BENNETT, WENDELL
    1939   *Archaeology of the North Coast of Peru.* Anthropological Papers of the American Museum of Natural History 37 (1): 1–153. New York.

BEST, FELIX
    1960   *Historia de las Guerras Argentinas,* vols. 1 and 2. Buenos Aires.

BINFORD, LEWIS
    1971   Mortuary Practices: Their Study and Potential. In *Approaches to the Social Dimensions of Mortuary Practices.* (James A. Brown, ed.). Memoirs of the Society for American Archaeology 25: 6–29. Washington, D.C.

BLAKELY, ROBERT L.
    1977   *Biocultural Adaptation in Prehistoric America.* Southern Anthropological Society, Proceedings 11.

BLOCH, MAURICE, AND JONATHAN PARRY (EDS.)
    1982   *Death and the Regeneration of Life.* Cambridge University Press, New York.

BRADLEY, RICHARD (ED.)
    1990   Monuments and Monumentality. *World Archaeology* 22 (2): 223–241.

BROWN, JAMES A.
    1981   The Search for Rank in Prehistoric Burials. In *The Archaeology of Death* (Richard Chapman, Ian Kinnes, and Klavs Randsborg, eds.): 25–37. Cambridge University Press, New York.

BUIKSTRA, JANE E.
    1990   Sumario de la Investigación de Restos Humanos de Omo, Moquegua y San Geronimo, Ilo. In *Trabajos Arqueológicos en Moquegua, Perú* (Luis K.

Watanabe, Michael E. Moseley, and Fernando Cabieses, eds.): 59–69. Programa Continsuyu del Museo Peruano de Ciencias de la Salud, Southern Peru Copper Corporation, Lima.

BULLOCK, DILLMAN
   1955 Urnas funerarias prehistóricas de la región de Angol. *Boletín del Museo Nacional de Historia Natural* 26: 73–157.

BUXTON, JEAN
   1963 *Chiefs and Strangers*. Clarendon Press, Oxford, England.

CABRERA, PABLO
   1934 Los Araucanos en Territorio Argentino. *Actas y Trabajos Científicos del XXV Congress de Americanistas*. Buenos Aires.

CANALS FRAU, S.
   1946 The Argentine Araucanians. In *Handbook of South American Indians* (Julian Stewart, ed.). Smithsonian Institution, Bureau of American Ethnology, Bulletin 143 (2): 761–766. Washington, D.C.

CANNON, AUBREY
   1989 The Historical Dimension in Mortuary Expressions of Status and Sentiment. *Current Anthropology* 30: 437–458.

CHAPMAN, RICHARD, IAN KINNES, AND KLAVS RANDSBORG (EDS.)
   1981 *The Archaeology of Death*. Cambridge University Press, New York.

CONA, PASCUAL
   1973 *Memorias de un Cacique Mapuche*. ICIRA, Santiago.

CONRAD, GEOFFREY
   n.d. Burial Platforms and Related Structures on the North Coast of Peru: Some Social and Political Implications. Ph.D. dissertation, Harvard University, 1974.

COOPER, JOHN M.
   1946 The Araucanians. In *Handbook of South American Indians* (Julian Stewart, ed.). Smithsonian Institution, Bureau of American Ethnology, Bulletin 143 (2): 687–760. Washington, D.C.

DILLEHAY, TOM D.
   1981 Visión actual de los estudios de la Araucanía prehispánica. *Boletín del Museo Nacional de Historia Natural de Chile* 38: 155–166.
   1985 La Influencia Política de los (los) Chamanes Mapuche. *Hombre, Cultura y Sociedad* (2): 141–157.
   1986 Cuel: Observación y comentaries sobre los tumulos de la Cultura Mapuche. *Chungará* 16–17: 181–193.
   1990 Mapuche Ceremonial Landscape, Social Recruitment, and Resource Rights. *World Archaeology* 22 (2): 223–241.
   1992 Keeping Outsiders Out: Public Core, Resource Rights, and Hierarchy in Historic and Contemporary Mapuche Society. In *Wealth and Hierarchy in the Intermediate Area* (Frederick W. Lange, ed.): 379–422. Dumbarton Oaks, Washington, D.C.

DILLEHAY, TOM D., AND AMÉRICO GORDON
  1977 El Simbolismo en el ornito-morfismo mapuche: La Mujer Casada y el *Ketru Metawe*. *Actas del VII Congreso del Arqueología de Chile*: 303–316. Santiago.

DONNAN, CHRISTOPHER B., AND CAROL MACKEY
  1978 *Ancient Burial Patterns of the Moche Valley, Peru*. University of Texas Press, Austin.

DONNAN, CHRISTOPHER B., AND DONNA MCCLELLAND
  1979 *The Burial Theme in Moche Iconography*. Studies in Pre-Columbian Art and Archaeology 21. Dumbarton Oaks, Washington, D.C.

ERIZE, ESTEBAN
  1987 *Mapuche 1–3*. Editorial Yepún, Buenos Aires.

ESTRADA, EMILIO
  1957 *Prehistoria de Manabí*. Publicación del Museo Victor Emilio Estrada, No. 4, Guayaquil, Ecuador.

FARON, LOUIS C.
  1961 *Mapuche Social Structure*. University of Illinois Press, Urbana.
  1964 *Hawks of the Sun: Mapuche Morality and Its Ritual Attributes*. University of Pittsburgh Press.

FLEMING, ANTHONY
  1972 Vision and Design: Approaches to Ceremonial Monument Typology. *Man* 7: 57–73.

GODELIER, MAURICE
  1977 *Perspectives in Marxist Anthropology*. Cambridge University Press, Cambridge.

GOODY, JACK
  1966 *Succession to High Office*. Cambridge University Press, Cambridge.

GORDON, AMÉRICO
  1975 Excavación de una sepultura in Loncoche, provincia de Cautín, Novena Región, Chile. *Boletín del Museo Nacional de Historia Natural de Chile* 34: 63–68.
  1978 Urna y canoa funerarias. Una sepultura doble excavada en Padre Las Casa, Provincia de Cautín, IX Región, Chile. *Revista Chilena de Antropología* 1: 61–80.
  1984 Huimpil: Un cementerio agroalfarero temprano en el centro-sur de Chile. *Cultura Hombre y Sociedad* 2: 86–112.
  n.d. Informe sobre la excavación de una sepultura in Loncoche, Depto. de Villarrica, Provincia de Cautín, 1973.

GORDON, AMÉRICO, JACQUELINE MADRID, AND JULIA MONLEÓN
  1972–73 Excavación de un cementerio indígena en Gorbea (Setio GO-3) provencia de Cautín, Chile. *Actas del congreso de Arqueología Chilena* 501–514. Santiago.

GUEVARA SILVA, TOMÁS
  1913 *Las últimas familias i costumbres araucanas*. Santiago.

Mounds of Social Death: Araucanian Funerary Rites and Political Succession

HERTZ, ROBERT
    1960   *Death and the Right Hand.* Cohen and West Publishers, Aberdeen.

HODDER, IAN
    1984   Burials, Houses, Women and Men in the European Neolithic. In *Ideology, Power and Symbolism* (Daniel Miller and Christopher Tilley, eds.): 46–62. Cambridge University Press, Cambridge.

HOUSSE, EMILE
    1939   *Une épopée indienne: Les Araucans du Chile.* Zig-zag Press, Paris.

HUNTINGDON, RICHARD, AND PETER METCALF
    1979   *Celebrations of Death: The Anthropology of Mortuary Ritual.* Cambridge University Press, Cambridge.

KOSSACK, GEORG
    1974   Prunkgräber. In *Studien zur vor und frühgeschichtlichen Archäologie.* (Georg Kossack and Günter Ulbert, eds.): 3–33. Münchner Beiträge zur Vor und Frühgeschichte. Beck, Munich.

LATCHAM, R.
    1915   Costumbres mortuarios de los indios de Chile y otras partes de América. *Anales de la Universidad de Chile* 136–137. Santiago.
    1928   *La Alfareria Indigena Chilena.* Imprenta La Bandera, Santiago.

LEÓN, LEONARDO S.
    1991   *Maloqueros y Conchavadores en Araucania y las Pampas, 1700–1800.* Ediciones Universidad de la Frontera, Temuco, Chile.

MEILLASSOUX, C.
    1968   Ostentation, destruction, reproduction. *Economie et Société* 2: 760–772.
    1972   From Reproduction to Production. *Economy and Society* 1: 93–105.

MENGHIN, OSVALDO
    1962   *Estudios de prehistoria araucania.* Studia Prehistoria 2. Centro Argentino de Estudios Historicos, Buenos Aires.

MOLINA, JUAN IGNACIO
    1795   *Compendio de la historia geográfica natural y civil del Reino de Chile.* (Primera Edición Bologna, 1776; Narciso Cueto, trans.). *Historia Colonial de Chile* 2, Santiago.

O'SHEA, JOHN
    1984   *Mortuary Variability: An Archaeological Investigation.* Academic Press, New York.

PINTO, JORJE (EDS.)
    1988   *Misioneros en la Araucania, 1600–1900.* Ediciones Universidad de la Frontera, Temuco, Chile.

POWELL, MARY L., ANN M. MIRES, AND PATRICIA BRIDGES (EDS.)
    1991   *What Mean These Bones?* University of Alabama Press, Tuscaloosa.

QUILTER, JEFFREY
    1989   *Life and Death at Paloma: Society and Mortuary Practices in a Preceramic Peruvian Village.* University of Iowa Press, Iowa City.

QUIROGA, JERONIMO
    1979   *Memoria de los sucesos de la Guerra de Chile*. Editorial Andrés Bello, Santiago.

RENFREW, COLIN
    1976   Megaliths, Territories and Populations. In *Acculturation and Continuity in Atlantis Europe* (Samuel De Laet, ed.): 198–220. de Tempel, Bruges.

RENFREW, COLIN, AND SHENNAN, S. (EDS.)
    1982   *Ranking, Resource and Exchange*. Cambridge University Press, Cambridge and New York.

ROSALES, DIEGO DE
    1989   *Historia general del reino de Chile* (Escrita 1674–?), 3 vols. Editorial
    [1877–78]   Benjamin Vicuña Mackenna, Valparaiso, Chile.

ROWE, JOHN H.
    1962   Warsaae's Law and the Use of Grave Lots for Archaeological Dating. *American Antiquity* 28 (2): 129–137.

SAHLINS, MARSHAL
    1961   The Segmentary Lineage: An Organisation of Predatory Expansion. *American Anthropologist* 63: 322–343.

STRONG, WILLIAM D., AND CLIFFORD EVANS
    1952   *Cultural Stratigraphy in the Viru Valley, Northern Peru: The Formative and Florescent Epochs*. Columbia Studies in Archaeology and Ethnology 4. Columbia University Press, New York.

STUCHLIK, MILAN
    1976   *Life on a Half-Share: Mechanisms of Social Recruitment among the Mapuche of Southern Chile*. St. Martin's Press, New York.
    1979   *Rasgos de la sociedad mapuche contemporanea*. Ediciones Nueva Universidad, Santiago.

TAINTER, JOHN
    1978   Mortuary Practices and the Study of Prehistoric Social Systems. *Advances in Archaeological Method and Theory* 1. Academic Press, New York.

TELLO, JULIO C., AND T. MEJÍA XESSPE
    1979   *Paracas: Parte II, Cavernas y Necropolis*. Universidad Nacional Mayor de San Marcos, Lima.

TITIEV, MISCHA
    1951   *Araucanian Culture in Transition*. University of Michigan Press, Ann Arbor.

TURNER, VICTOR
    1969   *The Ritual Process*. Aldine Press, Chicago.

UHLE, MAX
    1903   *Pachacamac*. University of Pennsylvania, Philadelphia.

VAN DE MAELE, MAURICIO
    1968   *Excavaciones en Cementerios, fogones y tacitas de la región de Valdivia*. Investigaciones Históricas e Investigaciones Arqueológicas. Universidad Austral de Chile, Valdivia.

VILLALOBOS, SERGIO
 1982   Tres siglos y medio de vidoc fronteriza. In *Relaciones Fronterizas en La Araucania* (Sergio Villalobos, ed.): 16–38. Ediciones Universidad Católica de Chile, Santiago.
 1989   *Los Pehuenches en La Vida Fronteriza*. Ediciones Universidad Católica de Chile, Santiago.

WILLEY, GORDON
 1953   *Prehistoric Settlement Patterns in the Viru Valley, Peru*. Smithsonian Institution, Bureau of American Ethnology, Bulletin 155. Washington, D.C.

"The Beautiful Grandparents": Andean Ancestor Shrines and Mortuary Ritual as Seen Through Colonial Records

FRANK SALOMON
DEPARTMENT OF ANTHROPOLOGY
UNIVERSITY OF WISCONSIN-MADISON

For a few regions and for short intervals, the Andean written record describes death, mourning, mummification, entombment, and ancestor[1] cult. As a sampling it is scarce, and as testimony it is deeply problematic because of its anti-Andean axiomatic foundations. Nonetheless, relating this information to ethnological and theoretical work from other world areas greatly enhances its value and, indirectly, its usefulness as a tool for interpreting material remains. The aims of this paper are to sketch the patchwork of written sources available (Part I); outline basic organizational traits and roles of Andean ancestor cult (Parts II and III); summarize Andean folk theories of mortality so as to make these traits more intelligible (Part IV) and locate them in relation to general ethnological discussion of such folk theories (Part V); follow descriptively the stages of Andean mortuary practice from experiences of the moribund to cycles of ancestor veneration, differentiating between Inka and provincial practice (Parts VI–IX); and finally, interpret total mortuary practice in terms of social reproduction and transformation (Part X). The final sections (XI–XII) develop an argument about ways in which rites combined an overtly conservative function with processes tending to alter the very social arrangements ritual pretends to put beyond time's reach.

The author cordially appreciates support from the National Endowment for the Humanities and the William F. Vilas Trust Estate, which made possible the research reported here.

[1] Meyer Fortes (1965: 124) defines the term: "An ancestor is a named dead forebear who has living descendants of a designated genealogical class representing his continued structural relevance. In ancestor worship such an ancestor receives ritual service and tendance directed specifically to him by the proper class of his descendants." To this William Newell (1976: 20) adds that "service and tendance" demand the existence of a sacrificer, a group who benefits from sacrifice, and a designated place of cult.

Frank Salomon

I. THE SOURCES AND THEIR SILENCES: DOCUMENTS ON
ANDEAN MORTUARY CULTURE

Written records offer important clues to Andean mortuary behavior and belief. But it is important to remember their limitations: above and beyond the evident bias inherent in hostile description, they make up a spotty sample of a cultural domain which is probably as ancient and as far-flung as Andean culture itself. The document-based perspective views Andean mortuary through a few narrow windows.

First, in the sacred capital Cuzco, Inka mortuary rite continued up to 1550 (Duviols 1977: 111). Early soldier-chroniclers glimpsed it, among them Pedro Pizarro, who in 1571 remembered some archaeologically relevant details, such as the pouring of libations for the dead through specially pierced or channeled stones. Descriptions of Inka rites are relatively numerous, but somewhat contradictory or hard to collate (see Part VII). Ransacking of sacred places, and the policies enacted by the First Council of Lima (1551), put an end to Inka public rites in fewer than 20 years after Spanish invasion.

However, from 1551 to the 1570s, the colonial assault on the Inka ancestors in Cuzco itself produced continuing testimony. In 1559 Juan Polo de Ondegardo, while *corregidor* of Cuzco, apparently sleuthed out the mummies of all but the oldest two sovereign Inkas. Garcilaso Inca and José de Acosta subsequently saw some in "a sort of mummy museum Polo had in his house" (Garcilaso 1966 [1609]: 306; Duviols 1977: 123). Debate on what happened to them after they were exhibited in Lima's Hospital San Andrés lingers inconclusively (Hampe 1982; Guillén Guillén 1983).

The second documentary vein is the record of persecution against the nativist movement Taki Onqoy in parts of modern Ayacucho, Huancavelica, and Apurímac (Varón 1990: 403). These papers afford some ethnographically coarse-grained information relevant to the reconceptualized and renascent worship of *huaca*s ca. 1560 (Millones 1990; a *huaca* was any tangible thing embodying a superhuman being). The earliest of the persecution manuals (Albornoz 1984 [1583?]) recounts the attack on Taki Onqoy. These sources, however, give the impression that Taki Onqoy revivalism was quite different from the highly localistic ancestor worship later and more copiously recorded in central Peru. Taki Onqoy emphasized "general" or regional superhumans as apical ancestors, more than the genealogy of local groups embodied in tombs, and its most copiously described foci are described as artifacts or natural landmarks rather than human bodies.

Third, to a limited but incompletely explored extent, records about looting and taxation of grave wealth afford data on the contents of tomb sites, sometimes in places where death customs were otherwise scarcely recorded. Cieza heard of a tomb with more than 50,000 pesos of treasure, a Peruvian north coast shrine yielded 427,735 *castellanos* in 1566, and later yields sur-

"*The Beautiful Grandparents*"

passed these (Duviols 1977: 375). Susan Ramírez Horton (n.d.) has discovered detailed documents on a tomb apparently inside one of the large Chan Chan platform complexes, looted starting in 1558 (see also Donnan, this volume). Even in poorer peripheries such as Cañar, in modern Ecuador, tombs yielded thousands of pesos (Salomon 1987). Sometimes such records itemize metal objects and conserve local native knowledge about them. From the initial pillagings of Pachacamac and Cuzco to about 1610, both civil and religious authorities condoned looting as a source of revenue (from 1561 onward, assessed at the uniquely high rate of 50%), a scourge to Andean worship, and a sop to pacify ambitious colonists. The church and state later tried to rein in clerical self-enrichment by looting. Nonetheless, grave-plundering claims and disputes occurred far into the colonial era.

Fourth, "geographical reports" (Jiménez de la Espada 1965; Caillavet 1988; Ponce Leiva 1992) and other papers on the implementation of Toledan and post-Toledan viceregal policies contain fragmentary allusions to mortuary practice, ancient and modern. This corpus forms the only wide sampling of provincial societies, extending to the outermost peripheries of the former Inka domains.

Fifth, the "Native chronicler" Felipe Guaman Poma de Ayala (1980 [1615]) took an intense interest in mortuary custom. His book contains drawings and descriptions of cult classified according to the *suyus* or geographic quarters of the Inka domain (see Figs. 1-6).

Sixth and most importantly, throughout a region corresponding to southern Ancash Department and most of Lima Department, the "extirpation of idolatries" campaigns from 1607 or 1608 (A. Acosta 1987) through the 1660s produced a rich and intensive record of persecution against ancestor worship (Duviols 1977: 317-320; Millones 1967).[2] Trials of mummy cult officiants also occurred, but rarely and less intensively, in Arequipa and Ayacucho (Duviols 1966; Millones 1984: 142). Duviols' *Cultura andina y represión* (1986a), a compendium of trials from the heavily persecuted province of Cajatambo, is the most important printed source for documents on ancestor cult. (Its index mentions more than 400 named mummies.) Mary Doyle's 1988 doctoral dissertation contains an exhaustive descriptive synthesis of Cajatambo and other trial data. Persecutors of the ancestors were

---

[2] It is possible that Peruvian clerics' intense hostility to mummy worship has to do with European worries about the ambiguously Christian and pagan meanings of corpse preservation. Among Roman Catholics of the sixteenth century, "natural mummification" (i.e., the spontaneous self-conservation of a corpse) was understood as odor of sanctity. The most famous case was Teresa of Avila, who died in 1582. It was, however, considered problematic that incorruption sometimes occurred with pagans as well. When, in Rome in 1485, quarriers uncovered a remarkably well-preserved girl in a Roman sarcophagus closed some 1500 years earlier, an enthusiastic crowd carried her in triumph to the Capitoline Hill. Pope Innocent VIII, "concerned at this enthusiasm for a 'pagan,' had the body removed in secret, and it has never been seen again" (Ragon 1983: 8).

Fig. 1 The November ritual in honor of the ancestors, Aya Marcai or "bearing the dead," as drawn by Felipe Guaman Poma de Ayala 1980 [1615], 1: 230). Bearers carry a mummy garbed in feather ruff, cloak, coca bag, and the headband signifying Chinchaisuyo in the artist's iconography.

Fig. 2 An *illapa aia* or royal Inka mummy his spouse receive the homage of descenda in the form of maize beer. The tomb in background is labeled *pucullo* (Guaman Po 1980 [1615], 1: 262).

moved by greed for grave wealth, frustration at the persistence of non-Christian devotion, and doctrinal habit. Clerics had been taught at least since Aquinas that "demons . . . were particularly fond of appearing in the guise, or under the accidents, of the dead" (MacCormack 1991: 29). Several persecutors (Hernández Príncipe 1923 [1622]; Arriaga 1968 [1621]) distilled lore about mummies in how-to literature for "extirpators."

Taken together with the unique Quechua Manuscript of Huarochirí (Taylor 1987; Salomon and Urioste 1991), which is probably a by-product of incipient "extirpation," "idolatry" literature offers the most graphic and detailed testimony on the lore of the dead. It is, however, a literature wholly circumscribed by the assumptions of compulsory Christian conversion. Torture and other coercions, as well as stereotyped reporting and tendentious translation, cast a veil over the intended meaning of natives' testimony. And

"The Beautiful Grandparents"

when the trials began, few if any people educated before the Spanish invasion were still living. Moreover, clandestinity affected everything, including the physical disposition of both ancient and recent ancestors. So archaeological analogies demand special caution.

Finally, for the centuries postdating the waning of "extirpation" campaigns, one can occasionally find trial records about political offenses which accusers saw as linked to leadership in mummy cults. Cases from scattered locales afford detailed images of cult as late as the later eighteenth century.

II. ORGANIZATIONAL CHARACTERISTICS OF ANDEAN ANCESTOR AND HUACA WORSHIP

The following ideal-typical image is founded mostly on seventeenth-century sources about provincial agricultural settlements of middle altitude on the central Peruvian west slope. The best documented cases come from

A Chinchaisuyo mummy on procession his mourning widow (*yquima*) passes a (*pucullo*) in Guaman Poma's reconstruc- f pre-Hispanic mortuary (1980 [1615], 1:

Fig. 4 An Antisuio (Amazonian) widow joins her husband (?) as he seals the bones of an endocannibalized corpse into a tree trunk (*uitaca*) according to Guaman Poma (1980 [1615], 1: 266).

319

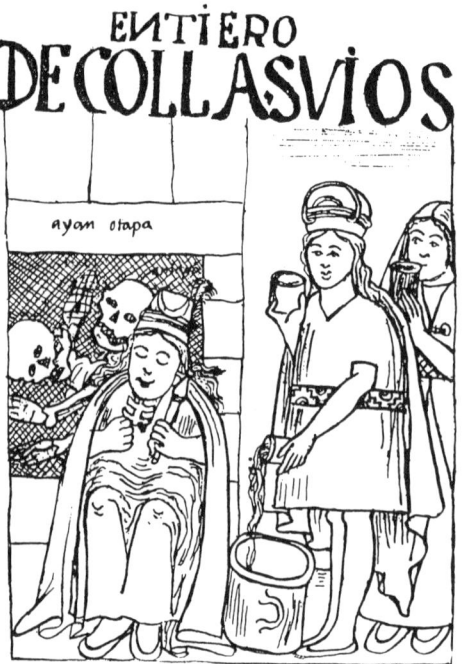 

Fig. 5 In Collasuio, an ancestor in cloak and *suyo* insignia receives maize beer from the living at the door of an *ayan otapa* or tower tomb (Guaman Poma 1980 [1615], 1: 268).

Fig. 6 Guaman Poma's Condesuio widows weep for a mummified man at his *amayanc utapnaca* ("house of the dead"). They cha "Wherein have you entered, lord?" The lal are in an Aymara-related language (1980 [16] 1: 270).

villages that had undergone forced resettlement but retained their outlying *pueblos viejos* (pre-Hispanic sites) as satellite residence centers and clandestine ceremonial centers. The churchmen ferreted out mortuary cult at a time when older customs had already been modified to meet colonial constraints. But the changes are not matters of acculturation, because it was precisely in the ritual domain that Andean people made distinctions between the ethnic and colonial sources of their culture. The description below emphasizes primarily the forms witnesses described as proper to an earlier time. It is frequently hard to tell whether they had in mind pre-Hispanic time or the several intervals between 1532 and 1608 when colonial neglect or connivance allowed older mortuary tradition to flourish.

The minimal element of ancestor cult was the veneration of at least one dead person as the source of entitlement among a group of people who shared rights or identity. As far as we know this behavior was characteristic

"The Beautiful Grandparents"

of all the collectivities styled ayllu in Quechua, from small agrarian communities to entire ethnic groups. For the most part the following discussion uses the word in its "micro" application, referring to small peasant clusters ranging (in colonial records) from a few households up to a few hundred people. Ayllus were typically localized, but not necessarily in a single contiguous space; many held dispersed "islands" of resources. The component households were preferentially to marry each other so as to keep durable resources within the immediate collectivity.

Ethnologically, it is typical of groups which depend on a circumscribed, inherited resource base to imagine ancestors as vigilant and jealous. When transmission of goods follows descent lines, it is felt, prosperity follows and ancestors are known retrospectively to have fostered good fortune. In the Andes, the building of permanent, highly visible, durable dwellings for ancestors symbolized and enforced commitment to a program of social organization through inheritance, apparently emphasizing local endogamy for common people except where elites sent commoners' daughters away as gift brides. Elites, with their politically freighted marital alliances, may have been more widely exogamous.

Each small ayllu was affiliated with a local ceremonial center. The set of ayllus whose cults, and whose entitlements of resources, were celebrated at such a center is typically the unit called *llacta* in colonial usage. Many ceremonial or *llacta* centers were still known and honorifically used ca. 1600. To what degree they had been permanent or seasonal residence centers in pre-Hispanic times is not clear from document records.

Such centers housed among other sacred things the mummified ancestors of one or more small ayllus. Sometimes the respective ayllu-"founding" ancestors had common parents, that is, mummies ancestral to the whole *llacta*, but more typically ayllu-founders were said to be descendants of superhuman beings, *huacas*, whose physical substance inhered in monoliths, statues, or other sacred objects. The *huacas* in turn were sometimes imagined as the progeny of major permanent land features or natural forces such as great snowcapped mountains or lighting. In this fashion, ancestry could be imagined as a seamless web expanding from family organization to geographic and even cosmological order.

The typical west slope, central Peruvian *llacta* center turned *pueblo viejo* had a small plaza close to, and often overlooking, an area of houses for the living. The plaza would be bordered by small stone chambers or cells described as "tiny lodgings," something "like storehouses." (They were called by the Quechua term *colca*, which also means "storehouse.") These contained preserved bodies. It was at this plaza, often called *cayan*, that the village's ayllu(s) jointly fêted their "founders." The small chambers in which mummies dwelled usually also contained collections of lesser holy objects, such as *conopas* or fertility "idols."

From the worshiper's viewpoint, the established local complex of holy objects and spaces was seen as the end product of a mythohistorical transit from *huaca* origin, to *huaca* actions in which remote hero-ancestors took part, to the political establishment of *huaca*s in their present sites (often involving migration and warfare), and finally to a stable order in which the living continually aggregate the recent dead to the heroic dead. All the places which a given ayllu saw as significant in this transit were ritually marked. Those which represented the remote, origin-time segments of the system were often so remote or so high as to lie outside the common round of activity. (Important ones were objects of pilgrimage.) A *huaca*'s or group's place of origin was called its *pacarina* or *pacarisca* (from a verb meaning "to begin"); a part of the dead which the Spanish called "spirit" (*anyma*) was thought to return and rest there after the mummy had been enshrined, but it could also be called back for consultation.

The dwellings of *mallquis* (founding ancestors, a colonial spelling), especially those sanctified as embodying the transition from *huaca* origins to genealogically recognized human individuality, were the object of constant attention. A mummy's dwelling was called *machay* (mummy cave); chullpa, "burial house or tower"; *pucullo*, "burial house"; or *aya huasi*, "house of the dead" (Bengtsson n.d.).

Villages which judged each other to have similar customs, similar status vis-à-vis foreign groups, and similar legendary memories described their respective *huaca*s and ancestors as kin to each other. A number of *huaca*s each emblematizing parts or wholes of several villages might be interpreted as a set of siblings who had together shaped the natural and social landscape. For example, several culturally similar ayllus resident in several villages that had in common a historical or legendary concept of themselves as recent conquerors would tend to see their respective *huaca*s as members of a set of invading superhuman siblings. Their respective mummified "founders" would therefore also be kin.

It was typical of the best documented *llacta*s to imagine some of their component ayllus as descended from ancient, valley-owning, agricultural heroes and ancestors (called *huari*, or *llactayoc*), and others as descended from immigrant conquerors whose origin lay in the camelid-herding heights. The latter were called *llacuas*. The set of mummies and *huaca*s housed in a typical western Andean ceremonial center may well have included members of both classes. The ritual regimen described in the Huarochirí manuscript carefully balances and articulates their respective cults within single ceremonial collectivities. One idolatry trial of 1621 (village of Ocros; Duviols 1986a: 467) speaks of the two populations as "interwoven."

Documents rarely clarify at exactly what level political or demographic aggregation corresponded to the transition from human (mummy) to superhuman genealogy. Human mummies of renowned antiquity may have been recognized as the common progenitors of multivillage collectivities, but the wide ethnic aggregations that Tristan Platt (1986) calls "maximal ayllus," which also attributed their own solidarity to common origins, seem to have vested their origin in superhuman figures such as animate mountains called *apu* ("lords"). Local groups which rendered devotion to great regional shrines such as Paria Caca defined their most ancient or most prominent human mummies as the "children" of these major powers. On the whole there existed a tendency to interpret the focalized members of ego's own social structure, and sacralized features of landscape or even cosmos, as nodes in a nested set of genealogically patterned and sometimes more broadly kin-like relationships extending in principle to the whole of the known world.

III. PRIESTLY AND LAY PRACTICE IN THE CULT OF ANCESTORS

To deduce the duties of pre-Hispanic priests from the mid-seventeenth-century sources is unsafe. While seniority in descent apparently weighed in recruitment, by midcolonial times this dangerous duty seems to have become partly a matter of vocation. The "extirpators of idolatry" claimed that "idolators" constituted a priestly hierarchy like that of Roman Catholicism (Huertas 1981; Cock 1980); if correct, this may have much to do with the natives' close acquaintance with, but exclusion from, Roman Catholic clerical careers. Colonial "ministers" (*ministros*) of the ancestors may, however, have sustained some pre-Hispanic practices, especially rites of purification and confession for those asking their dead to send rain, crops, and calves. Priests also gave "consultations" or oracular responses on behalf of mummies. Most importantly, they conducted annual rites to wine and dine, praise and reassure the ancestors. Since mummies were consulted via priests on all important matters including marriages, the "ministry" gave considerable leverage on processes of community reproduction.

It is possible, but not certain, that pre-Hispanic priesthood demanded the supranormal state of rapport with *mallquis*, which the famous and much-persecuted colonial priest Hernando Hacaspoma reached:

> [In the presence of the ancestors] this witness experienced ecstasy, was deprived of his senses, and heard inside himself that the said *malqui* was speaking to him . . . having made the sacrifices he embraced the idol Guamancama, and he experienced another ecstasy and he said that the *camaquen* [forceful spirit] of the said *malqui ratacurca* [Quechua: adhered to him] and descended to his heart and told him what to do in the matter on which they were consulting him. (Duviols 1986a: 143)

Accounts of worship from the viewpoint of lay participants are rare. A late-colonial account from Arequipa affords a close view, albeit one affected by clandestinity. The worshipers ascended to their ancestral caves by moonlight, in a group representing the whole kindred descended from the mummies. Arriving at the cave mouth, the worshipers whistled to ask entry. Inside the cave they greeted the ancestors, who sat or stood among their offerings in a lifelike tableau. Quechua-speakers in secular context, the worshipers invoked their ancestors in Aymara (AA/A [174(8?)–55: fol. 246r]). They mended the mummies' clothing "of ancient style" and served them offerings of coca, small flasks of specially made maize beer in three colors (white, yellow, and red; ibid.: fol. 244v), and lit candles of llama fat. Each member of the "family" then petitioned his or her ancestors for favors: a successful caravan, a profitable sale of wool, skill in learning to weave (fol. 16v-17r). To contract a marriage, prospective in-laws brought the bride and groom before the ancestors of each contracting "family" and asked for an augury. When children reached the age of seven, and had been instructed about clandestinity, parents presented them to the ancestors. Testimonies suggest a climate of solemn communion between newer generations and the ancient mothers and fathers, and at the same time one of affectionate intimacy.

IV. THE FUNCTION OF DEATH IN ANDEAN NARRATIVE

Fernando Fuenzalida Vollmar (1979) has pointed out that Andean societies, which frequently depend on tightly circumscribed resources, produce narratives poignantly evoking the dilemma of fertility that leads into Malthusian danger. The mythology of Huarochirí, for example, voices in four different passages the conviction that excess of fertility is disastrous.

These stories cast in negative terms the positive ideology of ancestry: that individual death is the source of collective life. When elders die they indebt their heirs profoundly. Since in an all but literal sense their death is the precondition of fertility and life, they are due the homage of the living. A code of reciprocity between dead and living was the simple central rule of ancestor cult: dispatching goods by destroying them from among the living, one compensated the dead.

This native exegesis, however, falls short of explaining why the dead were made to exist corporeally in the world instead of becoming metaphysical beings or altruistically disappearing. For such insights we turn to ethnological analyses.

V. THE DEAD, THE RENEWAL OF LIFE, AND THE RELATIONS BETWEEN MORTUARY AND STATECRAFT

Ethnology from its origins has focused and refocused on regularities in mortuary customs which span otherwise diverse peoples. Among these are theories of enduring personhood in the afterlife, models of death as prolonged transition rather than punctual transformation, images of the cemetery as the double of society, death rite as the commemoration of individuality or conversely as the submergence of individuality in the human condition, renderings of mortality as the obverse of fertility, and studies of the role of royal death in statecraft (Humphreys and King 1981; Cederroth and Lindström 1988). To varying degrees all these themes are relevant to Andean data, but few have been fully explored.

Andean peoples are anything but unique in representing mortality as the source of fertility. Probably the most influential recent sociocultural exploration of this perennially fascinating theme is Maurice Bloch and Jonathan Parry's *Death and the Regeneration of Life,* published in 1982.

Bloch and Parry inherited the theme from Sir James George Frazer and Johann Jacob Bachofen, but explain the phenomenon through theoretical terms strongly rooted in an analysis first propounded by Emile Durkheim's associate Robert Hertz in 1907 (1960). The argument is that what shapes customs about the dead is not folk theory about the fate of souls, but the functional imperative of mourning the disappearance of individuals while at the same time reshuffling and reassigning the deceased's roles and interests. It is in the process of reassigning them that society makes explicit and sacralizes patterns of transmission, and thereby comes to describe itself in terms of social structures such as lineage or ayllu:

> If we can speak of a reassertion of the social order at the time of death, this social order is a *product* of rituals of the kind we consider rather than their cause. In other words, it is not so much a question of Hertz's reified "society" responding to the "sacrilege" of death, as of the mortuary rituals themselves being an occasion for *creating* that "society" as an apparently external force. (Bloch and Parry 1982: 6)

Death disrupts the durable interests vested in a system of power (especially rights in land and water or political office). Those who share the dead's interests must reassert them within a new constellation of persons, with unforeseeable consequences. Mortuary rite minimizes the element of unpredictability by treating the physical putrescence of the person as the mere shedding of temporary qualities that inhere in soft flesh. Just as the hard, durable, bony mummy outlasts the fleshy body, so the social constitution of an ancestor results in the retention, with improved stability, of relationships reckoned from him or her. This transition occupies a period, often (as in the Andes) lasting one year after death. What remains is a permanent being made of harder or purer stuff. The ancestor newly enshrined is regarded as standing in unalterable, immortally ordered relationship to other persons. These relationships are the matrix on which the living represent social process as determined, regular, and structured, the model for normative action.

Because it is the embodiment of permanence, the means by which the collectivity creates an ongoing order, the set of ancestors is seen as "the source of the continuing fertility of the living" (Bloch and Parry 1982: 11). Accordingly all functions of reproduction tend to be ceremonialized in the presence of ancestors: planting, harvesting, marriage, and political succession. Because they embody and represent the predictable social bonds and rights on which the living rely—in whose permanence they must trust—the living credit the dead with holding or withholding the potential for future life.

The few well-described Andean mortuary complexes greatly elaborated this idea. Duviols, apparently independently of the Hertzian tradition, drew the conclusion that "These dead, these *mallquis*, are the ones who have given and continue to give life" (1977: 317).

The making and worship of Andean ancestors can (like many other mortuary complexes studied under the influence of Arnold Van Gennep's treatment of funeral as rite of passage) be seen as a double transition: from life to death through funerary rite, and from death to ancestorhood via secondary burial and enshrinement. A second major point at which the Andean case intersects the vast literature of mortuary lore is that of royal death and succession. Because of its long independent development, Inka mortuary stands in interesting comparative relationships to earlier-studied cases of royal transitions in power. Richard Huntington and Peter Metcalf's *Celebrations of Death* (1979) emphasizes the problem of why forms of centralized rule are associated with stupendous aggrandizements of mortuary rite and architecture.

In 1936 and later works A. M. Hocart suggested that the emergence of the early state was an epiphenomenon of the care of the dead:

> Beginning with the striking suggestion that "the first kings must have been dead kings" [Hocart] went on in later works to outline the proposition that "modern" bureaucratic government actually began in a ritual organization and only later took on the administrative function. In Hocart's view, "government" formed around a ritual specialist involved in, as often as not, the ghosts of important men, and the evolution of the state is merely the unintentional byproduct of the ritual attempt to secure life and well-being from supernatural powers." (Huntington and Metcalf 1979: 153)

Whether or not one imagines kingship emerging within the cult of the dead, it is clear regarding Inka as other kinship that the death of the ruler created a troublesome contrast between the overarching permanence which priestly and bureaucratic organization attributed to itself, and the perishability of its human substance. The period during which the royal corpse putresced coincided with the period during which the body politic, its metaphorical extension, had yet to be insured through stable succession. Royal mourning was therefore a period of danger, the one in which all political chickens came home to roost. Many kingdoms treated the anniversary of the royal funeral as a deadline; the foreseeable date for the corpse's transition to ancestorhood was ideally the time by which the appearance of stability had to be restored.

"The Beautiful Grandparents"

Various complex societies have invented differing ways to mitigate the stresses of postmortem turbulence. During the year leading up to the installation of the dead ruler as royal ancestor and the new one as live incarnation of political-cosmic order, at least one all-empire sacrificial cycle is typically called. The central collection, sanctification, and redistribution for sacrifice of homage from all provinces activated the myriad political ties of the center, adjusted them to recent changes in dynastic and regional interests, and thereby repaired the homology between polity and cosmos which would once again be presented as timeless under the rule of the succeeding sovereign. In Inka society the Capac Hucha ("opulent prestation"; see Part VII) did this service.

It is also a common tendency for states to treat royal death as the death of one who is in principle, or at least metaphorically, the kin of all subjects. Royal death is therefore a sort of *general death,* which, since it affected all, was the occasion for expressing feelings of common mortality. Inka ceremony insisted greatly on the replication at smaller local scales of rites performed at the sacred capital. As will be explained below, the Inkas even redistributed human sacrifices during the royal mortuary cycle so as to make local and imperial rites consubstantial. Royal death provided the occasion for demonstrating a microcosm/macrocosm relation between local shrines and the royal tomb, which claimed to stand in ancestor-like relation to all subjects.

This practice, however, entailed a political dilemma: if the dead Inka was ancestor to all, statecraft demanded a demarcator between his civic and his political-genealogical progeny lest sovereignty itself become diffuse. This purpose was answered by the distinction between the civic mummy and a second body, the exuvial vessel left in custody of the deceased's commemorative corporation (*panaca*). The Inkas' second bodies, like the mummies which served as civic ancestors, were indefinitely preserved. Each functioned after death as the token of a durable genealogical collectivity which would preserve the interests built up among political allies during one reign. The commemorative corporation was not, however, to transmit the mandate (for debate on this point see Conrad 1981, and a critique by Duviols 1986b; also Rostworowski 1988: 147; Zuidema 1990: 35–50, 78, 80–81). Other eligible divisions of the Inka caste would succeed (by competition, according to Rostworowski 1960) and create a new live instantiation of the Inka to coexist with the other, preserved ones.

Inka practice, relying as it did on the self-sufficiency and the diversified surpluses of it in innumerable subject villages, tended to impose ceremonial unification only on rare and costly occasions. Daily functioning generally encouraged the retention of signs of Inka separateness in dress, worship, and also mortuary rite, with attention more to arranging complementary and profitable relations among horizontally differentiated parts of the empire than to homogenizing them. Hence, diversity in archaeologically recovered tomb architecture and content does not preclude close integration into Inka rule.

VI. HUAÑUC: THE DEATH CONTINUUM

The colonial Quechua terminology of death distinguishes at least three simplex terms for dead people. They correspond in part to the distinctions inherent in double burial, and will be mentioned successively in that framework.

Intellectual descendants of Van Gennep including Victor Turner have emphasized the fact that death is widely seen as a prolonged process, in some ways coextensive with vitality itself, and mortuary is structured as a series of stages along its advance.

This perception is assuredly relevant to Andean death. *Huañuy* is a colonial and modern Quechua word meaning "to die, or expire, or faint." Its agentive form *huañuc*, "die-ers," was glossed by a Jesuit in 1608 as meaning "the dead, or mortal" (Gonçález Holguín 1989 [1608]: 178–179). Andeans share with many other cultures (and with modern biological science) the conviction that although the end of breathing is a discontinuity, nonetheless death is not an instantaneous event but a gradually manifested attribute of all life (Urioste 1981). Common colonial and modern usages of *huañuy* reflect this. A person is called *huañuc* when he is thought to be approaching death, or is dying, and continues to be called so after expiration for as long as mourning rites continue. The Huarochirí manuscript (Salomon and Urioste 1991: 73, 99, 100, 104, 123, 130) uses the word to mean both those on their deathbed and the lamented dead of recent times.

Expiration signifies that a person has become definitively rather than intermittently or proximately *huañuc*. Being *huañuc* marks passage from vital and fresh, but also formless and mutable, existence to the immutable type of existence typical of very old beings. Plants, animals, and people all pass from soft, juicy, unformed, and fast-changing life states (tender plants, babies) to dryer, harder, more lasting states (dry husks, trees, old people, and finally mummies).

Individuals partake of this process in cumulative, episodic ways long before they expire, for example, via evanescent deaths like fainting. Sleep, disease, and drunkenness also have some commonalities with death. Many Andean elders, as they approach the passage to ancestor status, undergo episodes of unconsciousness considered temporary deaths (Zuidema and Quispe 1973). Stereotyped narratives about these experiences are common. They generally include a stagewise journey at whose end the elder is bidden to stay a while longer among the living. Telling such stories implies putting oneself in a quasi-ancestral posture of authority. The elder, declining in economic and political power, and in all likelihood set about by juniors impatient for inheritance (as in the brilliant ethnographic film "Spirit Possession of Alejandro Mamani"), in effect borrows on his future ancestral standing to influence the reproduction of society while he or she still can. Seventeenth-century elders gave instructions and demanded promises about their own enshrinement and endowment (Duviols 1986a: 471).

Huañuc persons dead less than a year were in colonial times, and still are, considered likely to walk among the living. But even those already enshrined and transformed into permanent ancestors retained some of the powers of individual life and intermittently returned to individual functioning (see below).

The simplest generalization about theory of life and death compatible with consistent motifs in the documents is that a human being consisted of perishable soft parts (softer in younger people); a durable skeleton and hide, which became the lasting person or mummy; and a volatile personal shade or spirit, sometimes visualized as a flying insect, which departed from both soft and hard parts to return to the place of origin (*pacarina*) whence the person came. (This part was also apparently the entity called "*upani* or *camaquen*" [Duviols 1978, 1986a: 67, 92; Taylor 1980]. It could be visualized as a shadow.) Subsequent stages emphasize the parts' separation.

VII. AYA: THE BODY AND FUNERAL RITES

Although the two well-attested Andean mortuary complexes, the Inka and western Andean provincial variants, have commonalities of underlying structure, the details of behavior that leave behind archaeologically visible traits differed between them. For this reason the next three sections present Inka and provincial data under separate subheadings.

After expiration, the corporeal human became an *aya*. Spanish lexicographers rendered the term as "dead body" (Gonçález Holguín 1989 [1608]: 39) and court translators apparently rendered it "cadaver." These Spanish glosses were applied to the dead both during their mourning year and after their enshrinement. (The November rites in honor of mummies were entitled "bearing the *aya*s" according to Guaman Poma 1980 [1615], 1: 230–231; Duviols 1976; Molina [1575?] 1959: 132–135; see Figs. 1-2.)

Funerals in Provincial Society

When a man expired, his leading female mourners organized five nights of intense mourning featuring redistribution of hominy, toasted maize, maize beer, and coca. We have as yet found no detailed description of a woman's funeral. All the dead man's subjects and followers brought gourds of food and coca to lay around his body for his "viands" (*cocabi*) and for gifts to mourners.

At the start of the five nights the head mourners killed llamas or other large animals, sprinkled the deceased's feet and hands with blood, conducted auguries about possible anger or unatoned sins of the dead by inspecting the inflated lungs, and served the meat at dawn. Officiants collected the blood and sprinkled it in the streets during a sunrise procession. The sacrificial animal's head was served to the dead as a propitiation. Already-mummified ancestors received other meat portions and coca and would deliver responses to the survivors' questions. All the mourners sat around a bonfire enjoying coca and corn gifts throughout the five nights. The portion burned in the fire was said to be eaten by the dead (AA/L Idolatría y Hechicerías Leg. 5 exp. 23 1660: fol. 3r; Duviols 1986a: 276). Foods were eaten in the fashion proper to sacred context, that is, without salt or red pepper. Ash from sacrificed meat was nightly scattered at the doorway to detect the footprints of the deceased's "spirit" (*anyma*), which might come back to hear the weeping and praise-singing inside. During this time the deceased's best clothes were washed.

In colonial context, at some point during "the five" the body was buried in church.

> . . . after burying [his wife] and for days afterward, [the widower] went out in search of his wife saying that she was in the village, playing music and dancing the Bayllaco Mayor de Catauari, which was the style in the time of the Incas. . . . he passed the night weeping with Indian men and women who helped him weep (AA/L Idolatrías y Hechicerías Leg. 4 exp. 9–10 1659: fol. 3v).

At the end of the five days, the dead person's close kin swept the home, removed belongings of the deceased in a bundle, and took them away to a ravine. The disposal of the belongings lifted the obligation to grieve publicly. The end of this period was, and still is, associated with ritual gambling using a die-like marked bone (*wayru;* Hartmann 1980: 226–229; Harris 1982: 51; Pærregaard 1987. See also Valderrama and Escalante 1980). Ending "the five," mourners carried the deceased's clothing or wore it as they paraded weeping through streets to the portal of the church.

The hair and nails of the dead were borne to the cave of the mummified ancestors and left there for a year (Duviols 1986a: 198, 200). It is likely that this colonial measure substituted for ancient measures to mummify and purify the whole cadaver after "the five." Chapter 28 of the Huarochirí manuscript says that after "the five" a woman would take out certain clothing (of the dead person?) and conduct the dead to a special place called Yarutini, where she would wait until the "spirit" emerged. The passage is unclear but suggests that signs of putrescence in soft tissues such as the emergence of insects were taken to signify that the volatile part of the person was separating and beginning its journey back to its place of origin. This woman would turn back carrying a stone as token of the deceased's person to his house. He would be fêted for a last time and then dismissed from the society of the living. (See Duviols 1986a: 276 for a related colonial procedure.)

"The Beautiful Grandparents"

Women are described in trials and in the Huarochirí manuscript as playing a leading role in managing the phase during which the soft parts must be disposed of. Men tend to figure as leaders in postenshrinement cult, once the body assumes its rigid, permanent form. This may only reflect the prevalence of male ego/male deceased descriptions. But it may also reflect a phenomenon which Bloch and Parry consider general. These authors suggest that in many cultures the sexual and fleshy fecundity of women is opposed to the "mystical," vegetable-like fertility of ancestors; consequently, women are assigned to handle the decaying flesh so that men can later celebrate "death [as] a triumph over the necessity for affines and over the world of sexual reproduction" (1982: 21).

During the year following expiration the dead person was said to suffer hardships "until he (that is, his 'spirit') could go to his place of origin (*pacarina*)." The dead had to overcome many hazards, including a canyon bridged with human hair, and would curse the living if not helped along his route. Witnesses explained the journey as the return to "*upaimarca* . . . from whence his mummified ancestors came." *Upaimarca* and similar terms apparently refer to origin shrines understood to be the point at which the remotest apical ancestors emerged or branched off from *huaca*s and began their actions on earth. Survivors took measures to redirect the spirit should he stray back to his mortal village instead of going to his immortal home. For example, mourners would walk out on the road while trailing a two-colored string (*cuchica*) that would steer him toward his origin place (AA/L Idolatrías y Hechicerías Leg. 5 exp. 21 1660: fols. 8r, 9v).

Inka Funerals

Juan de Betanzos' recently recovered chapters 30 through 32 (1987 [1551]: 141–150) concern "the gentile rites which [Pachacuti] Ynga Yupangue ordered . . . at the time when he chose to die" (*se quiso morir*). One of many texts in which Pachacuti Ynga Yupangue is treated as culture-giver, this narrative may have conveyed a prototypical or ideal image of royal mourning.

The dying Pachacuti Ynga Yupangue ordered the inhabitants of his house to stop lighting fires or wearing ornaments. The day after his death, still keeping the death secret, the other royals would meet to choose a successor. Meanwhile, his agents would collect sacrificial animals from subject nobles. All the Inkas and residents of the royal house were to wash themselves and color themselves green with an herbal paint. Wives of the sovereign volunteered to accompany him by dancing festively and then letting themselves be strangled drunk. They would be buried at the door of the dead ruler's tomb together with lavish offerings of vessels, beer, coca, and treasures. John Verano's findings on the burial of retainers, in this volume, appear to settle the doubts raised by Carlos Araníbar (1969–70) as to whether Inkas really did inter servitors; they did, at the apex of society, but Araníbar was right in suspecting that the practice was more widespread among non-Inka societies, including those of the more remote past (Donnan, this volume).

According to Betanzos, after the publication of the death all the lord Inkas were to go out into a Cuzco plaza and weep and recite the famous deeds of the deceased. The *bulto* ("three-dimensional form," a term sometimes meaning a sculpture or apparition but in this case apparently meaning mummy bundle) was to be displayed as soon as it was seasoned (*curado*) and arrayed "with the past lords who were there" (i.e., other mummies of the dynasty). An all-empire sacrificial cycle or *capac hucha* was to honor the funeral (Duviols 1976; Molina 1959 [1575?]: 132–135). It required a thousand boys and girls gathered from all provinces, including children of non-Inka ethnic lords. They were dressed and then "married" to each other, and given servants. Officiant priests dispatched them to all regions where the Inka had been ceremonially received. The *capac hucha* children rode in litters carried by their servants, to the places where they would be buried alive, two by two. Each burial would constitute a new permanent shrine. An Inka official accompanied each *capac hucha* and directed the province's mourning for the sovereign. All sacrifices were to be synchronized on a single day. In 1621 Rodrigo Hernández Príncipe detected an Inka shrine created at Ocros by live burial in a *capac hucha,* and was able to recover the oral tradition of its consecration including the speech of a girl about to become a *huaca* (Zuidema 1973; Duviols 1986a: 471–474).

Initial mourning lasted ten days. After the first month, Inkas repeated rituals at each lunar conjunction and each full moon for one year.

At the end of the year they celebrated the anniversary of the death with recitations of deeds by specialist mourners. Commoners observed royal deaths with a simpler version of the same regimen.

In life, each Inka ruler possessed a statue containing his afterbirth, called his "brother," which traveled as his representative to the battlefront and to petitionary rites (J. Acosta 1954 [1590]: 146–148). At death, the ruler's collected hair and nails were united with it, and this "brother" lived on and was revered. (They survived Spanish invasion, but Polo de Ondegardo later sleuthed out and destroyed the "brothers" curated in Cuzco.) After the death of the Inka, it seems, the "brother" was conserved with the body, but served specifically as an emblem of the deceased's estate and commemorative corporation (*panaca*). Thus royal funeral process resulted at the end of one year in a double-bodied permanent Inka. The ruler's mummy proper would dwell in a royal cemetery. It would return to Cuzco for ceremonies and emblematize the continuity of the state. It appeared to embody his broad public relationships, stretching to the ends of Tawantinsuyu. The Inka's second self, containing the remains of his birth and the outgrowths of his body, emblematized his closer kin relationships and was enshrined as the focalized ancestor of a quasi-kin political corporation.

VIII. MALLQUI: ENSHRINED ANCESTORS AND THE COMMUNITY OF THE DEAD

The transformation of a mourned person into a permanent ancestor is perhaps the most revealingly recorded moment in mortuary process. *Mallqui* was a term referring to certain mummies held to be founders of collectivities. Doyle (1988: 95–105) argues that the term applied only to supreme focalized ancestors, in whose shrines the bodies of purported descendants were gathered.

Enshrinement in Provincial Society

In midcolonial times, one year after "the five," kinsmen carried the exuviae back to the house of the deceased (Duviols 1986a: 198) and put them onto the dead's own clothes. This likely corresponds to an older rite in which a purified and completed ancestor (mummy bundle?) was received. A llama was sacrificed. The kindred of the dead invited the community to drink chicha and dance with drums. They sprinkled llama blood on the exuviae, killed a guinea pig or two, and then burned the hairs with coca, maize flour, llama fat, and spiny oyster shell powder, all by way of "sacrifice" (the Spanish used this term; Duviols 1986a: 157, 227).

Exactly where the ancestors were enshrined is hard to tell. Documents refer most frequently to *machayes,* which were, caves or rock shelters on the heights. Some mummy caves were reported to contain several hundred mummies grouped around their respective progenitors, and this is easy to believe given the quantity of desecrated bones still in them today. Other mummies, however, seem to have resided in the small complexes of stone chambers (*colca*) mentioned above, adjacent to ritual plazas and "set slightly apart from the village" (according to a 1657 witness in Duviols 1986a: 200; see also Doyle 1988: 106).

Both types were reportedly in use in the seventeenth century. Guaman Poma took note of their coexistence, supposing the high shelters to be ancient and the "villages of the dead" to be more recent (1980 [1615], 1: 271). Both kinds of structure are clearly visible in the modern Huarochirí landscape, but their chronology is not known archaeologically.

The Huarochirí narrators ca. 1608 (Salomon and Urioste 1991: 73) said that just before the yearly pilgrimage to their great regional *huaca* Paria Caca, worshipers carried out divinations and atonements to make good on any pending duties or claims of the year's dead. Then they carried the year's dead to Paria Caca. Presumably this refers to mummified, not freshly dead, persons.

> On the eve of the day when they were to arrive to Paria Caca for worship, people whose kin, whether men or women, had died in the course of that year, would wail all night long, saying, "Tomorrow we'll go and see our dead by Paria Caca's side!"

> They said regarding their deceased of the year, "Tomorrow is the day when we'll deliver them there."
> They offered the dead food and even fed them that night, and spread out the ingredients for their rituals. They said,
> > "Now I deliver them to Paria Caca forever.
> > They will never come back any more!"
>
> (Salomon and Urioste 1991 [1608]: 173)

Presumably the mummies were then conducted back to their permanent residences.

Enshrinement in Inka Society

For the apex of Inka society, more is known about secondary burial. Betanzos (1987 [1551]: 145–146) closely detailed the rites for installing a new Inka ancestor mummy. One year after the death "they made for him a certain festival which is almost like canonization for a saint." At this month-long festival people put on "disguises." First all the lords and ladies exited the city, formed in "their squadrons" (representing corporate kin groups?), and painted their faces black. They also went to fields which the dead Inka had sowed. Each carried the arms and tools the dead Inka had used, and visited the places which in life he had frequented, calling him and chanting his deeds, and beckoning him by displaying his clothes, tools, and weapons. "They had to do this for fifteen days from morning to evening throughout the hills and lands and houses and streets of the whole city" until the "leading lord" assured them that the dead Inka had indeed reached "his father the sun." They also asked the deceased to give good weather and remove sicknesses.

Several sources purport to detail the splendid dwellings of the Inka dead in the Yucay Valley (J. Acosta 1954 [1590]: 146–148; Garcilaso 1966 [1609]: 323–324).

In Betanzos' account, at the end of the 15 days reserved for retracing the dead Inka's steps, the Cuzco Inkas performed a festival called *purucaya*. Betanzos observed Paullu Inka's *purucaya* in 1550 and saw his mummy enter the great plaza (Cieza de León was also in Cuzco at this time, but felt a scruple against describing such "paganisms"; 1985 [1550]: 178).

On the first day of *purucaya*, four men dressed in feathers and paints came out to the plaza. Betanzos thought them as frightening as devils. Each carried tied at his belt a long cord of fine wool and gold, and ten women in precious garments followed each, tied onto the cord. Two of the men with their retinues stood at one side of the plaza, two at the other. Each man also brought a boy and a girl, the boy with ayllus (*bolas*) and the girl with a golden coca sack. The four men would dance forward and back, gesturing to all sides. As they danced forward the women would release some cord, and as they retreated pull it in. Girl and boy dancers attended. Betanzos

"The Beautiful Grandparents"

understood the four dancers to represent warriors, and the 40 women the will of the ruler, who alternately loosed the warriors in combat or reined them in.

Then two squadrons of warriors representing the Hanan (upper) and Hurin (lower) moieties of Cuzco came out from opposite sides and fought. Hurin would be conquered by Hanan, signifying the sovereign's war victories. All the Cuzco lords joined hands and unanimously recited the dead lord's victories.

Two squadrons of women came out wearing men's garments over their own. One squadron carried rectangular shields and the other halberds. They went around the square at a measured pace. Some men marched among them with slings. This procession marked the Inka's successful arrival at what Betanzos chose to render "sky" or "heaven" (*cielo*).

Betanzos at this point returns from his own observations of 1550 to the culture-heroic dicta attributed to "Ynga Yupangue" (i.e., Pachacuti Inka). He has the great Inka commanding that all participants wash off their year's mourning and return to the plaza carrying the clothes in which they had mourned. All such gear was to be burned in a bonfire. Then those present were to bring a thousand llamas with "vestments" and sacrifice them in the fire, and likewise two thousand without "vestments." The meat was to be shared among the entire city's mourners. An all-empire human sacrificial cycle followed, as described in an earlier part of the same text: a thousand children, male and female, were to be buried in the places where the Inka had slept and rested. (It is not entirely clear whether Betanzos understood there to have been two such cycles for two phases of enshrinement, or whether doublet narratives have been spliced; the latter seems likelier.) All the Inka's treasure was to be buried "under the ground" with him, in his houses, and all his livestock and warehouses burned. At the end, "the new ruler was to make an effigy or bundle (*bulto*) of his body and keep it in his house where all could revere and adore it, because . . . it was canonized, and they held it as sacred."

The adoration of finished royal ancestors deeply impressed Spanish witnesses in the early years of conquest. Cristóbal de Mena, eyewitness to the first Spanish looting of the temples of Cuzco, saw Inkas visiting their dead:

> . . . in that house were many women, and two male Indians as if embalmed. Together with them was a live woman with a gold mask on her face, blowing away with a fan the dust and the flies. And [the dead] had in their hands very rich staffs of gold. The woman would not let anyone come in until the shoes were removed; taking off their shoes they went to see these dried-out bundles. . . . (de Mena [1534] quoted in Valcárcel 1964: 225)

Frank Salomon

In April 1535, Bartolomé de Segovia saw Paullu Inka preside over an eight-day solar and agricultural festival (Inti Raymi) at which several hundred Inka notables conducted a vigil, exhibited their ancestral mummies, and sang them chants of praise as the sacred day dawned (1968 [1553]: 82).[3] Miguel de Estete reported that when in 1537 Paullu Inka returned from the Almagro expedition to Chile, the Inkas initiated a 30-day festival in his honor by placing him at the head of a panoply of mummified sovereigns. Each mummy arrived in a litter with his "livery" to the sound of his own chants of remembrance, and sat in a tent where women and pages attended him with flywhisks. A "reliquary" displayed the exuviae each had left.

IX. MALLQUIS AND ANCESTORS IN CYCLICAL, TRANSITIONAL, AND CRISIS RITES

In principle, the rites described above resulted in the creation of an everlasting person whose presence throughout the annual round of celebrations would voice the claims of social structure.

Cyclical Cult Acts in Provincial Society

Modern rural culture conserves a shadow of the conviction that in conducting the routines of production one is treading the domain of the dead, and that this warrants ritual caution. "The beautiful grandparents" (*los hermosos abuelos*) is a phrase by which modern Huarochiranos refer to the despoiled bones of ancestors, common in local ruins and caves (see Figs. 7-8).

Although positive cult for the pre-Christian dead is rare if not extinct in the Andes, and although in some places the pre-Christian dead are now lumped with the frightful protohumans of remote antiquity, still Andean people regard the ancient dead as demanding at least negative consideration. If one disturbs a tomb, even accidentally, one ought to bring a gift (an animal, coca, liquor, etc.) to its offended tenant. (In Huarochirí, this author repeatedly heard it said that the ancestors sent the pioneer archaeologist and Huarochírano Julio C. Tello a horrible disease to punish him for putting the mummies of his home into museums.)

Certainly the mummies' participation in many annual rites was one of the practices "idolators" most energetically sheltered against colonial rule. If Hernando Hacaspoma's midcolonial testimony is any guide, a typical visit to ancestors began with salutations, offerings, and sharing of news with the dead, and climaxed in conversations between ancestors and the living, with response delivered by the "ministers" of mummies. During these rites, the dispersed parts of the dead person were felt to be temporarily reunited: the volatile spirit "descended" from its rest at its origin shrine to reanimate the

---

[3] Sabine MacCormack, whose *Religion in the Andes* contains details on how the Spanish perception of Inka mortuary developed, cautions that Segovia may have seen the dead Inkas' statuary doubles, not their bodies (1991: 78).

"The Beautiful Grandparents"

Fig. 7 A mortuary building at Llaquistambo near San Damián village in Huarochirí Province, Department of Lima, Peru.

dry mummified body. While the dead "adhered," the "minister" could transmit his or her voice to the living.

Proceedings like this sacralized all the major steps in social reproduction. In provincial society, annual agrarian transitions were conducted with appeals and sacrifices to the ancestors. When planting and harvesting, according to a witness in Cajatambo in 1663 (Duviols 1986a: 190, 198, 407), people offered guinea pigs, grease, coca, and beer to the *mallquis* and prayed saying "Grandfather, give me food and drink and increase my fields." When the maize began to ripen, Cajatambo peasants would sacrifice, confess, ask mummy priests to purify their heads with white maize, attend the tombs, offer first fruits, and abstain from seasonings and sex in honor of the ancestors (p. 204, 274). The festival *vecochina* included all-night contests between parties chanting the glories of their respective *mallquis* (p. 268). Occasional rites of renewal like house reroofing also partook of this regimen (p. 227).

Cyclical Cult Acts in Inka Society

The annual cult of Inka ancestors in Cuzco appears to have retained permanently the division between an inner cult embodying the shared inheritance of the *panaca* or commemorative corporation, which retained the image containing the dead ruler's exuviae, and the public cult celebrating his

Frank Salomon

Fig. 8 "The beautiful grandparents." Despoiled human bones abound in the mortuary buildings and caves of Huarochirí province.

mummy. The mummy was ordinarily lodged at a burial house in Patallacta (according to Betanzos 1987 [1551]: 149), in a large urn, under ground level, with a statue above it. When removed and paraded or displayed in Cuzco, the song dictated by the Inka before his death was sung by "los de su generación" (probably meaning his putative descendants).

X. THE COMMUNITY OF THE ANCESTORS, GENEALOGY, AND THE IMAGE OF SOCIAL ORDER

We return now from ethnographic description to the broader relation between mortuary rites and attributes of social organization. Because they were the tangible emblems of collectivities sharing inherited, localized interests (fields and canals, and sometimes political statuses or privileges), founder-*mallqui*s were focalized as the key reference points in genealogical reckoning. *Mallqui*s made up an ostensibly permanent society of ancestors standing in purportedly constant kin relationships to each other and the living. These relationships were archetypes of correct human relations among localized interest groups.

Mallqui genealogy at the time of the major extirpation research (usually the 1650s–60s) located the hero-ancestors a few generations anterior to Spanish invasion (sometimes as few as two or three and occasionally as many as seven; Duviols 1986a: 466). Although few full genealogies have survived, the known examples suggest a very detailed oral tradition of inheritance. One trial (Ocros 1621; Duviols 1986a: 464–465) contains a "book of the idolators' descent" (*Libro de la generación de idolatras*) which opens with the *huaca* founder of the Llacuases of Ocros, details his four sons as junior *huaca*s, and then switches from superhuman to apparently human genealogy covering three generations prior to Inka rule. The fourth-generation successor won Inka backing by giving his only daughter as a *capacocha*. His son was the last mummy accredited as a pre-Spanish ruler. Genealogy from Spanish conquest onward tends to be evasive as to whether specific post-1532 successors were rescued from the church and mummified, but "cuerpos de cristianos" were discovered in many ancestor shrines.

For reasons bound up with dynastic interests in colonial *curacazgo,* genealogy was recited in no less detail from 1532 onward. Genealogies connecting midcolonial humans to pre-Hispanic and pre-Inka ancestors also make up a substantial corpus in civil litigation over political offices. In these, reference to mummies is never explicit.

The degree of genealogical telescoping or "structural amnesia" involved in such accounts is unknown but probably substantial. Chronologizing is difficult because texts do not commonly contain direct chronological statements other than correlations to the reigns of certain Inka rulers. One reputedly ancient mummy, Tutayquiri, was described by Francisco de Avila's ally Fabián de Ayala as being 600 years old (1966 [1608]: 252).

The world of the ancestors is in many cultures imagined as an eternal version of society, a fixed and prototypical model. Funerary settlements are, therefore, utopias in the sense of being constructed perfect societies, the structural self-images of processual human society (Ragon 1983: 39). The totality of tombs on the landscape could therefore be interpreted as an image of normative social order (as opposed to settlement pattern, and later, to colonially reorganized society). Given enough chronological knowledge of artifacts, therefore, it should be partly possible for archaeologists to trace a *prehistory of ideal social organization.*

Archaeology is already in a fair position to address the cultural heterogeneity of tombs. Since the tomb is usually a symbol of the continuity of the resource-holding kinship group, one might expect that distinctions among groups would leave as their traces differences in mortuary architecture. When an assortment of endogamous groups self-described as ranked but similar in ethnicity and origin coexist, as seems to have been the usual case in pre-Hispanic villages, we might expect to find basically similar cemeteries, each with marked boundaries and similar outward features, but with something distinctive within the inner space. (These tokens of collective self-hood were, however, especially exposed to iconoclasm under Christian rule.) Grossly visible exterior differences of tomb architecture, on the other hand, seem to mark ethnic boundaries. Guaman Poma may have shared a widespread folk theory in taking mortuary customs as a ready index of cultural distance (1980 [1615]: 262–272), although he is atypical in reducing it to five grossly aggregated categories (the Inka center and the four quarters of Tawantinsuyu; see Figs. 3-6).

The local understanding of these constructions will always be hard to know, but perhaps not unguessable. In accord with the image of the cemetery as an ideal community celebrating organizational continuity, it is a common metaphor in Southeast Asia and elsewhere to treat entombed skeletons as symbols of social order (making salient their strength, rigidity, cleanness, and durability) while contrasting them to the perishable flesh, which is the stuff of softer and less enduring connections like sexuality, fellow-feeling, and dependency. Because of the close association of ancestry with the ideology of permanence through inheritance, the paradisiacal organization of ancestors tends to emphasize sibling and descent ties over alliance and affinity; it privileges what preserves the estate over what takes from it. Cult often idealizes descent and inheritance in an imaginary space of permanence "as if" unvitiated by the demands of marriage and affinity.

Bloch and Parry (1982: 27) note that this metaphor sometimes goes so far as to disconnect ancestors from the sexual and therefore affinal way of reproducing, and likening their power of fertility instead to vegetative vitality. The vegetative metaphor certainly pervades Andean mortuary complexes. Catherine Allen (1982) has documented in a modern Andean village a common metaphor likening the dried or shriveled but still life-bearing and life-giving parts of plants (seeds, rhizomes, or stored tubers) to dead people; one should ritually nourish dried tubers (*ch'uñu*) so that they will sustain live humans, and likewise ritually nourish dead humans so that they will sustain the crops. The well-known fact that the word *mallqui* means not only "mummified ancestor" but "the tender plant to be planted" of "any fruit tree" (Sherbondy 1986; Gonçález Holguín 1989 [1608]: 224) is part of a more pervasive vegetative metaphor. It has been pointed out that during the year when the dead body was drying and becoming a mummy, the volatile part called *anyma* in Spanish emerged from the deteriorating flesh, somewhat as living seed escapes a desiccating plant. It would eventually "go to rest at

"The Beautiful Grandparents"

their origins (*pacarinas*) in Upaimarca" (Duviols 1986a: 150, 269, 274, 276). Upaimarca was imagined as an eternal farm, wherein the escaping "anyma," replanted, would regenerate the fertility of its descendants. In the age of the epidemics, one witness said, "so many Indians had died that there's no more for each than a piece of field the size of a fingernail" (Duviols 1986a: 171).

This vegetative metaphor concerning the destiny of the soul constitutes one of the most durable elements of Andean cosmology. It remains clearly recognizable in the Kallawaya funeral complex described by Bastien in this volume. Today the Kallawaya term *uma pacha,* used in colonial times for a concept similar to Upaimarca, still means the high place to which the dead person's vivifying essence returns, and from which it emanates fertilizing energy.

XI. POLITICAL PROCESS AND HISTORICAL INNOVATION IN ANCESTOR CULT

The view of mortuary as a theater of social structure, in which the transgenerational collectivity invents itself as such, implies that ancestor cult fixes all minds on a notion of continuity. But the decisions involved in attaching people to the unchanging ancestral core, interpreting ancestral wishes, and regulating living people's access to ancestors, were freighted with unpredictable and mutable effects on group and personal interests.

Mortuary offices in themselves were fulcrums of power and wealth. Priests who served ancestors accumulated and disposed of substantial parts of the community production surplus, and constituted a managerial or even a propertied elite. They attained advantage in two ways. First, they disposed of large amounts of meat, coca, and perhaps silver offered in sacrifice. Among Paria Caca's Huarochirí worshipers, when *yanca* priests presented new ancestors to Paria Caca, they would assess mourners a fee:

> [Mourners] worshiped with the sacrifice of a small llama, or if they had no llamas, [mourners] would bring coca in large skin bags. . . . After completing these rituals, the *yancas* carried off the heads and loins of those llamas for themselves, no matter how many thousands there might be, declaring, "This is our fee!" (Salomon and Urioste 1991: 73–74)

Second, the mummies had their own endowments (Duviols 1986a: 127, 181, 197, 335). The famous 1657 confession of Pedro Hacaspoma (Duviols 1986a: 153, 162, 275) tells that the endowed fields for each ayllu in his village occupied two whole *tablas* (terraces?) worked by worshipers and reserved for producing maize beer to drink in rites. The ancestor priest in charge of an endowed camelid herd was entitled to half the product for personal use and might even take part of the herd along if he married elsewhere (Duviols

1986a: 158). Endowments fed people engaged in the five-day ritual period of sexual and condimentary abstinence prior to nearly all important ceremonies (Duviols 1986a: 140, 407). While from the believers' viewpoint these intervals may have been chances for people to live directly off the ancestors' generosity, the requirement of client-like relations to mummy shrines may also be read as levies through which priests directed the flow of goods and especially prestige goods through their own hands. Given such facts, could the politics of ancestor worship really have been as conservative as the ideology of genealogical continuity suggests?

Bloch and Parry exaggerate the element of automatism and permanence in the making and maintenance of ancestor cults. The initial establishment of ancestors must have been a product of political processes in the first year of their death. The size and dramatis personae of the exequies, the furnishing of tombs, and so forth, are likely to have been matters of decision and not necessarily of unanimity. Articles in this volume by Dillehay and Drennan stress how heavily the political contingencies facing a dead leader's kin conditioned their decisions about the design and scale of commemorative mounds. In the chiefdom-based cases Dillehay and Drennan study (Araucania and Colombian Alto Magdalena, respectively), funerary architecture appears to have been political successors' way of "banking" the otherwise transient prestige of personalistic leadership. At the village level, central Andean *curacazgo* was in many respects also a kin-based and lightly institutionalized form of leadership, despite Inka subsidies and manipulations,[4] and it is likely that the architecture it generated records the hazards of politics among living social actors more than the schematics of segmentation or other structural definitions of the dead person's role. The options of the living, as Jane Buikstra points out in this volume, range from "direct representation of the deceased individual's composite roles to deliberate distortion," and, as we will see below, there were strong incentives to distort by postmortem aggrandizement.

The rank and consequently the form of a tomb continued to change long after its establishment. A realistic theory of the archaeology of death has to recognize this fact as essential, not incidental, to the functioning of mortuary artifacts. After a resting place was built, the greatness of an ancestor's cult grew or shrank according to its perceived efficacy on descendants' behalf. A kindred's prosperity enhanced the authority of its founders' oracular spokesmen and women. Access to such ancestors became in itself a good worth striving for. The management of cult—from the officiant's position, the

---

[4] To take up Patrick Carmichael's terminology (this volume), the best documented local polities seem to have a double system of inequalities. Segments (typically ayllus) were "ranked" within the community on a continuous gradient of precedence. But those segments ranked highest also enjoyed Inka state privileges sufficient to set them apart as, in some contexts, a discontinuously "stratified" elite.

"The Beautiful Grandparents"

creation of a positive feedback loop amplifying the cult's social potency—may itself have enhanced, and not just reflected ex post facto, the emergence of dominant kinship groupings.

Moreover, Inka examples suggest that the idiom of ancestor worship could express disruption and factional aggression as well as piety and continuity. Betanzos (1987 [1551]: 209–210) explained a key turn of Inka history in terms of politically manipulated funeral rites: when Guayna Capac died in Quito, his body was taken to Cuzco, but Atahualpa and his allies, in Quito, wanted to perform the secondary funeral one year after death in their own right. "They wanted likewise to make certain likenesses or bundles (*bultos*) with certain hairs and fingernails which had been left to [Atahualpa] and of a certain piece of his father's flesh which he had left behind when they dressed him (*adobaban;* the word may also mean 'to tan a hide') to take him to Cuzco." Atahualpa had two "bultos" of the dead ruler made, one to carry with him and the other to leave in Quito at the deceased's own house. A second full ancestor cult was established there, and with it the second, insurgent, Inka political center which was on its way to triumph over Cuzco when the Spanish arrived.

At provincial and village levels the approach of death was the occasion for planning to heighten the affected kindred's standing. Andean *curaca*s prepared before their death tombs not only sufficient to aggrandize their own mummies, but extra vaults so that their descendants might come to be venerated in fealty to their persons (Duviols 1986a: 465).

A dead person was not at the end of his career but at the beginning of candidacy for ancestral greatness. Every death created the potential for mobilizing a faction, the consanguines of the dead, whose salience varied with the interest shared through the deceased.

In Andagua, near Arequipa, in the eighteenth century an incident of antitribute agitation among villagers brought under the spotlight of prosecution some clearly factional developments of ancestor cult (Salomon 1986; Marzal 1988). Each of the self-described "families" of Andagua maintained a mummy shrine, "holding it as a blazon or mark of honor so that others would respect them" (AA/A 174(8?)-54: fol. 173v). But while their ancestor cults, for reasons mentioned above, were usually sharply individuated, they were not so immune from affinal, economic, and factional entanglements as their public facade suggested. A "family" in Andagua was not a self-sufficient unit, neither endogamous nor economically autarkic. When a "family" enjoyed notable success in reproducing, in economic enterprises (dyeing and caravan trade), or in fending off Spaniards and other outsiders, it became more desirable for commercial, political, or marriage alliance. Affines, allies, and defenseless persons in need of patronage sought access to successful families' mummies as the "first and true owners . . . who give wealth and everything we need."

The ancestors of such a family became the foci of political factionalism as well (Newell 1976). Descendants manipulated loyalties by offering to transmit petitions to their mummies as a special favor. At least two factional and economic alliances formed in this way became anticolonial political forces, and successfully challenged not only the village representatives of the Spanish state but the militia sent by the provincial government.

Thus, while the "social structure" created and made visible in mummy shrines, viewed retrospectively, embodied a highly ideological normative order, the manipulation of that display in current social process ran on no preordained track of lineage or other structured reproduction. It was in colonial times politically plastic, open to innovation. It could well have functioned this way long before Spanish times.

Nor were such possibilities limited to princes and other lords. Being constructed as alternative societies, the villages of the dead could sometimes function to focus the hypothetical or critical viewpoint on ordinary society. Seventeenth-century churchmen and administrators found out to their disgust that nominally abandoned "old villages" with their ceremonial plazas and chambers (*aposentillos*) for the dead functioned as efficient redoubts for crypto-Andean and anticlerical belief. They constituted foci for revalidating autochthony and local entitlement as against entitlements conferred by authority in Lima. Places of the dead everywhere are usually marked with a visible threshold or ritual of entry or crossing (Ragon 1983: 65); in the colonial Andes the delimited space of the dead sometimes functioned as a metaphor for the boundedness of the autochthonous group with its immemorial and ancestral claim to resources. There is no obvious reason why they could not have served similarly resistant functions before 1532.

This possibility seems to have evoked imperial counteractions. In pre-Hispanic times mortuary process connected local ancestry to higher political powers. Established ancestors taken as apical to the ayllu, deme, or other group could become important to higher rulers, even at state or imperial level. The Inka state (so Huarochirí narrators told) appropriated and enshrined important local heroes as adoptive members of royal pantheons. Inkas attempted to coopt important descent groups by subsidizing their ancestors' cults, and by concurrently exalting submission to Inkas as a higher form of piety (Silverblatt 1988). The Spanish, as we have seen, set a dangerous goal in minimizing ritual articulation with the ancestry of their Andean subjects. In demanding the reproduction of a largely kin-structured agrarian society while narrowing the point of contact between Andean ancestry and Spanish genealogy to "spiritual kinship" alone, or the remote Adamic connection, they greatly narrowed the possible arena for reciprocal relations of moral economy.

An important negative facet of the problem of politics and the dead, insufficiently studied, is ancestor obliteration (Fortes 1965). We know that seventeenth-century depopulation caused neglect of some ancestors (and anxiety about their hunger), but we do not know what was considered the correct way of extinguishing a cult, nor the specific results of sacrilegious extinctions imposed from without.[5] Presumably when it became impossible to sculpt an image of society—the image known as social structure—from the physical substance of the people, folk theory of social order found other media. The consequences of this shift are the focus of the speculations which follow.

XII. SPECULATIVE CONCLUSIONS

It was in ancestor-venerating practice that Andeans brought into being the model which the Spanish bureaucratized as the colonial ayllu. All senses of the word ayllu denote a kindred reckoned from a focused person. The term ayllu could refer to the kindred of a living or recently dead person, but when it denotes larger units the focus is on ancestral "founders" or apical mummies. Groups self-recognized as culturally similar and historically linked considered their founders as siblings, and generally expressed common origin in terms of a non-mummy *huaca* who was parent to the sib and apex of a larger ayllu. Thus the structure ayllu could be extended to increasingly inclusive nested units focused on increasingly exalted origin figures.

Spanish intolerance of Andean mortuary, therefore, built a paradox deep into the Crown's attempts to utilize preexisting social structure. A regime that allowed ancestors no public and corporeal being, and thereby robbed the prime system for assigning rights and duties of its objective referents, incurred problems of definition. The malleability and manipulability of colonial ayllu categories increased slippage in the colonists' effort to administer purportedly permanent "native" political segments under the term ayllu, and made possible the creation of such paradoxes as "forastero" ("outsider") ayllus—ayllus of people who had no ancestral entitlements (Wightman 1990).

The phenomenon touches many peoples subjected to ancestor-intolerant imperial rule. To what degree are human bodies, as medium, their own message? Does suppressing the corporeal medium of ancestry change the sense in which social structure is itself taken as "real"? For example, if, due to Spanish attacks, known genealogical ancestors ceased to have a different physical nature from remote legendary or mythical or transcendent ones, did social structure by that token become a hypothesis rather than a "known" map of society?

Paul Connerton's distinction between "inscribing" and "incorporating"

---

[5] Victims of extirpation collected ashes of mummies that Spanish clerics had destroyed and reconstituted them in vessels as "burned parents" receiving cult similar to that of mummies.

social knowledge may be useful. An incorporating practice carries meaning through time by lodging it in movements and postures of the body itself; habit and partly unconscious transmission makes it durable, but transmission itself occurs only while bodies are present and enacting the practice. For example, rank has precise incorporative vehicles in most societies: gestures and body poses understood to indicate command, confidence, familiarity with elite custom, or conversely, submission and habituation to labor. Connerton suggests that, because they are more convincing the less conscious attention is paid to them, they tend inherently to get "backgrounded" in a society's reflexive interpretation of itself.

An "inscribing" practice, by contrast, is one which passes meaning through time by vesting it in objects other than living people, such as texts, monuments, etc. Because inscriptions unlike corporeal acts have independent physical existence beyond the moment when a meaning was expressed in them, "inscribed" objects can become problematic, enigmatic, or contradictory vis-à-vis each other and their context. Because they outlive their intelligibility, they tend to become "foregrounded" in a society's representation of itself, subjected to interpretation and redefinition (Connerton 1989: 100–102).

Mummified ancestors transmit both kinds of messages. "Extirpators" noted that in some shrines amazingly successful efforts had been made to give the anestors lifelike postures, gestures, and orientations. These communications from the dead "incorporated" inherited meaning in the most literal possible way. They carried out with special perfection the mission commonly entrusted to incorporating practice, namely, that of inculcating collective sentiments beneath the threshold of awareness and criticism (in this case, local solidarity, the real existence of a corporation outliving the individual, etc.).

On the other hand, in a different sense the makers of mummy shrines inscribed and textualized the meanings associated with the dead. The creation of a mummy display must have entailed propositional or programmatic purpose at the start, when the formal model of genealogy and entitlement was extended another generation: where was one to put the dead in relation to heroes and minor members? For the long haul, such curation vested genealogical propositions in manipulable objects—mummies—which endured long enough to invite and eventually demand interpretation as circumstances around them changed: had the mummy ranked as great, indeed proven great?

The conduct of ancestor cult was not a mechanical consequence of rules of descent but a product of interaction between the repetitive program of inheritance and the historical need to reconcile inherited interests with unpredictable current circumstances. The relative fortunes of corporate groups as time went by invited comparison about their respective ancestors' strength and disposition. Ancestors of kindreds which prospered were credited with power and attracted worship by remote kin, while others languished. Mummies had to be reclothed while fashion and technology changed among the living; their cultural attributes were ever interpreted and evaluated. Continuing commemorative rite in the Andes functioned to comment on and make an object of the same set of relational norms which the enshrinement of mummies proposed. To whatever extent such concerns can be applied to the archaeological record of burial, and especially of ritual treatment after burial, ancestor cult may be readable as the trace of critical and innovative cultural process—a tangible prehistory of a people's idea of itself.

BIBLIOGRAPHY

AA/A (Archivo del Arzobispado de Arequipa)
174(8?)–54 Proceso de Gregorio Taco y otros por haber incitado a los indios de Andagua contra la administración del tributo, y por idolatrías y hechicerías.

AA/L (Archivo del Arzobispado de Lima) Idolatrías y Hechicerías Leg. 4 exp. 9–10
    1659 Causa criminal por querella del fiscal de la visita contra don Juan Gonzales indio de la doctrina de San Juan de Lampian, Juana Caxa, y Leonor Lorica indias de la dicha doctrina por ser hechiseras.

AA/L Idolatrías y Hechicerías Leg. 5 exp. 21
    1660 Causa criminal de hechisera contra Maria Guanico mestisa del pueblo de Quinti y Cicilia Cancha Suyo del ayllo Curitupi.

AA/L Idolatrías y Hechicerías Leg. 5 exp. 23
    1660 Causa criminal de hechisera fecha de oficio contra Ines Chumbi Ticlla india del pueblo de San Lorenço de Quinti del ayllo Guancaya.

AA/L Idolatrías y Hechicerías Leg. 5 exp. 27
    1660 Causa criminal de hechisera fecha de officio contra Maria Pomaticlla del pueblo de Guarochiri y ayllo quiripa y de Catalina Chuquiticlla por otro nombre Calaguaya del pueblo de San Francisco de Calaguaya de los Olleros y de Juana Chuquiticlla del pueblo de Guarochiri = Catalina es del ayllo Lupo.

Acosta, Antonio
    1987 La extirpación de idolatrías en el Perú: Origen y desarrollo de las campañas. A propósito de *Cultura andina y represión*. *Revista Andina* 9: 171–195.

Acosta, José de
    1954 [1590] *Historia natural y moral de las Indias*. Ediciones Atlas, Madrid.

Albornoz, Cristóbal de
    1984 [1583?] Instrucción para descubrir todas las guacas del Piru. In *Albornoz y el espacio ritual andino prehispánico* (Pierre Duviols, ed.). *Revista Andina* 3: 169–222.

Allen, Catherine
    1982 Body and Soul in Quechua Thought. *Journal of Latin American Lore* 8 (2): 179–196.

Araníbar, Carlos
    1969–70 Notas sobre la necropompa entre los Incas. *Revista del Museo Nacional* 36: 108–142. Lima.

Arriaga, Pablo Joseph de
    1968 [1621] *The Extirpation of Idolatry in Peru* (L. Clark Keating, ed. and trans.). University of Kentucky Press, Lexington.

Avila, Francisco de
1966 [1608] Tratado y relación de los errores, falsos dioses y otras supersticiones y ritos diabólicos en que vivían antiguamente los indios de las provincias de Huaracheri, Mama y Chaclla. In *Dioses y hombres de Huarochirí: Narración quechua recogida por Francisco de Avila* [¿*1598?*]. José María Arguedas, trans.): 198–217. Instituto Francés de Estudios Andinos/Instituto de Estudios Peruanos, Lima.

Bengtsson, Lisbet
n.d. Grave Chambers at Kachiqhata and Markaqocha in the District of Ollantaytambo, Cusco Department, Peru. Paper presented at the 47th International Congress of Americanists, New Orleans, 7–11 July 1991.

Betanzos, Juan de
1987 [1551] *Suma y narración de los Incas* (María del Carmen Martín Rubio, ed.). Ediciones Atlas, Madrid.

Bloch, Maurice
1981 Tombs and States. In *Mortality and Immortality: The Anthropology and Archaeology of Death* (S. C. Humphreys and Helen King, eds.): 137–148. Academic Press, London.

Bloch, Maurice, and Jonathan Parry
1982 Introduction: Death and the Regeneration of Life. In *Death and the Regeneration of Life* (Maurice Bloch and J. H. Parry, eds.): 1–44. Cambridge University Press, Cambridge.

Caillavet, Chantal
1988 Una "relación geográfica" inédita de 1582 sobre Ecuador: Oyumbicho y Amaguaña del Valle de los Chillos. *Revista Andina* 12: 525–535.

Cederroth, S., C. Corlin, and J. Lindström (eds.)
1988 *On the Meaning of Death: Essays on Mortuary Rituals and Eschatological Beliefs*. Almqvist and Wiksell International, Uppsala Studies in Cultural Anthropology 8. Stockholm.

Cieza de León, Pedro
1985 [1550] *Crónica del Perú. Segunda parte* (Francesca Cantù, ed.). Pontificia Universidad Católica del Perú, Lima.

Cobo, Bernabé
1964 [1653] *Historia del nuevo mundo* 2. Biblioteca de Autores Españoles. Ediciones Atlas, Madrid.

Cock, Guillermo
1980 *El sacerdote andino y los bienes de las divinidades en los siglos XVII y XVIII*. Licenciatura tesis, Pontificia Universidad Católica del Perú.

Connerton, Paul
1989 *How Societies Remember*. Cambridge University Press, New York.

Conrad, Geoffrey
1981 Cultural Materialism, Split Inheritance, and the Expansion of Ancient Peruvian Empires. *American Antiquity* 46: 3–26.

Conrad, Geoffrey, and Arthur Demarest
　　1984　*Religion and Empire: The Dynamics of Aztec and Inca Expansionism.* Cambridge University Press, New York.

Doyle, Mary Eileen
　　n.d.　The Ancestor Cult and Burial Ritual in Seventeenth and Eighteenth-Century Central Peru. Ph.D. dissertation, University of California at Los Angeles, 1988.

Duviols, Pierre
　　1966　Un procès d'idolatrie. Arequipa, 1671. *Fenix, Revista de la Biblioteca Nacional* 16: 198–211. Lima
　　1973　Huari y Llacuaz: Agricultores y pastores, un dualismo prehispánico de oposición y complementaridad. *Revista del Museo Nacional* 39: 153–191. Lima.
　　1976　La Capacocha: Mecanismo y función del sacrificio humano, su proyección, su papel en la política integracionista, y en la economía redistributiva del Tawantinsuyu. *Allpanchis* 9: 11–57.
　　1977　[1972] *La destrucción de las religiones andinas (conquista y colonia)* (Albor Maruenda, trans.). Universidad Autónoma Nacional de México, Mexico D.F.
　　1978　'Camaquen, upani': Un concept animiste des anciens Péruviens. In *Amerikanistische Studien: Festschrift für Hermann Trimborn* (R. Hartmann and U. Oberem, eds.): 132–144. Collectanea Instituti Anthropos 20. St. Augustin, Switzerland.
　　1986a　*Cultura andina y represión: Procesos y visitas de idolatrías y hechicerías, Cajatambo, siglo XVII.* Centro de Investigaciones Rurales Andinos, Archivos de Historia Andina 5. Cuzco.
　　1986b　(Review of) Geoffrey W. Conrad and Arthur A. Desmarest [sic], *Religion and Empire. L'Homme* 99: 150–151.

Fortes, Meyer
　　1965　Some Reflections on Ancestor Worship in Africa. In *African Systems of Thought* (Meyer Fortes and G. Dieterlen, eds.). Oxford University Press, London.
　　1976　An Introductory Commentary. In *Ancestors* (William H. Newell, ed.): 1–16. Mouton Publishers, The Hague and Paris.

Fox, John W.
　　1987　*Maya Postclassic State Formation.* Cambridge University Press, New York.

Fuenzalida Vollmar, Fernando
　　1979　Los gentiles y el origen de la muerte. *Revista de la Universidad Católica* 5: 213–222. Lima.

Garcilaso Inka de la Vega
　　1966　[1609] *Royal Commentaries of the Incas and General History of Peru.* Part One (Harold V. Livermore, trans.). University of Texas Press, Austin.

Gonçález Holguín, Diego
　　1989　[1608] *Vocabulario de la lengua general de todo el Perú llamada lengua Qquichua o del Inca.* Universidad Nacional Mayor de San Marcos, Lima.

GUAMAN POMA DE AYALA, FELIPE
    1980   [1615] *Nueva corónica y buen gobierno*, 3 vols. (John V. Murra and Rolena Adorno, eds.; Jorge L. Urioste trans.). Siglo XXI, Mexico D.F.

GUILLÉN GUILLÉN, EDMUNDO
    1983   El enigma de las momias incas. *Boletín de Lima* 28 (5): 29–42.

HAMPE M., TEODORO
    1982   Las momias de los Incas en Lima. *Revista del Museo Nacional* 46: 405–418. Lima.

HARRIS, OLIVIA
    1982   The Dead and the Devils among the Bolivian Laymi. In *Death and the Regeneration of Life* (Maurice Bloch and J. H. Parry, eds.): 45–73. Cambridge University Press, Cambridge.

HARTMANN, ROSWITH
    1980   Juegos de velorio en la sierra ecuatoriana. *Indiana* 6: 25–274.

HERNÁNDEZ PRÍNCIPE, RODRIGO
    1923   [1622] Mitología andina: Idolatrías de Recuay, 1622. *Inca* 1: 25–78.

HERTZ, ROBERT
    1960   [1907] A Contribution to the Study of the Collective Representation of Death. In *Death and the Right Hand* (R. and C. Needham, trans.): 27–86. Free Press, Glencoe, Ill.

HUERTAS VALLEJOS, LORENZO
    1981   *La religión en una sociedad rural andina (siglo XVII)*. Universidad Nacional San Cristóbal de Huamanga, Ayacucho, Peru.

HUMPHREYS, S. C., AND HELEN KING (EDS.)
    1981   *Mortality and Immortality: The Anthropology and Archaeology of Death*. Academic Press, London.

HUNTINGTON, RICHARD, AND PETER METCALF
    1979   *Celebrations of Death: The Anthropology of Mortuary Ritual*. Cambridge University Press, New York.

JIMÉNEZ DE LA ESPADA, MARCOS (ED.)
    1965   *Relaciones geográficas de Indias*, 3 vols. Ediciones Atlas, Madrid.

MACCORMACK, SABINE
    1991   *Religion in the Andes: Vision and Imagination in Early Colonial Peru*. Princeton University Press, Princeton, N.J.

MARZAL, MANUEL
    1988   La religión andina persistente en Andagua a fines del virreinato. *Histórica* 12 (2): 161–181. Lima.

MILLONES, LUIS
    1967   Introducción al estudio de las idolatrías. *Aportes* 4: 47–82. Instituto Latinoamericano de Relaciones Internacionales, Paris.
    1984   Shamanismo y política en el Perú colonial: Los curacas de Ayacucho. *Histórica* 8 (2): 131–149. Lima.
    1990   *El retorno de las huacas: Estudios y documentos del siglo XVI* (ed.). Instituto de Estudios Peruanos, Lima.

MOLINA, CRISTÓBAL DE
　1959　[1575?] *Relación de las fábulas y ritos de los Incas* (Ernesto Morales, ed.). Editorial Futuro, Buenos Aires.

NEWELL, WILLIAM H.
　1976　Good and Bad Ancestors. In *Ancestors* (William H. Newell, ed.): 17–29. Mouton Publishers, The Hague and Paris.

PÆRREGAARD, KARSTEN
　1987　Death Rituals and Symbols in the Andes. *Folk* 29: 23–42.

PLATT, TRISTAN
　1986　Mirrors and Maize. In *Anthropological History of Andean Polities* (John V. Murra, Jacques Revel, and Nathan Wachtel, eds.): 228–259. Cambridge University Press, New York.

PONCE LEIVA, PILAR (ED.)
　1992　*Relaciones histórico-geográficas de la Audiencia de Quito (siglos XVI–XIX)*. Marka / Abya-Yala, Quito.

RAGON, MICHEL
　1983　[1981] *The Space of Death: A Study of Funerary Architecture, Decoration, and Urbanism* (Alan Sheridan, trans.). University Press of Virginia, Charlottesville.

RAMÍREZ HORTON, SUSAN
　n.d.　*Huaca* Looting on the Peruvian North Coast—A Tale with Two Perspectives. Manuscript, 1993.

ROSTWOROWSKI DE DIEZ CANSECO, MARÍA
　1960　Succession, Coöptation to Kingship, and Royal Incest among the Inca. *Southwestern Journal of Anthropology* 16: 417–427.
　1988　*Historia del Tawantinsuyu*. Instituto de Estudios Peruanos, Lima.

SALOMON, FRANK
　1986　Ancestor Cults and Resistance to the State in Arequipa, ca. 1748–1754. In *Resistance, Rebellion, and Consciousness in the Andean World, 18th to 20th Centuries* (Steve J. Stern, ed.): 148–165. University of Wisconsin Press, Madison.
　1987　Ancestors, Grave Robbers, and the Possible Origins of Cañari "Incaism." In *Natives and Neighbors in South America: Anthropological Essays* (Frank Salomon and Harald Skar, eds.): 207–232. Göteborgs Etnografiska Museum, Etnografiska Studier 38. Gothenburg.

SALOMON, FRANK, AND GEORGE URIOSTE (EDS. AND TRANS.)
　1991　*The Huarochirí Manuscript, a Testament of Ancient and Colonial Andean Religion*. University of Texas Press, Austin.

SEGOVIA, BARTOLOMÉ DE
　1968　[1558] Relación de muchas cosas acaesidas en el Perú. [Formerly attributed to Cristobal de Molina "cuzqueño".] In *Crónicas peruanas de interés indígena* (Francisco Esteve Barba, ed.): 57–95. Ediciones Atlas, Madrid.

SHERBONDY, JEANNETTE
    1986   *Mallki: Ancestros y cultivo de árboles en los Andes*. Ministerio de Agricultura/Instituto Nacional Forestal y de Fauna, Organización de las Naciones Unidas para la Agricultura y la Alimentación, Lima.

SILVERBLATT, IRENE
    1988   Imperial Dilemmas, the Politics of Kinship, and Inca Reconstructions of History. *Comparative Studies in Society and History* 30 (1): 83–102.

TAYLOR, GERALD
    1980   Supay. *Amerindia* 5: 47–63.
    1987   *Ritos y tradiciones de Huarochirí del siglo XVII*. Instituto de Estudios Peruanos/Instituto Francés de Estudios Andinos, Historia Andina 12. Lima.

URIOSTE, GEORGE
    1981   Sickness and Death in Preconquest Andean Cosmology: The Huarochirí Oral Tradition. In *Health in the Andes* (Joseph Bastien and John Donahue, eds.): 9–18. American Anthropological Association, Washington, D.C.

VALCÁRCEL, LUIS E.
    1964   *Historia del Peru Antiguo,* vol. 3. Editorial Juan Mejía Baca, Lima.

VALDERRAMA FERNÁNDEZ, RICARDO, AND CARMEN ESCALANTE GUTIÉRREZ
    1980   Apu Qorpuna (visión del mundo de los muertos en la comunidad de Awkimarca). *Debates en Antropología* 5: 233–269.

VARÓN GABAI, RAFAEL
    1990   El Taki Onqoy; las raíces andinas. In *El retorno de las huacas: Estudios y documentos del siglo XVI* (Luis Millones, ed.): 331–405. Instituto de Estudios Peruanos, Lima.

WIGHTMAN, ANN M.
    1990   *Indigenous Migration and Social Change*. Duke University Press, Durham, N.C.

ZUIDEMA, R. TOM
    1973   Kinship and Ancestorcult in Three Peruvian Communities: Hernández Príncipe's Account of 1622. *Bulletin de l'Institut Français d'Études Andines* 11 (1): 16–33.
    1990   [1984] *Inca Civilization in Cuzco* (Jean-Jacques Decoster, trans.). University of Texas Press, Austin.

ZUIDEMA, R. TOM, AND ULPIANO QUISPE
    1973   A Visit to God. In *Peoples and Cultures of Native South America* (Daniel Gross, ed.): 358–374. Doubleday/Natural History Press, New York.

The Mountain/Body Metaphor Expressed in a Kaatan Funeral

JOSEPH W. BASTIEN
UNIVERSITY OF TEXAS AT ARLINGTON

Andean burials, then and now, are performed with rituals that evoke metaphorical understandings of the living's relationships to the ancestors, land, ayllu, and community. An analysis of metaphor in a recent burial ritual of Guillermo Bautista, a Kallawaya of ayllu Kaata in Bolivia, illustrates this and provides an alternative methodology for scholars to interpret ancient grave sites.

According to Western funerary practices, scholars interpret ancient Andean burial as *memorials* that have functional significance for the living in regard to political and social aspects of the culture. Such an interpretation is limiting in the burial ritual of Guillermo. His funeral and the annual commemorative ritual, Feast with the Dead, aesthetically and symbolically present a metaphor for a cyclical process of life to death and death to life that is related to these people's understanding of their land. Rituals provide visual images that are analogies for Andeans' understanding of themselves, their land, society, and ayllu. The visual images provide experiences of metaphorical journeys and banquets with the living and the dead. Moreover, metaphors of journeys and banquets become parts of community metaphors, such as the mountain/body metaphor of ayllu Kaata.

Advantages of the metaphorical approach is that it provides anthropologists and art historians with a methodology that focuses on the function, context, and formal properties of grave objects. Grave artifacts are studied as representations with formal and aesthetic properties that require interpretation of relationships of Andeans to images, social memory, and metaphor. This relationship functions on several cognitive registers, ranging from perception through the conversion of visual experiences into metaphors for other kinds of experience: psychological solace, cosmological understanding, and cultural and social continuity.

Another advantage is that there are many forms of representations found in Andean burial sites: pictographs on weavings, ceramics, and tombs; positions and placement of bodies and tombs; adornment of clothing and jewelry; and architectural structures. Although each representation has its own biography, when they are clustered in funerary rituals they are subjects of a social memory or an inscribed modality of remembering (Connerton 1989).

Melion and Kuchler (1991: 30) describe social memory:

> In a preliterate culture, . . . (images) are remembered for themselves and are passed on to others as something to hold in memory. The very manner of their transmission, involving both remembering and forgetting, fashions the intellectual field of the culture that in turn responds to the concerns arising from socially and historically relevant situations.

Within the southern Andes social memory is frequently inscribed with images that are structured according to metaphors that correspond to configurations of the sky, land, mountain, body, and ayllu. Within Kaata, as illustrated in this article, a primary cognitive pattern shaping social memory is a mountain/body metaphor. Configurations in one area provide scholars with a key to understanding correspondences in other areas. Thus, clues to what metaphor(s) were evoked for the beholders by the visual images found at the ancient site can be found in spatial configurations of the village, ayllu structure, lineage patterns, and ritual paraphernalia.

Frequently these configurations have been reduced to basic structures that are mathematical or reciprocal, such as the binary, triadic, or quadripartite divisions so well-documented for Inka society and extrapolated for other communities throughout the southern Andes. Although these relationships can be found within metaphors, these simple structures do not adequately explain aesthetic, cognitive, experiential, and biographical aspects of representations nearly as well as metaphors. Andean metaphors are aesthetically more appealing and perceptual than structural paradigms. Metaphors enable Andeans to form elaborate systems of correspondence, richly textured by language, imagery, experience, cognition, and performance.

METAPHORS THROUGHOUT ANDEAN CULTURE

A distinctive mark of Andean culture is the application of metaphor to land, society, and the dead. Andeans think about their territory and communities according to anatomical paradigms of animals and people. Early Peruvians planned the space in their ancient cities according to metaphors of birds and animals (Schaedel, personal communication, 1978). They furrowed outlines of large animals into surfaces of the Nazca Valley between A.D. 200 and 600 (Mason 1968: 88). These metaphors served as maps oriented to high mountain shrines (Reinhard 1985a).

Along similar spatial-metaphorical orientations, ceremonial centers of Chavín (900–200 B.C.) and Tiwanaku (A.D. 400–1200) were located relative to the most sacred mountains in each region, and mountain worship was a principal reason for their construction. Priests at the Chavín complex used water channels for ritual purposes. The water originated from the melting snows of a sacred mountain—Huantsan (20,500 ft), whose rivers partake of the mountain's power and sacred character. In the central Andes, Tiwanaku is located near Mount Illimani (20,500 ft), seen as the most powerful mountain deity over the altiplano and mountains surrounding Lake Titicaca. According to the Inkas, Lake Titicaca supplied water to the mountains, which distributed the water to the animals, plants, and people. Tiwanaku was also important because it was centrally located between the sierra and Amazonian lowlands (Reinhard 1985b).

Mountains were, and still are, important metaphors in fertility as well as controlling deities in meteorological matters. They concentrate water that is needed for life. Like the body, they are centers that concentrate and disperse vital principles (Bastien 1987: 73–76).

During the fourteenth and fifteenth centuries, the Inkas designed Cuzco according to the metaphor of a puma (Rowe n.d.: 60). The spatial organization of Cuzco was also symbolic of their social structure (Zuidema 1964, 1968). The Huarochirí legends, preconquest oral traditions of the central Andes, depicted the mountain as a human body with the summit of the mountain as the head, the central slopes as the chest and shoulders, and the places where two rivers diverge below the central slopes as the crotch and legs.

Throughout the conquest, metaphors persisted, and today the Aymara people of Jesus de Machaca, a community near Tiwanaku, Bolivia, still refer to their land as divided and integrated according to the parts of a cougar (Albo 1972; Bonilla and Fonseca 1967). Aymaras in a community of the Department of Oruro perceive of the spread of disease in the body as similar to the rotational use of four *aynoqas* for planting, employing land use as a metaphor for body concepts and disease. Aymaras in a neighboring community refer to their ayllus as fingers (Oscar Velasco, personal communication, 1986). Quechuas in a community near Cuzco, Peru, continue to use astronomical metaphors for geographical and political organization of their community (Urton 1981).

Metaphors were, and still are, unifying principles between ecological levels and groups within the Andes. Moreover, performance and symbols of burial rituals continue to express these metaphors.

THE MOUNTAIN/BODY METAPHOR OF AYLLU KAATA

For the Kallawayas in the southern Andes, a mountain/body metaphor is evoked in rituals, toponyms, and body concepts to unite distant and distinct Andeans into an ayllu. Approximately 13,000 Kallawayas live in the Province of Bautista Saavedra, midwestern Bolivia, north of Lake Titicaca, and bordering on Peru. They live on extensive valleys that extend from 6,000 to 17,000 ft, which they refer to as *cabecera del valle*. Kallawayas distinguish their communities according to the mountain on which the community is located. They call these mountains ayllus, and each ayllu has communities on low, middle, and high levels of the mountain. Kallawayas have nine ayllus, namely, Amarete, Chajaya, Chari, Chullina, Curva, Inka, Kaalaya, Kaata, and Upinhuaya. Without calculating vertical relief, these ayllus cover 925 square miles (2,252 km square).

According to an ayllu division of labor, the communities on each mountain specialize in some profession. The ayllus exchange services and supply each other, as well as other parts of the Andes, with necessary resources. Ayllus Amarete, Chajaya, and Upinhuaya, for example, provide the potters, jewelers, tool and hat makers for the province. The people of ayllu Amarete mold pottery and carve wooden tools, and ayllu Chajaya, famous for jewelers, who once fashioned ornaments for ruling Inkas, furnishes jewelry for many Kallawayas. According to a unique technique, Upinhuayas press sheep wool into dress hats. Herbalists of ayllus Curva and Chajaya are experts in the use of medicinal plants. Diviners of ayllu Kaata are sought after for their ritual and prophetic skills.

The people of ayllu Kaata understand their ayllu according to a mountain/body metaphor (see Bastien 1978, 1987). Kaatans understand the ayllu as a vertical, triangular land mass divided into high, center, and low ecological zones in which communities live; its solidarity is formed by kinship ties, common earth shrines, exchange of resources, and a metaphorical understanding of places, communities, and levels reflecting body parts. Ayllu Kaata has three major communities of Niñokorin, Kaata, and Apacheta.

The people of Niñokorin are Quechua speakers who farm corn, wheat, barley, peas, and beans on the lower slopes (10,500–11,500 ft). The people of Kaata speak Quechua and cultivate oca, Oxalis species, and potatoes on rotative fields of the central slopes (11,500–14,000 ft). The people of Apacheta speak Aymara and herd sheep in the highlands (14,000–17,000 ft) of the ayllu.

Traditionally, people from the three levels exchange produce and provide each other with the necessary carbohydrates, minerals, and proteins for their balanced subsistence. And the members of these communities maintain social ties by marriage exchange and ritual kinship. People of the three communities use toponyms that correspond to different levels and parts of the mountain/body metaphor (Bastien 1987). The upper level has an *uma* (head), *ñawi* (eyes); the middle level has *sixa* (stomach) and *sonco* (heart); and the lower level has *chaquis* (legs) and *sillus* (toenails, which are indentations on the river). They use the metaphor of the human body to understand their ayllu: Apacheta corresponds to the head, Kaata to the trunk, and Niñokorin to the legs. Just as the parts of the human body are organically united, so are the three levels of ayllu Kaata. Rivers, underground streams, and tunnels link the levels together.

Social structure of ayllu Kaata corresponds to the mountain/body metaphor in that marriage is an exchange of spouses between people living on high, central, and low levels (Bastien 1973). There is a pattern of exogamous levels and virilocality within ayllu Kaata which is now being replicated in community Kaata, transforming it into a mini-ayllu with high, central, and low levels. This illustrates the flexibility and isomorphic properties of this metaphor. Women cross levels in marriage but equally inherit land according to bilineal inheritance patterns customary among Quechuas. Girls frequently marry a man from their mother's level where they have land and, all things being equal, are more attractive to boys needing access to land. Men remain on their level with a patrilineal claim to land. Their claim is an ancestral and permanent rite to property founded on a male descendant working the land and performing rituals to its shrine and to an ancestor buried in the community cemetery.

DEATH AND BURIAL OF GUILLERMO

Within burial rituals, Kaatans employ visual images and performances to express these relationships and to evoke a mountain/body metaphor for participants that perceptually and cognitively links them with ancestors, ayllu, and land. Metaphorically understood, land provides a more enduring reminder of proper ancestral behavior in regard to the ayllu than the living people who die. Ethnographically, this metaphorical process is illustrated in the funeral of Guillermo Bautista, at whose burial I participated.

On the second day of the Fiesta of the Holy Cross, 14 September 1972, Guillermo fell backwards from a wall where he sat intoxicated and enjoying the music. The house sat on a cliff, and the courtyard wall, which was only three-feet high inside the patio, dropped twenty feet to a gravel road. Guillermo's head and shoulders crashed against a sharp rock. Four men carried Guillermo home. Guillermo's wife, Refilda, sobered instantly when she realized his spinal column had been seriously injured. Guillermo was paralyzed from his neck to his toes. And for days they tried to cure him.

As everyone realized, Guillermo was dying. They considered taking him to a hospital in Ancoraimes, but decided not to because if he died on the journey or in Ancoraimes his body would be buried where he died. According to Andean custom, people are buried where they die, otherwise they take the harvest with them. Moreover, the Indians of ayllu Kaata believed that if Guillermo were buried away from Mount Kaata, then he could not reach the *Uma Pacha* (head place) of the mountain, neither could Guillermo banquet with his living descendants during the Feast with the Dead, the annual commemorative banquet for the dead.

Joseph W. Bastien

The *Uma Pacha* is the mythological place of origin and return for people, animals, time, and history in the highlands of ayllu Kaata. Kaatans associate *uma* with head and water, and *pacha* with space and time. The highland lakes of Apacheta are associated with the "eyes" of the mountain/body metaphor. During the Feast of All Colors, Apachetans perform rituals to these lakes which they symbolize as producing *illas* or reflections generative of humans and animals emanating from these lakes. The dead travel through the underground waterways up the three levels to the highland lakes where they are born again.

Guillermo's mortal accident brought into focus these metaphorical and cosmological considerations for Kaatans, and a diviner, Teodoro Yanahuaya, was summoned to read the coca leaves to decide whether Guillermo was going to live.

Teodoro placed coca over Guillermo's heart for several minutes. He selected several leaves and marked them by tearing pieces from the side of the leaf.

"*Manan allinchu!*" ("Not good!"), he said finally, and Guillermo's wife broke into loud crying. The diviner said that his blood was running out and that he would die away from the mountain if he went to Ancoraimes. To die in Ancoraimes would negate Guillermo's claim to the land that he once worked because he would be buried there and not within ayllu Kaata.

Guillermo began bequeathing his land to his relatives, asking that the Secretary of Education of Kaata register this in a notebook. Guillermo's wife, Refilda, sat close to him as he listed lands he had inherited from his father and his mother. He named the distinct places of the lower fields, and then his terrace in each rotative field: Waterhole for the Skunk (*Añas Unoyuh*), Two Faces (*Iskay Uya*), Rounded Terrace (*Muyupata*), and Lord of the Black Bull (*Yana Toroyuh*).

As Guillermo named the places where he had plowed, planted, and harvested since he was four years old, everyone relaxed and mentally made the journey with him through the lower and rotative fields. They were happy, not so much to receive land, as to know that Guillermo was associated with so many places. By cultivating these places, Guillermo had become a part of the mountain, which would remain forever. By burial, he would enter into its life- and death-giving forces.

Life comes from and returns to the earth. Kaatan children grow with the earth of which they become a part at death. Together with their parents, they feed the earth, put it to sleep, give it drink, plow, germinate, nurture, and harvest its gifts. When Kaatan children are able to do these things alone, they become adults. Each time this cycle of the earth involves them they become more of an adult (*runa*), an elder (*pasado runa*), and finally a completed person or ancestor (*machula*).

The Mountain/Body Metaphor Expressed in a Kaatan Funeral

The designation *runa* begins when adolescents assume leadership roles within the hierarchical cargo transformed to fit the secretary system of Bolivian Agrarian Reform laws in 1953 (see Bastien 1978: 61–62). *Pasado runa* is given to commoners who have completed secretarial roles within the community. This designation is more a function of role performance than age, and some young adult Kaatans deliberately seek these roles to become *pasado runa*, completed persons, so that they have greater authority within the community. *Machula* is sometimes used to designate ancestors of significance and at other times to refer to distinguished diviners (*yachajkuna*), because they feed the ancestors with ritual foods.

According to Kaatans, one becomes a person progressively throughout life and death. Within this process of becoming, Kallawayas consecutively perform agricultural, political, and ceremonial roles within the community that enable them to become elders and influential members of the community. Through ritual and metaphorical understandings, Kaatans believe that elders continue becoming and being after death as ancestors and that they affect agriculture, health, and social relations. Mediators between elders and ancestors are diviners (*yachajkuna*), especially the chief diviner (*machula watayuh purijchej*) (Ancestor, Lord of the Year, and He Who Guides). Sarito Quispe was the chief diviner in 1972 (see Bastien 1973 and 1978). Through coca divination and rituals, diviners communicate and mediate between the living and the dead. As rites of passage, funerals celebrate an elder becoming an ancestor, and as metaphors, funerals suggest a journey of the deceased within the ayllu climbing up its three levels.

Guillermo was an elder who had accumulated land that was bequeathed equally to his children. It was kept in trust for them by their mother and the eldest son. When they came of marrying age, it became their land, and they took care of their mother. The living Guillermo guaranteed his patrilineal claim to land in writing, and everyone knew that the dead Guillermo would haunt them if they failed to work this land.

JOURNEYING TO THE *UMA PACHA*

During the burial rite of Guillermo, clothes, food, coca, chicha, and alcohol were given to him for the journey to the *Uma Pacha* or Place of Origin. His body was turned toward the summit of ayllu Kaata and given a candle for this dark trip. The burial ritual prepared him for a journey along the underground rivers to the *Uma Pacha*. A similar journey is described in the Huarochiri oral tradition.

> When they captured a prisoner, they cut his face. "This is our strength," they said and made dance.... the prisoner said, "Brother, you are going to kill me. I was a man of influence, but you are going to make me a *wayu* (person to be sacrificially

hanged). When I am ready to go out to the field, you should feed me well and give me a lot to drink."

After they heard this, some people fed and gave drink to the *wayu*. "Today you will dance with us in the open," they said. Then they carried the *wayu* around in a stretcher for two days. On the next day they hanged him with the corn, potatoes, and all they had given him. Regarding the things they hanged, people used to believe and say: "Bringing along these things he will return to *Uma Pacha*. (Huarochiri manuscript 3169: fol. 94, translation mine)

In preparation for this journey, Guillermo was washed in hot water. A tight cord was then tied around his throat and cotton stuffed in his nose and mouth to stop the odors. Relatives dressed the body in new clothes and placed it on a table with two candles. Friends and relatives paid their respects by praying Hail Marys and Our Fathers and by putting coca into his bag for the journey.

The burial service began at noon the day after Guillermo had died. Refilda filled his medicine bag with cooked potatoes, oca, charqui, hot sauce, and llama fat, enough for a long day's journey. She wrapped him in his blankets and lead-colored poncho, customarily used for trips, for it would be cold inside of the earth as he traveled the underground waterways toward the highlands.

Four secretaries of the community carried Guillermo's body, stretched out on two large poles and two smaller crossbars to the cemetery, which is about 20 yards long and 15 yards wide, with an 8 ft adobe wall encircling it. All the dead are buried about 5 ft below the ground, close to the other members of their patrilineage. The wife is usually buried near her husband, or if she dies before him, she is buried in his patrilineal plot of the cemetery. Since the dead are believed to be journeying, after several years another dead relative may be buried on top of or in the same place as the other deceased.

Thirty-six men sat on benches along the wall of the cemetery. The leaders measured the coffin with a cord and instructed the diggers as to the size of the grave. The coffin was constructed of two large eucalyptus boards and alcohol crates. One man rapidly broke the earth with a hand plow and another shoveled. The grave digging was a relay race; they plowed and shoveled in pairs to the point of exhaustion and then were replaced by another pair. From the time of death to burial is the neither-here-nor-there phase within this rite of passage from·being an elder to becoming an ancestor that is dangerous to Kaatans. The sheriff invited new diggers when he saw that the old ones were tiring. The gravediggers struck buried coffins, whose tin edges from alcohol cans had rusted through. They uncovered the top of a skull and large femur bone, which was rapidly placed aside. Suddenly they all exclaimed, "Wajta!" ("Another One!"). A fetid smell filled the grave, and everyone stepped back, holding their noses with their ponchos

The Mountain/Body Metaphor Expressed in a Kaatan Funeral

and placing coca leaves inside their nostrils. They had opened a decomposed skull. They quickly covered it and passed around coca and alcohol. The coca quids were placed alongside the grave, as were the empty alcohol bottles. Some of the men were crying and others were laughing.

Only four women attended the burial: Guillermo's sisters and one classificatory mother, since his natural mother was dead. As is customary for all burials in Kaata, only the mother and sisters are permitted. Guillermo's wife and members of her lineage were not allowed to assist at the grave site, but remained at home to cook.

Only members of Guillermo's patrilineage could set him into the earth and secure his claim to the land by burying him within it. Guillermo's eldest son had arrived from La Paz shortly after his father had died. He served everyone alcohol and coca, and so assumed his responsibilities as head of his father's patrilineage. The living members of the patrilineage were the hosts of dead Guillermo, and they would feed him for the next three years, during the Feast with the Dead. After three years of ritual feeding, he would complete the cycle, by climbing up the three levels to the *Uma Pacha*.

The 12 leaders or secretaries of ayllu Kaata were present at the burial. Within this chain of roles lie hidden assumptions that they too are working toward completion as ancestors and that their leadership is sustained by relating to the dead.

The grave was dug in half an hour, and the Secretary General of Kaata approved it. Guillermo's body, wrapped in a lead-colored poncho, symbolic of night and journeys, was placed inside the coffin. They placed a candle in his hand and lit it. I took from my hat a white carnation, whose ruffled petals resembled a lazy cloud and whose two sisters, pink and red, inaugurate and terminate the day, and asked that it be given to Guillermo. They put it in his hand, saying, "This is a gift from Sebastian to take with you on your journey and to give to him."

Four men holding rope straps lowered Guillermo to begin his journey. They covered the coffin hastily, while the women wailed. The dirt was tamped down with a rock, and they made a large cross from the four poles and placed it at the head of the grave. A wreath of red gladiolas formed a circle around the cross. All of the participants washed their hands in a pot of water over the grave, and later flowers were placed inside the pot. The burial service ended with a silent prayer and, as rapidly as Guillermo was buried, everyone descended to the deceased's house.

As we entered the courtyard, Refilda passed incense beneath our hands, and prayed, "May your sorrow rise with the smoke." The women arrived with pots of soup and cloths filled with solid foods, which they gave their husbands. The husbands set the boiled food on the four sides of the courtyard where the men sat, and in the center of the circle of women. Everyone sampled the wide variety of potatoes, oca, and corn. The husbands then served us soup with rice, noodles, charqui, and barley. The Secretary General received the servings, lining them up in the courtyard. After he had drunk five bowls of soup, he served the rest to the other guests. We enjoyed each other's company and food.

When the meal was finished, the Secretary General called for a few minutes of silent prayer for Guillermo's journey. Then everyone shouted, "Have a good trip, Guillermo!" and we threw alcohol and coca in a rounded gesture toward the summit of Mount Kaata. We continued drinking until evening, when the Secretary General ended the funeral with his announcement that the sun had died in the highlands and Guillermo's journey had ended.

The ritualist at the burial service was the Secretary General of the community. Throughout this one-year term of office, he leads the secretaries and elders. He presides at burials where he symbolically sends dead elders on their journeys to becoming ancestors. Noticeably absent at the funeral was Sarito Quispe, *machula watayuh purijchej,* perhaps because he is considered an ancestor. In rituals throughout the year, Sarito feeds the ancestors as well as intercedes with them in behalf of their living descendants.

The Secretary General told Guillermo's patrilineage and Refilda's lineage that although they suffered the consequences of Guillermo's death, they remained members of a community which shared grief and food. His ritual activity was to serve drink and food to the bereaved and to dispatch Guillermo on his journey to the *Uma Pacha.*

The burial ritual emphasized the journey of the dead to the *Uma Pacha,* and this journey is contrapetally related to that of the sun. The living travel down the three levels of the ayllu above the earth from west to east, and the dead climb back up the ayllu within the earth from east to west (Bastien 1978: 171–187). The living and the dead travel in opposite directions to the sun but each propels the other in contrapetal movement. The sun rises in the east and travels up the three levels of the ayllu during the day and sinks into a highland lake in the west, where it travels to the east and is reborn in the morning.

WOVEN METAPHORS OF SNAILS AND SUNS

The style and pictographs of clothes in Kaata provide more visual images whose configuration into metaphors can be used to further understand the journey of Guillermo. Clothing in Kaata has distinct forms of representation: the biographical history of the person who wore it, such as objects found within medicine bags; functions of the garments, such as Guillermo being dressed in a lead-colored poncho used for journeys; political economy of the clothing, such as a coca bag used for exchanging coca; and interpretations of style and pictographs.

Style and pictographs reflect the distinct ayllus among the Kallawayas. Ayllus Chari, Chajaya, Inka, Amarete, Chullina, Curva, and Upinhuaya have similar clothing as in ayllu Kaata: mantles, medicine bags, petticoats, and headdresses, but each ayllu varies in the pictographs and stripes of these garments.

Clothing is a symbol for identifying the ayllus to which women belong. Spouses often meet at inter-ayllu saint fiestas, where the women are dressed in their finest weavings. Clothing expresses the availability of the woman for marriage and if she is from an ayllu with whom there is already an exchange of women.

Stripes on weavings are analogous to the levels of the ayllu. For illustration, the cloths of ayllus Chajaya and Kaata have similar pictographs, but the width and color of bands differ corresponding to each's ecological zones. Ayllu Chajaya's levels range from around 10,000 to 14,000 ft, whereas ayllu Kaata has a wider vertical range of from 10,000 to 16,000 ft. Ayllu Chajaya's weavings have two wide peripheral red bands and two central green bands. Ayllu Kaata's weavings have two peripheral red bands and two central maroon bands.

The two sets of weavings refer to the levels of land, as is symbolized by the multicolored stripes. Ayllu Chajaya is geographically distinct from Kaata and is located on both sides of a lower valley, which is represented by the two central green stripes, where corn, wheat, peas, and beans are grown. Above these lower fields on both sides are the intermediate level fields of potatoes, oca, and barley. The red stripes symbolize the light red earth beyond the green and fertile fields. Ayllu Chajaya's upper level does not extend far into the higher pastoral areas. Ayllu Kaata's weavings have two thin peripheral stripes referring to two thin layers of lower fields with corn, wheat, and vegetables; two red stripes, representing the central fields of potatoes, oca, and barley; and two maroon stripes representing the higher pastoral areas. In short, cloth is a visual metaphor of the fields and levels of the ayllu.

Pictographs on weavings are like notes of music written horizontally and vertically on a sheet (Fig. 1). Pictographs are woven along each stripe and with continuity from one stripe to the next. A traditional Kaatan and exclusive Quechua speaker, Carmen Quispe Yanahuaya read pictographs on a belt which she had woven for herself.

Carmen explained that pictographs of cones with spirals represent snails (see diagram of Snail Motif). Sets of these symbols are woven and intertwined into symmetrical stacks dividing all of the stripes. The most prestigious weavings in Kaata are those with only this symbol. Carmen wove a snail-motif poncho for husband, Marcelino, in eight months and said that she wouldn't do it again because of eye strain. (Similar ponchos sell for $150 in La Paz.) According to Carmen, the snail motif signifies that ayllu Kaata is a sacred place with many *yachajkuna* who perform rituals to the earth shrines.

Joseph W. Bastien

Fig. 1 Pictographs from Kallawaya weavings.

The Mountain/Body Metaphor Expressed in a Kaatan Funeral

Although Carmen did not explain this, the snail is an animal that is found on all levels of ayllu Kaata; it lives underneath the earth, on its surface, and above in trees, carrying its home wherever it goes. The snail comes out of a logarithmic spiral and returns to it, resembling the regenerative properties of plants, animals, people, and ayllu. Because these associations represent important cultural values about themselves and their ayllu, these people consider the snail motif as a sacred metaphor.

Crossculturally, the snail is frequently considered sacred because it represents the spiral. This spiral is found in nature in the beautiful conch shell *Nautilus pompilius,* which the dancing Shiva of the Hindu myth holds in one of her hands as one of the instruments through which she initiates creation (Lawlor 1991: 14–15). Around 500 B.C., Greek followers of Pythagoras believed that the spiral embodies the dynamics of the rhythmic generation of the cosmos, and through its harmonic principle represents universal love. The logarithmic spiral is analogous to the growth pattern of many plants, such as the distribution of seeds in the sunflower, and to the development of fetuses positioned within the womb, during birth, and subsequent development from the navel.

When Guillermo was buried, nobody wore ponchos or mantles with snail motifs, which are reserved for festive occasions, such as marriages, baptisms, and fiestas to the saints. However, the men wore belts and the women wore headbands with this motif, and Guillermo was buried with a coca bag embroidered with snail motifs. Another association with this motif was the spiral-like journey to and from the cemetery, and the circular sprinkling of alcohol toward the summit of Mount Kaata as a final farewell to Guillermo, but these parallels are speculative. Interpretations of the snail motif provide insights into Kaatan cosmology, which values a symbol that represents generation, regeneration, levels, and spirals. The burial of Guillermo also suggested the earth, like the snail, as the form from which Guillermo was generated and to which he was returning in cyclical motion, across, above, and below the levels.

Guillermo's journey can metaphorically be related to Kaatans' beliefs about the path of the sun as signified in pictographs on weavings. Carmen shared with me her understanding of time and universe when she explained pictographs of the sun on her belt. Sun motifs are composed of two triangles with a common base formed by a dividing line and apexes pointing up and down bordering on peripheral lines. She called the green central line "ch'aupi," emphasizing that the sun is divided into halves. This reflects divisions of the community into upper (*hanan*) and lower (*hurin*) moieties. Although people of ayllu Kaata exchange spouses between upper, center, and lower communities, the couple also represent above and below, in similar fashion as the ayllu has three levels, as well as above and below. Binary exchange and oppositions cut across apparently triadic divisions.

Joseph W. Bastien

Carmen differentiated suns according to types and numbers of rays on the outside and symbols on the inside: *Machu Inti* ("Elder Sun") has a beard formed by 44 lines protruding from the triangles, *Wayna Inti* ("Young Adult Sun") has the beginnings of a beard with 28 whiskers, and *Uña Inti* ("Miniature Sun") has four lines or none at all (Fig. 1). *Wayna Inti* is also depicted with triangulated rays, and *Uña Inti* with U-shaped extensions. Carmen proceeded to explain the analogies: whiskers of the beard correspond to rays of the sun. At the end of the day and in the western highlands, Elder Sun is covered with brilliant rays and carries Miniature Sun within it. When it dies in a highland lake and travels through the underground streams to the lowlands and eastern lake of Tuana, its fiery rays are extinguished and *Uña Inti* is born. *Uña Inti* arises from the lake near the far eastern earth-shrine (Chaqamita) of ayllu Kaata. *Uña Inti* travels to the zenith at high noon far above the central lands where it becomes *Wayna Inti*. In its descent from the zenith to the highlands of ayllu Kaata, *Wayna Inti* becomes *Machu Inti*, growing more whiskers and begetting *Uña Inti*. (See last pictograph of *Machu Inti* pregnant with *Uña Inti*.)

In comparison to the journey of Guillermo, travels and transformations of the sun are in contrapuntal motion. Guillermo arose from the western highland lakes, crossed the three levels eastward throughout his life, and after death entered the ayllu to begin an east-to-west journey to the highlands where he would arise anew. As the sun goes from birth to death in an east-to-west direction, humans go from birth to death in a west-to-east direction. Journeys of sun and people are related in that one propels the other, or as the one goes up, the other goes down.

Metaphors in the dance of rituals are helpful toward understanding these journeys around and within the ayllu. During New Earth ritual (see Bastien 1978: 77), flute players danced in their slow east-to-west spiral, which every so often reversed its direction and retraced its steps, until finally at the point of completion, the dancers turned and marched from the small field toward Kaata. As mysteriously as a sun being constantly reborn or a circle revolving in upon itself, the chain of musicians moved toward Kaata to the staccato beat of the drum and four recurring notes of the flute.

FEAST WITH THE DEAD

An annual commemorative ritual, The Feast with the Dead symbolizes a concurrence of the journeys of sun, ancestors, ayllu, and community. In November of 1972, Guillermo was invited to eat with the living for the Feast with the Dead. This feast coincides with All Souls' Day on the Roman Catholic calendar, but it also marks the end of the dry season and beginning of the rainy season. The rains cease in April and May, and the dry season continues until November. During this time of rest and relaxation, Kaatans

The Mountain/Body Metaphor Expressed in a Kaatan Funeral

harvest and celebrate. When the rains begin again in November, Kaatans plant their crops.

The living invite the dead when the harvest and festive times have ended and planting and agricultural rituals begin. The Feast with the Dead is an annual rite of passage from the dry to wet season and from the activity of the dead to that of the living. The dry season connotes resting, and the wet season, growth. Between this pivotal point within the Andean year, the dead visit the living, and then they are sent on another year's journey with their share of the harvest.

At noon on Wednesday, the Secretary General ignited a coffee can of dynamite. The explosion rocked the dead and announced their arrival to the living. Only those who had died within three years were invited to the feast. Inheritors of land are required to feed the dead from whom they have inherited the land for three years after the person's death. The dead are said to be present when a fly circles around the banquet table and alights upon the different levels.

The banquet was prepared on an elaborate table with three tiers of food and drink (Figs. 2, 3). The lowest was covered with lowland products of coca, apples, bananas, and chicha. A platform was set on this surface to symbolize the central lands, and a square wooden box formed the third level, upon which sat a wicker basket with bread figurines. The third level symbolized the *Uma Pacha* of ayllu and place of origin for all the produce of the ayllu. The llamas, birds, fish, and cows within the basket were symbolic products of the three ecological zones emerging from the lakes and waterholes of the *Uma Pacha*.

Bamboo was placed above the table, and a crossbar was positioned horizontally. Flowers were arranged over the center and a string of oranges was hung beneath the crossbar. The bamboo with the cross and the oranges symbolized the heavens of the saints and the sun.

The table's three levels symbolized ayllu Kaata, and its legs the netherworld. Kaatans imagine the mountain of their ayllu as a solid three-leveled center with an ephemeral heaven above a hollow netherworld foundation. The sun, living, and dead circulate above, below, and around the mountain.

Kaatans placed a glass of chicha on the dead's table, and when someone prayed for the dead they sprinkled chicha on the earth asking the dead to drink. Although cane alcohol was drunk at the feast, chicha remained the primary drink for both the living and the dead. Chicha was also the preferred Pre-Columbian drink of the dead in Huarochiri as the following tradition illustrates:

> In the olden times they used to bring the dead all kinds of food, all of them well-cooked. When a man died, they said, "Our dead will return after five days. We shall wait for them." They used to stay awake each night until the fifth day of their death.

Joseph W. Bastien

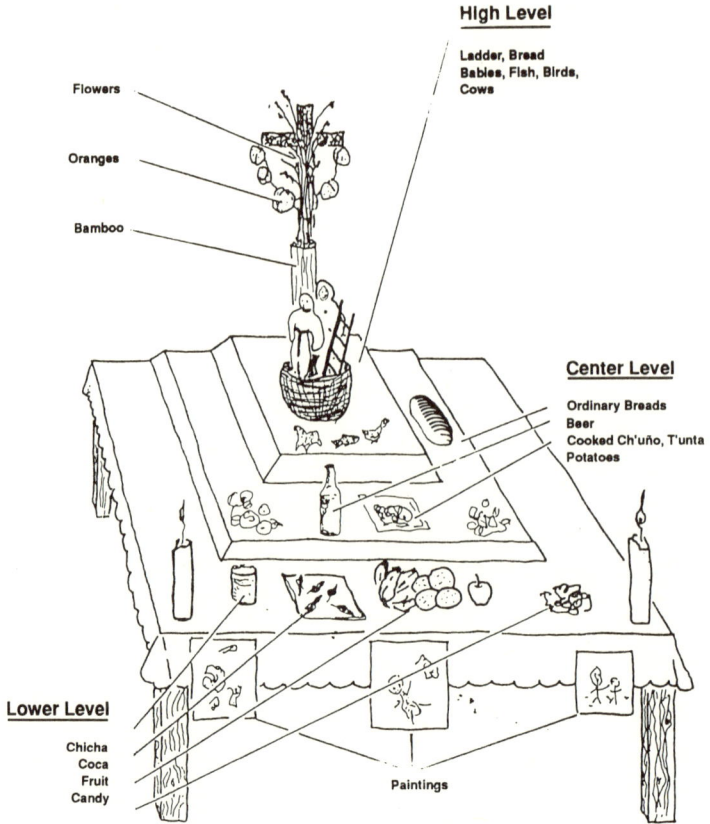

Fig. 2 Diagram of the table for the dead: correspondence of three levels of table to levels of the ayllu.

Already on the fifth day, a woman putting on her best clothes used to go to Yaru Tini saying, "I will wait for him," or "I will lead him." The woman went bringing food and chicha. In Yaru Tini when the sun was already rising, the dead ones used to arrive. In the olden times two or three flies used to sit on the garment she brought, and there they remained for a long time. When the other fly we call *wanquy kuru* left, she said to a small stone, "Come on, let us go to the village."

"This is he," she said to the stone, bringing it back with her. When she arrived, her home was swept clean and people began to serve food. Once they had offered the dead food, they gave the

The Mountain/Body Metaphor Expressed in a Kaatan Funeral

Fig. 3 Table for the dead. Table prepared for ancestors during annual commemorative ritual in southern Andes.

dead chicha. After the dead one had eaten, they ate. (Huarochiri manuscript 3169: fol. 98, translation mine)

Wherever banquets had been prepared for the dead in Kaata, friends and relatives visited, playing flutes and praying for the dead person, and in return they were given bread, fruit, and a glass of chicha for their prayers. Everyone exchanged coca bags and visited for a while.

By midmorning on Thursday, 3 November 1972, the son had carried Guillermo's table to the cemetery, where he placed it on his grave. The cemetery was filled with similar tables. About 40 people from the highlands of Apacheta were making the rounds, praying for the dead. They carried large sacks filled with bread and fruit. Those who prayed fervently and offered candles to the dead were given beautiful bread figurines, oranges, and bananas.

Many Kaatans had congregated in the cemetery around the tables of the dead. They spoke in whispers out of respect for the dead; occasionally someone wailed or laughed. Subdued silence and reverence were the communal emotions, rather than grief and fear. They were at home with their dead, or perhaps it is that the dead are at home both literally and figuratively with the living.

When the sun was overhead, the dead departed to the *Uma Pacha*. Relatives rapidly dismantled the tables and stuffed what was left into sacks. Everyone went from the cemetery to the homes of the sponsors, and by early afternoon the graveyard resumed its quietude.

The hosts sponsored departure banquets for the deceased, similar to that of the burial ritual. Once they had finished eating, people shared drinks, and the flute band, silent until then, played. The band was composed of six flute players, two drummers, and two playing the cowtail (*wacachupa*), which is a long wooden tube with a cow's horn and emits a low and resonating sound like a foghorn. The band zigzagged through the streets while the dancing couples were swinging back and forth until they completed the spiral, traveling as it were from the highlands to the lowlands.

After the festivities, I arrived a bit tipsy at the house of Godfather Marcelino Yanahuaya. Two Apachetans arrived at the gate and asked to pray for our dead. They did, and Marcelino consoled me about my mother who had died the month before:

> Your mother is one with the earth. She is like Mother Earth, and she is here with us now. The dead visit us and they assist us in our work. They provide many blessings. As the sun and moon live, so the dead accompany us. When the sun burns out at the judgment, then the dead will never return.

Later that afternoon, Marcelino and I ate one of the bread babies that had been placed on the Table of the Dead (Fig. 4).

ANIMATION OF THE DECEASED

Comparisons are found between Inka and Kaatan burial practices. Dead Inka rulers were not buried but mummified and placed in chambers (Rowe, this volume). These mummies were removed, carried around, and given food. Commoners considered the mummies divine and prayed to them. These practices created an animation of the deceased. In contrast, rulers of Chimu were buried in platforms. In the southern Andes animation of the dead is still practiced, as documented above.

The Mountain/Body Metaphor Expressed in a Kaatan Funeral

Fig. 4 Baking bread babies. Throughout the southern Andes figurines of babies are made out of dough and baked in ovens. Bread babies are given to people who pray for ancestors and are eaten in commemoration of the dead.

Differences are that Kaatans no longer use mummies and bury their dead in sacred cemeteries because of the Spanish conquest and its efforts to extirpate idolatry. Once mummies were burned and the dead were buried, visualization of the deceased was no longer possible and animation of the deceased assumed different forms. The burial ritual presented Guillermo as taking a journey within the ayllu in relation to the sun, and the Feast with the Dead forced the dead from inside the ayllu to join with the living for a banquet on a table that is a metaphor for the ayllu.

Animation of the deceased is represented within the ayllu and mountain/body metaphor. One can hypothesize that Kaatans transformed ideas of heaven and hell to those of above and below the ayllu, thereby changing the spiritual-Christian metaphor into a telluric-Andean metaphor based on their understanding of the body, ayllu, and sun. Basic Andean structure, however, is perdurable with Christian symbols fitting into these patterns of animation.

Kaatans do not view the deceased as detached animated figures but as personalities within their lives and ayllu. The rituals were not staged performances with distanced participants. Rather they became frenzies of involvement with the animated deceased. This intimacy with the dead and the earth was sexual and physical, experienced in digging the grave, entering the body into it, praying on knees, kissing the earth, and dancing until falling on the earth while others danced over them. This entering into the earth was related to loved ones inside of it. Kaatans banqueted with the dead, sharing bread babies with them in communion. They communicated with them through prayers in the cemetery and talked with them in front of the Table of the Dead.

METAPHORICAL CONTEXT

Animation of the deceased for Kaatans was explained within their metaphorical understanding of ayllu Kaata. The funeral and Feast with the Dead evoked for Kaatans a metaphorical understanding of their ancestors as journeying inside the mountain, up the three levels to the *Uma Pacha*. This journey is metaphorical in that it is the reverse of the journey from life to death when the baby arises out of the highland lakes, travels on top of the mountain, across the three levels to the lowlands, where he or she dies, is buried, and journeys once again the highlands. The Feast with the Dead is a break in the agricultural cycle when the living prepare a banquet for the dead; thereafter the dead will feed the living with a good harvest.

Death is a vital process for Kaatans, and rituals express metaphors that link them analogically with ancestors, burial sites, levels of land, ayllu, and Inti. These components fit into an elaborate system of metaphorical correspondence, which at times is synchronized and at others is not. Ritualists manipulate the terms of this metaphor to maintain agricultural, cultural, and social relationships vital to their land, ayllu, community, and family.

ACTIVE FORCES WITHIN THE AYLLU

Rituals and metaphors animate the deceased to such an extent that ancestors are active forces within the ayllu and lives of the living. Anthropologists are sometimes misled by the small populations of communities in the southern Andes and disregard the conceptual presence of the deceased. The deceased create some threats for peasants. Unbaptized dead babies cause hail storms. *Condenados* are the heads of the deceased, especially delinquents, who appear at night and cause sickness or death. *Chullpa tullu* (Ancestor sickness) is polio or osteomylitis and is believed to be caused by the ancestors for those disturbing a chullpa site. Many of these threats support community values: baptism, respect for chullpas, and conformity to community rules.

In Kaata, ancestors played an important role in inheriting and maintaining land. For three years after death, inheritors of land were required to prepare a table for the deceased. If someone died without descendants, then another person could inherit the land if he or she prepared a table for the deceased for three years. In either case, if these rituals were not performed, then the deceased would harm the harvest by climatic factors. Entitlement to land is associated with funerary practices. Salomon (this volume) also concludes from ethnohistorical sources that Andean mortuary practices involve moribund experiences that include cycles of ancestor veneration and the ayllu. Ancestors are symbols of death and fertility. The Kaatan funeral vividly illustrates that this ancient practice continues today.

Ambivalent ancestors, associated with life and death, relate to another theme that Salomon makes: Andean mortuary rites combine the contradictory function of altering the social arrangements that they pretend to conserve. Kaatans continually rearrange their ancestors, burying them in the cemetery, journeying them underneath the ayllu to the *Uma Pacha,* and resurrecting them at the Feast with the Dead. During these movements, living Andeans change political and social arrangements, but always reflecting as how these changes fit into Andean metaphors about body, land, and ayllu.

Some interpretive and methodological approaches can be derived from this ethnographic analysis. The most central point is the importance of metaphor for providing a systemic cultural context to understand Andean burial practices, past and present. Andeans employ metaphors to understand their communities, land, and ayllu, and within these metaphors they animate the deceased so that Andeans perceive of them as vital forces or continually present. Rituals perform these processes.

Working back in time for a methodology to interpret tombs of ancients, it is necessary to figure out the dominant metaphors from the props and stage settings of rituals whose actors are long since absent. Clues are given in the pictographs on weavings and ceramics, the placement of bodies and body parts, and in the architectural setting, such as John Rowe's conclusion about dead Inka rulers being set into a metaphor of animation that mimics living rulers. Christopher Donnan reports that a hand was found in the tomb at Sipán, which belonged to no one buried there. As a possible avenue of research, the hand may be a metaphor of a lineage or parcel of land, entrusted to the regal deceased. Ethnographic and ethnohistorical data could be examined to see if people within this region used body parts as metaphors for lineage and land.

Joseph W. Bastien

Another possibility for uncovering metaphors is the examination of motifs on walls, weavings, and ceramics. Common Andean metaphors are animals, body parts, mountains, levels, and stars. Frequently Andeans write their metaphors on the earth by earth shrines, pictographs, roads, and symbols. Use of land and irrigation layouts correspond closely to their metaphors and earth shrines.

To understand ancient and modern tombs, an interdisciplinary perspective is necessary that incorporates ethnographic research concerning contemporary burial practices; ethnohistorical examination by ethnohistorians and art historians of motifs on weavings and ceramics; and archaelogical analysis of architectural structures, chronology, and ritual paraphernalia. The objective, however, is not more disparate information but rather theoretical schemata that provide a broader contextualization of data, such as the mountain/body metaphor for understanding the burial of Guillermo. If, as Rowe suggests, the Inkas animated their deceased, scholars might at least provide tombs of the ancestors with a bit more flesh.

BIBLIOGRAPHY

ALBO, JAVIER
1972 Dinámica en estructura inter-communitaria de Jesús de Machaca. *América Indígena* 32: 773–816.

BASTIEN, JOSEPH W.
1973 *Qollahuaya Rituals: An Ethnographic Account of the Symbolic Relations of Man and Land in an Andean Village.* Latin American Studies Program, Cornell University, Ithaca, New York.
1978 *Mountain of the Condor: Metaphor and Ritual in an Andean Ayllu.* American Ethnological Society, Monograph 64. West Publishing Company, St. Paul. (Reissued by Waveland Press, 1985.)
1987 *Healer of the Andes: Kallawaya Herbalists and Their Medicinal Plants.* University of Utah Press, Salt Lake City.
1992 *Drum and Stethoscope: Integrating Ethnomedicine and Biomedicine in Bolivia.* University of Utah Press, Salt Lake City.

BONILLA, HERACLIO, AND CESAR FONSECA MARTEL
1967 *Tradición y conservadorismo en al área cultural del Lago Titicaca: Jesús de Machaca, una communidad Aymara del Altiplano Andino.* Instituto de Estudios Peruanos, Lima.

CONNERTON, PAUL
1989 *How Societies Remember.* Cambridge University Press, Cambridge.

HUAROCHIRI MANUSCRIPT
16 c. Manuscript 3169. Quechua text attributed to Francisco de Avila. Biblioteca Nacional de Madrid.

LAWLOR, ROBERT
1991 The Measure of Difference. *Parabola* 16 (4): 11–15.

MASON, J. ALDEN
1968 *The Ancient Civilization of Peru.* Penguin Books, New York.

MELION, WALTER, AND SUSANNE KUCHLER
1991 Introduction: Memory, Cognition, and Image Production. In *Images of Memory: On Remembering and Representation.* (Walter Melion and Susanne Kuchler, eds.) 1–46. Smithsonian Institution Press, Washington, D.C.

REINHARD, JOHAN
1985a *The Nazca Lines: A New Perspective on Their Origin and Meaning.* Editorial Los Pinos, Lima.
1985b Chavín and Tiahuanaco: A New Look at Two Andean Ceremonial Centers. *National Geographic Research* 1: 395–422.

ROWE, JOHN H.
n.d. What Kind of Settlement was Inca Cuzco? Paper presented at the 11th Annual Meeting of the Kroeber Anthropological Society, Berkeley University, 22 April 1967.

Joseph W. Bastien

URTON, GARY
    1981   *At the Crossroads of the Earth and Sky: An Andean Cosmology.* University of Texas Press, Austin.

ZUIDEMA, TOM
    1964   *The Ceque System of Cuzco: The Social Organization of the Capital of the Incas.* E. J. Brill Publishers, Leiden.
    1968   La relación entre el patrón de poblamento prehispanico y los principios derivados de la estructura social incaica. *Actas y Memorias de XXXVII Congreso de Americanistas* 1: 45–55.

Death in the Andes

PATRICIA J. LYON

INSTITUTE OF ANDEAN STUDIES

THE TOTALITY OF ANDEAN MORTUARY CUSTOMS cannot be encompassed in so limited a space as this volume; Andean cultures have existed through more than 10,000 years and thousands of kilometers of space. What the papers here present is a mere sample of the kind of material that archaeology has produced so far and some of the approaches to the study of that material. As large as some of the samples are (e.g., Chinchorro, Moche, Nasca), it is important to keep in mind that they are not necessarily, indeed probably are not, representative of the cultures from which they derive.

Very few cemeteries have been systematically excavated and recorded to the extent and in the detail necessary to permit discussion of their relationship to their associated communities, and in almost all such cases the cemeteries are part of or associated with Preceramic settlements (see Quilter 1989: 70–82, for a discussion of some of the more important work). Unfortunately, our chronological control at Preceramic sites is much less precise than that attainable at ceramic sites (e.g., Menzel 1976), and lack of a precise chronology severely limits the sorts of interpretations that can be made. After all, if we do not know the precise relationship of what is being compared, then comparison is meaningless.

Some ceramic sites have been rather well studied, however. At Ancon, the relative position of both the graves themselves and the objects within each grave has been recorded and, in large part, published, thus providing a large body of data for interpretation (Kauffmann Doig 1978: 504–506; Ravines 1979–83). In their analysis of a large group of graves from the Moche Valley, Christopher Donnan and Carol Mackey (1978) provide not only a longitudinal study of a limited area, with detailed descriptions of each burial, but also one of the few glimpses of some humble burials. These examples are exceptional in reflecting good recording as well as reasonably detailed publication. We do not, unfortunately, have similar information from the thousands of graves excavated by Gustavo Le Paige in 37 cemeteries around San Pedro de Atacama (Le Paige 1964), or from those that have been or are now being excavated around Arica and in the area of Tiahuanaco.

Even when graves have been properly excavated, all too often we find that the associations were lost when the materials were catalogued, although they can sometimes be retrieved (Julien 1994). While the artifactual remains of graves may be retained as grave lots, the human remains have often been either discarded or recorded separately with no way to connect them to the artifacts; thus, our ability to interpret sex and age differences in mortuary practices is severely limited.

If we wish to discuss prestige, social rank, social relations, etc., on the basis of mortuary patterns, we must know as much as possible about the individual people who are buried. Correct sexing and aging of the dead is crucial. The accuracy of skeletal sexing depends on both the condition of the remains and the skill and experience of the specialist doing the sexing. In the hands of amateurs (including archaeologists with only basic training in osteology), accuracy is likely to be very low, especially when dealing with an unfamiliar population. Since native Andeans tend to be small and very gracile, the non-specialist is likely to identify more females than are actually present. In order to be considered reliable, sexing must be done by a trained and experienced physical anthropologist, who must be identified in the publication, and a discussion of the criteria and methods used to determine sex must be provided. These are, of course, the same sort of criteria that should be applied when evaluating the identification of flora, fauna, and minerals. It should be kept in mind that in the past, sex was often ascribed to burials on the basis not of osteological analysis, but rather of the associated artifacts as interpreted through sexual stereotypes (e.g., weaving tools are female, fishing gear male).

Even in the absence of ideal data, much can be done with what we have. The extensive bodies of data presented by Donnan and Patrick Carmichael (this volume) are broadly comparable. Both date to the Early Intermediate Period (although that encompasses several hundred years), and the number of burials they include is roughly the same. The degree of geographical separation, close enough for sporadic contact but not for constant influence, provides an interesting contrast. The most obvious difference between the two samples lies in the quantity of material lavished on burials, especially in terms of metals. In the south, nothing even approaches the lavishness of the Sipán, La Mina, and San José de Moro burials. In this case there is even a way to check for sampling error.

Because of the sheer number of graves found by looters in the areas where the Moche and Nasca cultures flourished, we can be reasonably assured that the results of their vandalism is relatively representative of the total sample. While looters once melted down all or most of the precious metals they recovered, more recently such objects have been worth more on the art market than the intrinsic value of their metals. Most museum and virtually all private collections of ancient Andean art are the result of looting. Thus, an examination of these collections gives us a clue to the nature of the materials that might be expected to occur in heavily looted areas. Such appears to be the case for the Moche sample where looted material closely approximates that excavated by archaeologists in terms of materials and artifact classes. The fact that the Nasca style material that has resulted from looting also reflects that excavated by archaeologists suggests that it, too, is reasonably representative, and therefore the contrast between the samples described by Donnan and Carmichael is real. Only in the earliest phases of the Nasca style, those contemporary with the so-called Paracas embroideries, do we find fancy metalwork, largely in the form of gold mouth-masks and forehead ornaments.

This north-south contrast is to be expected since it has long been clear that Moche and other northern cultures are tied more closely to the artistic, and presumably cultural, traditions of Ecuador and Colombia than to the southern ones (e.g., Lumbreras 1981; Lyon 1991). It is, of course, to the north that we find an elaboration of fancy, ornamental metalwork in a tradition that extends from at least Panama into northern Peru. In contrast, in spite of the fact that the earliest evidence for metalworking comes from Andahuaylas (Grossman 1972), there is little such material in the south. Isolated finds, like the cache of Middle Horizon silver plumes found south of Cuzco (Chávez 1987) and the bronze plaques from northwest Argentina (González 1977), merely serve to underline its rarity. Whatever the precise significance of this difference, it does suggest that we cannot use the criteria for, say, wealth developed in one area to assess the status of the graves from another.

There are other disparities between the northern and southern burials. While the vagaries of preservation prevent a detailed comparison of the textile components of the burials, it is possible that elaborate textiles occupied the same position in the south during the Early Intermediate Period that goldwork held in the north. It should also be kept in mind that the elaborate polychrome ceramics of the southern tradition required a much greater labor investment than did the mono- and bichrome, mold-made pottery of the north (Lyon 1991).

The distinctions just noted, while only the most obvious between these two burial traditions, serve to emphasize the amount of cultural variability in the Andean region. From time to time there have been discussions of the degree of cultural unity in the Andes (e.g., Bennett 1948), most recently exemplified by the tendency to speak of *lo andino,* or "Andean," as though there were an immemorial tradition of cultural similarity. While there now exist a number of marked cultural parallels, at least in the central Andes, the time depth of such uniformity is questionable. In addition to the archaeological evidence, consider that the entire region was once ruled by the Incas, who practiced deliberate cultural mixing through the movement of *mitimas*. When the Europeans arrived, diversity was further reduced by the massive die-off, especially of coastal peoples, and by the Spanish policy that spread the Inca language beyond its preconquest bounds. More population mixture resulted from movement caused, both intentionally and unintentionally, by such institutions as the *mita* of Potosí. Finally, the overlay of Spanish religion and customs and some 500 years of culture change applied to this chaotic base could well yield the situation we see today with no need to invoke earlier uniformity.

"Burial customs change over time and from location to location, and all are demonstrations of 'the right thing to do' about a very important event" (Crabtree n.d.: 58). The precise nature of that event, however, can be problematic in the Andes. Certainly in Peru, and probably elsewhere in the Andean region, there has been a long and flourishing tradition of burying non-mortuary offerings, as noted by John Rowe, John Verano, and Frank Salomon in this volume. The best-known archaeological examples are probably those dating to the Middle Horizon, particularly the Pacheco offering with its tons of fancy polychrome pottery apparently smashed in a single event (Menzel 1964: 23–31). Other similar, though smaller, offerings from the highlands suggest that such events were far from rare in the Middle Horizon (Menzel 1964: 6; Ravines 1969, 1977; Isbell and Cook 1987; Cook 1987). An analogous event seems to have taken place in the Early Horizon in the Ofrendas Gallery at the site of Chavín (Lumbreras 1989: 183–216). Even today, most Andean offerings are ultimately buried.

An equally long tradition in Peru (and also likely elsewhere in the Andes) is that of human sacrifice, which may be extremely difficult to distinguish from a normal burial. The most obvious group of sacrificed individuals are those found in mountain-top shrines (Beorchia Nigris 1987), all apparently dating to the time of the Inca empire. From the same empire comes the group of sacrificed women excavated by Uhle at Pachacamac already mentioned by Rowe. The locations of the mountain sacrifices and the ropes around the necks of the women at Pachacamac, together with historical references to Inca custom, leave no doubt that these were sacrifices. Modern practice suggests that human sacrifice may have been more common than the historical sources indicate (e.g., Núñez del Prado B. 1974: 247). It is probable that human sacrifice was involved in the Ofrendas event of the Early Horizon (Lumbreras 1989: 206–216). It is also possible that many, if not all, of the isolated human heads and other body parts found here and there represent human sacrifice rather than simply war trophies, as is sometimes suggested (Hecker and Hecker 1992).

The discovery that some of the burials accompanying the elite Moche burials were secondary rather than primary raises the possibility of yet another burial category, the nature of which is not yet entirely clear. To these examples should be added some Inca burials from Ollantaytambo. These, too, were apparently reburied to accompany important personages whose tombs had long since been looted (Llanos 1936: 131–143). Since the disposition of the human remains in most other Inca burials from the Cuzco region has not been recorded (Julien 1994), it is impossible to say more about Inca practice at this time. Discovery of more such burials will require considerable attention to details of body position and evidence for articulation. The cases so far noted, however, seem to suggest that certain individuals, even though they had died earlier, were expected to accompany others in death. One wonders just how the bodies of these individuals were stored before reaching their final resting place, presumably as companion to someone more important than themselves.

None of these cases is what one normally considers a common burial, emphasizing yet again the care that must be exercised in recording and interpreting the precise nature of each burial. Certainly cases of buried objects unaccompanied by human remains need to be viewed with great caution. In some cases such buried artifacts may have been interred in lieu of a dead person whose body was either irretrievable or buried far from home. Given the common occurrence of buried offerings that are unrelated to death, however, it is perhaps best to consider that when no human remains are present the offering is not mortuary in nature. Even if such associations are discovered in an area that otherwise appears to be a cemetery, it may still be wise to consider the possibility that they represent some other sort of offering. While we may restrict the use of our cemeteries to the honored dead, some peoples may have simply set aside certain areas where one could bury anything that one did not wish to be disturbed: relatives; offerings; and perhaps sacrifices, human or not. Only proper excavation and recording of rather large portions of some of the known cemeteries will resolve this problem of definition.

While it may be difficult to identify a human sacrifice when it is buried in a cemetery, it should be easier to recognize those buried elsewhere. For example, given cemeteries at the site, why would a normal burial be placed under a ramp or one of the U-shaped structures at Chan Chan? Indeed, how would a burial be located in such a place without destroying the architecture? Such burials, which Verano notes were richly accompanied, may be interpreted more convincingly as dedicatory burials interred when the structure was built.

It is far too easy to ignore alternative possibilities once a line of interpretation has been established. As a case in point, let us consider the so-called burial platforms at the site of Chan Chan. Rowe points out that to interpret the *ciudadelas* in terms of Inca inheritance practices is to misconstrue those practices. If such an interpretation is incorrect, however, how should the enclosures and their "burial platforms" be interpreted?

In the following comments, unless otherwise noted, my evidence derives from the publication of Thomas Pozorski (1979) on his work at Las Avispas. This choice reflects not an attack on Pozorski, but rather the fact that his is the only "burial platform" excavation that has been published to the extent that it can be discussed, although excavations have been carried out at others (Conrad 1982: 99) and the Tschudi platform has been extensively excavated (Gutiérrez Rodríguez 1990: 101–114).

Most burials in Las Avispas were contained in a large platform area comprising 24 rectangular chambers and a single larger, T-shaped chamber. Not all the chambers were built at once. The T-shaped chamber and the 13 surrounding smaller ones were built first; the remaining 11 chambers were added in three units, which may or may not have been completed at about the same time (Rowe 1981: 81). Adjacent to the platform is a series of small rooms, one of which contained a "stone-lined bin containing crushed *Spondylus* species shell" (Pozorski 1979: 123). All of the platform chambers had been looted to a greater or lesser extent, and only one (a later addition) was completely excavated by Pozorski, although in five others "a narrow trench was excavated to the floor" (Pozorski 1979: 127). Fragments of pottery, cloth, wooden, metal, and shell artifacts as well as food remains were found in the platform area; only the textiles have been described in detail (Rowe 1981). Pozorski concluded that the T-shaped chamber was the tomb of an important male, probably a ruler, who was accompanied by sacrificed women. Of course the looting left no evidence of who or what had been buried in the T-shaped chamber. There is also no evidence that any or all of the people buried in the smaller chambers were sacrificed at the same time that the central burial took place; architectural evidence does indicate that some of the chambers (and presumably the burial of their contents) were not made at that time.

According to Pozorski, all bodies that could be sexed are female, and all bones that could be aged fall between 17 and 24 years of age. He estimated that at least 300 individuals were buried in the chamber. The textiles that were analyzed represent all those sufficiently well preserved to be studied that were decorated (some 50% of the total) and a representative sample of the plain-woven ones that were undecorated or had monochrome weft stripes (Rowe 1981: 82).

The contents of the rectangular chambers, human remains and some associated textiles, raise certain points of interest. Assuming that Pozorski's sexual identifications are correct, why were there male garments (tunics, loincloths, hats) deposited in the burial chambers (Rowe 1981: 103–107)? Ann Rowe comments that a number of textiles were found either rolled or folded, so that they apparently served as independent offerings rather than as garments or shrouds at the time of burial (Rowe 1981: 82). She also notes that the dimensions of one of the tunics are so small that it might have been woven solely as an offering (Rowe 1981: 103–104); no remains of children are reported from the platform. Equally puzzling is why three of the chambers that were trenched to the floor (17, 21, 25) contained no decorated textiles whatsoever, and one of them (7) yielded almost twice as many such textiles as did chamber 19, which was completely excavated. It is unlikely that previous looting can be invoked to explain such anomalies.

The fact that all the "burial platforms" share certain characteristics (a number of small chambers arranged around a larger one, similar orientation, etc.) suggests that they share the same function (cf. Conrad 1982). Nevertheless, only two of the platforms have undergone much excavation, and one of those, unfortunately the one from which we have the best information (Las Avispas), is atypical in that it is not enclosed within a larger compound. It is also unique in containing evidence of numerous camelid sacrifices (Pozorski 1979: 135). With these facts in mind, a comparison of the two is nonetheless instructive. The most striking contrast is that there seem to have been no human remains in the small chambers of the Tschudi platform, indeed, they are said to have contained baskets of seeds, fine cloth, and ornaments (Gutiérrez Rodríguez 1990: 106). Since some 21 of these cells were cleared, it is unlikely that no human bones would have been encountered had they been present originally. The four smaller, T-shaped chambers that Gutiérrez does identify as tombs were built in a separate structure abutting the platform.

Since neither the archaeological evidence nor historical analogy seems to support the common interpretation of the Chan Chan burial platforms, let us try another hypothesis. The platforms with multiple cells and adjacent structures were religious structures dedicated to the celebration of special ceremonies and sacrifices. These rites were held periodically and included a major sacrifice, which may or may not have involved humans, that was buried in the largest cell of the platform. The surrounding cells were designed to receive subsequent, smaller sacrifices that took place at regular intervals, upon certain specified occasions, or under special circumstances (e.g., marriage or death of a ruler, flood, pestilence, crop failure, a warlike undertaking). Perhaps the major sacrifice was intended to dedicate the compound in which it was buried (but then what about Las Avispas?). This suggestion might explain both the sequential construction and the fact that additional chambers were often added to the original platform; there was not yet a new area available for the necessary ceremonies.

How does the evidence square with this hypothesis? The items found on and around the platforms are those commonly used in important Andean offerings (humans of relatively uniform age, textiles, pottery and other artifacts, food, animals, *Spondylus*). The compound is an area with increasingly restricted access, but with open spaces suitable to the performance of ceremonies. Nearby storage space would serve to house religious tribute, paraphernalia, and sacrificial materials, like the crushed *Spondylus* in the Las Avispas storage bin. In the absence of more archaeological evidence, there is really nothing to choose between the two hypotheses. It would not be difficult to formulate others that would fit the evidence equally well. The less evidence available, the greater the number of possible interpretations. The way to reduce the number of hypotheses is to gather more evidence.

A lot of work lies between us and any detailed understanding of Andean mortuary customs. However elaborate mortuary rituals may be, little may remain for the archaeologist to discover and interpret (see, for example, Reichel-Dolmatoff 1974); and even what is left may be ambiguous. How can we determine to what extent the ostentation of a burial offering reflects not the status of the occupant of the grave but rather the social aspirations of his or her survivors? It is not, however, necessary to employ modern metaphors to interpret ancient burials. Indeed, such a procedure is likely to result in mere speculation unrelated to archaeological evidence. While keeping in mind as much ethnographic and historical data as possible, we must remember that we are archaeologists, and must work first and foremost with the evidence from the earth.

We must also consider that archaeologists, like ethnographers, are prone to work with a limited number of cultures and generally in a restricted area. Unlike ethnographers, however, we usually lack detailed cultural descriptions (in our case, site reports) from surrounding areas to aid us in interpreting our findings. Archaeologists, therefore, are given to interpreting their discoveries on the basis of known ethnographic or historical practices, simple logic, or some a priori schema such as cultural evolution. The results of this conference suggest the danger of such approaches. Clearly, we need more and better published site reports to aid us in broader comparisons of detailed archaeological contexts if we are to understand ancient beliefs and practices.

BIBLIOGRAPHY

BENNETT, WENDELL C.
    1948   *A Reappraisal of Peruvian Archaeology.* Society for American Archaeology, Memoir 4. Menasha.

BEORCHIA NIGRIS, ANTONIO
    1987   El Enigma de los Santuarios Indígenas de Alta Montaña. *Revista del Centro de Investigaciones Arqueológicas de Alta Montaña* 5 (año 1984 or 1985). San Juan, Argentina.

CHÁVEZ, SERGIO JORGE
    1987   Funerary Offerings from a Middle Horizon Context in Pomacanchi, Cuzco. *Ñawpa Pacha* 22–23 (1984–85): 1–48.

CONRAD, GEOFFREY W.
    1982   The Burial Platforms of Chan Chan: Some Social and Political Implications. In *Chan Chan: Andean Desert City* (Michael E. Moseley and Kent C. Day, eds.): 87–117. University of New Mexico Press, Albuquerque.

COOK, ANITA G. WYNN
    1987   The Middle Horizon Ceramic Offerings from Conchopata. *Ñawpa Pacha* 22–23 (1984–85): 49–90.

CRABTREE, KATHRYN RAE
    n.d.   Cemeteries in California and Nevada: A Western Thanatopsis. M.A. thesis, Sonoma State University, 1988.

DONNAN, CHRISTOPHER B., AND CAROL J. MACKEY
    1978   *Ancient Burial Patterns of the Moche Valley, Peru.* University of Texas Press, Austin.

GONZÁLEZ, ALBERTO REX
    1977   *Arte Precolombino de la Argentina: Introducción a su Historia Cultural.* Filmediciones Valero, Buenos Aires.

GROSSMAN, JOEL W.
    1972   An Ancient Gold Worker's Tool Kit: The Earliest Metal Technology in Peru. *Archaeology* 25 (4): 270–275.

GUTIÉRREZ RODRÍGUEZ, RODOLFO
    1990   *Chan Chan: Arquitectura e Implicancias Sociales del Palacio "Tschudi."* Colección "Arqueología y Pueblo," CONCYTEC, Lima.

HECKER, GIESELA, AND WOLFGANG HECKER
    1992   Ofrendas de Huesos Humanos y Uso Repetido de Vasijas en el Culto Funerario de la Costa Norperuana. *Gaceta Arqueológica Andina* 6: 33–53.

ISBELL, WILLIAM H., AND ANITA G. COOK
    1987   Ideological Origins of an Andean Conquest State. *Archaeology* 40 (4): 26–33.

JULIEN, CATHERINE JEAN
  1994 Las Tumbas de Sacsahuaman y el Estilo Cuzco-Inca. *Ñawpa Pacha* 25-26 (1987-88): 1-110.

KAUFFMANN DOIG, FEDÉRICO
  1978 *Manual de Arqueología Peruana*. Ediciones PEISA, Lima.

LE PAIGE, GUSTAVO
  1964 El Precerámico en la Cordillera Atacameña y los Cementerios del Período Agro-Alfarero de San Pedro de Atacama. *Anales de la Universidad del Norte* 3. Antofagasta.

LLANOS, LUIS
  1936 Trabajos Arqueológicos en el Depto. del Cuzco Bajo la Dirección del Dr. Luis E. Valcárcel. *Revista del Museo Nacional* 5 (2): 123-156, I-XV. Lima.

LUMBRERAS, LUIS GUILLERMO
  1981 *Arqueología de la América Andina*. Editorial Milla Batres, Lima.
  1989 *Chavín de Huántar en el Nacimiento de la Civilización Andina*. Instituto Andino de Estudios Arqueológicos, Ediciones INDEA, Lima.

LYON, PATRICIA J.
  1991 Andean Art and its Cultural Implications. In *Kodai Andesu Bijutsu* (Ancient Art of the Andean World) (Shozo Masuda and Izumi Shimada, eds.): 27-45. Iwamani Shoten, Tokyo.

MENZEL, DOROTHY
  1964 Style and Time in the Middle Horizon. *Ñawpa Pacha* 2: 1-106.
  1976 *Pottery Style and Society in Ancient Peru*. University of California Press, Berkeley.

NÚÑEZ DEL PRADO B., JUAN VÍCTOR
  1974 The Supernatural World of the Quechua of Southern Peru as Seen from the Community of Qotobamba. In *Native South Americans: Ethnology of the Least Known Continent* (Patricia J. Lyon, ed.): 238-250. Little, Brown and Company, Boston.

POZORSKI, THOMAS
  1979 The Las Avispas Burial Platform at Chan Chan, Peru. *Annals of the Carnegie Museum* 48: 119-137. Pittsburgh.

QUILTER, JEFFREY
  1989 *Life and Death at Paloma: Society and Mortuary Practices in a Preceramic Peruvian Village*. University of Iowa Press, Iowa City.

RAVINES, ROGGER
  1969 Un Depósito de Ofrendas del Horizonte Medio en la Sierra Central del Perú. *Ñawpa Pacha* 6 (1968): 19-46.
  1977 Excavaciones en Ayapata, Huancavelica, Perú. *Ñawpa Pacha* 15: 49-100.
  1979-83 Prácticas funerarias en Ancón. *Revista del Museo Nacional* 43 (1977): 327-397; 45 (1981): 89-166. Lima.

REICHEL-DOLMATOFF, GERARDO
    1974 Funerary Customs and Religious Symbolism among the Kogi. In *Native South Americans: Ethnology of the Least Known Continent* (Patricia J. Lyon, ed.): 289–301. Little, Brown and Company, Boston.

ROWE, ANN POLLARD
    1981 Textiles from the Burial Platform of Las Avispas at Chan Chan. *Ñawpa Pacha* 18 (1980): 81–148.

Andean Mortuary Practices in Perspective

JAMES A. BROWN

NORTHWESTERN UNIVERSITY

MORTUARY THEORY IN ANDEAN STUDIES

ANDEAN ARCHAEOLOGY IS FAMOUS for its well-preserved graves. Some of the driest environments known have fostered an extraordinarily well-preserved record of both cadavers and grave goods. The information potential provided by these mummified dead and their grave offerings is self-evident. It is little wonder that such well-preserved objects have attracted the most archaeological interest. Some of them have provided insight into matters that are unavailable outside of hyperdry environments. Others have led to a finely sequenced prehistoric chronology through the abundance of decorated pottery and other time-sensitive grave goods. But with increased attention that cemeteries around the world have received as documents of social organization, it is understandable that archaeologists should turn to the arrangement and outfitting of the graves themselves for the information they might hold about the organization of past societies. The potential for this line of research is amply indicated by the contributors to this collection of papers.

Unlike research on grave objects, study respecting the composition, arrangement, and location of graves is strongly affected by incompleteness in recovery, unsystematic reconnaissance and recovery, and other sampling problems. Although these problems have discouraged the study of graveyards, important archaeological goals can be attained only by the study of graves as members of graveyard populations. In the Andes alone, cemeteries offer some of our most direct avenues of information on certain issues respecting political and social-class development. As difficult and as problem-ridden as the study of graveyards is, experience has led to the development of useful research strategies. Frequently, specific questions offer plausible solutions because only a certain, limited range of information is required. On these and other matters most of the chapters in this book offer good examples of the use of archaeological grave research to inform on issues of social and political complexity in past Andean societies.

James A. Brown

MORTUARY ARCHAEOLOGY TODAY

Mortuary archaeology has developed as a method of social analysis along specific lines (Chapman, Kinnes, and Randsborg 1981; Morris 1987; O'Shea 1984). Certain features in the treatment of the dead have been singled out as having demonstrable significance in uncovering the specifically social factors underlying past practices. This has meant that such topics as the political contexts for monumental tomb building and the marking of social rank among burials can be approached within a worked-out theory. While other topics of potential interest remain relatively undeveloped theoretically, mortuary archaeology has emerged primarily as a research tool for uncovering the marking of political claims to control over critical resources through the planting of tombs and the existence of material marking of social differences within a population.

John Rowe's paper is at variance with the main perspective of this volume. His use of mortuary practices as a source of information on some monolithic body of behavior and belief—the customs of ancient Andeans, so to speak—is fundamentally normative in perspective. Other contributors are less avowedly normative, and most are committed to utilizing differences in the application of mortuary practices as a tool for social analysis.

Theoretical developments in mortuary archaeology have taken two separate perspectives to the interpretive significance of the material record of mortuary practices. One associated with the seminal work of Arthur Saxe (n.d.) and Lewis Binford (1971) views the dead as *individuals* and their mortuary treatment as somehow representative of some feature, aspect, or attribute they possessed before death. The oft-cited principle that treatment in death is determined by one's former status as a living individual is a restatement of this operating principle (Brown 1981; Peebles and Kus 1977; Tainter 1978).

Juxtaposed to this theoretical stance is the position that the dead are treated in accordance to the needs and wishes of the living (Pearson 1982; Shanks and Tilley 1982). This position is supported by certain forms of treatment of the dead that take on a strongly political aspect, such as the use of the dead to consecrate a monument, or the practice of determining the actual physical treatment of the corpse on criteria completely independent of the age, sex, or social standing of the deceased—such as the day on the ritual calendar or the stage of mound development and cemetery use. Particularly outstanding as instances of non-individual treatment are the ossuary accumulation of commingled bones and the collective burial in corporate facilities. In the case of contemporary Western practices, this perspective is particularly useful in explaining treatments based on the attitude of individuals having primary responsibility of conducting the funeral or memorial service (Pearson 1982).

Andean Mortuary Practices in Perspective

Although it is easy to cite cases that support both positions, recent developments in mortuary archaeology place greater emphasis on the second as logically the more encompassing (Trinkhaus 1984). While the "representationist" position, as I will call it here, has contributed toward some of the foundational thinking in the subject, a preponderance of evidence points to significant limitations to this thesis that make it a special case of more general principles. Individual representation is simply a common means for representation of the dead by the acts, practices, and beliefs on the part of a social community of living people. As it will be seen in the example below, groups that attempt to preserve the status quo of inherited rights typically use representationist means for symbolizing the treatment of the dead.

Once we begin to see the enactment of representation as a variable rather than as a constant, the power of mortuary archaeology increases as a tool for uncovering hidden dimensions of social organization. If a principle exists here, it is that mortuary practices exemplify the allocative principle in economics, in which any apportionment of time and effort inevitably concentrates on the few at the expense of the many.

SOCIAL CONSTRUCTION THROUGH MORTUARY PRACTICES

The position that the dead are treated to socially and culturally constructed rules is the more general of the two theoretical perspectives and can be illustrated by two examples in which a social world is constructed through monumental tomb building. The first of these is drawn from postreformation England, where monumental inscriptions were used to augment the investment in expensive material and craft labor in the creation of monumental tombs. These tombs, which were erected in churches to display the social importance of local landholders, contrast markedly in size, elaborateness, sculptural fixtures, visual impact, and locational exclusiveness with the monuments of the middling sector of society. To complete the impact of lordly tombs, the laboring classes usually were completely unmemorialized in durable materials. Nigel Llewellyn (1991) has shown that after the mid-1500s the nobility and gentry consciously used these monuments, particularly the life-sized effigies of the deceased, to create what he calls a "monumental body." This mortuary artifact was used to bolster the ideology that the upper classes were as enduring as the stone into which their images were transferred. Although death removed individuals unpredictably and leveled everyone before God, the monuments and effigies the elite invested in were regarded as instructive reminders of the endurance of a class-ordered social system. Thus, for several centuries in English society the grading of funerary dress, expense, and grieving behavior in accordance with the social standing of the dead was a customary means for reestablishing obedience to the social order more than it was an acknowledgement of the social persona of the deceased as the Saxe–Binford thesis would dictate. Thus, the principles that guided choice in funeral and tomb were ones that communicated the verities of upper-class domination: permanence of property and legitimacy of descent proclaimed through text and heraldic achievements. If one were to approach churchyard burials as an archaeological record, many features of this material record conform to expectations of the Saxe–Binford program, but what is crucial here is what happened to this material form of social construction in the twentieth century when obedience to the social order was abandoned by British society as a customary proscription. The very individuals who could afford conspicuous funerals and monumental tombs dropped them from consideration and rapidly adopted less conspicuous forms of material marking of the dead (Cannon 1989; Pearson 1982).

The second example taken from the Berawan of Borneo illustrates the political aspects to monumental tomb building in an entirely different way (Metcalf 1982; Metcalf and Huntington 1991). The Berawan monuments have changed from the traditional wood to modern concrete, but nonetheless the imperfect correspondence between the size of the monument and the social standing of the deceased remains as it was. Contrary to the expectations of the Saxe–Binford thesis, it is the social standing of the individual upon whose shoulders rests responsibility for the funeral feast and monument construction that corresponds most clearly to size and costliness of the funeral and tomb. And because of happenstance this responsibility often falls upon individuals whose economic resources are not in accord with that of the dead. As a consequence, high-standing individuals are sometimes marked by insignificant tombs and vice versa. The principle of graded response on the part of the funeral host toward the size and costliness of both the funeral and the tomb construction is in accordance with social standing, but that standing is of the host, not the deceased. Where there is social continuity between the deceased and survivors having funerary obligations, there is concordance between the status of the deceased and his or her tomb. Otherwise, discordance obtains. The Berawan are not an isolated case, but are part of a common pattern throughout Oceania.

The object of these two examples is not to cast up the obstacle of a "cautionary tale," but to emphasize the disconnection between the treatment of individuals (when they happened to be treated individually) and their social standing. Although the two may be very closely correlated in particular cases, this connection between treatment and social status has to be argued for separately. For instance, in her paper describing the sequence from the Osmore drainage, Jane Buikstra makes an argument for both representationist and non-representationist models in the treatment of the social persona of the deceased. Hence, any statement made about past social organization has to solve the problem of how the dead were primarily represented in any particular past society. Context and pattern are obviously very important to any determination.

A good example of how this problem can be reasonably resolved is provided by Christopher Donnan's analysis of Moche burial patterns. His study stressed the endurance of specific treatments of the dead. They were highly persistent whether they happened to be the richest known example or one of the poorest. Throughout his study sample of 291 burials, he found the telltale imprint of an invariant patterning in the burial treatments. Although the content of expression varied, the patterns were enacted with steadfast consistency, whether in rich elaborate materials or by cheap token ones. By demonstrating the strength of this set of Moche practices in all economic strata and in both sexes, we are in a good position to believe that Moche graves, grave furnishings, and grave locations conformed to an individual, representationist treatment of the dead. They were not treated as a collectivity, whose individual personae were submerged within an impersonal community of the dead. Nor were they furnished in a manner that seriously distorted or even "inverted" the status of the deceased for purposes of political manipulation. This is a very useful finding that prepares the way for certain kinds of fruitful analyses. However well this serves Moche studies, it does not necessarily apply to other cultures, as we shall see shortly.

TOMBS AS MARKERS OVER CRITICAL RESOURCES

One of the more useful applications of mortuary archaeology has been the thesis that the placement of the dead on the landscape is frequently used by families, descent groups, and whole societies to lay claim to the control of critical resources where other means are insecure or non-existent. Since Saxe's original development of this thesis as his Hypothesis 8, we have realized that a group's claims may be symbolized by funereal declarations that do not affect the burial itself (Chapman 1987; Charles and Buikstra 1983; Goldstein n.d.). Hence, the appearance and disappearance of planned cemeteries or mound construction, for example, cannot be used to faithfully trace the rise and fall of competition over critical resources. Nonetheless, the consistent use of some sort of formalized place for the interment of a group's dead usually points to uses of the dead for the purpose of laying some claim over important resources. Conspicuous examples are known in which the historical appearance of monumentalism of all kinds, including simple earthen mound building, can be attributed to a response to competition over resources and to a validation of claims to a range of different kinds of resources, from agricultural lands to urban citizenship (Bloch 1981; Morris 1991; Randsborg 1981). A couple of chapters in this volume draw upon this principle (Buikstra, Dillehay), while others beg for its application (Drennan, Rivera).

The most specific applications can be found in Buikstra's chapter. First, she champions the notion, not taken up by Rivera, that the Chinchorro mummy shrines were prima facie instances of the resource marking principles. She also argues that the Tumilaca, as initial settlers in a noncompetitive environmental setting, practiced casual disposal of the dead without conspicuous grave markings. The appearance of competitors at the P4 and P8 sites introduced collared tombs to the area as a means of expressing claims to land and resources. Thus, the appearance of grave architecture is less an expression of cultural diffusion than the emergence of new social stresses.

MORTUARY PRACTICES AND ANDEAN SOCIAL ORGANIZATION

Several of the papers strive specifically to seek evidence of ancient social structure from mortuary patterns (Buikstra, Carmichael, and Donnan). Carmichael and Donnan in particular make use of a promising strategy for investigating these patterns by pooling scattered burial records into a composite sample. Not only does this increase the effectiveness of their samples, but the strategy leads in theoretically viable directions with their investigation of the distributions of age, sex, location, wealth, and other factors. The distribution of burial treatments, grave wealth, and burial location among a population of groups of various age and sex happen to be what mortuary archaeology is all about theoretically: the allocation of resources (time, wealth, and effort) to alternative subgroups within a population of funerals. Since resource demand, potentially, can easily outstrip a group's tolerance or capacity, with any kind of pressure on these resources even the most common of allocations readily become differentially distributed and hence subtle measures of the effects of these pressures upon the local economy of mortuary practices.

The big problem confronting archaeologists is the fact that the physical burial is only one part of the total funeral. To the participants, symbols of social differentiation may or may not be marked in the burial. They need only be symbolized during the funeral. But once admitting this limitation to the theory of behavioral economy in mortuary practices, a virtue can be made out of this limitation by focusing upon the distribution of treatments among a representative sample of a biological population. Since the physical remains of the deceased retain crucial information on age and sex, the distribution of cultural treatments among various segments of the population divided by sex and age groups conveys the essentials respecting the economy of mortuary practices. To this can be added the vital information on health that Buikstra has indicated to be a silent but critical factor in social analysis.

NASCA SOCIAL COMPLEXITY?

An important application of mortuary theory is represented by Patrick Carmichael's critique of the supposed "complexity" of Nasca culture. This chapter illustrates the point that the benefits of mortuary theory have scarcely been tested in the Andes. New light can be shed on long-contested debates respecting the kinds of social and political complexity that occurred at various times in the past.

Carmichael's chapter is somewhat exploratory since the sample is somewhat meager (168) for the number of Early Intermediate Period epochs over which the Nasca burials are distributed. The problem of sample representativeness is acute, particularly with the locational contexts of the no. 4 graves. If they lie within cemeteries containing a normal range of lower categories, the question of the disconnection of status and ayllu affiliation has to be raised. Further investigations to clarify this point are clearly warranted. But the overall direction his conclusions take cast doubt on reconstructions that make the Nasca out to be a political state, at least on the presently available mortuary data. His conclusion that there is no evidence of discrete social classes, only a gradient of status positions, is reasonable, but open to revision, particularly if large, high-status graves are discovered.

Of great interest for its window to an unexplored world of secondary burial is Carmichael's case for the scavenging of skull and upper body parts from a large tomb at Cahuachi. He rightly raises the prospect of this as a source for a multiphased secondary burial. One alternative explanation that Carmichael did not address is the possibility that his large "reentered" tomb was the locus of collective graves, in which disintegration of individual corpses would be expected over time. The presence of collective burial in his high-status tombs would have changed his analysis considerably. Based on the absence of any indication of collective tombs elsewhere, I doubt that this single remarkable burial was a sign of hitherto overlooked graves of the communal sort.

Last, in answer to Carmichael's rhetorical question of whether status markers are represented among the Nasca grave attributes—yes, they are likely to have been identified considering the age distribution among various interment categories and the kind of standardized body position he describes. Measures of social differentiation he came up with are not surprising. They are ceramic volume (wealth), tomb construction (expense), and grave depth (labor investment).

THE MOCHE MORTUARY PROGRAM

In the case of the famous Moche, Donnan is faced with an interesting challenge. He develops an algorithm (decision tree) for the Moche funerary pattern based upon a burial sample of 291 that was unevenly distributed through the five periods—nearly half in the last phase. Donnan examines his sample in terms of five dimensions or variables: preparation of the corpse, encasing of the corpse, funerary chambers, quantity and quality of the grave goods, and location. He finds that four of the five are determinative, namely, ones in principle very similar to those identified for the Nasca. Some not unsurprising observations are the degree to which proximity of these graves to substantial sacred architecture (large pyramids and platforms) determines size and elaborateness. In this drop-off in scale of elaborateness with distance from large pyramids we have one of the classic means by which one's social standing is defined.

Donnan also observed that four cemeteries "appear to have been used exclusively for the burial of a distinct set of individuals." Males that he identified with the Bean Runner of Moche painting were placed together in a mud-brick platform. They had copper-disk headdresses resembling those worn by Bean Runners in Moche art. Although a distinct category of interments, it is instructive to his general thesis that the attributes of the Bean Runner grave type lay outside of those that defined the Moche social pyramid.

The richest known tomb from Sipán naturally dominates Donnan's discussion. What was important about this spectacular tomb was that it differed from others in degree, not in kind. Differences were along the dimensions of labor and raw material investment. Hence, this "apical" grave possessed a large, room-sized burial chamber that was simply an enlargement of the smaller, rectangular burial chambers. Numerous vessels were deposited in place of a single vessel. Expensive materials of copper and gold substituted for cheaper more accessible materials found in ordinary graves. The plank coffin was tied with copper strapping, whereas the lowly cane coffin was tied with sedge rope. A gold dish replaced the gourd plate commonly found beneath the head. Copper sandals were tied to the feet instead of the small sheets of copper placed beneath the feet of some burials. A gold ingot and silver, one in each hand, replaced the copper pieces commonly found in these positions. A gold mask was present where a sheet of copper was usual. Although the body was wrapped in the prescribed manner, it rested on a wooden instead of a cane frame. Donnan found the same adherence to prescribed custom operating even in the case of a very poor dead woman—where token items of cheap materials were substituted.

THE VERTICAL ARCHIPELAGO IN THE OSMORE DRAINAGE

In what is a review of the history of cemetery practices in a single river drainage, Buikstra offers refreshing counterproposals to the commonplace Andean practice of explaining all trade and development toward increasing complexity through time to the dynamics of the Vertical Archipelago thesis. Respecting the Middle Horizon Omo site, Buikstra rejects the view that the Omo site is an altiplano or Tiwanaku-inspired local production center or an administrative subordinate to Tiwanaku. She favors Omo as an autochthonous community that was the recipient of altiplano exotic items through trade. No strong indication of differential treatment is present that would signify strong vertical social distinctions. With respect to cranial deformation, this practice at Omo probably signifies different descent groups.

Late Intermediate Period Chiribaya sites indicate a localized, autonomous political entity. Trade is documented by the plentiful remains and products of camelids, with few exotic items to indicate strong foreign connections. Hence any vertical trade that may have existed was "attenuated." The elite became more visible at the end of the period with the construction of fortification walls at the Chiribaya Alta site. Many elaborate tombs were built overlooking the Osmore Valley in a manner suggestive of the politics of resource control through the placing of the dead.

When it comes to explaining the rise in Estuquiña phase Tumilaca of what is apparently a lineage-based organization of households, the appearance of graves in house floors is entirely consistent with the other evidence. A decline in the mortuary hierarchy from preceding Tumilaca phase times probably represents a loosening, if not an outright decline, in the importance of social ranking.

TROPHY HEADS AND ANCESTOR REMAINS

John Verano examines the varieties of non-mortuary treatment of the human body for parallels and divergences with mortuary treatment. Non-mortuary "treatment include[s] human sacrifice, dedicatory burial, secondary offerings of human remains and the collection and curation of human body parts." In so doing he returns to an ever-present theme in Andean studies, the trophy head. A variety of evidence leads one to believe that by the Middle Horizon the taking and display of trophy heads was commonplace. But this evidence does not mean that all isolated skulls were trophies. Quite the contrary. Mortuary practices that involve secondary treatment of the dead often include removal of skull or mandible from the skeleton. Just such practices have been indicated in two other chapters.

First, Carmichael has shown the possibility of ancestor worship being represented in the decapitated burial from Cahuachi. This is rather indirect evidence, but entirely reasonable given the evidence. More to the point are the instances of secondary skull removal practices summarized by Buikstra for Early Horizon and Early Intermediate sites. The instances of skull removal at the Wawakiki cemetery is particularly striking. One can conclude from these cases that a number of alternative forms of skull treatment existed, particularly prior to the Early Intermediate Period, that urge caution in assigning every loose skull as a trophy head.

Probably more interesting is the logical connection one can draw between the act of taking a head from an enemy and conserving the heads of the valued ancestors, often in shrines controlled by the descendants. In both cases—one "non-mortuary," the other part of secondary burial—the skull is regarded as the reservoir of potent human power. Conserving one's ancestor's power is important to the descendants, and depriving the enemy of their powerful bones further enhances one's own. In a sense then, the viability of trophy-head taking is seated, historically at least, in the practice of placing great significance upon the heads of the ancestors. Although ancestor head veneration may have lapsed in use long before the practice of trophy-head taking had waned, it is logical to see the former as a precursor of the latter practice, especially if it took place on a large scale.

All of this alerts us to the necessity for spelling out quite clearly the reasons for assigning human skulls to the category of trophies. Verano has been reasonable on this score. But when it comes to extending his argument to earlier periods and different areas, the problematic position of isolated skulls will have to be reexamined.

POLITICAL USES OF FUNERARY PRACTICES

In his focus on unusual historic funerary practices, Dillehay describes the political contexts in which earthen mound construction was undertaken among the Araucanians of south-central Chile. Elaborate mounds were constructed over the tombs of paramount chiefs in the late prehistoric and historic periods. The act of construction was part of what Dillehay describes as a postfuneral ritual that took place under certain circumstances only. In a relationship that bears certain similarities to the Berawan case cited above, new Araucanian leaders with the requisite resources and connections use the tomb of a high-ranking dead chief as the focus of prolonged rites of memorial, in which the assembled guests raise a monument over the tomb. In one sense the project is simply the occasion by which the new leader is legitimated and his authority over other lineages is cemented. In the end, however, the mound becomes emblematic of his political success. Dillehay makes the point clearly that the funeral only sets the stage for alliance building and the consolidation of authority. Other elements of personal drive and access to requisite resources are necessary to support the prolonged installation ritual that makes the difference between a mound construction or nothing at all. The political uses of the dead could not be more clearly exemplified as in this example. It should serve to brake the fascination with demonstrating a representationist relationship between the deceased and the size of the mound erected over the tomb.

Andean Mortuary Practices in Perspective

TOMBS FOR THE LIVING

In the absence of a sample of burials, and because of the poor preservation of skeletal remains, Drennan makes use of other lines of evidence to advance the thesis that leadership was personalized during the Regional Classic where the tomb and statue complex was found. He argues for this kind of leadership for two reasons. First, burial mounds are the sole forms of monumentality, and second, burial mounds are not integrated into plazas, residences, and other constructions. Although architecture did not have the permanent monumental character of mounds, we do not know anything about the "size, location, and character of spaces created for other public, ritual, or communal activities." Although little or no wealth differentiation is indicated, some sort of intensive field investigation of single communities is required to back up this inference.

Nothing approaching the monumentality of the tomb and statue complex appears in the preceding Formative. As for the post-A.D. 800 Recent period, the tomb and statue complex ceases without any demonstrable collapse of population, since levels do not seem to have changed at all. Patterns of population aggregation continue. Elite tombs become shaft graves without tumuli. Drennan sees two reasons for the changes: (1) "more complete institutionalization of positions of leadership"; and (2) expanded exercise of economic forms of control. For the former one might expect standardized symbols of office, which Drennan sees evidence for in ethnohistoric accounts of southern Colombia.

One missing aspect to this analysis is some notion of the strategy of placement with regard to critical resources. Are we dealing with a political placement of the dead as a means for exercising group claims, or do we have an instance of the Araucanian model? These and other possibilities come to mind.

CHINCHORRO MORTUARY SHRINES?

In his review of the Preceramic Chinchorro mummy complex of northern Chile, Rivera has emphasized exotic origins over local development. Despite the early age of the beginnings of the mummy tradition, he prefers to find the origins of mummies outside of the Pacific coast and to find refuge in a phylogenetic rationale for the mummy traditions throughout South America. The Chinchorro is thereby regarded as having eastern tropical forest connections. Only after 1000 B.C. (Chinchorro III) did the Andean or altiplano tradition reach the area, with connections to the circum-Titicaca area. I find this scenario to be thin. Connections may or may not have existed, but what is far more important is the natural and social environment of this early Preceramic tradition of treating the dead.

As Buikstra has indicated, the Chinchorro tradition became established when populations along the South Pacific coast became increasingly more numerous. This growth in use of marine resources was also made possible by increasing competition for limited supplies of fresh water and terrestrial resources (Wise n.d.). Under these pressures for control of precious land rights it is understandable that the ancestors would have been enlisted to assert a group's claim to those resources. Rivera's description of typical mummy sites suggests the use of ancestors to stake out claims to critical resources. They are found in small groups composed of both sexes and adults and children. The distribution of family-sized groups of mummies positioned on steep dunes facing the ocean points to the use of artificially preserved mummy stands as parts of shrines. Buikstra points out that these mummies show evidence of repainting of faces although the bodies reveal wear and surface cracking.

CONCLUSION

To varying degrees the principles of contemporary mortuary archaeology have been drawn upon by the authors in this volume. The contributors demonstrate the usefulness of mortuary archaeology as a method for bringing fresh perspectives to older problems and for questioning common ideas respecting the ubiquity of the vertical archipelago thesis, invasions of people, political takeovers, and effects of class structures that typically have been used to explain various features of the archaeological record and puzzling connections in art and culture.

Out of the many challenging problems raised by the "pan-Andean" perspective to mortuary practices, I would like to single out a few:

(1) How can the study of mortuary practices contribute to the identification of differences in social and political complexity?

(2) How uniform or prevalent is the ancestor shrine as a potent instrument of political organization? The evolution of this "institution" is a useful goal and one that potentially can shed great light on social history.

(3) Given the importance of the ancestor shrine in Preceramic and Early Horizon times, I think it particularly critical that the physical remains of the honored ancestors be distinguished from "trophy heads." The two go hand in hand. Where heads are collected ethnographically, the same body part is regarded as a reservoir of power to be used to legitimize actions and to confer on other centers of power some degree of sanctity.

(4) Carmichael raises the issue of how membership in a graveyard was determined. Related to this question is the connection of the ancestor shrines to cemeteries open to the majority of the population. Were the elite placed in locations separate and

disjunct from the majority? Were they part of a unified representation of society in a single location? Were they mixed—some being included within society-wide cemeteries but others clearly excluded? Or were they merely appended to sacredly charged shrines (much as medieval Christian church cemeteries)?

(5) A major problem in the Andes is how to recover representative burial samples for social analysis. False pictures of vertical status differentiation can be created by integrating parts of cemeteries that happen to have survived. John O'Shea (1984) has observed that non-status marking treatments of the dead are more likely to perish than those indicating status distinctions, and furthermore, non-status markers are likely to be confused with or conflated with status markers when most features of treatment disappear through decay. The presence of perishables only adds to the problem since so much information is provided by even the most ordinary of interments that one could be easily deceived into thinking that a small sample would suffice.

Of more immediate utility is the advantage to burial investigation that research priorities offered by mortuary archaeology provide in today's environment of diminished opportunities. There is no substitute for clarity of purpose in fostering effective research, and this is particularly true when faced with the daunting task of allocating scientific labor and resources to a shrinking pool of unravaged sites. The mass of material is simply too great to justify continued collection of graves without a programmatic rationale. In the past, burials have provided useful closed contexts for chronology construction. Although cemeteries have served Andean archaeologists well in this regard, much more information resides in the material record provided by burials. Given the shrinking supply of cemeteries, research agendas that tap the little-explored social dimension of mortuary practices ought to be given due attention. For these reasons, this collection of essays is all the more welcome as an exploration of the uses of mortuary archaeology to such a fertile field as Andean archaeology.

BIBLIOGRAPHY

BINFORD, LEWIS R.
    1971 Mortuary Practices: Their Study and Their Potential. In *Approaches to the Social Dimensions of Mortuary Practices* (James A. Brown, ed.). Memoirs of the Society for American Archaeology 25: 6–29. Washington, D.C.

BLOCH, MAURICE
    1981 Tombs and States. In *Mortality and Immortality: The Anthropology and Archaeology of Death* (S. C. Humphreys and Helen King, eds.): 137–148. Academic Press, London.

BROWN, JAMES A.
    1981 The Search for Rank in Prehistoric Burials. In *The Archaeology of Death* (Robert Chapman, Ian Kinnes, and Klavs Randsborg, eds.): 25–37. Cambridge University Press, New York.

CANNON, AUBREY
    1989 The Historical Dimension in Mortuary Expressions of Status and Sentiment. *Current Anthropology* 30: 437–458.

CHAPMAN, R.
    1987 Mortuary Practices: Society, Theory Building and Archaeology. In *Death, Decay and Reconstruction: Approaches to Archaeology and Forensic Science* (A. Boddington, A. N. Garland, and R. C. Janaway, eds.): 198–213. Manchester University Press, Manchester.

CHAPMAN, ROBERT, IAN KINNES, AND KLAVS RANDSBORG (EDS.)
    1981 *The Archaeology of Death*. Cambridge University Press, New York.

CHARLES, DOUGLAS K., AND JANE E. BUIKSTRA
    1983 Archaic Mortuary Sites in the Central Mississippi Drainage: Distribution, Structure, and Behavioral Implications. In *Archaic Hunters and Gatherers in the American Midwest* (James L. Phillips and James A. Brown, eds.): 117–145. Academic Press, New York.

GOLDSTEIN, LYNNE G.
    n.d. *Spatial Structure and Social Organization: Regional Manifestations of Mississippian Society*. Ph.D. dissertation, Northwestern University, 1976.

LLEWELLYN, NIGEL
    1991 *The Art of Death: Visual Culture in the English Death Ritual, c. 1500–c. 1800*. Reaktion Books, London.

METCALF, PETER
    1982 *A Borneo Journey into Death: Berawan Eschatology from Its Ritual*. University of Pennsylvania Press, Philadelphia.

METCALF, PETER, AND RICHARD HUNTINGTON
    1991 *Celebrations of Death: The Anthropology of Mortuary Ritual* (2nd ed.). Cambridge University Press, Cambridge.

MORRIS, IAN
    1987   *Burial and Ancient Society: The Rise of the Greek City-State*. Cambridge University Press, Cambridge.
    1991   The Archaeology of Ancestors: The Saxe/Goldstein Hypothesis Revisited. *Cambridge Archaeological Journal* 1: 147–169.

O'SHEA, JOHN M.
    1984   *Mortuary Variability: An Archaeological Investigation*. Academic Press, New York.

PADER, ELLEN-JANE
    1982   *Symbolism, Social Relations and the Interpretation of Mortuary Remains*. BAR International Series 130. Oxford.

PEARSON, MICHAEL PARKER
    1982   Mortuary Practices, Society and Ideology: An Ethnoarchaeological Study. In *Symbolic and Structural Archaeology* (Ian Hodder, ed.): 99–113. Cambridge University Press, Cambridge.

PEEBLES, CHRISTOPHER S., AND SUSAN M. KUS
    1977   Some Archaeological Correlates of Ranked Societies. *American Antiquity* 42: 421–448.

RANDSBORG, KLAVS
    1981   Burial, Succession and Early State Formation in Denmark. In *The Archaeology of Death* (Robert Chapman, Ian Kinnes, and Klavs Randsborg, eds.): 105–121. Cambridge University Press, New York.

SAXE, ARTHUR ALAN
    n.d.   Social Dimensions of Mortuary Practices. Ph.D. dissertation, University of Michigan, 1970.

SHANKS, MICHAEL, AND CHRISTOPHER TILLEY
    1982   Ideology, Symbolic Power, and Ritual Communication: A Reinterpretation of Neolithic Mortuary Practices. In *Symbolic and Structural Archaeology* (Ian Hodder, ed.): 129–154. Cambridge University Press, New York.

TAINTER, JOSEPH A.
    1978   Mortuary Practices and the Study of Prehistoric Social Systems. *Advances in Archaeological Method and Theory* 1: 105–141.

TRINKHAUS, K. MAURER
    1984   Mortuary Ritual and Mortuary Research. *Current Anthropology* 25: 674–679.

WISE, KAREN E.
    n.d.   Late Archaic Period Maritime Subsistence Strategies in the South-Central Andes. Ph.D. dissertation, Northwestern University, 1990.

Index

Prepared by Lisa deLeonardis

An "f" following a page number indicates a figure.

Acarí, 177–178, 180, 210–211
Acha, 46, 236
Admapu, 304
Adobaban, 343
Adobe, 161, 178. *See also* mud bricks
Age distinction in burials, 7, 13, 15, 27–28, 30, 36, 51, 54–55, 65–66, 82, 123, 143, 154, 162, 167–168, 170, 176, 194, 197, 199–202, 213–214, 218, 236, 240, 247–248, 250–251, 260, 263–264, 266–267
   importance of, 380, 384
Agriculture, 9, 44, 63, 67, 233
Aguazuque burial complex, 6
Aja B (site), 171
Akapana, 201, 243, 245
Algarroba, 142. *See also* wood
Altiplano tradition, 46, 258, 263, 401
Alto de las Piedras, 100
Alto de Lavapatas, 100–101, 103f
Alto de los Idolos, 82, 85, 86f, 87f
Alto Magdalena, 79–80, 81f, 82–83, 89, 95–96, 98–100, 105–107, 342
Alto Ramirez Phase, 51, 62, 64, 67, 241
Amarete (ayllu), 358, 364. *See also* ayllu, Kaata
Amayanacan utapnaca, 320f
Amaya 'uta. See corpse house
Amazon, 203
Ancestor, vii, 8, 10, 67, 321, 324, 333, 355, 361, 368–369, 372, 374
   cult, 17, 285, 315, 317, 319–320, 324, 342, 347
   definition, 321n
   feeding of, 364, 374

monument, 17
shrine, 402–403
sickness, 374–375
veneration, 63, 315, 375
worship, 13, 17, 63, 177, 182, 202, 219, 343, 399. *See also machula*
Ancon, 28, 379
Ancoraimes, 359–360
Andagua, 17, 343
Andahuaylas, 381
Animal, viii, 264, 386
   alpaca, 44
   bird, 261, 369
   blood, 292, 297, 333
   bone, 142, 147
   camelid, 142, 146–147, 260–261, 264–267, 329, 335, 341, 385
   cougar, 357
   cow, 369
   crocodile, 96
   dog, 147
   fang, 96
   guinea pig, 44, 147, 333, 337
   llama, 44
   monkey, 261
   puma, 357
   sea lion, 147
   sheep, 292
   skin, 62, 178
   snake, 147
   teeth, 61, 63
   vulture, 190, 192, 194f, 195. *See also* animal sacrifice; bird; camelid; ceramics; leather; llama; reptile; skin; textile

Index

Animal sacrifice, 163, 283, 294, 297–298, 307, 329–331, 333, 335, 341, 385. *See also* human sacrifice; llama
Antofagasta Hipodromo, 44
Anyma, 322, 330, 340–341
Apacheta (ayllu), 358, 371–372
  lakes, 360. *See also* ayllu; Kaata
Aposentillos, 344
Apu, 323
Apurímac, 316
Aragón, 60
Araguaya River, 64
Araucanian, 238, 285–287, 289, 292, 294, 300, 302, 307, 342, 400
  culture area, 282, 282f
  link between living and dead, 283–284, 297, 300
  society, 286–289. *See also* Chile; Mapuche
Arawaks, 64
Archaic period, 5–7
  Middle Archaid, 5–6
  in North America, 237–238
  premonumental cemeteries, 5–7
Architectural models, 142. *See also* clay
Architecture, 14, 342
  ceremonial, 194f, 202, 212, 215, 245, 255
  circular houses, 46, 89, 103, 105
  monumental, 229–230
  niche, 142, 147f
  round structures, 240
  sacred, 398
  semisubterranean, 46, 62. *See also* platform; plaza; tomb architecture
Arequipa, 317, 323, 343
Argentina, 5, 62, 64, 190, 283, 302, 381
Arica, 49, 54, 229, 380
Arms. *See* weapon
Arriaga, Pablo Joseph de, 3
Art, 14
  representational, 6. *See also* Moche art
Asia (Peru), 62–63, 202–203, 219
Atahualpa, 192, 196, 343
Audencia, 199–200
Awn, 296, 301
Aya, 329
Ayacucho, 247, 316–317
  basin, 202
  Uchurracay hamlet, 247

Aya marcai, 318f
Ayan otapa. *See* tomb architecture: tower tomb
Ayllu, 243, 252–253, 264, 321–322, 325, 334, 341–342, 344–345, 355, 357–359, 363–365, 367–369, 372–375
  community divisions, 367
  ecology, 358
  metaphor, 357
  maximal, 323
  structure, 356
Aymara, 2f, 16–17, 28, 320f, 324, 357–358
Aynoqa, 357

Bajo Molle, 44, 45f, 50, 60
Bamboo, 369
Bandurrias, 62
Barranquilla, 101, 103f, 104f, 105
Basketry, 44, 46, 51, 54, 60, 62, 67, 120, 150, 168, 240, 248, 260
  cache, 239
  coiled, 51
  throne, 177
  wicker, 369. *See also* fiber; matting
Bautista Saavedra, 357
Bawden, Garth, 263–264, 266
Bead. *See also* bone; jewelry; shell; stone
Bean Runner, 147, 153: ceremony, 143, 144f, 153
  sacrifice, 148, 154
Berawan, 394, 400
  burial monument, 394
Binford, Lewis, 10, 66, 162, 231, 284, 392
  Saxe-Binford School, 232, 394
Bird, 261, 369
  bone tube, 67
  condor motif, 168
  flamingo motif, 248
  hummingbird motif, 168
  skin, 51, 67
  vulture, 190, 192, 194f, 195. *See also* animal; feather; headdress, mutilation; scavenger
Bird, Junius, 43
Body curation techniques, 5, 7, 9, 51, 54–55, 60–63, 66–67
  red ochre, 5, 54–55, 59f, 62–63, 67, 123, 176, 203, 236, 248

408

Index

salt, 7
wrapping, 7, 9. See also Aymara; Chinchorro; Inka; Mapuche; Moche; mummification; mummy; Nasca; Paracas; San Agustín
Body/head orientation, viii, 7, 27, 123, 152, 155, 164, 166, 197
  face down, 28, 197, 247
  facing east, 258
  facing mountain, 261, 361
  facing northwest, 236
  facing sea, 51
  facing south, 152, 258
  facing southwest, 152
  facing west, 152
Body posture
  extended, 6, 27–28, 51, 55, 60–62, 66, 123, 176, 199, 236
  flexed, 6, 27–29, 55, 60, 197, 258
  seated and flexed, 28–29, 34, 166
  side flexed, 178
  standing, 61. See also mummy
Bolivia, 7
Bone (animal), 147, 200
  ankle bracelet, 240
  artifacts, 236, 240
  beads, 240
  bird-bone tube, 67
  camelid, 259–260
  dog, 147
  ear ornament, 149
  figurine, 54
  fragments, 240
  guinea pig, 211, 248, 267
  hollow tubes, 236, 240
  llama, 146–147, 248, 263, 267
  mallero, 150
  ornament, 6
  sea lion, 147
  sea mammal, 54, 63, 68f
  whale, 62, 67. See also animal, animal sacrifice
Bone (human), 338f
  burned, 62, 200, 219
  flute, 192
  isolated find, 34, 200
  necklace, 203
  pin, 203. See also head; human sacrifice; jewelry; musical instrument; skin: human
Borneo, 394

Brazil, 61, 203
Bread baby, 372, 373f, 374. See also figurine; food
Bronze, 381. See also metal
Bulto, 332, 335, 343. See also mummy
Burial accoutrements: placement of, viii, 7, 27
  and political structure, 15
  renewal of, 37
  sparcity of, 7, 11, 37. See also basketry; bone; ceramics; clothing; copper; feather; figurine; fishing implements; food; gold; hallucinogens; metal; plant; shell; silver; spinning and weaving implement; *Spondylus;* stone; textiles; weapon; wood
Burial compound, 29
Burial construction types. See tomb architecture
Burial records, 3, 29
Butalmapu, 287, 300, 302, 306

Cabeccera del Valle, 358
Cahuachi, 171, 174, 177, 180, 209f, 211, 239, 397, 399
Cajatambo, 317
Calancha, Fray Antonio de la, 192
Calca, 201
Caleta Huelén, 42, 44, 45f, 46, 60
Caliche, 211
Camaquen, 323, 329
Camarones-14 (site), 44, 45f, 46, 50, 60, 65, 237
Camarones-15 (site), 44, 45f, 50, 53f, 54, 61, 65f, 67
Camelid, 260–261. See also llama
Cañar, 317
Canastos-3 (site), 44, 45f, 50
Candle, 361–363, 372
  llama fat, 324, 333
Cane, 46, 62, 103, 167, 229
  alcohol, 369
  beam, 137
  coffin, 120, 130, 131f, 132f, 133, 135–137, 146–147, 151, 153–155
  covering, 167, 178
  frame, 125, 127f, 135, 152, 398
  grave marker, 142, 168
  pan pipe, 248
  roof, 178

409

Index

splint, 125, 126f
stretcher, 206
tube, 125, 128f, 129f, 135, 146, 152. *See also* tomb architecture
Cannabalism, 105, 200
Capac hucha (cycle), 190, 327, 332
Capac Yupanqui (Inka), 193f
Carrizal, 236
Castellanos, 316
Castillo de Tomoval Site 1, 130n
Cayan, 321. *See also* plaza
Ceja de selva, 44. *See also* tropical forest culture
Cemeteries, 153, 178, 202, 219, 238, 242–247, 257–258, 281, 282f, 291f, 299f, 331, 340, 362, 371, 379, 383, 391
  cemetery culture, 161
  community, 247
  formal, 6–7, 70, 236, 238, 258, 262, 264, 266–267, 269
  group, 292
  multistratified group, 11
  patrilineal, 362
  planned, 44
  premonumental, 5
  in relation to residential sites, 6–7, 168
  specialized, 153–154. *See also* Aymara; Chinchorro; Inka; Mapuche; Moche; Nasca; Paracas
Central coast burials, 28
Ceramics, 85, 96, 142, 146, 156, 200, 215f, 217f, 243, 260, 264, 267, 289, 385
  as encasement, 125, 130
  fiber-tempered, 240
  flaring bowl, 143
  food marks on, 31
  iconography, 143
  jar, 143, 167
  as mask, 146
  miniature, 32, 171
  mold-made, 32, 381
  offerings, 85, 89, 101, 142–143, 155, 164, 168, 170f, 171, 174, 177–178, 200, 212, 259, 385
  olla, 167, 210–211, 218, 239
  overfired, 32
  painted bowls, 239
  pairs, 143, 171–173
  polychrome, 381–382
  sand and algae temper, 60
  stirrup spout bottle, 143
  urn, 34, 164, 167, 178, 255, 338
  wear patterns, 31. *See also* clay; Moche; Nasca
Ceremonial center, 320–322, 356
Ceremonial sites, 92, 105
Cerro Carapo, 204, 212
Cerro de la Cruz, 210
Cerro El Plomo, 190
Cerro Guacas, 89
Cerro Max Uhle, 210
Cerro Sechin, 14, 219
Chajaya (ayllu), 358, 364–365
Chancay Valley, 32
Chan Chan, 10, 19, 29, 198–199, 219, 317, 383, 385. *See also audencia; ciudadela*
Chaquis, 358. *See also* Niñokorin (ayllu)
Chari (ayllu), 358, 364
Chaviña, 178, 211, 213
Chavín de Huantar, 14, 200–201, 356–357, 382. *See also* Galería de las Ofrendas
Chemamüll, 288–289, 291f, 294, 297, 303. *See also* statuary; wood
Chibcha Indians, 61
Chicha, 292–293, 297, 307, 333, 361, 369–371
  jar, 293–294, 307
  maize beer, 318f, 320f, 324, 329, 331, 337, 341
  mudai, 297
  vessel, 297. *See also* corn; drink; feasting: festival
Chiefdom, 4, 7, 18–20, 92, 94–96, 100, 106, 161, 179, 181–182, 286, 342
  chief, 96, 162, 197, 283, 285–288, 292–298, 300–306
  chiefly burials, 98, 101
  group-oriented chiefdoms, 95
  individualizing chiefdoms, 95
  paramount chief, 16, 283, 288, 304, 400
  symbols of, 288. *See also* elite burial; Nasca; political power
Chilca Valley, 62
Chile, 38; 43–44, 190, 202, 233, 236, 239–240, 242, 302, 336
  south-central, 281, 282f, 289, 302, 400

Index

Chimor, 29, 30
  kings, 198. *See also* Chimu
Chimu, 2f, 10, 29, 151, 161–162, 164, 179, 199–200, 219, 372
  iconography, 192, 195
Chincha, 32–33
Chinchorro, 6, 15, 43–68, 269, 379, 396, 401
  architecture, 46
  body curation, 60–61, 236
  cultural phases, 47f
  fishermen, 48f
  link between living and dead, 43, 63
  mortuary practices, 6, 44–70, 236–239, 241, 269
  mummy, 53f, 54, 55, 56f, 57f, 58f, 59f, 60–62, 64f, 66
  sites, 44–45, 50
  tradition, 43–44
  type-site, 44, 45f, 49, 54, 60. *See also* Archaic period; Preceramic period
Chiribaya, 12, 246, 248, 254–257, 261, 270
  cemeteries, 255–261
  sites, 254–255, 258, 399. *See also* Late Intermediate Period; Omo; Osmore
Chiribaya Alta, 246, 255, 256f, 258–261, 399
Chiribaya Baja, 255, 258, 261
Chiripa, 240
Chol-Chol, 298, 300
Chongos, 37
Christian burials, 27
  Christianity, 33
  Roman Catholicism, 19, 323
  symbols, 374. *See also* idolatry: extirpation of
Chueca, 293
Chullina (ayllu), 358, 364
Chullpa, 28, 229–230, 258, 263, 267–269, 322, 375
  proto-chullpa, 230, 258, 262–263. *See also* Inka; Late Intermediate Period; Omo; tomb architecture
Chullpa tullu, 374–375. *See also* ancestor
Cieza de Léon, Pedro de, 96, 103–104, 163, 192, 196, 316
Ciudadela, 199, 384
Clay
  baked tablet, 63

black, 55
  as body covering, 54, 55, 60
  body organs modeled in, 55
  corpse treatment (facial), 55, 60
  as fill for orbital cavity, 55, 60
  mask, 54, 56f, 57f, 59f, 238
  plaster facial coating, 60
  white, 55. *See also* ceramics; Chinchorro; mask
Cliff burials, 14
Clothing, 96, 123, 133, 229, 259, 292, 324, 330, 333–335, 361, 370, 385
  belt, 334
  blanket, 362–363
  cloak, 236, 318f, 320f
  coca bag, 364, 367
  cotton garment, 103, 166
  cotton loincloth, 123, 236
  fiber hat, 236
  hat, 384
  headband, 318f, 367
  headdress, 365
  llama wool tunic, 190
  loincloth, 384
  mantle, 365, 367
  medicine bag, 364–365
  new, 362
  petticoat, 365
  poncho, 288, 362–364, 367
  shirt, 123
  shroud, 124, 385
  symbolism and function, 365
  tunic, 384–385
  turban, 60
  twined cloak, 203
  wool, 266. *See also* cotton; fiber; headdress; head covering; shroud; textiles; wool
Cobo, Bernabé, 3, 173, 190
Coca, 66, 190, 240, 248, 261, 324, 329–331, 333–334, 336–337, 341, 360–364, 369. *See also* clothing; plant; textiles
Cocabi, 329
Cohen, Ronald, 11
Colana, 268
Colca, 321, 333
Colla, 262–263
Colombia, 3, 6, 11, 61, 94–96, 381, 401. *See also* San Agustín; Alto Magdalena

Index

Colonial Period burials, 33
Colonial records, 29, 38, 95–96, 316.
   See also Arriaga; Cobo; Garcilaso; Guaman; Poma; Huarochirí
Common burials, 152–153, 155, 164, 253, 266, 292, 383, 398
Condendados, 374. *See also* head
Conopa, 321. *See also* fertility; idol
Conspicuous consumption, 97. *See also* covert consumption
Copper, 44, 398
   disk headdress, 153
   fish hook, 150
   gilded, 147, 155
   ingot, 155
   jewelry, 147
   mask, 147
   nose ornament, 149
   as offering, 135, 142, 147, 156, 164
   ornament, 239
   ring, 240
   sandal, 398
   sheet, 147, 155, 398
   strap, 133, 155, 398
   tupu, 202. *See also* fishing implement; jewelry; mask, metal
Cordage, 120, 173, 334
   cotton textile, 205
   hair, 205
   knotted ligature, 190
   neck, 362
   twined vegetable fiber, 204–205
   suspensory, 206f, 208f, 212. *See also* fiber; textiles
Corn, 146, 292, 362–363, 365
   chicha, 292–293, 297, 307, 333, 361, 369–371
   cob, 146, 156
   leaves, 211
   maize, 101, 146, 240, 267, 329
   maize beer, 318f, 320f, 324, 329, 331, 337, 341
   maize flour, 333. *See also* chicha; drink; food; plant
Corpse house, 28–29
Corregidor, 35, 316
Cotton, 123, 150, 156, 168
   sash, 150
   stuffing, 62, 362. *See also* textiles
Covert consumption, 97. *See also* conspicuous consumption

Cranial deformation, 166, 171, 213, 218, 240, 243, 247–248, 249f, 250f, 251–253, 399
   annular, 239, 250
   tabular erect, 239, 250
   pads used in, 249–251. *See also* head
Cremation, 200–201
Cross, 369
Cuchica, 331
Cuel, 283, 288, 296, 298
   cuelku, 305n
   cuel'un, 285, 296, 301
   kuifil cuel, 305n. *See also* earthen mound
Cuiluene River, 64
Cultural developmental periodization, 3. *See also* Rowe, John
Cupisnique burials, 31
Curacautin, 290f
Curacazgo, 182, 339, 342
   curacas, 343. *See also* chiefdom; señorío
Curva (ayllu), 358, 364
Cuzco, 10, 35, 190, 192, 316–317, 332, 334–335, 337–338, 343, 357, 381, 383

Decapitation, 195, 198, 215f, 217–219, 399. *See also* head; trophy head; mutilation; torture
Dedicatory burials, 14, 189, 199–201, 243, 383, 399
Delayed burial, 151, 195, 238. *See also* secondary burial
DNA, 66
Doig, Federico Kaufmann, 14. *See also* cliff burials
Drink
   alcohol, 38, 361, 363–364, 369
   chicha, 292–293, 297, 307, 333, 361, 369–371
   libation, 316
   maize beer, 318f, 320f, 324, 329, 331, 337, 341. *See also* chicha; corn; feasting: festival
Dune burial, 49

Early Ceramic, 239, 251, 269
Early Horizon, 9, 13, 15, 35–37, 178, 241, 382, 399, 402. *See also* Chavín de Huantar; Paracas

Index

Early Intermediate Period, 35–37, 161, 164, 176–178, 180–182, 241, 243, 380, 397, 399–400. *See also* Moche; Nasca
Earthen barrow, 85–86, 88–89, 92, 99
Earthen mound, 283, 285, 288–289, 290f, 293–294, 296, 302, 304–305, 400. *See also* cuel; tomb architecture
Ecological complementarity, 44
Ecuador, 6–7, 61, 197, 203, 261, 317, 343, 381
Elite burial, 8–12, 29–30, 33, 37, 123, 149–155, 163, 171–172, 174, 177, 179, 197–200, 211, 219, 242, 248, 251–252, 261, 263, 266, 268, 270, 292, 326–327, 393, 401. *See also* common burials; Inka; Moche; Nasca
El Plomo, 38
Eltun, 296
El Yaral, 246, 255, 257f, 258–261, 263, 268
Embroidered mantle. *See* textiles
Endogamy, 359
England, 393
Estuquiña, 246, 248, 258, 262–268, 265f, 267f, 268, 399
Evisceration, 54–55, 61
Extended burial, 6, 27–28, 51, 55, 60–62, 66, 123, 155, 176, 199, 236. *See also* body posture; mummy
Eyes
 artificial, 61
 open, 28

Faldas, del Morro, 240
Farfán, 200
Farming, 360
 distribution of land at death, 361
 Kallawaya, 358
Feasting, 15–16, 283, 293, 300, 363–364, 369, 371–372, 374
 Feast of All Colors, 360
 Feast with the Dead, 182, 355, 359, 363, 368–369, 373–375
 festival, 182, 294, 334, 336–337
 Festival of First Fruits, 182
 fiesta, 365
 Fiesta of the Holy Cross, 359
 Inti Raymi, 336
 puru caya, 334

vecochina, 337. *See also* chicha; drink; food
Feather, viii, 46, 54, 64–65, 103, 120, 168, 179, 203, 239, 318f, 334. *See also* headdress
Feline, 149
 cougar, 357
 fur, 67
 motif, 248
 pelt, 54
 puma, 357. *See also* animal
Fertility, 6, 16, 182, 324
 cult, 6, 69
 and death, 325, 375
 and mountains, 357
Fetus
 human, 51, 152, 247, 367
 llama, 245, 252
Fiber, 236
 boat, 259
 body stuffing, 55
 ceramic temper, 240
 hat, 236
 pit, 236
Figurine, 6, 32, 54, 69–70, 190
 bread, 369, 372
 Spondylus, 190. *See also* bone; bread baby; shell; stone
Fingernail clippings, 190, 330, 332, 343
Fish, 369
 bead, 88
 bone, 67
 bones and skin, 147
 fishing implements, 54, 150
 gold bead, 88
 as offering, 146
 shrimp, 267
 star fish, 245, 252. *See also* food; shell
Fishing and gathering, 46, 60
 late Preceramic fishing, 236, 238
Fishing implement, 150, 380
 harpoon, 46, 54, 60, 259
 harpoon shaft, 236
 hook, 54, 60, 150, 239, 259
 line, 54, 60, 259
 mallero, 150
 net sinker, 150
 as offering, 150
 weight, 60, 259
Flexed burial, 6, 27–29, 55, 60, 123, 197, 258

413

Index

seated and flexed, 28–29, 166
side flexed, 178. *See also* body posture; extended burial
Flower
  carnation, 363
  gladiola, 363
  sunglower, 367
Food, 96, 146, 260, 293–294, 329, 334, 361–362, 369–370, 384, 386
  apples, 369
  bananas, 369, 372
  barley, 364
  beans, 146
  bread, 371–372
  bread baby, 372, 373f, 374
  charqui, 362, 364
  chicha, 260
  coca, 369
  corn, 146, 292, 362–363
  fish, 146–147
  flour, 292, 333
  fruit, 371–372
  gourd, 177, 240, 329
  hot sauce, 362
  llama fat, 362
  maize, 329
  meat, 292, 330, 341
  noodle, 364,
  oca, 362–363
  orange, 369, 372
  rice, 364
  seaweed, 146
  soup, 364. *See also* bread baby; coca; corn; fish; plant; seed
Formative period, 13, 99–101, 106, 192, 202, 401
Fried, Morton, 11, 162
Fruit. *See* food

Galería de las Ofrendas, 200–201, 382. *See also* Chavín de Huantar
Gallinazo, 27
Garcilasco de la Vega, 38, 190, 248, 316
Gender distinction in burials, 7, 13, 15, 27–28, 30, 51, 54–55, 60, 62, 65–67, 82, 123, 143n, 150–151, 153–155, 167–168, 170, 174, 176, 196–201, 213–214, 218, 236, 240, 247–248, 250–252, 259–260, 263–264, 266–267, 289, 380, 384
Geoglyph, 180, 356

Gold, 44, 82, 85, 88, 96, 135, 229, 334, 398
  beads, 88, 149
  bowl, 192
  dish, 34, 398
  dish-shaped object, 155
  ingot, 155, 398
  inlay, 149
  jewelry, 37, 147, 177
  kero, 242
  mask, 147, 335, 398
  mouth mask, 381
  nose ornament, 149
  as offering, 147, 162–163, 178, 190
  ornament, 89, 96, 103
  staff, 335. *See also* jewelry; mask; metal
Goldstein, Paul, 245–252, 262
Gourd, viii, 177, 240, 259, 329
  container, 120, 143, 145f, 146, 150, 168, 264, 266
  dipper, 248
  fragment, 267
  plate, 125, 146, 155–156
  spoon, 150. *See also* food; plant
Grave markers
  abode, 168
  logs, 168
  poles, 168, 247–248
  sticks, 168
Guaman Poma de Ayala, Felipe, 191f, 192, 193f, 317, 318f, 319f, 320f, 329, 332, 340
Guayna Capac, 343

Hair (human), 54, 66, 123, 173, 190, 192, 203, 330–333, 343
  braid, 123
  bundle, 168, 173
  cordage, 205
  offering, 168, 173–174
  stuffing, 54
  tresses, 173
Hallucinogens, 6, 46, 60, 63, 238, 242
  plants, 6
  rapé snuff tubes and palettes, 242
  snuff tray, 46
  snuff tubes, 46, 63. *See also* plant
Head, 103, 111n, 151, 374
  burial in olla, 211, 217
  disembodied, 194f, 202, 219, 239, 399

of enemies, 103, 192, 193f, 203, 213, 400
false, 28
as metaphor, 358
mummified, 61
shrunken, 61, 203
trophy, 14, 63, 123n, 189, 203–204, 205f, 206f, 207f, 208f, 209f, 210–211, 382, 399–400, 402. *See also* cranial deformation; decapitation; skull; trophy head
Head covering, 149–150
fiber cap, 150
four-pointed hat, 260
hat, 259
reed cap, 150
tapestry weave, 150. *See also* clothing; fiber; headdress; textiles
Headdress, 149, 153, 260, 365. *See also* clothing; feather; head covering; metal; textiles
Herder, 358
Hodder, Ian, 15, 284, 306
Horizontal strategy of social and economic organization, 12, 254–255, 261. *See also* Rostowrowski de Diez Canseco, Maria; Murra, John
Horticulture, 62
Huaca, 316, 321–322, 331–333, 339, 345
Huaca de la Cruz, 142–143, 149–150, 152, 155, 197
Huaca Prieta, 6, 62
Huachichocana Cave-7 (site), 62
Huana Putina, 239n
Huancavalica, 316
Huanchaco, 150, 152, 202
Huantsan, 357
Huañuc, 228, 329
huañuy, 328
Huaracane
phase, 268
residential terraces, 239
river, 233, 262
site cluster, 239–242, 245–246, 251–252, 259, 268. *See also* Osmore
Huari. *See* Wari
Huarmey, 120n
Huarochirí, 324, 330–331, 333, 336, 337f, 338f, 341, 344, 357, 369

link between living and dead, 324, 336
oral tradition, 361
Quechua Manuscript of, 318, 322, 328, 362
Human sacrifice, 13–14, 38, 150–151, 154, 176, 194f, 195, 199–200, 202, 215, 217, 219, 331–332, 361–362, 382–383, 399
children, 38, 150–151, 154, 190, 191f, 192, 214
as offerings, 189, 199, 202
women, 38, 190, 384. *See also* head; mutilation; retainer burial; torture
Hunting and gathering, 44, 60, 238

Ica, 29, 33, 163–165, 178–179, 181, 202, 210
Idol (fertility), 321. *See also conopa*
Idolatry
extirpation of, 35, 295, 317–319, 323, 336, 339, 346, 373. *See also* Christian
Illapia aia, 318f
Illimani, 357
Ilo, 238
Inca. *See* Inka
Incense, 363
Individual burial, 27, 236, 239, 246, 258, 263
Infant, 51, 62–63, 67, 123, 130, 133, 143, 149–150, 152–154, 202, 236, 240, 266–267, 374
Ingenio Valley, 180, 212
Inheritance rules, 321
Initial Period, 9, 13, 28, 201–202, 219
Inka, 10, 18, 29, 33, 38, 61, 161–164, 182, 189–190, 192, 196, 219, 283, 294, 315–317, 326–329, 331–332, 334–337, 339–340, 342–344, 356–358, 372, 382–383
mummified kings, 10
rulers, 29–30, 34. *See also* clothing; Cuzco; elite burial; human sacrifice; Late Horizon
Inka (ayllu), 358, 364
Insect, 195, 329, 330, 335
fly, 369–370

Jequetepeque Valley, 118, 119f, 135, 142, 152, 192, 196f, 201
Jewel, placement in corpse, 61

415

Index

Jewelry, 6, 34, 61, 147, 149, 241
  ankle bracelet, 240
  beads, 33, 54, 62, 88, 149, 236, 240
  bead string, 149
  bracelet, 149
  ear ornament, 147, 149
  earspool, 248
  necklace, 147, 149, 192, 203
  nose ornament, 147, 149
  pendant, 202–203
  pin, 203. *See also* bone; copper; gold; metal; silver; stone
Jivaro, 61
Jujuy, 62

Kaalaya (ayllu), 358
Kaata, 355, 358, 362–363, 374–375
  cosmology, 367
  Kaatan, 360–361, 367–369, 372–373
  mortuary ritual, 360, 372
  mount, 359, 364, 367. *See also* Kallawaya
Kaata (ayllu), 355, 358–360, 365, 367–369, 374
Kallawaya, 355, 357–358
  ayllus, 358
  Kallawayan, 361
  weavings, 366f
Kamaiura, 64
Karaya, 64
Kilometer-4 (site), 236
Korikancha, 10
Kroeber, A. L., 31, 172, 174, 211

La Argentina, 91f
Laberinto Compound, 198
La Calera de Jegoan, 32
La Calera de Lauren, 32
La Estacíon, 105
La Florida, 197
Lake Titicaca, 28–29, 46, 253, 263, 357, 401
Lake Tuana, 368
La Leche, 120n
La Mina, 32, 120n, 142, 380
La Paloma, 7
La Paz, 363, 365
Lapis lazuli, *See* stone, semiprecious
Las Avispas, 29–30, 198–199, 384–386
Las Haldas, 62

Las Vegas (Ecuador), 6, 61–62
Late Horizon, 28–29, 33–34, 163–165, 179, 201–202. *See also* Inka
Late Intermediate Period, 9, 12, 28, 163, 195, 254–255, 260–261, 262–263, 269–270, 399. *See also* Chiribaya
Late Period, 230, 262
Lauricocha, 27
Leather, 120, 190
  animal-hide bag, 236
  animal skin, 239
  sewn furs, 67. *See also* animal; animal sacrifice, skin
Life cycle, 1
Lineage, 288–289, 298
Lithic
  blade, 63
  cryptocrystalline quartz knife, 267
  projectile point, 6, 236
  quartz projectile point, 248. *See also* stone tools; weapon
Litter (funerary), 260
Living and dead, relationship between, vii, 1, 6, 8–9, 16–17, 19, 43, 63, 161, 172–173, 182, 283–284, 297, 300, 325, 336
Llacta, 321–322
Llactayoc, 322
Llacuas, 322
Llama, 44, 146, 369
  blood, 333
  bones, 142
  caravan, 242, 261
  fat, 333, 362
  feet, 264, 267
  motif, 248
  partial skeletons, 146–147
  sacrifice, 329, 335, 241, 385. *See also* animal; animal sacrifice; camelid
Llaquistambo, 337f
Lo Andino, 381
Lonko, 287–288, 292, 296–298
Looting, vii, 3, 29–30, 82, 85, 95, 100–101, 111, 142, 177, 179, 189, 198–199, 210–212, 239–241, 246–247, 267, 316–317, 336, 380–381, 384–385
Los Canastos, 61
Los Morrillos, 62
Lumaco, 290f, 296–297, 305

Index

Machay, 322, 333
Machi, 287, 295–298
Machula, 360–361. *See also* ancestor; *runa*
Magdalena River, 64, 89
Maize. *See* corn
Mallquis, 322–323, 326, 333, 337, 339–340
Mannequin, 192
Mapuche, 2f, 16–18, 20, 106, 232, 285–286, 288n, 289, 291f, 292, 294, 295f, 296, 298, 299f, 300, 304–307
  ethnography/archaeology, 296
  ethnohistory, 292–295
  Mapuche-Huelliche, 287
  mortuary analysis, 283–285. *See also* Araucanian; Chile
Mapudungun, 283
Mask
  clay, 54, 56f, 57f, 59f, 238
  copper sheet, 147, 155
  gold, 147, 155, 335
  gold mouth, 381
  metal, 147
  silver, 34. *See also* clay; copper; gold; metal; silver
Mass burial, 192, 196f
Matting, 46, 54, 66, 125, 133, 202
  with hair, 54
Melanesia, 210
Menzel, Dorothy, 32–33, 38, 163–164, 179, 202
Mesita A (site), 82, 83f, 84f, 90f
Mesita B (site), 82, 88f
Metal, 147, 241, 247–248, 266, 317, 380–381, 384
  coin, 317
  dish, 34
  forehead ornament, 381
  head band, 260
  mask, 147
  plaque, 381
  plate headdress, 260
  plume, 381
  sandal, 147, 149, 155
  sheathing, 163
  sheet, 147
  spike, 202
  work, 381. *See also* bronze; copper; gold; jewelry; mask; silver
Metallurgy, 44, 381

Metaphor, 355–356, 367–368, 374–376
  fertility, 357
  journey and banquet, 355, 374
  land, 359, 369
  land-society-dead, 356, 369
  mountain-body, 357–359, 369, 373
  sacred, 365. *See also* feasting; fertility; mountain
Middle Bronze Age chamber tombs, 34
Middle Horizon, 9, 13, 28, 164, 178, 201, 230, 242–243, 246–247, 252, 262, 269, 381–382, 399. *See also* Omo; Wari
Mirror, 203
Mita, 382
Mitima, 392
Mitmaquna, 243
Moche, 2f, 8, 12–13, 18, 27, 31–32, 111, 118, 189, 197, 202, 219, 379–382, 395, 397–398
  art, 192, 195, 219
  corpse encasement, 125, 130–136, 152
  corpse preparation, 121, 123–124
  culture, 111
  funerary chambers, 135, 138–142, 151, 153
  funerary practices, 111, 121, 122f
  grave goods, 142–150
  link between living and dead, 8–9
  method of interment, 27
  multiple burial, 151–152
  royal burials, 10
  Site F, 31
  valley, 118–119f. *See also* Early Intermediate Period
Moiety, 11, 162, 367
Monumental burial, 5, 8–10, 80, 94, 106, 180, 232, 267, 285, 304, 393 401. *See also* elite burial; Inka; San Agustín
Moquegua Valley, 2f, 8, 233, 241, 253–255, 264, 270
Moro, 120n, 147, 236
Morro-I (site), 44, 45f, 46, 54–55, 57f, 58f, 60, 66–68, 237
Mortuary archaeology, 392–393, 402–403
Mortuary data
  approaches to, 4
  discrepancies in, 3
Mortuary practice, vii, 1, 4, 10, 27

417

Index

Mortuary ritual, 1, 10, 16, 34. *See also* rite; ritual
Mountain, 361, 369
  as ayllu, 358
  body metaphor, 357–358, 369, 373–374
  sacred, 9, 357
  shrine, 38, 356, 382
  worship, 357. *See also* metaphor
Mourning, 96, 121, 173, 325–326, 328, 331–333, 335, 362–363, 372
  mourner, 232, 241, 260, 269, 292–293, 319f, 320f, 329–330, 332, 341. *See also yquima*
Mudai. See chicha
Mud bricks, 136, 139f, 142, 153, 155, 211. *See also* adobe
Multiple burials, 51, 63, 123, 136–137, 151–152, 164, 175–176, 197, 239–240, 266–267. *See also* cemetery; mass burial; monumental burial
Mummification, 6, 10, 44, 196
  artificial, 55, 61
  natural, 55, 317n. *See also* Chinchorro; Inka; Moche; mummy; Nasca; Paracas
Mummy, 6, 35–37, 54–55, 62, 66
  artificial eyes, 61
  bundle, 35–37, 54–55, 62
  covered with clay, 37
  furs, 62, 67
  masks, 56f, 57f, 59f
  placement of, viii, 7, 27
  preparation of, 55, 60
  wigs, 55, 57f. *See also* body curation; burial accoutrements; Chinchorro; clay; Inka; mask; Moche; Nasca; Paracas; textiles
Mummy cult, 17
Mundurucú, 61, 203
Murra, John, 12. *See also* vertical strategy of social and economic organization
Musical instrument
  bell, 147
  cowtail, 372
  drum, 192, 333, 368, 372
  flute, 192, 368, 371–372
  pan pipe, 248
  rattle, 147. *See also* bone (human); musician; *wacachupa*
Musician, 368, 372

Mutilation, 13–14, 192, 195, 203. *See also* mass burial; torture; vulture

Ñache. *See* animal: blood
Narrative, 324
Nasca, 2f, 8–9, 12–13, 29, 161, 189, 202–204, 205f, 206f, 207f, 208f, 209f, 210–214, 215f, 216f, 217f, 218–219, 238–239, 252, 379–380, 397–398
  basin, 164, 177–178, 180–182
  burials, 8, 29, 164, 165f, 173, 181
  burial patterns, 12, 29, 164–168
  grave goods, 168
  link between living and dead, 8–9, 161, 172–173, 182
  mortuary correlates, 162–163
  polity, 180
  social structure, 162
  style, 381
  valley, 356. *See also* Early Intermediate Period; Middle Horizon
Nawi, 358. *See also* Apacheta (ayllu)
Nazca. *See* Nasca
Necropolis. *See* Paracas Necropolis
Ñguillatun, 288, 288n, 290f, 303
Niche, 137, 141f, 142, 155
Niñokorin (ayllu), 358

Oceania, 394
Ocucaje, 164, 178, 210
Ollantaytambo, 383
Omo, 230, 240–242, 248, 252, 399
  cemeteries, 242–253
  phase, 243, 245
  site group, 243, 244f, 245, 269
  site M-10, 245, 246f, 247, 248f, 250f, 251–253, 262, 268
  type site, 245. *See also* Goldstein, Paul; Middle Horizon; Moquegua; Osmore
Oruro, 357
Osmore
  chronology, 235f
  community, 254
  drainage, 230, 231f, 232–233, 234f, 236, 242, 258, 260–261, 268, 394, 398–399
  river, 232, 255
  sites, 241

418

Index

valley, 12, 233, 243, 245, 255, 261, 268–270, 399. *See also* Chiribaya
Ossuary, 13, 35
Otora
  community, 263
  phase, 258, 268
  valley, 233, 255, 258, 262–263, 267

Pacarina, 322, 329, 331, 341
Pacarisa, 322
Pacatnamu, 118, 119f, 120n, 135–136, 142, 149–151, 154–155, 192, 195, 200–201, 219
Pachacamac, 38, 190, 191f, 317, 382
Pachacuti Inka, 335
Pachacuti Ynga Yupanque, 331
Pacheco, 382
Paloma, 62
Palpa, 204, 211–213
Palta, 248
Pampa Blanca, 152
Pampa de Descanso, 261
Panaca, 327, 332, 337
Panama, 64, 381
Paracas, 2f, 3, 9, 13, 35, 62, 178, 203–204, 210, 213, 218–219, 240, 381
  Cavernas, 9
  Necropolis, 9, 35–37
  peninsula, 9, 37. *See also* Early Horizon; Early Intermediate Period; Nasca
Paria Caca, 323, 333–334, 341
Partial bodies, 13, 61, 63, 111, 123n, 150–151, 176–177, 189, 192, 198, 201–202, 219, 240
  foot, 123
  hand, 123, 150
  headless burial, 63, 201
  isolated skull, 201, 219, 399–400. *See also* decapitation; head; human sacrifice; mutilation; skull; torture; trophy head
Patallacta, 338
Patillos, 44, 45f, 50, 59f, 60, 64f
Patrilineality, 17, 359, 362–363
Passageway, 86
Paucarcancha, 65
Paullu Inka, 334, 336
Pendant, 96
  shell, 203
  tooth, 202. *See also* jewelry

Peru, 2f, 7, 119f, 121, 189, 316–317, 319, 381–382
  central coast, 180, 197, 202, 219
  formalized cemeteries, 7
  north coast, 180, 192, 201, 219
  south coast, 161, 177, 197, 202–204, 207, 218–219. *See also* Chimu; Cuzco; Moche; Nasca; Paracas; Recuay
Pictograph, 355, 364–367, 375–376
Pigment, red, 31, 34, 236. *See also* red ochre
Pigment box, 248
Pikillacta, 201–202
Pisagua, 61, 66
Pisagua Viejo-1 (site), 44, 45f, 46, 50, 60
Pisco Valley, 37, 180
Piura Valley, 120n, 135n
Plant
  avocado, 146
  barley, 365
  bean, 146, 365
  cactus spine, 211, 267
  chili pepper, 146, 211
  corn, 365
  cotton, 44
  gourd, 146, 240
  grass, 239
  hallucinogenic, 6
  huarango spine, 204, 211
  lucuma, 146, 240
  maize, 44, 63, 146
  manioc, 60
  pea, 365
  peanut, 146, 211
  oca, 365
  potato, 44, 365
  quinoa, 44, 60
  reed, 239
  seaweed, 146
  tuber, 44
  vegetables, 365
  wheat, 365
  yucca, 63. *See also* coca; corn; flower; food; red ochre; seed
Platform, 29, 153, 198–199, 211, 240, 253, 369, 372, 384–385
Playa Miller-7 (site), 44, 45f, 61, 65
Playa Miller-8 (site), 44, 45f, 46, 49, 50, 56, 60

419

Index

Plaza, 29, 104, 230, 321, 332–334, 344, 401. *See also* cayan
Political power, 11, 14, 16–17, 32–33, 288. *See also* chiefdom; elite burial; social rank; state organization
Popayán, 82
Porobaya, 267
Potosí, 382
Potrero de Lavapatas, 105
Pottery. *See* ceramics
Pouroupouroyu. *See* Arawaks
Prayer, 362–364, 369, 371, 374
Preceramic period, 13, 44, 63, 65, 202, 219, 233, 236–238, 269, 379, 401–402
Premonumental cemeteries, 5, 8. *See also* Archaic period
Pucullo, 318f, 319f, 322
Pueblo, 94
Pueblos viejos, 320–321
  Pukara, 241
  Purucaya, 334. *See also* feasting
Pyramid, 143, 149, 152–153
  of moon, 153
  of sun, 153

Quechua, 321, 324, 328, 357–359, 365
Quetru metave, 289
Queule, 298
Quiani-1 (site), 45f, 50, 60
Quiani-2 (site), 44, 45f, 50
Quiani-7 (site), 44, 45f, 50, 61, 236
Quijo, 61
Quinchana, 105

Recent period, 100–103, 105, 401
Recuay, 8
Red ochre, 5, 54–55, 59f, 62–63, 67, 123, 203, 236
Reducción, 289, 295
Regional Classic period, 80, 92, 93f, 94–100, 105–106, 401. *See also* San Agustín
Regional Developmental period, 197
Regues, 293
Re-interment, 6, 163–164, 175, 177. *See also* delayed burial; secondary burial; secondary offering
Renfrew, Colin, 67, 95, 284, 287, 304, 306

Reptile
  crocodile, 96
  face, 240
  snake, 147. *See also* animal
Reque Valley, 152, 197
Resources, natural
  competition over, 395–396
  control over, 70
  stress on, 396, 401–402. *See also* ayllu; chiefdom; mountain; water
Retainer burial, 28, 30, 137, 149, 153–154, 176, 196–197, 198f, 331, 383. *See also* delayed burial; elite burial; Moche; secondary burial
Rio Grande de Nasca, 164. *See also* Nasca
Rio Magdalena. *See* Magdalena River
Rite, 299f, 301, 304, 315–316, 323, 325, 336–337, 384
  funerary, 13, 16, 283, 326–327, 361–362
  mortuary, vii, 16, 20, 375
  of passage, 362, 369
  post funerary, 16, 283, 400. *See also* feasting; ritual
Ritual, 6, 8, 12, 16–17, 34, 66, 255, 355–356, 361, 364, 374–375, 385
  agricultural, 369
  burial, 1, 10, 16, 361–362
  coca, 361
  feeding, 363
  and lakes, 360
  mortuary, 18, 34
  New Earth, 368
  paraphernalia, 356
  public, 46. *See also* feasting; rite
Ritual death, 14
Ritualist, 364–365, 374
Rope, 125, 133, 155, 195, 212, 363, 382
Rostworowski de Diez Canseco, Maria, 12. *See also* horizontal strategy of social and economic organization
Rowe, John, 3. *See also* cultural developmental periodization
Runa, 360–361
  pasado runa, 360–361. *See also* ancestor; *machula*

Sacrifice. *See* animal sacrifice; human sacrifice
Salinar, 27

420

Index

Sambaquies Cabezuda, 65
San Agustín, 2f, 3, 11, 14, 18, 79, 82, 89, 103f
   culture, 79
   distribution of tombs and statuary, 89–92
   sites, 81f
   social organization, 92
   tombs, 83f, 85–89. *See also* Colombia; earthen barrow; Regional Classic period; statuary
San Gerónimo, 255, 258–260
San José de Moro, 135–136, 151–152, 155, 380
San Pedro de Atacama, 242–243, 252, 380
Santa Elena Peninsula, 61
Santa Gertrudis, Fray Juan de, 82
Santa Valley, 152
Saqsawaman, 192
Sarcophagus, 317n
   stone, 85, 87f
   wooden, 100
Sarito Quispe, 364
Saxe, Arthur A., 70, 230–231, 266, 392, 395
   Saxe-Binford School, 232, 236, 394. *See also* Binford, Lewis
Scavenger, 192, 195. *See also* vulture
Secondary burial, 5–6, 8, 197, 201–202, 219, 326, 334, 383, 399–400. *See also* ancestor cult; re-interment; secondary offering
Secondary offering, 51, 189, 399
Seed, 385
   cotton, 146
   pacay, 177
   squash, 146, 240
   sunflower, 367. *See also* food; plant
Sendero Luminoso, 247
Señorío, 182. *See also* chiefdom; *curacazgo*
Service, Elman, 11
Settlement pattern, 79–80, 89, 92, 93f, 94, 101, 105, 161, 168, 180, 236, 245, 255, 266
Sex. *See* gender distinction in burials
Shell, 200
   bead, 54, 62, 236
   cache, 239
   conch, 367

   fish hook, 54, 60
   fragments, 267
   inlay, 149
   midden, 49
   mussel, 236
   ornament, 6
   pendant, 203
   snail, 364–365, 367
   spiny oyster powder, 333
   Spondylus, 149, 190, 261, 384, 386. *See also* figurine; fish; jewelry; snail; *Spondylus*
Shell-fishing culture, 49
Shroud, 121, 124f, 130, 133, 146, 155–156, 166
   wrap encasement, 125, 135, 152. *See also* clothing; textiles
Shrunken head, 61, 203. *See also* cranial deformation; decapitation; head; trophy head
Shuar, 203, 205
Sillus, 358. *See also* Niñokorin (ayllu)
Silver, 44, 135, 147, 162–163, 190, 229, 341
   bead, 149
   dish, 34
   earspool, 248
   ingot, 155
   jewelry, 147
   mask, 34
   nose ornament, 149
   plume, 381
   spout, 192. *See also* jewelry; mask; metal
Sinu Indians, 61
Sipán, 20, 120n, 140f, 147, 149, 151–155, 197, 198f, 375, 380, 398
Sixa, 358. *See also* Apacheta (ayllu)
Skin (animal), 62, 178, 239, 260
   bird, 67
   camelid, 62, 67
   fish, 147
   sea lion, 54, 67. *See also* animal; animal sacrifice; leather
Skin (human), 192
   bandage, 55, 57f
   burned, 51
   defleshed, 207, 210
   dried, 55, 61–62
   flayed, 203, 213
   resinous coating, 61

Index

stuffing, 61. *See also* body curation
Skull (human)
 drinking vessel, 192
 isolated, 201, 219, 399–400
 trophy, 207. *See also* head; trophy head
Snail, 54, 364–365, 367
 black sea, 67. *See also* shell
Social distance, 16
Social memory, 356
Social order, 1, 325
Social organization, 16, 92, 99, 393
Social personae, 66, 232, 266, 394
Social rank, 9–10, 12–13, 15, 32–33, 51, 135, 154–155, 162, 174–175, 181, 380, 399. *See also* chiefdom; elite; burial; Inka; Nasca
Social status, 12, 14, 29, 34, 67, 123, 149, 156, 182
 ascribed, 181
 and communication of leader, 94–96, 101, 301
 status hierarchy, 162
Social stratification, 10, 162, 179
Social structure, 12, 16, 162, 164, 175, 178, 181, 357, 359, 396
Sodalities, 8, 162
Sonco, 358. *See also* Kaata (ayllu)
Soniche, 34
Spanish, 29, 34–35, 101, 182, 196, 203, 239n, 283, 286, 295, 302, 316, 319, 322, 329, 335–336, 339–340, 343–345, 373, 382. *See also* Christian; Cuzco; idolatry; Inka; Late Horizon
Spear throwers, 46, 54, 63, 64f, 177. *See also* weapon
Spinning and weaving implements, 150, 247, 264, 380
 spindle whorl, 150, 156, 247–248, 259, 264
 weaving staff, 150. *See also* wood
Spiral, 365, 367–368, 372. *See also* snail
Splayed body, 194f
Spondylus, 261, 384, 386
 figurine, 190
 inlay, 149. *See also* figurine; shell
Stanish, Charles, 262–263, 267–268
State organization, 4, 18, 19, 106, 161, 163, 179–181. *See also* chiefdom; Inka; Nasca
Statuary, 11, 82–83, 84f, 85–86, 88–89, 92, 95–96, 98–100, 294, 304, 321, 338, 401
 supernatural, 96. *See also chemamüll;* San Agustín; stone; wood
Stone bead, 85, 88–89, 96, 149, 326
 basalt, 236. *See also* jewelry
Stone (building material), 153, 229, 247
 chamber, 8, 166, 178
 fieldstone, 20, 267, 294
 rocks in tomb construction, 137, 138f
 roof, 247
 slab cist, 247
 slab tombs, 11, 82–83, 84f, 85, 88f, 89, 90f, 91f, 92, 178, 247
 storehouse, 321. *See also* tomb architecture
Stone objects, 96, 142, 200, 240, 370
 figurine, 54
 sarcophagus, 85, 87f
Stone (semiprecious)
 iron pyrite, 149
 lapis lazuli, 54, 149
 malachite, 149
 turquoise, 149. *See also* jewelry
Stone tools
 blade, 63
 celt, 89
 cryptocrystalline quartz knife, 267
 grinding stone, 46, 54
 mallero, 150
 mano, 101, 260
 metate, 101, 260
 mortar, 46
 polishing pebble, 88, 239. *See also* lithic; weapon
strangulation, 38, 150n, 190
Succession, leadership, 16, 342. *See also* chiefdom; Inka; state organization
Sun, 364, 367–369, 372
 Inti, 368
 symbolism with death, 364
Suyo, 320f
Suyu, 317

Table for the dead, 370f, 371f, 372, 374–375
Tainter, Joseph, 66, 163, 181, 284
Taki Onqoy, 316
Taltal, 44
Tambo Veijo, 178, 210

Index

Tatoo, 67
Tawantisuyu, 340
Teeth (animal), 61
  fang, 96
  shark, 63
Teeth (human), 54
  deciduous, 190
  necklace of, 192
Tello, Julio, 35, 203, 213
Temple del Sol. *See* Korikancha
Temple of the Sun (Pachacamac), 38
Temuan, 266
Témuco, 294
Textiles, 9, 63, 67, 146–147, 149, 156, 168, 177, 179, 199–200, 202–203, 207f, 209f, 212, 236, 240–241, 248, 260, 264, 267, 381, 384–385
  belt, 260, 367
  belt loom, 60
  burned, 201
  coca bag, 318f, 334, 367
  cordage, 205
  cotton, 211, 236, 239
  embroidered mantle, 37
  headband, 318f, 367
  head wrap, 125, 151
  Kaatan weaving, 365, 366f, 367
  Moche, 120
  Paracas, 9
  plain cloth, 166, 177
  plain weave, 207, 210, 384
  repp geometric design, 60
  shroud, 121, 124f, 125, 133
  stuffing, 204
  tapestry weave, 150
  wool, 236, 241, 265, 334. *See also* clothing; shroud; spinning and weaving implements
Tiahuanaco. *See* Tiwanaku
Titia, 294
Tiwanaku, 12, 65, 201, 242–243, 246, 252, 254–255, 261, 356–357, 380, 399
  Chen Chen, 230, 245, 248, 252, 262
  Tiwanaku-V, 240, 245, 247, 253, 262, 264, 269. *See also* altiplano tradition; Middle Horizon; Omo; Osmore
Toledo, Viceroy Francisco de, 35, 317
Tomb architecture
  adobe cist, 178
  boot-shape, 135, 136f, 151, 153, 240, 245
  cane and mud, 178
  chullpa, 28
  cist, 88, 177–178, 229
  clay-lined pit, 210
  cylindrical cist, 247, 263
  deep shaft, 3, 167, 178, 197
  dome-shaped chamber, 9
  earthen mound, 16, 237–238, 283, 285, 288–289, 290f, 293–294, 296, 302, 304–305, 400
  fiber-lined pit, 236
  fieldstone, 36
  in floor, 7, 46, 153, 210–211, 260
  grass-lined pit, 239
  laced-cane, 178
  log, mud and stone, 166
  log roof, 177–178
  in midden, 236, 255, 258
  mud and stone, 168
  mud plaster, 178
  in olla, 167, 211, 218
  ossuary, 35, 201
  oval pit, 89, 212
  pit, 28, 82, 135, 153, 156, 164, 167, 176, 202, 210, 289
  platform mound, 29
  rectangular chamber, 134, 138f, 139f, 140f, 141f, 142, 146, 151, 153
  rectangular pit, 9, 89
  in refuse, 36–37, 105, 153, 236
  rock-lined pit, 210
  round, semisubterranean, 239, 240
  slab cist, 247
  stone chamber, 8, 166, 178
  stone-lined tomb, 247
  stone roof, 247
  stone slab, 11, 82–83, 84f, 85, 88f, 89, 90f, 91f, 92, 178
  storage pits, 7
  tomb chambers with wooden pole roofs, 29, 166
  tower tomb, 35, 320f
  unlined pit with surface rings, 247
  in urn, 164, 167, 178, 289, 292. *See also* cane; cemetery; Chinchorro; *chullpa; cuel;* Inka; Mapuche; Moche; mud brick; Nasca; Paracas; stone; wood
Tomb re-entry, 177. *See also* secondary

Index

burial; secondary offering; re-
interment
Tongue (human), 205, 208f
Topa Inka Yupanqui, 193
Toqui, 287–288, 292–294, 296, 301–303
toquicura, 288, 294
Torata River, 233, 262
Torture, 318, 361. *See also* human sacrifice; mutilation; scavenger
Trapiche, 241–242, 262
type site, 242
Tres Ventanas, 62
Trokinche, 288, 288n
Trophy head, 13–14, 63, 123n, 189, 203, 204, 205f, 206f, 207f, 209f, 210–215, 216f, 217f, 218, 382, 399, 400 402
curation of, 217
skull, 207. *See also* decapitation; head; shrunken head; skull
Tropical forest cultures, 6, 46, 61, 65, 401
Tschudi platform, 384–385
Tumilaca
cemetery, 247, 258, 268
culture, 263, 396
phase, 251, 255, 262–264
river, 233, 262
site, 264, 266, 399
tradition, 263

Uhle, Max, 31–34, 38, 43, 49, 54, 190, 192, 203, 238, 382
Ulmen, 287
Uma, 358. *See also* Apacheta (ayllu); head
Uma Pacha, 341, 360–364, 369, 372, 374–375
Upani, 329
Upinhuaya (ayllu), 358, 364

Valle de Laboyos, 101
Valle de la Plata, 80, 81f, 82, 89, 91f, 92, 93f, 94, 99, 101, 102f, 103f
Vanuatu, 61
Vecochina, 337
Venezuela, 61
Vertical strategy of social and economic organization, 12, 242–243, 252, 254–255, 264, 399. *See also* Murra, John

Villa del Mar, 236, 239
Virilocality, 359
Viru Valley, 149, 152, 197
Volcano, 239n, 298
Vulture, 190, 192, 194f
sacrificed, 195. *See also* mutilation; scavenger
Vutanmapu, 287

Wacachupa, 372. *See also* musical instrument
Wall mural, 142
Wankarani, 240
War, 192, 213, 288
captive, 104, 154, 190, 192, 194f, 195, 219, 293, 361
enemy, 214–215
trophy, 192, 213
warfare, 300, 322. *See also* head; mass burial; mutilation; torture; trophy head
Wari, 17–18, 28, 161, 201
Water
lakes and the dead, 360, 368–369
ritual use, 357, 362–363
underground waterways, 362
Wawakiki, 238, 239, 399
Wax, 61
Wayru, 330
Wayu, 361–362
Waywaka, 28
Weapon, 96, 149, 292, 334
atl-atl, 149
club, 149
dart, 54, 177
halberd, 335
shield, 335
sling, 335. *See also* spear thrower
Wenumapu, 296
Weupin, 287
Wichquana, 202
Wig, 54–55, 57f, 173. *See also* hair
Wood
algarroba, 142
beam construction, 16, 142
box, 369
canoe, 289, 292
carbonized, 101
carving, 163–164, 242
coffin, 120, 133, 134f, 289

Index

cradle, 54
cross, 363
cup, 240
ear ornament, 149
eucalyptus plank coffin, 363
figurine, 54
frame, 155, 398
huarango, 204, 211
kero, 247, 259
mallero, 150
plank coffin, 133, 134f, 135, 137, 154–155
post 142
roof, 240
spindle, 150
splint, 123
spoon, 259, 267
statue, 294

Xesspe, Toribio Mejía, 35–36
Xingu River, 64

Yachajkuna, 364–365
Yanacona, 162
Yanca, 341
Yarn, 123, 147, 150
Yarutini, 330
Yquima, 319f. *See also* mourning
Yucay Valley, 35, 334

Zonal complementarity, 243. *See also* ecological complementarity